Catechist Manual
Catechumenate
Year A

Foundations in Faith

Bob Duggan • Carol Gura
Rita Ferrone • Gael Gensler
Steve Lanza • Donna Steffen
Maureen A. Kelly

RESOURCES FOR CHRISTIAN LIVING®

Allen, Texas

Contents

Nihil Obstat
Rev. Msgr. Glenn D. Gardner, J.C.D.
Censor Librorum

Imprimatur
† *Most Rev. Charles V. Grahmann*
Bishop of Dallas

July 27, 1998

The Nihil Obstat and Imprimatur are official declarations that the material reviewed is free of doctrinal or moral error. No implication is contained therein that those granting the Nihil Obstat and Imprimatur agree with the contents, opinions, or statements expressed.

Copyright 1998
RCL • Resources for Christian Living®

Foundations in Faith is registered in U.S. Patent and Trademark Office.

ACKNOWLEDGMENTS
Scripture excerpts are taken from the *New Revised Standard Version Bible* Copyright © 1993, 1989, by the Division of Christian Education of the National Council of the Churches of Christ in the U.S.A. Used by permission.

Send all inquiries to:
RCL • Resources for Christian Living
200 East Bethany Drive
Allen, Texas 75002-3804

Toll free 877-275-4725
Fax   800-688-8356

Printed in the United States of America
12705 ISBN 0-7829-0759-8

3 4 5 6 7 8 9 10
04 05 06 07 08 09

Catechist Manual
Introduction

"According to the hopes of the Second Vatican Council, sacred scripture will then be a perpetual source of spiritual life, the chief instrument for handing down Christian doctrine, and the center of theological study."

(Pope Paul VI, Apostolic Constitution of the Roman Missal)

What you have before you is a great adventure. Each week the living God speaks to us—who could believe it?—a Word that turns the world upside down, calling us to conversion and newness of life. This manual is a companion to that process by which God reaches us and changes us through the gospel of Jesus Christ.

What is this resource, and who is it for?

The *Catechist's Manual* is a resource to help catechists involved in the Rite of Christian Initiation of Adults as they prepare to lead sessions with catechumens, candidates, and their sponsors during the period of the catechumenate. It is the result of a collaborative effort by seven writers, all of whom have had extensive experience in various pastoral settings implementing the Rite. While this manual is intended primarily for catechists, it could conceivably be used also by homilists, especially those who are preaching to an assembly that is home to a catechetical group. Catechists who use this manual will find that in the Foundations in Faith series there is a corresponding resource for catechumens and candidates and their sponsors: the Participant Book to be used in conjunction with it.

Why a catechetical resource based on the Liturgy of the Word? This resource is based on the Liturgy of the Word celebrated at Sunday Mass, because the initiation process, as revised by the Second Vatican Council, clearly mandates that catechesis be wedded to the Word of God, experienced in the Sunday liturgy and the seasons of the Church year. Catechumens and candidates become more familiar with the Christian way of life in the midst of the community of the Church which proclaims, celebrates, and reflects upon the gospel. By encountering the Word proclaimed in the community of faith, they truly meet the Word

who is Christ. The community also assists them in performing those acts of service and apostolic witness that show they take to heart the Word they hear (RCIA 75–89).

The *Catechism of the Catholic Church* declares that the liturgy itself is the privileged place for catechesis (CCC 1074). This declaration reflects the teaching of the Church as expressed in the *Introduction to the Lectionary* which insists that when the assembled People of God hear the Word proclaimed and reflect upon it they are made new in the promises of the covenant (*Lectionary for Mass: Introduction*, 7 & 8). In their "full, conscious and active participation in liturgical celebrations," the "true Christian spirit" is promoted and the Church lives up to its stature as "a chosen race, a royal priesthood, a holy nation, a redeemed people" (SC 14). Thus, the liturgical cycle itself is catechetical.

According to the *Rite of Christian Initiation of Adults*, the catechumenate period requires "a suitable catechesis . . . provided by priests or deacons, or by catechists and others of the faithful, planned to be gradual and complete in its coverage, accommodated to the liturgical year, and solidly supported by celebrations of the word" (RCIA 75.1). This "catechesis leads . . . to an appropriate acquaintance with dogmas and precepts but also to a profound sense of the mystery of salvation . . ." (RCIA 75.1). The design of the *Catechist's Manual* takes its cue from this understanding of the relationship between liturgy and catechesis.

When do I use this book?

The period of the catechumenate, for which this resource is tailored, is an ongoing, year-round process. One enters the period of the catechumenate by celebrating the Rite of Acceptance (for catechumens) or the Rite of Welcome (for candidates). The period concludes with the Rite of Election. It is the longest of the four periods of initiation described in the *Rite of Christian Initiation of Adults*, and may last several years if necessary (RCIA 76). There is a *Catechist's Manual* for each year of the lectionary cycle. There are separate resources for the Lenten period of Purification and Enlightenment, the inquiry period, or Precatechumenate, and the period between Easter and Pentecost, or Mystagogia.

Within the catechumenate period, this resource is used weekly on two occasions: after the dismissal, and at a subsequent session for catechesis. The rite asks that catechumens be "kindly dismissed" from the Sunday assembly after the homily (RCIA 75.3), and usually the baptized but uncatechized candidates leave along with them. When they are dismissed, they go together with their catechist to a session called "dismissal catechesis," which lasts as long as the remainder of the liturgy. Then they reconvene with sponsors and others for another, longer catechetical session, which is somewhat different in style, either that same day or on a day later in the week. This second session is called "extended catechesis," because it takes more time than the dismissal session.

What is in this book?

The *Catechist's Manual* incorporates five basic sections that illuminate each Sunday, Holy Day, and solemnity of the Church year. The first three are found on the background pages titled *Understanding this Sunday*. The rest form the actual catechetical plan, and are found on the next two pages, titled *Session Plans*.

The Word in Liturgy

This section interprets the Sunday (or feast day) Word in light of its liturgical and seasonal context. While historical, critical, and literary exegesis as well as other scholarly materials bearing on the scriptures have been used in interpreting the readings, the main concern of this work has been to present the Word in a way that is faithful to its liturgical proclamation. In each liturgy the Church combines several readings in such a way that they effectively interpret each other, and their meaning is heightened and focused by the seasons, feasts, and fasts of the liturgical year. The interpretations of the readings offered here always bear these elements in mind.

The Word in Liturgy as much as possible weaves all four scripture passages of the day (the first reading, the psalm, the second reading, and the gospel text) into a coherent whole, and identifies one doctrinal theme which arises from all of them. On some occasions, especially during Ordinary Time, when the second reading is not thematically connected with the other texts, commentary on each of the readings is offered, and the doctrinal theme is selected from either the gospel or the second reading. With the help of the *Catholic Doctrine* section

following, the catechist may then naturally proceed from catechesis upon the Word to open up the riches of Church teaching.

Catholic Doctrine

Given the identification of a particular doctrine in association with these particular scripture readings, a summary of relevant Catholic teaching and understandings is then presented. The monuments of faith—scripture itself, the writings of the Fathers of the Church, the prayer texts found in the *Sacramentary* and in the other ritual books, magisterial pronouncements found in papal writings and in conciliar documents, the work of theologians, the *sensus fidelium*, and writings of the saints—all have been employed to present this summary of Catholic teaching. This presentation is in keeping with the *Catechism of the Catholic Church*. The catechist will note that, where appropriate, reference is made both to the *Catechism* and to other documentary resources.

Catholic Culture

This section contains a brief collection of significant cultural artifacts that express the Catholic faith. Its content is related to either the readings of the day, the season of the liturgical year, the feast day, or the doctrinal theme. It is not meant to be exhaustive, for the Church is heir to a vast treasury of culture. It does, however, describe some notable Catholic works of art, architecture, hymnody, popular prayers and devotions, literature, and the lives of the saints to enhance the understanding of that Sunday or feast day.

Dismissal Catechesis

This section is meant to be used by the catechist immediately after the catechumens and candidates are dismissed from the liturgical assembly and thus the material presented is fashioned for about a half-hour time period. It consists of four parts: (1) "Getting Started," which proposes an action which will focus the attention of the group, (2) "First Impressions," which outlines a process or gives questions and activities to help the group share their experience of what just happened in the liturgy, (3) "Making Connections," which offers two or three sample questions or processes that elicit the link between the catechumens' and candidates' life experience and the day's liturgy, and (4) "Closing Prayer," which provides directions for a concluding prayer to the dismissal catechesis.

Extended Catechesis

This section always indicates a focus which relies upon the doctrinal theme identified in the *Word in Liturgy* and amplified in the *Catholic Doctrine* section. This focus may reiterate the theme or it may reformulate it in order that the catechetical process may flow with ease from the doctrine.

The material in this section is designed to be used in one of two ways: either immediately after the dismissal catechesis (after the catechumens and candidates are joined by their sponsors and friends and have shared some hospitality), or later in the week. (Please note: It is always used *after* the Sunday celebration, not *before*.)

The first part of this extended catechesis, "Gathering," reflects this dual usage and describes either the action which integrates the new participants (sponsors and friends) or the action which focuses the attention of the group later in the week as the Word is liturgically recalled and proclaimed. After this initial "Gathering," the extended catechesis consists of four parts: (1) "The Word," which describes a process using questions and activities connecting the scripture with Christian living, (2) "Catholic Teaching," which proposes a user-friendly process to help participants assimilate the doctrine of the Church which flows from this Sunday or feast day, (3) "Putting Faith into Practice," which outlines a process that links parts one and two with life and may include a tip on how to help participants decide to act according to what they have heard, and (4) "Prayer," which suggests a way to conclude this entire session using either a prayer text, a prayerful activity, or one of the minor rites of the catechumenate.

How do I prepare to lead a session?

Prepare by first reading the scriptures of the day, praying over them, reflecting upon them, and hearing them in your own heart, with the needs of the particular catechumens and candidates of the parish in mind. Next, read the background page, *"Understanding this Sunday,"* noting significant insights that you want to remember from the Word, Doctrine, and Culture sections. You will want to have a copy of the *Catechism of the Catholic Church* nearby to consult when reading the Doctrine section.

Then read through both the *Dismissal Catechesis* and the *Extended Catechesis*, making note of any materials you will need to conduct the activities. Remember that the environment for catechesis is important, and requires attention and preparation. Suggestions are offered throughout the manual for how to set up the space where catechesis will take place. Visualize what you will do, and how you will do it. How will you need others to help you? Visualize what the participants will do and how they will do it. What will they need from you and others in order to do their part?

Read any prepared texts you plan to use (including scripts and prayer texts) aloud several times until you are comfortable with them, and can make eye contact easily while using them. If you feel ready to express the script or prayer in your own words, great! The texts in this book are intended to help you, not tie you down.

Many times the catechist is called upon to facilitate a discussion. Be aware that listening, drawing out responses, clarifying, and summarizing are some of the most important things you do as a catechist. As you prepare, one of your goals should be to become so familiar with your catechetical plan that you are free to relax, listen, and pay full attention to the participants as you facilitate their sharing in the course of the session.

One final note: If you are a first-time catechist, or unfamiliar with the catechumenate, you owe it to yourself and to the people you serve to acquire some orientation and preparation beyond what is provided in this book. Your parish religious education director or pastor can help you to find an appropriate workshop or institute to attend in your diocese. Ongoing education and formation is desirable for everyone who ministers in the Church, so you will be starting out on the right foot. The *Catechist Manual* will then be of great assistance to you in your "on-the-job training."

May I adapt what is written here?

Absolutely. While every effort has been made so that the catechist may use this manual "as is" to facilitate a session, nevertheless, given the power of the Spirit and the special needs and character of one's own catechetical group, adaptation will certainly be required and is encouraged by the multifaceted style in which this book is created. Throughout the catechetical plan, options are offered, and you are always free to substitute questions, activities, and prayers of your own. The prayer context and the basic elements of the catechesis, however (Word—Doctrine—Action), we do recommend that you keep. If any of these fundamental elements is missing, the participants will be shortchanged.

In the preparation of the manual the authors have attempted without manipulating the scriptures to choose a single doctrinal theme each week and also to present a comprehensive treatment of Church teaching throughout the year. Catechists may choose to adapt this material to the needs of their own groups, including changing the doctrinal theme, but in doing so they should be careful to include a complete and comprehensive presentation of Church teaching throughout the year. The analytical index of doctrinal themes (which appears on pages 300–302) is a tool to help you find whatever you may need to respond to particular questions and to ensure this complete coverage.

What other books will I need?

You will need the ritual text, *The Rite of Christian Initiation of Adults*, which is referenced often in the *Catechist's Manual*, especially for prayers. (We have used the paragraph numbers from the U.S. edition.) You will need the *Lectionary for Mass*, from which to proclaim the readings. You will also want to have on hand the *Catechism of the Catholic Church*, an invaluable resource for assuring a sound presentation of Catholic doctrine. Participants will need the Participant Book, which contains many exercises to complement the plans included in this manual.

Excelsior!

Now you are ready to begin. As each Sunday unfolds, may it bring you lasting joy.

ADVENT
SEASON

First Sunday of Advent

The Word in Liturgy

Isaiah 2:1–5
Psalm 122:1–2, 3–4, 4–5, 6–7, 8–9
Romans 13:11–14
Matthew 24:37–44

One feels the edge of tension and excitement in all the readings today, but nowhere more than in the gospel. Here, on the first Sunday of the liturgical year, we are called to attention, to alertness, to vigilance—not for the first coming of Christ in the weakness and vulnerability of a human child, but for the second coming of Christ, in judgment and in glory. How unflattering a comparison it seems at first sight: as householders watch out for thieves, who may rob them at any time without notice, so we must watch out for the return of our Lord! How frightening the notion of a coming as sudden and devastating as the flood in Noah's time! Yet these are images typical of Christian apocalyptic literature, meant to stress the unexpected nature of the Lord's return and our need for attentiveness to the ultimate end of human history: Christ.

The gospel writer is making a comparison that definitely involves an element of trepidation. No domesticated God here. No smug and self-satisfied people who rest assured of their own salvation. Rather, Matthew unsettles us with the possibility that we may not have everything "all sewn up" with God. To human eyes one man plowing a field looks much like another. One woman milling wheat looks much like another. But to God, who knows how each appears? "One will be taken and one will be left." The implicit question to the hearer of this word is: Which would you like to be? The passage puts us on edge. It calls for decision. If we would like to be ready to meet the Lord when he comes, we must begin now to get ready. We must stay alert. This is a strong Advent theme, which persists throughout the season.

Paul's letter to the Romans develops this theme of readiness in moral terms. Christians live in a time of tension. We know Christ has come already, but we still live in a world which has not

embraced the fullness of his coming. As we wait for the final consummation to be found in his second coming, we are to live good lives and so embody the message of his death, resurrection, and glorification in the present. Paul uses the contrast of darkness and light to make his point. Darkness and light are not merely external conditions over which we have no control, but are qualities of our lives that we may choose with God's help. Thus, we are exhorted to "put on the armor of light." Protected by goodness, we are defended against evil, and become ready to meet the Lord. "The day draws near" sounds a note of Advent hope.

The first reading, from Isaiah, uses a very old image of the nations coming together to God on a mountain to describe in eschatological terms the final fulfillment of the hopes of Israel. The passage tells us that not just Israel but all peoples will be drawn to God, whose teaching, the Torah, will bring about both judgment (understanding, wisdom) and true peace. The word for peace here, *shalom,* suggests complete well-being, the wholeness of life with God, and is an element of the name of Jerusalem. The passage belongs to the early career of first Isaiah, whose prophecies began before the Assyrian invasion and were oriented toward the moral and spiritual reform of the people. His glorious vision of God-given peace descending on all nations and resulting in weapons being turned into farm equipment is truly an amazing word. For us, its liturgical proclamation on this Advent Sunday is especially poignant as an invitation to "Come . . . climb the Lord's mountain" today. We—the nations brought into peace with God through Christ—continue to yearn for the ultimate fullness of peace promised by God's Word. The psalm, which follows perfectly, complements Isaiah's vision for, as a psalm of pilgrimage inviting us to Jerusalem, it echoes the themes of peace, judgment, and blessing that are captured by the holy place of God's dwelling. Both remind us of our ultimate hope and destiny, and so fit in well with the Advent theme of the second coming.

Catholic Doctrine

The Second Coming of Christ

The very idea of a second coming—or, for that matter, a first coming—of Christ depends on a sense of time, that is, the progression of one moment to the next and a "before, during, and after" to people's lives. The Bible itself begins and ends with references to time (the statement "In the beginning . . ." of Genesis 1:1 and the prayerful cry "Come, Lord Jesus" of Revelation 22:20). The starting and ending points of sacred scripture are the God who creates time (and yet who stands outside of time and is eternal) and the expectant hope of believers who long for the return of Christ in glory to judge the living and the dead.

As the season of Advent opens, the Catholic Church looks toward the end of historical time, in which all the moments from the beginning of creation to its fulfillment are achieved in the reign of Christ. This forward-looking stance gives meaning to all the days and years of individual believers and to the life of the whole community of the faithful as celebrated in the liturgical cycle. Speaking from this forward-looking stance and citing Philippians 2:12, the Second Vatican Council affirmed: "The promised and hoped-for restoration, therefore, has already begun in Christ. It is carried forward in the sending of the Holy Spirit and . . . continues in the Church in which . . . we learn the meaning of our earthly life, while we bring to term, with hope of future good, the task allotted to us in the world by the Father . . ." (LG 48).

The realization that there will be a certain end which includes judgment—that how we behave here and now has consequences in the hereafter—gives a definite purpose not only to each person's history but to the history of the world. Since that moment in time when Christ ascended in glory to the right hand of God, the world has been on the verge of his imminent return. While no one knows the day or the hour, it is coming soon—so much so that the Church characterizes these days as the final hour of the history of the world (CCC 673).

This should not be seen as a type of "winding down" or cause for gloom, but just the opposite. That we live on the verge of the end times is understood by believers as a source of hope. All creation and thus all time will be renovated and renewed in Christ (CCC 1047). The Second Vatican Council described the Catholic Church, therefore, as a pilgrim traveling forward,

striving in holiness for that day of the Lord when "will come the time of the renewal of all things." The Council went on to say, "At that time . . . the universe itself . . . will be perfectly reestablished" (LG 48). Therefore, the pilgrim Church, looking forward to the second coming of Christ, calls all people to conversion. It is not too late to commit to the kingdom of justice which has been ushered in not only by Jesus' preaching, but by his death and resurrection, and which will be fully revealed at the second coming of Christ (CCC 1041).

The seeds of the kingdom have been planted by Jesus, and the final harvesting of that Word sown in justice and truth by the cross and resurrection will be realized when Christ comes again. Thus, the Church proclaims at the Easter Vigil that all time belongs to Christ, and in that joyful vision we pilgrims pray during Advent: "Now we watch for the day, hoping that the salvation promised us will be ours when Christ our Lord will come again in his glory" (*Sacramentary,* Preface 1).

Catholic Culture

Marana tha is an Advent prayer. The next-to-last verse of the Book of Revelation (the final book of Christian scriptures) ends with the exultant prayer, "Come, Lord Jesus!" This is a rendering of the Aramaic *marana tha,* which also can be found in 1 Corinthians 16:22 and in a very ancient text, the Didache (which literally in Greek means "teaching" and is the shorthand title for "The Teaching of the Lord to the Gentiles through the Twelve Apostles"). The Didache was probably composed in either the first or second century A.D. and includes instructions on the "two ways" (good and evil), liturgical matters, disciplinary matters, and the Eucharist. The last verses in its chapter ten read: "Let grace come, and let this world pass away. Hosanna to the God of David! If any one is holy, let him come; if any one is not so, let him repent. Marana tha. Amen" (*Revelation,* Wilfrid J. Harrington, O.P., Sacra Pagina series, vol. 16, The Liturgical Press, Collegeville, Minnesota, 1993, p. 224).

The original reason the Church encouraged pilgrimages to the holy sites of Jerusalem, Rome, and Santiago de Compostela (Spain) was the difficulty of travel. Pilgrimage was seen as a penitential journey to safeguard one from future sinning— one's place in the coming kingdom was better served by this ascetical practice (EncyCath 1001). Catholics today still make pilgrimages to these and other holy sites and derive great spiritual benefits from the inner journey of conversion that this outward travel fosters.

In the 1960s, a group of Catholic peace activists in the United States, including the Berrigan brothers, invoked the imagery of today's reading from Isaiah by calling themselves the "Plowshares Eight." They gained national attention through public demonstrations against war and weapons production.

Dismissal Catechesis (30 min.)

Getting Started

1. Prepare the space ahead of time with a circle of chairs around a centerpiece arranged on the floor consisting of a purple cloth, a wreath of evergreens and four candles, three purple and one pink, to form an Advent wreath. Be sure to secure the candles in a substantial holder to avoid the danger of fire.
2. Lead the candidates and catechumens to the circle and place the Lectionary on a stand upon the cloth, lighting one Advent candle. Remain standing as you lead them in singing the response to Psalm 122: "I rejoiced when I heard them say; let us go to the house of the Lord," after the proclamation of each verse. Invite all to be seated and remain quiet, recalling their experience of today's Liturgy of the Word.

First Impressions

1. Invite the catechumens and candidates to name their impressions of the Church environment, the music, and the scriptures. Explain Advent in these or similar words: *The new liturgical year begins today with the season of Advent. The word "advent" means "coming." This liturgical season—meaning a season of the Church year—is celebrated for four weeks and is marked by joyful anticipation. There is a twofold thrust to our waiting. Advent is a preparation for the celebration of Jesus' birth—his incarnation—and also a time to prepare for his second coming at the end of the world, which is today's emphasis.* Continue in the large group, inviting the participants to discuss: What do your impressions and observations at today's Liturgy of the Word reveal about this season of Advent?
2. Help the participants get in touch with some of the deep meanings of the Advent season by asking them to close their eyes and listen as you recall some of the images found in today's scriptures: *The mountain of the Lord's house—All nations shall stream toward it—Swords into plowshares—Spears into pruning hooks—Go up to the house of the Lord—Night is far spent—The armor of light—The days before the flood—Noah entered the ark—Two men in the field—One is taken—Two women grinding meal—One is taken—The thief was coming—Watchful eye—Stay awake*
3. Gather the participants into small groups to reflect on these questions: *What did you feel as you listened to these images? What response do they evoke in you? What else do these images reveal about this season of Advent?*

Making Connections

1. Invite the participants to summarize their small group discussion for everyone. As they name the deeper meanings of the Advent season ask them to recall times when they have had to be alert or vigilant. Encourage them to share these experiences in the large gathering. Conclude this discussion by asking the group to name several adjectives that describe what it means to be alert. These can be listed on newsprint or on an overhead.
2. Encourage everyone to return to their small groups to discuss these questions: *What does it mean to be spiritually alert?*

How can we prepare for the coming of Christ, both at Christmas and at the end of time? Then ask each small group to share their ideas. Distribute a purple slip of paper to each person and ask them to write one practical thing they can do this Advent to be more watchful and vigilant.

Prayer

Invite everyone to call to mind that God is present. Then ask each person to read what they have written as the group responds, *"Prepare us for your coming, Lord, by giving us a watchful eye and a hopeful heart."* Conclude with this prayer: *God of the past, the present, and the future, be with us as we begin our Advent journey. Make us aware of your presence in one another and in all of your creation. Prepare us to celebrate your birth and to anticipate your coming at the end of time. Protect us from the deeds of darkness and shed your light upon us. We ask this in Jesus' name. Amen.*

Extended Catechesis

SESSION FOCUS: *The Second Coming of Christ*

Gathering

A. Sunday:
1. Greet and welcome the sponsors and team members. Invite them to join the circle of catechumens and candidates.
2. After all are seated, lead the group in singing a few verses of the Gathering Song used at today's liturgy. Ask a team member to proclaim the first reading, Isaiah 2:1–5, followed by a period of silence. Proclaim the gospel, Matthew 24:37–44. Close with this prayer: *God of Jerusalem, your Word goes out from your holy mountain, teaching us your ways, that we might walk the path of light. Help us to discard our deeds of darkness and put on the armor of light. Clothe us in Christ, that we might become a people of peace and justice. As we prepare to celebrate Christ's second coming, fill us with eager anticipation. Form us into a people who walk in your marvelous light. Let us rejoice in Jesus' name as we go up to the house of the Lord. Amen.*

B. Weekday:
1. Use the same centerpiece as in the Dismissal Catechesis.
2. As the participants gather in the circle, warmly welcome each person. Invite a few of them to share one Advent experience they have encountered in the past few days.
3. Lead this celebration of the Word:
   - Song: "Maranatha" (G. Westphal, K&R Music, 1981.)
   - Greeting and lighting of one Advent candle
   - First Reading: Isaiah 2:1–5
   - Silence
   - Second Reading: Romans 13:11–14
   - Sing the Gospel Alleluia
   - Gospel: Matthew 24:37–44
   - Closing Prayer: Same as section A, 2

The Word (30 min.)

1. Invite everyone to close their eyes and allow this meditation to enter their depths: *Move into the depths of your heart and soul by relaxing your body and freeing your mind to imagine yourself climbing the mountain of the Lord. You are not alone. People of all nations are streaming toward the summit. While the climb is arduous, there is lightness to your feet; you seem to be buoyed up by a marvelous light. You are dressed in dazzling white; the garment of Christ covers you and protects you as you climb. Finally, you reach the top, the house of the Lord. A voice thunders across the mountain: "I will instruct you in my ways. You must put aside your swords, spears, and weapons of war. Melt and hammer them, remaking them into the tools for life—plows and pruning hooks." You are caught short by these ominous words. In your mind's eye you see the ways you have used the tools of violence in the past—words that pierced another like a sword; actions that slashed and crushed the dreams and concerns of people you love. What else do you see? How have you brought peace, justice, and life to others? As you stand on this holy mountain, you feel like you have been awakened from a deep sleep. Deep within, you know that you must cast off your deeds of darkness and be transformed by the light of Christ. The voice speaks once again more urgently: "Stay awake, the Lord is coming. You must be prepared, for the Son of Man is coming at the time you least expect."*

2. Gently and slowly ask everyone to open their eyes and take up their Participant Book, turning to page 5, to write their feelings and insights flowing from this meditation.

3. After time for quiet reflection explain the gospel in these words: *This passage is a bit unsettling. It stresses the unexpected nature of the Lord's return and our need for vigilance—not for the first coming of Christ in the weakness and vulnerability of a human child, but for the second coming of Christ, in judgment and in glory. It is frightening to imagine this second coming as sudden as the flood, which purged the people in Noah's time. Matthew reminds us that while we may think we are right with God, there is the possibility that we may not be ready for this coming.*

4. Ask everyone to turn back to the Participant Book and discuss the questions presented there in the same small groups. When they have finished, invite a few responses in the large group.

Catholic Teaching (30 min.)

1. Remain in the large group to discuss the ways we mark time. Use these or similar words to open the discussion: *We use the concept of time to mark events as past, present, and future. Name some ways we use time to mark events in our families.* Gather experiences like births, weddings, anniversaries, deaths, graduations, and relocations. Then continue: *The Bible itself is framed in time. It begins with the words "In the beginning . . ." and concludes with the prayerful cry "Come, Lord Jesus." As the season of Advent opens, the Catholic Church looks toward the end of historical time, in which all the moments from the beginning of creation to its fulfillment are achieved in the reign of Christ. This forward-looking stance gives meaning to all the days and years of the individual believer, as well as the life of the whole community of the faithful.*

2. Invite the participants to discuss the following question in small groups: *How does the way we live in the here and now have consequences for the future?* After some time in the small groups, focus their attention back to the large group. Gather comments and insights from their discussions.

3. Continue to explain the Church's teaching on the second coming of Christ in these words: *Since Christ ascended in glory to the right hand of God, the world has expected his return. While no one knows the day or the hour, the Church characterizes these days as the final hour of the history of the world. That we live on the verge of the end times is a source of hope. All creation and all time will be renovated and renewed in Christ. The seeds of the kingdom have been planted by Jesus, and the final harvesting of that Word sown in justice and truth by the cross and resurrection will be realized when Christ comes again.*

4. Focus the discussion in the small groups on this question: *In what ways will the unexpected second coming of Christ change our living?* You may choose to invite the groups to report on their discussion in the large gathering.

Putting Faith into Practice

1. Review the instructions for making an Advent wreath: four candles (3 purple, 1 rose-colored, to mark the four Sundays of Advent)—evergreen (a sign of life and hope)—purple cloth (as a sign of waiting)—placed in a circle (to remind us that God's love is never ending). Suggest that they make an Advent wreath for their home and light it for family prayer each day.

2. Share some of the ways in which the parish prepares for Christmas during Advent, for example, Vespers (Evening Prayer from the Liturgy of the Hours), a Blessing Tree, collecting gifts for children and families in need, talks, evenings of reflection, and small faith sharing groups.

3. Invite everyone to share practical ideas of how to deal with the overwhelming consumerism that fills this season. Some examples: making Christmas gifts; placing an empty crèche in a prominent place in the home and adding a figure or two each week leading to Christmas; spending family and private time reflecting upon the daily scripture readings for this season; volunteering in a nursing home; or helping someone discover the gift of reading. These suggestions can be written on slips of purple paper, copied, and distributed at the parish liturgies next week, or noted in the parish bulletin.

Prayer

Draw the participants' attention to the Advent wreath. Ask everyone to respond to each invocation by praying, "Come, Lord Jesus."
Into our world searching for peace . . . Come, Lord Jesus.
Into the lives of the poor, the hungry, and the homeless . . . Come . . .
Into our city (town) . . . Come . . .
Into gangs, prisons, and those who suffer addictions . . . Come . . .
Into our parish . . . Come . . . .
Into our family . . . Come . . .
Into our hearts . . . Come
(Continue to add your own petitions to this list.)
Close by leading the group in singing "Maranatha."

Second Sunday of Advent

Understanding this Sunday:
Background for Catechesis

The Word in Liturgy

Isaiah 11:1–10
Psalm 72:1–2, 7–8, 12–13, 17
Romans 15:4–9
Matthew 3:1–12

The prophecies of Isaiah celebrated in the Lectionary these four weeks are a hallmark of the Advent season. In today's beautiful, lyrical description of a future, messianic king, the prophet Isaiah gives us a vision of justice and peace that embraces Israel, the human community, and all of creation as well. Taken from a section known as the "Book of Emmanuel," this passage begins with the promise of a king in the line of David, continues with a description of his reign, and concludes with the consequences to be expected in terms of a peace-filled new world order harking back to the Garden of Eden. The virtues of the king described by Isaiah are what the Christian tradition was later to identify as "gifts of the Holy Spirit." The reign of the king is marked by justice, with a right ordering of relationships in society, and championship of the poor as its key ingredients. And the signs of the messianic era found in reconciliation within creation itself enlarge the vision presented to include peace in all its forms. The passage is eschatological, and ends on a note of universalism. In other words, its promise is not bound to current events as if this or that successor to Israel's king will prove or disprove the prophecy. Rather, it is God's Word pulling all who hear it forward into an ultimate future. Christians have interpreted the passage to refer to Jesus the Christ, whom we regard as the messianic king and the fulfillment of God's promises.

The psalm continues today's emphasis on justice and peace. This royal psalm with messianic overtones emphasizes the wide extent and eternal nature of the justice and peace that will come with the reign of God's elect king. Its placement in the liturgy of Advent again suggests a christological interpretation: the kind of king we must expect in Jesus is one whose concern for the poor and the afflicted issues forth in lasting justice and in a peace that is worldwide.

Today's Pauline reading is a summons to the Christian community in Rome to live in unity and harmony in everyday life. Differences between Jewish Christians and those of Gentile origin caused tension within the community. Paul sees each group as having a part in God's plan nevertheless and exhorts all to accept one another. This sense of unity and acceptance is naturally expressed in heartfelt common worship and giving glory to God. Advent is a time of waiting. Given this context, a theme of "patience and encouragement" (vv. 4 and 5) also emerges strongly from this reading. Paul cites the scriptures as a font of patience and encouragement, but then reminds the Romans that it is God indeed who is the source of these things which are necessary ingredients of unity and harmony within the community.

In Matthew's gospel, John the Baptist symbolizes the end of the era of patriarchs and prophets and sets the stage for a new era which begins with Jesus. His clothing of camel's hair is reminiscent of Elijah, his desert food of the Exodus, and his preaching of the call of Deutero-Isaiah. Although John's baptism of repentance is mentioned, the passage focuses more on his preaching, which is eschatological and centers on the coming Messiah and the moral conversion necessary to welcome his reign. Pharisees and Sadducees are both mentioned, though the two groups were enemies of one another, presumably because representatives of both were later opposed to Jesus' message.

John announces the coming of a new age in which no inherited privilege or mere external observance can substitute for true conversion or save an individual from the judgment of God. His fearful eschatological images of fire, wrath, the ax, and the winnowing fan (which separates wheat from chaff) remind us of the painful wrenching required to free the world from the grip of sin, even as the idyllic vision of Isaiah offers us hope of the ultimate outcome of such an effort.

Catholic Doctrine

Justice and Peace as a Sign of the Messianic Era

Last Sunday's doctrine section explored the Catholic understanding of time. Today's doctrine section continues that discussion, focusing on the messianic era: a new time or age begun by Christ's coming into the world.

God is a God of promises. A promise is, necessarily, future-oriented. Catholics affirm that the relationship of promise God initiated with humanity, first broached in the covenant with Abraham and then developed throughout the time of Moses and the prophets, comes to its definitive fulfillment in Jesus Christ. Something new and vital has entered human history with the event of the incarnation. The Savior who entered our humanity and our history (and thus time) inaugurated the kingdom of God that will culminate in the final judgment and the fullness of the divine dominion. Thus, for believers, history from the time of Christ onward can be characterized as having entered the messianic era.

Two very important contemporary Church documents, both promulgated as a result of the Second Vatican Council, help to flesh out the Catholic understanding of this messianic era. In the document that dealt with the nature of the Church, the Council fathers asserted: "The promised and hoped-for restoration [of the world], therefore, has already begun in Christ. It is carried forward in the sending of the Holy Spirit and . . . continues in the Church in which . . . we learn the meaning of our earthly life, while we bring to term, with hope of future good, the task allotted to us in the world by the Father. . . . Already the final age of the world is with us (cf. 1 Corinthians 10:11) and the renewal of the world is irrevocably under way. . ." (LG 48). Second, in the pastoral constitution which dealt with the relationship between the Church and the modern world, the Council fathers forthrightly proclaimed that in his life, death, and resurrection, Christ sums up the meaning of history. They described Christ as the perfect human being who "entered world history, taking that history into himself and recapitulating it" (GS 38). Through the Holy Spirit, Christ continues to work in the world, providing believers with a future orientation and hope, and, indeed, animating the faithful toward that future (GS 38).

As the perfect human being, Jesus embodies God's justice and peace. Through his ministry, Jesus planted the seeds of God's reign, which Isaiah's prophetic vision extols. It is through Christ that this promised vision will come to its full stature—

a kingdom that does not merely pay lip service to the Most High, but whose subjects are imbued with divine qualities and live those qualities in their relationships and actions. Thus, the flowering of justice and peace are signs of the messianic era. Justice, in this context, is not something abstract, but consists of relationships in harmony with God's will and law, always founded on solicitude for the poor and weak. Peace is not just the absence of war, but total well-being grounded in friendship with God, centered in the human community but also extended to harmony with the whole created order.

The Catholic Church teaches that by putting on Christ, and living as Jesus would live, believers hasten the full advent of the kingdom of God (CCC 2046), a kingdom of "justice, love and peace" (*Sacramentary,* Preface xx). To live in this messianic era does not mean that people must abandon their tasks in this world: Rather, they enter into those activities even more ardently, with the mind of Christ, animated by the Spirit.

Catholic Culture

Frederic Ozanam (1813–1853), while a law student at the Sorbonne (Paris), along with others who were like-minded, defended Catholicism from attacks by certain professors at the university. However, he was challenged to put into practice the message he was, in effect, preaching. In May of 1833, he and his friends formed a Conference of Charity which emphasized outreach to the poor of Paris, especially visitation of the needy in their homes. Two years later, the conference was formally organized as the St. Vincent de Paul Society, in deference to this saint who was considered by his social outreach and actions a great friend of the poor. At the time of Ozanam's death, the society boasted fifteen hundred conferences and almost fifteen thousand members. At the turn of the century, the society had branches throughout the world dedicated to preparing for the fullness of the kingdom of God by helping the poor and needy (NDictSoc 695).

Jesse trees are a traditional Advent decoration sometimes found in Catholic schools, churches, and catechetical centers. Using either an evergreen or a deciduous tree, the faithful hang ornaments on it that are symbolic of the Messiah's "lineage," beginning with Adam and Eve, continuing through Moses, and ranging through the rest of salvation history up to Mary and Joseph. Another popular Advent decoration is called a "giving tree." This is a Christmas tree on which is displayed ornament placards that indicate a needy child. Families and individuals take the placard, purchase either a toy or an article of clothing for the child, and replace the placard with an ornament from their home. In both instances, a Jesse tree and a giving tree, the trees of Advent prepare for the tree of Christmas and symbolize through our recalling of salvation history or our gift giving to the poor that we are in a new age, the messianic age whose signs are justice and peace.

Dismissal Catechesis (30 min.)

Getting Started

1. Prepare the space ahead of time with a circle of chairs around a centerpiece. The arrangement consists of a purple cloth, upon which is placed the Advent wreath and a barren branch with new shoots.
2. Lead the candidates and catechumens to the circle and place the Lectionary on a stand upon the cloth, lighting two purple Advent candles. Remain standing and lead the participants in singing the fourth verse of "O Come, O Come, Emmanuel." Indicate that all be seated as you pray:
Come, Emmanuel, to us and to our world. Where there is hatred and division, bring your peace and harmony. Where there is discouragement, bring your hope. Where there is deception and falsehood, bring your truth. Come, open our hearts to your Spirit. Prepare our hearts and all the people of the world for the coming of Jesus, the Messiah, who is peace. We pray in Jesus' name. Amen.

First Impressions

1. Invite the group to listen as you repeat the rich images from today's first reading, Isaiah 11:1–10. Encourage the participants to notice those images that ring true for them:
A shoot shall sprout from the stump of Jesse—The Spirit of the Lord shall rest upon him—A Spirit of wisdom, understanding, counsel, strength, knowledge, and fear of the Lord—Not by appearance shall he judge—Justice shall be a band around his waist, and faithfulness a belt upon his hips—The wolf shall be a guest of the lamb—the baby shall play by the cobra's den—There shall be no harm or ruin on all my holy mountain.
2. Ask the group these questions, one at a time, inviting them to share their feelings and thoughts: *Which of these images speaks to your heart? What do you hear in them?* Repeat the images, once again asking the participants to pay attention to their feelings. Then ask: *What feelings and impressions well up within you as you hear these words?*
3. Invite the participants to turn to the person on their right and share their impressions of the whole Liturgy of the Word, asking: *What message do you perceive in today's scriptures, the music, the church environment, and the mood of the gathering?* Invite responses and insights in the large group.

Making Connections

1. Help the group move deeper into the meaning of the reading from Isaiah: *Close your eyes and imagine Isaiah's lyrical description of the future reign of God. You find yourself in a garden that appears dead, but as you look closely the tree branches and plants are bursting with new buds and shoots. Animals play and rest with one another. The wolf and the lamb, the leopard and the goat are together. All are in harmony in this Eden-like place. The poor and the sick are being cared for. The goodness and sense of purpose you observe surprises you. There is a strong feeling of justice and connectedness, compassion and care.*

2. Gently, invite them to return to the present time and place. Ask the participants to share their responses to these questions in the same pairs: *What is your reaction as you imagined this vision of life in God's kingdom? How did this meditation inspire you? What in your own life was challenged as you imagined this glimpse of the future reign of God?* When the sharing seems to be finished, gather the attention of the participants back to the large group to present their thoughts. Summarize this discussion in a few sentences.

Prayer

Encourage the participants to look at the barren branch with new shoots or buds, a reminder of God's promise to bring about a new era of justice and peace through Jesse's offspring. Invite them to reflect upon how they themselves are like the barren branch, ready to burst forth and bloom. After a time of silence, distribute copies of Psalm 72:1–2, 7–8, 12–13, 17 to each person. Lead them in praying this psalm. Conclude by asking all to stand and sing "O Come, O Come, Emmanuel," verse 4.

Extended Catechesis

SESSION FOCUS: *Justice and Peace as a Sign of the Messianic Era*

Gathering

A. **Sunday:**
1. Greet the sponsors and team members as they arrive. Invite them to join the circle of catechumens and candidates. Help the group to center themselves by inviting all to focus on the lighted candles of the Advent wreath.
2. Begin by leading the participants in singing two verses of the Gathering Hymn used at today's liturgy. Invite all to close their eyes and imagine the scene of today's gospel:
Imagine yourself in the Judean desert. The air is hot and dry. You are standing in the midst of a crowd of people waiting to hear the noted preacher, John. As the heat of the day wears on you, you catch a glimpse of a ragged-looking man walking out of the stony wilderness. He is dressed in a garment made of camel's hair and wears a leather belt around his waist. You can see that this man is a holy person. Imagine his eyes, his face, and the way he looks at you. You are mesmerized by his appearance and listen as he speaks.
Proclaim the gospel, Matthew 3:1–12. After a short silence, conclude with the prayer of St. Francis.

B. **Weekday:**
1. Use the same centerpiece as in the Dismissal Catechesis.
2. As the participants gather in the circle, greet each person. Invite the participants to share an experience of anticipation from their Advent journey during this past week.
3. Lead this celebration of the Word:
   • Song: Gathering Song from Sunday's liturgy
   • Greeting and lighting of Advent wreath (two purple candles)

- First Reading: Isaiah 11:1–10
- Sing Psalm 72
- Meditation: same as in section A
- Gospel: Matthew 3:1–12
- Silence
- Closing Prayer: same as in section A

The Word (30 min.)

1. Invite the participants to share their insights into the gospel passage in the large group by asking: *What did you experience as you placed yourself into the passage?* When they have expressed some reactions, invite a candidate or catechumen to share their impressions of the first reading from Isaiah from the Dismissal Catechesis.
2. Explain the relationship between these two readings: *In the gospel, John the Baptist uses strong language urging the people to prepare for the coming of the Messiah. The substance of his message is, "Reform your lives. The reign of God is at hand." In the first reading, the prophet describes this future reign of God: In the messianic era, children and wild animals will dwell together; there will be peace; the poor will be cared for; and justice will reign. John the Baptist preaches good news, but also a warning— this era is upon us, prepare its way. He presents fearful images of fire, wrath, the ax, and winnowing fan to remind everyone that neither external observances nor privileged status will be of help in this new era. Preparing for this future restoration of the garden of harmony, justice, and peace is a painful, wrenching reform.*
3. Gather the participants into small groups to share their insights on the following questions (Ask each group to record their insights on a large newsprint or poster board): *What words, phrases, and images would you use to describe the restoration of God's reign of harmony, peace, and justice among humanity and all of God's creation? Knowing that John's message was accompanied by frightening images, what attracted people to follow him? What in society needs to be reformed in order to further God's reign?* Invite each group to post their newsprint or poster as they present a summary of their discussion to the large group.

Catholic Teaching (30 min.)

1. Invite the large group to name words and phrases that come to mind when they hear the word "peace." Record their responses on an overhead or newsprint. Then have them do the same with the word "justice," recording these phrases on an overhead or newsprint.
2. Present the Church's teaching on justice and peace as a sign of the messianic era from the Catholic Doctrine section found in Understanding this Sunday, including these points:
   - With the coming of Christ the messianic era has begun. The promise God made at the time of Isaiah is brought to fulfillment. This messianic era, known as God's kingdom, will be brought to completion at the end of the world when Christ has dominion over everything.
   - The Second Vatican Council document on the Church (*Lumen Gentium*) states that the restoration of the world begun in Christ is moved forward by the Holy Spirit, and continues through the Church, giving our lives meaning.

- In the document on the Church in the Modern World (*Gaudium et Spes*), the bishops gathered at the Council state that the life, death, and resurrection of Christ sums up the meaning of history. Christ continues to work in the world through the Holy Spirit, and provides hope for all believers that God's reign will surely be fulfilled.
- The sign of the messianic era is justice and peace. Justice is right relationship between and among God's people and indeed all creation, with particular care for the poor and weak. Peace, more than the absence of war, is grounded in friendship with God.

3. Invite the participants to turn to the Reflection and Questions in the Participant Book on page 6. After responding to these exercises, ask everyone to share one thing with a partner. Sponsors and candidates or catechumens may pair together.

Putting Faith into Practice

1. In the large group, ask all the participants to brainstorm how they can cooperate with God to bring about the fullness of God's reign of peace and justice. List their ideas on a large poster board or newsprint. Some examples include reconciling with alienated family members, working on specific environmental issues, and advocating the rights of the poor.
2. Invite the participants to look over the list and spend a few minutes in silence, during which they ask God to direct them to select an action as part of their Advent journey. Encourage them to write their decision in the Participant Book on page 7, in the section "I want to put my faith into action by."
3. Describe the Church traditions of the Jesse tree and the giving tree in the following manner: *The Church has two Advent traditions using trees. The symbol of the Jesse tree flows from the Isaiah scripture verse, "a shoot shall sprout from the stump of Jesse." Jesse was King David's father. Both were part of Jesus' family tree. To make a Jesse tree you can use a tree branch and hang symbols of the Messiah's "lineage," beginning with Adam and Eve through Mary and Joseph, to be reminded of the story of salvation.* Here you may stop and show the participants of a Jesse tree and the symbols used. Continue by stating: *Each symbol represents a scripture passage, one for each of the twenty-five days before Christmas. In addition, many parishes provide a "giving tree" as a way of caring for the poor. Names and ages of children or families in economic need are placed on ornaments and hung on the tree. Families and individuals select an ornament and purchase a toy or an article of clothing for the person and follow the directions for delivery of the gift.* Invite the group to participate in one or both of these Advent traditions.

Prayer

Close the session by asking the participants to name the global and local situations where justice and peace need to reign more fully. As they name these places, invite everyone to respond, "Come, Lord Jesus, bring your peace and justice," following each naming. Conclude by inviting all to sing "Let the God of Glory Come" (Michael Joncas, NALR, 1979) or a familiar Advent song.

Third Sunday of Advent

Understanding this Sunday:
Background for Catechesis

The Word in Liturgy

Isaiah 35:1–6, 10
Psalm 146:6–7, 8–9, 9–10
James 5:7–10
Matthew 11:2–11

Today's passage, which links first and second Isaiah, describes the coming redemption of Israel in glowing terms of nature restored and human beings made whole. The prophet's message in first Isaiah was devoted mainly to decrying Israel's infidelity and announcing God's judgment. In this section, however, the emphasis shifts to news of a coming rescue by that same God—a strong theme of second Isaiah. The people, scattered and sent into exile by the destruction of the kingdom through the Assyrian invasion, will be ransomed and brought back into their land. They will be helped along their journey of return by visions of a saving God, by a transformation of the desert land, and by divine strengthening and healing. Lebanon, Carmel, and Sharon in their dryness are symbols of God's wrath (see 33.9); here they bloom to betoken God's mercy. The passage ends on a note of joy.

The psalm continues to celebrate the grace and merciful favor of God. It is focused on the way in which God sustains those who are in any way dispossessed or without help and protection, such as the poor and downtrodden, foreigners, orphans, and widows. The expression that God "keeps faith" explicitly suggests keeping the covenant, offered freely to the people.

In the second reading, James counsels the Christian community to practice patience: first, because the second coming of Christ did not come as soon as they expected; second, because of friction within the community; and third, because they were subjected to injustice by the rich (5:1–6). James uses the comparison of the farmer and the soil to suggest a total dependence upon God. As the farmer is subject to the elements, and must cooperate with them, so the Christian must practice patience, trusting God for what human beings alone cannot provide. Furthermore, he suggests that Christians can learn from

the prophets of the Old Testament. The trials the prophets suffered for bearing the Word of God to their contemporaries can be an inspiration to Christians in times of difficulty and persecution. Christians, in their sufferings, are elsewhere in the New Testament compared with prophets as well (Matthew 5:12).

Today's gospel comes from a different tradition than the one Matthew used in recounting the story of Jesus' baptism. Hence, John inquires about Jesus as if he did not know him. Much of the passage concerns the kind of Messiah Jesus is. In contrast with the gospel read last week, which emphasized the eschatological judgment that the coming Messiah would bring ("the wrath to come," a baptism of fire, the winnowing fan to separate wheat from chaff, and so on), today's passage focuses on the qualities of mercy that mark the Messiah's reign. He brings healing to the blind and lame, to lepers and the deaf. He raises the dead and preaches glad tidings to the poor. Those who can accept this Messiah are blessed. The passage then goes on to reflect on John the Baptist—his extraordinary ascetic personality and powerful mission. Scripture scholars have speculated that followers of John may have persisted after the coming of Jesus, and that this passage is one of several which attempt to reconcile John's ministry with that of Jesus. In any case, John's identity as prophet and forerunner of the Messiah is lauded here in the highest possible terms. In a surprising twist, the calling of the followers of Jesus is said to surpass even that of John. A new age has truly dawned with the coming of Jesus the Messiah.

Our doctrinal focus on the charism of prophecy can help to illuminate the meaning of all three of today's readings. Isaiah's prophetic message, present throughout the Advent season, reaches beyond its immediate historical context and still speaks to us today. The prophets, as James suggests, serve as models of faithfulness in spite of hardship and persecution. And John the Baptist, the last of the prophets of old, sets the stage for the coming of Jesus. We Christians, who are "born into God's reign," can reflect with awe and joy today on our own calling to share in the charism of these prophets.

Catholic Doctrine

The Charism of Prophecy

The Catholic understanding of prophets and prophecy rests upon the testimony of Old Testament scriptures. These sacred texts show that a prophet is one called by God to speak God's message in a specific historical situation. The message of the prophet Isaiah, for example, is characterized by the strong theme of God's future that will be accomplished through the agency of the messiah. Jeremiah is known for his forthright stance before God, resisting the call at first but then persevering in the face of continual rejection by the people. These Old Testament books paint a picture of the prophet that represents both challenge and hope for the people of God. Prophets communicated God's judgment, but they also conveyed God's promise of mercy and revitalization in times of decline or confusion. Because their message was often unwelcome, they suffered hardships and persecution in fulfilling their calling.

Catholics consider John the Baptist as the last great prophet in the Old Testament line, even though he did not accept this description of himself or his ministry, saying only that his was a voice crying in the wilderness (John 1:9–23). St. Augustine, in reflecting upon John the Baptist, preached, "John is the voice, but the Lord is the Word who was in the beginning. John is the voice that lasts for a time; from the beginning Christ is the Word who lives forever. . . . Do you need proof that the voice passes away but the divine Word remains? Where is John's baptism today? It served its purpose, and it went away. Now it is Christ's baptism that we celebrate. It is in Christ that we all believe; we hope for salvation in him. This is the message the voice cried out." *(Sermo* 293, 3: PL 1328–29 found in LitHrs vol. 1, p. 261). The Baptist functioned in a way that clearly was prophetic, calling the people to repentance and pointing the way to the Messiah, Jesus.

For Catholic Christians, any portrait of prophets or prophecy must also include the time after the Old Testament and John the Baptist. For the Christ, the Messiah, has inaugurated a new age, the final age of this world. The gift of God's prophetic Spirit is proclaimed by Peter to have been bestowed upon the disciples at Pentecost (Acts 2:14–21) for the birth and growth of the Church. While the full extent of the exercise of prophecy in the early Christian Church is unknown to us, what is clear from the New Testament scriptures is that prophecy did function in the community. Thus, prophecy is named as a charism (or gift) of the Holy Spirit by Paul and he sets up regulations for the exercise of this gift (1 Corinthians 14:29–33).

Today, believers do not function as did Old Testament prophets and yet, by baptism, all Christians share in Christ's identity as priest, prophet, and king. As one rises from the baptismal waters, the Church prays: "God, the Father of our Lord Jesus Christ, has freed you from sin and given you a new birth by water and the Holy Spirit, and welcomed you into his holy people. He now anoints you with the chrism of salvation. As Christ was anointed Priest, Prophet, and King, so may you live always as a member of his body, sharing everlasting life" (RBC 98). Clearly, as the prayer text indicates, this share in the identity of Christ as prophet is given collectively to the entire people claimed for God in Christ by this sacrament. Thus, the Second Vatican Council taught: "The holy People of God shares also in Christ's prophetic office: it spreads abroad a living witness to him, especially by a life of faith and love and by offering to God a sacrifice of praise, the fruit of lips praising his name . . ." (LG 12). In referring to the mission of Christ and the laity's share in that work, Pope John Paul II has written: "People today put more trust in witnesses than in teachers, in experience than in teaching, and in life and action than in theories. The witness of a Christian life is the first and irreplaceable form of mission: Christ, whose mission we continue, is the "witness" *par excellence* (Revelation 1:5, 3:14) and the model of all Christian witness. The Holy Spirit accompanies the Church along her way and associates her with the witness he gives to Christ . . ." (*Redemptoris Missio,* December 7, 1990, # 42.1).

Therefore, prophecy is far from dead. It continues in the Church, as believers are given a new birth in Christ through baptism and are initiated into the holy work of the Messiah and the kingdom (CCC 2045). This Advent theme is worthy not only of meditation but of commitment in word and deed.

Catholic Culture

There are many fine programs in use today in Catholic parishes which not only promote reflection upon the gospel message and the person of Christ, but also encourage the believer to work as a witness in the world to the kingdom of God. An example of this type of program is Renew, originally a three-year process engaging not only the parish at large through Sunday Masses but also small faith sharing groups. Another example is Christ Renews His Parish, which entails an initial weekend retreat experience with witness talks by parishioners, followed by many weeks of formation devoted to a variety of subjects. The goal is the commitment of these adults in a variety of parish ministries, especially to the poor and needy.

While artists still produce icons and portraits of the Mother of God and of saints, there are some who also depict what are described as contemporary "prophets," such as Archbishop Oscar Romero and Dorothy Day, who challenged others to live the gospel message and to put it into practice in concrete social situations.

Dismissal Catechesis (30 min.)

Getting Started

1. Prepare the space ahead of time with a circle of chairs around a centerpiece on the floor consisting of a purple cloth upon which is placed an Advent wreath. For this third Sunday of Advent, place a smaller rose-colored cloth over the purple one. You may add a cactus plant or other succulent in bloom.

2. Lead the candidates and catechumens to the circle and place the Lectionary on the table. Begin the prayer by lighting three candles on the wreath, two purple and one rose. Lead the group in singing verses one and two of "Every Valley" (Bob Dufford, NALR, 1970). Then pray:
   God of history and time, you promised to send us a Savior who will bring healing and sight, singing and dancing, freedom and justice. Give us eyes and ears to be attentive to the fulfillment of these promises in the world around us. Empower us to speak your Word in our home, workplace, and city. Open our minds and hearts that we might hear this Word proclaimed in our midst. We pray in the name of Christ, who brings new life, now and forever. Amen.

First Impressions

1. Begin the session by making the following comment about this, the third Sunday of Advent: *This third Sunday of Advent is traditionally called* Gaudete *Sunday.* Gaudete *is a Latin word meaning "rejoice." The third candle we lighted today is rose colored, to indicate the joy we experience; knowing that the Messiah's coming is near.*

2. Gather the participants into small groups to discuss the following: *What words or images in the Gathering Hymn, prayers, scriptures, or homily give you a sense of hope and joy?* When they have had sufficient time to discuss the question, ask the participants to share some of their responses with the large group. Summarize the input of the participants in a few sentences.

3. Continue to provide a brief overview of the scriptures in these words: *Today's passages present us with many signs of God's action in the midst of brokenness. The parched, dry desert breaks forth into abundant bloom, feeble hands are strengthened, the blind see, the deaf hear, the lame not only walk but also dance, and the mute not only speak but sing. The Lord's promised salvation is fulfilled in Jesus who is reputed for many wonders: lepers are cured, the dead are raised to life, the poor have the Good News preached to them, the hungry are fed, and captives are set free.* Invite the same small groups to deepen their sharing by asking them to discuss what hope and joy they find in these scriptures.

Making Connections

1. Gather the insights of the small groups and focus the sharing on the source of our joy.

2. Invite the whole group to offer their insights on God's promises in terms of our lives, asking: *What does it mean for us that the desert will bloom? The blind will see? Etc.*

3. Ask the participants to return to their small groups to discuss this question: *What signs of God's action, in the light of these promises, do you see in your family, workplace, or city today?* Invite a few groups to offer their insights and summarize these responses in a few sentences.

Prayer

Invite the participants to join in singing the response to Psalm 146, "Lord, come and save us," as you pray the verses. Begin this prayer for redemption, inviting the participants to think of and pray for specific people as you pray: *For all who are blind, open their eyes to the light of your promises. For all who are feeble or lame, strengthen their limbs that they might follow the path of truth and justice. For all who are dried up, quench their parched throats that their voices might bloom with songs of praise to you. For all who are deaf and mute, loosen their tongues and open their ears that the Good News might be ever on their lips and in their hearing. For those who are decaying with leprosy, inside or externally, cleanse their minds, spirits, and bodies with your anointing. For the broken and depleted, the crushed and downtrodden, lift and raise them from death's clutches. Amen.*

Extended Catechesis

SESSION FOCUS: *The Charism of Prophecy*

Gathering

A. Sunday:
1. Greet and welcome the sponsors and team members as they arrive. Invite them to join the circle of catechumens and candidates. Allow time for introductions if the group does not yet know one another.

2. Spend a few moments in quiet as the participants focus on the lighted Advent wreath. Ask one of the candidates or catechumens to share a brief summary of the Dismissal Catechesis.

3. Begin the prayer by asking all to sing two verses of the Gathering Hymn used at today's liturgy. Provide song-books in order that all may join in the singing. Proclaim the gospel, Matthew 11:2–11. Pray Psalm 146:6–7, 8–9, 9–10 with a sponsor reading the verses, and all saying or singing "Lord, come and save us" after each set of verses.

B. Weekday:
1. Use the same centerpiece as in the Dismissal Catechesis.

2. As the group gathers in the circle greet each participant. Light three candles on the Advent wreath. Allow time for introductions if the group does not yet know one another. Invite everyone to sit in quiet and think about the past few days. Ask them to share a sign of God's saving action that they recently experienced.

3. Lead this celebration of the Word:
   - Song: Gathering Hymn from Sunday's liturgy
   - Greeting and lighting of the Advent wreath

- First Reading: Isaiah 35:1–6, 10
- Sing Psalm 146:6–7, 8–9, 9–10
- Gospel: Matthew 11:2–11
- Silence
- Prayer: *God of all life, you come to save us. You send prophets to prepare the way, and speak your Word. We thank you for the prophets Isaiah, John the Baptist, and your greatest prophet, Jesus. Help us understand our call to be part of your saving action as we speak your Word in our world today. We ask this through Christ, the living Word. Amen.*

The Word (30 min.)

1. Invite a catechumen or candidate to share some of the ways in which the images of God's action in the scriptures are a cause of joy for us today. This summary of the Dismissal Catechesis can be deepened by asking everyone to offer their insights on this question: *What signs of God's action, in the light of these promises, do you see in your family, workplace, or city today?*

2. Prepare a presentation on the background of the sacred scriptures. These points and the information on the Word in Liturgy in the section Understanding this Sunday will help.
   - In the first reading from Isaiah, the prophet offers the people of Israel hope and joy: promising that God will ransom and bring them back to their land; help them along this difficult journey of return; and transform their desert (God's wrath) into full and abundant flowering (God's mercy).
   - The psalm celebrates the grace and mercy of God, who will be faithful to the covenant with Israel.
   - The gospel passage from Matthew occurs at the time when John the Baptist is in prison, during the ministry of Jesus. In answer to John's question as to the true identity of Jesus, Jesus points to signs of God's healing and mercy through the ministry of Jesus.
   - In contrast to the gospel reading last week, which emphasized the judgment of the Messiah, today's passage focuses on the qualities of mercy that mark the Messiah's reign.
   - The extraordinary personality and powerful mission of John the Baptist is lauded in this passage. Surprisingly, the calling of the followers of Jesus is said to surpass even that of the prophet John.

3. Ask the participants to gather into small groups to discuss the following questions: *What signs of God's mercy have you experienced in your own faith journey? In the light of your experiences, how would you describe Jesus to another? What is your reaction to the words of Jesus in this gospel, "Yet the least born into the kingdom of God is greater than he [John]?"* Invite the small groups back to the large gathering to share their insights.

Catholic Teaching (30 min.)

1. Continue in the large group, asking the participants to name the descriptive words and phrases that come to mind when they hear the word "prophet." Encourage them to name some of the prophets that they can think of either from the scriptures or persons they consider prophets in our day. These can be listed on newsprint, writing large enough for all to read.

2. Then present the following teaching on the charism of prophet, drawing upon their insights:
   The Old Testament scriptures recount the words and deeds of such prophets as Jeremiah, Isaiah, Ezekiel, and Daniel. Prophets are called by God to speak God's message in a specific historical situation. Prophets often speak a difficult word, calling people to change their ways and live in accordance with God's design. They also speak a word of hope that God will bring about justice, mercy, and new life. John the Baptist is the last great prophet in the Old Testament line. John is the greatest of prophets because he pointed and prepared the way for the Messiah.
   As we have learned in the past weeks, Christ, the Messiah, inaugurated a new final age with his coming. Through baptism all Christians share in Christ's identity as priest, prophet, and king. In this sacrament, we are part of a community of people who share in this responsibility of prophet. Jesus reveals that the mission of his followers will surpass even that of John. We exercise this prophetic call through the witness of our lived experience in Jesus.

3. Invite the participants to spend time responding to the Reflection and Questions found in the Participant Book on page 8. Encourage them to share their insights in pairs, sponsors and godparents with their candidates or catechumens.

4. In the large group, take time to listen to the reflections of the pairs as to the practical ways each person had experienced or witnessed to the prophetic call of the faithful.

Putting Faith into Practice

1. Invite a parishioner who is involved in prophetic activity on behalf of others—ministry of peace and justice, support for widows, widowers, or single parents and children—to present a witness on his or her lived experience of this prophetic activity.

2. This is a good week to explain the "O Antiphons" to the group. Use these or similar words:
   The "O Antiphons" are a series of seven antiphons or short verses sung in praying the Liturgy of the Hours, the public prayer of the Church for praising God and sanctifying the hours of the day. The antiphons are used at Vespers— Evening Prayer—and also before the gospel at Mass from December 17 to December 23. Taken from the prophetic and wisdom books of the Bible, the "O Antiphons" include these titles for Jesus: O Wisdom; O Lord of Lords; O Root of Jesse; O Key of David; O Radiant Dawn; O King of All Nations; and O Emmanuel (God with us). The antiphons invoke Christ to come and dwell in our lives.

Prayer

Invite the participants to pray in their same small groups. Direct them to ask God to prepare them to live out the prophetic role of the baptized. You might suggest that they pray silently or aloud, that sponsors place their hands upon their candidate or catechumen as they pray, or that the small groups hold hands as they pray. After sufficient time, lead the Prayer for Exorcism, (RCIA 94E), inviting the sponsors to place their hand on the shoulder of their catechumen or candidate as he or she bows or kneels. Close by leading the song "God Has Chosen Me" (Farrell, OCP, 1990).

Fourth Sunday of Advent

Understanding this Sunday: Background for Catechesis

The Word in Liturgy

Isaiah 7:10–14
Psalm 24:1–2, 3–4, 5–6
Romans 1:1–7
Matthew 1:18–24

Divine messages figure prominently in today's readings. In the first reading, the prophet Isaiah speaks to Ahaz, the king of Judah, on behalf of God. The context is that of state turmoil in the face of possible foreign invasion. The northern kingdom, Israel, has allied with Syria in hopes of fending off the Assyrians. When they attempt to enlist the support of Judah, however, Isaiah counsels King Ahaz to ally with no one, but trust God alone. This advice proves difficult for Ahaz to accept, frightened as he is by the great powers around him. His reluctance to ask for a sign (covered up by a pious suggestion that he does not wish to tempt God) suggests his fear of being drawn further into the counsels of Isaiah. To abandon political and military alliances no doubt seemed like madness. To trust God alone and refuse other forms of security represented a great risk to his kingdom and himself.

The sign the prophet gives him is the birth of a child to a young girl. (The Hebrew word for young girl was later translated into the Greek word for virgin. This Greek translation from about 150 B.C., the Septuagint, would have been known by Jesus and his contemporaries.) The name of the child is highly significant: Immanuel, which means "God is with us." The fulfillment of this sign was expected to occur within a short time and would point to the truth of the prophet's word from God. The king's wife, or someone in his harem, would become pregnant, and this would indicate that the king's line would continue and God would protect the kingdom. Christians, however, in looking back on this passage, saw in this sign a prefiguration of the virgin birth of Jesus. Through the mystery of the incarnation "God is with us," and one of his traditional titles indeed has been Emmanuel (the Greek spelling for the Hebrew Immanuel).

Joseph, in today's gospel, also receives a summons to trust God and be obedient in fearful circumstances. In first-century Palestine, betrothal was considered binding, and even though the couple did not yet live together, any sexual infidelity was regarded as adultery and was punishable by death. Mary's unexpected pregnancy was more than a cause for social embarrassment. It was a breach of sacred law. In his decision to divorce Mary quietly, Joseph's concern for the law was combined with mercy. Matthew then shows that, like the patriarch Joseph (whose interpretation of dreams played a significant role in the fate of the chosen people), this Joseph changed the course of his plans because of a communication he received in a dream. The figure of Joseph is crucial to Matthew's infancy narrative. His genealogy establishes Joseph in the line of David. His acceptance of Mary thus gives Jesus legal paternity and human lineage going back to David. His acceptance of the message of the angel (an annunciation) shows the child is the Son of God.

The name Jesus, from Joshua, means "God saves," indicating the child's mission. The miraculous events surrounding Jesus' conception and birth are elaborate commentaries on the identity and mission of the adult Christ we meet in the rest of the gospel.

Today's passage from Paul's letter to the Romans draws our attention to the person and mission of Jesus, and the "obedient faith" to which the Gentiles are called through the preaching of Paul, a messenger of the Good News. By way of introducing himself, Paul recapitulates the whole gospel message in a succinct fashion. Jesus is both God and man. His birth and earthly life show his humanity; his resurrection through the power of the Spirit shows his divinity. Thus, all three readings point to who Jesus is: the sign of God's presence with his people (Isaiah), true God and true man (Romans), the Son of God who has come to save us (Matthew). The focus of today's catechesis, as the Advent season draws to a close, concerns one aspect of his identity traditionally affirmed by the Church and echoed in today's readings: the virgin birth.

Catholic Doctrine

Virgin Birth

To say that the phrase "virgin birth" describes something unique is to engage in understatement. But that is precisely the suggestion, and more, which is being made by the Catholic Church when it espouses this teaching. It is important to note that while many people mistakenly associate this phrase with the birth of the Virgin Mary, virgin birth actually describes the entrance of *Jesus* into this world. The Spirit is responsible for Jesus' conception in the womb of Mary. The virgin birth, thus, is a unique manifestation of God's power and grace breaking into the world in an almost unfathomable mystery, rich in significance for believers. What is that significance?

To understand the significance of this mystery, one must see how the Church has articulated this teaching. This mystery has been more precisely described in three distinct aspects, that is, Mary retained her virginity (1) before, (2) during (or in), and (3) after the birth of Jesus. Each of these specific aspects illuminates a reality significant for the Church. The first aspect, virginal conception, underscores the core belief surrounding the Christian faith that the Messiah has only one father, his heavenly Father. Therefore, Jesus is truly God. He has an earthly mother, Mary, and therefore is also truly human. The second aspect, Mary remaining a virgin even during the birth itself, relies on the implication of Matthew 1:25 and underscores Mary's bodily integrity and her having been spared the pains of childbearing. The theologian Karl Rahner has described this second aspect, saying that because Mary herself is immaculately conceived (without stain of original sin), every moment from Jesus being conceived to the birth itself has been graced with distinction, is different, and is blessed. The third aspect, her perpetual virginity even after the birth, underscores Mary's continuing wholehearted commitment to Jesus and his mission and ministry (NDictTheol 1077–81).

New Testament scriptures attest to the virginity of Mary in Matthew 1:18–25 (today's gospel) and Luke 1:26–38. Both gospel accounts are primarily interested in what this indicates about Jesus, more so than Mary (as suggested above). Other texts (such as Mark 6:3) which speak about the "brothers and sisters of Jesus" are not in conflict with this teaching when it is understood that in that time and culture the expression "brothers and sisters" meant either cousins or the offspring of Joseph's widowed *sister,* who would be required by Jewish law to be taken in and raised by him (ModCathE 900).

As the great christological debates of the first centuries raged, the Fathers of the Church gave continual witness to the virgin birth, starting as early as St. Ignatius of Antioch (martyred in about 110 A.D.) and continuing with Clement of Alexandria (d. 215), Hilary of Poitiers, (d. 367), St. Athanasius (d. 373), St. Augustine (d. 430), St. Leo the Great (d. 461). Later commentators and teachers, such as St. Thomas Aquinas (d. 1274), affirmed this teaching as well. St. Augustine best sums up this train of thought, writing that Mary "remained a virgin in conceiving her Son, a virgin in giving birth to him, a virgin in carrying him, a virgin in nursing him at her breast, always a virgin" (*Sermo* 186, 1: PL 38, 999).

Contemporary Catholic Church teaching relies on this constant tradition. The Second Vatican Council reaffirmed this tradition, hailing Mary with words from the Eucharistic Prayer, saying that "the faithful must in the first place reverence the memory 'of the ever Virgin Mary, Mother of God and of our Lord Jesus Christ'" (LG 52).

Why is it important that Catholics uphold with great reverence Mary, the one who remains a virgin before, during, and after the birth of Jesus? Because this particular tradition in the Catholic experience proclaims both the role of Mary in salvation and the ministry of Jesus as Messiah. To uphold the virginity of Mary bespeaks God's absolute act in the incarnation (CCC 503) and positions Christ as the "new Adam" spoken of in scripture (CCC 504), who inaugurates the kingdom that produces new sons and daughters of God by adoption (CCC 505). The virginity of Mary also highlights her undivided devotion to God's plan (CCC 506). The affirmation of this unique event of virgin birth in world history is not a Catholic denigration of the female sex or of the conjugal act, nor is it considered a means by which the newborn Christ avoids the stain of original sin.

The concept of virgin birth is seen by the faithful as revealing the unique, miraculous action of God in the savior's entrance into this world, the intimate relationship between God and God's Son sharing in the same divine nature, and Mary's wholehearted cooperation in the plan of redemption. It has nothing to do with modern understandings of biology and everything to do with God's loving miracles astounding us and saving us.

Catholic Culture

The Virgin Mary has been the object of countless artistic depictions. In illustrating her perpetual virginity, artists have used the symbolic device of the walled garden, in Latin, the *hortus conclusus* (DictSymb 226).

The esteem with which Catholics hold Mary is indicated in the lyrical prayer of the Litany of the Blessed Virgin Mary that begins by referring to Christ, then to God (the Father, Son, and Spirit), and continues with titles for Mary as mother, virgin, and queen. The titles extolling her virginity read, "virgin most wise, virgin rightly praised, virgin rightly renowned, virgin most powerful, virgin gentle in mercy, faithful virgin . . ." (CathHous 344).

Dismissal Catechesis (30 min.)

Getting Started

1. Prepare the space ahead of time with a circle of chairs around a centerpiece arranged on the floor consisting of a purple cloth upon which is an Advent wreath. Encircle the wreath with white votive candles in glass holders, one for each participant. If available, place a painting, sculpture, or icon of Mary pregnant with the child Jesus in the center of the cloth.
2. Lead the candidates and catechumens to the circle and place the Lectionary in a stand upon the cloth and light all four of the Advent candles. As the group is seated, invite everyone to reflect briefly upon the centerpiece. Then lead them in singing the first three verses of "The King of Glory" (Willard F. Jabusch, Traditional Israeli Folk Song).

First Impressions

1. Invite the participants to recall a time when they were present at the birth of a child or a baptism. As they focus on one such event, ask them to name some of the traditions that surround these celebrations. Draw them into describing such things as (1) naming the child, (2) expression of future hopes for the child, and (3) stories that reveal the nature or traits of the child.
2. Explain the traditions surrounding the birth of a significant person in the Hebrew culture in these words: *In the Bible, a specific form of writing announced the birth of important persons. This included (1) an announcement of the birth by an angel—a messenger of God, (2) the naming of the person and the significance of the name, and (3) the name reflected the role that this person would play in the course of salvation history.* Invite all to recall the sacred scriptures in today's Liturgy of the Word and name those elements. Point out that Immanuel (Hebrew) and Emmanuel (Greek) mean "God Is With Us" and that Jesus means "God Saves."
3. Encourage the participants to continue their discussion in small groups, responding to these questions: *What is one thing that impressed you as you experienced the scriptures, the music, and the Church environment this morning? What in the scripture passages made you uncomfortable? What did you find enlivening?* In the large group gather a few responses to the questions and summarize their insights.

Making Connections

1. Remaining focused on the large gathering, share the background on the second reading from Romans 1:1–7 in these words: *Paul draws our attention to the person and mission of Jesus. He is clear in pointing out that Jesus is both God and man. His birth and earthly life indicate his humanity, Son of David, and his resurrection through the power of the Spirit shows his divinity, Son of God. Those who recognize Jesus and follow him, like the Romans, are called to holiness and obedient faith.*
2. Encourage everyone to discuss these questions in their same small groups: *What are some ways to cultivate holiness? When have you encountered obedient faith in a follower of Jesus? What characterized their life?* Invite the small groups to share their responses and begin to write with a gold or silver pen the attributes of holiness and obedient faith on labels (these can be name-tag size). Ask them to paste these labels, denoting the attributes of holiness, on the outside of the glass votive candle holders, replacing them around the center arrangement.

Prayer

Ask each person to search his or her heart to determine what attribute they feel called to pray for and act on as they anticipate Christmas. Then invite them to come forth and light their selected votive candle, bearing the attribute they have called to act upon, from one of the Advent candles. While each person approaches to take their candle, lead them in singing "The King of Glory Comes." The votive candle may be taken home as a reminder of their decision to grow in holiness.

Extended Catechesis

SESSION FOCUS: *Virgin Birth*

Gathering

A. **Sunday:**
1. Greet and welcome the sponsors and team members as they arrive. Invite them to join the circle of catechumens and candidates. Allow time for introductions if the participants do not as yet know one another.
2. Begin the prayer by inviting all to sit in silent prayer as you reverently name the following titles for Jesus: *O Wisdom—O Holy Word of God—O Sacred Lord—O Flower of Jesse's stem—O Key of David, O Royal Power of Israel—O Radiant Dawn—Splendor of Eternal Light—Sun of Justice—O King of All the Nations—Joy of Every Human Heart—O Keystone—O Emmanuel—King and Lawgiver—Desire of the Nations—Savior of All People—Jesus, God Who Saves.* Pause and invite a sponsor to proclaim the first reading from Isaiah 7:10–14. Lead the group in singing the refrain, "Let the Lord enter, he is king of glory" after each verse of Psalm 24:1–2, 3–4, and 5–6. Follow this by inviting all to stand and sing the Gospel Alleluia and hear the proclamation of the gospel, Matthew 1:18–25.

B. **Weekday:**
1. Use the same centerpiece as in the Dismissal Catechesis.
2. As the participants gather in the circle, greet and warmly welcome each person. Allow time for introductions if the participants do not as yet know one another. Invite the candidates and catechumens to share an experience of enacting the attributes of holiness and obedient faith over the past few days.
3. Lead this celebration of the Word:
   • Song: Gathering Song from Sunday's liturgy
   • Greeting and lighting of the Advent wreath
   • First Reading: Isaiah 7:10–14

- Sing Psalm 24:1–2, 3–4, 5–6
- Gospel Alleluia
- Gospel: Matthew 1:18–24
- Gospel Alleluia

The Word (30 min.)

1. Encourage the candidates and catechumens to name one thing that impressed them from the Dismissal Catechesis. Invite everyone to offer their thoughts, experiences, and feelings about "messengers from God." When they have finished, explain that God communicates to us through others, in the stillness of our heart, in something we read or hear, and through creation.

2. Continue to explain the first reading and the gospel in these words or your own words:
   These scripture passages describe the experiences of two men confused by the events surrounding their lives. The first, king of Judah, Ahaz, faces the probability of foreign invasion and finds himself and his nation in a state of turmoil. God speaks to him through the prophet Isaiah. Isaiah offers a message that seems folly to the king—trust in God alone and abandon all foreign alliances. Ahaz struggles, afraid that he will put his kingdom at risk. In the gospel, Joseph is also troubled. The young maiden to whom he is betrothed is pregnant. This was a breach of sacred law, for their betrothal was binding and any sexual infidelity was considered adultery. Joseph's heart went cold at the thought of putting Mary to death so he decided to divorce her privately. God speaks to the conflicted heart of Joseph through an angel who appeared in a dream. The message was clear, yet difficult to believe: "[F]or the child conceived in her is from the Holy Spirit. She will bear a son, and you are to name him Jesus, for he will save his people from their sins."

3. Ask everyone to reflect upon these messages from God by spending time in quiet with the exercise and questions in the Participant Book on page 10. After sufficient time, encourage the sponsors and godparents to gather with their catechumen or candidate to share the stories described in the Reflection exercise. In the large group invite the participants to discuss the faith of Mary and Joseph in the light of our own developing faith. Summarize the responses and explain that it takes great faith to believe in the God of the impossible.

Catholic Teaching (30 min.)

1. Continuing in the large group, point out the Church's teaching on the virgin birth, using the Catholic Doctrine section found in Understanding this Sunday:
   - The term "virgin birth" seems a contradiction, yet the teaching of the Catholic Church on this doctrine is not about biology but concerns a unique manifestation of God's power and grace breaking into the world in an unfathomable mystery.
   - The virgin birth refers to Mary's perpetual virginity before, during, and after the birth of Jesus.
   - The significance of Mary, Virgin and Mother, is this: first, it underscores the traditional belief that Jesus, the Messiah, has only one Father in heaven and is thus truly God; second, Mary, a virgin even in birth, indicates that she, conceived without sin or the effects of sin, did not suffer the pains of childbirth; and third, her perpetual virginity after the birth of Jesus indicates Mary's wholehearted commitment to Jesus' mission and ministry.
   - This tradition, upholding the Virgin Mary, Mother of God and our Lord Jesus Christ, has been constant throughout Catholic history from the earliest days of the Church.
   - The virginity of Mary reveals the unique and miraculous action of God in the birth of Jesus, the Savior; the intimate relationship shared by the Father and the Son; the integration of full humanity and full divinity in Jesus; and Mary's full cooperation with the plan of redemption.

2. This would be a good time to allow the participants to raise any questions as to the Church's teaching on Mary and its significance for our faith life. You may choose to have a panel from the parish staff—priest, deacon, and/or pastoral minister—to help you respond to the questions.

Putting Faith into Practice

1. Encourage the participants to gather in the same pairs to brainstorm specific ways in which they can grow into the faith demonstrated by Joseph and Mary. Ask them to choose one action they feel God is calling them to take as a "leap of faith" and write it in the Participant Book on page 11, in the section entitled "I want to put my faith into action by."

2. Have some books on display about the lives of people who have taken a similar "leap of faith." Talk a little about each book and encourage the participants to borrow one of these to read during the next weeks. Some possible titles include:
   - *Butler's Lives of the Saints,* eds. Herbert Thurston and Donald Attwater (Allen, TX: Christian Classics, a division of Thomas More Publishing, 1995).
   - Norris, Kathleen, *The Cloister Walk*, and *Dakota: A Spiritual Geography* (New York: Riverhead Books, 1996).
   - Durka, Gloria, *Companions for the Journey Series: Praying with Julian of Norwich, Praying with Hildegard of Bingen* (Winona MN: St. Mary's Press, 1989 and 1991).
   - Meehan, Bridget Mary, *Praying with Passionate Women*, (New York: Crossroad Publishing Company, 1995).
   - Bielecki, Tessa, *Holy Daring: An outrageous gift to modern spirituality from St. Teresa the grand wild woman of Avila*, (Rockport, MA: Element Press, 1994).

Prayer

Focus the attention of the group upon the artwork depicting Mary, pregnant, virgin. If the piece is small you may choose to pass it around the circle as you play some instrumental Marian music. Then pray in these or similar words:
Virgin Mary, Mother of God and our mother, we ask you to intercede for us that we might have the courage to risk everything as we step out in faith and follow the message of the Lord. Just as you gave your assent to the announcement of the angel and walked the impossible journey toward the birth of Jesus, let us walk this same road with you at our side. Steep us in holiness. Inspire us to be obedient to the angels God sends to us. Complete in us the birth of Jesus to a world that awaits his coming once again. We ask you all this, Mary, in the name of your Son and our Brother, Jesus. Amen.

CHRISTMAS SEASON

Christmas, Mass during the Day

Understanding this Feast:

Background for Catechesis

The Word in Liturgy

Isaiah 52:7–10
Psalm 98:1, 2–3, 3–4, 5–6
Hebrews 1:1–6
John 1:1–18 [or (short form) 1:1–5, 9–14]

The liturgical books provide four Mass formularies with which to celebrate the Solemnity of Christmas: a vigil Mass on Christmas eve, and then one at midnight, one at dawn, and one during the day. Different historical factors and pieties are responsible for the development of each of these celebrations, but it is the Mass during the day that is the most ancient celebration. The perceptive observer will note that this original observance is focused less on the details of the historical event of Jesus' birth and more on the timeless meaning of the Incarnation for the believer. Consistent with this insight, we focus today especially on the reason behind the birth of the Word made flesh: "for our salvation." The wonderful truth of the Incarnation is that because of Christ's coming in human flesh, we can be drawn to the Father through him.

The first reading's joyful proclamation of Good News is an announcement of Yahweh's return to Zion, a triumphant return from exile which reveals God's salvation in the sight of the nations (Psalm 98). The image we are given is of a messenger bringing the news to Jerusalem that the God of Israel reigns over all peoples. In the midst of the "ruins of Jerusalem," the people experience the comfort of a God who has "redeemed Jerusalem" (v. 9). The scene is regal in scope: No focus on the homeless child in a manger, but a victorious king reclaiming his royal city. Psalm 98 echoes those same images, a joyful victory chant at God's triumph revealed before all people.

The letter to the Hebrews stresses the revelatory character of the Incarnation, with God described as speaking to us in this the final age through the Son, the "reflection of God's glory." God spoke to our ancestors "in many and various ways" (v. 1), but now the superiority of God's full revelation is shown forth in Jesus, who has cleansed us from our sins. Once again, the meaning of the Incarnation is described in terms of its redemptive impact on the human condition. Here, too, Christ is portrayed in royal splendor "at the right hand of the Majesty on high" (v. 3) rather than in the humble conditions of his birth.

The prologue of John's gospel has long been recognized as our most profound meditation on the meaning of the Incarnation. It proclaims the theme of God's self-disclosure in the Word made flesh, who comes as light in the darkness, the "glory as of a father's only son, full of grace and truth" (v. 14). This understanding of the Incarnation as God's self-disclosure in the human flesh of Jesus is a fundamental aspect of the Incarnation. In Jesus we see divine love revealed as saving grace. The Son, who is "the reflection of God's glory and the exact imprint of God's very being" (Hebrews 1:3), is now proclaimed as the fulfillment of the ancient prophecy of "Good News," a message that brings comfort and redemption to God's chosen people. The Church's doctrinal assertion of the divinity of Jesus becomes, in its liturgical proclamation, an experience of saving grace, the "power to become children of God" for all who have "received him" and "believed in his name" (v. 12).

Dismissal Catechesis (30 min.)

Getting Started

1. Prepare the space ahead of time with a circle of chairs around a table draped with a white cloth, covered with a smaller gold fabric. On the table place several white taper candles and a Christmas crèche.

2. Lead the candidates and catechumens to the circle and place the Lectionary on the table, lighting the candles. Remain standing as you lead the group in singing several verses of the Gathering Hymn used at today's liturgy. Invite all to be seated as the first reading from Isaiah 52:7–10 is proclaimed. Encourage all to join in singing the response to Psalm 98, "All the ends of the earth have seen the saving power of God," as you pray the verses, or the song, "All the Ends of the Earth" (Bob Dufford, New Dawn Music, 1981). Then pray in these or your own words:
   Most powerful God, you sent your Son, Jesus, to be born among us and dwell with us. We are filled with joy as we behold your salvation. The fullness of your revelation, spoken through the prophets, is completed in Jesus, your Word. Give us the eyes to see and the ears to hear the Good News celebrated in this feast. We ask this through your Word made flesh, Jesus. Amen.

First Impressions

1. Begin by inviting all to close their eyes and to recall what they saw, heard, smelled, or felt as they celebrated the Liturgy of the Word today. You may choose to mention some of the images, words, or music that were part of the parish liturgy to help the participants remember their experience. After a time of silence invite all to share the one impression that stood out for them today, in the large group.

2. Offer this presentation on the scriptures, adding whatever is appropriate for your group from the Word in Liturgy section of Understanding this Feast:
   On this feast of Christmas we celebrate the Incarnation. This wonderful truth means that because of Christ's coming in human flesh, we are drawn to the Father through him. This feast proclaims God's self-disclosure in the Word made flesh, Jesus, who comes as light in the darkness, the "glory as a father's only son, full of grace and truth." The celebration of this mystery of the Incarnation goes on for many weeks in the liturgical calendar, beginning today and concluding with the Baptism of our Lord.
   Invite the participants to listen as you slowly and prayerfully name several images from the scriptures:
   Imagine the beautiful feet of those who proclaim the Good News.
   Imagine the people so joyful at their return from exile that they break out in song.

Imagine the beginning of creation, as the Word, with God brought all things into being.
Imagine Jesus, Son of God, the Word made flesh, born among us.
Remember the deeds of Jesus, revealing the fullness of the Father's love for humankind.
Remember that Jesus came and brought light in our darkness.
Remember the Word made flesh died for our sins and rose from the dead.
Remember the glory of the risen Jesus, who now sits at the right hand of the Father.

Making Connections

1. Encourage the participants to turn to the Reflection and Questions found in the Participant Book on page 14. Give them enough time to prayerfully reflect upon these exercises. When they have finished, ask each person to share one insight into the meaning of the Incarnation with their partner. In the large group invite the pairs to complete this sentence as a way of summarizing their discussion: *In my life the Incarnation is Good News because. . . .*

2. Deepen their understanding of the Incarnation by preparing a presentation on the Incarnation. Emphasize the following points:
   • Jesus is Son of God, promised Messiah and Redeemer.
   • Jesus is the Word of God, the "logos." Because he came in human flesh we are drawn to the Father through him.
   • The Word, Jesus, is God's revelation—self-disclosure—who came to be light in our darkness.
   • The Son is a "reflection of God's glory, an exact imprint of God's very being" (Hebrews 1:3).

3. Invite the pairs to share their insights and ideas on this question: How are we to respond to this gift of God's own self in human flesh? After they have had time to brainstorm several possibilities, invite each pair to write one way of responding to the Incarnation on a slip of gold paper.

Prayer

Focus the attention of the gathering on the lighted candles and the crèche. Encourage the pairs to read aloud their responses. When they have finished, direct each pair to approach the center of the circle and place their gold slip of paper on the table near the crib scene. Invite a team member to proclaim the gospel, John 1:1–18, indicating that all stand for the proclamation. Conclude by singing "Joy to the World" (Melody, George Friedrich Handel; text, Isaac Watts).

Feast of the Holy Family

SUNDAY WITHIN THE OCTAVE OF CHRISTMAS

Understanding this Sunday:
Background for Catechesis

The Word in Liturgy

Sirach 3:2–7, 12–14
Psalm 128:1–2, 3, 4–5
Colossians 3:12–21 [or (short form) 3:12–17]
Matthew 2:13–15, 19–23

The Feast of the Holy Family is a modern addition to the universal calendar of the Roman Church (since 1921, when it was placed as the First Sunday after Epiphany). Like many feasts added in modern times, its emphasis tends to be more on a doctrinal theme than some specific action of God or event in the life of Christ. Its contemporary character is also shown by the way it seeks to instruct and inspire through an obvious appeal to sentiment and emotion. The relocation of Holy Family Sunday to the Christmas season is an even more recent adjustment to the calendar, stemming from the reform of 1969. Situated so closely to Christmas, today's celebration cannot help but resonate with overtones of the incarnation. By highlighting the family as the context into which Jesus was born, today's liturgy underscores the fact of his full humanity. We proclaim that the Word made flesh sanctifies everything that he has taken upon himself: our full human nature including, today, the reality of family life. The family, made holy by virtue of Jesus' life with Mary and Joseph, becomes a source of holiness for every Christian. The fourth commandment, today's doctrinal focus, is crucial to both Jewish and Christian understandings of family life, and thus is a suitable teaching to reflect upon on this feast.

The Book of Sirach (also known as Ecclesiasticus) is part of the Wisdom literature, written most likely during the second century (circa 180 B.C.) in Jerusalem by Joshua Ben Sira, a member of the scribal class. Today's reading is considered by many scholars to be a commentary on the fourth commandment. The author's concern lies with the quality of relationships that must characterize family life. His suggestion that filial piety "will be credited to you against your sins" (v. 14) should be regarded as a way of offering encouragement to the reader to show reverence and care for one's parents, not as a guarantee of divine forgiveness.

However, the comment does support the sense of today's celebration that family life can be a source of holiness when lived within God's commandments.

The reading from Colossians has been interpreted as part of an ancient baptismal catechesis (3:5–4:1). Paul's admonition to "put on love" is suggestive of the ritual clothing of the newly baptized in a white garment, an early Christian custom expressive of new life and holiness. Because of baptism, a Christian is recognized as "chosen . . . holy . . . beloved" (v. 12) and therefore one's behaviors and relationships must reflect those qualities. Paul's list of behaviors which characterize family members is called a "household code." Such lists were common in Greek philosophical writings of the day. Paul's "household code" is transformed into specifically Christian teaching, however, by his insistence that family relationships be carried on "in the Lord" (vv. 18, 20). Thus, the reading recognizes the family as a place where faith is formed and holiness achieved.

Today's gospel reading belongs to the specialized literary form known as "infancy narrative." The author's concern is not primarily to supply historical details from Jesus' childhood (although it is obviously important to him to establish Nazareth as the place of Jesus' upbringing), but rather it is to proclaim to the reader the theological truth of Jesus' identity as Messiah, Son of God and Savior. Using a technique known as *midrash,* and surely familiar to his Jewish audience, Matthew skillfully weaves together a series of allusions to people and events from the Hebrew scriptures designed to show that Jesus is the new Moses and the new Israel of God, called out of Egypt. Joseph, an interpreter of dreams—as was Joseph in the book of Genesis—guides his family with divine help through perils to safety. Jesus, in his human destiny, recapitulates the entire history of the chosen people.

The connection of this text with today's feast and with the doctrinal theme chosen for our catechesis must not be overstated. It is clear that Jesus' reverence toward his parents is not the direct point of this passage. But as one fully human like us, Jesus' way to holiness surely would have included observance of this commandment of the Law.

Catholic Doctrine

The Fourth Commandment:
Honor Your Father and Mother

The idea of law in the Old Testament derives from the companion notion of divine election. Israel is chosen by God because of divine love. Thus, the commands of God are not meant to be a burden, but a light, a guide. The most commonly used Hebrew term for law is *torah*, which means instruction or guidance. There are many laws given in the Old Testament, but the Decalogue is considered the foundation of all other commandments and instructions.

The evangelists indicate that when Jesus is asked which commandment is the greatest, he responds with the twofold instruction to love God and to love one's neighbor, much as did Rabbi Hillel. (See Mark 12:29–31, and parallel versions in Matthew 22:34–40 and Luke 10:25–28.) While Jesus himself embodies the New Law and the New Covenant, he does not seek to abolish the old. Indeed, Jesus specifically preaches that he has come to fulfill the law (Matthew 5:17). His attitude toward the law is thus one of reverence and respect—even if his contemporary critics accused him of not following all its prescriptions. The portrait painted in the New Testament is that Jesus not only fulfills the law, but follows it more closely in its intent than those who claimed to follow it and who, in turn, criticized him.

Jesus upheld the responsibility enjoined by the fourth commandment (Mark 7:10–12). This commandment, in its original context, addressed adult Israelites concerning the needs of their aged parents. The aged were not to be judged on the basis of their functionality but on their intrinsic worth as human beings. The fourth commandment not only addresses adult children in their relationship to their aged parents, but also extends to the relationship between young children and their parents, and, by extension, treats a broad range of issues related to the individual's submission to proper authority (CCC 2199).

Catholic teaching treats this commandment in the broadest sense because the family is seen as the basic unit of society (CCC 2207), established as such by God's plan (CCC 2203). Echoing the Second Vatican Council, John Paul II describes the family as the "domestic church" (FC 21). In a letter addressed to families, John Paul II examines the fourth commandment

and writes, "The family is a community of particularly intense interpersonal relationships: between spouses, between parents and children, between generations. It is a community which must be safeguarded in a special way. And God cannot find a better safeguard than this: "Honor." . . . *The fourth commandment* is closely linked to the *commandment of love*. Honor cannot be explained fully without reference to love: the love of God and of one's neighbor" (Letter to Families from Pope John Paul II, February 2, 1994, #15, Vatican translation, St. Paul Books & Media, Boston, MA).

Catholic teaching on the fourth commandment enumerates the duties of family members. Children are to respect their parents (CCC 2215) and obey them (CCC 2216). Parents are to provide for their children's education (CCC 2221), regarding them as God's children and full human beings (CCC 2222). Through the grace of marriage, they also bear the responsibility to evangelize them (CCC 2225).

Recognizing the many pivotal roles of the family, on this feast the Church prays, "Father in heaven, creator of all . . . teach us the sanctity of human love, show us the value of family life, and help us to live in peace with all . . . that we may share in your life for ever" (*Sacramentary,* Feast of the Holy Family, Alternate Opening Prayer).

Catholic Culture

The Holy Family as depicted in art represents Jesus, Mary, and Joseph, usually in a domestic setting or in traditional scenes taken from the infancy narrative, such as the birth of Jesus, the adoration of the Magi, or the flight into Egypt. Artists have also represented Mary feeding the infant Jesus and Joseph working with a young Jesus in a carpentry shop. The Middle Ages witnessed a burst of popularity in artistic depictions of the Holy Family and often expanded the grouping to include Elizabeth or Anne, with some artists going so far as to represent the kinship of Jesus with dozens of figures. By the time of the Counter-Reformation, however, there was a reaction against such domesticity and a different approach was taken in representing the Holy Family by depicting in the same work two trinities, that is, the earthly Jesus, Mary, and Joseph, and the heavenly Father, Son, and Holy Spirit (OxA&A, 231).

Pope Paul VI wrote that the Holy Family in Nazareth is "a kind of school where we may begin to discover what Christ's life was like and even to understand his Gospel. . . . First, we learn from its silence . . . [and] how to meditate in peace and quiet, to reflect on the deeply spiritual. Second, we learn about family life. May Nazareth serve as a model of what the family should be. May it show us the family's holy and enduring character. . . . Finally, in Nazareth, the home of a craftsman's son, we learn about work and the discipline it entails" (Pope Paul VI, address, Nazareth, January 5, 1964, found in LitHrs, vol. 1, Feast of the Holy Family, Office of Readings, pp. 426–28).

Dismissal Catechesis (30 min.)

Getting Started

1. Prepare the space ahead of time with a circle of chairs around a table draped with a white cloth, covered with a smaller gold fabric. Place a work of art (painting, icon, or statue) of the Holy Family on the table next to several white taper candles.
2. Lead the candidates and catechumens to the circle and place the Lectionary on the table and light the candles. Lead the participants in singing the refrain to Psalm 128, *"Happy are those who fear the Lord and walk in his ways,"* as you pray the verses.

First Impressions

1. Help the group recall the Liturgy of the Word by calling to mind these images from the scriptures. Invite them to close their eyes and listen as you slowly name the following: *A father is set up in honor before his children—A mother's authority is confirmed by the Lord—Take care of your father when he is old—Even if his mind fail, be considerate—Your wife shall be like a fruitful vine—Clothe yourselves with heartfelt mercy, kindness, humility, meekness, and patience—Over all these virtues put on love, which binds the rest together—Children, obey your parents in everything—Get up, take the child and his mother, and flee to Egypt—An angel of the Lord appeared in a dream to Joseph—They settled in a town called Nazareth—The prophecy "He shall be called a Nazarean" was fulfilled.*
2. Invite the participants to gather into small groups to discuss these questions. *What image from the scriptures did you find affirming? How was Joseph able to lead his family to safety? Name some ways God has protected your family.*
3. As you focus the attention of the catechumens and candidates back to the large group, invite them to share a few of their responses. Summarize their comments briefly.

Making Connections

1. Ask the participants to define "family" by naming a phrase that comes to mind when they think of family life today, in its various forms and structures. Record their insights on newsprint, writing large enough for all to read. Then refocus the discussion on the scriptures by asking this question: *What qualities of family life are offered as an ideal in the scriptures heard today?* List these ideas on another newsprint.
2. Gather the participants into small groups and invite them into a discussion of these questions: *What are some practical ways that this parish could enhance family life? What can each of us do to transform the quality of our own family?* Invite the groups to record their practical ideas on two sheets of newsprint—one entitled "Parish" and the other "My Family"—hanging on the wall. When all have finished, review the responses of the small groups with everyone.
3. Encourage the catechumens and candidates to write their individual action in the Participant Book in the section entitled "Things I want to remember." Make a list of the ideas listed for the parish to act on and save these to be used in the Extended Catechesis session.

Prayer

Invite everyone to reflect in silence, thinking of one blessing they would like to ask God to pour out upon families today. After sufficient time, create a Litany for Families by directing the participants to name their petition, after which all will respond, *"Jesus, Mary, and Joseph, teach us love by your model of family life."* Close with the proclamation of Colossians 3:12–21, followed by a brief silence.

Extended Catechesis

SESSION FOCUS: *The Fourth Commandment: Honor Your Father and Mother*

Gathering

A. Sunday:

1. Greet and welcome the sponsors and team members as they arrive. Invite them to join the circle of catechumens and candidates.
2. Ask the participants to offer their feelings and reactions as they look at the art piece of the Holy Family or think about the Holy Family. Then pray in these or your own words: *God, you call us to be one family bound together in love. As a model for that love, you sent your Son to this earth, born into the human family of Mary and Joseph. As Joseph protected his family from the evil plots of wicked leaders, you reassure us that family life today is within your protective embrace. Let us be slow to judge the new forms and shapes of family life today. Open us to reconcile with members of our own family. Help us as we strive to live in holiness and love with parents and siblings, offspring and in-laws, and all our extended family. Amen.*
3. Ask a sponsor to proclaim the first reading from Sirach 3:2–6, 12–14. Lead the group in singing the refrain to Psalm 128 and the Gospel Alleluia. Invite all to stand as a team member proclaims the gospel, Matthew 2:13–15, 19–23.

B. Weekday:

1. Use the same centerpiece as described for the Dismissal Catechesis.
2. As the participants gather in the circle, greet and warmly welcome each person. Invite everyone who wishes to share something they observed this week about the holiness of family life today.
3. Lead this celebration of the Word:
   - Song: Gathering Song from Sunday's liturgy
   - Greeting and lighting of the candles
   - Opening Prayer: Use prayer in section A. 2.
   - First Reading: Sirach 3:2–7, 12–14
   - Sing Psalm 128
   - Gospel Alleluia
   - Gospel: Matthew 2:13–15, 19–23

The Word (30 min.)

1. Ask a catechumen or candidate to share some of the insights from the Dismissal Catechesis, using the newsprint as a guide.

2. Invite the participants to close their eyes and place themselves into the context of the gospel through this meditation: *You are a good Jew trying to decide whether or not to join this humble sect that call themselves Christians. You are torn between the faith of your ancestors and the marvelous hope of the Messiah preached by the apostles. You join a small group of Christians led by Matthew, a follower of Jesus, for their special meal called the "breaking of the bread." There they gather and share food and clothing and give money to be used for the poor. You are impressed by their generosity. They begin to share stories about this Messiah whom they call Jesus. You hear the story of his earthly father, Joseph the carpenter, a good, holy, and hardworking man, and his mother, Mary. The tale begins with Jesus' birth in a cave in Bethlehem and a visit by astrologers from the East. They tell of Joseph visited by a messenger of God in a dream, warning him to flee the slaughter of the male babies by King Herod. You begin to see the significance of this Jesus as the new Moses, the new Israel, who is also God's Son. Finally, when the story relates another visit by an angel to Joseph and his conse-quent settling in the region of Galilee in a town called Nazareth, you are convinced. This Jesus must be the promised Messiah, for the prophets said, "He shall be called a Nazarean" (Luke 2:40).*

3. Invite the participants into small groups to share their insights on these questions: *In portraying Jesus as the new Moses, what message did Matthew offer the early believers? What does this mean for us today? What does Joseph's dependence upon God's protection indicate for your family life?* In the large group gather a few insights from the discussions.

4. Offer this explanation of the first reading from Sirach 3:2–6, 12–14: *This passage from the wisdom literature of the Hebrew scriptures is part of a larger section on family life, considered to be a commentary on the fourth command-ment. The scribe Joshua Ben Sira is concerned with the quality of relationships that must characterize family life. It is especially focused upon the manner in which adult children are to respect and honor their elderly parents.* Elicit some of the characteristics of family relationships mentioned in this passage.

Catholic Teaching (30 min.)

1. Continue the discussion on familial relationships by inviting all to name the qualities implied by the word "honor." These can be listed on newsprint, writing large enough for all to see. Then invite the participants to turn to their Participant Book and spend some time responding to the Reflection and Questions on page 16.

2. In the same small groups invite everyone to share their insights on the questions. After allowing sufficient time for this discussion, invite several responses from the small groups in the large gathering.

3. Present the Church's teaching on the fourth commandment, "Honor Your Father and Mother," emphasizing these points:
   - The law presented in the Hebrew scriptures flows out of the notion of being chosen. Thus, the commands of God are a light or guide, rather than a burden.
   - In its original context, the fourth commandment was addressed to adult Israelites concerning the needs of their aged parents. Later, the fourth commandment was extended to include the relationships between young children and their parents, spouses and generations of family members.
   - The core of honor is the practice of justice, bound together in love. Thus, honor includes respect, obedience, care, nurture, guidance, and selflessness.

Putting Faith into Practice

1. Invite the participants to name some of the structures that threaten family interpersonal relationships in today's society. List these on newsprint. Ask everyone to gather back into the same small groups to brainstorm practical ideas on how this faith community can strengthen family relationships by "honoring" one another. Point out the work of the candidates and catechumens from the Dismissal Catechesis as a starting point for the brainstorming. Emphasize the concept of "honoring" family members and "honoring" family life. Ask the groups to determine one action and share their suggestion in the large gathering. Write their responses on a second sheet of newsprint.

2. Invite a guest either from the parish staff or a parish ministry to speak about the ways your parish strengthens family life today. Have them mention ministries to divorced and separated families, engaged couples, senior families, and single-parent families. Encourage a participant to summarize for the speaker the recommendations of the small groups to strengthen the quality of family life in the parish. Offer an opportunity for the candidates and catechumens to become involved in one of the ministries already in place. Determine a few recommendations for new family life events or ministries and prepare a letter to the pastor and pastoral council asking that these recommendations be considered.

Prayer

Invite everyone to pray in silence for family life today. The partic-ipants may choose to pray for their own families and the specific families they know who are struggling. Then proclaim the second reading, Colossians 3:12–21. Close with this prayer:
Jesus, God and man, you were born into a human family to model for us the sanctity of family life. Teach us the sanctity of human love that binds all families together in you and in God. Show us the way to respect, honor, and trust our aged parents and our newborn family members alike. Break down the barriers to forgiving one another, drawing us instead to love your image present in every human heart. Move us to act for the sake of family life, to create a better society and a more perfect church. Amen.

Epiphany

Understanding this Sunday:
Background for Catechesis

The Word in Liturgy

Isaiah 60:1–6
Psalm 72:1–2, 7–8, 10–11, 12–13
Ephesians 3:2–3, 5–6
Matthew 2:1–12

The Solemnity of the Epiphany has an extremely rich liturgical tradition, stemming from the earliest Christian centuries. In the churches of the East, this day has occupied a place of even greater prominence than Christmas. Rome has assimilated it into the Christmas season where too often many think of it only as a commemoration of the historical visit of the Magi to the newly born Christ child. However, the richer meaning of the feast is suggested by translating its name, *epiphania,* which means "revelation." Associated with this feast historically are several "revelations" of Christ—to the Magi, at his baptism in the Jordan, and at Cana in Galilee as he worked the first of his "signs." We draw attention today to the way in which the feast continues to unfold the Christmas mystery, highlighting the revelation of God's saving love in Jesus. We focus in a particular way on the universality of God's offer of salvation, symbolized by the presence of the Gentiles, alluded to in all three readings.

The first reading reflects the joy felt by the inhabitants of Jerusalem after their return from the Exile. God's promise of deliverance has been fulfilled and that saving act is like a beacon of light shining before the entire world, revealing the compassion and love of the Lord. It is that splendid act of mercy that has drawn even the Gentiles to the Holy City, proclaiming the praises of the Lord as they stream toward Jerusalem from every corner of the earth. The refrain of the responsorial psalm ("Lord, every nation on earth will adore you") underscores the universal import of God's deliverance of the chosen people.

Paul sees in his own ministry to the Gentiles a similar manifestation of God's gracious offer of salvation to all people. He calls it a "mystery" that the Gentiles have become "sharers in the promise" (v. 6), a mystery "made known to me by revelation" (v. 3). Nothing in Paul's background as a Pharisee, a strict observer of the Law, could have prepared him for such a startling revelation. Convinced as he had been of the privileged place of the Jewish people in God's plan of salvation, and remembering how fixated he was on the importance of a careful observance of the Law in order to be righteous in God's eyes, Paul writes now with wonder that Jew and Gentile alike are "members of the same body" (v. 6).

This same motif is echoed in the gospel, where the Magi—foreigners—are drawn to the Savior by the light of a star. These pagans, unschooled in the Law and ignorant of the prophets, nonetheless find the Christ and adore him. Matthew makes a point of contrasting their attitude with that of King Herod, the chief priests, and scribes, and indeed "all Jerusalem" (v. 3). The Gentile astrologers who follow the light of the star are seen as the truly enlightened ones. "Enlightenment" in early Christian parlance referred to baptism. Catechumens preparing for baptism are in a unique position to appreciate the journey toward enlightenment represented in today's readings and lived out by them in their catechumenal process.

Catholic Doctrine

Universal Offer of Salvation

Reflecting on the mystery of the Church, the Second Vatican Council wrote, "Christ is the light of all nations; and it is, accordingly, the heartfelt desire of this sacred Council . . . that, by proclaiming his Gospel to every creature (cf. Mark 16:15), it may bring to all . . . that light of Christ which shines out visibly from the Church" (LG 1). The Church's self-understanding described in the dogmatic constitution on the church, *Lumen Gentium*, is embodied in today's feast which proclaims that all people are attracted to and find salvation in the radiance of God's light. In *Lumen gentium* nn. 15–17, the bishops addressed the Church's relationship with other Christians (15) and with non-Christians (16), emphasizing that the Church's mandate from the Lord himself is ultimately to preach God's offer of salvation to the very ends of the earth (17). Epiphany means "showing forth" or "manifestation." In the context of the Christmas season, it is Jesus, the Word made flesh, who is shown as the light of all people (John 1:4).

The special preface for this day also reiterates: "Today you revealed in Christ your eternal plan of salvation and showed him as the light of all peoples" (Preface for Epiphany, Roman Missal). Several eucharistic prayers also illuminate and carry forward this theme of universality: "From age to age you [God] gather a people to yourself, so that from east to west a perfect offering may be made to the glory of your name" (Eucharistic Prayer III); and "You [God] have gathered us here around the table of your Son, in fellowship with the Virgin Mary, Mother of God, and all the saints. In that new world where the fullness of peace will be revealed, gather people of every race, language, and way of life to share in the one eternal banquet with Jesus Christ the Lord" (Eucharistic Prayer for Masses of Reconciliation II).

The Church's missionary impulse derives from the conviction that all are meant to share in the banquet of God's love. The Council asserted, "The Church's essential nature is universal . . . preaching the Word of God and proclaiming the kingdom throughout the whole world" (AG 1).

St. Leo the Great preached: "The loving providence of God . . . decreed that all nations should be saved in Christ. . . . A promise had been made to the holy patriarch Abraham in regard to these nations. He was to have a countless progeny, born not from his body but from the seed of faith. His descendants are therefore compared with the array of the stars. . . . Let the full number of the nations now take their place in the family of the patriarchs. . . . Dear friends, now that we have received instruction in the revelation of God's grace, let us celebrate with spiritual joy the day of our first harvesting, of the first calling of the Gentiles. . . . This came to be fulfilled . . . from the time when the star beckoned the three wise men out of their distant country and led them to recognize and adore the King of heaven and earth. The obedience of the star calls us to imitate its humble service: to be servants, as best we can, of the grace that invites all . . . to find Christ" (*Sermo* 3 in *Epiphania Domini*, 1–3, 5: PL 54, 240–44, found in Liturgy of the Hours, Office of Readings for Epiphany).

Catholic Culture

The coming of the Magi to Bethlehem has been depicted in Christian art throughout the centuries. One unusual such depiction was commissioned by Ludovico Gonzaga for the small chapel in the family chapel at Mantua, Italy (1464 A.D.) and is now on display at the Uffizi Gallery, Florence. The panel upon which this scene is painted is slightly curved inward, that is, it is concave. This perspective device employed by the artist, Andrea Mantegna, is the same as that which enhances perspective in modern times for large cinema movie screens. If the viewer stands at the center of the circle of which this painting forms the arc, then the "picture plane, equidistant from [the viewer] at all points, will seem to disappear and the effect of the illusion will be greatly enhanced" (HistItal 390). A seated Mary holds the infant Jesus in her lap at the mouth of a dark cave surrounded by a multitude of cherubs. A winding road leads down out of the horizon from which the procession of Magi are arriving. The elder magus is already on his knees, paying homage to the Christ child as the others still make their way down the long road. An unexpected element has been added to this unique depiction: the shape of the star directly above the cave is seven-pointed, symbolic of the Seven Joys of Mary (one of which is the Adoration). The bottom-most ray of the star is the longest, arrowing down directly above Mary's (and the infant's) head, perhaps in reference to the scriptural prophecy given by Simeon, "and you yourself a sword will pierce" (Luke 2:35).

Catholic custom associated with this joyful season of the year, in spite of the festive nature of Christmas, nonetheless includes that which is celebrated later: the saving passion and death of Jesus. Gloriously decorated and adorned Christmas trees are a relatively modern practice derived from medieval mystery plays which depicted the tree of paradise and the Christmas light or candle symbolizing Christ, light of the whole world. The tree is usually set up just before Christmas and remains in its prominent place until after this feast of the Epiphany. The prayer which the Church offers in blessing the Christmas tree includes references not only to the joy of this season but looks forward to the Lenten and Easter seasons when the death and resurrection of Jesus is celebrated. One form of the Christmas tree blessing exults, "Holy Lord, we come with joy to celebrate the birth of your Son, who rescued us from the darkness of sin by making the cross a tree of life and light. May this tree, arrayed in splendor, remind us of the life-giving cross of Christ, that we may always rejoice in the new life that shines in our hearts" (BB #1587).

Dismissal Catechesis (30 min.)

Getting Started

1. Prepare the space ahead of time with a circle of chairs around a centerpiece arranged on the floor. On a white cloth covered with a smaller gold cloth arrange the figures of the Magi within the Christmas crèche and place several white votive candles around the scene. You will need to have songbooks available for the prayer times.

2. Lead the candidates and catechumens to the circle and place the Lectionary on the table. Ask all to join in singing "We Three Kings" (John H. Hopkins Jr.) as you light the votive candles. Continue to pray in these words:
O Light of Lights, you showed forth the light of God's love to all nations. In your coming, God's saving love is revealed from east to west. You have made us co-heirs and sharers in the promise of salvation. Illuminate our minds and hearts with your love. May we, as the Magi, always seek and search for you. Enlighten us as we contemplate your Word today. We pray in your light and in your love. Amen.

First Impressions

1. Invite the participants to share their insights into the following: *What stood out for you in today's celebration? (Note that some parishes read the Epiphany Proclamation on this day.) Is the story of the Magi following the star to the place where Jesus lay new or familiar to you? What in this story touched your heart?*

2. Present this background on today's feast:
Today's feast of the Epiphany continues to unfold the rich meaning of Christmas. The name Epiphany is derived from epiphania, *which means "revelation." Today, the Church celebrates the revelation of God's saving love in Jesus, given for all nations and peoples of the world. In churches of the east, this day has occupied a place of even greater prominence than Christmas. The feast of the Epiphany falls on January 6, the twelfth day or fullness of Christmas yet it is celebrated on Sunday because of its importance.*

3. Invite the group to listen as you proclaim the second reading, Ephesians 3:2–3, 5–6. Invite the whole group to offer their interpretation of the phrases *co-heirs, members of the same body,* and *sharers of the promise.* As they offer their insights to each phrase, encourage them to probe deeper by articulating the significance of these expressions in their own lives and in the world today.

Making Connections

1. Continue by explaining the first reading from Isaiah 60:1–6 in these or similar words:
Today's reading from Isaiah presents the joy of Israel upon their return from the Exile. This is a marvelous saving act, symbolized as a beacon of light. Close your eyes and imagine yourself in total darkness and envision a strange and radiant light piercing the darkness. Steep yourselves in the beautiful and poetic images as I proclaim the first reading from Isaiah. Proclaim Isaiah 60:1–6.

2. Invite participants to reflect on and discuss the following questions in small groups: *As you heard this passage once again, what did you notice that was new for you? What feelings did the images evoke in you? Recall a time when you experienced something similar to the experience of the returning exiles. How would you describe your experience of light illuminating your darkness?* Invite some of the small groups to share their reflections on the questions with everyone.

3. Continue in the large group by asking everyone to look at the lighted votive candles in the center of the circle. Ask them to think about the significance of light in their lives. After sufficient time for silent reflection, ask each participant to share his or her ideas and thoughts. Then move the discussion to a deeper level, asking: *Why is God's saving presence depicted as light? How does the light of God illuminate your thoughts, feelings, and decisions? In what ways do you bring the light of God's saving presence to the world?* Summarize the discussion in a few sentences.

Prayer

Gather the participants for prayer by asking them to close their eyes and imagine God's light surrounding and filling their whole being. Ask them to name some of the gifts that this light of God brings as it illuminates their hearts, minds, and souls. Then invite the participants to imagine God's light shining on all people of the world. As they meditate on God's light on all peoples, name some places in the world where God's light is needed to light the way out of the darkness of war, violence, and evil. When you are finished, lead the group in singing "Arise, Shine" (Marty Haugen, GIA Publications, 1987).

Extended Catechesis

SESSION FOCUS: *Universal Offer of Salvation*

Gathering

A. **Sunday:**

1. Greet and welcome the sponsors and team members as they arrive. Invite them to join the circle of catechumens and candidates.

2. Invite everyone to sing "We Three Kings of Orient Are," verses 1 and 2. Then pray:
Lord of Light, scatter the darkness of our lives with your radiant presence. Just as the stars led the Magi to Jesus, lead and guide us to embrace your Son.

We are co-heirs with the Jews, members of one body, sharing in the promise of salvation. As we walk this journey of faith, enlighten our hearts and minds in the witness of these Gentile astrologers. Lead us to appreciate the wonderful light of baptism, transforming us into a People of Light. All this we ask in the name of Jesus, the holy one. Amen.

B. Weekday:

1. Use the same centerpiece as described for the Dismissal Catechesis.
2. As the participants gather in the circle, greet and warmly welcome each person. Invite participants to give examples of how they have experienced an Epiphany of God's light in the world over the last few days.
3. Lead this celebration of the Word:
   - Song: "We Three Kings of Orient Are," verses 1 and 2.
   - First Reading: Isaiah 60:1–6
   - Sing Psalm 72
   - Alleluia
   - Gospel: Matthew 2:1–12
   - Pray the prayer as in A.2 above.

The Word (30 min.)

1. Invite the candidates and catechumens to share their insights gained at the Dismissal Catechesis. Ask all of the participants to name their impressions and insights as to the meaning of God's marvelous light described in the scripture passages for the feast of the Epiphany. State the following:

   The Magi were astrologers who studied the stars. They did not have the advantage of knowing the messianic descriptions found in the scriptures or Jewish traditions. Yet they came to see and understand the truth of Jesus' birth through the natural study of the stars. In this passage from Matthew, the Gentile astrologers who follow the light of the star are depicted as the truly enlightened ones.

2. Ask the group to name some of the qualities these Magi had to possess in order to embark on the long journey and pursue the folly of following a star. List these on newsprint, writing large enough for all to read.

3. Invite the participants to move into their small groups and discuss these questions: *From this story, what does it mean to be enlightened? How would you compare your journey of faith to the seeking and searching of the Magi?* After sufficient time for discussion, invite the small groups to report on their discussion. Summarize their insights in a few sentences.

Catholic Teaching (30 min.)

1. Ask each small group to continue by sharing their thoughts on this question: *What is the main message of the journey and visit of the three Magi to the Messiah King?* Allow enough time for the discussion; then encourage them to share their insights with the large group as you record their ideas on newsprint or an overhead.

2. Present the Church's teaching that God's salvation is offered to all people using the background found in the Catholic Doctrine section of Understanding this Sunday and emphasizing the following points:
   - The feast of Epiphany proclaims that all people are attracted to and find salvation in the radiance of God's light. Jesus, the Word made flesh, is the light of all people. The light of Christ shines on everyone. No one is excluded from God's offer of salvation in Jesus.
   - The Church by its very nature is universal and not exclusive. This implies that all people are meant to share in the banquet of God's love.
   - At the Second Vatican Council, the bishops of the world addressed the Church's relationship with other Christians and non-Christians in the document known as *Lumen gentium* (Light of the Nations). This document presents the Church's self-understanding as a sign and instrument of communion with God and of unity among all people.
   - The Church stands at the service of Jesus' universal and reconciling mission to the world. Thus, the Church is called to give witness and to bring about this unity and reconciliation in the world. We are the People of God, the Church, with the responsibility to share in this ministry.

3. Invite the participants to turn to the Reflection and Questions found in the Participant Book on page 18. When they have finished writing their thoughts, ask them to gather back into the same small groups to share one insight they gained from this reflection exercise.

Putting Faith into Practice

1. Focus the attention of the participants back to the large gathering. Encourage them to share their sense of the baptismal challenge to bring unity and reconciliation to the world. After the group has had a chance to brainstorm practical ideas, ask each person to pause in silence, decide upon one action they wish to take, and write it in their Participant Book on page 19, in the section called "I want to put my faith into action by."

2. Invite the participants to brainstorm ways in which the faith community is challenged to be a light for peace and reconciliation in the world. Note the practical suggestions on large newsprint. Encourage the participants to determine one action they will take as a group to bring about this unity and reconciliation of all people in God's marvelous light. Spend the rest of the session planning and organizing this activity.

Prayer

Direct the participants to look at the light emanating from the candles and to silently invite God's light to dispel any darkness in their hearts and burn brightly in them. After a moment of silence, invite catechumens and sponsors to stand, and sponsors to place a hand on the shoulder of the catechumen. Pray Exorcism (RCIA 94C), making any needed adaptations. Conclude by inviting everyone to sing verses 1 and 5 of "Lord, Today" (Balhoff, Ducote, Daigle, Damean Music, 1978).

Baptism of the Lord

Understanding this Sunday:
Background for Catechesis

The Word in Liturgy

Isaiah 42:1–4, 6–7
Psalm 29:1–2, 3–4, 3, 9–10
Acts 10:34–38
Matthew 3:13–17

Today's celebration marks the end of the Christmas season. Since the scene at the Jordan is presented as the beginning of the public ministry of Jesus, today also serves as a bridge into Ordinary Time, which traces the historical unfolding of the ministry of Jesus through a continuous reading from the gospel of Matthew. Because we are still in the Christmas season, the theme of the incarnation remains important in today's celebration. Jesus' baptism is a sign that he has embraced our full humanity. Prominent in today's readings, and closely associated with last Sunday's celebration of the Epiphany, is the theme of the revelation of God's saving action in the person of Jesus. The gospel presents his baptism as the time when Jesus is revealed as God's Son, the beloved. It is clear from the ensemble of readings selected for today that the baptism of the Lord is also fundamental for our understanding of the sacrament of baptism as the source of our Christian mission.

The text from Isaiah is one of the "Servant Songs," passages describing a chosen one who will deliver God's people from slavery by his suffering and death. Originally intended as a prophecy of consolation and hope for the Jewish people during the Exile, these poems became messianic texts understood to speak metaphorically of the broader salvation that God would offer to the people in the midst of their moral slavery to sin. Christian tradition has found here allusions both to Jesus' ministry of reconciliation and to his redemptive suffering and death. This passage fits well with today's gospel, both because of its references to God's chosen servant, echoed in Matthew's voice from heaven, and because its imagery is so strongly suggestive of the ministry of Jesus which serves as the paradigm for every Christian's mission, rooted in baptism.

The redemptive ministry of Jesus is expressed in a more theological manner in the reading from Acts, an excerpt from a speech of Peter in which he reminds his listeners how Jesus went about "healing all who were oppressed by the devil" (v. 38). The setting for Peter's sermon is the home of Cornelius, a pivotal scene in Luke's theology, because it revealed the divine will to call even the Gentiles to salvation through faith in Jesus and baptism. Peter proclaims of Jesus, "God was with him," an affirmation that expresses powerfully the Christmas season's message of the incarnation.

Matthew's description of the baptismal scene alludes only indirectly to the actual water rite at the hands of John, no doubt because of continuing tension in Matthew's day between the disciples of the Baptist and the early Christian community. Even before baptizing him, John recognizes Jesus' messianic identity. Matthew further highlights Jesus' messiahship by his answer to John that his baptism must be done to "fulfill" God's plan. Central to Matthew's gospel is the notion of the prophecies of the Messiah being fulfilled in the person of Jesus. The sky opening, the dove descending, and the voice from heaven all resonate with messianic prophecies that are fulfilled in Jesus. God's favor resting on him and his "anointing" with the spirit are Matthew's way of authenticating that Jesus is the Messiah foretold in today's first reading from Isaiah. Catechumens seeking to be disciples of Jesus are presented with a vision of their own destiny, as they prepare for the waters of baptism, from which they will emerge as God's beloved, freed from sin, filled with the Spirit and "anointed" with the Spirit to share in the mission of Jesus.

Catholic Doctrine

Baptism and Mission

The Catholic Church describes the effects of baptism in various ways. These not only illustrate a rich theological understanding but also convey the breadth and depth of this first sacrament. In this section, after some general remarks, the relationship between baptism and mission will be explored.

Baptism incorporates the believer into the mystery of Christ, it joins one to the Church, and it provides for us a share in the mission of Jesus. A key phrase, developed by the Council of Florence (fifteenth century) helps focus these theological understandings about baptism. The Council proclaimed that baptism is the gateway to life in the Spirit (*vitae spiritualis iannua*). Thus, baptism marks a new beginning, whereby the person is regenerated and made whole by this sacrament, and is made ready by the gift of God for a new life which will be lived in the Spirit (CCC 1213).

The term itself, "baptism," comes from the Greek word for "plunge" or "immerse," which refers to the use of water, the main symbolic element which conveys the sacrament, along with the words "I baptize you in the name of the Father, and of the Son, and of the Holy Spirit." That triple plunging or immersing into the depths, where the body of the baptized is overwhelmed by water, symbolizes dying to the old self. Coming up out of the water corresponds symbolically to being born as a new person in Christ (CCC 1239–40).

St. Gregory Nazianzus (d. 390 A.D.) reflected on the sacrament of baptism, writing, "Baptism is God's most beautiful and magnificent gift. . . . We call it gift, grace, anointing, enlightenment, garment of immortality, bath of rebirth, seal, and most precious gift. It is called *gift* because it is conferred on those who bring nothing of their own; *grace* since it is given even to the guilty; *Baptism* because sin is buried in the water; *anointing* for it is priestly and royal as are those who are anointed; *enlightenment* because it radiates light; *clothing* since it veils our shame; *bath* because it washes; and *seal* as it is our guard and the sign of God's Lordship" (*Oratio* 40, 3–4: PG 36, 361C).

Baptism forgives all sin and incorporates one in the life of the Trinity. In this way, believers are given a share in the divine nature. In addition, baptism makes one a member of the body of Christ and of the visible manifestation of that body, the Church.

Thus, as reborn members of the ecclesial communion, those who are baptized are responsible for witnessing to the faith and participating in the mission of the Church. The Second Vatican Council described this as the "priesthood of the faithful," saying, "The baptized, by regeneration and the anointing of the Holy Spirit, are consecrated to be a spiritual house and a holy priesthood, that through all the works of Christian[s] they may offer spiritual sacrifices and proclaim the perfection of him who has called them out of darkness into his marvelous light. . . . They should everywhere on earth bear witness to Christ and give an answer to everyone who asks a reason for the hope of an eternal life that is theirs" (LG 10). The priesthood of all the faithful is not the same as the ordained priesthood, although as the Church teaches, "each in its own proper way shares in the one priesthood of Christ" (LG 10). The whole Church—ordained priests and the priesthood of all the faithful—is called in baptism to live, through sacraments, prayer, holiness of life, self-denial and active charity, the priestly, prophetic and kingly mission of Christ.

The Second Vatican Council reiterated its understanding of the foundational nature of baptism as the source of the believer's call to mission, in its document focusing on the laity. The Council exhorted, "From the fact of their union with Christ . . . flows the [laity's] right and duty to be apostles. Inserted as they are in the Mystical Body of Christ by baptism . . . it is by the Lord himself that they are assigned to the apostolate. If they are consecrated a kingly priesthood and a holy nation (cf. 1 Peter 2:4–10), it is in order that they may in all their actions offer spiritual sacrifices and bear witness to Christ all the world over" (AA 3).

Therefore, while Catholics believe that the sacrament of baptism is imparted in a particular moment and by discernable sacramental signs, it is also understood that baptism is meant to be lived and celebrated throughout the believer's life. Those who rise out of the baptismal waters are charged with the responsibility to lend themselves personally and communally to the mission of Jesus, participating in the apostolic witness of the People of God (CCC 1270). Baptism and mission go hand in hand.

Catholic Culture

The prayer used in blessing the baptismal waters employs images not only of rebirth and of the People of God but also of mission. The text declares, "Father, God of mercy, through these waters of baptism you have filled us with new life as your very own children. . . . From all who are baptized in water and the Holy Spirit, you have formed one people, united in your Son, Jesus Christ. . . . You have set us free and filled our hearts with the Spirit of your love that we may live in your peace. . . . You call those who have been baptized to announce the Good News of Jesus Christ to people everywhere . . . " (RCIA 222C).

Dismissal Catechesis (30 min.)

Getting Started

1. Prepare the space ahead of time with a circle of chairs around a table draped with a white cloth. On the white cloth position several white tapers upon a smaller green cloth. Arrange several evergreens at the base of the table.

2. Lead the candidates and catechumens to the circle and place the Lectionary on the table and light the candles. Begin the session by praying in these or your own words:
   God of victory and justice, you have offered to humankind your servant, Jesus the Messiah. His coming to dwell among us opened our eyes to the light of justice, peace, and salvation. Jesus is your beloved Son, who is Lord of all. Just as you anointed him with the Holy Spirit at his baptism in the Jordan, anoint and empower us to hear and heed your living Word. We ask all in Jesus' name, through the same Holy Spirit. Amen.

3. Lead the participants in singing a few verses of the Gathering Song from today's liturgy.

First Impressions

1. Explain this celebration as a culmination of the Christmas season in these words: *Today, the Church celebrates the baptism of Jesus in the Jordan by John the Baptist. This feast marks the close of the Christmas season and serves as a bridge into the liturgical season known as Ordinary Time. This last Sunday of the season of Christmas still celebrates the incarnation—the coming of Christ, Son of God, born into a human family, one like us in everything but sin, and servant-savior of us all. Yet, in the baptism event, Jesus begins his public ministry and his mission of redemption, which will be unfolded for us in the continuous reading from the gospel of Matthew during Ordinary Time.*

2. Invite everyone to turn to the person on their right and share three things that caught their attention at today's Liturgy of the Word. Then invite the pairs to mention one thing that stood out for them and state the reason for that in the large group.

3. Invite the pairs to focus upon completing this statement: *"Jesus' baptism was significant because. . . ."* In the large group ask everyone to offer their insight on Jesus' baptism. Summarize their insights in a few words or phrases.

Making Connections

1. Encourage the pairs to then complete this statement: *"My baptism is/will be significant because, like Jesus, I will be/am. . . ."* After sufficient time for sharing, ask the pairs to share their insights on the significance of baptism for the believer today.

2. Create a parallel chart either on an overhead or newsprint in which you take the insights of the participants on Jesus' baptism and on our baptism and compare the significance of both. Encourage the candidates and catechumens to offer additional ideas on the relationship between the two. If these are not mentioned in the discussion, add them to the comparison:

Jesus is the beloved Son of God	We are the beloved sons and daughters of God
Jesus was chosen by God to redeem us	We are chosen by God to continue Jesus' mission of redemption
The Spirit came upon Jesus	The Holy Spirit is poured upon us baptism

3. Invite the same pairs to look at this comparison and discuss the following questions: *What is my reaction to discovering the similarities between Jesus' baptism and my (anticipated) baptism? What can I do to better prepare for initiation into the Catholic community of faith?* Then invite everyone to write one thing they would like to do to prepare more fully for initiation in their Participant Book on page 21, under the section entitled "I want to put my faith into action by."

Prayer

Focus the attention of the group on the centerpiece of lighted candles and the white cloth, covered by a smaller green cloth. Explain liturgical use of color in these words:
Each liturgical season has a focus and specific liturgical color to symbolize that focus. The color white is used in the celebrant's vestments and has been part of our centerpiece during this season of Christmas. As we anticipate the season of Ordinary Time, symbolized by green vestments, today's centerpiece has a smaller green cloth over the white table covering. As we gather our thoughts and experiences of the Word in prayer, look at these colors and allow the fullness of their symbolism to bring to mind a variety of images. First look at the white cloth and recall the many things that this color brings to mind. Pause to allow time for this. *Now look at the green cloth and let it call forth from within you what green represents.* Pause to allow time for this.
Close by leading the participants in singing the refrain to Psalm 29, *"The Lord will bless his people with peace,"* after you pray each verse of the psalm.

Extended Catechesis

SESSION FOCUS: *Baptism and Mission*

Gathering

A. Sunday:
1. Greet and welcome the sponsors and team members as they arrive. Invite them to join the circle of catechumens and candidates.
2. Begin the prayer by leading the participants in singing the Gathering Song from today's liturgy. Invite a godparent or sponsor to proclaim the first reading from Isaiah 42:1–4, 6–7. Prepare for the proclamation of the gospel with this meditation:
   Relax and close your eyes. Release the worries that hover around your mind and become aware of your heartbeat and each breath that fills your lungs. Move

deep into the center of your being and allow your imagination to take you back to the time of Jesus. You are among the crowd of people gathered around John the Baptist. You feel the heat of the sun and your eyes linger on the cooling waters of the Jordan River. You listen to John's message of repentance and you long to reform your ways and feel the guilt of your sins released. Linger for a moment and experience this deep longing. You notice a rabbi approaching John. These two men seem to know one another. You strain your ears to listen as they speak to one another. This is what you hear: Proclaim the gospel, Matthew 3:13–17. Pause in silence, allowing enough time for the participants to take in the fullness of this Word of God.

B. Weekday:

1. Use the same centerpiece as described for the Dismissal Catechesis.
2. As the participants gather in the circle, welcome each person warmly. Ask them to name some ways they have experienced God's blessing over the past few days.
3. Lead this celebration of the Word:
   - Song: "Rise Up In Splendor" (Daigle, Ducote and Ault, NALR, 1986)
   - Greeting and lighting of the white candles
   - First Reading: Isaiah 42:1–4, 6–7
   - Sing Psalm 29:1–2, 3–4, 3, 9–10
   - Second Reading: Acts 10:34–38
   - Meditation on the gospel as in part A
   - Gospel: Matthew 3:13–17
   - Silence

The Word (30 min.)

1. Invite the participants to offer their responses to these questions in the large group: *What does the conversation between Jesus and John the Baptist evoke in you? What do you understand by Jesus' insistence that he be baptized? What image in the baptism of Jesus do you find particularly engaging and why?*
2. Offer this background on the first reading from Isaiah 42:1–4, 6–7 and its correlation with the gospel:
   This passage describes a chosen one who will deliver God's people from slavery by his suffering and death. God's chosen servant would be recognized in terms of the servant's mission. For the Israelites, the mission of the servant could be understood to be embraced by another prophet, the poor ones of the nation or the nation of Israel itself. For Christians today, the mission of the servant was fulfilled in Jesus. Thus understood, this passage is a messianic text, revealing the salvation that God would offer through the reconciliation and redemptive suffering and death of Jesus. In the light of Matthew's provocative "opening in the sky from which the Spirit of God descends" and anoints the beloved Son for the mission of redemption, these scriptures present the Christian with a paradigm for baptismal mission.
3. Gather the participants into small groups and ask them to discuss the following questions: *What links do you discover in comparing these two passages? How would you describe*

the relationship between God and Jesus based upon the imagery found in the baptismal scene? What does this imagery reveal about the transformation that occurs at your own (anticipated) baptism? Focus their attention back to the large group and gather some insights on this last question from each small group.

Catholic Teaching (30 min.)

1. Present the Church's teaching on baptism in these words: *Baptism is the gateway to life in the Spirit. When we are immersed into the waters of baptism we are incorporated into Christ, into the life of the Church and empowered to share in the mission of Jesus. The action of the Holy Spirit makes this new beginning in Christ and his Church a reality. This same Spirit gifts and graces us to continue the mission of Jesus in the world today. Union with Christ transforms us and carries us beyond our selves, making us a holy people sent forth into the world. The power of baptism is a gradual unfolding of what it means to take up the personal and communal responsibility to participate in the mission of Jesus.*
2. Invite the participants to spend time in prayerful thought on this baptismal mission with the help of the Reflection and Questions in the Participant Book on page 20. Encourage the sponsors and godparents to gather with their candidate or catechumen to share their reflection and the responses to questions one and two. You may choose to call upon the small groups to share some insights from the Reflection with everyone.

Putting Faith into Practice

1. In the same small groups, ask everyone to share the third question: *Name one specific way you are being prepared for mission through this journey toward full initiation.*
2. Continue the small group discussion by directing the attention of the participants to the Quotable Quote section in the Participant Book on page 20. Invite the participants to share their insights on these questions: *What does it mean to be clothed in Christ through the sacrament of baptism? What will need to be discarded—thrown off—to "put on" Christ?*
3. Invite the group to decide on what they choose to "put aside" in preparation for taking up the mission of Christ. This can be recorded in the Participant Book of page 21, in the section called "I want to put my faith into action by."

Prayer

Ask the participants to silently ask God's help in their decision for faith. Prayerfully and slowly read these images for baptism as the group sits in silence: *anointing, enlightenment, garment of immortality, bath of rebirth, seal, most precious gift, outpouring of the Spirit, precious in the eyes of God, heirs of the kingdom, sons and daughters of God, regeneration, consecrations, out of darkness into his marvelous light, formed as one people, incorporated into Christ.* Add any other images as you see fit. Conclude the session by inviting all to stand and sing "We Are Called" (David Haas, GIA Publications, 1988).

LENTEN SEASON

Ash Wednesday

The Word in Liturgy

Joel 2:12–18
Psalm 51:3–4, 5–6, 12–13, 14, 17
2 Corinthians 5:20–6:2
Matthew 6:1–6, 16–18

The evolution of Lent as a time of preparation for Easter began as a very modest few days of preparation before the annual celebration of the Paschal Vigil. By the end of the fourth century, those days had expanded to a forty-day period of prayer and fasting that began on a Sunday, with an emphasis mainly on the preparation of catechumens for initiation at Easter.

In subsequent centuries, with the decline and virtual disappearance of the catechumenate, the focus of Lent shifted to those doing public penance in anticipation of being reconciled to the Eucharist for Easter. The public penitents had ashes placed on their heads as an outward sign of their mortification. When public penance disappeared, the custom grew up of all the faithful asking for penitential ashes at the start of Lent. At the beginning of the sixth century, the start of Lent was shifted from Sunday to the preceding Wednesday so that there would be exactly forty days of fasting (since Sundays were not observed as days of fast), and during the next two centuries a preparatory period of three weeks was added prior to Ash Wednesday. By the end of the eleventh century, Ash Wednesday was observed throughout Christendom, and by the thirteenth century even the Pope himself accepted ashes as part of the papal liturgy on Ash Wednesday.

Among the reforms of the Second Vatican Council was the elimination of the three weeks of preparation for Lent and the placement of the blessing and distribution of ashes within the eucharistic liturgy rather than before the start of Mass (as it had been for centuries). The custom is retained of burning palm branches from Passion (Palm) Sunday of the previous year in order to obtain the ashes. Most importantly, the

Council re-established the primary focus of Lent as a time when the whole Church joins in penance, not merely out of personal piety but in order to help in preparing those to be initiated at Easter.

There is a considerable amount of scholarly disagreement as to when the Book of Joel was composed, but a date in the fourth or fifth century B.C. seems likely. The author writes at a time of devastation in Israel from locust plague and drought, which the prophet sees as a sign of divine judgment. He calls upon the people to repent and return to Yahweh. The Lord, for his part, is presented as "rich in kindness and relenting in punishment." The call to conversion of heart is extended to everyone in the community, even infants at the breast. And, the passage ends on a hopeful note, indicating that the Lord "took pity on his people." The reading's emphasis on conversion of heart is highlighted by the choice of Psalm 51, traditionally considered the great prayer of repentance of King David after his infidelity with Bathsheeba.

Paul's letter to the Corinthians offers a solid theological rationale for why we ought to reform our lives as Joel has suggested. Christ took on our sins by his death on the cross, so that "we might become the very holiness of God." This is the ultimate Good News of Paul's gospel, that we have been "reconciled to God" in Christ. The urgency of our response to this grace of God is unmistakable in Paul's words: "Now is the acceptable time! Now is the day of salvation!"

The section of Matthew from which we read today has no direct parallels in other gospels. This is the third part of the Sermon on the Mount, in which Jesus discusses almsgiving

(vv. 2–4), prayer (vv. 5–8), and fasting (vv. 16–18), traditional acts of Jewish piety. The reading omits a section on the Lord's Prayer (vv. 9–13) and forgiveness of sins (vv. 14–15). Jesus' emphasis is on the purity of one's interior dispositions, a way that he underlines the depth of conversion to which his disciples are called. He is not criticizing such acts of piety in themselves, nor is he speaking out against all public manifestations of piety. Rather, it is the ostentatious public display of one's personal piety that receives his negative critique. Presumably, this teaching was occasioned by perceived problems in certain Jewish circles, known to Matthew's community as well as in Jesus' day. But the advice that is offered is as important in our own time as it was for the first generations of believers.

SESSION PLAN: Ash Wednesday

Dismissal Catechesis (30 min.)

Getting Started

1. Prepare the space ahead of time with a circle of chairs around a table with a purple cloth and a bowl of ashes in the center.
2. Invite the candidates and catechumens to sit in the circle and reflect on the ashes they have just received. Play soft instrumental music in the background.
3. Begin the session by singing the Gathering Hymn used at today's liturgy. Proclaim the first reading from Joel 2:12–18. Allow a period of quiet after the reading. Follow this with the following prayer:
God of our Longing, you have marked us with the sign of your cross. May this ashen cross be a reminder of your call, 'Return to me with all your hearts.' During these days of Lent, show us how to repent from our sinful ways. Teach us how to pray and offer you the work of our hands in a way that is fitting. Guide us as we act in love and justice for those in need. We ask that you receive our willing and repentant hearts through Jesus who suffered and died for our sake. Amen.

First Impressions

1. Ask the participants to share the following: *What did today's liturgy awaken in you? How do you understand the meaning of being signed with ashes?* Offer this brief explanation of the meaning of Ash Wednesday:
In the early church, those who needed forgiveness for grave sin (apostasy, murder, and adultery) did public penance as a sign of repentance. Their return to the table and the community involved placing ashes on their heads as an outward sign of their mortification. When public penance disappeared, the custom grew of all the faithful asking for penitential ashes at the start of Lent. The palms of the previous year's Palm Sunday are burned to obtain the ashes. These are blessed and placed on the forehead of the faithful in the sign of a cross with the words (here use the form used at your parish liturgy).
2. Help the participants recall some of the key images from the readings used at the liturgy by asking: *What images and ideas do you recall from today's readings?* As the images are named, ask the individual to print that image on a large poster or paper. Prepare your own list prior to the session and add to those named by the group when they seem finished. Ask them to gather into small groups to discuss: *How would you summarize the meaning of today's scriptures? What did you find confusing?* Invite the small groups to present their responses in the large gathering.
3. Explain the scriptures in these words:
This penitential theme flows throughout all of the scriptures used at today's liturgy. The first reading from the Book of Joel is a call for conversion of heart for all of the community. Paul offers a theological reason for reforming our lives in the second letter to the Corinthians. Paul urges and exhorts us, "Now is the acceptable time! Now is the day of salvation." The passage from the gospel of Matthew flows from the previous section in which Jesus emphasizes the purity of one's interior disposition for conversion. Thus, it follows that this section of the gospel continues to criticize public displays of personal piety, urging the follower of Jesus to perform acts of prayer, fasting, and almsgiving in private.

Making Connections

1. Invite the participants to gather in small groups to discuss: *How do our interior motives affect our spiritual practices? From Matthew's gospel, what does God require of us as we journey toward conversion?*
2. Ask the participants to share their insights in the large group. When they have finished, invite them to brainstorm some of the ways they can make their penitential journey this Lent more authentic. You may choose to record their ideas on a large poster or paper. Summarize their discussion and pause, asking everyone to think of one action they will take this Lent.

Prayer

Allow a brief period of silence for each person to make their resolution. Proclaim the gospel, Matthew 6:1–6, 16–18. Ask the group to write their resolution on a slip of paper and place it on the table with the ashes as an offering to God. Close by praying Psalm 51 together. Copies of the psalm will need to be available for each person.

First Sunday of Lent

The Word in Liturgy

Genesis 2:7–9, 3:1–7
Psalm 51:3–4, 5–6, 12–13, 14, 17
Romans 5:12–19 or 5:12, 17–19
Matthew 4:1–11

The season of Lent begins with readings that unfold the drama of primordial sin, grace, and divine election. Today's first reading from the second chapter of Genesis, detailing the temptation by the serpent of the first man and woman in the Garden of Eden, is the story which is known classically as "the Fall." To contextualize the passage, a few lines concerning creation are included (vv. 7–9). The first human being created is brought to life by God's breath, showing the absolute dependence of the creature on the Creator. Without God's breath, the first human is no more than inert matter. The setting of the garden, coming from the hand of God, is one of beauty and nourishment for the human creature. Yet, through the cunning of the serpent, the woman and man are led to disobey God's command and eat the forbidden fruit of the tree of the knowledge of good and evil. The result of their transgression is an immediate realization of shame. Its long-range consequence is alienation from God.

By omitting the subsequent passages where, by God's judgment, the first man and woman are also evicted from the garden and bear as a curse all the hardships of human life, the reading focuses more narrowly on the sin itself. It is not a sexual sin, but a sin of presumption—of wanting to be "like gods," as the serpent describes it. Although a single creature personifies the temptation to sin, various aspects of the goods of creation are enlisted to support the temptation: the attractiveness of the fruit itself, the offer of the fruit to one person from another. The sin itself is simple. Part of the subtlety of the story lies in how little horror the action itself inspires. Yet the mythic nature of the story assigns to this one action a universal significance: the beginning of human rejection of God in favor of self. And it is this very act that unleashes all the evils of suffering and death upon the world.

The penitential psalm, Psalm 51, is attributed to David after he repented of his adulterous and murderous acquisition of Bathsheba as his wife. The psalm displays full consciousness both of the depth of sin, and the power of the compassion of God to redeem from sin those who have fallen.

Paul's letter to the Romans draws our attention to the universal consequences of the sin which is described in the first reading. Sin is pervasive. It exists even when there is no law to convict us of it. Paul goes on, however, to announce that the redemption won by Christ has the power to completely acquit the human race from all its sin. His comparison of Christ to Adam (better drawn, though more complicated, in the long form of the reading) accentuates the overflowing mercy of God in Christ. In today's liturgy, Paul's passage is pivotal.

Against this backdrop, then, the gospel story illuminates how God has entered our history of sin and changed it. Matthew's account of the temptations of Jesus in the desert displays his characteristic interest in Jesus as the Son of God. Jesus epitomizes God's revelation through the chosen people of the Old Testament and completes it in his own person. Each of the temptations which Jesus undergoes in the desert is parallel to a temptation suffered by the chosen people during the wandering in the wilderness after the Exodus. Although they are several—hunger, testing God, idolatry—all may be seen as manifestations of the sin described in the first reading, for they all describe ways that the Messiah might be tempted to exalt himself rather than to walk the path of obedience to God. The responses that Jesus makes to the devil are taken from the Book of Deuteronomy, which is the charter document of the Mosaic covenant. They underline key features of the faith of the chosen people, perfectly exemplified in Jesus: complete reliance on God's word, total humility before God, and single-hearted worship. The newly baptized Jesus, by choosing this path, rejects "the glamour of evil," and reveals the mercy of God.

As catechumens this Sunday experience the Rite of Election, and candidates and the faithful renew their commitment to ongoing conversion, they may see in Jesus how their own election is to be realized: in trust, humility, and devotion to God.

Catholic Doctrine

Divine Election

Our dignity as human beings rests in the truth that we are called to communion with God. The desire within us that draws us out of ourselves into communion with God is "built in," as it were, by the Creator. We cannot live an authentic human life without freely acknowledging the love God has for us and then entrusting ourselves to that love (CCC 27). The Second Vatican Council described this loving relationship as an "intimate and vital bond of [humanity] to God," initiated and sustained by the divine (GS 19). However, this relationship is indeed forgotten or rejected by people, through an attitude of sin which moves one to hide from God out of shame and fear and thus flee from the divine call (CCC 29).

God, however, refuses to give up on us. In spite of human sinfulness, God continued to reveal divine love by freely choosing a people, Israel, to be a sign of the relationship that God seeks with all. This revelation was not accompanied by overwhelming displays of power, but by paradox: a weak, small, and insignificant nation bears within its life the revelation of the Most High. This mystery is termed "divine election." The Church, called "a chosen people," participates in the mystery of divine election in a new way because of Christ. In Christ, those who "were no people . . . now . . . are 'God's people'" (1 Peter 2:10). One writer reflects, "Next to covenant, and intimately related to it, the concept of election is perhaps the most decisive one for the religion of Israel. And for the Christian, the idea that Jesus is the elect of God and the idea that the Church is elect in Christ are fundamental. Election has been called 'the heart of the Church.'" (*On the Rite of Election*, Rita Ferrone, Chicago: Liturgy Training Publications, 1994, p. 37).

Thus, Christians believe that the old covenant is fulfilled in Christ and that what had been prefigured in the people of Israel is now made new and perfect by God's Chosen One. The temptations in the desert, symbolic of the challenges faced by Israel during the formative period of wandering in the wilderness after the Exodus, are faced victoriously by Jesus. His victory is a victory of humility over pride, trust over presumption, and fidelity over faithlessness. Jesus, the poor, humble, and suffering servant of God, walks along the path of

obedience to the divine will and plan for salvation. Chosen to redeem humanity from sin, Christ surrenders himself to the paradox of the cross. In that obedience and surrender, the Lord shows us the right response to divine election (CCC 606, 615).

All those who follow the example of the Son and believe in Jesus can, therefore, say "yes" to God in Christ. The Church expresses this belief in its prayer on this First Sunday of Lent: "Father . . . we . . . give you thanks through Jesus Christ our Lord. His fast of forty days makes this a holy season of self-denial. By rejecting the devil's temptations he has taught us to rid ourselves of the hidden corruption of evil, and so to share his paschal meal in purity of heart, until we come to its fulfillment in the promised land of heaven." (*Sacramentary*, Preface Prayer 12).

We, the Church, caught up in the mystery of divine election, affirm the experience of a persistent God who continues to love the world in spite of sin and who chooses us in Christ. God's election sends us forth into the world, as Christ was sent, to be a living sign of hope and love. As the Second Vatican Council reflected, those who are chosen, the people of God, are "a most sure seed of unity, hope and salvation for the whole human race" (LG 9).

Catholic Culture

In the Genesis account of the Fall, Adam and Eve ate from the fruit of the tree of knowledge. The fruit itself is not specified in the biblical text; however, artistic convention usually depicts it as an apple, perhaps because the Latin *malus* can mean either "apple" or "evil," given the context of the sentence within which it is used. The convention of the apple, therefore, in Christian art usually symbolizes temptation, the Fall, and original sin (DictSymb 28).

The grand portals of cathedrals and the simpler doors of parish churches traditionally are constructed to symbolize some aspect of faith, to depict a scriptural message, or to illustrate an episode from the life of a saint. The oldest church in Tucson, Arizona, Mission San Xavier del Bac, founded in 1692, has a door handle in the shape of a serpent. Those who enter must grasp the serpent in order to pass through the threshold into the Church—an eloquent commentary on the struggle with primordial sin that marks our entry into the people of God.

G.K. Chesterton in his writings noted that the central notion in the doctrine of election is more often better understood, in literature and in life, by its opponents than its adherents. He referred to the idea that election should, above all, produce humility in the elect, since those chosen do nothing to merit it. That reversal, the preaching on "the last shall be first and the first, last" (see Matthew 20:16), finds its motivation in the doctrine of divine election (BibTrad 232).

Dismissal Catechesis (30 min.)

Getting Started

1. Prepare the space ahead of time with a circle of chairs around a low table (a milk crate will work well) draped with a purple cloth. Upon the table arrange sand, rocks, or a barren branch, using a symbol that is included in the church environment.

2. Lead the candidates and catechumens to the circle and place the Lectionary on the table. Invite everyone to be seated. After a few moments of quiet, pray in these or similar words: *Good and gracious God, each year you give us this holy season of Lent. During this season Christians around the world pray, fast, and give to the poor in order to renew their lives. Help these candidates and catechumens in a special way this year as they walk with us here at (name of the parish) through this Lenten season. We ask this through Jesus Christ, our Lord. Amen.*

First Impressions

1. Invite everyone to close their eyes and remember their impressions as they entered the church today. With their eyes still closed, ask them to name aloud what they saw, heard, or sensed as they came into church and participated in the Liturgy of the Word.

2. After everyone has had an opportunity to respond, invite the catechumens and candidates to further reflect on these images from today's scriptures:
God blew into Adam's nostrils the breath of life—God planted a garden in Eden and placed the man there—The serpent was the most cunning of all the animals—The woman saw that the tree was good and pleasing—They hid themselves from God, for they were naked—Through one person, sin entered the world—The grace of God through Jesus overflowed for the many—Through the obedience of Christ the many will be made righteous—The Spirit led Jesus into the desert—After forty days of fasting the tempter approached him—The devil left him and the angels began to minister to him.

3. Gather the group into pairs and ask them to discuss this question: *From these images presented in today's scriptures, what is your understanding of Lent?* In the large group, encourage the candidates and catechumens to name some of their understandings. Record key words and phrases on newsprint, large enough for all to see.

Making Connections

1. Revisit today's poetic first reading from Genesis 2:7–9; 3:1–7 through this reflection: *Imagine yourself at the scene of today's first reading from Genesis. You are Adam, this first human being, brought to life by God's breath. Breathe in now and visualize the very breath of God, giving you life. Inhale . . . Exhale . . . Inhale . . . Exhale . . . . God places you in a garden filled with variety and beauty. Walk with God and see the different trees ripe with fruit, waiting to be eaten. Picture the garden. Everything in this Eden is to be enjoyed except the tree in the middle.*

Remember what tree that is? How does this tree appear in your imagination? This tree of the knowledge of good and evil is a curiosity. The serpent is cunning: "You will be like gods." You want to know and understand everything. Would you be tempted? What do you do? It's only fruit. What harm can there be in eating it? What harm is there in knowledge? Adam and Eve's story is our story. We begin to choose our way, rather than God's way. The gap between God and humankind is widened each time we sin.

2. Ask the participants to return to the small groups to discuss these questions: *What similarities do you detect between the first parents and your own life? When have you been faced with a similar choice? How does the breath of God, giving you life, affect your choices?*

3. Invite some responses from the small groups. Summarize their insights in a few sentences.

Prayer

Encourage everyone to reflect in silence about his or her experiences of sin and evil, grace and love. You may choose to play some soft instrumental music as a background to their silence. Instruct the group to quietly speak to God in their heart about the choices they have made in the recent weeks. Create a prayer of petition by inviting the participants to name aloud a word or phrase that names some evidence of sin or evil in the world. Direct them to respond to each naming with the prayer, *"God, strengthen us when we are tempted."*

Extended Catechesis

SESSION FOCUS: *Divine Election*

Gathering

A. **Sunday:**

1. Greet and welcome the sponsors, team members, and additional participants as they arrive. Invite them to join the circle of catechumens and candidates.

2. Ask the group to focus their attention upon the sand, rock, or barren branch upon the table and reflect upon their understanding of this season of Lent. You may wish to hear some of their thoughts spoken aloud. After a time, ask all to stand and join in singing the first two verses of the Gathering Song used at the parish liturgy. While standing, encourage all to listen as a team member proclaims the second reading, Romans 5:12–19, and the gospel, Matthew 4:1–11. Allow silent reflection after the proclamation of the Word.

B. **Weekday:**

1. Use the same centerpiece as in the Dismissal Catechesis.

2. Ask the participants to gather in the circle as you greet and warmly welcome each person. Select one or two participants to share an experience of God's strengthening grace during a time of temptation (or difficult decision) during the past few days.

3. Lead this celebration of the Word:
- Song: Gathering Song from Sunday's liturgy
- First Reading: Genesis 2:7–9; 3:1–7
- Sing Psalm 51
- Second Reading: Romans 5:12–19
- Silence
- Gospel: Matthew 4:1–11

The Word (30 min.)

1. After a time of silence, ask a catechumen or candidate to briefly summarize the sharing during the Dismissal Catechesis, using the newsprint on the meaning of Lent and their discussion as an aide. Encourage others in the group to add their insights on the Genesis passage. Summarize their comments and share this important insight: *The first human beings are created and brought to life by God's breath, indicating the absolute dependence of each human person on the Creator. The setting of the garden, coming from the hand of God, is furthermore one of beauty and nourishment for humankind.*

2. Continue to open the meaning of the second reading, Romans 5:12–19, in these or similar words: *As we know, humankind became alienated from the Creator by falling prey to the tempting presumption of wanting to be "like gods." St. Paul focuses upon the universal consequences of this breach which is so poetically described in the first reading. When we look around at the world and at our own lives we know that sin is pervasive. Yet God's mercy is greater. Paul assures us that the redemption won by Christ has the power to completely acquit humankind from sin. Our keen sense of sin is overshadowed by the magnanimous love of God.* Gather the participants into pairs to share their responses to this question: *When have you experienced God's mercy and love as a power greater than sin and evil?*

3. Continue expanding the meaning of the gospel, Matthew 4:1–11, in these or your own words: *Jesus' temptations in the desert parallel the temptations suffered by the chosen people during their wandering in the wilderness. The temptation to be ruled by our physical hungers, to test God, and to engage in idolatry—placing a creature, ideal, or object above God—are universal temptations. They describe the ways that the Messiah will be tempted to exalt himself rather than walk the path of obedience to God. The response that Jesus makes to the temptations, however, shows us some of the key features of the faith of the chosen people. That faith is rooted in complete reliance on God's Word, total humility before God, and single-hearted worship of God.* Continue the discussion in pairs with these questions: *How does reliance (trust and obedience) upon God's Word satisfy your hunger? In what ways can you foster total humility (surrender to God's mercy and love) toward God? What priorities need to shift?*

Catholic Teaching (30 min.)

1. Ask the participants to focus upon the Reflection exercise in the Participant Book on page 24. Allow enough time for them to examine their relationship with God.

2. In these or similar words, describe the notion of "divine election" using the background material found in Understanding this Sunday, in the section on Catholic Doctrine: *Our life experience parallels that of our mythic first parents. Like them our eyes are opened, we are aware of our sinfulness and we are ashamed. Just as God did not give up on them, God refuses to give up on us. Our dignity as human beings lies in the fundamental truth that we are created for communion with God. In spite of human sinfulness, God continued to reveal divine love by freely choosing a people, Israel, to be a sign of the relationship that God seeks with all. This revelation was not accompanied by displays of power but by paradox: a weak and insignificant nation bears within its life the revelation of the Most High God. This mystery is termed "divine election." The Church participates in the mystery of divine election in a new way because of Christ. The testings of Israel in the desert are faced by Jesus in his desert experience. He is victorious, overcoming pride with humility, presumption with trust, and faithlessness with fidelity. Chosen to redeem humanity from sin, Jesus surrenders himself to the paradox of the cross. In that obedience and surrender, the Lord shows us the right response to divine election.*

3. Invite the participants to continue the conversation in pairs by discussing the first two questions on page 24 of the Participant Book. Elicit a few insights from the pairs in the large group gathering.

Putting Faith into Practice

1. Ask the pairs to share their practical ideas on the third question on page 24 of the Participant Book. When they are finished sharing, focus the attention of the participants back to the large group and ask each pair to write their practical ideas for responding to God's loving relationship of "divine election" on a newsprint large enough for all to read.

2. Invite each participant to reflect on their relationship with God, their relationship with others, and their relationship to things. Direct them to look at the ideas for responding to God's mercy and unfathomable love on the newsprint and select two that they wish to cultivate this Lent. This resolve can be recorded in the Participant Book, on page 25, under the heading "I want to put my faith into action by."

3. Take time to describe the various parish opportunities for Lenten renewal and encourage the sponsors to accompany their catechumen or candidate to some of these events. Explain the Lenten practices of prayer (worship, praise, and surrender to God's loving providence); fasting (emptying ourselves to make room for God); and almsgiving (giving of our time, talent, and treasure for the sake of justice).

Prayer

Invite everyone to close their eyes and to take a few deep breaths, imagining the breath of God enlivening their hearts and spirits. Then lead them in singing "Psalm 51: Be Merciful, O Lord," (Marty Haugen, GIA Publications, 1983) or "Psalm 51: Create in Me" (David Haas, GIA Publications, 1987). Conclude the prayer with Minor Exorcism (RCIA 94G).

Second Sunday of Lent

The Word in Liturgy

Genesis 12:1–4
Psalm 33:4–5, 18–19, 20, 22
2 Timothy 1:8–10
Matthew 17:1–9

The entire Period of Purification and Enlightenment is a call to holiness—a call directed to catechumens, elect and faithful alike—to share God's life in the Christian community, living in obedience to God's will and preparing to celebrate the sacraments of initiation. Each year on the second Sunday of Lent, the Church begins the Liturgy of the Word with the story of Abraham's call, a call to holiness in which countless generations of believers have recognized the contours of their own call. Chapter 12 of Genesis marks a turning point, not only in the literary structure of the Book of Genesis but in the whole story of salvation. After eleven chapters dealing with human sinfulness and rebellion, the patriarchal history begins here with a stark summary of God's initiative on Abraham's (and our) behalf: A call and a promise, a mission and a blessing are what God offers. Abraham's call is to holiness, a life lived in covenanted relationship with the Lord; Abraham's blessing is holiness, the faithful promise of the Lord that he will be given immortality in his progeny. The terse phrase, "Abram went as the Lord directed him," is epigrammatic of the entire saga of tested and proven fidelity on Abraham's part that will be told in the succeeding chapters. As such, it is also a wonderful summary of the essence of holiness—living as the Lord directs us.

The psalm today emphasizes that God's word (promise) is trustworthy, and that God protects us in our time of need. This is the heart of what Abraham (and every believer) discovers about God: that when we put our hope in the Lord, God's "kindness" will always be upon us (v. 22).

The second letter of Paul to Timothy is one of the so-called Pastoral Epistles, reflecting the maturing pastoral situation of the young Christian Church as it struggled with persecution and issues of leadership. The author here reminds his reader(s) that God "has called us to a holy life, not because of any merit of ours." The emphasis is on this holiness as a gift of God, described as "the grace held out to us in Christ Jesus." That gift, that grace, is ultimately "life and immortality." But it is not the vague immortality promised to Abraham in his descendants. Rather, it is an immortality that has been "brought into clear light through the gospel," the Good News of the resurrection of Jesus that has "robbed death of its power." Our call to holiness is, ultimately, a call to share in the eternal life of the Risen One to whom we have been joined in baptism.

In all three years of the liturgical cycle, the gospel reading on this day is that of the transfiguration of Jesus. The previous readings have already provided the key to understanding this text in light of our Lenten pilgrimage. Jesus, his divinity revealed in splendor on the mountaintop, offers to his disciples (ourselves included) a glimpse of the promised glory that awaits all who share his life in baptism. The psalm refrain echoes in our hearts: "...as we place our trust in you." Our trust, our hope, is that we will share Christ's very holiness by virtue of the astounding gift of eternal life offered in baptism. The Church invites us to gaze on our promised destiny today, so that the rigors of the Lenten season—indeed, the rigors of discipleship—will not lead to discouragement. Abraham's call led to trials. Paul's letter to Timothy admonishes Christians to "bear your share of the hardship which the gospel entails." And at the end of Matthew's account of the transfiguration, Jesus warns of his impending death. The path to holiness passes through the refining fires of suffering, and so today we are reassured that the promise is firm and will surely lead to fullness of glory with Christ.

Catholic Doctrine

Christ, Our Hope of Glory

God alone is holy. And yet, humans can participate in the holiness of God. The path to sanctification ("to make holy") in a believer's life begins with awe. The human creature realizes there is a "Greater One," the Creator. Even though this leads to the realization of one's unworthiness, a simultaneous sense of attraction to the positive, to God's glory, is experienced. In this gospel passage depicting the transfiguration, the disciples fall forward, hiding their faces, in awe of the divine manifestation. At the same time, the experience is a positive one, leading Peter to exclaim how good it is.

Much has been written in the scriptures about the holiness of God and our participation in or striving toward that holiness. Theologians in the early Church also contributed to an understanding of what was variously called sanctification in the western tradition or deification in the eastern tradition. The Second Vatican Council made it very clear that not only priests and religious are called to sanctity, but all—whatever their vocation or station in life—should strive toward holiness by a continued participation in the sacramental life of the Church and in its mission. The Council stated: "The forms and tasks of life are many but holiness is one—that sanctity which is cultivated by all who act under God's Spirit and, obeying the Father's voice and adoring God the Father in spirit and in truth, follow Christ, poor, humble and cross-bearing, that they may deserve to be partakers of his glory" (LG 41).

Thus, all Christians, no matter their station or their walk of life, are challenged to heed the divine voice and accept the good news to "get up," to cast off fear and conform their lives to Christ, God's beloved Son (Matthew 17:1–9). The transforming effect of God's grace enables this sanctification or holiness in the lives of believers. The Second Vatican Council teaches that God will indeed provide the necessary grace for this progression in holiness if one surrenders to and trusts in the divine will—as Christ conformed himself to the will of his heavenly Father. In that trusting attitude and by the actions motivated by that trust, Christians will manifest the power of God's love (LG 41–42).

Jesus' life, poured out for our sake in his selfless ministry and his passion and death on the cross, is the fountain welling up within the hearts of believers which provides for our very life and the possibility of entering into God's holiness. By his obedience to the will of God the Father, Jesus, the Son, makes of us all children of the kingdom and heirs to the crown of glory achieved by his sacrifice. Thus, the Master whom we follow is the image in which believers' lives are conformed (CCC 2012).

Yet the Christian path to holiness and progress toward perfection is marked by struggle (CCC 2015). The allure of sin, the seductions of Satan, must be fought and the way of self-sacrifice (the cross) must be embraced. In that spiritual battle, the disciple of Jesus takes heart in knowing that Christ has led the way in rejecting the kingdom of darkness and has paid the price for us in advance.

St. Leo the Great (pope from 440 to 460), contemplating this gospel passage of the transfiguration, preached:

The Lord reveals his glory in the presence of chosen witnesses. His body is like that of the rest of mankind, but he makes it shine with such splendor that his face becomes like the sun in glory, and his garments as white as snow.

The great reason for this transformation was to remove the scandal of the cross from the hearts of his disciples, and to prevent the humiliation of his voluntary suffering from disturbing the faith of those who had witnessed the surpassing glory that lay concealed.

With no less forethought he was also providing a firm foundation for the hope of the holy Church. *The whole body of Christ was to understand the kind of transformation that it would receive as his gift.* The members of that body were to look forward to a share in that glory which first blazed out in Christ their head. (*Sermo* 51, 3–4, 8: PL 54, 310–311, 313 found in LitHrs, vol. 2, p. 149, emphasis added.)

Catholic Culture

The glory of holiness to which we followers of Jesus are called has frequently been symbolized in Christian art by the halo. The halo or a nimbus of light shining around the head of the saint or of the divine were used as an artistic convention beginning about the fifth century. The most common depiction of a halo is circular. But Christ's and God the Father's may be shown in triangular form to represent the Trinity. Artists have also incorporated a cross within the circular form of Christ's halo—combining this hint of glory with this sign of suffering. Finally, an *aureole* or *mandorla,* that is, a much larger area of light surrounding the whole figure, is sometimes used by artists in depicting God the Father, Jesus Christ, or Mary, the mother of God (DictSymb 108).

Dismissal Catechesis (30 min.)

Getting Started

1. Prepare the space ahead of time with a circle of chairs around a table covered with a purple cloth. Place a white cloth in folds across the table and add a large white candle.
2. Lead the candidates and catechumens to the circle and place the Lectionary on the table. Invite the candidates and catechumens to gather and be seated quietly within the circle. Then light the candle and pray in these or similar words: *Loving God, you called Jesus "your beloved Son." We, too, are your beloved daughters and sons. Just as you allowed the disciples to see Jesus as one filled with light, you desire to fill us evermore with your light. Enlighten us now with your life and spirit. Fill us today with your light and love. We ask this through Jesus, the transfigured Christ. Amen.*

First Impressions

1. Invite the participants to listen as you reverently recall the following scenes from today's scriptures:
   In Genesis we heard the words of Abraham's call, his invitation to go forth, the promise that his name would be great and that he would receive God's blessing. In faith, Abraham and his wife Sarah went as God directed them.
   In the psalm we heard the prayer "Let your mercy be on us, as we place our trust in you."
   Paul's letter to Timothy reminded us that God has saved us and called us to a holy life.
   In Matthew's portrayal of the Transfiguration of Jesus, we saw Jesus become as dazzling as the sun, his clothes as radiant as light. We heard God say, "This is my beloved Son on whom my favor rests. Listen to him."
2. When you have finished, ask the participants to respond to this question: *Which of these scenes speaks most strongly to you?* Move around the circle, allowing each person an opportunity to respond or pass. Then invite them to share in pairs their reasons for choosing that particular image.
3. Bring the participants back to the large group and elicit responses from each pair. Briefly summarize the sharing.

Making Connections

1. Using these or your own words explain the kernel of truth found in today's first reading from Genesis 12:1–4:
   Like Abraham and Sarah, we are called by God's promise to embark on a journey of faith. Remember that last week we explored what it means to be the "elect" or chosen of God. God's love for us is freely given according to God's promise. Out of this love we are called, as were Sarah and Abraham, to go forth to a new place, a new way of holiness. Our willing response to God's call is a life lived in a covenant relationship with the Lord. Like Abraham and Sarah, we will be blessed with holiness as we live out that call.
2. Invite everyone to discuss these questions in pairs: *How do you understand God's call to holiness? How have you experienced God's blessing as you respond to God's call? When have you been aware that you were a blessing for others?*

3. In the large group, elicit some insights from the pairs. Ask participants to note something they want to remember from this session. After a moment of quiet, invite the participants to share their insight with the group.

Prayer

Invite everyone to sit comfortably, to close their eyes, and to take several deep breaths. Direct the participants to inhale and exhale slowly. As they breathe in invite them to silently say, *"God."* As they exhale, silently say, *"May your blessing live in me."* Spend a short time in silence as they pray in this manner. Then close the prayer time by saying *"Amen."* Invite them to open their eyes.

Extended Catechesis

SESSION FOCUS: *Christ, Our Hope of Glory*

Gathering

A. **Sunday:**
   1. Greet and welcome the sponsors, team members, and additional participants as they arrive. Invite them to join the circle of catechumens and candidates.
   2. Briefly summarize the insights of the catechumens and candidates during the Dismissal Catechesis.
   3. Invite everyone to sit in silence. Then pray in these or similar words: *God, you called Jesus your beloved Son. Help us know in the depth of our being that we are truly your beloved daughters and sons. Let us see ourselves filled and surrounded by the light of your love. As Christ was filled with radiant glory on the mount of the transfiguration, help us to understand that you call us to a life of holiness. We pray in the name of Jesus, on whom your favor rests. Amen.*
   4. Invite the participants to close their eyes as they prepare to hear once again today's gospel. Introduce the proclamation of this gospel with this meditation: *Imagine walking up a mountain with Jesus and some of his disciples. You converse and notice the dusty path and feel the heat of the sun. When you arrive at the top, you each sit down to rest and get a drink of water. After a few minutes, you realize Jesus has walked ahead. You and the other disciples follow him and have an unusual experience.* Proclaim the gospel, Matthew 17:1–9.

B. **Weekday:**
   1. Welcome and greet the participants as they arrive. Invite all to gather in the circle around the same centerpiece used for the Dismissal Catechesis.
   2. Ask the participants to name an experience of being a blessing these past few days. Summarize the insights of the catechumens and candidates during the Dismissal Catechesis in a few sentences.
   3. Lead this celebration of the Word:
      - Song: "Jerusalem, My Destiny," verse 1 (Rory Cooney, GIA Publications, 1990).

- Greeting, sign of the cross.
- First Reading: Genesis 12:1–4
- Psalm: Sing the refrain to Psalm 33, "Let your mercy be on us, as we place our trust in you."
- Meditation: Invite the participants to close their eyes as they prepare to hear, once again, Sunday's gospel.
- Introduce the proclamation of this gospel by leading the same meditation as above (A.4).
- Proclaim the gospel, Matthew 17:1–9
- Concluding Prayer: You may use the prayer above (A.3) or one of your own.

The Word (30 min.)

1. Invite the participants to share whatever comes to mind when they hear the word "holiness." Based upon their spontaneous input and the scripture passages ask them to define "holiness."
2. Offer a background on today's gospel in these or your own words (The Word in Liturgy section of Understanding this Sunday will be of help in your preparation.):

   Every year on the second Sunday of Lent the Church presents the gospel of Jesus' transfiguration. Matthew places this event following Peter's profession of faith and Jesus' prediction of his passion and death. At the end of Matthew's account, Jesus warns the disciples once again of his impending death. The transfiguration is a glimpse for the disciples and for us of the glory that is to come. Through baptism we all share in the life of the glorified Christ. This life is the blessing of holiness, promised to Abraham by God and made possible through the transformative grace of Jesus' suffering and death.

   Baptism is the focus of Lent. For the baptized, Lent is a time to renew their baptismal commitment. For the elect, who will be baptized at Easter, Lent is an intense period of purification and illumination to prepare for baptism. The transfigured Christ, filled with light and wearing white clothing, is an image of the transfiguration that takes place in each of the baptized through the grace of the sacrament.
3. Invite everyone to gather into small groups to discuss this question: *What correlation do you see between the transfiguration and our call to holiness?* You may ask a few of the small groups to share their insights in the large gathering.
4. Encourage the participants to move deeper into the call to holiness using the Reflection exercise in the Participant Book on page 26. After they have sufficient time to reflect, write, and respond to the questions, ask the participants to discuss the paradox between suffering and glory in their small groups. Then invite some large group sharing of the ways the participants have experienced this light through suffering.

Catholic Teaching (30 min.)

1. Develop a presentation on Christ, Our Hope of Glory, using the background in the Catholic Doctrine section of Understanding this Sunday, including the following points:
   - God alone is holy, yet we participate in the holiness of God through baptism. We strive toward holiness by participating in the sacramental life of the Church and in her mission.
   - The very holiness of God is shown forth in Christ at the transfiguration and following his death and resurrection. Christ was glorified before the three apostles and sits now

and forever at the right hand of God in glory. The word "glory" connotes beauty and splendor, as in "a glorious morning," as well as a place of honor. The Church attributes both of these meanings to Christ who is glorified.
   - The transforming effect of God's gift of self—called grace—empowers the believer to grow in holiness. One need only surrender to and trust in the divine will. Christ is our model for conforming to the will of his heavenly Father.
   - Like the three apostles, we feel small and unworthy in the face of God's glory. But this experience of awe before God draws us into union with God.
   - We all are called to share in the very holiness of God—priests, religious, and laity alike—by virtue of being created in God's image and likeness, and by our baptism into Christ.
2. In the large group, ask the participants to respond to these questions: *Who are some people you know personally or have heard about that you consider holy? What are some of the qualities of "holiness"?* List their responses on newsprint, large enough for all to read.

Putting Faith into Practice

1. Gather the participants into small groups to share their thoughts on the following: *What is your hope for holiness? How have you experienced the blessing (grace) of holiness? What is your reaction to your personal call to holiness?* Allow several minutes for sharing. Then ask participants to offer a few responses to the questions in the large group.
2. In the same small groups, ask the participants to reflect on and share their response to these questions: *What is one concrete way you are able to live your call to holiness this week? What specific help/grace from God do you need to do this?* Participants may wish to write their action down in the Participant Book, page 27, in the section entitled "I want to put my faith into action by."

Prayer

Gather the group in silent reflection and prayer that they might have what they need to live as God's holy ones this week. Introduce the prayer with this explanation:

Christians have long imagined the holiness of Christ, Mary, and the saints with a halo, or circle of light around their head, or surrounding their entire body. With your eyes closed, picture such a circle of light around you and around each one of the people gathered here. Brief pause. *Now imagine this light of Christ moving into your being. It fills your mind, your heart, and the very core of your being.* Brief pause. Then, pray in these or your own words: *Let us pray. God, fill us and surround us with your light. Let us truly see ourselves as your holy ones. Let your love enlighten our minds, soften our hearts, and sustain us in the depth of our being. Clothe us in your light. Give us the grace to live as your holy people. When we are afraid, let us recall that we are your beloved, and that your favor rests on us. May the crosses we encounter on our journey of faith be transformed into the light of your glory. Keep us close to you. Mold us into Christ so that one day we may share in the fullness of the glory of Christ, who lives with you in full splendor and honor, now and forever. Amen.* Close by inviting all to sing "Jerusalem, My Destiny" (verse 2).

Third Sunday of Lent

Understanding this Sunday:
Background for Catechesis

The Word in Liturgy

Exodus 17:3–7
Psalm 95: 1–2, 6–7, 8–9
Romans 5:1–2, 5–8
John 4:5–42 [or (short form) 4:5–15, 19–26, 39, 40–42]

On the first two Sundays of Lent, all three years of the Lectionary cycle focus on important events in the life of Jesus: the temptation in the desert (Lent 1) and the transfiguration (Lent 2). However, for the next three Sundays, each year has its own particular focus. The readings chosen for Year A during these three weeks have ancient associations with the catechesis given to candidates for Easter baptism. Prior to Lent's expansion to a forty-day period, when it lasted only three weeks, today's gospel was read on the first Sunday of Lent, next Sunday's gospel (the man born blind) on the second Sunday, and the following Sunday's (Lazarus) on the third Sunday. The theme of water that is so prominent in today's texts is an unmistakable reflection of the baptismal focus of these readings, yet there is a richness to them that is much broader than catechesis for baptism.

The particular focus we suggest for the catechesis based on today's readings has to do with our understanding of faith as God's gift. In the gospel, Jesus invites the woman to come to faith in him. Exegetes have suggested that the woman is an image of faithlessness—that of Israel, Samaria, and indeed all of us. She is an image of every infidelity borne of trying to quench our cravings on something other than the "living water" of God's love. Jesus links his offer of "living water" with his offer of the gift of faith: the opportunity he presents for the woman to recognize him as the Messiah ("I who speak to you am he"). Jesus alone can give this gift of life-giving water, water that elsewhere in John's gospel is identified as being "the Spirit that those who came to believe in him were to receive" (John 7:39). The many-layered meanings to be discovered in John's gospel are nowhere more dense than in this passage that juxtaposes the symbolism of living water and the gift of faith.

The first reading teaches by way of contrast. The grumbling, mistrust, and lack of gratitude shown by the Israelites in the desert is the antithesis of the attitudes called for in those who have accepted God's gift of faith. Moses, the great intercessor, in whom Christian tradition has discerned an image of Christ the mediator, is contrasted with the Israelites. In the face of their mistrust, he believes in God's power to save; in the face of their grumbling, he lifts his hands in prayer; in answer to their testing ("Is the Lord in our midst or not?"), he proves God's presence by striking the rock to bring forth water. Today's responsorial psalm contains an indictment of the people's hardened hearts in the desert, but it also calls us (and every generation) to faith: "Come, let us sing joyfully . . . greet him with thanksgiving . . . joyfully sing psalms . . . oh, that today you would hear his voice."

This section of Paul's letter to the Romans reminds the reader of the central theme of the letter, that we have been "justified by faith." Faith has come to us as God's gift in Jesus ("Through him we have gained access by faith"). All of the spiritual benefits that have come to us as God's gift are summed up by Paul in his image of "the love of God [that] has been poured out in our hearts by the Holy Spirit who has been given to us." One commentator enumerates the benefits that Paul names as ours in this passage: (1) peace with God, (2) access to divine grace, (3) hope in sharing God's glory, (4) The Holy Spirit as God's gift, and (5) God's love manifested in Christ.

Catholic Doctrine

Faith as a Gift

While faith is the believer's response to God, that response is prompted by the initiative of God's action in reaching out to us. In other words, God acts first. It is only because of God's initiative that a relationship can develop between the human person and the divine. The theological term for this is grace. God acts graciously toward us, extending to us an offer of being in relationship. We, in turn, are given the freedom to respond, accepting or rejecting this offer. In a sense, it is upon the meeting ground of faith that God's grace and human freedom intersect.

An individual can believe only because God's grace is active in that person's life through the Spirit. But, at the same time, a believing stance is only possible because a person is free to choose. This ability to choose another in freedom, which is characteristic of our deepest relationships, such as friendship or marriage, is also true of our relationship with God in faith. This choice can only be effective if it is authentic, a true human act which surrenders to the promise of the other. To trust in the promises of God is not an evacuation of our human will or instincts but the truest sign of our human dignity (CCC 154).

It is not so much that we have faith in God because we are able to investigate and grasp truths independently or to process intellectually what is proposed to us by divine revelation. It is rather that our whole self is grasped by the illuminating power of God which draws us or immerses us into intimacy and friendship with the divine. In our Catholic way of conceiving of faith, it is a way of being, a whole way of life in concert with the God who prepares the ground for this relationship in love (EncyCath 512).

The Second Vatican Council asserts that Jesus Christ reveals the mystery of our own human nature and our divine calling. Human beings are a riddle to themselves, and given our human experience of finitude and incompleteness we search for answers, for meaning. The Council teaches that it is in and through Christ that light is shed on who we are and to what we are called. It also affirmed, "All this holds true not for Christians only but also for all . . . of good will in whose hearts grace is active invisibly. For since . . . all . . . are in fact called to one and the same destiny, which is divine, we must hold that the Holy Spirit offers to all the possibility of being made partners, in a way known to God, in the paschal mystery" (GS 22).

In reflecting upon the gospel episode of the woman at the well, St. Augustine wrote:

A woman came. She is a symbol of the Church not yet made righteous but about to be made righteous. Righteousness follows from the conversation. She came in ignorance, she found Christ, and he enters into conversation with her. . . .

She found faith in Christ, who was using her as a symbol to teach us what was to come. . . .

He asks for a drink, and he promises a drink. He is in need, as one hoping to receive, yet he is rich, as one about to satisfy the thirst of others. He says: *If you knew the gift of God.* The gift of God is the Holy Spirit. But he is still using veiled language as he speaks to the woman and gradually enters into her heart, (*Tract.* 15, 10–12. 16–17: CCL 36, 154–56, found in LitHrs, vol. 2, pp. 212–13).

St. Augustine emphasizes that she finds faith in Christ and that this faith is a gift. The gift is given by the Lord who initiates the conversation and who speaks to her heart, eager to satisfy the thirst which is there. As the Church prays on this Sunday, "When Christ asked the woman of Samaria for water to drink, Christ had already prepared for her the gift of faith. In his thirst to receive her faith he awakened in her heart the fire of your love." (*Sacramentary*, Preface for Third Sunday of Lent).

Catholics believe that faith is a gift. We act freely toward God, and yet that response is made possible by the divine love revealed to us in Jesus, the Messiah, who thirsts to receive our faith.

Catholic Culture

The subject of the conversation between the woman of Samaria and Jesus is depicted as early as the art of the catacombs of St. Callistus (third century). It also is illustrated by one of the panels on the sixth-century ivory throne of Maximian, which was probably made in Constantinople and is now found in the Archbishop's Palace Museum in Ravenna, Italy. This chair is covered by exquisitely carved delicate ivory panels depicting the four evangelists, John the Baptist, and scenes from the life of Christ. It is the only bishop's chair to survive from the early centuries of the Christian Church (OxA&A 317–18).

Prior to entering a Carmelite monastery in Paris, Brother Lawrence (d. 1691) was a soldier and a hermit. In the monastery he worked in the kitchen. His writings reflect a depth of interior spirit. Brother Lawrence is known for his simple, profound prayer: "Lord, I cannot do this unless you enable me." (*Prayers of the Saints*, Woodeene Koenig-Bricker, HarperCollins Publishers Inc., 1996, p. 72).

Dismissal Catechesis (30 min.)

Getting Started

1. Prepare the space ahead of time with a circle of chairs around a table that is covered with a purple cloth. Place a large clear vessel (bowl, pitcher, or tureen) of water on the table.
2. Lead the candidates and catechumens to the circle and place the Lectionary on the table near the bowl of water. As they stand in place around the circle, invite all to sing the first two verses of the Gathering Song used at your Sunday liturgy. Ask the participants to be seated and invite everyone to remain silent for a moment and focus their attention on the bowl of clear water. Encourage the catechumens and candidates to sing the refrain of Psalm 95 in response to your proclamation of verses 1–2, 6–7, and 8–9: "If today you hear his voice, harden not your hearts."

First Impressions

1. If catechumens and candidates were present for the celebration of the Scrutiny, invite them to share their insights as to the meaning of the ritual. (Details on celebrating and reflecting upon this ritual can be found in the *Purification and Enlightenment Manual,* which is part of the *Foundations in Faith* library.)
2. Assist the participants in recalling the Liturgy of the Word by inviting them to focus their attention on the vessel of water as you slowly repeat some of the images from the scriptures:
   "Give us water to drink"—The people grumbled against Moses, "Why did you ever make us leave Egypt?"—"What shall I do with this people?"—"Strike the rock, and water will flow from it for the people to drink"—"Give me a drink"—"How can you, a Jew, ask me, a Samaritan woman, for a drink?"—". . . he would have given you living water"—"Sir, you do not even have a bucket and the cistern is deep"—"Whoever drinks the water I shall give will never thirst; the water I shall give will become in him a spring of water welling up to eternal life"—"Sir, give me this water, so that I may not be thirsty."
3. Invite the participants to share their responses to the following questions in pairs: *What does God seem to be saying to you through the Liturgy of the Word today? What are some insights you have about water from the first reading and the gospel?*
4. In the large group encourage each pair to share their ideas from the discussion. Comment briefly. Then summarize the variety of responses.

Making Connections

1. Remaining in the large group, invite the participants to discuss these questions: *What are some ways you have experienced thirst? How do you try to satisfy your thirsts? What similarities do you find between your ways*

of quenching your thirsts and the reactions of the Israelites or the Samaritan woman?
2. Gather them once again into pairs and ask the participants to share their responses to these questions: *What has your journey of faith in the Catechumenate taught you about satisfying your thirst for meaning, community, and God? How have you changed on this journey?* Invite some responses from the pairs in the large group. As they respond be sure to encourage a free flow of ideas. Briefly summarize the main points of the sharing.

Prayer

Invite everyone into silence, asking that they think about those thirsts which they are experiencing right now in this journey of faith. After an appropriate time, direct the participants to name their thirst, using the phrase, *"God, I thirst for. . . ."* After each petition, instruct the group to respond, *"You alone fill our thirst."* At the conclusion of this litany, sing the third verse of the Gathering Song used at your parish liturgy.

Extended Catechesis

SESSION FOCUS: *Faith as a Gift*

Gathering

A. **Sunday:**
   1. Greet and welcome the sponsors, team members, and additional participants as they arrive. Invite them to join the circle of candidates and catechumens. After a time of silence, ask a catechumen or candidate to briefly summarize the sharing during the Dismissal Catechesis.
   2. Invite the participants to focus their attention upon the vessel of water and think about their own thirst for God. Invite all to stand and sing "Give us living water, give us living water" (David Haas, GIA, 1992). Ask a team member to proclaim the gospel, John 4:5–42. As the proclamation ends, intone the refrain, "Give us living water, give us living water." Pause in silent reflection.

B. **Weekday:**
   1. Use the same centerpiece as used for the Dismissal Catechesis.
   2. Ask the participants to gather in the circle. Greet and warmly welcome each person. Ask them to share an experience of thirsting for God over the last few days.
   3. Lead this celebration of the Word, after pausing for a time of silence:
      - First Reading: Exodus 17:3–7
      - Sing Psalm 95
      - Gospel: John 4:5–42
      - Silence
      - Prayer: *God, you are the one for whom we long, the one whom our hearts seek. We are thirsty for healing, for an end to poverty and hatred. We are*

*thirsty for forgiveness and an end to competition.
We are thirsty for acceptance and meaning in our
lives. In our heart of hearts, we are thirsty for you,
our God. Quench our thirst. Fill us with the life-
giving water that only you can give. For you are
our God, now and forever. Amen.*

The Word (30 min.)

1. Offer the following background to today's gospel:
*On the third Sunday of Lent the Church proclaims Jesus'
encounter with the Samaritan Woman. Today's gospel
passage, and those of the next two weeks, that of the Man
Born Blind and the Raising of Lazarus, all found in
John's gospel, have ancient associations with the catechesis given to those preparing for Easter baptism. They
each include someone coming to belief in Jesus, and
present a particular facet of Jesus' identity. In today's
passage, Jesus invites the Samaritan woman to believe
in him, the source of living water. She represents every
infidelity borne of trying to quench our cravings on
something other than the "living water" of God's love. As
Jesus offers her the "living water" he links it to his offer
of the gift of faith. Her response is to profess her faith in
the marvelous realization, unfolded in their conversation, in which she recognizes this rabbi as the Messiah.*

2. As you finish this explanation move to the vessel of water.
Quietly lift some water with your hand, letting the sound of
the water fill the silence as it falls through your fingers
back into the vessel. Invite the group to quietly reflect on
this gospel by using the exercise on page 28 of the
Participant Book. Ask them to answer the questions that
follow. When they have had sufficient time, gather them
into small groups to share any insights from this exercise.
Encourage the sponsors and their catechumen or candidate
to join together in the same group.

3. Then focus their attention back to the large group. Invite
someone from each group to share their thoughts on this
question: *Name some of your experiences of God taking
the initiative to invite you to a closer relationship. How
did you respond?*

Catholic Teaching (30 min.)

1. Invite the group to define "faith" in a word or phrase that
comes to mind. Record the responses of the group on
newsprint, writing large enough for everyone to see. Post
the newsprint when the group has finished.

2. Recall for the group that while faith is the believer's
response to God, that response is initiated by God's action
in our lives. Continue to share the teaching of the Church
on the gift of faith and cover the following points:
   - Faith is a gift. It is God's gracious offer to be in relationship with us. God freely gives us the gift of faith. We do
not do, nor can we do, anything to merit faith. God
simply and freely gives the gift of faith.
   - God acts first. Just as Jesus approached the Samaritan
woman and engaged with her, God enters our lives and
invites us to open to the gift of faith.
   - We respond to God's gift by choosing to enter freely into
this relationship with God. More than an intellectual

ascent to the truths revealed by God, faith immerses us
into intimacy and friendship with the divine. By the
grace of faith we are grasped by the illuminating power
of God.
   - Each individual is free to choose their response to God's
initiative. For a relationship to be authentic, it has to be
entered freely. We choose not only whether to enter a
relationship with God, but how much of ourselves to
invest in this relationship.
   - Faith is a way of being, of living in communion with
God, of surrendering to this relationship of intimacy
with God. Upon the ground of faith, we discover
meaning and identity through the light of faith shed in
the power of the Holy Spirit.

3. Once again, ask the participants to define "faith" in the
light of the Church's teaching. List their descriptive phrases
on a second sheet of newsprint and compare them to the
first responses of the group.

4. Invite the participants to pause and silently reflect upon
where they are "today" in their faith relationship with God.
They might wish to think about some of the obstacles that
keep them from a deeper surrender to the gracious gift of
intimacy with God.

Putting Faith into Practice

1. Make the following observation: *In today's gospel passage
the Samaritan woman lets go of her water jar and then
runs freely into town, proclaiming, "Come and see
someone who told me everything I ever did!" She is
freed in being fully known and accepted by the Lord.*

2. Ask participants to move back into their small groups and
discuss these questions: *What obstacles hold you back
from responding to God's gift of faith? In what way are
you being invited to surrender to deeper relationship
with Jesus/God? What is one concrete way you will
commit yourself to moving into a deeper relationship
with God this week?* Encourage participants to write their
response in the Participant Book on page 29 in the section,
"I want to put my faith into action by."

Prayer

Invite everyone to silently reflect on his or her desire for the
living water of faith in Jesus. When the group is ready
encourage them to sing the first verse of "Come to the Water"
(John Foley, GIA, 1978). Prayerfully read St. Augustine's reflection on the Samaritan Woman from the Liturgy of the Hours
provided in the Catholic Doctrine section of Understanding
this Sunday. Invite each participant to move to the center and
dip their hand into the vessel of water, and through some
symbolic gesture (for example, sprinkle the water on your face
or neck) bring their desire for the "living water" of faith to the
Lord. Continue singing the remaining verses of "Come to the
Water" as the participants engage in this ritual action. Close
by praying: *Pour your living water of faith upon all who
gather here today. Bless us with the water of life as we
together journey in faith. Let these thirst-quenching waters
bring each of us into a deeper intimacy with you, Our God
and Gracious Faithful One. Amen.*

Fourth Sunday of Lent

Understanding this Sunday:
Background for Catechesis

The Word in Liturgy

1 Samuel 16:1, 6–7, 10–13
Psalm 23:1–3, 3–4, 5, 6
Ephesians 5:8–14
John 9:1–41 [or (short form) 9:1, 6–9, 13–17, 34–38]

The themes of blindness/sight and darkness/light so prominent in this week's readings continue the Lenten tradition of catechesis aimed at preparing for Easter baptisms. It is not coincidental that this time has been designated as the Period of Purification and Enlightenment. Like the theme of water in last week's readings, today's themes can be understood on multiple levels. We choose to hear them against the backdrop of the Church's teaching on original sin and social sin.

The description of God's choice of David over his brothers that is found in 1 Samuel is a tale of human blindness, our inability to see spiritual truth as God sees it. David is portrayed as the least likely of his brothers to be chosen for greatness—it never even occurs to his father to present David to Samuel as a candidate for divine election. But God sees into the heart and directs the prophet to anoint David, causing the spirit of the Lord to rush upon him. The gesture of anointing signifies both God's choice of David and his consecration for the mission entrusted to him, shepherding God's people as king. The blindness of those around David to his potential for being an instrument of God's power is a symbol on many levels of how sin can blind us to God's will for us and for the world. The responsorial psalm connects David the shepherd boy with the Lord as shepherd; or, better, it reveals that David as king is but an instrument that the Lord uses to shepherd his people.

Although it would not be until several centuries later that Augustine would formulate the doctrine of original sin, the author of today's second reading certainly knew and described that reality in functional terms. "There was a time when you

were in darkness," he says, using that evocative metaphor to capture the desperate situation of the human race without Christ. The works of darkness are not explicitly named, though they are certainly alluded to in suggestive language: "vain deeds . . . shameful . . . condemned. . . ." Chapters 1–3 of the letter to the Ephesians deal with God's plan to save all people; chapters 4–6 aim at calling the readers to turn away from their former sinful ways and follow the way of Christ. Quoting what was most likely an ancient Christian hymn, the author reminds his audience of the fundamental Christian truth regarding how we are saved from the darkness of sin: "Christ will give you light." The fruits of Christ's saving light ("goodness and justice and truth") eradicate the effects of what contemporary theology calls social sin.

The figure of a man blind from birth is a fitting image of the human condition known as original sin. Without personal fault or responsibility, the man is nonetheless truly "in the dark" of a sinful world. John tells the story of the man's cure by Jesus in a way that reveals who it is that is truly blind—those who stubbornly refuse to accept Jesus as the light of the world (John 8:12). Social sin is not the same as original sin, but flows from it, and is the cumulative result of human choices to turn away from the light. The dramatic unfolding of John's story gives eloquent expression to the way individuals in a community compound their blindness, to their own and others' detriment. Everyone gets involved—the man's neighbors, his family, those who had seen him begging, the Pharisees—and the evil grows until, in an act that is surely filled with Johannine irony, the man is expelled from the synagogue for acknowledging Jesus as the Messiah.

Catholic Doctrine

Original Sin and Social Sin

The inescapable fact that from the dawn of time men and women have sinned led St. Augustine to pose his famous question, "Whence evil?" and prompted this great writer to reflect upon the account of Adam and Eve's fall from original holiness as portrayed by Genesis. By turning away from God and choosing to go against the divine prohibition they not only shattered the harmony of body and soul but experienced alienation from their creator and all creation (CCC 400).

The Adam and Eve account in Genesis may very well be figurative, and yet the Second Vatican Council affirmed that "at the very start of history" humanity abused its freedom and sought to place itself on a par with God. In reflecting upon the experience of the world, the council fathers noted that we are "drawn toward what is wrong and sunk in many evils which cannot come from [our] good creator." The Council acknowledged, therefore, the revelation which the Church has reflected upon since its inception, that God is not the author of sin but is the author of our redemption in Christ (GS 13.1)

Indeed, it is precisely because of our being offered salvation in Jesus that we are enabled to more clearly identify our original alienation from God. The very notion of a fallen state, a harmful captivity, a loss which is termed "original sin" is the opposite pole of the Good News of our release and liberation through the life, death, and resurrection of Jesus (CCC 389).

Born into a state of alienation from God, we are offered a way out by the generous mercy of our Creator through the new birth of baptism. And yet, the primeval event of original sin permeates this world. Born again to the new life of grace, we nevertheless find ourselves on a battleground, struggling against the powers of evil, and must constantly strive to do what is right. Assisted by God's grace, the human person can achieve an "inner integrity" (GS 37.2).

This inner integrity, however, does not spare the individual from committing sin from time to time. Why? The very inclination to sin, concupiscence, is a result due to the tragedy of original sin and is stirred up by communal situations, social structures, and institutions that are in conflict with divine graciousness (CCC 408).

John Paul II describes these communal situations, social structures, and institutions which are expressions of and the accumulated effects of personal sin as "social sin." He writes: "Whenever the church speaks of situations of sin or when she condemns as social sins certain situations or the collective behavior of certain social groups, big or small, or even of whole nations and blocs of nations, she knows and she proclaims that such cases of social sin are the result of the accumulation and concentration of many personal sins." (John Paul II, *Reconciliatio et Paenitentia* 16, December 2, 1984, Vatican translation, published by St. Paul Books and Media, Boston).

Not only each individual, but the world itself—as a result of original sin, the personal sins we commit, and structures of social sin—is in need of Christ, our physician, for healing. This is how St. Augustine described the Lord in reflecting upon "the sin of the world" (John 1:29). "Faith in Christ, made possible by grace, offers a "comfort against sin" (Julian of Norwich) and a passage from sickness to that state of health known . . . as holiness. It is the process of healing which is primarily revealed: we know of the disease partly from human experience but mainly, and salvifically, from what Jesus Christ has done for us by his life, teaching, death and resurrection" (NDictTheol 731).

Thus, on this fourth Sunday of Lent, the Church proclaims in the eucharistic gathering, "Father . . . we do well always and everywhere to give you thanks through Jesus. He came among us as a man, to lead mankind from darkness into the light of faith. Through Adam's fall we were born as slaves of sin, but now through baptism in Christ we are reborn as your adopted children" (*Sacramentary*, Preface for Fourth Sunday of Lent).

Catholic Culture

Writers in modern times have shown a renewed interest in the notion of original sin. Albert Camus, C.S. Lewis, J.R.R. Tolkien, Flannery O'Connor, and Walker Percy all explore "its meaning in the persistence of the will to evil despite every apparent social advance of reason" (BibTrad 579).

Dismissal Catechesis (30 min.)

Getting Started

1. Prepare the space ahead of time with a circle of chairs around a table upon which is draped a purple cloth. Place a large candle on the table and have matches handy for its lighting.

2. Lead the candidates and catechumens to the circle and place the Lectionary on the table. Light the candle, while the participants remain standing. Lead them in singing the first verse of the Gathering Song from the parish liturgy. Invite all to be seated and pray in these or similar words: *God of light and darkness, illuminate our minds and hearts that we may understand your Word this day. Your light penetrates the darkness of our lives, shining forth in goodness, righteousness, and truth. We long to become children of this light, good and pleasing in your sight. Therefore, we seek your light as we gather in your presence today. We ask you all this in the name of Christ our light. Amen.*

3. Ask the participants to remain silent and recall their impressions of today's Liturgy of the Word.

First Impressions

1. If the catechumens and candidates were present for the celebration of the Scrutiny, invite them to share their experience of the ritual.

2. Invite the participants to name some of the images of blindness that they heard in the scripture passages proclaimed today. List these on a flip chart, printing large enough for all to read.

3. Gather the group into pairs to explore these questions: *What was the blindness of Jesse, David's father? In what ways are we blinded by outward appearances? How did this shepherd boy have the makings of a king?* Invite the pairs to share their insights with the whole group. Summarize their insights in a few sentences.

Making Connections

1. In the large group, ask the participants to share their experiences of God choosing the least likely or most improbable person for greatness. Be ready to begin the sharing with your own story.

2. Ask the same pairs to discuss the differences between God's way of seeing and our human blindness.

3. Return the attention of the participants to the large group, asking these questions: *What are the obstacles that continue to blind us from seeing the heart of another as God does? What are the consequences of our human blindness?* These may be listed on the flip chart.

Prayer

Encourage the participants to sit quietly and reflect upon the consequences of their own blindness. Pray Psalm 23 together by asking the group to sing the response, *"The Lord is my shepherd, there is nothing that I lack,"* as you pray verses 2–3, 4, 5, and 6. Close with this prayer: *God, you are our shepherd. Though we are blind, you lead us. Though we misunderstand our brothers and sisters, you forgive our human weakness. Though we lack confidence and faith, you anoint our heads with oil. Though our sins are many, you pursue us with your love. Shed your light of love into the darkness of our living. We ask you this through Jesus, our Lord. Amen.*

Extended Catechesis

SESSION FOCUS: *Original Sin and Social Sin*

Gathering

A. Sunday:

1. Prior to the session prepare and practice proclaiming John 9, by asking team members to read the parts of the following characters: narrator, Jesus, blind man, and the parents of the blind man. The whole team and/or sponsors can divide into three groups, acting as the disciples, the Pharisees, and the neighbors.

2. Greet and welcome the sponsors and team members as they arrive. Invite them to join the circle of catechumens and candidates.

3. Invite all to stand and sing two verses of the Gathering Song from today's liturgy. Invite everyone to be seated and reflect upon the contrast between light and darkness in their own lives as they meditate upon the lighted candle. After a period of silent reflection, indicate to the team and sponsors that it is time to stand and proclaim the scripted gospel, John 9:1–41. Following the proclamation of the gospel, ask one of the candidates or catechumens to share a few insights from the Dismissal Catechesis, using the flip chart as an aid. Close the prayer with the third verse from the Gathering Song.

B. Weekday:

1. Use the same centerpiece as described for the Dismissal Catechesis and prepare the gospel script as indicated in section A.

2. As the participants gather in the circle, greet and warmly welcome each person.

3. Lead this celebration of the Word:
   - Song: Two verses from the Gathering Song used at last Sunday's liturgy
   - First Reading: 1 Samuel 16:1, 6–7, 10–13
   - Psalm: Sing Psalm 23
   - Second Reading: Ephesians 5:8–14
   - Gospel: John 9:1–41 proclaimed in parts
   - Closing Song: Third verse of the Gathering Song

The Word (30 min.)

1. Invite the participants to share their experiences of "seeing with the light of Christ" over the past few days. Following the group discussion, ask one of the candidates or catechumens to share a few insights from the Dismissal Catechesis, using the flip chart as an aid.

2. Share this presentation on the background to the readings, emphasizing the gospel:

   We were indeed once "the children of darkness," described in the second reading, in a similar state as the blind beggar. But the disciples' question, "Whose sin was it?" is as irrelevant today as it was for Jesus' followers in the gospel passage. Rather, for Jesus, the question is, "Why do you persist in your blindness, insisting that you can see?" We are moved from darkness to light, blindness to sight, by the radiant light of Christ's glory and truth. Turning toward Christ involves a putting off or rejecting all that is not Christ and turning toward, putting on and accepting Christ's way. As the blind man is healed with spittle and clay and the washing in the pool of Siloam, we regain our sight (our spiritual vision) by faith and baptism. Just as his faith and healing were questioned by neighbors, the religious leaders, and even by his frightened parents, our insight and faith will be tried and tested. Unable to believe in the healing, the whole community eventually rejects the blind man, now restored to sight. His only recourse is to turn to Jesus in complete surrender and worship, "I do believe, Lord." Cumulative blindness compounded by weak faith results in darkness and evil. But the light of Christ came "so that those who do not see might see."

3. Invite the participants to gather into small groups to discuss the following questions: *Where in this gospel passage do you find yourself? What are some signs of blindness all around you? How does Christ bring light in your personal darkness? What is the correlation between sight and faith?*

4. In the large gathering, invite a few responses from each of the small groups. Brainstorm with the large group: *What are the possible consequences of our common participation in blindness?* You may wish to record these in large writing on a flip chart.

Catholic Teaching (30 min.)

1. Using the poem on page 30 in the Participant Book, focus the attention of the participants on the notion of original sin. Gather the group into pairs and invite them to share their stories of being faced with a similar choice as that described in the poem. Continue the discussion with the questions following the poem. In the large group ask the pairs to share their insights as to the nature of human weakness.

2. Present the following points concerning original sin and social sin, using the background on Catholic Doctrine as a guide:

   - Humanity is radically and thoroughly flawed, drawn toward evil that widens the rift between the Creator, creation, and humankind. That we are born into this

situation is known as original sin. The effect of this sin impedes our capacity to choose salvation.

   - This original alienation from God and creation has been redeemed by the saving action of Jesus. We are born again into this redeemed nature—a new creation—in baptism, through the overarching grace of God's mercy and love.
   - While we still struggle with the inclination toward sin, this wounded human nature, the mystery of grace is at work, accomplishing all that Christ intended. Both sin and grace are at work in the human spirit. We are indeed graced sinners.
   - Social sin is the consequence of personal sins, which culminate in patterns of evil and injustice that become institutionalized and systematized.
   - By the faith, hope, and love given at baptism, we struggle to live out the grace of our salvation in Christ. Cooperation with the mystery of grace at work in the world is the continual responsibility of the baptized. Moments of triumph over evil systems are signs indicating the as-yet-to-be-completed victory of grace at work.

Or . . .

Use the Participant Book, page 31. Ask the group to read the section "The Church Says" and discuss the meaning of original and social sin in small groups. Field the responses of the groups in a large group discussion.

3. Invite the small groups to discuss: *What signs of God's grace are visible, amidst the evil structures and unjust systems at work in the world?*

Putting Faith into Practice

1. Focus the attention of the participants back to the large group and invite their responses and insights to this question.

2. Ask the group to return to the small groups to share their responses to these questions: *What is our responsibility to bring the light of Christ into the darkness of unjust social structures? How can we respond to corporate evil as a corporate body?* Instruct each group to determine one concrete action that can be taken by the group and/or the parish community. These suggestions can be succinctly described on large newsprint and posted around the room.

3. Ask each group to read their suggestion aloud. Determine, as a group, the action you will take over the next week and the suggestion you will make to the Parish Pastoral Council for parish consideration in the future.

Prayer

Gather the participants in silence around the lighted candle. Invite each person to name a social sin that comes to mind. After each naming, indicate that the group respond: *"Awaken, O sleeper, and arise from the dead, and Christ will give you light."* Close with a sung version of Psalm 23 that is familiar to your group.

Fifth Sunday of Lent

The Word in Liturgy

Ezekiel 37:12–14
Psalm 130:1–2, 3–4, 5–6, 7–8
Romans 8:8–11
John 11:1–45 [or (short form) 11:3–7, 17, 20–27, 33–45]

Today's gospel reading completes the ancient triad of Johannine texts chosen specifically for use in preparing candidates for Easter baptism. The death-resurrection motif so strong in the Lazarus story is also found in the prophecy of Ezekiel and in today's selection from Paul's letter to the Romans.

Ezekiel writes during the time of the Babylonian captivity, when his countrymen were on the brink of despair. They had lost the promised land, seen the destruction of the temple, and found themselves an enslaved people in a foreign land. In the face of such grim prospects, Ezekiel's famous prophecy of dry bones coming to life is meant to restore hope to the dispirited Israelites. In this section of the prophecy, the imagery shifts to dead bodies rising from the grave, and Yahweh speaks words of promise ("I will put my spirit in you that you may live") designed to reassure and comfort the people that God has not abandoned them. Ezekiel is a master of evocative images, and it is clear that the poetry of this passage is meant to be interpreted symbolically in terms of the nation's ultimate fate. Not surprisingly, Christian tradition has expanded the application of this imagery to embrace the paschal mystery of Jesus, the promise of personal resurrection to every Christian, and even the moral renewal of one who has sinned. In the psalm we hear further words of comfort, namely that when we cry to God "out of the depths," we will be heard, forgiven, and healed.

In the thinking of St. Paul, "flesh" was a term that referred not just to our physical body, but to that part of our human nature which had become enslaved to sin. Our "spirit," in this context, was the principle of life and freedom that allowed us to choose God's will over our sinful cravings. But our choice is possible only because we have received the gift of the Holy Spirit who dwells in us. For Paul, that Spirit was the life-force behind Jesus' resurrection from the dead and is the same Spirit that will raise our mortal bodies from death to life also. It is our incorporation into Christ that makes possible our share in the dynamic power of Christ's resurrection. That incorporation, for Paul, was a sacramental event rooted in baptism and sustained in Eucharist. Earlier, in chapter 6, Paul clearly linked this process of dying and rising with Christ to our baptism, an event in which we die to sin and rise to new life "in Christ."

The miracle of Jesus in today's gospel may be regarded as a kind of enactment of the theological vision of Paul contained in the second reading. In the raising of Lazarus from death to life, Jesus proves the truth of what he says in verses 25–26: "I am the resurrection and the life: whoever believes in me, though he should die, will come to life; and whoever is alive and believes in me will never die." This miracle is the seventh and greatest of the "signs" that Jesus works in John's gospel. Exegetes have long noted the deep sacramentalism underlying the Johannine theology of Jesus' "signs." The narrative we read today is most appropriately interpreted in the context of the Church's celebration of the sacraments as events which insert us into the dynamism of Christ's dying and rising, his paschal mystery.

Catholic Doctrine

The Paschal Mystery in the Sacraments

The paschal mystery is a term which encompasses the saving event of Jesus' suffering, death, entombment, resurrection, ascension, and sending of the Spirit. Jesus' paschal mystery is the primordial saving event experienced by Christians which opens for us the redemption of God in Christ.

The life of Jesus which led to the saving events of the paschal mystery, his mission and ministry, anticipated the power unleashed by and experienced in the redemption accomplished in his suffering, death, resurrection, ascension and sending of the Spirit. Thus, the entire life of the Lord can be understood as the foundation of what would later be experienced in the sacraments, which communicate his saving grace to believers today. What was made flesh in the life and saving event of Jesus is passed over to the Church in the celebration of the mysteries, the sacraments (CCC 1115).

The Second Vatican Council teaches: "Thus, for well-disposed members of the faithful, the liturgy of the sacraments and sacramentals sanctifies almost every event of their lives with divine grace which flows from the paschal mystery of the Passion, Death and Resurrection of Christ. From this source all sacraments and sacramentals draw their power. There is scarcely any proper use of material things which cannot thus be directed toward the sanctification of [people] and the praise of God." (SC 61). In other words, not only the seven sacraments, but the use of sacramentals, such as holy water, other types of blessings, rituals, and devotions, all assist in making us believers holy because the Son of God became flesh and in that very "material" of this world along with the "worldly event" of the paschal mystery accomplished our salvation.

Indeed, one contemporary author has described sacraments as the "doors to the sacred" in reflecting their effect and meaning in the lives of the faithful. The very presence of Christ is not only expressed, but tangibly communicated in the way in which they are celebrated. Therefore, they "open up" a doorway onto the experience of the saving event of Jesus Christ here and now in the life of the believing Church. "In these seven [sacraments] the Christian community recognized that the redemptive power of Christ was present, and that those who participated in these ritual actions could encounter the source of all salvation" (*Doors to the Sacred*, Joseph Martos, expanded edition, Triumph Books, Liguori, Missouri, 1991, p. 112).

The passage of time itself is able to raise our minds, our thoughts, and ourselves to the holy. The Council also teaches that the Lord's Day, Sunday, is to be observed as a holy memorial, a moment in the midst of the passage of days that commemorates the resurrection of the Christ (the apex of the paschal mystery). In the course of the year, Easter is the prime moment when the paschal mystery is celebrated. But it is not only on Sunday and Easter that the paschal mystery is made real in the life of believers who celebrate the liturgy—it is also in the very unfolding of the seasons as one progresses through the entire liturgical year that the saving event of Jesus is realized. The Second Vatican Council asserts, "In the course of the year, moreover, [the Church] unfolds the whole mystery of Christ from the incarnation and nativity to the ascension, to Pentecost and the expectation of the blessed hope of the coming of the Lord. Thus recalling the mysteries of the redemption, she opens up to the faithful the riches of her Lord's powers and merits, so that those are in some way made present for all time; the faithful lay hold of them and are filled with saving grace" (SC 102).

Catholic Culture

In the breathtakingly beautiful early Christian churches of Ravenna, Italy, one stands in the nave looking toward the sanctuary (or altar area) and the eye is drawn upward to gaze upon the magnificent mosaics of the domed ceilings. Almost always, Christ is depicted at the apex of the arch or at the top of the dome and as the eye travels downward, the whole panoply of Christian life, in the depiction of evangelists, saints, and the heavenly vision of a "new Eden" or new life through baptismal waters is presented. Because of simple architectural placement, eventually one's gaze comes to rest at eye level upon the altar table. There is a not-so-subtle message here, in the use of artistry and architecture, that the sacraments celebrated in these spaces and the spaces themselves convey the holy and saving action of Christ. In analyzing the holy images and icons of Ravenna, one author writes that these "were not seen as mere 'artists' impressions' of what Christ or the saints might have looked like: they were held to be versions of 'true' images of these figures and thus to contain or transmit—and not just represent—the presence of divinity or supernatural power. Artists were commissioned to produce work that would impress God and the saints by its religious truth. . . ." (*Early Christian and Byzantine Art,* John Lowden, Phaidon Press Limited, London, 1997, p. 7).

Dismissal Catechesis (30 min.)

Getting Started

1. Prepare the space ahead of time with a circle of chairs around a low table that has a purple cloth draped over it. On the table place some symbol of "new life"—a flower, a butterfly, or a budding branch.
2. Lead the candidates and catechumens to the circle and place the Lectionary on the table.
3. Remain quiet for a few moments and then lead them in this prayer or one of your own creation:
   God of all creation, we gather today to seek hope in your living Word. In your Spirit we cling to the promise that we are your children, the first fruits of your Spirit. Lift us out of our graves and restore us to life as you raised Lazarus, our brother. Allow your Word to penetrate our hearts and minds, that we might, with Martha, be able to confess, "Yes, Lord, I believe!" Amen.

First Impressions

1. Begin by asking the catechumens and candidates to name words or ideas they can recall from the hymns, psalms, prayers, and readings from today's liturgy. Write these on newsprint, large enough for all to read. After a few minutes of quiet, direct the group to look over the list.
2. Invite the participants to name the feelings or thoughts these words, ideas, or phrases evoke in them. These can be written alongside the list on the newsprint.
3. Gather the participants into small groups to discuss the following questions: *Considering Ezekiel's words of hope, Paul's description of what it means to belong to Christ, and the raising of Lazarus—what do you find puzzling? What in these readings is a consolation for you? How do these scripture passages challenge you?* After adequate time for discussion, invite the small groups to share their insights in the large group. Briefly summarize their comments.

Making Connections

1. Continue the discussion in the same small groups by asking the candidates and catechumens to share a recent experience of "new life." You may wish to begin the discussion by preparing a brief account of some "new life" that you have experienced.
2. Focus the attention of the participants back to the large group and invite a few participants to share their stories of "new life." After hearing the responses, ask the group to discuss this question: *How does death often lead to new life?* Summarize their insights and invite the group to remain quiet as they determine one thing they wish to remember. They may jot this down in their Participant Book on page 33, in the section entitled "I want to remember."

Prayer

Conclude the session by encouraging prayerful reflection as you proclaim the first reading, Ezekiel 37:12–14. Invite participants to recall those people who have given them "new life." Ask them to show their gratitude to God for these people by naming them aloud in the circle. After each naming, ask the group to respond, "Spirit of God, we give thanks for the new life that has raised us from death."

Extended Catechesis

SESSION FOCUS: *The Paschal Mystery in the Sacraments*

Gathering

A. Sunday:
1. Welcome the sponsors, team members, and additional participants as they arrive. Invite them to join the circle of catechumens and candidates.
2. Invite the catechumens and candidates to share briefly with the new arrivals the focus of the Dismissal Catechesis, using the newsprint as an aid.
3. Lead the group in singing Psalm 130 "Out of the depths I call to you, Lord; Lord, hear my cry." Invite one of the sponsors to proclaim the gospel, John 11:17–27. Pause for quiet. Continue with John 11:39–45. Pause again for quiet. Then pray in these or your own words:
   Jesus, when you heard about the death of your friend Lazarus, you wept, for your spirit was troubled. The powers of darkness, sickness, and death touched this man whom you loved dearly. Yet you saw in his death a moment to reveal the glory of God, the purpose of your whole life and ministry. In raising Lazarus from death, you desired that all would know that you are the resurrection and the life. Deepen our faith that we might know "life in you" is more powerful than death. Help us to realize the many ways in which death leads to life. Show us the way, Jesus, that we might believe. Amen.

B. Weekday:
1. Use the same centerpiece as in the Dismissal Catechesis.
2. As the participants gather in the circle, warmly welcome each person. Guide them through a brief relaxing silence by asking them to take a few deep breaths and let go of the busyness of the day. Invite them to name some signs of life and death they have noticed since Sunday.
3. Lead this celebration of the Word:
   - Song: Gathering Hymn from Sunday's liturgy
   - Sign of the Cross
   - Greeting: *The Lord be with you. And also with you.*
   - First Reading: Ezekiel 37:12–14
   - Sing Psalm 130
   - Second Reading: Romans 8:8–11, then quiet reflection
   - Gospel: John 11:17–27, 39–45, then quiet reflection
   - Closing Prayer: Use the prayer found in section A, or create your own concluding prayer.

The Word (30 min.)

1. In the large group ask the participants to name significant phrases or ideas that gave them a sense of "new life" as they listened to the gospel.

2. Using these or similar words, explore the gospel reading:
This story of the raising of Lazarus is the seventh and greatest of the signs that Jesus works in John's gospel. It is a turning point in that Jesus, the Lord of life, is going to his death. From this point onward, the plot to get rid of Jesus mounts. In raising Lazarus from death to life, Jesus proves the truth that he is the resurrection and the life. If we believe in Jesus, even though we should die, we will be raised to life. Belief in Jesus means we will never die. The believer, through the power of Jesus, will pass from death to life. Our physical death is a passing over, an exodus into eternal life. Martha responded to Jesus' question with a resounding "I do believe." She declares that Jesus is the messiah.
Encourage the participants to reflect on the meaning of the resurrection of Lazarus and Jesus. Invite them to share their understanding of the statement that Jesus is the resurrection and the life. After some quiet reflection, invite one or two people to share their insights in the large group.
Call the group's attention to Martha's words in response to Jesus' statement. Ask them to place themselves into the story and think about how they would respond to the death of a loved one. Could they say, "I do believe"? Ask a few participants to share their beliefs about death and resurrection with everyone. Summarize their beliefs and conclude with these or similar words:
Through the death and resurrection of Jesus we are saved—set free. All our dying is raised by Jesus, yielding renewed life. Just as Martha believed Jesus, so, too, we express our belief in Jesus by the way we live. If we do believe, we shall never die.

3. Ask a team member to proclaim the second reading, Romans 8:8–11. After a few moments of quiet, continue to explore the meaning in these or your own words:
The raising of Lazarus is a visual encounter with Paul's theology of Christian life, rooted in the resurrection of Jesus. In the thought of St. Paul, "flesh" is a term that refers not just to the physical body, but to that part of our human nature which has become enslaved to sin. Our "spirit" in this context is the principle of life and freedom that allows us to choose God's will over our sinful cravings. For Paul, the Spirit is the life force behind Jesus' resurrection from the dead and is the same Spirit that will raise our mortal bodies from death to life. It is our incorporation into Christ that makes it possible for us to share in the dynamic power of Christ's resurrection. That incorporation is a sacramental event rooted in baptism and sustained in Eucharist.
After this explanation ask the group to reflect upon the meaning of this scripture passage in their life.

Catholic Teaching (30 min.)

1. Ask the participants to write their responses to the Reflection and Questions in the Participant Book on page 32. When they have finished, invite them to share their responses in pairs, encouraging sponsors to join their candidate or catechumen. You may wish to elicit a few ideas from their sharing in the large group.

2. Then present a teaching on the paschal mystery in the sacraments to the large group. Using the Catholic Doctrine section of Understanding this Sunday to prepare, be sure to include the following points:
   - The paschal mystery encompasses the saving event of Jesus' suffering, death, resurrection, ascension, and sending of the Sprit. Jesus' paschal mystery is the primordial saving event experienced by Christians, which opens for us the redemption of God in Christ.
   - The entire life of Jesus can be understood as the foundation of what would later be experienced in the sacraments, which communicate his saving grace to believers. What was made flesh in the life and saving event of Jesus is passed over to the Church in the celebration of the sacraments, the mysteries.
   - The Second Vatican Council teaches: "Thus, for well-disposed members of the faithful, the liturgy of the sacraments and sacramentals sanctifies almost every event of their lives with divine grace which flows from the passion, death and resurrection of Christ" (SC 61).

3. Gather the participants back into the same pairs to discuss these questions: *How have you experienced the paschal mystery (dying and rising with Christ) in your own journey of faith? In the light of this teaching, what is the meaning of "sacrament" for you? How have you experience "the sacred" in the ordinariness of your daily life?*

Putting Faith into Practice

1. In the large group encourage the participants to share their responses to the last question, experiencing the sacred in the ordinary. These can be listed on a sheet of newsprint, large enough for all to see. Ask them to name practical ways they can become more aware of the sacred.
Some suggestions include:
   - helping a child, an aging parent, a neighbor, or a colleague and discovering in them the face of Christ;
   - cultivating a deeper awareness of the beauty of creation, leading to a response to respect the earth through recycling efforts, walking, using less water;
   - practicing patience with another who is in despair or is a chronic complainer and offering the hope of rising with Christ;
   - listening to another's story to discover the power of the Spirit.

2. Challenge participants to become more aware this week of their surroundings and to search out the presence of God in ordinary things and events. Ask them to write down their decision to live the paschal mystery in the Participant Book on page 33, in the section entitled "I want to put my faith into action by."

Prayer

Invite all to pause for a time of quiet to recollect their thoughts. After a few minutes, invite the candidates and catechumens to remain seated and invite everyone else to stand and to place their hand on the shoulder of a candidate or catechumen while you pray using the prayer of Minor Exorcism (RCIA 94F).

Palm Sunday of the Lord's Passion

Understanding this Sunday:
Background for Catechesis

The Word in Liturgy

Isaiah 50:4–7
Psalm 22:7–8, 16–17, 18–19, 22–23
Philippians 2:6–11
Matthew 26:14–27:66 [or (short form) 27:11–54]

We celebrate the entire paschal mystery of Jesus (i.e., his suffering, death, and resurrection) every time we gather for Eucharist. At certain times, however, one particular dimension of that single reality is focused upon more prominently than others in a given liturgical celebration. The many celebrations of Holy Week, starting with today's, exemplify how the liturgy is able to celebrate the entire paschal mystery, even while commemorating one or another historical moment of its unfolding. Today, our focus is first on the Lord's triumphal entrance into Jerusalem, and then on the events of his passion and death. Nonetheless, we also celebrate his resurrection, as we recognize in the breaking of the bread the presence of the Risen One in our midst.

The second part of the Book of Isaiah, written during the exile in Babylon, was intended as a word of consolation and hope to the Jewish people in a time of severe national trial. Particularly in the so-called Songs of the Servant, the author attempts to make sense out of the suffering which Israel was undergoing. Many scholars believe that the unnamed servant represents Israel (although there may have been an individual whose actual experience became in these poems a metaphor for the nation's suffering). Today's reading is from the third of the Servant Songs. The servant's sufferings, graphically portrayed here, are ultimately seen as redemptive. It is little wonder that the early Christian community identified Jesus with the servant, and even shaped their narrative of his passion and death in light of the descriptions found here. The gospels describe Jesus quoting from today's responsorial psalm as he hung on the cross. Although today's psalm refrain ("My God, my God, why have you abandoned me?")—taken from the psalm's opening verse—expresses utter desolation, the later verses show that the prayer is ultimately one of unshaken trust in God's deliverance.

Our second reading today is believed to be an early Christian hymn incorporated by Paul into his letter to the Philippians. Some have seen it as a Christian equivalent to Isaiah's Servant Songs. In any event, it contains a magnificent theology of divine abandonment in the incarnation, an abandonment that includes even an embrace of suffering and death. That self-emptying of the godhead is redemptive, as is seen in the resurrection of Jesus and in his exaltation at God's right hand. This is a crucial feature of Paul's theology, in which he stresses time and again that our being "in the Lord" is salvific. Because of our union with his dying, we know also his rising. It is our union with Christ that, for Paul, transforms the meaning of all human suffering.

While the other readings are the same every year, the gospel reading changes in each lectionary cycle. In year A we read from Matthew's account of the passion. Despite the many similarities of all of the passion accounts, each evangelist tells the story in ways that reflect his particular concerns. One of the distinctive features of Matthew's account is his deliberate citation of the Jewish scriptures in order to show that Jesus was indeed the promised Messiah. Writing for Jewish Christians at a time when they still felt keenly their recent break with the synagogue, Matthew wants to reassure them that Jesus' passion fulfills the Jewish scriptures. In addition, Matthew wants to "make sense" out of the suffering and shameful death that Jesus endured. He does so by emphasizing that the passion of Jesus is part of God's redemptive plan for the world.

Catholic Doctrine

Christ's Obedience as a Model for Believers

The gracious gift of Jesus to us is that he takes upon himself the weight of our sinful nature. In this liturgy we proclaim that the suffering of Christ is not without purpose, but is entered into willingly for our sake (CCC 602). On this Passion Sunday, the Church extols Christ in prayer, "Though he was sinless, he suffered willingly for sinners" (*Sacramentary,* Preface Prayer for Passion Sunday).

Jesus accepts death because he places his life in conformity to the plan of his heavenly Father. The whole purpose of his taking on our fleshly existence is to accomplish the will of the One who sent him (CCC 606). The sacrifice he embraces is not an indictment of his mission, but just the opposite—it is expressive of the depth of his own loving union with God. Jesus lays down his life freely because of this loving union. Thus, on this Passion Sunday, the church asserts in prayer, "Though innocent, he accepted death to save the guilty" (*Sacramentary,* Preface Prayer for Passion Sunday).

This willing sacrifice on the part of the Son did not require anything in advance from humanity. His death was offered while we were yet in sin. This alone proclaims the love God has for us, a love that does not require any merit on our part, but which is a free, overwhelming gift that the Savior gives to us (CCC 604). This gift is offered to every person. Christ dies for all, without exception. The Council of Quiercy teaches, "there is not, never has been, and never will be a single human being for whom Christ did not suffer" (DS 624). Thus, on this Passion Sunday the church holds in prayer, "By his dying he has destroyed our sins" (*Sacramentary,* Preface Prayer for Passion Sunday).

The suffering, death, and resurrection of the Lord which is celebrated on this day has two aspects. The first aspect has already been discussed—Christ liberates us by freely sacrificing himself for our sinful selves from that which enslaves us, sin. The second aspect of the paschal mystery is that his resurrection opens the way for us to new life, a wholeness and salvation that we could not achieve on our own, for we were mired in sin (CCC 654). We believe that by being joined to his own death in baptism we are therefore joined to his rising and are enabled to walk in newness of life. Thus, on this Passion Sunday the Church sings in prayer, "By his rising he has raised us up to holiness of life" (*Sacramentary,* Preface Prayer for Passion Sunday).

The fruitfulness of Christ's mission and the efficacy of his suffering, death, and resurrection are made possible because in his passionate love for God and for us, the Lord Jesus is obedient to the will of the Father (Latin, *oboedire,* "to give ear, to hear"). On the way to Jerusalem and the events of his passion and death, Jesus is transfigured in the presence of his disciples. He who hears and is obedient to God the Father's plan of salvation is, in turn, the one to whom the disciples are then instructed on the mountain of Transfiguration, "This is my beloved Son with whom I am well pleased; listen to him" (Matthew 17:5). Christ is *the* model of obedience for believers.

As the Second Vatican Council affirmed, "Just as Christ carried out the work of redemption in poverty and oppression, so the Church is called to follow the same path if she is to communicate the fruits of salvation. . . . Likewise, the Church, although she needs human resources to carry out her mission, is not set up to seek earthly glory, but to proclaim, and this by her own example, humility, and self-denial (LG 8).

Catholic Culture

Thomas à Kempis (c. 1380–1471) was born near Cologne and after study took vows in the early 1400s and was ordained in 1413. He remained in the monastery of Agnietenberg, writing, practicing spiritual direction, and copying manuscripts. His motto is said to be, "Everywhere I have sought rest and found it nowhere, save in tiny nooks with tiny books." His major work is the *Imitatio Christi* (Imitation of Christ), a manual detailing how to progress in the spiritual life (ECathHist 833–34).

"The Taking of Christ," a painting by Caravaggio which now is on display in the National Gallery of Ireland, is described by Sister Wendy Beckett in this way: "The taking of Christ is a violent picture . . . the disciples flee in open-mouthed terror, the soldiers surge forward angrily intent on seizure, Judas grasps his Lord grimly and terribly, intent upon betrayal. Only Jesus stays quiet, surrendering himself to his passion. . . . Only a willing surrender to love can truly 'take' us, and those who come to 'take' are unwitting instruments of that love. Judas 'takes' Jesus to the death that will be his own redemption as well as ours." (*The Mystery of Love,* Sr. Wendy Beckett, HarperCollins Publishers Inc., New York, 1996, p. 68).

Dismissal Catechesis (30 min.)

Getting Started

1. Prepare the space ahead of time with a circle of chairs around a table upon which is draped a red cloth. Place a plain cross in a stand next to the table. On the table arrange several palm branches.

2. Lead the candidates and catechumens, carrying their blessed palms, to the circle and place the Lectionary on the table. Encourage the candidates and catechumens to remain standing, lift their palms high, and once again sing the Gathering Song from today's liturgy. When everyone is seated, pause and then begin to pray by calling out some of these invocations, derived from the first reading. Pray the words and pause between each invocation:
   Suffering Servant, you speak to our weary hearts!
   Suffering Servant, you speak a word that rouses us!
   Suffering Servant, you did not turn back or rebel!
   Suffering Servant, you gave your back to those who beat you!
   Suffering Servant, you did not shield your face from buffets and spitting!
   Suffering Servant, you set your face like flint!
   Suffering Servant, you shall not be put to shame!
   The Lord God is our help; we shall not be disgraced!

First Impressions

1. Focus the attention of the candidates and catechumens on the palms, inviting them to offer their insights as to their meaning as part of today's liturgy. (The palms are a sacramental, blessed and used at today's liturgy to commemorate the triumphal entrance of Jesus into Jerusalem.)

2. Invite the participants to discuss the following questions: *What about today's Liturgy of the Word did you find challenging or confusing? What images, phrases, or descriptions evoke a sense of desolation in your heart? How do the Scriptures for today call out a sense of trust in God for you?*

3. Ask the participants to gather in pairs to further discuss the above questions. When they are ready, direct the pairs to write one image of desolation on a strip of paper (this can be red), large enough for everyone to read. On another strip of paper (if possible, use yellow- or gold- colored paper), instruct them to write a phrase that indicates a reason Jesus trusted in God's fidelity. Invite the pairs to hang the strips around the room one at a time as the group prays in silence.

Making Connections

1. Introduce the second reading in these terms: *The apostle Paul encouraged the Philippians to put on the mind of Christ. Verse 5, "Have among yourselves the same attitude that is also yours in Christ Jesus," precedes the beautiful, early Christian hymn that is today's second reading.*

2. In small groups, ask the catechumens and candidates to share their thoughts on this question: *What does it mean to have the attitude of Christ, particularly in difficult times?* Invite their responses in the large group.

Prayer

Focus the attention of the participants on the cross and invite them to pray Psalm 22:7–8, 16–19, and 22–23, either by singing the verses or a familiar song based upon this psalm. Encourage them to spend time in silence reflecting upon the meaning of the cross and the events leading up to Jesus' death, from the triumphal entry into Jerusalem to the hill of Golgatha. Close this time of silence with this short invocation, "Jesus, by your cross and resurrection, you have set us free; you are the Savior of the world!"

Extended Catechesis

SESSION FOCUS: *Christ's Obedience as a Model for Believers*

Gathering

A. Sunday:

1. Greet and welcome the sponsors, spiritual companions, and team members as they arrive. Invite them to join the circle of catechumens and candidates around the centerpiece of cross and palms.

2. Ask one of the catechumens or candidates to explain the meaning of the red and gold strips hanging around the room as a way of summarizing the Dismissal Catechesis.

3. With the attention of the participants focused upon the cross and palms, begin by inviting all to stand, holding their blessed palms as you pray: *Christ, our triumphal King, you did not use your divinity to escape the plan for our salvation. Rather, you humbled yourself in obedience even to the point of death. You emptied yourself for our sake, taking on the humiliation of a common criminal. You are worthy of our praise and adoration. We exalt you and bow low (indicate that all bow) before you. Your self-giving love is cause for our worship. Amen.* Ask all to be seated as a team member proclaims the reading from Philippians 2:6–11.

B. Weekday:

1. Use the same centerpiece as described for the Dismissal Catechesis.

2. Ask the participants to gather in the circle; greet and warmly welcome each person. Ask one of the catechumens or candidates to explain the meaning of the red and gold strips hanging around the room as a way of summarizing the Dismissal Catechesis. Ask the participants to continue the discussion by sharing how they experienced God's presence this week, particularly in times of anxiety or struggle.

3. Lead this celebration of the Word:
  - Song: Gathering Hymn from the Palm Sunday liturgy
  - First Reading: Isaiah 50:4–7
  - Psalm: Sung version of Psalm 22
  - Second Reading: Philippians 2:6–11
  - Closing Song: "Jesus the Lord," (Roc O'Connor, GIA Publications, 1981)

The Word (30 min.)

1. Explain the background to the first two readings in these or your own words: *In the first reading for Passion Sunday, Isaiah presents the Suffering Servant, whose graphic portrayal of suffering is later understood as redemptive. While the unnamed servant most likely represented the exiled Israel, for the early Christians the servant is identified with Jesus. Standing parallel to the Servant Song is Paul's theology of the saving Jesus in his use of the early Christian hymn to exhort the Philippians to take up the attitude of Christ. Christ transforms the meaning of human suffering by his willing obedience to God's plan of salvation.*

2. Ask the participants to reflect quietly upon the parallels between these two scripture passages as outlined in the Participant Book on page 34. When they have had time to follow the reflective process, invite them to gather into small groups to discuss the questions on the same page of the Participant Book. These include:
What are some specific ways of Jesus that give evidence of his obedience to God's plan for our salvation?
How has your obedience or willingness to accept God's plan for your life transformed difficulties into blessings?
Based upon your reflection on Jesus' obedience and the root meaning of obedience, "to hear," how can you better hear God's will in your life?

3. In the large group invite the participants to share some insights from their reflection and discussion.

Catholic Teaching (30 min.)

1. Present the Church's teaching on Christ's obedience in these or your own words:
The suffering and death of Christ has a purpose. For our sake, for the sake of our salvation, Jesus willingly entered into the suffering and death so graphically illustrated in the narrative of Matthew proclaimed at Sunday's liturgy. Jesus is totally in union with the Father. Therefore, the suffering he embraced is an expression of his loving union with the Father. That God offered his only begotten Son to suffer and redeem fallen humanity is the ultimate revelation of the depths of God's love for humankind. In Jesus the human and divine come together in complete obedience, without restraint. Christ suffered and died for all without exception. This willing action of Jesus opens the way for us to live a new life in wholeness and holiness. We are thus redeemed, lifted out of the mire of sin, because of Jesus' obedience to the will of the Father. Through and in Jesus' sacrifice, our sufferings, pains, and struggles are also transformed. As we join our suffering to Christ's redemptive action in the world we continue the unfolding redemption of the world. Christ is our model of obedience to the will of God, in all things.

2. Encourage the participants to gather into small groups to discuss the following questions: *How have you been challenged to follow the example of Jesus and obey what seemed to be God's will, even when that meant suffering? What was the outcome of your willingness to conform to the image of Christ? How can you more fully take on this attitude of obedience in your life?*

Putting Faith Into Practice

1. Focus the attention of the participants back to the large group. Encourage a few sponsors to share their stories of obedience to God's will.

2. Invite each small group to name some practical ways that they can model the obedience of Christ in their daily living experiences.

3. Explore the topic of how our personal sacrifice and suffering can have an impact on the lives of others. You may wish to begin the open discussion by telling a story of someone who, for example, offers his or her pain to God as a prayer for someone in dire need.

Prayer

Ask the participants to stand with their palms raised and prayerfully listen to the proclamation of the passion according to Matthew. Pre-select team members to proclaim the passion, having prepared and rehearsed prior to the session. Indicate that everyone should be seated and reflect upon the tremendous impact of Jesus' suffering and death. Dismiss the group in silence.

Holy Thursday

Understanding this Feast:
Background for Catechesis

The Word in Liturgy

Exodus 12:1–8, 11–14
Psalm 116:12–13, 15–16, 17–18
1 Corinthians 11:23–26
John 13:1–15

The General Norms for the Liturgical Year and the Calendar (Washington: USCC, 1976), revised as part of the liturgical reform mandated by the Second Vatican Council, emphasizes the unity of "the Easter triduum of the passion and resurrection of Christ [which is] the culmination of the entire liturgical year" (#18). "The Easter triduum begins with the evening Mass of the Lord's Supper, reaches its high point in the Easter Vigil, and closes with evening prayer on Easter Sunday" (#19). A sense of the unity of these days is found early on in the Church, as is evident from a letter of St. Ambrose (d. 397) regarding the celebration of Easter: "We must observe both the days of the passion and resurrection, so that there may be a day of woe and a day of joy, a fast-day and a feast-day . . . This is the holy Triduum . . . during which Christ suffered, was buried and rose again" [Letter 23, in J. P. Migne, *Patrologie latine,* 16, col. 1030. Cited in Days of the Lord, vol. 3, p. 3. (Collegeville: Liturgical Press, 1993)]. At the time of Ambrose, the three days were considered to be Friday, Saturday, and Sunday. But by the seventh century, a liturgical celebration had been added on Holy Thursday and the Triduum was considered to start with the Mass of the Lord's Supper.

The liturgy of Holy Thursday allows the symbolic action of washing feet to take place after the homily, but it is important not to see this merely as a historical reenactment of Jesus' action, any more than this or any other Eucharist is just a re-enactment of the Last Supper. Rather, the liturgy is a commemoration of Jesus' passion, death, and resurrection within the context of a ritual meal. Our theology of the liturgy holds that the saving reality of Christ's entire paschal mystery is actualized in the celebration, not that one discrete

moment of his life is rendered present, as if in a kind of liturgical "passion play." This understanding of how today's celebration is a "memorial" of the Lord's death and resurrection is rooted in the Jewish understanding of "zikkaron" (memorial or "anamnesis" in Greek). One of the best examples of this practice is found in the Passover meal, a memorial of the events of the Exodus which in some real way rendered the saving power of the Lord present in every age. Today's reading from Exodus describing the origins of the Passover meal even concludes by saying, "This day shall be a memorial feast for you." The reading is taken from the narrative of the tenth plague, into which the sacred author has inserted traditional material describing the rituals which Israel was to observe in remembrance of the events of their liberation from Pharaoh.

The psalm refrain is taken from 1 Corinthians ("Our blessing cup is a communion with the blood of Christ")—an appropriate choice given the content of today's second reading. In this part of 1 Corinthians, Paul is emphasizing the traditional nature ("I received . . . I handed on") of the teaching which the Corinthians were given about the origins and meaning of the eucharistic ritual. Paul's assertion that "every time" they perform this ritual they "proclaim the death of the Lord until he comes" is an excellent example of the continuity of the Jewish notion of zikkaron with our Christian understanding of how the Eucharist is a "memorial" of the Lord's saving death and resurrection, rendered present to us in every Eucharist.

The gospel helps us to understand how every liturgical commemoration also contains an implicit ethical imperative. Jesus tells his disciples that they "must wash each other's feet" and that what he has done is meant as an example for them to follow. Every ritual celebration that is done "in memory of" Jesus—whether it contains his proclamation of the gospel, a repetition of his classic actions of taking . . . blessing . . . breaking . . . sharing, or a symbolic washing of feet— because it renders present again in our day the saving reality of the event, also requires that we live in conformity with its meaning, lest we engage in the ritual without authenticity. That is why the foundational stories in the gospels are always so important—because in them are embedded the deep

meanings that lie behind the ritual memorials we celebrate. This helps us to see the key role played by today's Johannine text, which some scholars feel functions as an equivalent to the "institution narrative" missing in John but found in all the other gospels. The meanings that are contained in this story are about self-emptying service for the sake of others, redemptive identification with the lowly as a "suffering servant," discipleship as willingness to share the mission and ministry of Jesus, and a host of other themes that make up the dense content of today's feast.

SESSION PLAN: Holy Thursday

Dismissal Catechesis (30 min.)

Getting Started

1. Prepare the environment ahead of time with special care. On a table in the center of a circle of chairs place a white cloth, a large pitcher with water, a bowl and towel.

2. Ask the candidates and catechumens to gather in the circle and quietly reflect upon their experience of the Liturgy of the Word.

3. Pray in these or similar words:

Gracious God, you gather us for this great feast of your love. From the time of the first Passover, we continue to gather as we remember your saving power. Jesus, our Passover Lamb, taught us the meaning of Eucharist as he washed the feet of his disciples. We ask that we might be encouraged to serve one another, following the example of Jesus. Open us to hear your word as we gather this evening of the Lord's Supper. Amen.

First Impressions

1. Ask participants to find one or two words that describe what they observed or felt during the Liturgy of the Word this evening. Write these words on poster board or paper, large enough for everyone to read.

2. In the large group continue the discussion by asking: *What did you notice that was different or new to you at this evening's celebration?* Take the time to allow the participants to ask questions about the various liturgical actions that they experienced at your parish liturgy, for example, washing of the feet, renewal of priesthood, ringing of bells.

3. Using the information found in Understanding this Feast, explain that this evening's Mass is the beginning of the Easter Triduum—the three days.

Making Connections

1. Offer the following explanation of this feast:

This liturgy is a commemoration of Jesus' passion, death, and resurrection within the context of a ritual meal. Just as the Passover meal is a memorial of the Exodus event, each Eucharist is a memorial of the Lord's saving death and resurrection. The gospel John 13:1–15 also contains an imperative that all who partake of this meal—all who would profess to follow Jesus—must wash one another's feet.

2. Ask the participants to gather into small groups to discuss: *What does the action of Jesus—washing the feet of his disciples—mean for you? What is the challenge of Jesus' action for you?*

3. In the large group gather a few insights from the small group discussion. Tell the group about some of the service activities—foot washing—that take place in your parish.

Prayer

Invite the group to join in singing the "Servant Song" (Rory Cooney, NALR, 1987). Ask each participant to think about an action they wish to serve others following the call of Jesus. These can be written on pieces of paper, folded, and placed in the empty bowl on the table. Close leading Psalm 116 in the following manner—Pray verses 12–13, 15–16 and 17–18 and invite the participants to sing "Our Blessing Cup" (Michael Joncas, NALR, 1979) as a response.

Good Friday

Understanding this Feast: Background for Catechesis

The Word in Liturgy

Isaiah 52:13–53:12
Psalm 31:2, 6, 12–13, 15–16, 17, 25
Hebrews 4:14–16; 5:7–9
John 18:1–19:42

The Triduum is a single feast, and each day's liturgy celebrates the entire paschal mystery (see the Word in Liturgy for Holy Thursday for a full explanation). This is true of Good Friday, although our attention today is certainly focused on the events that transpired on the day of the Lord's passion and death as a way of understanding and celebrating their meaning in the larger context of the whole Triduum. Today's liturgy consists of three parts: Liturgy of the Word, Veneration of the Cross, and Communion. The history of these distinct segments is quite diverse, but the most ancient element of the Roman tradition is certainly the Liturgy of the Word with its proclamation of the narrative of the Passion at its heart. The veneration of the Cross was first celebrated in Jerusalem after the discovery of the True Cross, and only later incorporated into liturgies elsewhere in the Christian world. Reception of Communion on this day was sometimes observed and sometimes not, depending on differences of time and locale.

The text from Isaiah is the fourth Servant Song, one of a series of poems celebrating a mysterious figure whose vicarious suffering for the people is ultimately redemptive. Christian tradition has from the beginning seen in this text a remarkable foreshadowing of the suffering and death of Jesus. Its influence on the formulation of the gospel accounts of the passion has long been noted by scholars. It would be hard to overstate the influence of this text on Christian understanding of the meaning of Christ's death. The graphic descriptions of the physical sufferings of the Servant make the text a natural selection to accompany today's gospel reading. But even more to the point are its interpretation of the meaning of the Servant's death: ". . . he gives his life as an offering for sin . . . my servant shall justify many . . . he shall take away the sins

of many." The redemptive nature of the Servant's fate is suggested by the author's allusion to the Jewish custom of sacrificing a lamb for the sins of the community ("like a lamb led to the slaughter"). It is important to note also that the text contains its share of expressions which Christian tradition has seen as allusions to the resurrection ("He shall be raised high and greatly exalted . . . he shall see the light in fullness of days"). Reflective of this, the responsorial psalm proclaims a vision of deep trust in God ("Father, I put my life in your hands"), peace, and confident praise in God's ultimate vindication ("You will redeem me, O Lord, O faithful God").

In contrast to Isaiah's unnamed Servant, the reading from Hebrews boldly proclaims the name of him from whom our deliverance has come: "Jesus, the Son of God." The text alludes clearly to the human sufferings of Jesus ("with loud cries and tears . . . from what he suffered"), but it is also unequivocal in its insistence that "perfected, he became the source of eternal salvation for all who obey him." Written to a Jewish Christian community in danger of lapsing from their Christian faith, the letter is straightforward in its insistence that "we must hold fast to our profession of faith" if we are to be saved. For a community undergoing the trials of persecution and the temptation to defect, the author has reassuring words of encouragement, urging his readers to "confidently approach the throne of grace to receive mercy and favor and to find help in time of need."

John's account of the passion is strikingly different from that of the synoptics. Throughout his gospel, John portrays Jesus as eager for his "hour" to come. When the time does come, Jesus is shown not merely to submit to his fate, but rather to be master of his destiny, freely ascending the cross as if it were a royal throne from which he will rule. The theological themes so carefully woven throughout the earlier chapters of the gospel all come together in the passion narrative. Jesus is revealed to be a true king, as the prescription over his head will proclaim and as Pilate is forced to acknowledge; the new Passover Lamb willingly offers his life for sinners, just as the lamb is being sacrificed in the Temple; from the cross he gives his mother, the new

Eve, to his followers in the person of the beloved disciple; and also from the cross, he breathes forth his spirit in death as if in a new creation of the world, just as the blood and water flowing from his side are seen as the source of the Church's sacramental life. The Johannine account of the passion seems ideally suited for Good Friday, when the Church celebrates not only the dying of Jesus but also his glorious triumph in the resurrection and sending of the Spirit.

SESSION PLAN: Good Friday

Dismissal Catechesis (30 min.)

Getting Started

1. Prepare the space ahead of time with a circle of chairs around a table. The table should have a red cloth upon which is a cross (not a crucifix) and a candle.

2. Invite the candidates and catechumens to stand in a circle around the table.

3. Begin the prayer by lighting the candle. Pray the words of the Entrance Antiphon for Good Friday:

   "We should glory in the cross of our Lord Jesus Christ, for he is our salvation, our life and our resurrection; through him we are saved and made free."

First Impressions

1. Invite the participants to spend several minutes seated in silence as they look at the centerpiece. Invite them to share their thoughts and feelings by asking: *What did this experience of the liturgy evoke in you?*

2. Ask them to continue their reflection by sharing in small groups: *What did you observe about today's liturgy? What images, words, and actions were particularly meaningful for you?*

Making Connections

1. Ask the participants to name some of the people involved in the Passion of Our Lord. Write these on a large poster board. Ask each person to choose one of these people. Direct a prayerful meditation on the Passion in these words:

   Allow yourself to enter the Passion of Jesus through the mind and heart of this person. As you watch Jesus being tried, mocked, and sentenced to death like a criminal, what do you observe?

   You continue to follow this man Jesus as he walks the hill to the place of crucifixion. What are you feeling as you watch?

   You are at the foot of the cross as he speaks and eventually dies. What is happening in the quiet of your heart? What are your fears?

   Jesus has died and is being taken from the cross. What questions would you ask the character you chose? What would you change in the story of the passion if you could? Why?

2. Gather the participants into small groups, inviting them to share their experience of the Passion of Jesus through the eyes of one of the people in the account.

3. Continue with the participants in small groups, asking them to think about an action they can take or a change they wish to make in their lives in response to Jesus' passion and death. These ideas can be shared in the groups.

Prayer

1. Invite everyone to enter into a time of prayer. Begin by asking them to join in singing, "Jesus Remember Me" (J. Berthier, Taize, 1982). Hold up the cross. Invite the group to reflect silently on the great love Jesus has for each person.

2. Once again ask everyone to sing "Jesus Remember Me." Take the cross to each person. Encourage each one to reverence the cross: hold the cross or bow to it or kiss it.

3. After several minutes encourage the participants to sing "Jesus Remember Me."

EASTER
SEASON

Easter Sunday

Understanding this Sunday:
Background for Catechesis

The Word in Liturgy

Acts 10:34, 37–43
Psalm 118:1–2, 16–17, 22–23
Colossians 3:1–4 or 1 Corinthians 5:6–8
John 20:1–9

"This is the day the Lord has made. . . ." Psalm 118 rings out in the Church on this day of days that celebrates the resurrection. The liturgy is imbued with paschal, baptismal joy, for Christ has passed over from death to life, and the faithful, through baptism, pass over with him. The liturgy may begin with a blessing and sprinkling of water, or, in the United States, include a renewal of baptismal promises and sprinkling with water after the homily. A sequence praising the Risen Christ, our Paschal Lamb, is sung or recited before the gospel reading: "Christ indeed from death is risen, our new life obtaining. . . ."

Peter's preaching in the first reading presents the entire scope of the life, death, and resurrection of Jesus and its meaning for the world. Beginning with John the Baptist, Peter recounts the essential story of Jesus' coming, preaching, overthrow of the powers of evil, his passion, death, and resurrection, and the forgiveness of sins which results from these events. He speaks as one of the chosen witnesses who ate and drank with Jesus after his resurrection, thus emphasizing the real, physical nature of the resurrection.

In its context in Acts, Peter's speech is momentous. It provokes an outpouring of the Holy Spirit upon its hearers. Peter delivers it to Gentiles gathered in the home of Cornelius, who is a virtuous and devout non-Jew. In the context of its Easter Sunday proclamation, the passage retains its urgency and eruptive power. It both announces the whole message of the Good News of Jesus, centering on his resurrection, and states the universal import of that message in the Good News of forgiveness of sins for Jew and Gentile alike.

The two alternative epistle readings of the day declare that the resurrection is the foundation of new life for those who believe. Paul reminds the Colossians that they have died and have been raised up (in Greek, "co-raised") in the company of Christ—a reference to their baptism—and urges them to live accordingly.

The passage from 1 Corinthians draws its imagery from the Jewish practice of sweeping the house before Passover to assure that no yeast remained in it. Yeast, a mysterious living thing spoken of figuratively as a corrupting influence, was thought unsuitable in bread made for sacrifices. Unleavened bread, on the other hand, was a metaphor for purity and holiness. The context of the passage is Paul's pastoral response to a conflict caused by a case of incest tolerated by some in the community. Paul will have no accommodation with "corruption and wickedness," but expects the community to sweep its house clean in order to truly celebrate (live) Christ's Passover.

Set in the darkness of Mary Magdelene's early morning pilgrimage to the tomb, the gospel passage is an account of several lights dawning: daybreak itself, the disciples' discovery that the tomb is empty and their dawning awareness of what that fact meant, and, finally, the beloved disciple's coming to believe that Jesus has been raised from the dead.

Most striking in this account is the role of the beloved disciple (assumed in the tradition to be John). Having heard the story of Mary, he outruns Peter to the tomb, yet allows Peter to enter first. Both enter the tomb, but the beloved disciple alone is described as believing. Why is John the first to reach the tomb and to believe? The simplest explanation is the most likely one: the author of John's gospel wished to show the power of love to put the believer in touch with the truth of the resurrection. The figures of Peter and John are not in competition with one another. The beloved disciple, however, because of his love for Jesus, comes more quickly to discern and to believe that Jesus is risen.

The empty tomb, though important, is not the sole basis for Christian belief in the resurrection. John's account, like that of the synoptics, shows that the disciples did not expect the resurrection, and found it hard to believe on the evidence of the empty tomb alone (for "they did not yet understand the scriptures . . ."). Crucial to their faith in the resurrection were their subsequent personal encounters with the Risen Christ, encounters described in various ways in the gospels proclaimed throughout the Easter season. Thus we have, alongside the full proclamation of the resurrection in Acts, a gospel account today that is something like the first act in a longer drama.

The mystery of the resurrection, celebrated every Sunday, and *par excellence* at Easter, may be the doctrinal focus of today's catechesis.

Catholic Doctrine

"On the third day he rose again, in fulfillment of the scriptures . . ."

The unconditional and overwhelming love of God for us made visible in the incarnation does not disappear and fade with the death of Jesus on the cross. That passionate love of God for us is enthroned upon the cross which becomes the pulpit of God's truth. That message of divine love is deepened in the death and entombment of Jesus. That love transcends the tomb in Jesus' resurrection from the dead. The Church exults: "Jesus Christ broke the chains of death and rose triumphant from the grave!" (*Sacramentary,* Easter Vigil, Exsultet, Roman Missal).

The chains of death are truly broken. Just as the divine nature took on our humanity (in all things but sin), so too the resurrection of Jesus was accomplished in a real human body. The Risen Lord is not a ghost who returns to haunt the disciples, nor some sort of resuscitated corpse (CCC 645). The resurrection of Jesus is a passing over from death into a new life, a new existence. The Church sings: "Exult, all creation around God's throne! Jesus Christ, our King, is risen! Sound the trumpet of salvation!" (Exsultet)

The resurrection is a glorious mystery that deserves a full-throated "alleluia" from every believer. And yet this wonderful gift from God to us comes at a price that Jesus is willing to pay (CCC 649). It is continuous with the mystery of the cross. Jesus Christ is the crucified, Risen Lord, in whose resurrected body wound marks are visible. The Church gives thanks: "This is our passover feast, when Christ, the true Lamb is slain, whose blood consecrates the homes of all believers!" (Exsultet)

That Jesus rose from the dead is an actual historical event and not a psychological or spiritual experience of the disciples (CCC 643). This is not some myth or wish fulfillment on their part, or ours. Those first disciples witnessed something totally unexpected and surprising and which they only gradually understood. And in understanding it, they were willing to be martyred in telling the Good News of the resurrection. The Church proclaims: "What good would life have been to us, had Christ not come as our Redeemer?" (Exsultet)

The implications for us believers is that by the resurrection God ratifies Jesus' whole life and teaching (CCC 651). Baptized into his death by our plunging beneath the waters of the font, we rise as adopted children of God whose inheritance is the resurrection. Even now we taste the promise of new, risen life in the Eucharist. The Church glories in this mystery: "Christians everywhere, washed clean of sin and freed from all defilement, are restored to grace and grow together in holiness!" (Exsultet)

Catholic Culture

Some of the earliest artistic renditions of the resurrection of the Lord can be found in the catacomb of Domitilla in Rome which dates back to about the fourth century of the Christian era. A sarcophagus (a rectangular marble tomb) in this particular catacomb is engraved with a "wreath encircling the sacred monogram, above a cross, with two guards below" (OxA&A 430). Many of these early depictions of the resurrection show the guards (Matthew 27:66), who were supposed to be guarding the tomb of Christ, asleep.

While artists developed many other ways to depict the resurrection, from the Risen Christ meeting Mary Magdalene in the garden to the triumphant Lord who tramples evil beasts underfoot after rising, this theme of the resurrected Jesus rising above the sleeping guards persists in art. In about 1460, Piero della Francesca shows the Risen Lord stepping up out of a conventional tomb (that is, not a cave cut in the side of a hill, but a sarcophagus), the wound marks clearly visible. The guards are deep asleep, with their weapons laying about them, oblivious to the Christ who, as he is stepping out of the tomb, holds a banner emblazoned with a cross. The Risen Lord is looking directly at the viewer with a piercing gaze, his burial clothes cover only half of his chest—the exposed side reveals the wound where droplets of blood still are seen (OxA&A 431).

In pre-Christian times, the egg became a symbol of spring and fertility—something living comes forth from a seemingly "dead" shell. The custom of decorating special Easter eggs evolved soon after Christianity found a foothold in northern Europe and Asia. Eggs were included in the Lenten fast and for this reason they were also associated with the Easter season. Easter eggs were mostly colored with vegetable dyes. The Syrians and Greeks dyed the eggs crimson to suggest the blood of Christ. Slavic Easter eggs are lavishly and painstakingly decorated. Armenian Easter eggs are decorated by hand-painted religious pictures or scenes. In Germany, Easter eggs were hung from trees and bushes, much like Christmas trees (*Catholic Traditions in Crafts,* Ann Ball, Our Sunday Visitor, Inc., Huntington, Indiana, 1997, p. 54).

Dismissal Catechesis (30 min.)

Getting Started

1. Prepare the space ahead of time with a circle of chairs around a table draped with a white cloth upon which is placed a bowl of water. Place Easter flowers at the base of the table, along with a large white candle in a stand.
2. Lead the candidates and catechumens to the circle and place the Lectionary on the table. Light the candle and remain standing as you lead the group in singing Psalm 118: "This is the day the Lord has made" or "Jesus Christ is Risen Today" (EASTER HYMN).

First Impressions

1. After everyone is seated, invite them to close their eyes for a few moments of quiet and to recall what they saw, heard, smelled, or felt as they entered the church today and celebrated the Liturgy of the Word. Ask them to turn to the person next to them and describe their experience.
2. Allow several minutes for sharing before gathering their responses in the large group. Anticipate descriptions of feeling alive; seeing water; hearing alleluias; sensing beauty, joy, excitement, celebration; smelling incense, chrism, spring flowers, and Easter lilies. Ask the candidates and catechumens what the smells, sounds, and surroundings reveal about the Easter season. Summarize their responses and explain Easter in these or similar words: *Today is the feast of the resurrection of Jesus Christ. We rejoice that he rose from death. Our cause for rejoicing lies in the belief that with Christ we have passed from death to life, from slavery to freedom, and from sin to glory. So great is this glorious mystery that the Church celebrates the joy of the resurrection for fifty days.*
3. Introduce the focus of the first reading from Acts 10:34, 37–43 in these or similar words:
In the first reading from Acts, Peter addresses the Gentiles in the home of Cornelius and announces the whole message of the Good News of Jesus' resurrection by recalling his earthly ministry. After describing Jesus' baptismal anointing by God, Peter recalls the healing and teaching of Jesus, under the power of that anointing in the Holy Spirit. Peter then centers on the significance of Jesus' death and resurrection, "They put him to death by hanging him on a tree. This man God raised [on] the third day and granted that he be visible, not to all the people, but to us, the witnesses chosen by God in advance, who ate and drank with him after he rose from the dead" (Acts 10:39–41).
Gather the participants into small groups and ask them to discuss these questions: *What is the significance of eating and drinking with Jesus after he rose? Why is the resurrection such Good News?*

Making Connections

1. Focus the attention of the participants back to the large group and invite some responses to the above questions. Summarize their input in a few sentences.

2. Invite a sponsor or team member to witness to the Good News of Jesus' resurrection by relating an experience of Jesus' lifting him or her out of "death" into "new life." Encourage the participants to reflect upon similar experiences of Good News during the next week.

Prayer

After a brief silence, begin to pray in these or similar words: *Jesus, by your cross and resurrection, you have set us free. As you have been raised from the dead by the power of God, lift us out of the darkness of sin, oppression, and suffering. Raise us, renew us, and empower us to live in the light. Make of us a new creation. As we anticipate the blessed waters of baptism or look forward to our profession of faith in you and your Church, guide us by the light of your resurrection. Amen.* Conclude the prayer by inviting all to stand and sing the first few verses of the Gathering Hymn used at the parish liturgy or the Easter Alleluia.

Extended Catechesis

SESSION FOCUS: *"On the third day he rose again, in fulfillment of the scriptures . . ."*

Gathering

A. **Sunday:**
1. Greet the sponsors and other team members. Invite them to join the circle of catechumens and candidates. Ask everyone to stand and join in singing "Sing a New Song" (Daniel L. Schutte, New Dawn Music, 1972) or another Easter hymn familiar to the participants. Invite all to be seated as you pray in these or similar words: *"God, source of all power and love, we gather this day to give you thanks and praise for the great gift of your Son, Jesus Christ, who rose from the dead on the third day. Through his resurrection we have been freed from sin and death and given new life. Help us to grow in our understanding of this great act of love and instill in us a desire to follow Jesus, the Way, the Truth, and the Life. Amen.* Ask a team member to proclaim the gospel, John 20:1–9, as the group stands. Lead all in singing the Easter Alleluia after the proclamation.

B. **Weekday:**
1. Use the same centerpiece as described for the Dismissal Catechesis.
2. Welcome everyone and invite the participants to gather in a circle around the lighted candle. Ask anyone who wishes to share the signs of Easter's "new life" they have observed in the past few days.
3. Lead this celebration of the Word:
   - Song: Gathering Hymn from Easter Sunday
   - Sign of the Cross and greeting
   - Opening Prayer: See section A

- First Reading: Acts 10:34, 37–43
- Sing Psalm 118
- Second Reading: Colossians 3:1–4 or Corinthians 5:6–8 (whichever was proclaimed on Sunday)
- Gospel Alleluia
- Gospel: John 20:1–9
- Repeat Gospel Alleluia

The Word (30 min.)

1. Ask several catechumens and candidates to name some of the insights on the reading from Acts gained during the Dismissal Catechesis. Encourage all to share his or her understanding of the significance of the Easter season and the power of the resurrection in their own lives.
2. Gather the attention of the whole group by leading them in singing the Gospel Alleluia once again. Then invite everyone to take a few deep breaths and close their eyes, as you lead this meditative reflection:
   It is very early in the morning. The sun is rising on this the first day of the week. Imagine yourself, along with Mary Magdalene or the disciples Peter and John, as you make your way to the tomb where you witnessed the burial of Jesus on Friday. What are you feeling as you climb the hill to the tomb? . . . You had so hoped that Jesus was the messiah. Why would the messiah have to die? What now, you wonder? . . . He said he would rise on the third day—that's today. What questions and perplexities fill your thoughts? . . . As you near the tomb you see that the stone has been moved. What has happened? Your heart clenches with fear. You look into the darkness of the tomb and see the burial wrappings lying on the ground. What is your first impulse as you see the tomb is empty? . . . What has happened to Jesus? What does it mean for you? What about this Easter event causes believers to sing "Alleluia"?
3. Sing "Alleluia." Encourage the participants to reflect on their experiences of Easter and respond to the questions posed on page 38 in the Participant Book. When they have finished, ask them to share one insight from their reflection in small groups. Then focus the attention back to the large group and invite a few participants to offer insights from the reflection and their responses to the questions.
4. Continue to explore the gospel in these or similar words:
   This gospel passage is an account of several lights dawning: daybreak; the disciples' discovery that the tomb is empty; their dawning awareness of what that fact meant; and finally, the beloved disciple's coming to believe that Jesus has been raised from the dead. John describes the Easter morning events to show that the power of love places the believer in touch with the truth of the resurrection. Peter and John are not in competition with one another. Because of his love for Jesus, the beloved disciple quickly discerns that Jesus has risen. The disciples did not expect the resurrection. They found it hard to believe on the evidence of the empty tomb alone. Their faith in the resurrection grew with the subsequent personal encounters with the Risen Christ.

Gather the participants into the same small groups to discuss these questions: *What do you find challenging about Jesus' resurrection? How is the resurrection a source of comfort for daily living?*

Catholic Teaching (30 min.)

1. In the large group, invite insights as to the meaning of the resurrection from each small group.
2. Present the Church teaching on Jesus' resurrection from your reading of the Catholic Doctrine section found in Understanding this Sunday. Include the following points:
   - The resurrection of Jesus is a passing over from death into new life and a continuance of the mystery of the cross, wherein the passionate love of God for us is revealed and the chains of sin and death are broken.
   - The first disciples witnessed something totally unexpected and surprising, but the full import of Jesus' resurrection was only gradually understood.
   - God ratifies Jesus' whole life and teaching in the resurrection.
   - Through baptism, the believer is plunged into the waters of baptism (death) to rise as adopted children of God whose inheritance is the resurrection.
   - The believer continues to taste the promise of new, risen life in the Eucharist.

Or . . .

Encourage the participants to read the section in the Participant Book entitled The Church Says on page 39.

3. Gather the participants into the same small groups to discuss these questions: *What is your understanding of the significance of the death and resurrection of Jesus? How have you experienced Jesus' resurrection—breaking the chains of sin and death—in your own life?*

Putting Faith into Practice

1. Invite a parishioner or a team member to present a witness talk on their personal experience of dying and rising with Christ.
2. In the large group, encourage the participants to share ways in which they might cultivate their faith in the Risen Jesus as they deepen their journey toward full initiation. Write these three headings on a large newsprint: SCRIPTURE, PRAYER, and COMMUNITY. Jot down their responses under the appropriate heading, encouraging them to name activities that are practical and attainable. Invite everyone to decide on a few ways in which they will cultivate their faith in the resurrection during these fifty days of the Easter season. This resolution can be noted in the "I want to put my faith into action by" section of the Participant Book on page 39.

Prayer

Invite all to silently pray for the help of the Holy Spirit to keep their resolution to grow in faith. Then lead the group in singing Psalm 118 or another song used in the Easter liturgy in your parish. Refer the participants to the Prayer for the Week found in the Participant Book on page 39. Invite all to stand and pray this poetic Easter Sequence together.

Second Sunday of Easter

Understanding this Sunday:
Background for Catechesis

The Word in Liturgy

Acts 2:42–47
Psalm 118:2–4, 13–15, 22–24
1 Peter 1:3–9
John 20:19–31

Following an ancient tradition, the Church regards the eight days from the Paschal feast to the second Sunday of Easter as a single unit of joyful celebration (an octave). Today the Church sings again Psalm 118, the psalm for Easter day, which proclaims: *"This is the day* the Lord has made. . . ."* The preface for Easter day is prayed again today as well: "We praise you with greater joy than ever *on this Easter day* . . ." even though that day is already a week behind us. All the prayers of the liturgy and the tone of the celebration are unmistakably full of paschal, baptismal joy. The readings are to be understood in this spirit.

Throughout the Easter season, the first reading of the liturgy is taken from the Acts of the Apostles in order to illuminate the mystery of the church as it developed from its beginnings at Pentecost. Today's passage is the classic description of the Spirit-filled life of the disciples, centering on four paradigmatic features of the early church: the apostles' instruction, the common life, the breaking of bread, and the prayers. The community of goods practiced by these early Christians continues the Lucan emphasis on the use of possessions to indicate the reign of God, and is accompanied by a warm account of sharing table fellowship and prayer in each other's homes. And, finally, the evangelical dimension of the life of the early Christians (leading to the presence of increasing numbers of new members) is presented as a divinely generated abundance, not as the result of activism or a particular program for spreading the faith.

The second reading during Year A is always taken from 1 Peter, a text particularly rich in baptismal imagery. Thought by some scholars to have been based on an ancient baptismal hymn or liturgy, at times the letter bursts into

prayer and praise, as it does at the outset of the present passage. The community to which the letter is addressed faced persecution. The gold of its faith was "fire-tried" by suffering. Yet the overwhelming sense of joy associated with the resurrection and the "new birth" of baptism, with its "imperishable inheritance," is undimmed by the trials to which the faithful are subjected. The passage concludes with reference to the kind of faith blessed in today's gospel: one that loves and believes without seeing.

The gospel for today is constant in all three years of the Lectionary cycle. It is a story of mission, forgiveness, and faith. The Risen Lord appears to his followers on the evening of the resurrection, when they are gathered behind locked doors, afraid. He speaks a greeting of "peace" and at once commissions them to continue his own saving work: "As the Father has sent me, so I send you." As God breathed on the waters at creation, so Jesus now breathes on the disciples in this scene and gives them the Spirit, with an immediate creative effect. In the giving of the Spirit, Jesus imparts a particular power for reconciliation: "If you forgive sins they are forgiven; if you hold them bound they are held bound." Just as the earthly Jesus exercised a power to forgive sins, now his followers are given that power in the Spirit. The story concludes with the apostle Thomas, who, confronted by the resurrected Jesus, comes to a profound articulation of faith. He calls Jesus "My Lord and my God." At the end of the passage, the words of Jesus seem to speak directly to its hearers. We have not seen as Thomas did, but are called upon to believe.

The focus of today's catechesis may therefore be upon faith: the faith of the early Christian community described in Acts, the faith "more precious than the passing splendor of fire-tried gold" lauded in the first letter of Peter, the faith of doubting Thomas who finally sees and believes, and the faith of generations of believers who have not seen the Risen Lord but who rely on the word of the original witnesses to the resurrection.

Catholic Doctrine

Faith

Faith invites us into a relationship of love, for "God is love"(1 John 4:8 referred to in CCC 221). The hidden, triune God is fully revealed in Jesus Christ, who embodies divine love and who communicates that love to us by his life and mission and by his suffering, death, and resurrection. That divine love is freely given, and our free response is how Catholic teaching describes "faith" (CCC 142 and 166). The gift of faith is therefore a relationship wherein we trust the truth of that which has been revealed in Jesus Christ, handed down by those first witnesses, and afterwards, from generation to generation in the church.

Old Testament scriptures speak of faith in terms of one's personal obedience to the Word of God. There are several Hebrew words for faith, all of which refer to something "solid" or "trustworthy," to which we pledge our loyalty. Our word "amen" comes from a Hebrew word for faith (aman). From this perspective, faith is understood as "I believe you," a relationship of trust.

New Testament scriptures continue this understanding of faith and add to it. The Greek verb *pisteuein* means not only "to trust" or "to show confidence in" but also "to accept as true." St. Paul thus writes about the "obedience of faith" (Romans 1:5, 16:26) and in a variety of places he summarizes the content of his preaching on the faith (Romans l0:9–10; 4:24–25). For Paul, faith is not just an interior reality, believing in the heart, but also confessing with one's lips. In other words, the experience of faith includes doctrinal content, "the faith" (EncyCath 513).

It is through the community that the individual first receives the gift of faith from God. Faith comes through "hearing" and depends on witnesses who hand it on, who "speak it." By the action of the Holy Spirit tongues are loosened to tell the Good News and ears are opened to hear what is told (CCC 153).

A heritage of faith is entrusted to the whole church (CCC 84). The Catholic genius understands this inheritance to be contained in both Scripture and Tradition. Indeed, the development of the New Testament shows the process of the living Tradition at work (CCC 83). The function of authoritative

church teaching is to explain and guard this "deposit of faith" (1 Tim. 6:20).

Our relationship to God in faith can be shaken. We experience evil, suffering, and injustice in this world, and we question God, we doubt, and we struggle in our belief (CCC 164). In times of doubt and struggle, individuals can turn to the community of faith for support.

Through baptism we are born within, nourished by, and are members of a living tradition handed down from the time of the apostles to the present day, in a pilgrim church walking by the light of faith. St. Augustine, bishop and teacher, preached to the newly baptized:

> [Y]ou . . . are the new offspring of the Church, gift of the Father, proof of Mother Church's fruitfulness. . . . You are walking now by faith, still on pilgrimage [to] the Lord; but he to whom your steps are directed is himself the sure and certain way for you. . . . This is the octave of your birth. Today is fulfilled in you the sign of faith . . . (*Sermo* 8 in octava Paschae I, 4: PL 46, 838. 841; LitHrs, vol. 2, pp. 635–36).

Catholic Culture

Andrea Del Verrocchio (Andrea di Michele Cioni, 1435–88) is most noted for his painting of the Baptism of Christ now found in the Uffizi gallery, Florence. His skill and artistry also extended to sculpture and is best seen in his work "The Doubting of Thomas," found in the Orsanmichele in Florence. The figures of Jesus and Thomas are arranged in a marble niche which was designed by Donatello originally meant for a gilded statue of St. Louis of Toulouse commissioned by the then leading political and economic party of the Parte Guelfa. With the eclipse of this leadership by the Medici, their niche was sold to the magistrates of the Mercanzia (or merchants' guild) and Donatello's statue was moved elsewhere. The new subject may have been prompted by the magistrates' insistence that in all their decisions, they required tangible evidence, as did Thomas in the gospel account (HistItal 324).

The gospel of John refers to Thomas (counted as one of the Twelve) in three episodes: (1) where he promises to follow Jesus to Bethany and die at 11:16; (2) when he asks Jesus about "the way" at 14:5–6; and (3) when he doubts the others as they tell him of the Risen Lord and eventually cries out "My Lord and my God!" at 20:28. According to an early church historian, Eusebius of Caesarea (d. 340), Thomas preached the Good News to the Parthians and eventually traveled to India. He is considered the founder of the Malabar Christians (also known as the St. Thomas Christians). His relics are venerated in Ortona, Italy, and his feast day is July 3 (ECathHist 832–33).

Dismissal Catechesis (30 min.)

Getting Started

1. Prepare the space ahead of time with a circle of chairs around a table draped with a white cloth. Arrange several Easter flowers at the base of the table, along with a large white candle in a stand.

2. Lead the candidates and catechumens to the circle and place the Lectionary on the table. While the participants remain standing, light the candle and ask all to pray with arms extended upward as did the early Christians. Pray in these or similar words:
   O God, we gather in joy on this day of Easter. Breathe your Spirit upon us. By the grace of your Spirit, help us to recognize the Risen Christ who stands among us. We ask that we, your community of believers, be of one mind and heart. Strengthen us to give witness to the resurrection of Christ, who is Lord, now and forever. Amen.

3. Close by leading the group in singing the Gospel Alleluia.

First Impressions

1. Begin the large group sharing by asking these questions: *What signs of Easter did you hear, see, and experience at today's Liturgy of the Word? What phrases or images from today's scriptures remind you of the power of this season of resurrection?* Listen carefully to the observations of the candidates and catechumens.

2. Ask the participants to turn to the person next to them and share their response to these questions: *How did your experience at the Liturgy of the Word comfort you? What roused your spirit or thrilled your heart?*

3. Focus the attention of the participants back to the large group, inviting them to share their reactions with everyone. Summarize their insights in a few phrases.

Making Connections

1. Encourage everyone to discuss these questions with their same partners: *What examples of the power of the resurrection in the early Church did you hear in today's scriptures? In what ways does the meaning of resurrection have consequences for your life? For the life of the Church? In the world? What signs of the resurrection do you continue to notice in the life of believers today?*

2. Draw the attention of the participants back to the large group. Ask them to share one way they have seen signs of the resurrection in their personal lives or in the world today. You may choose to record these on newsprint, writing large enough for everyone to see. After allowing some time for discussion, ask the participants to discuss this question: *What significance do these signs of the resurrection have for you personally?* Continue to note their responses on another sheet of newsprint.

Prayer

Begin the prayer by inviting all to reflect quietly upon a specific way in which the resurrection has changed his or her life. Then lead them in praying a Litany of Thanksgiving.

As they express their gratitude for a specific and personal experience of power of the resurrection, ask them to use the form, "Jesus, I give thanks for . . ." Instruct the group to respond to each expression by saying, "We give thanks, for God's love is everlasting." Begin this litany yourself. Allow time for those who wish to express their gratitude. Close the litany by praying: *Loving and gracious God, your goodness and love abounds in our world. We are grateful for you, for these signs which we have named, and for all of the many ways you share your life with us. May we live daily in your love and never fail to see your wondrous works. This is the day you have made. We give thanks and rejoice. Amen.* Then invite all to stand once again, and sing the Gospel Alleluia.

Extended Catechesis

SESSION FOCUS: *Faith*

Gathering

A. Sunday:

1. Welcome the sponsors, team members, and additional participants as they arrive. Invite them to join the circle of catechumens and candidates.

2. Ask a catechumen or candidate to give a brief summary of their first insights on the Liturgy of the Word in the Dismissal session. The insights recorded on the newsprint might be of help.

3. Begin the prayer by asking all to stand and lead the group in singing a few verses of the Gathering Song used at today's liturgy. Invite a team member to proclaim the first reading from Acts 5:12–16. After a moment of quiet, invite all to imagine themselves among the early disciples gathered in fear, after their experience of the empty tomb. They are gathered on the first day of the week with the doors locked. Proclaim the gospel, John 20:19–31. Then sing the last verse of the same song.

B. Weekday:

1. Use the same centerpiece as described for the Dismissal Catechesis.

2. As the participants gather in the circle, greet and warmly welcome each person. Invite them to share some sign of the power of the resurrection that they have experienced over the past few days.

3. Lead this celebration of the Word:
   - Hymn: "Jesus Christ is Risen Today" (EASTER HYMN)
   - Sign of the Cross, Greeting
   - First Reading: Acts 2:42–47
   - Sing Psalm 118
   - Gospel Alleluia
   - Preparation: Invite all to place themselves in the locked room as described in section A.
   - Gospel: John 20:19–31
   - Gospel Alleluia

The Word (30 min.)

1. In the large group invite a few responses to the following question: *In listening to this first reading from the Acts of the Apostles, how did the early Christians express their faith in the Risen Lord?* After hearing some ideas, probe deeper into the question of faith by asking this question: *What expressions of faith have you observed in this parish community?*

2. When the sharing has subsided offer the following background to today's scripture readings:
   This passage from the Acts of the Apostles helps us understand what life was like in the early Church after the resurrection. Four significant features formed the faith life of these early Christians: the apostles' instruction, the communal life, the breaking of the bread, and the prayers. Today, these actions include listening to the scriptures and the teachings of the Church, experiencing the support of the faith community, sharing in the Eucharist, and developing the practice of prayer. Today's gospel takes us back in time to the account of one of Jesus' early resurrection appearances: Jesus' greeting of "Peace" in his first post-resurrection appearance to the disciples, gathered in fear behind locked doors, signaled the beginning of the messianic era— the dawning of a new age. This new age of change is marked by Jesus' immediate commissioning of the followers to continue his saving work. Just as God breathed on the waters at creation, Jesus enters and breathes on the apostles, giving them the Holy Spirit. This giving of the Spirit signifies that the power of reconciliation is given to the Church. The gospel then shifts to a similar, behind-locked-doors scene, one week later. Here, the resurrected Jesus confronts Thomas. His articulation of faith is spontaneous. Thomas no longer needed to touch the wounds of the Lord to believe. This is a profound moment for all believers. The faith of generations of believers who have not seen the Risen Lord is acknowledged and blessed by Jesus.

3. Invite the group to reflect upon their faith in the Risen Jesus with the help of the reflection exercise and questions found in the Participant Book on page 40. When they have finished, gather the participants into small groups to share something of their stories of faith and their responses to the first two questions. After the small group sharing, ask each group to present some insights on faith from their sharing in the large group.

Catholic Teaching (30 min.)

1. Continuing in the large group, ask participants to describe what it means to believe in Jesus. Summarize their responses and invite each small group to share one insight from their discussion of the third question in the Participant Book, regarding their response to faith in Jesus.

2. Present the Catholic teaching on faith, including the following points from your own reading of the Catholic Doctrine section found in Understanding this Sunday:
   - Faith is a living relationship with God, who communicates love to us through the life, death, and resurrection of Christ in the Holy Spirit.
   - Faith includes, but also goes beyond, knowledge or statements of truths taught by the Catholic Church. Faith is grounded in one's relationship with God.
   - Faith in what has been revealed to us in Jesus Christ is handed down to us by the first witnesses of the resurrection—the disciples through the faith community—the Church.
   - Faith is a gift from God and is, therefore, not earned by good works. Living one's faith—believing in the heart and confessing with one's lips—is necessary to keep faith alive.

   The Catholic faith is not only personal, it is lived, shared, and professed within the community of the Church and beyond. Through baptism we are born into, nourished by, and made members of a living tradition of faith, handed down from the apostles to the present day. We live daily by the light of faith.

Or . . .

Draw the attention of the participants to the section in the Participant Book entitled "The Church Says" on page 41. Expand on this understanding of faith as you read this section.

3. Invite the participants to gather into small groups to share their insights into these questions: *Since you began this process of initiation, how has your understanding of the meaning of faith changed? In a time of fear, suffering, or sin, how has the Spirit empowered your faith? What role has this faith community played in the development of your faith?*

Putting Faith into Practice

1. In the large group ask the participants to share their understandings of faith in the light of these scriptures and the Church's teaching.

2. Distribute some letter-writing materials to the participants and invite them to write a note to the parish community describing a specific way in which the witness of the parish has led to a deepening of his or her faith. These can be printed from time to time in the parish newsletter or bulletin.

3. Ask the participants to turn to the person next to them and share one way they could support another's faith over the next week. Encourage each person to write this action in the Participant Book on page 41.

Prayer

Focus the attention back to the large group and invite everyone to reflect silently upon their own faith in Jesus as their Lord and God. Then ask a sponsor to proclaim the second reading, 1 Peter 1:3–9, as the participants listen prayerfully to this baptismal hymn from the early Church. After a short silence, invite all to stand and raise their hands in prayer, as did the early Christians, saying, "Let us proclaim our joy in the Risen Christ, singing Alleluia!" Lead the group in singing the last verse of "Jesus Christ is Risen Today" or the Closing Hymn from Sunday's liturgy.

Third Sunday of Easter

The Word in Liturgy

Acts 2:14, 22–33
Psalm 16:1–2, 5, 7–8, 9–10, 11
1 Peter 1:17–21
Luke 24:13–35

Week by week, as the Easter season unfolds, various facets of the great gift of Easter are cherished and explored by the Church through its liturgy. The season of Easter is a time for reflecting on the mysteries that were celebrated on Holy Saturday night at the Easter Vigil. In other words, it is a time of mystagogy. Today in the readings we hear a bold proclamation of the resurrection (Acts), a moral exhortation for the newly baptized (1 Peter) and the story of an appearance of the Risen Jesus to two disciples on the road to Emmaus (Luke). Each text illumines a different feature of the Easter mystery in which believers are immersed during this season.

In the first reading, set on the day of Pentecost, Peter's proclamation to the people of Jerusalem explains that the crucifixion and resurrection are part of the plan of God, foretold by sacred scripture. We see here the Spirit in action, empowering Peter to speak fearlessly (a common theme in Acts). Psalm 16, which Peter quotes in this passage, is our responsorial psalm of the day. It stresses confidence in God, and a communion with God which lasts beyond death. Yet it finds a new level of interpretation when Peter offers it as a description of the resurrection of Jesus. Peter's preaching presents the resurrection experience in light of the sacred text and he also reads the sacred text in a new way because of this experience.

Today's reading from 1 Peter contains a moral exhortation to the newly baptized. Though they call God "Father" (a reference perhaps to the Lord's Prayer), they cannot presume to receive special treatment, because by nature God will be an impartial judge of their behavior. This is a sobering message. Our time on earth is a "sojourn" or pilgrimage in "a strange land" for those whose true home is heaven, and so the imperative to obey God faithfully surpasses any pull toward a return to former pagan ways. The ancient custom of manumission (buying a slave his freedom) or ransoming captives in time of war is alluded to as a metaphor for the spiritual redemption of baptism. When proselytes were received into the Jewish religion at that time, they were baptized, circumcised, and an animal sacrifice was offered. Here the sacrifice which accompanies baptism is that of Christ "the lamb without blemish"—an allusion to the lamb prepared for the Passover.

Luke's power as a storyteller is richly illustrated in today's gospel by the sense of place, drama, and vivid psychological details of the narrative. Like Peter in today's reading from Acts, the disciples on the road are reflecting on recent events concerning Jesus. But here the Risen Lord himself interprets these events in a way that stirs their deepest convictions and emotions ("Were not our hearts burning within us. . . ?")

Like other resurrection appearances, this one is marked by delayed recognition. The actions in which the disciples recognize Jesus are the familiar ones which accompanied any Jewish meal, and which are highlighted in the feeding of the five thousand, and the last supper: taking, blessing, breaking, and giving. These four actions continue to be essential to the celebration of the Christian Eucharist. In fact, the entire story—including the dialogue with Jesus in which he explains the scriptures, the meal in which "their eyes were opened" (an expression used six times in Luke, to indicate insight), and their joyful haste in going forth to share the Good News of the resurrection—offers the pattern of the Eucharist that was to develop in the early Church.

The disciples' invitation to the stranger they have met on the road ("Stay with us") has rich overtones of meaning in this context as well. In Luke's narrative, it indicates the openness of the disciples to receiving a further revelation. And in a larger context, it points toward the eucharistic mystery, in which Jesus indeed continues to stay with us.

Catholic Doctrine

The Celebration of the Eucharist

Even though it is not the first sacrament celebrated in the life of the believer, the Eucharist is considered by Catholics as preeminent among all the seven sacraments. Indeed, the Eucharist is described by the Second Vatican Council as "the source and summit of the Christian life" (LG 11). In addition, the Council strongly asserted the centrality of the Eucharist in Catholic life, saying: "The other sacraments, and indeed all ecclesiastical ministries and works of the apostolate, are bound up with the Eucharist and are oriented toward it. For in the blessed Eucharist is contained the whole spiritual good of the Church, namely Christ himself, our Pasch" (PO 5).

Although Jesus himself instituted this sacrament on the night before he died, it is not a drama reenacting the Last Supper with the disciples. The Eucharist celebrates the whole of the paschal mystery: the suffering, death, and resurrection of Jesus Christ in which we continue to share by faith and baptism. In other words, the celebration of the Eucharist expresses our whole faith, in a unique ritual summation.

The Eucharist is ritually celebrated in one liturgy consisting of two parts, the Liturgy of the Word and the Liturgy of the Eucharist. In the first part, the assembly hears and responds to the Word of God proclaimed and preached. In the second part, those gathered give thanks and remember what God has done for us in Christ by sharing a meal (CCC 1346). The very arrangement of Catholic churches reflects the great dignity of these two actions. The attention of the assembly is focused on the pulpit where the Word is proclaimed and preached and on the altar where the meal is prepared and from which it is offered. As the Second Vatican Council explained, the Liturgy of the Word and of the Eucharist together form "one single act of worship" (SC 56), for the eucharistic table which is set before the worshipping assembly consists of both the table of God's Word and the table of the Body of the Lord (DV 21).

This single act of worship, the Eucharist, contains such a richness and depth that Catholics understand and discern various ways in which Christ is truly present in it. The Church believes and teaches that this real presence of Christ is experienced in four ways: (1) in the very people who are gathered, in the worshipping assembly, the household of the faith; (2) in the priest, the one who is acting in the person of Christ (*in persona Christi*); (3) in the proclamation of the Word, the sacred scripture; and (4) substantially and permanently in the elements of bread and wine (GIRM 7).

In celebrating the Eucharist, we make present again the sacrifice of Jesus on the cross. By his own action and by the power of the Holy Spirit the gifts of bread and wine are transformed into the body and blood of Christ, the self-sacrifice which he offered on our behalf to save us by his suffering and death (CCC 1357). At the same time, the celebration of the Eucharist is also a banquet of praise and thanksgiving. The very word in Greek, *eucharistein*, means "to give thanks." In the Eucharist, the Church expresses gratefulness to God for all the blessings shown us, first, through creation, and, more importantly, through the redemption accomplished in Christ. Every celebration of the Eucharist recalls the banquet feast of heaven.

Sent forth from the Eucharist, we are encouraged to carry on the mission of Christ. The common name for the celebration, the Mass, comes from *missa,* the Latin word meaning "to send." Thus, this liturgy which expresses and celebrates the mystery of our salvation in Christ concludes with the faithful being sent forth to offer their lives for the sake of the gospel, to be a leaven of Good News in the world, transforming agents, and, as St. Augustine wrote, to become what we are, members of the Body of Christ.

Catholic Culture

The earliest artistic depiction of the Emmaus story can be seen in a series of mosaics in Sant'Apollinare Nuovo in Ravenna, fashioned sometime before 540 A.D. Caravaggio (c. 1598) also depicts this episode. Christ is seated between the two disciples, both of whom are frozen in the act of finally recognizing who is present with them. One disciple's arms are flung out on either side in surprise, the other disciple's hands are grasping the chair as he begins to raise himself out of it, leaning slightly forward toward the Lord who is serenely looking down at the food upon the table, one hand extended over the bread as if in blessing. Even the servant at the inn is caught up in the drama of the moment. The painting is now in the National Gallery in London (OxA&A 163–64).

The importance attached to our Catholic understanding of Eucharist is signified by the number of paragraphs in the *Catechism of the Catholic Church* which deal with this subject: almost one hundred.

A standard feature of many Cursillo weekend retreats is the "Emmaus walk" where a retreatant signs up with one of the team members giving the retreat or with a priest or religious who then spends time in conversation (and walking) with them.

Dismissal Catechesis (30 min.)

Getting Started

1. Prepare the space ahead of time with a circle of chairs around a table draped with a white cloth upon which is placed a whole loaf of bread. Place spring flowers at the base of the table along with a large white candle in a candle stand.

2. Lead the candidates and catechumens to the circle and place the Lectionary on the table. Light the candle and remain standing as you lead the group in singing the Gospel Alleluia. Pray in these or similar words:
Spirit of God, fill us as you did Peter and the other disciples. Take away our fears and empower us to boldly proclaim your resurrection. Guide us as we try to live in a reverent manner, grateful for the price paid by the unblemished lamb who redeemed us. As the disciples recognized Jesus in the breaking of the bread, open our eyes to see Jesus each day. Fill us with gratitude for the gift of the Good News of the resurrection. Enlighten our minds and convict our hearts as we interpret these scriptures proclaimed in our midst today. We ask this through Christ, our Risen Savior. Amen.

First Impressions

1. Begin by making this comment on the Easter season:
Easter is a time to reflect on the mysteries celebrated at the Easter Vigil. It is called a time of mystagogy. During this period of fifty days, the parish community, the newly initiated, and those received into the Church will pray and meditate upon the resurrection. We join them in anticipation of our own initiation into the community of faith. Invite all to name the symbols, images, and phrases in today's Liturgy of the Word that helped their comprehension of the mystery of the resurrection. Record these on large strips of yellow or gold paper large enough for all to read. Post these around the room.

2. Invite the candidates and catechumens to gather into small groups to discuss the following questions: *What caused the change in Peter, from denying Jesus out of fear to his bold proclamation of the Good News? What does Peter mean by the phrase "conduct yourself reverently," taken from the second reading?* After sufficient time, ask the small groups to share their responses with everyone.

Making Connections

1. Remaining in the large group, move the discussion on this last question to a more practical level. Ask the candidates and catechumens to name specific actions that would be a loving response to God's gift of salvation through Jesus' death and resurrection. Write these practical suggestions on green strips of paper and post them around the room.

2. Gather the participants in the same small groups to share their insights on this question: *How has the Holy Spirit strengthened you as you attempt to live out God's gift of redemption?* You may begin this discussion by offering a personal experience in which you have been changed and empowered by the Spirit. After hearing their insights in the large group, briefly summarize the sharing.

Prayer

Prior to the session, make copies of Psalm 16 for everyone. Begin the prayer by inviting all to sing the Gospel Alleluia. Pray Psalm 16 by inviting each person to proclaim one verse at a time, moving around the circle until the psalm is completed. Complete this psalm prayer with the Gospel Alleluia.

Extended Catechesis

SESSION FOCUS: *The Celebration of Eucharist*

Gathering

A. Sunday:

1. Greet and welcome the sponsors, team members, and additional participants as they arrive. Invite them to join the circle of candidates and catechumens.

2. Begin the prayer by asking all to stand as you lead them in singing the first two verses of "Song of the Body of Christ" (David Haas, GIA Publications, 1989). Pray in these or similar words:
Gracious and ever living God, you make us into your holy people and call us to be the body of Christ. Enlighten our minds that we know you in the stories of faith given to us in the sacred scriptures and those stories of this faith community. Open our eyes that we recognize you in the breaking of the bread and the pouring of the wine. Inspire us to believe that you are really present in the eucharistic meal. Fill us with zeal to go out into the world to proclaim your Good News. We ask this through our Risen Savior. Amen.

3. Ask a team member to proclaim the first reading, Acts 2:14, 22–28. Allow for some silence, then invite a sponsor to proclaim the gospel, Luke 24:13–35, while the participants stand. Close the prayer with the Gospel Alleluia.

B. Weekday:

1. Use the same centerpiece as in the Dismissal Catechesis.

2. As the participants gather in the circle, greet and warmly welcome each person. Open the discussion to all the participants, asking them to share their experiences of God's Spirit empowering them to live the resurrection during the past few days.

3. Lead this celebration of the Word:
   - Song: "Song of the Body of Christ" (David Haas, GIA Publications, 1989)
   - First Reading: Acts 2:14, 22–33
   - Sing Psalm 16
   - Gospel: Luke 24:13–35
   - Sing "Alleluia"
   - Closing Prayer: See prayer in section A.2

The Word (30 min.)

1. Invite a catechumen or candidate to give a brief summary of the Dismissal Catechesis, using the posted strips of gold and green paper as help.

2. Ask everyone to close their eyes and imagine that they are walking along the road to Emmaus with the two disciples. Then prayerfully name some of the images from the gospel, pausing after each:

   Two disciples were walking and discussing all that had happened—Jesus approached and began to walk with them—"Are you the only one who does not know the things that went on in Jerusalem these past few days?"—"Jesus, a powerful prophet, was condemned to death and crucified. We were hoping he was the one who would set Israel free."—"Some women of our group were at the tomb before dawn and failed to find his body"—"How slow you are to believe all that the prophets have announced!"—He interpreted for them every passage of scripture that referred to him—He acted as if he was going farther. But they pressed him: "Stay with us!"—He took bread, pronounced the blessing, then broke the bread and began to distribute it to them—With that their eyes were opened and they recognized him—"Were not our hearts burning inside us as he talked to us on the road and explained the scriptures to us?"—They got up immediately and returned to Jerusalem where they found the eleven and the rest of the company assembled.

   Invite the participants to turn to the person next to them and name those images that stirred their hearts, telling their partner why the image had that effect.

3. Present the following background to the gospel:

   In this powerful story, Luke begins with two disciples who are disillusioned and despondent after the events in Jerusalem. Their feelings are summed up in the words, "We were hoping!" The stranger on the road is none other than the Risen Lord, whom the disciples failed to recognize. Even when the stranger opens the meaning of the scriptures for them, they do not understand. This story peaks when the disciples express their emotions again, "Stay with us!" Their plea hints at the loss the disciples felt as well as an openness to hear more. The phrase also points to the Eucharist in which Jesus does "stay with us." In Jesus' action taking the bread, blessing it, breaking and giving it to the disciples, their "eyes were opened." In hindsight, they realize that their hearts burned within as he explained the scriptures. This burning excitement causes them to retrace their steps to tell the others their Good News.

4. Encourage the participants to look at their own faith journey in the light of this passage by writing their responses to the Reflection section found in the Participant Book on page 42. Invite the sponsors and godparents to pair up with their catechumen or candidate, to share their faith reflection and responses to the questions.

5. Then invite the pairs to share one way that the presence of Jesus has been of help in living their faith.

Catholic Teaching (30 min.)

1. Begin the teaching on the Eucharist by pointing out that this gospel passage contains the two parts of the Eucharist: the Liturgy of the Word and the Liturgy of the Eucharist. Refer to the Catholic Doctrine section of Understanding this Sunday for a fuller explanation.

2. Continue this teaching on the Eucharist, including these points:
   - [Hold the loaf of bread] The four actions of the Eucharist—taking, blessing, breaking, and giving the bread—are essential to the celebration of the Eucharist.
   - The Eucharist is considered the preeminent Sacrament, called by the Second Vatican Council document on the Church "the source and summit of the Christian life." The entire life of a Christian flows from and is oriented toward Eucharist.
   - The real presence of Christ is experienced in four ways at the Eucharist: in the gathered assembly, in the presider, in the proclamation of the Word, and in the blessed bread and wine.
   - The Eucharist celebrates the whole of the paschal mystery: the suffering, death, and resurrection of Jesus. Each time we celebrate the Eucharist we make present again the sacrifice of Jesus on the cross. By the action of the Holy Spirit the gifts of bread and wine are transformed into the body and blood of Christ.
   - Eucharist sends us out to continue the mission of Christ in the world.

3. Invite the participants to discuss these questions in small groups: *In this teaching on Eucharist, what do you find comforting? What is still troublesome or difficult to accept?* You may choose to have a pastoral minister or priest present to discuss the teachings that pose a problem among the participants.

Putting Faith into Practice

1. Ask the group to name some ways they can continue the mission of Jesus in their daily living. Write the ideas on strips of orange paper and post them around the room. Encourage everyone to notice the gold, green, and orange strips, which summarize their responses to this living Word. They may choose to record these insights in their Participant Book on page 43, under the heading, "I want to remember."

2. In small groups encourage a discussion on those blessings for which they are grateful. Ask each small group to prepare another strip of blue paper by writing down their expression of gratitude for Jesus' saving death and resurrection.

Prayer

Focus the attention of the participants back to the large group. In a prayer of gratitude, ask each group to present their expression of gratitude by reading the blue strips and posting them on the wall. As they finish each expression, pass around the loaf of bread and invite all to tear off a piece and eat it as a sign of unity and gratitude. This is not Eucharist, merely a sharing of one loaf as a sign of unity in our common journey of faith. Close by leading the group in singing the last verses of "Song of the Body of Christ."

Fourth Sunday of Easter

Understanding this Sunday:
Background for Catechesis

The Word in Liturgy

Acts 2:14, 36–41
Psalm 23:1–3, 3–4, 5–6
1 Peter 2:20–25
John 10:1–10

Although at this point in the liturgical calendar the Church has not yet celebrated Pentecost, the entire Easter season is marked by readings from Acts concerning events that occurred after the giving of the Spirit. This is no accident, but it demonstrates that the whole season is Spirit-filled, from the Easter Vigil to Pentecost. Today's reading is taken from Peter's sermon on the day of Pentecost itself, continuing the passage read last Sunday. In response to his proclamation of the Good News (narrated last week), some of the crowd are struck by the message and ask "What are we to do?" This question is the same as the one asked by those who heard the preaching of John the Baptist (Luke 3:10). The truth cannot be entertained passively, but demands a response in action. Peter's command—to believe and be baptized—highlights the mission of the Church, which is also illustrated by the three thousand who were baptized. Thus, the proclamation of the resurrection provokes a crisis in people's lives, demands decision, and results in rapid growth of the new community of faith.

In addition to the persecution of the Roman Emperor Domitian (81–96 A.D.), which afflicted the Christians of Asia Minor to whom the first letter of Peter is written, the evils of slavery also produced sufferings in that early community, as many of the new converts were slaves. The injunction to patient endurance, in imitation of Christ, here is coupled with an expression of gratitude for the continuous caring presence of Christ as "shepherd and guardian of your souls." Chosen no doubt for this last verse, which connects the passage with the gospel that follows, the reading is both a theological meditation on reconciliation through the cross, and a pastoral exhortation to a community under fire.

The complex imagery of shepherd and sheep contained in the tenth chapter of John's gospel gives the fourth Sunday of Easter its customary name ("Good Shepherd Sunday") and has many reference points. The image of the shepherd is well known in the Old Testament literature as an image for God and for leadership of the community. The reference to others who are "thieves and marauders" may reflect the condemnation in Ezekiel of the "false shepherds" whose corrupt influence will be replaced by God's own shepherding. The contrast between the shepherd who is Jesus and other, hostile influences may also reflect the tension which developed between Christians and the leaders of the Jewish communities from which the early Church sprang. Continuing conflicts made it necessary to look to and trust Christ alone, the true shepherd.

The text also relies on a common understanding of shepherding practices in first-century Palestine. The sheep were gathered for the night in an enclosed area which had but one opening, and no gate. The shepherd would lay across the opening during the night, to protect the sheep from any possible predators, and so was himself the gate. Several flocks would be mixed together, but the sheep would recognize the shepherd's voice and respond to none other when called. Last of all, rather than walking behind the sheep and using dogs and other animals to keep the flock together as is done today, the shepherd would walk in front of the sheep and lead them. In today's gospel passage, the description of Jesus through these metaphors may be summed up as follows: he protects his followers daily by laying down his own life for them, he gathers them into a unique relationship with himself, and he guides them by leading the way. The focus of today's catechesis may therefore be on Jesus the Good Shepherd, caring companion and leader of his people.

Catholic Doctrine

Jesus, the Good Shepherd

The person of Jesus reveals God the Father. His words and deeds, his whole life, open to us the mystery of God (CCC 516). Similarly, the many titles of Jesus illuminate for us particular aspects of his identity: Christ, Messiah, Lord, Son of God, Son of Mary, Lamb of God, King of the Universe, and so on. The fourth gospel, in particular, is characterized by vivid and direct statements made by Jesus ("I am . . .") describing who he is, for example, "the light of the world," "the bread of life," "the way, the truth and the life," "the living water," and "the good shepherd." These metaphors provide a rich imaginative framework for understanding the mystery of Jesus and the relationship of the believer to Christ.

The image of shepherd suggests a number of meanings, building upon Hebrew scripture (for examples, see Genesis 48:15, Psalm 23, Ezekiel 34:11). The Good Shepherd is the leader who lays down his life for the sheep, his flock. He is the caring companion, who protects them, whose voice they recognize and who provides pasture and life for them. The believer is thus offered a relationship of trust and safety because of the action of the shepherd. The use of this image indicates the intimate and close bond between the members of the flock, the Church, with Jesus, the shepherd (see John 10:15). The Second Vatican Council used the image of the Good Shepherd in its document on the Church to illustrate the close connection between believers and the Lord, who guides his Church (LG 6).

In addition, the gospel of John also extends this powerful and multileveled metaphor to the disciple Peter. In a post-resurrection encounter, the Christ asks him to "feed my lambs" and "tend my sheep" (John 21:15–19). The disciple who three times denied the Lord now pledges three times to act as Jesus would in caring for the flock, his Church. The image of shepherd has thus been used in our Catholic tradition as an image of the pastor. John Paul II has crafted an apostolic exhortation concerning the formation of priests in the world today, the title of which is "I Will Give You Shepherds" (*Pastores Dabo Vobis*, March 25, 1992, Vatican translation, Pauline Books and Media, Boston). His starting point is the scriptural image of shepherd and the flock.

St. Gregory the Great (pope from 590–604) challenged his hearers in a homily to plumb their own relationship to Jesus, the Good Shepherd. He preached, "Ask yourself whether you belong to [Jesus'] flock, whether you know him, whether the light of his truth shines in your minds. I assure you that it is not by faith that you will come to know him, but by love; not by mere conviction, but by action. John the evangelist is my authority for this statement. He tells us that *anyone who claims to know God without keeping his commandments is a liar*.... So our Lord's sheep will finally reach their grazing ground where all who follow him in simplicity of heart will feed on the green pastures of eternity. . . . Let us stir up our hearts, rekindle our faith, and long eagerly for what heaven has in store for us. To love thus is to be already on our way" (Gregory the Great, *On the Gospels* 14, 3–6: PL 76, 1129–30 found in LitHrs, vol. 2, pp. 753–54).

God, revealed in Jesus, is thus truly the shepherd of Psalm 23. But Jesus also shows us that God is the one who lays down his life for us, who knows us personally, guides us, protects us, and offers believers the abundance of eternal life.

Catholic Culture

Shepherd and sheep abound in early Christian art. Some of the earliest representations of Christ depict the Lord as a shepherd carrying a sheep on his shoulders and can be seen in the frescos of the catacombs of Domitilla, Priscilla, and Commodilla (Rome).

Contemporary scripture scholar Sofia Cavalletti and her colleagues have developed a catechetical method using the parable of the Good Shepherd with children worldwide. Cavalletti writes, "Once begun, the relationship with the Good Shepherd never ceases; the parable will grow slowly with the child, revealing its other aspects and satisfying the needs of the older child, adolescent and adult. . . . The development is from the love that protects, to the love that forgives, and finally, to the *imitatio Christi* . . . [that is, its dynamic unfolds as] early childhood, sensitive period for protection; later childhood, moral sensitive period; adolescence, sensitive period for heroism" (Sofia Cavalletti, *The Religious Potential of the Child*, Liturgy Training Publications, Chicago, IL, 1992, p. 75).

The practice of reading the Good Shepherd gospel during the Easter Season is an ancient custom. The Lectionary of Wurzburg (seventh century) assigns this gospel passage from John to the Second Sunday after Easter. This passage may have been used even earlier, since St. Gregory the Great preached on this passage in an Easter homily (see above).

Dismissal Catechesis (30 min.)

Getting Started

1. Prepare the space ahead of time with a circle of chairs around a table draped with a white cloth. Place a large white candle in a candle stand next to the table, upon which you have placed an artwork, carving, or icon of the Good Shepherd.

2. Lead the candidates and catechumens to the circle and place the Lectionary on the table and light the candle. Pray in these or your own words:

Jesus our Shepherd, lead us out of our wanderings and set us on the path of holiness. Guard us against the lure of easy answers and quick fixes, strengthening us instead with patient endurance as we struggle to know you. Attune us that we might recognize your voice and follow you. Light our path each day and open our hearts this day that we might come to know you through your Word proclaimed in our midst. Amen.

First Impressions

1. Invite all to listen in silence and notice their reactions as you read these phrases taken from the scriptures used at today's liturgy:

They were deeply shaken.
What are we to do?
You must reform and be baptized.
The Lord is my shepherd.
You anoint my head with oil and my cup overflows.
By his wounds you were healed.
At one time you were straying like sheep.
Now you have returned to the shepherd, the guardian of your souls.
I am the sheep gate.

2. Ask the candidates and catechumens to think of one word or phrase that captures their impression of today's Liturgy of the Word. Record these on newsprint, large enough for all to read.

3. Then gather the participants into small groups to discuss these questions: *What does the imagery found in today's scriptures say about the nature of Jesus? What do the scriptures call forth as a response from the followers of Jesus and us?* Ask that each small group print their response to the second question on an index card.

Making Connections

1. When the groups have had sufficient time to share their responses, focus their attention back to the large gathering. Encourage each small group to name some of the responses of the believer to the saving action of Jesus, by reading their index card.

2. Continue by guiding the discussion toward practical suggestions for responding to Jesus' death and resurrection. Open the discussion even further, saying: *If you were among the crowd gathered on the day of Pentecost,*

listening to the proclamation of Peter, how would you respond to the question, "What are we do to?" Encourage the group to be realistic and practical; for example, instead of "reform your life," invite them to name some ways to do that, such as, "I will try to see the face of Christ in the people I meet each day." Encourage participants to write each response on a separate index card. These can be gathered and placed on the table.

Prayer

Ask everyone to stand and sing Psalm 23, using either the refrain, "The Lord is my shepherd; I shall not want," or the song, "Shepherd Me, O God" (Marty Haugen, GIA Publications, 1987). While they are singing, ask each person to take a card from the table and try to act on that particular response over the next week. Close with a short period of quiet, directing the attention of the group to the lighted candle and the image of the Good Shepherd.

Extended Catechesis

SESSION FOCUS: Jesus, *The Good Shepherd*

Gathering

A. Sunday:

1. Greet and welcome the sponsors and team members as they arrive. Invite them to join the circle of catechumens and candidates.

2. Gather the group by inviting all to stand and sing a few verses of the Gathering Song used at today's liturgy. Continue by setting the context for the gospel reading with this meditation, after everyone is seated:

Close your eyes and imagine yourself back among the followers of Jesus in his day. You are outside the small town where you live in the Galilean country-side. It is twilight and the hills are scented with the aroma of newly cut grass. You are among several others who are shepherds, just like you. After a lazy day watching your flock of sheep in the bright sunlight, you now hurry the flock into a rock-walled enclosure. Each sheep hears the distinctive whistle or call and comes to you as you lead them into the pen. Your sheep bleat and scamper amidst the other flocks. That night you will be on duty, guarding the flocks by lying across the stony opening. The next morning you will call and the sheep of your flock will follow as you lead them to a new, green pasture.

3. Ask one of the sponsors to proclaim the gospel, John 10:1–10, as the group stands to listen.

B. Weekday:

1. Use the same centerpiece as described for the Dismissal Catechesis.
2. As the participants gather in the circle, greet and warmly welcome each person. Invite the group to share some examples of good leadership that they have noticed over the past few days.
3. Lead this celebration of the Word:
   - Song: Gathering song from Sunday's liturgy
   - Greeting: *May the peace of Christ fill you with joy, Alleluia*
   - Response: *You are the cause of our joy, O Risen Christ, Alleluia*
   - First Reading: Acts 2:14, 36–41
   - Sing Psalm 23
   - Second Reading: 1 Peter 2:20–25
   - Meditation: Use the meditation found in A.
   - Gospel: John 10:1–10

The Word (30 min.)

1. Invite the catechumens and candidates to share some insights from the Dismissal Session.
2. Then ask the participants to name some qualities and characteristics of a shepherd that they gleaned from the meditation and the gospel proclamation. List these on newsprint, writing large enough for all to see.
3. Present this background on the readings, using these or similar words:

   Traditionally known as Good Shepherd Sunday, this fourth Sunday is part of the Easter season. The reading from Acts is a continuation of the preaching of Peter to the crowds on the day of Pentecost. In this particular passage, the crowd is so moved by the message, they ask, with urgency, "What are we to do?" This is the perennial question of the believer as he or she grows in understanding the full power of the resurrection. The response is simple enough: believe and be baptized in the name of Jesus that your sins may be forgiven and your life reformed. The gospel pushes us deeper into the lifelong process of reform. For in proclaiming Jesus as the Good Shepherd, we are challenged to reform—conform our lives—to that of this Christ. As we move deeper into a relationship with the Good Shepherd, we will recognize his voice and will be reformed (changed) through this intimacy with Jesus. The Good Shepherd leads and guards, with the best interest of the flock in mind. As we are led and protected by the Good Shepherd, so too we will be challenged to lead and guard others, who ask, "What are we to do?"

4. Direct the group to turn to page 44 in the Participant Book and spend time reflecting on their images of Jesus. Encourage them to share this description of Jesus with a partner. The candidates and catechumens will want to pair up with their sponsor and/or godparent.

Catholic Teaching (30 min.)

1. Ask the pairs to continue sharing the questions presented on page 44 of the Participant Book. In the large group invite a few to offer some suggestions on how to come to know the Good Shepherd more intimately.
2. Explain the teaching of the Church on the Good Shepherd, covering these key points:
   - The metaphor of the Good Shepherd, along with others found in the scriptures, is a framework for helping the believer to understand the intimate relationship of the believer to Jesus.
   - The Good Shepherd is the leader who lays down his life for his flock, the caring companion who protects them and the provider of sustenance and life for the sheep.
   - Jesus offers the believer a relationship of trust, safety, sustenance, and life. The bond between our Redeemer and us, the redeemed, is close and intimate.
   - The disciple, through baptism, is challenged, as was Peter, to become a leader, a Good Shepherd for others. Upon forgiving Peter for his triple denial, Jesus thrice calls Peter to "feed my lambs" and "tend my sheep," indicating the mission of all believers.
3. Invite the pairs to discuss these questions: *How does this new understanding of Jesus as the Good Shepherd challenge you? From your experiences of intimate relationships, what is it you desire, as you grow closer to Jesus? Where are you being challenged to lead in the model of Jesus? Where are you called to protect and guard, as does the Good Shepherd?*

Putting Faith into Practice

When the pairs have had adequate time to share their thoughts, invite them to focus back to the large group and spend time listening to their responses. Encourage the participants to note those things they wish to remember from the discussion in their Participant Book on page 45. Offer some examples of current leaders in your parish, in the Church, or in the world who give witness to the model of the Good Shepherd.

Prayer

While remaining seated in the circle, prepare the group to hear once again the Good News of Peter. Invite them to imagine themselves in the crowd on the day of Pentecost, captivated by the preaching of Peter. Then ask them to raise the question, as did the crowd, by repeating after you, "What are we to do?" Continue by proclaiming the response of Peter, Acts 2:38–41. Ask the participants to think about their own response to the Good Shepherd and make a commitment to carry that out this next week. Close by praying Psalm 23 together.

Fifth Sunday of Easter

The Word in Liturgy

Acts 6:1–7
Psalm 33:1–2, 4–5, 18–19
1 Peter 2:4–9
John 14:1–12

As the Easter season progresses, our attention is drawn from intimate encounters with the risen Jesus and relationships within the young community of faith to a more outward-looking focus. Today's passage from Acts forms the connection between the ministry in Jerusalem, and the spread of the gospel to Samaria and beyond. Although the dispute between the Hellenists (Greek-speaking Jews) and Hebrews (Aramaic-speaking Jews) is reportedly concerned with the impartial distribution of charity to widows, the actual function of the seven who are appointed to see to these needs seems later in Acts to be prophetic ministry rather than table service. A link between the two may be found, however, in Luke's persistent association of authority over material goods with spiritual authority. Those who are chosen to serve at table are *ipso facto* spiritual leaders. The imposition of hands by the apostles suggests a passing of power to the seven chosen for service *(diaconia)*. It is worth noting that authority rested with the Twelve, yet the community's approval was sought and the community actually chose the seven. Although the sacrament of Holy Orders is a later development in the Church, passages such as this one—where service to the community is empowered by a laying on of hands—would later in Christian history be seen as prototypes of ordination.

Today's reading from 1 Peter beautifully describes the identity of the Christian people given in baptism and continually discovered throughout the living of the Christian life. Those who formerly were only isolated individuals are made into a people. They rise to the dignity of Israel, being called "chosen." And in the Christian people the benefits and functions of priests and kings are distributed to all. The image of Christ as the "living stone," an image shared with all the faithful who are likewise living stones, suggests solidity and strength, yet vitality as well. Christ the stone is chosen (eklectos) by God, even as the believers are elect. Yet this stone is also rejected by faithless humanity ("rejected by men," v. 4) as well as by "the builders" (the Jewish leaders who put Jesus to death), and is an obstacle and source of confusion for those who do not believe. The author nevertheless consigns even the role of the enemies of Christ's reign to the care and keeping of God.

Our gospel passage is taken from the Farewell Discourse at the Last Supper, and addresses concerns of the disciples that arise because of the departure (i.e., death) of Jesus soon to occur. In the context of its liturgical proclamation at this point in the Easter season, this reading also invites us to reflect on the coming "departure" of Jesus in the Ascension and the impact on us believers of the physical absence of Jesus. What are the disciples to do without him? What do *we* do without this reassuring presence? First of all, the passage assures us that Jesus will return and take his followers with him. The reference seems to be to the parousia, though it may also be interpreted as a reference to being reunited with Jesus at death. The immanent departure of Jesus is presented not as a loss but as a preparation for the future. The expression "many dwelling places" of the Father's house ("mansions" is a mistranslation) suggests not a diversity of place within heaven but that there will be room enough for everyone in God's eternal presence. Jesus, who is "the way" of salvation, will lead to the Father, who is one with Jesus.

At the conclusion of the passage, Jesus promises another benefit of his leaving: those who believe in him will do works as great, and greater, than his. The future ministry of his followers depends upon him going, thus suggesting that the events of his glorification will bestow on them a power to be like him in an outstanding new way. The passage begins and ends with faith—not the pale assent of fearful followers, but the confidence of those who are empowered do great works because they have immersed themselves in "the way" who is Jesus.

Catholic Doctrine

The Sacrament of Holy Orders and the Common Priesthood of the Baptized

There is one priesthood: that of Jesus Christ. The Lord is the one high priest, and his ministry is accomplished as a servant (CCC 1551). The Son has been made holy and sent by the Father to serve the needs of the world and to accomplish our redemption in humility (LG 28).

Jesus Christ himself sends the Holy Spirit upon the whole body of the Church and endows the community of the faithful with a share in his servant nature. Thus, as the Second Vatican Council teaches, Jesus makes the whole Church a sharer in the Spirit in which he has been anointed, that is, "all the faithful are made a holy and kingly priesthood, [for] they offer spiritual sacrifices to God through Jesus Christ, and they proclaim the virtues of him who has called them out of darkness into his admirable light" (PO 2). It is by baptism that the members of the Church are privileged to share in the priesthood of Jesus Christ (CCC 1591).

Founded upon this common priesthood of all believers and directed to its service, there is yet another form which participates in the priesthood of Jesus. This is the ministry given as a gift through the sacrament of Holy Orders. This is called the ministerial priesthood. While the priesthood of all believers is worked out in a life of faith, hope, and love, the ordained (or ministerial) priesthood exists in order to assist and serve the full flowering of the baptismal call of all. Those who are ordained to the ministerial priesthood enable the Church to be built up into its full baptismal stature (CCC 1547). As Pope John Paul II has observed, ". . . because their role and task within the Church do not replace but promote the baptismal priesthood of the entire People of God, leading to its full ecclesial realization, priests have a positive and helpful relationship to the laity. . . . They recognize and uphold, as brothers and friends, the dignity of the laity as children of God and help them to exercise fully their specific role in the overall context of the Church's mission" (*Pastores Dabo Vobis,* March 25, 1992, #17, Vatican translation, Pauline Books and Media, Boston).

The center and high point of the ministerial priesthood is the celebration of the Eucharist. The Second Vatican Council reminded us, "The purpose then for which priests are consecrated by God . . . is that they should be made sharers in a special way in Christ's priesthood and, by carrying out sacred functions, act as his ministers who through his Spirit continually exercise his priestly function for our benefit in the liturgy" (PO 5).

There are three hierarchical degrees of Holy Orders: the episcopate (bishops), the presbyterate (priests), and the diaconate (deacons). In our Catholic understanding, bishops receive the fullness of the ministerial priesthood, for they, by ordination, exercise the office of sanctifying, teaching, and ruling (CCC 1558). The very word *episcopoi* (Gk) means "overseer." Priests are considered co-workers of bishops, who have given to them, in a subordinate degree, a share in the ministry of bishop so that the mission of Christ might be accomplished. Priests assist their bishop in preaching, celebrating the liturgy, and shepherding the faithful (CCC 1562–63). Deacons are ordained not to the priesthood itself but are gifted by the sacrament of Holy Orders for ministry or service. Deacons assist bishops and priests in the celebration of the Eucharist, the proclamation of the gospel and preaching, presiding over funerals, weddings, and baptisms, and in charitable outreach to those in need, as depicted in the first reading for today's liturgy. The very word *diakonia* (Gk) means "service" (CCC 1569–70).

Catholic Culture

Vestments are the special garments worn by ministers at the celebration of liturgy. They originated in the time of the late Roman Empire. The ordinary clothing for men at this time was a long tunic tied at the waist (the origin of the present-day alb and cincture) and a large serape-like over-garment (the origin of the present-day chasuble). While everyday garments changed after the fall of the Empire, clergy continued to use these styles in the celebration of liturgy— hence, they took on symbolic meaning. Priests wear the alb, chasuble, and stole (a narrow band of cloth worn across the back of the neck and hanging down the front, as did Roman judges and other officials as a sign of their office). Bishops also wear the same vestments but with the addition of a mitre (a pointed hat, to symbolize their office of ruling, like a crown). Deacons wear albs, dalmatics (similar to a chasuble but closed on the sides), and stoles worn over only one shoulder (ModCathE 898). Laypersons who minister at liturgy sometimes wear an alb, the white garment which symbolizes baptism.

Dismissal Catechesis (30 min.)

Getting Started

1. Prepare the space ahead of time with a circle of chairs around a table draped with a white cloth on which is placed a large stone. Place a large white candle in a stand next to the table and arrange spring flowers at its base.

2. Lead the candidates and catechumens to the circle and place the Lectionary on the table and light the candle. While standing, lead the catechumens and candidates in singing the Gospel Alleluia. When the participants are seated, pray in these or your own words: *Jesus, you are the cornerstone of our faith. Like your first followers, we place our faith in you, our eternal priest. Send your Spirit upon us that we might be your chosen people, a royal priesthood. Help us to follow you in faith, for you are the Way, the Truth, and the Life. Nurture us with your Word that we might do your works in a hungry and hurting world. We ask this in your name. Amen.*

First Impressions

1. Invite everyone to be seated and to take a few deep breaths. Invite them to close their eyes and quietly to recall words, phrases, or images of the Liturgy of the Word just celebrated. After several minutes, and with their eyes still closed, ask one person at a time to speak aloud these words, phrases, or images. Record them on newsprint, writing large enough for all to see. When all have been recorded, slowly repeat all the words, phrases, and images.

2. Offer the following insight on the second reading from 1 Peter 2:4–9: *The image of Christ as the "living stone" is shared with all the faithful who are likewise "living stones." This suggests unity, strength, and vitality. Through Jesus' resurrection we have been changed from isolated individuals and made into a holy people, a royal priesthood. Our strength is derived from faith in Jesus. Our vitality flows from following him, the Way, the Truth, and the Life.* Invite the participants to look at the stone and name further insights into today's scripture passages that come to mind as they reflect upon this symbol of Jesus, the "living stone." Use another sheet of newsprint to record their insights.

3. Invite them to discuss these questions with the person sitting to their right: *What do you find enlivening in today's scriptures? How is this stone an obstacle or source of confusion for you?*

Making Connections

1. Listen to the responses of each pair in the large group. Then ask these same pairs to discuss these questions: *How is Jesus a source of strength as you journey in faith? What does it mean to be called a holy people, a living stone, a royal priesthood by Jesus? How can you respond to this call as did the early deacons who were appointed to serve the widows and orphans?*

2. Invite each pair to share their ideas about responding to the challenge of being a living stone, a holy people, a royal priesthood. Ask each participant to write down one way they might act this week in light of that challenge in their Participant Book in the section entitled "I want to put my faith into action by" on page 47.

Prayer

Encourage the participants to sit quietly in the circle and pass around the stone. Invite them to ask, when they have an opportunity to handle the stone, for strength to keep their resolution. They may choose to articulate their petition aloud or offer it in silence. When all have had an opportunity to pray, lead the group in singing Psalm 33, using the same melody used at today's Liturgy of the Word.

Extended Catechesis

SESSION FOCUS: *The Sacrament of Holy Orders and the Common Priesthood of the Baptized*

Gathering

A. Sunday:

1. Greet and welcome the sponsors, team members, and others as they arrive. Invite them to join the circle of catechumens and candidates.

2. While the group remains seated, lead them in singing the first few verses of the Gathering Song used at today's liturgy. Proclaim the first reading, Acts 6:1–7. Intone the Gospel Alleluia, indicating that all stand. Ask a team member to proclaim the gospel, John 14:1–12. Close with the Gospel Alleluia.

B. Weekday:

1. Use the same centerpiece as described for the Dismissal Catechesis.

2. As the participants gather in the circle, greet and warmly welcome each person. Invite the participants to share their experiences of encountering Jesus among the "holy people" they met in these past few days.

3. Lead this celebration of the Word:
   - Song: Opening Song from Sunday's Liturgy
   - First Reading: Acts 6:1–7
   - Sing Psalm 118 "This is the Day. . . ."
   - Second Reading: 1 Peter 2:4–9
   - Sing the Gospel Alleluia
   - Gospel: John 14:1–12
   - Sing the Gospel Alleluia

The Word (30 min.)

1. Invite the catechumens and candidates to summarize the insights gleaned during the Dismissal Catechesis.

2. Ask the group to name some key words or phrases from the scriptures, as you list them on newsprint, writing large enough for all to read. If the group does not name the following, add them to the list.

*Look for seven men acknowledged to be spiritual and
    prudent.
They prayed over them and then imposed hands on them.
The Word of God continued to spread.
Exult, you just in the Lord.
Come to the Lord, a living stone, precious in God's eyes.
The stone is of value for you who have faith.
You, too, are living stones (a chosen race, a royal
    priesthood, a people claimed by God,
Do not let your hearts be troubled.
I am going to prepare a place for you.
I am the way, the truth, and the life.
I am in the Father and the Father is in me.
If you have faith in me you will do the works I do and
    greater far than these.*

3. Continue to explore the scriptures by presenting these insights
   expanded in the Word in Liturgy section found in
   Understanding this Sunday:

   *As the Easter season progresses, our attention is drawn
   from intimate encounters with the risen Jesus and relationships within the young community of faith to a more
   outward-looking focus.*

   *Today's first reading from the Book of Acts forms the
   connection between the ministry in Jerusalem and the
   spread of the gospel to Samaria and beyond.*

   *Those chosen to serve are the spiritual leaders. The imposi-
   tion of hands by the apostles indicates a passing of power
   to the seven chosen for service.*

   *The second reading from 1 Peter describes the identity of
   the Christian people given in baptism and gradually
   discovered in living the journey of the Christian life.*

   *Both readings converge in the union between Jesus and
   his holy people, who share in the royal priesthood by
   sharing in the ministry of a servant. Priesthood is forever
   directed to and linked with service.*

   *The gospel passage from the Farewell Discourse at the Last
   Supper addresses the disciples' concerns because of the
   departure of Jesus soon to occur (his death). Jesus promises
   to return but says that he must go.*

   *This passage begins and ends with faith. This faith is not the
   pale assent of fearful followers, but the confidence of those who
   are empowered to great works because they have immersed
   themselves in "the way, the truth, and the life" who is Jesus.*

4. Invite the participants to gather into small groups to discuss
   these questions: *In what ways have you experienced union
   with the "holy people, the consecrated nation" of the
   faithful in this parish? How has your faith helped you to
   trust in Jesus, the living stone, the way, the truth, and the
   life? What life changes has this brought about for you?*
   When they have had adequate time for discussion, focus the
   attention back to the large group and invite a few responses
   from the small groups.

Catholic Teaching (30 min.)

1. Continuing in the large group, invite all to name some words or
   qualities that come to mind when they think of royal priesthood.
   Record these on newsprint, writing large enough for all to see.

2. Build on their responses by presenting the Catholic understanding of the common priesthood of the baptized and the
   sacrament of Holy Orders in these or your own words:
   *Jesus Christ is the one high priest who was sent by the
   Father to serve the needs of the world and to accomplish
   our redemption in humility through his death on the cross
   and his resurrection. According to the teaching of the
   Second Vatican Council, Jesus makes the whole Church a
   sharer in the Spirit in which he has been anointed, making
   all the faithful into a holy priesthood. Through baptism we
   share in the priesthood of Jesus Christ. In baptism, the
   believer is anointed priest, prophet, and king with the oil of
   chrism. Thus, through the sacrament of baptism we are all
   called to exercise the common priesthood of all believers.
   There is yet another form of priesthood, which is called the
   ministerial priesthood. While the common priesthood of all
   believers is worked out in a life of faith, hope, and love, the
   ordained priesthood exists in order to assist and serve the
   full flowering of the baptismal call of all. The center and
   high point of the ministerial priesthood is the celebration of
   the Eucharist. The Second Vatican Council also states that
   the ordained priest acts as Christ's minister and carries out
   sacred actions for the benefit of all baptized believers.*

3. Invite the participants to raise any questions that they might
   have regarding this Church teaching. You may choose to have
   a pastoral minister, deacon, or priest present to respond to
   their questions.

4. Invite one of the ordained deacons or priests at your parish to
   briefly elaborate upon the three degrees of Holy Orders—the
   episcopate (bishops), the presbyterate (priests), and the
   diaconate (deacons). Ask the minister to use the Catholic
   Doctrine section found in Understanding this Sunday to
   explain these hierarchical degrees.

Putting Faith into Practice

1. Invite everyone to turn to their Participant Book and write
   their responses to the Reflection and the Questions found on
   page 46. After allowing sufficient time to reflect, ask the
   participants to share their responses in their small groups.

2. Encourage a few responses in the large group, particularly on
   the first question on ways to get involved with outreach to the
   poor and homeless. You may choose to suggest some organizations in the parish that serve in these areas and encourage
   the sponsors to help their candidate or catechumen get
   involved.

3. Give them a copy of the diocesan newspaper and point out
   some of the ways in which the common priesthood is
   exercised by the lay faithful and the ministerial priesthood is
   exercised by the bishops, priests, and deacons.

Prayer

While gathered in the circle around the table, pray Blessing B
(RCIA #97). Proclaim again verses 1, 2, and 6 from John 14: "Do
not let your hearts be troubled. Have faith in God and have faith
in me," and "I am the way, the truth, and the life." Allow these
words of Jesus to sink in; close by leading the group in singing
the last verse from the Closing Song used at Sunday's liturgy.

Sixth Sunday of Easter

Understanding this Sunday:
Background for Catechesis

The Word in Liturgy

Acts 8:5–8, 14–17
Psalm 66:1–3, 4–5, 6–7, 16, 20
1 Peter 3:15–18
John 14:15–21

This Sunday's gospel continues the farewell discourse of Jesus. Whereas last Sunday's passage centered on believing in Jesus, this week's gospel centers on loving him. Those who love Jesus keep his commandments. In other words, covenant fidelity is an outpouring of love. To those who love him, Jesus also promises his abiding presence by means of "another paraclete" whom he will send. The term "paraclete," unique in the New Testament to the writings of the evangelist John, has both the juridical meaning of "advocate," and a more general meaning of teacher or guide. Christian tradition has identified this paraclete as the Holy Spirit. Jesus himself has been the first paraclete to his followers during his time on earth; the paraclete whom Jesus will send ("another paraclete") will continue to be an advocate and guiding presence just as Jesus himself has been. The paraclete, moreover, will dwell in the believer. In typical Johannine fashion, the passage warns of a contrast to be expected between "the world" of hard-hearted unbelief, which will not see and recognize the paraclete, and the minds and hearts of faithful followers, who will know and accept this one whom Jesus sends.

The second reading concerns the persecution. The Christian communities of Asia Minor to which the first letter of Peter is written are living in tension with the world around them. The sufferings alluded to in the letter may be the result of an official, governmental persecution, because of which Christians must defend themselves in court. Or they may simply be the mockery and bullying of hostile neighbors. In any event, the author of 1 Peter advises those who are suffering to conduct themselves with gentleness and humility, and not to descend to the level of viciousness that their

accusers adopt. The passage begins with an invitation to spiritual wholeness: to revere the Lord in one's heart—an attitude consistent with the baptismal tone of the whole letter. This expression is reminiscent of the Lord's Prayer: "Hallowed be thy name." The passage concludes with a theological reflection which relates the persecution of Christians to the Passion of Christ. Jesus is not merely an example of guiltless suffering for the faithful to emulate. More importantly, his unique, expiatory suffering effects our redemption and so brings us to God. Sufferings because of persecution find their place within this greater mystery of redemption.

The passage from the Acts of the Apostles is edited to omit the story of Simon the Magician, who is converted by Philip's preaching but then tries to buy with silver Philip's wonder-working power! The narrative that remains, once this colorful story has been excised, is a simple, straightforward account of the spread of the gospel into Samaria. Presented in Acts as the result of the expulsion from the synagogues in Jerusalem, the expansion of the mission into new territory shows God working in unexpected ways to make known the Good News to an ever-widening circle of believers. The sending of Peter and John to lay hands on those whom Philip baptized links the Jerusalem community with the new Christians in Samaria. The relationship between baptism, hand-laying, and the giving of the Spirit varies throughout Luke-Acts. Sometimes the Spirit is received before a sacramental action, sometimes afterwards. The Spirit is not subject to a rigid program, but operates in free and varied ways. Nevertheless, the separation of Philip's baptism from the laying on of hands and giving of the Spirit hints at the beginning of a distinction between baptism and confirmation. Psalm 66, following this joyful reading from Acts, sings praise for divine deliverance through the Exodus, but with a universalizing thrust.

Catholic Doctrine

The Sacrament of Confirmation

The Catholic Church teaches that the Spirit promised in today's gospel as advocate, helper, and guide is associated with the followers of Jesus in a variety of ways. First, the Church as a whole is a messianic people and community of the Spirit. The Second Vatican Council asserted that Christ "has shared with us his Spirit who, being one and the same in head and members, gives life to, unifies, and moves the whole body" (LG 7). Second, in the celebration of liturgy and the sacraments, the Spirit is also at work, animating and giving life to divine worship. The Council also asserted that: "It is not only through the sacraments and the ministrations of the Church that the Holy Spirit makes holy the People, leads them and enriches them with his virtues. Allotting his gifts according as he wills . . . he also distributes special graces among the faithful of every rank" (LG 12). Last of all, the individual believer is gifted with the Spirit through the sacrament of confirmation.

Confirmation is one of the three sacraments of initiation. The sign of confirmation is the laying on of hands and the anointing with chrism. The anointing of confirmation is consecratory. Similar to the anointing received by priests, prophets, and kings, the anointing of confirmation signifies a noble status. When the newly baptized are confirmed, this consecration with sacred chrism imparts a unique, indelible spiritual mark, sealing and strengthening their baptism. What is the purpose of this consecration? It seals the newly baptized for their mission to be a witness to Christ in the world. The term "Christ" means "anointed one," and therefore believers sealed with chrism at confirmation are rightly called "Christians," those who are anointed to profess their faith in Jesus, the Christ, and witness to the Lord in their daily lives (CCC 1294).

The perfumed oil used in the sacrament of confirmation is itself consecrated by the bishop on Holy Thursday at the cathedral for use throughout the year. The richness of the sacred chrism, the perfumed oil, expresses symbolically the richness of the gifts of the Spirit poured out upon the believer in confirmation. The prayer which accompanies the laying on of hands during the celebration of the sacrament expressly mentions seven gifts of the Spirit: wisdom, understanding, right judgment, courage, knowledge, reverence, and wonder and awe (RC 25).

The text of the bishop's prayer consecrating oil to be used in confirmation (and also in dedicating churches and altars) celebrates the richness of God's grace manifested by the Spirit. He prays, "By anointing them with the Spirit, you strengthen all who have been reborn in baptism. Through that anointing you transform them into the likeness of Christ your Son and give them a share in his royal, priestly, and prophetic work. And so, Father, by the power of your love, make this mixture of oil and perfume a sign and source of your blessing. Pour out the gifts of your Holy Spirit on our brothers and sisters who will be anointed with it. Let the splendor of holiness shine on the world from every place and thing signed with this oil. Above all, Father, we pray that through this sign of your anointing you will grant increase to your Church until it reaches the eternal glory, where you, Father, will be all in all . . ." (RC 25).

Catholic Culture

Bathing in the ancient world included anointing. Even today, body oils and scents after a bath are a sign of refreshment and luxury. In confirmation, the anointing with perfumed chrism prepares the newly bathed, the baptized, to come with great dignity to the banquet table of the Eucharist and gather around that table to join with saints, apostles, and witnesses.

Prior to the Second Vatican Council and the revision of the rites of the Church, the bishop would slap confirmands in the face at confirmation. The practice may have originated historically because of a misunderstanding about the rubric for the laying on of hands. It developed a rationale, however, likening the newly confirmed to a "soldier for Christ" who needed to be toughened up for battle. Today the image of "soldier for Christ" has been replaced by the idea of "witness for Christ" and there is no slap, however gentle.

In Catholic churches, the place where the sacred chrism is kept, along with the oil of catechumens and the oil of the sick, is called the ambry. It can be a prominent shelf or pedestal near the baptismal font or a glass case in which the containers of oil are displayed and honored.

Dismissal Catechesis (30 min.)

Getting Started

1. Prepare the space ahead of time with a circle of chairs around a table, draped with a white cloth upon which is placed the chrism oils. Next to the table place a large white candle in a stand, with an arrangement of spring flowers.
2. Lead the candidates and catechumens to the circle and place the Lectionary on the table and light the candle. After all are seated, lead them in singing Psalm 66, "Let all the Earth Cry Out to God with Joy." Invite the participants to reflect in quiet upon all that God has done in their lives, for which they are joyful. After a period of quiet reflection, once again lead the singing of Psalm 66.

First Impressions

1. Invite those who are willing to share some of the ways God has worked in their lives that evoked a sense of joy.
2. Focus the discussion on the readings by asking the candidates and catechumens to name some of the causes of joy among the first followers of Jesus as proclaimed in today's Liturgy of the Word. Include the following ideas: *Philip was able to proclaim the Messiah and perform miracles among the Samaritans—The Samaritans accepted the Word of God and received the Holy Spirit— The early Church spread, in spite of, and perhaps because of, persecution and suffering—We have been given the Spirit of Truth—This Spirit remains within us and with the Church—That God loves us compels us to respond in love for God through Jesus.*
3. Explain the background for the second reading from 1 Peter 3:15–18 in these words: *The first letter of Peter was addressed to Christians living in the communities of Asia Minor during a time of tension and persecution. Some experienced official political persecution and others endured the hostility and mockery of their neighbors. The author advises that those who are suffering conduct themselves with gentleness and humility.* Gather the candidates and catechumens into small groups to discuss these questions: *What would your response be if you were persecuted or mocked because of your beliefs? What is your reaction to the writer's advice that we venerate the Lord in our heart?*

Making Connections

1. Continue the small group discussion by asking them to share ways in which they have experienced suffering on a daily basis in the normal course of trying to live out their faith. In the large group invite a few participants to share some of these daily struggles. Encourage them to bring up ordinary ways we struggle to respond as Jesus would: when criticized, tempted, asked to go out of our way, misunderstood, cheated, or when confronted with prejudice.
2. Ask the participants to brainstorm several responses to these ordinary situations which express gentleness and respect when we encounter the misunderstanding and hostility of others as we try to live out our faith. These can be recorded on newsprint, large enough for all to read. [For example, when we encounter a co-worker who laughs at our refusal to cheat our employer by using work time for personal business, we could respond with a smile and the line, "I am trying to be honest with my time because I want to be treated honestly."]

Prayer

Focus the attention of the participants upon the lighted candle, the flowers, and the holy oils and invite them to allow these symbols to enter their hearts and fill them with Easter joy. Then pray in these words:
Christ, the anointed one, bless us, your people, and strengthen us as we struggle to live our faith each day. Empower us with your love that we might live more wholly conformed to your image. Let your light and holiness shine forth from us upon the world, in order that some day all will know of your abundant love. Unite us with you and your Father through the power of your abiding Holy Spirit. May your Spirit continue to abide with your Church, granting her wisdom, truth, and fidelity. All this we ask in your name, Jesus the Christ. Amen.

Extended Catechesis

SESSION FOCUS: *The Sacrament of Confirmation*

Gathering

A. Sunday:

1. Greet and welcome the sponsors and team members as they arrive. Invite them to join the circle of catechumens and candidates.
2. Invite all to stand and sing the first few verses of the Opening Song used in today's liturgy. When the participants are seated, ask a sponsor to proclaim the first reading from Acts 8:5–8, 14–17. After a short silence, lead the group in singing the Gospel Alleluia as they stand. Ask another member of the team to proclaim the gospel, John 14:15–21, and close with the Gospel Alleluia.

B. Weekday:

1. Use the same centerpiece as described for the Dismissal Catechesis.
2. As the participants gather in the circle, greet and warmly welcome each person. Ask a few participants to share some ways that they experienced the presence of the Holy Spirit during these last few days.
3. Lead this celebration of the Word:
   - Song: Opening song from Sunday's liturgy
   - First Reading: Acts 8:5–8, 14–17
   - Sing Psalm 66
   - Gospel Alleluia
   - Gospel: John 14:15–21
   - Gospel Alleluia

The Word (30 min.)

1. Encourage several catechumens or candidates to summarize the insights from the Dismissal Catechesis regarding the response of the faithful to everyday experiences of suffering or hardship.

2. Invite everyone to offer his or her ideas about the presence of the Holy Spirit, either personally or in the community. You might ask the question, "When have you observed the presence of the Holy Spirit in your life or in the life of this parish? Record their ideas on newsprint, writing large enough for all to read.

3. Continue by sharing these insights from the first reading and the gospel:

   Jesus promised to remain with his followers through "another Paraclete," the Holy Spirit. This promise is another manifestation of the outpouring of God's love upon all people for all times. As we respond to God's love in a covenant or relationship of love freely offered, the Holy Spirit will show us the way, reveal the truth, and impart us with life. For our part, we are to love God by keeping God's commands, recognizing the Lord in all things and making God's truth known to the world. The abiding presence of the Holy Spirit is observed in the first reading from the Book of Acts, wherein the infidel Samaritans incredibly came to believe the Good News and were baptized by Philip. Later, Peter and John prayed and imposed hands upon these people, rejected by the Jews, and they received the Holy Spirit. His disciples, through the outpouring of the Holy Spirit, continue Jesus' tolerance and love for the Samaritans. It is this Holy Spirit who bridges the gap of human limitations to overcome centuries of prejudice.

4. Encourage the participants to gather in pairs, sponsors and godparents with candidates and catechumens, to share their thoughts on these questions: *What does Jesus' promise to remain with us for all time through the sending of the Holy Spirit mean in your life? How has the Spirit empowered you and helped you overcome your human limitations? What role has the Holy Spirit played in the Church, the community of God's People?*

Catholic Teaching (30 min.)

1. Focus the attention of the participants back to the large group and invite each group to share one insight on the Holy Spirit with everyone. Record their responses on newsprint, using one paper entitled "The Spirit abides in the church by _" and another page entitled "The Spirit abides in each of the faithful by _." [Add the following to their responses if they are not mentioned: unifies, gives life, motivates, inspires, guides, and leads the church; animates, transforms, and freely gives the gifts of wisdom, understanding, right judgment, courage, knowledge, reverence, and wonder to the faithful.]

2. Present a teaching on the sacrament of confirmation, making sure to include the following points from the Catholic Doctrine section found in Understanding this Sunday:

- Confirmation is one of the three sacraments of initiation, along with baptism and Eucharist. The sign of the sacrament is the laying on of hands and the anointing with chrism.
- The anointing with holy oil or chrism at confirmation is a consecration, imparting a unique, indelible spiritual seal on the confirmed, strengthening their baptism. Through confirmation the baptized are anointed and empowered to be a witness to Christ in the world.
- The Holy Spirit, at work in the faithful, pours out the gifts of wisdom, understanding, right judgment, courage, knowledge, reverence, and wonder and awe upon us in the sacrament of confirmation, making us a holy people, transformed and ready to partake of the banquet of the Eucharist. From the table the fully initiated are sent forth as apostles and witnesses to the ends of the earth.

3. Gather the participants into small groups to discuss these questions: *What outpouring of the Holy Spirit do (did) you anticipate at your own confirmation? Describe your heart reaction to the notion of being consecrated, sealed with the Spirit through the anointing with chrism.*

Putting Faith into Practice

1. Ask each person to turn to page 48 in the Participant Book and write a letter to the Holy Spirit, asking for whatever is needed to respond to Christ with love and to live in faith and holiness. When they have finished the letter, encourage them to respond to the questions posed on the same page.

2. Invite the participants to share their responses to the questions in the same small groups. The candidates and catechumens may wish to share their letter to the Holy Spirit with their sponsor and godparent.

3. Invite an adult parishioner, newly confirmed, to present a witness to the power of the Holy Spirit in their life.

Prayer

Focus the attention of the participants back to the large group by leading them in singing "Send Us Your Spirit" (David Haas, GIA Publications, 1982). Invite the sponsors and godparents to place their hands upon the shoulders of their candidate or catechumen and pray silently for the outpouring of the Holy Spirit. Then pray in these words:

Spirit of truth, be our source of strength as we journey to the sacraments of initiation. By the gift of God, the Risen Christ abides with us, your chosen people, through you, most Holy Spirit. May we be purified and made holy in your sight, overcoming our human limitations through your abiding presence. At the dawn of each new day, fill us with joy, that we may be called your consecrated, your holy ones. Guide our path that we may walk each day in the newness of your life. Inspire us to share the Good News of Jesus dying and rising for all of humankind to the ends of the earth. As we celebrate the joy of the Risen Jesus, we anticipate with hope his return in glory at the end of time. Let us live with, in, and for you, Spirit of Jesus. Amen.

Seventh Sunday of Easter

The Word in Liturgy

Acts 1:12–14
Psalm 27:1–4, 7–8
1 Peter 4:13–16
John 17:1–11

Today's reading from Acts very simply depicts the Church, after the ascension of Jesus and before the coming of the Spirit, united in a state of prayerful expectancy. The eleven, so important to Luke's narrative, are named, as is Mary the mother of Jesus. As this is the first time Mary is referred to by name in Luke since the infancy narratives, the mention of her brings to mind a parallel between the Spirit's overshadowing of Mary at the conception of Jesus, and the Spirit overshadowing her and the other disciples at the birth of the Church. Other women and Jesus' "brothers" (an expression, common in that culture, which indicates all male relatives) are also present, thus illustrating that the community was neither all-male nor limited to the eleven. In saying that they are gathered together in prayer, Luke employs one of his favorite words to point toward spiritual unity: *homothumadon*. In other words, his vocabulary (nuances of which may be hard to detect in translation) suggests that not only individuals but also this gathering "together" is significant.

The psalm which follows is full of joyful confidence springing from contemplation of God's own loveliness and the beauty of God's dwelling place. In its liturgical setting it underscores both the prayer motif of the first reading and the anticipation the Church feels as Pentecost approaches.

The injunction to "rejoice" in suffering which we hear in 1 Peter is not a counsel of masochism. Rather, it is an accurate description of Christian experience. The experience of faithful suffering is a gateway to some of the most profound aspects of the mystery of our redemption (such as the radical trustworthiness of God, and the development of our own capacities for compassion and solidarity with others). Christ himself is the font of rejoicing. But the way to Christ is through the cross. The author is careful to point out that there are two kinds of suffering: one

which we bring on ourselves by doing evil and another simply because of our adherence to Christ and all that it implies. The first is to be avoided absolutely. The second is to be embraced unconditionally. It is the Spirit who enables us to do this.

The "priestly prayer" of Jesus at the Last Supper (first so-called by Cyril of Alexandria in the fifth century), of which today's gospel is a part, has a highly charged immediacy that draws the listener into the dialogue of Jesus with his heavenly Father. In this lengthy prayer, reminiscent of Moses' last words, he speaks about his coming death and glorification as a present reality, as if we have stepped into the "eternal now" of God.

Both the first part of the reading, pertaining to Christ himself, and the last, pertaining to his followers, are important because his coming glorification and the fulfillment of his mission are intertwined with the fate of his disciples. He prays in an intimate way about the disciples whom he will leave behind. They remain present to God because they belong to God, have been personally entrusted to Jesus, and have received the message Jesus came to share. In a passage which so frequently speaks of glory as an attribute of God and the works of God, it is particularly striking that Jesus says his *followers* are the ones in whom he is glorified. Drawn into full intimacy with God the Father by the Son, these treasured disciples have become part of the mystery of God's love and are thus the place where Jesus is glorified.

Our doctrinal focus today may therefore be the mystery of the Church—gift of the Father (John), glory of the Son (John), and work of the Holy Spirit (1 Peter). It is the Church, gathered *together* in prayerful anticipation of the Spirit's ever-new advent (Acts), which shows forth the gift of unity that is both the sign and the instrument of the coming kingdom.

Catholic Doctrine

Christian Unity

The Nicene Creed, formulated by the Council of Constantinople (381 A.D.), proclaims our Catholic belief that the marks or characteristics of the Church are fourfold: unity, holiness, catholicity, and apostolicity—all of which are a gift from on high through Christ (CCC 811). In today's gospel, Jesus prays to the Father, and in his prayer entrusts to the disciples everything that had been entrusted to the Son. Because the last verses of the gospel passage emphasize the relationship between the Father and the Son, and between believers and the Son, this essay will focus on the first characteristic of the Church, unity.

The Church is characterized by unity because the source of the Church is One: the Father, Son, and Holy Spirit are intimately united, three persons in one God. This characteristic of the Church, unity, is a gift given by the Holy Spirit and is of the very essence of the people of God who are bound together as one in Christ (CCC 813). St. Clement of Alexandria (d. 215 A.D.), wrote, "What an astonishing mystery! There is one Father of the universe, one Logos of the universe, and also one Holy Spirit, everywhere one and the same; there is also one virgin become mother, and I should like to call her 'Church.'" (*Paedagogus* 1, 6, 42: PG 8, 281).

As Catholic teaching holds, the significance of the characteristic of Church unity is that to be fully what the Church is meant to be, believers must maintain harmony and union among themselves. Every divisive instinct or practice must be minimized, such as prejudice and factionalism. In other words, overcoming those divisions within the body of the Church is an essential task because an essential mark or characteristic of the Church is unity (ModCathE 544). The Second Vatican Council extolled and challenged the Church, saying, "Hence that messianic people, although it does not actually include all . . . and at times may appear as a small flock, is, however, a most sure seed of unity, hope and salvation for the whole human race" (LG 9). Thus, the Church, which is described as "the seed" sown among the peoples of the world, cannot fulfill this mission for unity unless the very body of believers within the Church is visibly striving for union among its own members.

Unity or communion within the Church is a result of the redemption achieved by Christ which restores our relationship with God and with one another (CCC 766). This gift of unity, as Jesus indicates in the gospel, is entrusted to us. Yet, historically, Christians have experienced division into different denominations, churches, and communions. These separations are caused by sin, although those today who are raised in and baptized into separated churches are not responsible for this sin. They are brought up believing in Jesus and baptized into Christ—and the Catholic Church accepts them as separated brothers and sisters in the Lord who are gifted with the name

"Christian" (CCC 818). These divisions, however, create scandal and diminish Christian witness in the world. The Second Vatican Council noted that there is ample historical record which indicates that the responsibility for these divisions must be shared (UR 3).

Regardless of the historical record, the Church is called as a whole body and as individuals to heal divisions and work for unity. First, we must live faithfully within our own Catholic communion and to put our own house in order, striving for a deepening of our own conversion and living out the gospel message (UR 6). Second, we must develop proper attitudes, striving in our lives and in our public and private prayer for a change of heart and strength to assist in the ecumenical movement (UR 8). Third, we must work to understand the outlook of our separated brothers and sisters, as the Council says, to treat each other "on an equal footing" (UR 9). Fourth, an organized dialogue is encouraged between us and our separated brothers and sisters "comparing doctrines with one another," and searching for the truth, with love and humility (UR 11). Finally, prayer for Christian unity should consume us all as we cooperate and collaborate where we can for the coming of the kingdom of God (UR 8).

Catholic Culture

In 1935, Abbe Paul Couturier, a Catholic priest in France, advocated a "Universal Week of Prayer for Christian Unity" which had been begun by the Society of the Atonement earlier in this century.

In 1984, a report was published of the various bilateral talks that had, up to that point, taken place between the Catholic Church and various Protestant denominations. This 514-page report shows many areas of agreement as well as some continuing differences between the Catholic Church and the Anglicans, the Baptist-Reformed, the Lutherans, and the Disciples of Christ (*Growth in Agreement*, Harding Meyer & Lukas Vischer, eds., Paulist Press, New York, and World Council of Churches, Geneva, 1984).

The Second Vatican Council was the watershed moment in the history of the Catholic Church which represents a turning point in ecumenical relations. As a result of the Council and the actions of both Paul VI and John Paul II, dialogue has continued between the Catholic Church and Protestant denominations and the Orthodox churches. After the Council, a department of the Curia was set up to assist in these dialogues, and was named the Pontifical Council for Promoting Christian Unity (begun in 1960 to assist the Council and organized as a pontifical council in 1988). In 1993, John Paul II issued an updated "Directory for the Application of the Principles and Norms of Ecumenism" (ECathHist 282–83) to further assist the Church in its continuing efforts to promote unity.

Dismissal Catechesis (30 min.)

Getting Started

1. Prepare the space ahead of time with a circle of chairs around a table that has been draped with a white cloth upon which are arranged some spring flowers. Near the table place a large white candle in a stand.

2. Lead the candidates and catechumens to the circle and place the Lectionary on the table and light the candle. Invite the group to sing the response to Psalm 27: "I believe that I shall see the good things of the Lord in the land of the living." Pray in these or similar words: *All loving God, you have given us the greatest gift, your Son, Jesus, who showed us how to live as your adopted sons and daughters. Be with us in a special way this day, as we reflect on these readings and their meaning for our lives. Send your Spirit to be our guide. We ask this in the name of Jesus Christ, who lives and reigns with you, one God, forever and ever. Amen.*

First Impressions

1. Lead the participants in taking a few deep breaths before asking them to sit quietly as you name some images from today's Liturgy of the Word. Encourage them to notice their feelings as you prayerfully name the following images: *The apostles went to the upstairs room—They devoted themselves to constant prayer—There were some women in their company and Mary—Rejoice insofar as you share Christ's sufferings—Happy are you when you suffer for the sake of Christ—Father, the hour has come—Give glory to your Son—Eternal life is this: to know you—I have given you glory by finishing the work you gave me to do—I have made your name known—For these I pray—It is in them that I have been glorified.*

2. After a time of silence, encourage the catechumens and candidates to form small groups to share their feelings and experience of the liturgy. These questions may be helpful: *What were some of the emotions you experienced as you listened to these images from the scriptures? What is your general impression of today's Liturgy of the Word? What did you find difficult to accept? What was a source of hope and comfort for you?*

3. Focus everyone's attention back to the large group and invite them again to become quiet as you prayerfully repeat these same images. Then in the large group ask each small group to share what they heard as the overarching message of the Liturgy of the Word. Briefly summarize their comments.

Making Connections

1. Proclaim the second reading, 1 Peter 4:13–16. In the large group invite the participants to share their understanding of the divisions caused by religious beliefs using these questions: *What divisions have you experienced among Christians? Among people of different faiths?* After the group names specific incidents caused by religious differences, gather them back to their small groups to discuss these questions: *What attitude does this second reading from the first letter of Peter call forth from Christians? What actions are condemned in*

this passage? How can we take on the posture of the early Christians who were persecuted for their beliefs?

2. In the large group, invite responses to the question regarding the posture of the early Christians. Summarize their responses.

3. You may use this time to tell the story of Archbishop Oscar Romero, Saint Maximilian Kolbe, or Blessed Edith Stein, all of whom suffered and died for their beliefs.

Prayer

Invite each person to name a place where religious persecution is occurring right now. Then pray: *God of glory, look upon your people and show us the way to respect the differences and diversity among people. In Jesus' suffering and death we were made one with you and one another. Let us take on the attitude of your early followers, that of waiting with hope for the Lord Jesus to return. For then we will partake of your glory as one family, united in your powerful Spirit. We ask you to forgive our intolerance and our prejudices in the name of Jesus who rose from the dead that we may have life. Amen.*

Extended Catechesis

SESSION FOCUS: *Christian Unity*

Gathering

A. Sunday:

1. Welcome the sponsors, team members, and other participants as they arrive. Invite them to join the circle of catechumens and candidates.

2. Lead the participants in singing the first few verses of the Gathering Song used at today's liturgy. Invite a sponsor or godparent to proclaim the first reading, Acts 1:12–14. After a short silence intone the response to Psalm 27: "I believe that I shall see the good things of the Lord in the land of the living." Indicate that all stand to hear the gospel, John 17:1–11, proclaimed by a team member.

B. Weekday:

1. Use the same centerpiece as in the Dismissal Catechesis.

2. Warmly welcome the participants as they gather in the circle. Invite a few participants to share their experience of hopeful anticipation over the past few days.

3. Lead this celebration of the Word:
   • Song: Gathering Song from Sunday's liturgy
   • First Reading: Acts 1:12–14
   • Sing Psalm 27
   • Silent Reflection
   • Gospel Alleluia
   • Gospel: John 17:1–11
   • Gospel Alleluia

The Word (30 min.)

1. Encourage a candidate or catechumen to share a few insights from the Dismissal Catechesis.

2. Begin to open up the meaning of the first reading from the Book of Acts with these or similar words: *Today's reading*

from Acts refers to the interlude between the ascension of Jesus and before the coming of the Spirit at Pentecost. The apostles and those gathered with them, including Mary and the women, gather in an upper room to wait, to pray, and to hope. This posture of prayerful expectancy is a model for all believers. The eleven, so important to Luke's gospel, are named, as is Mary the mother of Jesus. This is an indication of the parallel between the Spirit's overshadowing of Mary at the conception of Jesus, and the Spirit overshadowing her and the other disciples at the birth of the Church. In saying they are gathered in prayer, Luke employs one of his favorite words to point not just to a physical assembly, but a true, spiritual unity: homothumadon. His vocabulary suggests that there is great significance in the coming together of Jesus' followers, not only as individuals but also as one body.

3. Gather the participants into pairs to share their insights to these questions. Encourage the candidates and catechumens to join their sponsor and/or godparents for this sharing: *What experiences of gathering together with family and friends during times of confusion or anticipation have you had? Why was it important to be together? What was the result of your coming together?*

4. Invite everyone to turn to page 50 in the Participant Book to reflect on the gospel, John 17:1–11, and respond to the questions. Then invite them to share their thoughts in the same pairs.

5. Focus the attention of the participants back to the large group and ask a few pairs to share their responses.

Catholic Teaching (30 min.)

1. Continue by introducing the Catholic teaching on Christian unity in these or similar words: *Our focus today is the mystery of the Church—gift of the Father, glory of the Son, and work of the Holy Spirit. The Church, gathered together in prayerful anticipation of the Spirit's ever-new coming, shows forth the gift of unity. This unity is both the sign and the instrument of the coming kingdom. The Nicene Creed proclaims our Catholic belief in the fourfold characteristics of the Church: unity, holiness, catholicity, and apostolicity. In the gospel, Jesus prays to the Father and entrusts to the disciples that which had been entrusted to the Son. This handing on continues in the life of the Church.*

2. Encourage the participants to compile a list of the visible ways in which the Church is a sign of unity. Use newsprint, writing large enough for all to read. Add the following to the list if they are not mentioned: the sacraments, Lectionary, celebration of the Eucharist, works of charity and justice, centrality of governance in the Vatican, and the mission of the Church in the world. Ask the participants to compile a second list on newsprint naming ways the Church is divided. Add the following if not mentioned: prejudice against cultures or races, treatment of the divorced and separated, differences in spiritual practices among Catholics, differences among Christian denominations, and divisions caused by lifestyle choices, such as single people, homosexuals, or adolescents.

3. Allow some quiet time for people to look over the two lists before continuing with these or similar words:
The Church teaches that the mark of unity calls all members to maintain harmony and unity among themselves. Every divisive instinct or practice must be minimized. Overcoming divisions within the body of the Church is an essential task because the source of Christian unity flows from the redemption achieved by Christ. In and through Christ we were made one with God and with one another. This gift of unity is entrusted to us. Yet Christians experience division. The Second Vatican Council noted that our history as a people indicates that the responsibility for the divisions among all the Christian churches must be shared among the generations. The Church is challenged as a whole body and as individual members to heal divisions and to work for unity.

4. Allow questions regarding Christian unity to arise from the group. You may choose to invite a priest or pastoral minister to be present to respond to these questions.

Putting Faith into Practice

1. In the large group, point out the five ways in which we can work for unity, as named in the Catholic Doctrine section of Understanding this Sunday.
   - Live out the faith and deepen our conversion journey as we try to conform our lives to Christ, thus modeling Jesus' attitude of acceptance, openness, and unity.
   - Develop an attitude of unity rather than competition with other Christian traditions.
   - Treat our separated brothers and sisters with understanding, that is, "on equal footing."
   - Encourage dialogue among the Christian churches as we search for the truth with love and humility.
   - Pray for Christian unity.

2. Gather the group into pairs to share these questions: *What divisions among God's People have I experienced? How can I work toward greater unity in my everyday life? How can this parish promote Christian unity?* Invite the pairs to share a few responses in the large group. Ask everyone to reflect on one thing that they could do this week to promote unity within the Catholic faith community and among the Christian churches. Encourage them to write their resolution in the Participant Book on page 51, under the heading "I want to put my faith into action by." Continue the sharing by asking them to offer ideas that the parish might adopt to promote Christian unity. These can be written and given to the pastoral council and/or the parish staff.

Prayer

Invite everyone to gather around the table. After a few moments of silence, ask everyone to pray as you proclaim the gospel, John 17:1–11. Conclude with this prayer: *God of us all, you made us to be one with you and with each other. In the act of creation you graced us with a basic unity. In our humanness we created conflict, competition, and comparisons which led to division and separation. As your Son Jesus prayed that we may be united as one family, his death and resurrection restored us to that original union. Strengthen and empower us by your Holy Spirit to live in this redemption of loving relationship with you and all people. Grant us the courage and love to overcome all that separates us from our brothers and sisters. We ask this in Jesus' name. Amen.*

Pentecost

Understanding this Sunday:
Background for Catechesis

The Word in Liturgy

Acts 2:1–11
Psalm 104:1, 24, 29–30, 31, 34
1 Corinthians 12:3–7, 12–13
John 20:19–23

Today's feast of Pentecost celebrates the sending of the Spirit upon the Church. It is the last Sunday of Easter, and brings the season to a close. The liturgical year honors the chronology of Luke by placing our celebration of the Spirit's descent fifty days after the Resurrection. The Christian Pentecost in Luke coincides with the Jewish Feast of Weeks, fifty days after Passover, which was a time of prayer for a good harvest, and later became a commemoration of the giving of the Law. Against this background, Luke's presentation of the Pentecost event calls our attention both to the way in which the descent of the Spirit resembles the *theophany* at Mount Sinai (fire, sound, and word), and to the effects of Pentecost as the "harvest" of the paschal mystery.

The liturgy does not bind itself to Luke's chronological unfolding of the events of Easter in every respect, however. All the readings from Acts that have been proclaimed in previous Sundays of the Easter season are about events that took place *after* Pentecost. In other words, the effects of Pentecost have been the subject of our reflection and our celebration *throughout* the fifty days of Easter. In today's gospel passage from John, read every year on Pentecost, Jesus gives the Spirit on the evening of Easter day itself. Thus, in a certain sense, the liturgy draws the whole fifty days of Easter into one.

The first reading tells in very few words the story of the Spirit's descent and how it was manifested: a loud sound (like wind), tongues (like fire) coming to rest on each disciple, and bold proclamation of the Good News thereafter by the disciples. *Glossolalia*, a form of ecstatic speech-like babbling known in the ancient world and attested to in the New Testament, here

is presented as intelligible speech, understood by listeners from around the world as communication in their own languages. By naming the geographic origins of all the diaspora Jews living in Jerusalem at the time of Pentecost, Luke paints a vivid symbolic picture of the worldwide proclamation of God's great works.

The psalm reminds us of the role of the Spirit in creation, and the dependence of all earthly things on the Spirit of God for life and sustenance. The second reading develops the theme of the Spirit's diverse but united gifts. First making the point that the Holy Spirit mediates the believer's confession of faith in the exalted Lord, Paul goes on to explain that the multiplicity of gifts in the Church is united by their source—the Spirit—and that indeed the body of people that is the Church is also diverse and yet one because of baptism and the Spirit.

The gospel passage, introduced by the description of the disciples gathered in fear behind locked doors, draws our attention to the reversal of their fear to joy and their transformation from frightened followers to apostolic witnesses ("apostle" means "one sent"). At the heart of this change is the presence of the Risen Lord, the command to go forth, and the giving of the Spirit. In a gesture that recalls God's act of creation, Jesus gives the Spirit by the action of breathing on the disciples. His imparting of the Spirit is from his own wounded and risen body. The giving of the Spirit is thus a new act of creation, by the crucified and glorified Christ. Last of all, as in Luke's gospel, reconciliation is central to the mission entrusted to them and enabled by the Spirit.

Catholic Doctrine

The Holy Spirit

The Holy Spirit in Catholic doctrine is the third person of the Trinity. Both Hebrew and Christian scriptures bear witness to the presence and activity of the Holy Spirit by many names, such as "Spirit of God," "Breath of God," "Paraclete," and "Advocate." As the Church developed its understanding of the Trinity, it clarified the existence of the divine third person, called the Holy Spirit, who proceeds from the Father and the Son. This teaching is proclaimed every Sunday by Catholics who gather to celebrate the Eucharist: "We believe in the Holy Spirit, the Lord and Giver of Life, who proceeds from the Father and the Son. With the Father and the Son he is worshiped and glorified. He has spoken through the prophets" (*Sacramentary*, Profession of Faith). Thus, the Sunday liturgy is where this teaching of the Church is reaffirmed for every Catholic and is a reminder of the initial liturgical context where faith is professed—at infant baptisms or during the Easter Vigil as adults renounce Satan and the power of evil and confess their commitment to God the Father, Son, and Holy Spirit.

The Holy Spirit mediates the continuing presence of Jesus in the Church and in the world. To be in contact with Christ means that the believer must first be moved or under the influence of the Spirit (CCC 683). Thus, the Holy Spirit kindles faith in the hearts of those who are moved to confess their belief in Jesus. As St. Irenaeus wrote: "And it is impossible to see God's Son without the Spirit, and no one can approach the Father without the Son, for the knowledge of the Father is the Son, and the knowledge of God's Son is obtained through the Holy Spirit" (*Demonstratio apostolica* 7: SCh 62, 41–2).

The work of the Spirit can be characterized in two ways: as sustainer and as surprise. In the first instance, the Holy Spirit can be understood as the sustaining presence of God in our individual lives and in the life of the Church. The Spirit thus gives the gifts of healing, unity, and love (Paul's letters). The Spirit is the architect of the Church and a guide to those who pray (Luke-Acts). The Spirit is also the teacher and advocate (John's gospel). The Spirit is the animating breath of liturgy and sacramental life. And yet, in the second instance, the Holy Spirit can also be understood as a source of discontinuity and surprise. Scripture refers to tongues of fire and the driving wind of Pentecost which shook the apostles and changed them. Jesus cast out demons by means of the power of the Spirit (Mark's gospel). New and sometimes very radical movements throughout the history of the Church have claimed a basis in the Holy Spirit. The Second Vatican Council even asserted that the work of the Spirit takes place outside the bounds of the Church. The Council fathers observed, "For since Christ died for all, and since all . . . are in fact called to one and the same destiny, which is divine, we must hold that the Holy Spirit offers to all the possibility of being made partners, in a way known to God, in the paschal mystery" (GS 22).

Thus, in the life of the believer, the Holy Spirit is all these things: sustainer and giver of manifold gifts, architect of the church, animator of liturgy and heart of sacrament, and yet the Holy Spirit is also the source which pushes believers out of complacency, empowers us to move beyond where we are at the present, surprising us with the amazing grace of God's challenge.

Catholic Culture

See the Sixth Sunday of Easter for a listing of the seven gifts of the Holy Spirit. In addition, St. Paul (Galatians 5:25) mentions "fruits" of the Holy Spirit: love, joy, peace, patience, self-control, kindness, goodness, faithfulness, and gentleness.

Twelfth-century abbess, Hildegard of Bingen, is much studied today for her poetry, music, preaching, and compilations of scientific lore. She is considered by many to be a mystic, and is the earliest known female composer in Europe. She wrote the following "Antiphon for the Holy Spirit":

> The spirit of God
> is a life that bestows life,
> root of the world tree
> and wind in its boughs.
> Scrubbing out sins,
> she rubs oil into wounds.
>
> She is glistening life,
> alluring all praise,
> all-awakening,
> all-resurrecting.

(From *Symphonia,* translated and edited by Barbara Newman, Ithaca: Cornell University Press, 1988, p. 141.)

Dismissal Catechesis (30 min.)

Getting Started

1. Prepare the space ahead of time with a circle of chairs around a table draped with a red cloth. Next to the table place a large white candle on a stand, along with an arrangement of spring flowers.

2. Lead the candidates and catechumens to the circle and place the Lectionary on the table and light the candle. As they prepare to pray state the following: *The Church uses the color red on the feast of Pentecost as a sign of the Holy Spirit. This feast of Pentecost concludes the Easter season. The Hebrew word for "spirit" is* ruah, *meaning "breath."* Then invite everyone to breathe in and out several times, conscious of their breath and imagining the Spirit filling their very being as they breathe. Ask them to become aware of their own longing for the Spirit to come more fully into their lives. After a time, lead them in singing the chant "Veni Sancte Spiritus," which means "Come Holy Spirit" (Taize, 1979), several times.

First Impressions

1. In the large group, help the candidates and catechumens reflect upon their experience of the Liturgy of the Word with these or similar questions: *What did you notice as you entered the church today? What feelings did the music, the environment, and the scriptures evoke in you? From your experience, what significance did today's celebration of this great feast mean for you?*

2. Remaining in the large group, invite all to offer their ideas about the Holy Spirit. Keep in mind that the participants will bring different understandings and experiences of the Holy Spirit. These or similar words may be of help in starting the discussion: *Today's feast of Pentecost celebrates the outpouring of the Holy Spirit on Jesus' first followers and, indeed, on the whole Church throughout the ages. What words, phrases, or images do you associate with the Holy Spirit? From the scriptures heard today, what characteristics of the Holy Spirit come to your attention?*

3. Invite them to write these initial images, words, and characteristics of the Holy Spirit on pieces of red paper cut out in the shape of flames. These can be posted around the room.

Making Connections

1. Present this background on the significance of Pentecost: *The first Pentecost coincided with the Jewish Feast of Weeks, fifty days after Passover. Pentecost brings the Easter season to fulfillment and celebrates the outpouring of the Spirit on the apostles, Mary, and the women and men who followed Jesus. The word "apostle" means "one who is sent." Pentecost is a time of mission, of being sent, of spreading the Good News of Jesus' resurrection and redemption to others through the action of the Spirit. In the first reading from the Acts of the Apostles, the symbols of the "noise like a driving wind" and the "tongues, as of fire" resting on each person present, reveal that the Holy Spirit is experienced, but is mysterious and unpredictable.*

2. Gather the participants into small groups to share their thoughts on this question: *What influence did the outpouring of the Holy Spirit have on the first followers of Jesus? Describe a time when you witnessed the presence of the Holy Spirit in your life, or in the life of another.* Invite each group to share their insights on the Holy Spirit in the large group. Summarize their ideas in a few sentences.

Prayer

Invite all to quietly reflect upon one way in which they desire to experience the outpouring of the Holy Spirit. After a few moments, ask each person to name aloud the outpouring of the Spirit they desire. Then create a spontaneous prayer that includes all of the desires for the Spirit mentioned, using this formula: *Loving God, send your Holy Spirit upon us. Gift each one of us with the particular manifestation of the Spirit we need at this time in our lives. Fill our yearning for the Holy Spirit by granting us these graces . . . (summarize the desires named by the participants). Make us ever aware of your Spirit at work in us, so that we may go forth and be apostles of your Good News to others. We ask this trusting in the power of your Spirit. Amen.*

Extended Catechesis

SESSION FOCUS: *The Holy Spirit*

Gathering

A. Sunday:

1. Welcome the sponsors, team members, and additional participants as they arrive. Invite them to join the circle of candidates and catechumens.

2. Begin the prayer by asking all to stand and sing the first two verses of "Send Us Your Spirit" (David Haas, GIA Publications, 1984). Then pray: *God, send your Holy Spirit into our lives with the power of a mighty wind. Enflame our hearts with your love. Enlarge the vision of our minds. Loosen our voices to proclaim your praise. We pray to you, giver of every gift, now and forever. Amen.*

3. Invite a team member to proclaim the gospel, John 20:19–23, while the group remains standing. Close by leading all in singing the Gospel Alleluia.

B. Weekday:

1. Use the same centerpiece as in the Dismissal Catechesis.

2. As the participants gather in the circle, welcome each person warmly. Light the candle and be sure the Lectionary is in place. Ask a few participants to share their experience of presence of the Holy Spirit over the last few days.

3. Lead this celebration of the Word:
- Song: "Send Us Your Spirit," verses 1 and 2 (David Haas, GIA, 1984)
- First Reading: Acts 2:1—11
- Sing Psalm 104 or the refrain of "Send Us Your Spirit"
- Second Reading: 1 Corinthians 12:3—7, 12—13
- Sing: Alleluia
- Gospel: John 20:19—23
- Silence
- Closing Prayer: Pray the prayer in section A.

The Word (30 min.)

1. Ask a catechumen or candidate to give a brief summary of the Dismissal Catechesis, using the display of flames to aid them in recalling the discussion. Invite the participants to express one emotion they experienced as they heard the scriptures proclaimed and prayed in word and song. Add these feelings to the flames posted around the room.

2. Present this background for Pentecost and the gospel in these or similar words: *Today, the scriptures present us with two different accounts of the sending of the Holy Spirit upon the early Church. The story of the Pentecost event, occurring fifty days after the resurrection, is presented in the reading from Acts, written by the evangelist Luke. Here, Luke's account calls to mind the covenant scene on Mount Sinai in which fire, sound, and word are signs of God's presence. Today's gospel presents the sending of the Spirit on the evening of the day of the resurrection. The fearful disciples hid behind closed doors. Jesus breathed on them, thus imparting the Spirit. Their fear was transformed into joy as these frightened followers became apostolic witnesses. As part of the imparting of the Spirit through his own breath, Jesus entrusted the mission of reconciliation to the Church.*

3. Gather the participants into groups, asking them to discuss the following questions: *How does the image of breath and wind help you in understanding and sensing the presence of the Holy Spirit? When have you experienced the power of the Spirit in forgiving someone who has hurt you? What signs of the Spirit's presence have you perceived in this Church community?* In the large group invite some responses from the small groups. Then direct each group to write several signs of power of the Holy Spirit at work in the Church and the world on additional red papers cut into the shape of a flame. Add these to the collection around the room.

Catholic Teaching (30 min.)

1. Pause and invite the participants to look around the room and reflect upon the various manifestations of the Spirit named in the tongues of fire hung around the room. You may play a recording of "Spirit, Come" (Gregory Norbert, OCP Publications, 1988) as they walk around the room prayerfully reading the posted flames.

2. Present the Church's teaching on the Holy Spirit, making sure to include these points:
- The Holy Spirit, the third person of the Trinity, worshiped and glorified, has acted since the time of creation, filling

Adam with the breath of life, hovering over the waters of chaos, and speaking through the prophets.
- The activity of the Spirit is revealed in the many names for the Spirit, "Spirit of God," "Breath of God," "Paraclete," and "Advocate."
- The Holy Spirit mediates the presence of Jesus in the Church and in the world. It is through the Holy Spirit that the hearts of believers are moved.
- The work of the Spirit is sustaining. The Spirit is the sustaining presence of God in the life of the believer and the Church. Through the Spirit we receive the grace of healing, unity, and love. The Spirit prays in us, teaching us how to pray and interceding for us. The Spirit is the animating breath of liturgy.
- The work of the Spirit moves us beyond self-imposed limits, and thus is a source of unpredictable surprise. The gifts of the Spirit are given for the common good, moving us to reach out to others.
- Galatians 5:25 names the "fruits" by which the presence of the Spirit is evident: love, joy, peace, patience, self-control, kindness, goodness, faithfulness, and gentleness. The "gifts" of the Spirit named in scripture and honored in the tradition are: wisdom, understanding, counsel, fortitude, knowledge, piety, and fear (awe) of the Lord.

3. Invite the participants to turn to the Reflection section in the Participant Book on page 52 and point out the list of fruits and gifts.

Putting Faith into Practice

1. Ask each person to reflect upon possible manifestations of the Spirit in his or her own life and to respond to the questions presented on the same page. Encourage the small groups to share their insights from this exercise. Then encourage each group to share their responses with everyone.

2. Invite the participants to reflect on these questions: *How does the Holy Spirit challenge you to change your life at this time? In what ways is the Holy Spirit surprising you with unexpected circumstances and unpredictable gifts?* After several minutes of silence, ask participants to share their responses in their same small group.

3. Encourage everyone to write down one way in which they will respond to the transforming, surprising ways of the Spirit during the next week. This can be noted in the Participant Book on page 53, in the section called "I want to put my faith into action by."

Prayer

Ask each small group to pray together, saying: *I invite you to pray together in your small groups that God's Spirit will gift you with all you need to live this summons of the Spirit that you have just named. You may choose to pray in your own words or in the silence of your heart. As you pray use some gesture to express the unity of your small group. You might hold hands, or place your right hand on the shoulder of the person to your right. When your group finishes the prayer, remain silent and continue praying until all groups are finished.* As the groups are finished, pray together the poetic Sequence from the Pentecost liturgy found on page 52 of the Participant Book.

ORDINARY TIME

Second Sunday in Ordinary Time

Understanding this Sunday:
Background for Catechesis

The Word in Liturgy

Isaiah 49:3, 5–6
Psalm 40:2, 4, 7–8, 8–9, 10
1 Corinthians 1:1–3
John 1:29–34

The second Sunday in Ordinary Time functions in the liturgical cycle as a kind of bridge, linking what has gone before with what is to come. Last Sunday's celebration of the Baptism of the Lord marked the close of the Christmas season, and began the first week in Ordinary Time. On this Sunday, in each year of the lectionary cycle, the gospel is taken from John. These Johannine readings always connect in some way with the mystery of the incarnation which has been to the fore throughout the Christmas season. On the following Sunday (Ordinary Time 3), the Lectionary allows the respective synoptic gospels to begin to tell the story of Jesus' ministry from the unique perspective of each of the evangelists. Introducing catechumens and candidates to this logic of the Lectionary at the beginning of Ordinary Time can help to orient them and deepen their understanding of how the Church "unfolds the whole mystery of Christ" (*Constitution on the Sacred Liturgy* 102).

The focus of today's readings is intensely christological. From the very beginning of Ordinary Time, our attention is directed to Jesus whom we hope to come to know ever more deeply as the Christ. During Israel's period of exile in Babylon, the author of this section of Isaiah included among his prophetic oracles a series of poems about an unnamed Servant who, by his sufferings, would bring deliverance to Israel and to all the nations. Contemporary scholars are not in agreement whether the author had in mind a single individual, or if the Servant may be a collective figure representing Yahweh's chosen people. Regardless of its specific original referent, the text remains a powerful statement of hope in the face of adversity and a confident announcement of the pivotal role to be played by the One who will be a "light to the nations." The text's christological significance is heightened by critical evidence in the gospels that the

historical Jesus did indeed identify himself and his mission with the Servant mentioned in this series of poems.

The refrain to today's responsorial psalm ("Here I am Lord, I come to do your will") supports an interpretation of the Isaiah text as a prophetic call narrative. The Christian community puts on its own lips words of acceptance, words which would have characterized both Jesus and the mysterious Servant. The sentiment expressed in the actual verses chosen for today is a prayer of thanksgiving for God's deliverance and acceptance of God's call.

The beginning of Paul's first letter to the Corinthians starts a semi-continuous series of readings that will be of seven weeks' duration. The carefully chosen words that are used in Paul's formal opening to this letter are dense with significance: "called . . . an apostle . . . Christ Jesus . . . consecrated . . . a holy people . . . grace and peace . . . God our Father . . . the Lord Jesus Christ." Paul's words allude not only to his own status as an authoritative witness; he also points to the dignity of his audience, a status they enjoy due to the grace they have received in Christ Jesus.

Such care in choosing the words one uses to refer to important personages was typical of ancient authors. John's gospel today heaps one clue upon another as to the deep truth of Jesus' identity. The evangelist presents Jesus to us as: "The Lamb of God who takes away the sin of the world . . . he was before me . . . [the Spirit] came to rest on him . . . God's Chosen One." Each of these descriptive phrases resonates with the rich imagery of the Jewish scriptures and invites further reflection from our Christian perspective. The symbol of the lamb, for example, surely evoked the paschal lamb whose blood saved the Israelites from the destroying angel, as well as the lamb (who bears the sins of others) that is mentioned in the fourth Servant Song of Isaiah.

Members of the Qumran community, known to the Baptist and his followers, spoke of a warrior lamb who protected the flock by dispersing its enemies. The book of Revelation uses the title "Lamb of God" twenty-nine times. From the abundance of images in today's lessons, we can readily construct a Christology of great breadth and depth.

Catholic Doctrine

Names of Jesus

In confessing Jesus as the Savior, the New Testament writers not only used contemporary cultural images to describe his unique significance, they also reached back into the rich heritage of Hebrew scripture and used Old Testament titles and designations to illuminate the identity of Jesus. The Christian community, for whom the New Testament authors wrote, continued to explore the profound mystery of Jesus in the immediate post-biblical times, especially in the christological discussions held at the councils of Nicea (325), Constantinople (381), and Chalcedon (451). Christology is the term used by the Church to delineate attempts to plumb the mystery of Jesus' identity, a task that continues today, although modern teachings regarding the nature of Christ still rest upon these early councils.

In today's gospel text, John the Baptist, pointing out Jesus, refers to him as "Lamb of God" and "God's Chosen One." These scriptural titles, and other adopted titles of Jesus from the Old Testament (such as those in today's first reading—"servant," and "light to the nations") express belief in Jesus' unique identity. The fourth gospel also employs other descriptions for Jesus: "eternal Word" (*logos*), "light of the world," "the way, truth, and life," "bread of life," "living water," "good shepherd," "sheep gate," and "vine." But among all the titles bestowed on Jesus in the New Testament, four stand out: "Lord," "Christ," "Son of God," and "Son of Man." In this brief survey, we will focus on these four titles.

The term "lord" or *kyrios* is employed as an honorific title (in the sense of "sir") by a variety of persons. The Samaritan woman at the well addresses Jesus as such (John 4:11). However, in the context of the epistles and in Revelation, the term "Lord" takes on a deeper meaning, connoting the second coming of the one who is now exalted by God and will usher in the end times (1 Corinthians 16:22, 1 Thessalonians 4:17, and Revelation 22:20).

The term "Christ" or Messiah, which literally means "anointed," referred to a consecrated person, usually in Old Testament times a king called by God to rule. But it could also refer to a priest called to serve God in a special way, or, in rarer instances, a prophet divinely called for a special mission. In the New Testament episodes found at Mark 8:29 and Luke 9:20, the use of this title by Peter is a confession of faith in Jesus as the

one who saves. The title, as applied to Jesus, describes his status as the promised one of God, the Savior, whose messianic mission is uniquely that of priest, prophet, and king (CCC 436).

In the New Testament accounts of the baptism and transfiguration, Jesus is described as "my beloved Son" by a divine voice (Matthew 3:17 and 17:5). Additionally, the title "Son of God" is spoken by the soldier at the foot of the cross immediately upon the death of Jesus (Matthew 27:54 and Mark 15:39). The Catholic Church thus teaches that this title indicates the unique relationship of Jesus who is God's only Son and who shares in the divine nature (CCC 444).

The description "Son of Man" is used in a variety of places in the New Testament. This phrase originates with Daniel 7:13–14 where arrogant earthly kingdoms will be judged by "one like the son of man." This agent of God will receive dominion, glory, and everlasting kingship. The use of this description in Daniel also carries with it the sense of vindication by God. Jesus himself uses this title in describing his mission (Mark 2:10, 28), his suffering and death (Mark 8:31, 9:31, 10:33, 10:45), and his return at the end of time (Mark 13:26 and 14:62). Thus, the crucified Jesus who came not to be served but to serve and gave his life as ransom for many, is vindicated by God the Father in the resurrection and is proclaimed by Peter as such in Acts 2:36 (CCC 440).

The modern Catholic Church has not sought to redefine its understandings of the early christological councils. But contemporary Catholic reflection upon the significance of the Savior has employed many other descriptions for Jesus, some of which are: liberator (CCC 1741), new creation (CCC 349), and physician (CCC 520). Thus, the many different descriptions of the Lamb, the Chosen One, found in scripture and in prayer texts, point to the rich depth of mystery which God offers believers in the person of Christ, Savior, Lord, and only Son of the Most High.

Catholic Culture

Luis de Leon was an Augustinian monk and professor who lived in late sixteenth-century Spain (d. 1591). His family background (Jews forcibly converted) along with his criticism of the Latin translation of the Bible drew the attention of the Inquisition and he spent some time in prison. He was a gifted translator (Hebrew, Latin, and Greek) and is most noted for his prose work "On the Names of Christ" (*Divine Inspiration: The Life of Jesus in World Poetry*, Robert Atawan, George Dardess, Peggy Rosenthan, eds., Oxford University Press, New York, 1998, p. 566).

The "Litany of the Holy Name" ascribes to Jesus many titles. A sampling of those titles are: "dawn of justice, prince of peace, pattern of patience, model of obedience, seeker of souls, refuge, courage of martyrs and crown of saints" (*Catholic Household Blessings & Prayers* 336–37).

Dismissal Catechesis (30 min.)

Getting Started

1. Prepare the space ahead of time with a circle of chairs around a small table draped with a green cloth. On the table place a green flowering plant and a candle.
2. Lead the participants to the circle, place the Lectionary on the table, and light the candle. Remain standing as you lead them in singing the refrain to Psalm 40:2, 4, 7–8, 8–9, 10, "*Here am I, Lord; I come to do your will.*" Or lead them in singing, "Here I Am, Lord" (Daniel Schutte, GIA Publications, 1981). Invite everyone to be seated and remain quiet as they recall their experience of today's Liturgy of the Word.

First Impressions

1. Ask the participants to describe the differences in the environment, music, and vestments that they observed from last week (last Sunday of the Christmas season) and this Sunday (second Sunday in Ordinary Time).
2. Explain the season of Ordinary Time: *Today we observe the liturgical season called Ordinary Time, which began during the past week. This is the second Sunday—there is no first Sunday of Ordinary Time since the Christmas season concluded with the feast of the Baptism of our Lord and Monday began the first week of Ordinary Time. "Ordinary" does not indicate that these Sundays and weeks are unimportant. Rather, ordinary comes from the Latin word "ordinal," meaning number. Ordinary Time means numbered Sundays and numbered weeks.*
3. Continue in the large group, asking the participants: *What do your observations and impressions from today's Liturgy of the Word reveal about Ordinary Time?* Assist the participants in a recalling of the scriptures by slowly naming the phrases and words listed below as they close their eyes and reflect: *you are my servant —a light to the nation—called to be a holy people—look—the Lamb of God—the Spirit descended—came to rest on him—God's Chosen One.*
4. In the large group ask: *What message do you hear in these words and phrases? What emotions do they evoke in you?* As the participants respond, listen and affirm their insights. Summarize the large group discussion in a few sentences.

Making Connections

1. Ask the group: *What is the significance of a person's name? What might a name reveal about the person?* Invite everyone to recall the names found in today's scriptures: Paul—an apostle—Sosthenes—our brother—church of God—a holy people—Lamb of God—God's Chosen One. Then ask them to describe what these names communicate about each of these scriptural characters: *What significance is there in Paul's name, changed from his former name, Saul? What can we learn about the Corinthians from their name? What comes to mind when you hear the name, Jesus? What do you know about Sosthenes from his name?*
2. Direct the participants to reflect on the meaning of their own names. Invite each person to turn to the person on his or her

right and share the meaning of their name. Then gather the large group and ask everyone the significance of their name.

Prayer

Invite everyone to stand around the candle. Lead them in prayer in these or similar words: *Good and gracious God, you call each of us by name* (slowly and deliberately speak each person's name aloud). *You know us by our name given to us at our birth. You have called us and we are yours. Open our ears to hear your call that we might discover all that you desire of us. We pray this in the name of Jesus, our brother, who lives and reigns with you and the Holy Spirit, one God, forever and ever. Amen.*

Extended Catechesis

SESSION FOCUS: *Names of Jesus*

Gathering

A. Sunday:

1. Greet and welcome the sponsors and team members as they arrive. After all are seated, ask the catechumens and candidates to summarize the reflection and discussion from the Dismissal Catechesis.
2. Invite the sponsors and team members to gather with a catechumen or candidate and share the significance of their names. After a few minutes gather everyone together. Invite a team member to proclaim the first reading, Isaiah 49:3, 5–6. Then lead the group in singing the refrain of "Here I Am, Lord" (Daniel Schutte). Ask a sponsor to proclaim the second reading, 1 Corinthians 1:1–3. Once again, sing the refrain of "Here I Am, Lord." Invite all to stand as you proclaim the gospel, John 1:29–34. Conclude with the refrain of "Here I Am, Lord." Leave time for silent reflection on the Word before beginning the session.

B. Weekday:

1. Use the same centerpiece as in the Dismissal Catechesis.
2. As the participants gather in the circle, greet and warmly welcome each person. After all are seated, ask the catechumens and candidates to summarize the reflection and discussion from the Dismissal Catechesis.
3. Lead this celebration of the Word:
   - Song: Gathering Song from Sunday's liturgy
   - First Reading: Isaiah 49:3, 5–6
   - Sing Psalm refrain: "Here I Am, Lord"
   - Second Reading: 1 Corinthians 1:1–3
   - Sing Psalm refrain: "Here I Am, Lord"
   - Gospel: John 1:29–34
   - Sing Psalm refrain: "Here I Am, Lord"
   - Silence

The Word (30 min.)

1. During the silence following the readings, invite everyone to speak the name "Jesus" in the silence of their hearts. Ask the participants this question: *What is evoked in you when you hear or speak the name "Jesus"?* Continue by stating this

background to the season of Ordinary Time: *On this Sunday each year, the gospel is taken from John. The readings always connect in some way with the mystery of the incarnation which dominated the Christmas season, while pointing to and introducing Jesus the Incarnate One as he begins his public ministry. Next Sunday, we will continue with our synoptic writer, Matthew. Today's readings are intensely christological. From the very beginning of Ordinary Time, our attention is directed on Jesus whom we hope to know ever more deeply as the Christ.*

2. Ask the participants to move into small groups and lead them in the following reflection: *In the first reading from Isaiah, we heard the words, "You are my servant." This servant was formed by the Lord from the first moment of life in the womb. This servant is called to be a light to the nations so that the good news of salvation might reach the whole world. Christian tradition has from the earliest centuries identified the mysterious servant with Jesus. By suffering, this unnamed servant would bring deliverance to Israel and to all nations. The text is a powerful statement of hope in the face of adversity.* Pause for a short time and lead the group in singing the psalm refrain, "Here I Am, Lord." Then ask the participants to gather into small groups to discuss the following questions: *Who is this servant? How did Jesus fulfill this description of the servant?* After a time, invite them to briefly summarize their discussion in the large group.

3. Invite everyone to close their eyes as you slowly and deliberately recall words and phrases from the second reading, 1 Corinthians 1:1–3. These might include: *called—an apostle—Christ Jesus—consecrated—a holy people—grace and peace—God our Father—the Lord Jesus Christ.* Gather them into small groups, directing them to discuss this question: *What do these words and phrases convey about Paul and about his audience?* Invite the small groups to share their discussion with everyone. Summarize their comments and again sing the psalm refrain "Here I Am, Lord."

Catholic Teaching (30 min.)

1. Invite everyone to close their eyes as you slowly recall several words and phrases from today's gospel. You may choose to include: *Lamb of God—who takes away the sins of the world—ranks ahead of me—he was before me—the dove from the sky came to rest on him—God's Chosen One.* Gather everyone into the same small groups to discuss this question: *What do these words and phrases reveal about Jesus and his role?* After sufficient time, gather responses from the groups. Summarize their comments: *These words express what we believe about Jesus' unique identity. The early Christian community continued to explore the profound mystery of Jesus' humanity and divinity. "Christology" is the term used by the Church to name the attempts to plumb the mystery of Jesus. Many titles reach back into the rich heritage of Hebrew scriptures.*

2. In the large group, brainstorm a list of all the titles associated with Jesus and write them on newsprint or an overhead. Make sure to include such titles as Lamb of God, God's Chosen One, servant, light to the nations, Lord, Christ, Son of God, and Son of Man. Explain the titles as follows: *"Lord" is derived from the Greek* kyrios *and is an honorary title in the same sense*

as "sir." *It is used by the Samaritan woman and by others who request healing from Jesus. In the context of the epistles and in Revelation, "Lord" takes on a deeper meaning, connoting the second coming of the one who is now exalted by God and will usher in the end times.* Invite the participants to articulate their understanding of Jesus as "Lord" by writing their response in the Participant Book on page 56.

3. After sufficient time, continue to elaborate on the title of Jesus the Christ: *The term "Christ" literally means "anointed" and referred to a consecrated person, a king called by God to rule, or a priest called by God to serve in a special way and, on rare occasions, a prophet called by God for a special mission. Applied to Jesus, this title describes his status as the promised one of God, the Savior and Messiah whose mission is that of priest, prophet, and king.* Invite the participants to articulate their own understanding of the title "Christ" and write their response in the Participant Book on page 56.

4. Then explain the meaning of the titles "Son of God" and "Son of Man": *A divine voice claims Jesus as "my beloved Son" and the soldier at the foot of the cross acclaims that truly this was "the Son of God." "Son of God" indicates the unique relationship of Jesus who is God's own Son and who shares in the divine nature. The title "Son of Man" originates in the book of Daniel. This "Son of Man" will receive dominion, glory, and everlasting kingship. Jesus uses this title in describing his mission, his suffering and death, and his return at the end of time. Thus, the crucified Jesus who came not to be served but to serve and gave his life as ransom for many is vindicated by God in the resurrection and proclaimed by Peter as such in Acts 2:36.* Ask everyone to articulate in their own words their understanding of the titles "Son of God" and "Son of Man" by writing their responses in the Participant Book on page 56.

Putting Faith into Practice

1. Gather the participants into the same small groups to discuss the following questions: *What new insights have you gained from this discussion on some of the titles of Jesus? Which title is most revealing for you, illuminating the mystery of his nature?* After time for this discussion invite each group to offer a summary of their discussion in the large gathering.

2. Invite any questions on the titles of Jesus and encourage the participants to use the name for Jesus that is most meaningful for them as they pray this week. You may ask everyone to name the most significant title for Jesus in the large group.

Prayer

Invite everyone to gather in a circle around the lighted candle. Lead them in the following prayer (After each title invite all to respond, "*Lead us.*"): *Jesus, you are the Christ . . . Jesus, you are Lord . . . Jesus, you are the Messiah . . . Jesus, you are Son of God and Son of Man . . . Jesus, you are the light to the nations . . . Jesus, you are the Chosen One of God . . . Jesus, you are the servant of God . . . Jesus, you are the eternal Word . . . Jesus, you are the light of the world . . . Jesus you are the way, the truth, and the life . . . Jesus, you are the bread of life . . . Jesus, you are the good shepherd . . . Jesus, lead us to know you more and more each day so that we will be your faithful followers in all that we do. Amen.*

Third Sunday in Ordinary Time

Understanding this Sunday:
Background for Catechesis

The Word in Liturgy

Isaiah 8:23–9:3
Psalm 27:1, 4, 13–14
1 Corinthians 1:10–14, 17
Matthew 4:12–23 [or (short form) 4:12–17]

The scholars believe that the historical setting for today's first reading was a period during the eighth century during which the Northern Kingdom was overrun by the forces of Tiglath Pileser III, and many in the Kingdom of Judah to the south were fearful that they would be the next to fall before the Assyrian might. Isaiah offers instead a vision of hope, based on what he sees as the certain intervention of Yahweh on behalf of Jerusalem. Some feel that the occasion for this hopeful prophecy may have been the accession to the throne of a new monarch, one who would be God's instrument to defend and protect the land and its people. The optimism of the text is impressive, heightened by Isaiah's lush imagery of a bright dawn, blazing torches of victory, a harvest festival, and the revels of soldiers dividing spoils after a victory. The refrain to today's responsorial psalm puts on our lips the words of every believer who has come to experience this same, saving action of God in the ministry of Jesus: "The Lord is my light and my salvation."

The Church reads this text of Isaiah as a preparation for our hearing Matthew describe the beginning of Jesus' public ministry. Matthew quotes this passage of Isaiah directly, thus invoking its aura of triumphant expectation as an appropriate response to the messianic age ushered in by Jesus, whose vocation and destiny it is "to fulfill what had been said through Isaiah the prophet." Today's pericope from Matthew concludes the first of the five "books" of his gospel by offering a summary of the entire ministry of Jesus: He proclaims the arrival of God's reign, calls disciples to join him, preaches and works deeds of power throughout the land. In 9:35,

Matthew repeats this same framework to summarize the ministry of Jesus who preaches (5:3–7:27, the Sermon on the Mount) and works wonders (8:1–9:34), and immediately thereafter (10:1–42) calls the Twelve by name and sends them out on a mission to share in his own messianic ministry. Our catechetical focus today on the notion of vocation is rooted, as we see, in the very structure of Jesus' ministry, which he deliberately chose to share with those whom he called as his disciples. And the ministry of Jesus, in turn, sinks deep roots in the prophetic soil of Israel, as Matthew repeatedly demonstrates by his frequent mention that what happened with Jesus was "to fulfill what had been said" of old, in the Jewish scriptures. Jesus' vocation is rooted in God's call to Isaiah and all the prophets like him. Our vocation, in turn, is rooted in that of Jesus.

Today's reading from 1 Corinthians is an important introduction to one of the major reasons why the apostle wrote to his struggling young community. Paul recognized clearly how the factions that were already dividing them threatened the very core of the gospel, the union in love that all are called to share "in Christ." What is at stake is nothing less than the very nature of our Christian existence, rooted in our being immersed into the death-resurrection experience of Jesus in baptism. So profound is the life we share "in Christ," that anything which threatens to divide us strikes at the heart of our Christian vocation. In subsequent weeks we will continue to hear how Paul attempts to reach his audience with the critical nature of reconciling their differences and finding their true unity "in Christ" and in him alone.

Catholic Doctrine

Vocation

The word "vocation" derives from the Latin *vocare*, which literally means "to call." Catholics believe that all human beings are called by God to share divine life and ultimately eternal happiness and that this calling has come to us in a privileged way in Jesus Christ. Through divine unconditional love, humanity has not only been created but gifted with a redeemer and savior, Jesus, who opens the way for all to be transformed in the Holy Spirit as adopted children of God and therefore as inheritors of a graced life (CCC 1).

Being graced does not imply passivity, but just the opposite. The Church teaches that being immersed in and experiencing divine love through baptism not only celebrates God's care and providence for us, but moves the believer to actions of love. Thus, the Church exults in prayer, "Love is [our] origin, love is [our] constant calling, love is [our] fulfillment in heaven" (*Sacramentary*, Preface 74).

In any discussion of our calling from God it must be noted that historically the concept of vocation was usually exclusively applied to the clergy and religious life. But, in modern times, drawing from the scriptures themselves and from its reflection upon the nature of the Church itself, the Second Vatican Council expanded the theological concept of vocation to all believers, rightly understanding that the model for discipleship as seen in the gospels applies to all men and women who are baptized. In examining the role of the laity in furthering the mission of Jesus, the Second Vatican Council asserted, "By their secular activity they help one another achieve greater holiness of life, so that the world may be filled with the spirit of Christ and may the more effectively attain its destiny in justice, in love and in peace . . . by their activity, interiorly raised up by grace, let them work earnestly in order that created goods through human labor, technical skill and civil culture may serve the utility of all . . . according to the plan of the creator and the light of his word" (LG 35). Therefore, Catholics understand that in speaking of a vocation, *all* are called—not just ordained ministers and religious—to contribute as disciples and followers of Jesus, given their own particular gifts and abilities and the circumstances of their lives.

John Paul II uses the scriptural image of the vine and branches to examine the nature of the calling of the laity. He teaches that all the members of the Church are in union with Christ and therefore with one another, even though their state of life (ordained, religious, and lay members) may be different. He writes, "The states of life, by being ordered one to the other, are thus bound together among themselves. They all share in a deeply basic meaning: that of being *the manner of living out the commonly shared Christian dignity and the universal call to holiness in the perfection of love*. They are *different yet complementary* . . ." (*Christifideles Laici*, The Lay Members of Christ's Faithful People, 30 December 1988, #55, emphasis in original).

The Church teaches that the faithfulness of all those who are baptized is the fundamental condition for the very proclamation of the gospel. In other words, the lives of believers witness to the truth of the sacrament celebrated in the font. From that font should issue forth a great company of witnesses which, in turn, draw others to the love, mercy, and grace of God (CCC 2044). In this way, the Church is built up by many holy men and women working in communion with one another (CCC 2045) and thus the world is prepared for the fullness of the kingdom of God (CCC 2046).

Catholic Culture

The prayer attributed to St. Francis of Assisi (d. 1226) focuses on the active engagement of the believer in following Christ. The text is revered and well known: "Lord, make me an instrument of your peace; where there is hatred, let me sow love; where there is injury, pardon; where there is doubt, faith; where there is despair, hope; where there is darkness, light; where there is sadness, joy. O Divine Master, grant that I may not so much seek to be consoled as to console, to be understood as to understand, to be loved as to love. For it is in giving that we receive, it is pardoning that we are pardoned, it is in dying that we are born to eternal life." It is significant that the bishops of the U.S. Catholic Conference suggest that this prayer text be used at the start of the new year by households of the faithful, as if to say that throughout the days and months of the coming year believers would strive for these actions in their following of Christ (CathHous 124).

The Greek word used in the New Testament to denote Jesus' call to his disciples has a sense about it that connotes "invitation," as in an invitation to a feast (ModCathE 902).

Dismissal Catechesis (30 min.)

Getting Started

1. Prepare the space ahead of time with a circle of chairs around a centerpiece arranged on the floor. Place a green cloth in the center of the circle, setting several candles of various heights and colors on the cloth. Add a seasonal arrangement of flowers, branches, and greens if you wish.

2. Lead the candidates and catechumens to the circle, place the Lectionary on the table, and light the candles. Invite them to join you in singing the refrain to Psalm 27 after you proclaim each verse. Then pray in these words:
God of light, penetrate our hearts with your rays of truth and justice. Light the darkness in our lives and the gloom of this world with the light of your love. Open us to hear your call in the depths of our hearts today. Grant us the wisdom to understand your Word as we gather in your name. We ask this in the name of Jesus, Savior and Messiah. Amen.

First Impressions

1. Ask the participants to recall their impressions of today's Liturgy of the Word as they sit in silent contemplation of the centerpiece. Then invite them to complete these sentences spontaneously in the large gathering:
Today's scriptures left me with a sense of . . .
I particularly noticed the phrase that went something like this . . .
The Gathering Hymn prepared me to . . .
The main insight I got from the whole experience of the Liturgy of the Word was . . .
In the homily I discovered . . .

2. Present this insight into the second reading from 1 Corinthians 1:10–13, 17:
This passage from 1 Corinthians describes one of the struggles that threatened to divide this early Christian community. Four competing groups of Christians claimed their leader was superior to the others. Paul realized that these divisions would destroy the very core of the gospel—the union in love that all are called to share "in Christ." He is very clear, reminding them of their basic union in Christ. The call to make unity with one another in Christ a priority, superceding human preferences, remains a challenge for Christians even today.

3. Ask the participants to gather in pairs to discuss the following questions: *What situation in your life can be compared to the factions among the Christians of Corinth? When has preference for one leader over another caused divisions in your experiences at home, work, or in community settings?* Focus the attention of everyone back to the large group and invite several pairs to share their responses.

Making Connections

1. Continue the discussion among the pairs, asking this question: *What does the phrase "union with one another in Christ" mean to you?* After sufficient time for discussion, ask the pairs to offer their ideas in the large gathering.

2. Then invite everyone to name some of the things that tend to divide people today, even religious people. Write these on large newsprint or an overhead so that everyone can see the list.

3. Introduce this concept to the group: *Our basic unity in Christ is preserved by the love that we have for one another. God expressed love for humankind by gifting us with God's own self, made flesh in Jesus, who expressed this love in the contradiction of the cross.* On a second newsprint or overhead list the participants' responses to this question: *How can we express this love for one another in Christ?* Summarize their insights in a few sentences. Encourage the participants to think about one thing that they want to remember from this session. They can write this in their Participant Book on page 59 under the heading "I want to remember."

Prayer

Gather the group, inviting them to stand as they pray for the unity among Christians and all peoples of the world. Using the newsprint or overhead list of those things which divide people, instruct the participants to pray aloud for unity, using the formula, *For the divisions caused by . . ."* Ask all to respond, *"Lord, hear our prayer."* Lead the group in singing "I Have Loved You" (Michael Joncas, New Dawn Music, 1979) or a familiar song with a similar meaning.

Extended Catechesis

SESSION FOCUS: *Vocation*

Gathering

A. Sunday:

1. Greet and welcome the sponsors and team members as they arrive. Invite them to join the circle of catechumens and candidates.

2. Begin the prayer by inviting all to listen to a recording of "By Name I have Called You" (Carey Landry, NALR, 1980) or a similar song as they pray silently, contemplating the centerpiece candles. Ask a team member to proclaim the first reading from Isaiah 8:23–9:3. Pause for silent reflection on the Word, inviting the participants to bring to mind any darkness in their lives in order to invite the light of God's presence to illuminate their gloom. Indicate that all stand to listen as a sponsor proclaims Matthew 4:12–23.

3. Invite the participants to be seated and reflect in silence upon Jesus, the promised light, saying to us today "Reform your lives! The kingdom of heaven is at hand."

B. Weekday:

1. Use the same centerpiece as described for the Dismissal Catechesis.

2. As the participants gather in the circle, greet and warmly welcome each person and light the candles. Ask the participants to share any experiences they have had this week of darkness transformed into light through God's presence.

3. Lead this celebration of the Word:
- Song: Gathering Song from Sunday's Liturgy of the Word
- First Reading: Isaiah 8:23–9:3
- Reflection: described in part A
- Sing Psalm 27:1, 4, 13–14
- Gospel: Matthew 4:12–23
- Reflection: described in part A

The Word (30 min.)

1. In the large group, invite one or two candidates or catechumens to summarize the Dismissal Catechesis. Ask the group to respond to this question: *What significance do these scriptures have for you?*

2. Present this background on the first reading and the gospel, adding your own words from the information in the Word in Liturgy section found in Understanding this Sunday:
The darkness of the collapse of the Northern Kingdom is the image of gloom used to describe the Assyrian defeat of Zebulun and Naphtali. This put fear into the Southern Kingdom of Judah who thought that they would be next to fall. Amidst the fear of hostile forces, the prophet Isaiah offers Israel a word of hope. Light will break forth in the darkness, heavy yokes will be lifted, and the crushing rod of the oppressor will be smashed. This passage prepares the way for the gospel, which is Matthew's description of the inauguration of Jesus' public ministry. In fact, the gospel begins with a quotation from this passage of Isaiah. The writer intended to set up an aura of expectation and hope, for the messianic age ushered in by Jesus marked his universal mission. Jesus' ministry begins in Galilee near the land of Zebulun and Naphtali along the sea in Gentile (heathen) territory. It is in Galilee that Jesus preaches his basic message of radical reform for the sake of the kingdom. The passage continues, describing a typical day in the life of Jesus' ministry. He calls his disciples to abandon everything and follow him; travels throughout the region of Galilee; teaches in their synagogues; proclaims the Good News of the inauguration of God's reign; and cures people of illness and disease.

3. Invite the candidates and catechumens to gather with their sponsor and/or godparent to discuss these questions: *What situations of darkness in your life cry out for the light of Christ? What is Christ calling you to reform in your life, for the sake of the kingdom? What are your expectations as you anticipate baptism or your profession of faith in the Catholic community?*

Catholic Teaching (30 min.)

1. Continue the discussion in the same pairs, asking this question: *In the light of these scripture passages, what does it mean to be called to follow Jesus?* After the pairs have had time to share their thoughts, invite them to summarize their insights in the large group.

2. Present the Church teaching on vocation using the Catholic Doctrine section found in Understanding this Sunday as a guide. Include the following points:
- Another word for "call," which is commonly used in the Catholic community, is "vocation." The vocation or call of all believers derives from baptism.

- All people are called by God to share divine life and eternal happiness with God. In response to this relationship with God, the baptized are called to further the mission of Jesus in the world. The mission of Jesus is the mission not only of ordained and vowed priests, deacons, brothers, and sisters, but also of *all* the baptized.
- An image used by Pope John Paul II to portray this relationship is that of the vine and the branches. As members of the Church, we are in union with Christ and therefore with one another, bound together in love.
- This love compels us to follow and imitate Jesus, using the unique gifts and graces, freely given to us by God, to build up the community of believers and proclaim the Good News of Jesus' death and resurrection throughout the world.
- The call is a summons that comes in the ordinariness of daily living. It comes as a light illuminating our lived experiences to grace us with the wisdom to see the Good News of Jesus dying and rising with us, raising us out of darkness and death. The call flowers and bears fruit as we proclaim this Good News in word and in the holiness of our living to those we meet in the course of our ordinary lives.

3. Encourage the pairs to gather again to share their ideas on the following questions: *What new insights did you gain from hearing this Church teaching on vocation? What implications does the call of the baptized have for you as you journey toward full initiation?*

Putting Faith into Practice

1. Ask the participants to turn to the Reflection and Questions found in the Participant Book on page 58. When they have finished reflecting and writing, direct them to share their responses in the same pairs.

2. Gather the attention of the participants and invite them to offer some examples of ways in which the Good News was proclaimed to them. Be prepared to begin this sharing with your own experiences. Stress that God calls us in ordinary ways and we are gifted to respond for the sake of the whole.

Prayer

Invite the participants to reflect for a short time on their call to carry on the mission of Jesus. Then pray in these words:
God of light, you lift us out of the darkness of sin and the gloom of our fears by sending your Son Jesus to die and rise for us. We proclaim the Good News that Jesus dies with us each time we die through failure, suffering, or despair. Through the power of his marvelous resurrection, he gathers us and lifts us up out of the trials of this life and we are renewed and re-formed. We are a graced and gifted people, called to share our dyings and risings with others, that they may come to believe in the resurrection and the life. Strengthen us to live in holiness that we might bring your wonderful light into our world. Give us the courage to share our stories of Good News with those who seek the light. Abide with us as we journey in faith, anticipating the fountain of living waters and the table of living bread. Amen.
Close by inviting all to join in singing "We Are Called" (David Haas, GIA Publications, 1988).

Fourth Sunday in Ordinary Time

Understanding this Sunday:
Background for Catechesis

The Word in Liturgy

Zephaniah 2:3; 3:12–13
Psalm 146:6–7, 8–9, 9–10
1 Corinthians 1:26–31
Matthew 5:1–12

Despite being one of the shortest books in the Bible (only 53 verses), Zephaniah is used four times in the Lectionary, and it proclaims a spiritual vision that is central to the people of the covenant. Writing at a time of religious reform, during the reign of Josiah (640–609), the prophet brought to the people of Judah words of both warning and promise. His teaching reflects an awareness, born of Israel's history, that times of moral decadence and covenant infidelity inevitably bring ruin upon the nation. He threatens a "day of the Lord" which will bring down God's wrath upon all evildoers, Gentiles as well as those in Judah.

In today's reading we hear words not of threat but of promise. "Shelter" is promised on the day of the Lord's anger, offered to the *anawim*, the "little ones" who are among the "humble of the earth" and who have "observed [God's] law." This notion of God's special favor toward the poor and lowly will continue to be developed by other prophets, as well as in the teaching of Jesus (cf. today's gospel), in the theology of the gospel writers (cf. Luke's Magnificat), and in subsequent ecclesiastical writers down to our own time (cf. current teaching on the Church's "preferential option" for the poor). In Zephaniah's words of promise, the Lord offers to protect a "remnant" of the people who, by their actions, prove themselves faithful to the covenant. Living the moral life, we are told, is the foundation of one's right relationship with the Lord.

In today's selection from Paul's letter to the Corinthians, the apostle addresses a community that apparently had little appreciation for the special place in God's heart for the poor and lowly. It appears that members of the community were boastful of their learning, their worldly wisdom and wealth, and their spiritual gifts. Still reflecting attitudes typical of the gnosticism and other Hellenistic philosophies of the day, Paul's converts need to be reminded of the spiritual vision reflected in Zephaniah's praise of the poor and lowly. Even more, they need to understand the centrality of the cross of Jesus, both for their own salvation and as a paradigm for their own lives of faithful self-emptying. Paul emphasizes God's action, God's "choice" (used three times in vv. 27–28), as opposed to the Corinthians' boasting in their own accomplishments. Their greatness comes from what God has done for them in Jesus, not from any of their own empty boasts. Echoing Jeremiah 9:23–24, Paul commands, "Let him who would boast, boast in the Lord."

Scholars believe that the gospel of Matthew was written in the first generation after the destruction of the temple in Jerusalem (70 A.D.) following the formal expulsion of Jewish Christians from the synagogues of Palestine. This setting helps to explain Matthew's deliberate portrayal of Jesus as the new Moses, giving the people the new commandments of the new Covenant from the mountaintop, just as Moses had done to an earlier generation. The Sermon on the Mount is the first of five sections of Jesus' teachings in Matthew's gospel, all of which conclude with the same formula (7:28, 11:1, 13:53, 19:1, 26:1), a technique clearly reminiscent of the five books of Moses in the Jewish scriptures. Here, the first four commandments of the new law refer to the "little ones" or *anawim* referred to in Zephaniah's text, and pronounce them "blessed" in God's kingdom. The next set of four highlights those whose actions help to usher in the kingdom. Matthew clearly intends his readers to understand the importance of this scene for all successive generations. Not surprisingly, this text has long been thought to articulate a foundational Christian ethic, which is one of the reasons why our focus today is on the foundations of Christian morality.

Catholic Doctrine

Foundations of Christian Morality

The Church contends that Catholic morality arises out of God's law, which is planted within the hearts of human beings. This "natural law" is knowable by all people, not just the Christian faithful. Indeed, the exercise of one's reason opens the human person to the ways of God.

Since the natural law is knowable, the question for theologians is whether there is a specific Christian morality. The answer is that there definitely is a specific Christian morality because its motivation and impetus lies in pleasing and loving God. Created, redeemed, and sanctified by God in Christ, the believer may very well say and do the same things as nonbelievers, but from a different perspective—which makes all the difference.

The recognition that one is saved and reformed by Christ's life, death, and resurrection assists the believer in following the example of the redeemer and choosing the way of life (CCC 1692). In this vein, St. Leo the Great preached, "Christian, recognize your dignity and, now that you share in God's own nature, do not return to your former base condition by sinning. Remember who is your head and of whose body you are a member. Never forget that you have been rescued from the power of darkness and brought into the light of the kingdom of God" (*Sermo* 21 in nat. Dom., 3: PL 54, 192C).

St. John Eudes likewise wrote, "Our Lord Jesus is your true head, and . . . you are one of his members; all that is his is yours: his spirit, his heart, his body and soul, and all his faculties. You must make use of all these as of your own, to serve, praise, love and glorify God. . . . And so he longs for you to use all that is in you, as if it were his own, for the service and glory of the Father" (*Tract. De admirabili corde Jesu*, 1, 5). The Christian moral life is supported by Christ himself.

How is the moral person formed? Morally responsible Christians are formed by baptism and a whole set of experiences, values, and symbols that shape conscience and, indeed, consciousness. It is not reason alone that forms a Christian conscience. The whole human person—a mysterious complex of emotions, understandings, and sensibilities, transformed by Christ—takes part in the moral life. Indeed, Catholicism forms a certain kind of character. The community itself has a vital role to play in this character formation because of the witness it hands on regarding Jesus. This witness is a powerful message about "creation, liberation, covenant, incarnation, death and resurrection" (NDictTheol 684).

The formation of moral character is not something nebulous, which can be referred to but whose dynamic cannot be explained and therefore remains only some sort of Christian instinct. Rather, the Church holds that there are objective norms of morality available to us that express the rational order of good and evil (CCC 1751). These objective norms are provided by scripture, tradition, the living witness of the community and, above all, the example and preaching of Christ. In articulating these norms, Catholic moral theology holds that for an action to be judged as morally good, three elements must be ascertained as good: the object itself, the intention, and the circumstances. A good intention cannot transform an intrinsically bad behavior into something that is good. In Catholic moral theology, therefore, the end does not justify the means (CCC 1753).

Every believer bears the responsibility of informing his or her own conscience in order to act rightly and justly in the world. Various elements assist the believer in forming conscience. Good preaching, sound religious education, an understanding of scripture, spiritual direction, the witness and example of other Christians, and the authoritative teaching of the Church help to form one's conscience. This formation is a lifelong process wherein the believer sifts through experience and with the grace of the Holy Spirit pursues the path of right (CCC 1785). Staying on the path of right, one avoids the way of sin.

Catholic teaching makes a distinction between mortal and venial sin. Venial sin is less grave and does not totally destroy one's relationship with God. Mortal sin is grave or deadly sin that ruptures one's relationship with God completely. For a sin to be grave or deadly, the Church holds that it must meet three conditions: the object itself is grave matter, and it is committed with full knowledge and deliberate consent (CCC 1857).

Precisely because we are free to choose either good or evil, we are moral subjects. We are, in freedom, the author of our actions. We can choose to follow Jesus' teaching and live the way of the blessed, the Beatitudes, or we can choose a way which is contrary to Jesus' law of love.

Catholic Culture

Saint Elizabeth Ann Seton (1774–1821), born in the United States, was a wife and mother. When her husband died, she continued to care for her children, even after she established a religious order, the American Sisters of Charity. Her prayer expresses the desire to walk along the paths of right, in spite of our human weakness: "Almighty and Giver of all mercies, Father of all, who knows my heart and pities its weaknesses: you know the desire of my soul to do your will. It struggles to wing its flight to you its creator and sinks again in sorrow for that imperfection which draws it back to earth. How long will I contend with sin and morality . . . Redeemer of sinners! Who gave your life to save us, assist a miserable sinner who strives with the corruption and desires above all things to break the snares of the enemy" (Woodeene Koenig-Bricker, Prayers of the Saints, Harper SanFrancisco, 1996, pp. 33–4).

Dismissal Catechesis (30 min.)

Getting Started

1. Prepare the space ahead of time with a circle of chairs around a table draped with a green cloth, upon which is placed a candle.
2. Invite the candidates and catechumens to be seated in the circle. Place the Lectionary on the table and light the candle. Pray in these words: *Loving God, You are a God who values the humble and the simple of this world. You are our true wisdom and strength. Our happiness lies in you. Give us open and simple hearts to allow your word to find a home in us. Help us hear your word now, in our own hearts and in the words of one another. Amen.*

First Impressions

1. To begin the discussion, name three images from today's readings that were important for you. These may include: *"Seek the Lord, all you humble of the earth. . . . Seek justice, seek humility"(Zephaniah 2:3). "God chose those whom the world considers absurd to shame the wise" (1 Corinthians 1:27). "How blessed are the poor in spirit: the reign of God is theirs" (Matthew 5:3).*
2. Invite everyone to add the images or phrases that appealed to them from today's scripture readings.
3. Gather the participants into small groups to discuss: *What did you find comforting about God's word to us today? What did you find challenging in today's scripture readings?* When they have finished, gather the participants back to the large group. Invite individuals to share their experience of today's scripture readings. Briefly summarize their comments.

Making Connections

1. Ask the group to name the kinds of people they consider to be the humble of the world. Then make these points: *The word "humble" comes from the word "humus," which means "earth." To be humble is not self-abnegation, but rather simply being who we are, grounded in the truth that we are both sinners and made in God's image and likeness.*
2. Invite them to think about the humble people they have named as they return to their small groups. Provide these questions for discussion: *In what way is the scriptural phrase, "the humble will shame the wise," true? What effect does true humility have upon you?*
3. Direct the small groups to continue the discussion with these questions: *Recall a time when you felt humble and describe the experience. What was this experience like? Use an image or a metaphor to describe your feelings. Was God present to you at this time?*
4. Gather the attention of everyone and invite each of the small groups to give a summary of their responses.

Prayer

Invite the participants to focus their attention within as you provide a time of silence. Invite them to move deeper to that place where they find their truest self. Then proclaim the second reading, 1 Corinthians 1:26–31. Conclude with this prayer: *God, you are all wisdom and holiness. Guide us to our truest self—sinner and made in your image—as we seek your presence. We pray that, like the apostle Paul, we might be empowered to say with honest and open hearts that we boast in the Lord alone. Amen.*

Extended Catechesis

SESSION FOCUS: *Foundations of Christian Morality*

Gathering

A. Sunday:

1. Greet and welcome the sponsors and team members as they arrive. Invite them to join the circle of catechumens and candidates.
2. Spend a few moments in quiet. Begin the prayer by asking all to sing three verses of "Blest Are They" (Haas, GIA, 1985). Provide songbooks so that all may join in the singing. To prepare the participants to hear the gospel, use these or similar words: *Open your hearts to hear the gospel by placing yourself into the scene. You are with a crowd of people on a hillside. Jesus is getting ready to speak. All becomes still as he lifts his eyes in prayer. Then he begins and you listen with rapt attention.* Proclaim Matthew 5:1–12. Pause for a period of reflection on the words of the Beatitudes.

B. Weekday:

1. Use the same centerpiece as described for the Dismissal Catechesis.
2. As the group gathers in the circle greet each participant. When you are ready to begin, light the candle. Invite everyone to sit in quiet and think about his or her week. Ask them to share an experience from the past few days of meeting a person of true humility or of experiencing a sense of humility themselves.
3. Lead this celebration of the Word:
   - Song: "Blest Are They," verses 1–3. (David Haas, GIA Publications, 1985)
   - Greeting, Sign of the Cross
   - First Reading: Zephaniah 2:3; 3:12–13
   - Sing Psalm 146:6–7, 8–9, 9–10
   - Introduction to today's gospel: same as in section A
   - Gospel: Matthew 5:1–12
   - Silence

The Word (30 min.)

1. Ask one of the candidates or catechumens to share a brief summary of the Dismissal Catechesis.
2. Present this background on the gospel passage:
   Today's gospel from Matthew is commonly known as the Beatitudes. The word "beatitude" means blissful, blessed, and happy. Matthew begins to reveal a summary of Jesus' teaching to his followers with this passage. The gospel writer, whose community included Jewish Christians, presents this teaching on a mountain, to indicate the parallel between Jesus and Moses. The giving of the law to Moses on the sacred mountain, Sinai, is no doubt in the mind of the evangelist and his hearers as he describes Jesus giving the new law on this mount of the Beatitudes. The first four Beatitudes or commandments of the new law of Jesus refer to the "little ones." These little ones are blessed in God's kingdom even though they are the humble of the earth in this world. In the next set of four Beatitudes or commandments of Jesus, the actions of the follower of Jesus to help bring about this kingdom of God are delineated.
3. Gather the participants into small groups to share their insights on the gospel, using the following questions as a guide for the discussion: *What paradoxes do you find in the new law of Jesus? How do these Beatitudes express your ethic for life?* Ask each group to share a summary of their discussion with the entire group.
4. Invite the participants to turn to page 60 in the Participant Book and think about their responses to the Reflection exercise. When they are ready, invite them to share whatever they think is significant from their reflection in the large group.

Catholic Teaching (30 min.)

1. Continue to work with the Participant Book, inviting the participants to write down the underlying values that are implied by each beatitude. When they have finished, invite them to name some of these values and list them on newsprint.
2. Present the Church's teaching on Christian morality, including the following points:
   - The natural law of God is in the heart of each human. The "natural" law is knowable by all people through the exercise of reason.
   - Believers in Christ have a specific Christian morality because they are motivated by love for God.
   - Christians are morally formed by baptism and a whole set of experiences, values, and symbols that shape their conscience and consciousness.

Stop and invite the participants to respond to this question: *What difference is there between natural law and the Christian ethic?* At this point, clear up any misconceptions that may pervade the understanding of the group.

3. Continue to develop this teaching, stressing these points and clarifying your own understanding by using the Catholic Doctrine section found in Understanding this Sunday:
   - The Church presents objective norms of morality that are knowable through scripture, tradition, and the community. Every believer is responsible to inform his or her own conscience in order to act rightly and justly in the world. This lifelong formation process occurs with the grace of the Holy Spirit.
   - Catholic moral theology holds that three elements are necessary for an action to be morally good: the action itself, the intention, and the circumstances.
   - Catholic teaching makes a distinction between mortal and venial sin. Venial sin is less grave and does not destroy one's relationship with God. Mortal sin is grave or deadly sin that ruptures one's relationship with God completely.
   - We are the authors of our actions because God made us free to choose either good or evil. The Beatitudes outline a way of life that is in total accord with Jesus' law of love. Invite the participants to raise any questions on the foundations for Christian morality.

   If you wish, you may choose to have another catechist or staff member present to help respond to these questions.

Putting Faith into Practice

1. Invite the participants to turn to the questions posed on page 60 in the Participant Book. Encourage them to write their responses. When they seem finished, gather them into the same small groups to share their insights. Ask each small group to offer a summary for everyone to hear.
2. Present an example of a parishioner or local church leader who exemplifies one of the Beatitudes. Tell their story and invite the team members to add their own examples. Ask the participants to write down one change they will make in their life as a result of the scripture on beatitude living in the "I want to put my faith into action by" section of the Participant Book.

Prayer

Gather the participants around the lighted candle and invite them to focus their attention on the candle as you once again proclaim Matthew 5:1–12. Close by inviting the group to pray Psalm 146 antiphonally, alternating right and left sides of the space. You will need copies of the entire psalm for each participant.

Fifth Sunday in Ordinary Time

Understanding this Sunday:
Background for Catechesis

The Word in Liturgy

Isaiah 58:7–10
Psalm 112:4–5, 6–7, 8–9
1 Corinthians 2:1–5
Matthew 5:13–16

The theme of light shining in the darkness is found in three of today's four readings. The metaphor of a dawning light suggests a public presence, a social reality that is available to and can be experienced by all inhabitants of the earth. This suggestive image is a powerful reminder of how deeply ingrained in our Judeo-Christian tradition is the notion that God's chosen people are called to be a force for good in society. Today's catechetical focus on the Church's social doctrine, specifically on our preferential option for the poor, reflects the way our Catholic tradition has captured this scriptural teaching.

The historical setting of today's reading from third Isaiah (cc. 56–66) is the late sixth century, following the return from Exile, when the inhabitants of Jerusalem were experiencing considerable disillusionment over the social and religious chaos to which they had returned. Their penitential fasts had not yet won God's favor, apparently, and they were asking why their prayers were not being heard. The prophet answers them (in the verses immediately preceding today's reading) with a powerful indictment of their self-serving piety. Then, as we hear in verses 7ff., he tells them just what kind of fasting God actually wants: action to alleviate the suffering of the poor and powerless. The evil the prophet deplores is societal—systemic ills afflict the nation—even if the focus of his remarks seems to be on what each individual must do. Feed the hungry; shelter the homeless; clothe the naked; remove injustice—these are the concrete actions that constitute a "fast" pleasing to Yahweh, and that will result in light dawning for the entire nation.

Psalm 112 reflects the view of the Wisdom tradition that good is rewarded with prosperity and evil is inevitably punished. The image in verse 4 of light dawning on the upright is a virtual echo of verse 8 from Isaiah's text ("your light shall break forth like the dawn"). The glory of the Lord shines on and through the lives of those who are just and who give "lavishly" (v. 8) to the poor.

Against this background, it is not hard to understand that Jesus' teaching in the Sermon on the Mount that his disciples must be the "salt of the earth" and the "light of the world" would have been recognized by his Jewish audience as an invocation of concern for action on behalf of the poor ("so that they may see goodness in your acts"). Even more, in the context of Matthew's theological perspective, the new Moses (Jesus) is here speaking to the new Israel (his disciples), telling them that they "are" (not "will be") what the ancient prophets called Israel of old to be. By observing the commandments of the new Law (these verses follow immediately on the Beatitudes), the disciples of Jesus become the light that has dawned on the world. Thus, the Church's social teaching is not about mere humanitarianism. Rather, in our concern for the poor, we actually become agents of the in-breaking of God's reign, an intrinsic part of the power of love which will, we believe, transform all reality.

Today's reading from 1 Corinthians is the fourth of seven in the series and follows directly on last week's text, in which Paul reminded his readers that they have no reason to boast of their own accomplishments, since it is by God's grace alone that they have been saved. Here, Paul applies the same truth to his own ministry: it was by God's power alone, not by any eloquence or wisdom of Paul's, that the gospel he preached bore fruit in their conversion. As he did in the previous chapter, Paul here points to the centrality of Christ crucified—the folly of the cross—as the focal point of his message. Paul's awareness of that "absurdity" (so it surely seemed to the "worldly wise" philosophers of his day) makes it all the more clear that their coming to faith can only be the result of "the power of God" (v. 5).

Catholic Doctrine

The Social Teaching of the Church: Preferential Option for the Poor

The Church has always been concerned with the problems and potentials of human society. In the nineteenth century, however, with the growth and expansion of the modern industrial society, the Catholic Church developed a more detailed social teaching. This teaching is concerned with the fundamental rights of persons and how the temporal goods of society are ordered toward not only the common good but God and the kingdom in the light of the gospel of Jesus (CCC 2419–20).

Catholic social thought and teaching upholds a preferential option for the poor as a key characteristic. What is this preferential option? It is the commitment on the part of individual believers, of communities of the faithful and the institutional Church itself, to not only work for the alleviation of poverty but to assist all those in society who are marginalized and oppressed. Thus, in making moral decisions in any particular circumstances, the needs and concerns of the poor should be given priority over others. In addition, the preferential option for the poor goes beyond economic terms to include all those who are exploited or who have been robbed of their basic human dignity.

It is important to note that this option or choice for the poor is being made by those who have greater material wealth or possessions, that is, those who are not stricken by poverty or oppression. Individuals and groups who are relatively well-to-do exercise this option when they make a free choice to give up some of their wealth or privileged state in order to more closely (to some degree) identify with those less fortunate. Those who are already poor may also exercise a preferential option for the poor by identifying with other groups who are oppressed or marginalized or who lack the basic human necessities.

A preferential option for the poor is not something new in the history of God's people. As indicated in the accompanying essay on the scriptures of today, this option arises out of the experience of the God who liberates the chosen people from slavery in Egypt and who continued to call that same people through the prophets to alleviate the suffering poor. In his life and death, in his mission, Jesus Christ sums up the Old Testament promises and challenges of deliverance and thus is described by the Church as the liberator of humanity for freedom (CCC 908 and 1741).

Through baptism all believers share in the mission of Jesus the liberator. In speaking of the laity, the Second Vatican Council asserted, "By their competence in secular disciplines and by their activity . . . let them work earnestly in order that created goods through human labor, technical skill and civil culture may serve the utility of all . . . according to the plan of the creator and the light of his word. May these goods be more suitably distributed among all . . . and in their own way may they be conducive to universal progress in human and Christian liberty. Thus, through the members of the Church, will Christ increasingly illuminate the whole of human society with his saving light" (LG 36).

This assertion, that the laity work toward universal progress in liberty, was further reflected upon by the South American bishops when they met at their general conferences, especially Medellin (1968) and Puebla (1979), where the bishops spoke of the Church as being allied with the poor. The Vatican has expressed some concern over the writings of various liberation theologians, especially those seen as Marxist influenced, although the term "preferential option for the poor" is accepted and used by Rome. John Paul II insists, however, that an option for the poor does not mean that those who are better provided for materially are excluded. In his view, the Church is a community that includes all (NDictSoc 757).

As members of a Catholic community that is inclusive and that exercises a preferential option for the poor, how does an individual or a group make a commitment in taking action to overturn structural injustice in society? There are four steps involved. First, careful analysis must be made of the situation being addressed so that before action is taken energy is not wasted on superficial change without addressing root causes of the injustice. Second, this analysis should stop collusion with the causes of oppression and thus promote a distancing of the individual or group from those others who are causing the injustice or who contribute to it. Third, concerted and organized actions should be planned and entered into at the political level, gradually escalating in scope and intensity, in order to challenge the injustice. Fourth, realistic alternatives to inhumane and unjust structures should be designed and brought to birth in society by believers (NDictSoc 758).

Thus, the modern social teaching of the Catholic Church, especially its preferential option for the poor, enjoins upon believers that they truly become salt of the earth and light for the world. This is not a poetic image alone, but a clarion call to concrete action in society.

Catholic Culture

Numerous Catholic parishes around the world engage in activities to alleviate the plight of the poor and oppressed. Soup kitchens, food pantries, and shelters for the homeless are examples of some of these activities. Indeed, many Catholic churches in the northern hemisphere open their doors in bitter winter weather to shelter the homeless. The Campaign for Human Development was established by the Church to collect money for programs of education and self-help that specifically address the root causes of poverty and oppression.

St. Joseph, whose feast always falls within Lent (March 19), is considered the patron saint of the poor. Many parishes host "St. Joseph tables," inviting those in any material need to celebrations of free, meatless food and drink.

Dismissal Catechesis (30 min.)

Getting Started

1. Prepare the space ahead of time with the chairs in a circle around a centerpiece on the floor, using a rug or cloth of green upon which is set a bowl of salt and a large candle.
2. Lead the candidates and catechumens to the circle and place the Lectionary into the centerpiece or on a separate stand in a prominent place. Light the candle and sing either the opening song from the liturgy or "Bring Forth the Kingdom" (Marty Haugen, GIA Publications, 1986).
3. After everyone is seated, play instrumental music. Carry the bowl of salt to each person, pause, and direct them to touch, smell, or taste it. Next, take the candle to each person, pause, then direct them to look into the burning flame and/or hold the candle. Return to your seat for a few moments of quiet. Stop the music.

First Impressions

1. Recall some of the words from today's scriptures, inviting the participants to remember what they observed and heard. You might include these phrases and images, feeling free to add to this list: *share your bread—shelter the oppressed and the homeless—clothe the naked—light in the darkness—salt of the earth—light of the world—your light must shine.* Then invite the catechumens and candidates to add phrases and images that they can recall.
2. Direct the participants to join with a partner to discuss these questions: *What do these images say about the life of a follower of Jesus? Which images encourage you as you journey in faith to become a follower of Jesus? How are you challenged by today's Liturgy of the Word?* Return the focus of the participants to the large group and invite responses. Briefly summarize their insights.

Making Connections

1. Encourage them to recall an experience of a storm or power outage when a candle or lantern or flashlight was the only source of light. Ask them to reflect upon: *the contrast between the darkness and the light—their feelings and thoughts in the darkness—the manner in which their eyes focused on the light and its brightness—their relief or joy when light was restored or a new day dawned.* Then ask them to share their experience of light and darkness with the same partner. Elicit from the pairs some of these responses.
2. In the large group open a discussion of this question: *What did Jesus imply when he told the disciples that they were to be a light for the world?*
3. Continue to guide the participants to connect the scripture with their life experience by asking them to name all the characteristics and benefits of salt, particularly in Jesus' time. Conclude their comments by reiterating: *Salt is a preservative, a flavoring, it has healing properties, it buoys up floating objects.* Continue by enumerating all that was mentioned. Then direct them to share their

thoughts on this question: *What was Jesus trying to uncover when he said we were to be salt for the earth?* Summarize their input and invite them to write down one idea they wish to remember in their Participant Book on page 63 under the section "I want to remember."

Prayer

Begin the instrumental music. Proclaim the gospel, Matthew 5:13–16. After a few moments, again carry the bowl of salt to each person, pausing for them to touch or taste it. Again, take the candle to each person, pausing for him or her to observe or hold it. Return to your seat; then pray: *Jesus, our brother, you came among us to show us the way to live. You want us to be the salt of the earth and the light of the world not for our own glory but in order that our actions might give praise to our God in heaven and lead others to follow your way. Help us to be the salt and the light that is needed in our world today. We ask this in your name. Amen.*

Extended Catechesis

SESSION FOCUS: *The Social Teaching of the Church: Preferential Option for the Poor*

Gathering

A. Sunday:
1. Greet and welcome everyone as they arrive. Invite them to join the circle of catechumens and candidates.
2. Begin the prayer by leading all in singing the refrain to the Gathering Song used at today's liturgy. Then, slowly and deliberately proclaim Isaiah 58:7–10. After a short silence, lead them in singing the psalm refrain, *"The just man is a light in darkness to the upright."* Ask one of the team members to proclaim Matthew 5:13–16.

B. Weekday:
1. Use the same centerpiece as in the Dismissal Catechesis.
2. As the participants gather in the circle, greet and warmly welcome each person and light the candle.
3. Lead this celebration of the Word:
   - Song: Gathering Song from Sunday's liturgy
   - First Reading: Isaiah 58:7–10
   - Sing Psalm 112:4–5, 6–7, 8–9
   - Second Reading: 1 Corinthians 2:1–5
   - Alleluia
   - Gospel: Matthew 5:13–16

The Word (30 min.)

1. Invite one or two of the catechumens and candidates to share something they learned during the Dismissal Catechesis. Invite the participants to share any experiences they might have had of being light or salt for another.
2. Lead the participants in the following meditation: *Close your eyes and relax. Take a deep breath. God is in our midst. As you breathe in and out, remember that*

the Spirit of God is breathing life into your being. Think back to an experience of encountering a person who was poor or homeless. Recall your impressions at the time. How did you react? What feelings emerged as you looked into the eyes of this person on the margins of our society? How did you react? Did you pretend not to see? Did you offer money? Did you talk with the person? Did you recoil from the person? Allow time for reflection. Then ask the participants to write about this experience in their Participant Book on page 63. When they finish, direct them to share their experience in the large group.

3. Proclaim Isaiah 58:7–10. From the Word in Liturgy background found in Understanding this Sunday, prepare a similar presentation: *Today's reading occurs after the return of the Israelites from the Babylonian exile. Isaiah addresses the societal and systemic evils that oppress the hungry, homeless, and those without the basics of life. Feed the hungry; shelter the homeless; clothe the naked; remove injustice—these are the concrete actions that constitute a "fast" pleasing to Yahweh. These actions will result in light dawning for the entire nation, order coming from chaos. The prophet is not speaking against worship; rather, he deplores the hypocrisy of those who gather for elaborate ritual but neglect or exploit the poor and the oppressed. It renders their prayer worthless.*

4. Invite the participants to review their encounter with a person on the margins of today's society. Then ask them to share their reactions to this question with a partner: *How does this passage affirm or challenge your response?* From the Word in Liturgy background, share this information: *The glory of the Lord shines on and through the lives of those who are just and who give "lavishly" to the poor. In Matthew's perspective, the new Moses (Jesus) is speaking to the new Israel (his disciples). That we are to become salt of the earth and light of the world is directly connected to the prophetic challenge. In our concern for the poor and the oppressed, we actually become agents of the in-breaking of God's reign, an intrinsic part of the power of love which will, we believe, transform all reality.* Invite everyone to share their reactions: *What power do these two scriptures have to transform your daily experience and actions?*

Catholic Teaching (30 min.)

1. Divide the participants into small groups. Distribute a secular newspaper, a Catholic newspaper, and some magazines to each group. Ask them to look for headlines/articles that address the poor, the homeless, the oppressed, the marginalized. Then direct them to select one article and respond to the questions posed in the Participant Book on page 62. Encourage the group to discuss their responses; then invite them to briefly share some of their insights.

2. Present the Church's teaching on the Preferential Option for the Poor, using the Catholic Doctrine section to help you develop the following points:
   - The Church has always been concerned with the problems and potential of human society. Rapid economic growth and expansion has caused Church leaders to develop a more detailed social teaching.
   - The Church exhorts all believers to commit themselves to assist the marginalized and oppressed. Thus, in making moral decisions, the needs and concerns of the poor are to be given priority over other issues.
   - This option for the poor arises out of the experience of the God who liberated the chosen people from slavery in Egypt. Jesus sums up the Old Testament promises and challenges of this liberation in his life, death, and mission to the poor.
   - Through baptism, all believers share in the mission of Jesus the liberator.

3. Invite the groups to turn again to the headlines/articles which they chose and ask them to discuss these questions: *What insight or new understanding does the Church's teaching about preferential option for the poor shed on these headlines/articles? In light of the Church's preferential option for the poor, what could we do to address the issues/concerns contained in these headlines/articles? In what ways might we be changed as we struggle to make decisions in light of the poor, the oppressed, and the marginalized?* Gather insights and challenges from the groups and take note of any recommendations that arise. These could be recorded and offered to the parish pastoral council for their consideration.

Putting Faith into Practice

1. Ask this next question in the large group and outline the four steps to include the Preferential Option for the Poor in their decision making. You may find an overhead helpful: *As members of a Catholic community that is inclusive and yet exercises a preferential option for the poor, how does an individual or a group make a commitment to take action against structural injustice in society?*
   - *First, careful analysis must be made of the situation so that energy is not wasted on superficial change without addressing root causes of the injustice.*
   - *Second, this analysis should stop collusion with the causes of oppression and thus distance the individual or group from those who contribute to it.*
   - *Third, concerted and organized actions should be planned and entered into at the political level, gradually escalating in scope and intensity, in order to challenge the injustice.*
   - *Fourth, realistic alternatives to inhumane and unjust structures should be designed and brought to birth in society by believers.*

2. Review with the group the corporal works of mercy (see page 62 in the Participant Book) and challenge them to reflect on how they already live these works of mercy, and how they could strengthen their commitment to them.

Prayer

Direct the participants to form two circles: an inner one with the catechumens and candidates and an outer one with sponsors and team members. Ask the outer circle—sponsors and team—to place their hands on the shoulders of the catechumens and candidates as you pray an adapted form of Minor Exorcism (RCIA 94D). Lead all in singing "Bring Forth the Kingdom" (Marty Haugen, GIA Publications, 1986).

Sixth Sunday in Ordinary Time

Understanding this Sunday:
Background for Catechesis

The Word in Liturgy

Sirach 15:15–20
Psalm 119:1–2, 4–5, 17–18, 33–34
1 Corinthians 2:6–10
Matthew 5:17–37 [or (short form) 5:20–22, 27–28, 33–34, 37]

The Book of Sirach is part of the Wisdom literature, a corpus of writings dedicated to show how the wise person can live in harmony with God's plan for the world and thus fulfill the prescriptions of the Law. Sirach was written in Hebrew at the start of the second century before Christ, but the work as we know it was translated into Greek some years later following the Maccabean revolt. The translation reflects the concern of pious Judaism to counter the attractions of Hellenistic culture, both in Palestine and in the diaspora, by reasserting the superiority of a wisdom based on Yahweh's Covenant with Israel. Sirach was not accepted into the Jewish canon of scripture and Protestantism considers it an apocryphal work, but Catholics regard it among the deutero-canonical, inspired books of sacred scripture. Early Christianity used Sirach extensively in the instruction of catechumens. Today's excerpt stresses human freedom and our ability to choose between good and evil. The context is an exhortation to choose wisely by following God's commandments, which connects the reading to today's gospel.

Psalm 119 is the longest and most complex of the three major psalms that celebrate the place of the Torah in the life of Israel (see also Psalms 1 and 19). After the reading from Sirach has urged us to choose rightly, Psalm 119 highlights the blessings that come upon us when we do so ("Happy are they . . ."). The verses selected show how the Torah was considered to be a precious gift of the Lord, a sure guide pointing the way to happiness by living in accord with God's plan.

The scribes and Pharisees of Jesus' time were renowned for their study of the Torah and for their scrupulous observance of its 613 prescriptions. Jesus' insistence that his disciples' holiness must surpass that of the scribes and Pharisees in order for them to enter the kingdom of God was deliberately shocking. So, too, Matthew's careful structure of six antitheses (four this week and two next) highlights what surely seemed like an unattainable ideal. First, he juxtaposes the Torah and Jesus' demands; then, he offers a practical illustration of what is being asked; and, finally, he gives Jesus' command. In every case, what Jesus asks of his followers requires an extraordinary interior conversion of heart. Mere external compliance seems impossible; only love as the basis for action could render possible the ethic proposed here by Jesus. Exegetes point out that the use of hyperbole here is integral to understanding the rhetoric of Jesus' message, and we must be careful not to become entangled in a literalistic interpretation of any of his injunctions. What is most important is the overall thrust of Jesus' teaching, how he deliberately pushes his hearers beyond mere observance of the Law to a way of following the commandments that springs from a radical love of God and neighbor (cf. Matt. 22:34–40).

Today's reading from 1 Corinthians picks up where last week's left off. Paul has been contrasting the folly (i.e., the wisdom) of the cross with worldly wisdom, and admitting that what he preaches has none of the persuasive force of the polished Greek rhetoricians of his day. Rather, the power of Paul's wisdom rests solely on its origin: the Spirit, through whom "God has revealed this wisdom to us" (v. 10). Paul is not hesitant to point out that the wisdom which the Christian receives from the Spirit surpasses that of "the rulers of this age" who are "headed for destruction" (v. 6). He is here cleverly laying the groundwork for his attempt to correct the errors of certain members of the Corinthian church. They were caught up in self-importance over their gnostic fascination with the hidden mysteries to which they believed themselves privy and had forgotten the basic law of Christian love.

Catholic Doctrine

Human Freedom and Christ's Law of Love

Human freedom is the ability we possess from God to choose how we wish to act or not act, to decide for or against something or to engage in specific actions wholly according to one's own responsibility. In traditional Catholic moral theology, this is described as exercising one's free will. Free will is the mechanism by which we grow and mature in truth and goodness, for when free will is focused on and disciplined for the kingdom of God (as opposed to being totally spontaneous and absolutely self-centered) it achieves a blessedness of life and holiness (CCC 1731).

This general analysis, however, must take into account the record of salvation history. For, without a doubt, we were created by God with freedom to do as we wished. And we failed. Adam and Eve are the scriptural symbols expressive of our failure to attune our free will to the design of God. Human history is replete with examples of individuals and groups who chose evil and evil-doing again and again, which has led to all sorts of diabolical and wretched situations and outcomes. This is why the Second Vatican Council began its discussion of human freedom saying, "The people of our time prize freedom very highly and strive eagerly for it. In this they are right. Yet they often cherish it improperly, as if it gave them leave to do anything they like, even when it is evil. But that which is truly freedom is an exceptional sign of the image of God in [humanity]" (GS 17).

Jesus Christ is that most exceptional sign. He has exercised his own freedom in complete obedience to the will of his heavenly Father. Jesus reveals the mystery of God's love for us and how we might respond to that loving kindness of the Most High (CCC 1701). The Savior is the summation of the law of Moses. Indeed, he proposes a new, more perfect law, the law of love as found in the gospels and in the very person of Jesus—whose promised Spirit guides and animates the Church as it interprets and hands on that law of love to every generation. This gospel law of love is therefore not so much codified in a series of prescriptions as it is brought to life by the action of the Holy Spirit in the life of the Church. The law of love proclaimed by Christ cannot only be spoken of, but must be preached in detail. By baptism and incorporation into the people of God, and throughout a lifetime of religious formation, the new commandment of love is etched upon our hearts as believers partake of the living tradition of discipleship.

There are two ways in which believers can fail to live up to God's Law. The first is legalism, whereby the letter of the Law is emphasized to the detriment of the Spirit of the Law. The second is antinomianism, which overemphasizes the Spirit to the exclusion of the letter of the Law. The Catholic Church teaches, however, that faith and good works go hand in hand. It is not enough to talk about the particulars of the law of love or the commandments of Christ as given in the gospels. Nor is it enough to claim that one possesses the Spirit. In freedom, the believer chooses actions (or non-actions) in the concrete situations of life which live up to and embody the law of love given to us by the life, death, and resurrection of Jesus Christ.

In fulfilling the law of love, the central focus becomes the person: in Old Testament times, God the Father, and in New Testament times (including our own), Jesus, the only Son of God. And in our own persons we participate, then, in this central focus—which is precisely the communion toward which Catholics strive as they internalize and manifest the law of love by "fostering integrity, justice, community, and transcendence," as they "bring human beings through authentic self-appropriation to that union which is the restoration of all things in Christ" (NDictTheol 569).

Catholic Culture

St. Thomas More (1478-1535) was born in London, educated at Oxford, eventually earning his law degree, and was elected to Parliament. In 1529 King Henry VIII named him Lord Chancellor of England. Three years later, he resigned his position because of his opposition to the king's divorce. Refusing to take the Oath of Succession, he was sent to the Tower of London and was tried. He made good use of his legal abilities, defending himself, hewing a fine line between respect for the office of the king and yet never budging in defending the faith and the position of the pope in the matter of the divorce of King Henry's wife. More was deeply spiritual and is an exemplar of the believer who lives the law of Christ's love with introspection, wit, and decisive choice of action—no matter the consequences. In July 1535, he was beheaded.

St. Thomas More is the patron saint of lawyers.

The stage play and the movie *A Man for All Seasons* details the last years of St. Thomas More, his unflinching conviction to live up to his faith in the face of the king's wrath and his eventual martyrdom.

Dismissal Catechesis (30 min.)

Getting Started

1. Prepare the space ahead of time with a circle of chairs around a table draped with a green cloth, upon which is placed a candle. You will need printed copies of Psalm 119:1–2, 4–5, 17–18, 33–34 and songbooks for this session.

2. Invite the candidates and catechumens to be seated in the circle. Place the Lectionary on the table and light the candle. Pause for a moment of quiet. Then pray in these or your own words: *Loving God, you created and formed us, and have given us the commandments out of love. Teach us your way of love. Fill us with your wisdom. Guide us during our time together today, that we might come to know and understand your Word. We pray in the name of Jesus. Amen.* Lead the participants in singing the refrain of the song "Eye Has Not Seen" (Marty Haugen, GIA Publications, 1982).

First Impressions

1. Invite the participants to silently recall their experience of today's Liturgy of the Word. Ask them to offer their comments on these questions: *What are some of your feelings and insights from today's readings, homily, prayers, and hymns? What message did you hear repeated throughout the liturgy?* Affirm each person who offers a response.

2. Proclaim the first reading, Sirach 15:15–20, in a slow and deliberate manner. Then direct them to find a partner to share these questions: *What do you understand by true wisdom? How would you interpret the verse, "Eye has not seen, ear has not heard, or has it so much as dawned on [humankind] what God has prepared for those who love [God]"? What is the role of the Spirit in order to mature in wisdom? How does keeping the commandments animate us with wisdom?* In the large group review each question and encourage a few pairs to offer their insights.

3. Summarize their responses in a few sentences.

Making Connections

1. Invite the catechumens and candidates to think of a wise person. Ask a few participants to describe this person, indicating some of the characteristics of wisdom, particularly as they relate to the reading from Sirach.

2. Direct them to return to the same pairs to share their insights on these questions: *How does the law of love, offered by Jesus, transform us with the wisdom of God? What are some ways to grow more spiritually mature?* Encourage the pairs to make a list of the ways to mature in wisdom. When the discussion seems finished, ask each pair to read their list for everyone to hear.

3. Conclude by asking each participant to name God's invitation to him or her from today's Liturgy of the Word. Encourage them to write this invitation in their Participant Book on page 65, under the section "I want to remember."

Prayer

Distribute copies of Psalm 119. Lead this prayer by proclaiming the verses and direct the participants to respond by singing the psalm response, *"Happy are they who follow the law of the Lord!"*

Extended Catechesis

SESSION FOCUS: *Human Freedom and Christ's Law of Love*

Gathering

A. Sunday:

1. Greet and welcome the sponsors and team members as they arrive. Invite them to join the circle of catechumens and candidates.

2. Spend a few moments in quiet. Begin the prayer by asking all to sing "Eye Has Not Seen" (Marty Haugen, GIA Publications, 1982). Pray: *O Source of Wisdom, open us to your life. Give us eyes to see your ways. Help us know and trust in your gifts that far surpass the gifts this world offers. Give us hearts that delight in your laws and your commands. Open us to hear your word to us now. We ask this through Jesus, who taught us your ways. Amen.* Invite the participants to listen to today's gospel from Matthew. Proclaim Matthew 5:17–37.

B. Weekday:

1. Use the same centerpiece as described for the Dismissal Catechesis.

2. As the group gathers in the circle, greet each participant. Light the candle. Invite everyone to sit in quiet and reflect on the past few days. Ask them to share a time from the past few days when they interacted with another person who had wisdom or a time when they thought they acted wisely.

3. Lead this celebration of the Word:
   - Song: "Eye Has Not Seen" (Haugen, GIA Publications, 1982)
   - Greeting, Sign of the Cross
   - First Reading: Sirach 15:15–20
   - Sing Psalm 119 or the Psalm used at Sunday's liturgy
   - Gospel: Matthew 5:17–37
   - Silence
   - Closing Prayer: same as in section A

The Word (30 min.)

1. Ask one of the candidates or catechumens to share a brief summary of the Dismissal Catechesis. Then invite the participants to name the words or phrases that come to mind when they hear the word "commandment."

2. Present the following background on this week's gospel passage:

   For the Israelites, keeping God's law was a way of life that indicated they were indeed God's people. Today's gospel reading from Matthew is a continuation of Jesus' teachings to his disciples. The scribes and Pharisees of Jesus' time would have known the Jewish law very well. In fact, they scrupulously observed its prescriptions. Jesus shocked the disciples by stating that their holiness had to surpass this way of living by the prescriptions of the law. Jesus brought the keeping of the law to a new dimension as each time he used the phrases, "You have heard it said. . . . What I say to you is. . . ." In every case what Jesus asks of his followers requires an extraordinary interior conversion of heart. The use of hyperbole here is integral to understanding the rhetoric of Jesus' message, and we must be careful not to interpret his injunctions literally. The message of this gospel is that Jesus deliberately pushes his hearers beyond mere observance of the law to a way of following the commandments that springs from a radical love of God and neighbor.

3. Then invite the participants to discuss the following questions in small groups: *Which of Jesus' statements most surprises you? Which of Jesus' statements seem the most demanding for you? How is the law changed by love?* When they have finished, ask each group to give a summary of their responses in the large group.

4. Then invite the participants to turn to page 64 in the Participant Book to spend time reflecting and writing their responses to the questions presented in Part I. When they have finished invite them to share their insights to the questions with a partner. Pair sponsors and godparents with their catechumen and candidate.

Catholic Teaching (30 min.)

1. When the sharing is finished, invite a few pairs to offer their insights on this question in the large group: *What is Jesus' message to you as you reflect upon your life and the law of love?*

2. Present the following points regarding human freedom and Christ's law of love:

   - Humans are born with free will, the ability to choose right or wrong. Free will is the mechanism by which we grow and mature in truth and goodness, for when free will is focused on and disciplined for the kingdom of God it achieves a blessedness of life and holiness.
   - Jesus Christ is the sign of this holiness in that he exercised his own freedom in complete obedience to the

will of his heavenly Father. Jesus reveals the mystery of God's love for us and how we might respond to that loving kindness of the Most High.

   - Christian believers can fail to live up to God's Law through legalism, observing the letter of the Law to the detriment of the Spirit of the Law, or, on the other hand, by overemphasizing the Spirit of the Law to the exclusion of carrying out its specific aims.
   - Christians fulfill the commandment of love not merely because it is a duty, but as a response to God's love.
   - Christians desire to live in faithfulness to their relationship to God in Christ.

3. Ask the participants to use the reflection exercise presented in Part II on page 64 of the Participant Book. Guide them through this exercise, explaining:

   Think of the vertical line on the page as a continuum, with the left side signifying disobeying God's laws, the middle signifying obeying God's laws out of duty, and the right side signifying responding to God's ways out of love. Where do you put yourself on this line? Give concrete examples of how you have changed in the past year. What is different in the experience of responding out of love rather than out of duty?

   When the groups are finished, invite some sharing and discussion in the large group.

Putting Faith into Practice

1. Explain the importance of an attitude in keeping Jesus' commands in these or your own words:

   There is a great difference between keeping laws merely out of a sense of duty, and keeping the commandment because we love God and our brothers and sisters. Our attitude makes all the difference in the interior spirit that leads us to true holiness. The wise person is constantly aware that he or she must examine interior motives for choosing and acting on the laws of God and the church. The law of love is an attitude that permeates our whole self. The law of love is a response of the heart to God and God's people.

2. Invite the participants to offer suggestions of how they can further live out the law to love. Ask each person to decide one way they will commit to doing this during the coming week. Encourage them to write their resolve in the Participant Book in the section titled "I want to put my faith into action by" on page 65. Have them share this commitment in the same pairs.

Prayer

Begin the closing prayer by asking everyone to recall his or her resolve to respond to God's call to love. Invite everyone to place a hand over his or her heart, and sense that this law of God and desire to respond out of love is in their heart. Encourage them to pray in the silence of their hearts for what they need to respond to God's commands. Sing the refrain of "Eye Has Not Seen" two times (Marty Haugen, GIA Publications, 1982).

Seventh Sunday in Ordinary Time

The Word in Liturgy

Leviticus 19:1–2, 17–18
Psalm 103:1–2, 3–4, 8, 10, 12–13
1 Corinthians 3:16–23
Matthew 5:38–48

The literary setting for the Book of Leviticus is the Sinai event with Moses and, as such, it belongs to the Pentateuch or Torah. In actuality, the book reflects the hands of many editors and many centuries of layered traditions, including cultic rules and customs as well as other ethical imperatives. The fourth part of the book (vv. 17–26) is called the Holiness Code, and the heart of its message is captured in verse 2 of today's reading: "Be holy, for I, the Lord your God, am holy." In ancient Israel God's holiness and the holiness of the people were inextricably linked, as a gift on God's part and as a task to be accomplished on Israel's part. Today's reading also shows another important linkage in its directives about social justice and love of neighbor: Our relationships with one another are a constitutive element in our quest to share God's holiness, for God has irrevocably bound himself to us—first in the covenant with Israel of old and definitively in the new covenant forged with all humanity in the flesh and blood of Jesus. Paul makes virtually the same point in today's second reading when he reminds the Corinthians, "the temple of God is holy, and you are that temple" (v. 17). Jesus, too, in the gospel links love of neighbor with the same command to share God's holiness. Today's psalm offers an image of the God whose holiness we are called to imitate: "He pardons all your iniquities . . . not according to our sins does he deal with us. . . ." These words of the psalmist find an echo in the gospel's injunctions to offer no resistance to injury, to love one's enemy, and to pray for one's persecutors.

Today's gospel continues the reading from last week, with Jesus pronouncing his fifth and sixth antitheses, which culminate with a reiteration of the holiness command of

Leviticus. In a sense, it is that final verse, "you must be perfected as your heavenly father is perfect" (v. 48), which provides the key to all that has gone before in chapter 5. The seemingly unattainable ethic that Jesus imposes as his gloss on the commandments truly is as lofty as the very holiness of God. And that is indeed the point Jesus wishes to make: as those who have entered into the reign of God, his disciples do have a share in the very holiness of God. As was the case with today's reading from Leviticus, so also in Matthew's gospel our relationships with one another are constitutive of our sharing in the holiness of God. Not only is social justice demanded and a limit set on the law of retaliation; Jesus pushes even further in demanding love for one's enemies, and he grounds that command in the image of a God whose sun shines on both the bad and the good without discrimination.

Earlier in chapter 3, Paul uses the metaphor of a building to describe his work in establishing the community at Corinth and to remind his readers that Jesus Christ is the sole foundation of their community. He then expands the metaphor, speaking of the temple that they are, evoking the image of the Holy of Holies, the innermost sanctuary of the temple that is filled with the presence of the Lord, reminding the Corinthians that God dwells in the midst of their community. To destroy the unity and harmony of the community is tantamount to defiling the very holiness of God. This reading, then, contributes to a deeper understanding of today's catechetical focus by reminding us that holiness is not only an individual quality, but it is also a communal reality.

Catholic Doctrine

Universal Call to Holiness

Prior to the Second Vatican Council, the trend in theological circles and in the preaching of the Church was to emphasize that only special persons were described as holy. These special persons were called to a distinct way of life which constituted holiness, namely, those who were members of religious communities of men and women who vowed to live chaste, celibate lives cloistered and apart from the "ordinary" world. But it was the revolutionary decision of the fathers of the Second Vatican Council to speak, instead, of the universal call to holiness before upholding the holiness of any single group (for example, priests and religious). The decision of the Council to first treat the universal call to holiness grew out of the Church's recovery of the foundational importance of the sacrament of baptism.

In baptism, believers are incorporated into Christ, and as such, they are gifted with a share in the mystery of Jesus, the Holy One of God. Thus, holiness is always a grace given from God—who alone deserves the description "holy." (One of the reasons the Catholic Church practices infant baptism is precisely because holiness of life is a gift received from God, not something that humans achieve all on their own.) The Reformation polemic portrayed Protestants as saying holiness is from faith and is given as pure grace while Catholics emphasized holiness as coming from works. Neither extreme is correct, however, and today's Catholic theology starts out with an assertion of holiness as God's gift to us.

The Second Vatican Council asserted that this gift of holiness is given to the Church itself. Christ sacrificed his life, so much did he love the Church. In doing so, he sanctified the Church and was joined to it as a groom to a bride, bestowing upon the community the gift of the Holy Spirit. Thus, the Council referred to 1 Thessalonians 4:3 and taught, "Therefore all in the Church, whether they belong to the hierarchy or are cared for by it, are called to holiness, according to the apostle's saying: 'For this is the will of God, your sanctification.'" The Council went on to declare, "It is therefore quite clear that all Christians in any state or walk of life are called to the fullness of Christian life and to the perfection of love, and by this holiness a more human manner of life is fostered also in earthly society" (LG 39). Then the Council examined the various states of life and how they might work with the grace of God's holiness, cultivating it in their particular callings. The Council examined how bishops, priests, deacons, lay ministers, married couples and parents, widows, single people, the poor, the sick, and those persecuted for the sake of justice are called "in the

conditions, duties and circumstances of their life . . . will sanctify themselves more and more if they receive all things with faith from the hand of the heavenly Father and cooperate with the divine will, thus showing forth in that temporal service the love with which God has loved the world" (LG 41).

How can diverse people strive to deepen their holiness? Participation in the sacraments, in a life of devotion shown through faith, hope, and love, and in ascetical practices are all ways that believers try to cooperate with God's grace and grow in holiness. The moral life, living the Commandments and putting into practice Jesus' Beatitudes are thus seen as a response to and cooperation with the grace of holiness (CCC 1719).

In summary, two important characteristics of the Catholic teaching on holiness, as it has been refined and developed in the contemporary Church, can be highlighted. First, that while holiness is a gift from God, it requires that we cooperate with that gift—and that all are called to do so, no matter their state or walk in life (CCC 2013). Second, members of the Church learn to walk in the way of holiness by looking to the example of Mary, the Mother of God, and by the witness given by the saints (CCC 2030).

Finally, by cooperating with the gift of God's holiness in Jesus, believers not only participate and are united in the mystery of Christ, they progress ever more deeply into the mystery of the Holy Trinity, the total and complete communion of love experienced between Father, Son, and Spirit. In this sense, the view of holiness as proposed by the Church today is founded upon an understanding of relationships—the quality of relationships within the Trinity and the quality of our human relationships.

Catholic Culture

A traditional Catholic devotional practice is the holy hour—an hour of prayer before the exposed Blessed Sacrament. Those who attend holy hours do so not only to honor the Blessed Sacrament but as a specific form of prayer to energize themselves in pursuing the call to holiness in life.

The Church document "Justice in the World" (November 30, 1971) is the first on social teaching to derive from a synod of bishops. One of its great contributions is how it links the gospel message of loving one's neighbor to the pursuit of justice. In the view of the synod these two things are inseparable. The mission of the Church (and of individual members) is not just a striving toward a spiritual wholeness and holiness, but working in the world for a holiness of right relationships.

Dismissal Catechesis (30 min.)

Getting Started

1. Before gathering, provide a circle of chairs with a table covered with a green cloth in the center. Place a candle, a bowl with charcoal for incense, and a container of incense on the table. The incense is used at the conclusion of the Extended Catechesis. You will need copies of Psalm 103 printed in stanzas as in the Lectionary. Provide a place for the Lectionary.
2. Invite the catechumens and candidates to gather in the circle of chairs. After a moment of quiet, pray in these or your own words: *God, you are holy, indeed! You invite us to share in your holiness. Help us to know that we truly are holy, as we are, and as you have created us. As we share today, may your word deepen in us. We pray this in confidence and in love. Amen.*

First Impressions

1. Ask the group to brainstorm images and phrases or words from the gathering hymn and each of the readings from today's Liturgy of the Word. Then ask them to share their responses to these questions in the large gathering: *Which of these images or words are you most drawn to? Which of the images or words seem to touch your heart today?* Briefly summarize the variety of their responses.
2. Point out that each of the scripture passages proclaimed today contains some reference to holiness. Use these examples:
   Be holy, for I, the LORD your God, am holy (Leviticus 19:2).
   For the temple of God is holy, and you are that temple (1 Corinthians 3:17).
   You must be perfect as your heavenly Father is perfect (Matthew 5:48).
3. Invite the participants to discuss these questions in pairs: *What does God's holiness mean for you? What qualities characterize God's perfect holiness?* Then ask each pair to share some of their responses with the entire group.

Making Connections

1. Invite everyone to envision himself or herself as holy. Have them touch their head, face, eyes, mouth, heart, hands, legs, knees, and feet while imagining the very holiness of God permeating their being. Ask the participants to discuss this question in pairs: *In thinking of yourself as a temple of God, what feelings and insights arise in you?*
2. Ask each pair to express something of their sharing with the entire group. Then, remaining in the large group, ask the participants this question: *What does your sense of being God's temple call forth from you in terms of your daily living?* Affirm and encapsulate their responses as this discussion proceeds.
3. Continue to deepen the discussion by saying: *God dwells within each person. Therefore, how does this knowledge change your feelings and thoughts regarding the potential for holiness in others? Consider your family members, co-workers, parents, children, neighbors, and other people you know.*
4. Conclude the discussion by clarifying and summarizing the group's insights regarding the holiness of God, others and us. Then invite the participants to name something from the scriptures of the day and the Dismissal Catechesis that they wish to remember. Encourage them to write this in their Participant Book on page 67, under the section "I want to remember."

Prayer

Distribute printed copies of Psalm 103. Invite participants to place a hand on their heart or abdomen to be conscious of God's indwelling as they pray. Pray the verses of Psalm 103 together and sing the refrain *"The Lord is Kind and Merciful"* between each verse.

Extended Catechesis

SESSION FOCUS: *Universal Call to Holiness*

Gathering

A. Sunday:
1. Greet and welcome the sponsors, team members, and other participants as they join the group. Invite them to gather in the circle.
2. Invite everyone into a moment of quiet. Sing the refrain of "Ubi Caritas" (Taize, GIA Publications, 1979) several times as a meditative prayer. Then pray: *God, you are love. Your love fills and surrounds us. Your presence is made known in love. Help us to be aware of your love. Make us bearers of your love for others. Mold and fashion our hearts in your love. We pray in Jesus' name. Amen.* Proclaim Matthew 5:38–48.

B. Weekday:
1. Welcome and greet the sponsors, team members, and additional participants. Invite them to gather in the circle with the same centerpiece as the Dismissal Catechesis.
2. Ask everyone to reflect on the last few days and respond to this invitation: *Share an experience of what happened to you as you were more aware of being a temple of God.*
3. Lead this celebration of the Word:
   - Gathering Song: "Ubi Caritas" (Taize, GIA Publications, 1979)
   - First Reading: Leviticus 19:1–2, 17–18
   - Sing Psalm 103:1–2, 3–4, 8, 10, 12–13
   - Second Reading: 1 Corinthians 3:16–23
   - Sing Alleluia
   - Gospel: Matthew 5:38–48
   - Silent Reflection
   - Closing Prayer: Use the prayer from A.2 above

The Word (30 min.)

1. Ask a catechumen or candidate to briefly summarize the Dismissal Catechesis.

2. Present this introduction to the gospel: *Today's passage from Matthew is a continuation of last Sunday's reading. Jesus tells us to not only obey God's commandments, but to be perfect, which some scholars translate as whole or complete. Listen again to the gospel and, after I read it, I will ask you to simply state some words or phrase that stay with you.* Proclaim the gospel, Matthew 5:38–48.

3. Invite participants to call out the words that remain with them. Then have the participants share in pairs an aspect of this gospel that is difficult for them to live. Encourage them to use specific examples.

4. Ask the participants to brainstorm examples of people who they consider their "enemies" or "persecutors." Then invite them to share in pairs: *What can we discover from the scriptures regarding Jesus' understanding of love? God's love? What, then, does it mean for us when we are told to love our enemies?* Allow sufficient time for this sharing. Then ask the pairs to share some of their responses with the entire group.

5. Using examples from the sharing, make these statements about this Sunday's scripture readings: *This week's readings from Leviticus and Matthew link together personal holiness with love of neighbor. Jesus presents not only a demand for social justice and a limit on retaliation, but also a love even for one's enemies. The love of a Christian is to be like that of God, whose sun shines on both the bad and good without discrimination. This is Jesus' invitation to us today in all the examples already mentioned.*

Catholic Teaching (30 min.)

1. Ask the participants to reflect on the following questions: (Participants may wish to write this reflection in the Participant Book page 67.) *Jesus says we must be perfect, like God. What kinds of attitudes and actions does Jesus envision? Knowing that you are human, do you feel that is Jesus asking the impossible?* After sufficient reflection time, invite them to share in pairs.

2. Ask the participants to share examples of the attitudes and actions they named. List these on newsprint. Then make the following points about the universal call to holiness:

   • Before the Second Vatican Council, 1962–1965, the Church emphasized that priests and women and men in religious life were called to holiness. The Council taught, however, that all people are called to holiness by reason of their baptism.

   • Married couples, parents, widows, single people, the poor, sick, and all baptized are called to express God's love in their particular way and situation.

   • Participation in the sacraments, prayer, and ascetical practices, looking to Mary and the witness of the saints as examples, as well as the strength and support of the Christian community, are all helps and supports to living a life of holiness, to living the call of love.

   • The call to holiness is a gift from God, yet it requires a response in action. Making moral choices, living the commandments, and practicing the Beatitudes are ways of cooperating with God's grace and call to holiness.

   • Believers are united with Christ and with the entire Trinity by cooperating with God's gift of holiness.

3. Encourage the participants to brainstorm ways they, as parents or children, married or single, neighbor or friend, are able to live the call of holiness—loving one another. List these possibilities on newsprint.

Putting Faith into Practice

From this list, ask participants to choose one way they feel God is calling them to holiness in an action that involves loving another person this week. They may wish to record this action in the section "I want to put my faith into action by" of the Participant Book on page 67. Then have each person share her or his commitment to this action with one other person.

Prayer

Light the charcoal for the incense several minutes before they will be needed. Give this direction:
Incense often brings an awareness of the holy, the sacred. As we remember that we are in the presence of God, who hears our prayers, I invite you one by one to take a grain of incense and place it on the coal, either stating your prayer of what you need to live your call to holiness aloud or praying it in your heart. After everyone has prayed aloud or silently and placed the grain of incense on the charcoal, we will sing the refrain "Ubi Caritas" several times. As we sing I will bring the bowl of incense around before each of you, and invite you to use your hands to bring some of the incense over your head, face, as a gesture of taking in God's holiness.
After everyone has prayed in this manner, place more incense on the charcoal. With a hand gesture invite everyone to stand. Then, by silent gesture, invite everyone to hold hands. After a moment of silence, say "Amen" to end the prayer.

Eighth Sunday in Ordinary Time

Understanding this Sunday:
Background for Catechesis

The Word in Liturgy

Isaiah 49:14–15
Psalm 62:2–3, 6–7, 8–9
1 Corinthians 4:1–5
Matthew 6:24–34

Today's first reading comes from the second part of the Book of Isaiah (chapters 40–55), also known as the Book of Consolation due to its setting at the time of Israel's return from the Babylonian Captivity. Historians have helped us to understand something of the disillusionment felt by the exiles upon their return to the chaos of the ruined city of Jerusalem. After generations of longing to be restored to Zion, what they actually found was far from their hopes. One can easily imagine how the refugees might well have lamented, "The Lord has forsaken me; my Lord has forgotten me" (v. 14). Yet the message of the prophet is clear and without hesitation. No more than a mother could forget her child will Yahweh ever forget the chosen city, Zion. The prophet's choice of feminine imagery to portray the nature of the deity ought not to be passed over lightly. Too often the predominance of patriarchal images that the scriptures use for God leads us to forget the importance of balancing our picture of God as Father with that of God as Mother. Here, the prophet's choice of a mother's love for her child represents his inspired understanding of the enduring quality of God's love for us.

Psalm 62 contains some of the strongest language of trust in God to be found anywhere in the Psalter. The images are powerful and fairly tumble from the psalmist's pen: our soul is "at rest" in God; God is "rock" and "salvation . . . stronghold . . . safety . . . glory . . . strength . . . refuge." Little wonder that the psalmist exhorts the people to trust in God "at all times" and to "pour out your hearts" before God. The ancient foundations of our Catholic teaching on divine providence are to be found in the evocative power of such images, forged over the centuries in the hearts of those who have come to know in a deeply personal way this God of steadfast covenant love.

The admonition that is put on our lips in the refrain to today's responsorial psalm ("Rest in God alone, my soul") is a fitting introduction to the teaching of Jesus in today's gospel reading. Still part of the Sermon on the Mount, chapter 6 is the setting in which Matthew has placed Jesus' instruction of his disciples on how to pray the Lord's Prayer. Some scholars believe this pericope may be a commentary on the fourth petition in that prayer, "Give us this day our daily bread." Whether one accepts that interpretation or not, what is clear is that the heart of Jesus' teaching here is the radical choice he demands of his followers: to rely completely on divine providence as they go about their everyday lives. One is reminded of how the Israelites in the desert were taught to rely completely on Yahweh for their survival by the daily gift of manna. That this teaching is not merely a superficial instruction on how we should relate to material things is shown by Jesus' command to "seek first [God's] kingship over you, his way of holiness." Ultimately, what is at stake is our ability to be part of the reign of God which Jesus announced with such single-minded intensity.

Today's selection from 1 Corinthians offers us the example of how St. Paul lived out that radical dependence on God in his everyday life. Here, no doubt defending himself against the attacks of those who had questioned his apostolic authority, he uses two terms to describe himself and his ministry. He is to be regarded as a "servant" and "administrator." Both terms, of course, describe someone whose whole life work is dependent upon the direction and continuing authority of another. In Paul's case, of course, that other is divine, and Paul reminds his readers that the ultimate judge of his life (and theirs as well) will be God. Paul's assertion, "I have nothing on my conscience," is not an idle boast. Rather, it is the appropriate expression for one whose whole life has been lived with a constant reliance on God's provident care and direction.

Catholic Doctrine

Divine Providence

The term used by Catholic theology to describe God's care for us and for all creation is "providence," which is derived from Latin and literally means "foresight." We believe that which God creates—the entire universe—has a goal and while characterized as "good" (Genesis 1:31), it is incomplete. Creation travels toward a perfection yet to be attained and which will be fully revealed according to God's plan. Divine providence thus refers to how God guides all of creation to this perfection (CCC 302).

While the term itself (providence) does not appear frequently in the Bible, scripture gives a powerful witness throughout, in both the Old Testament and New Testament, that God exercises care and solicitude to all of creation and to us creatures: a covenant was established through Moses with the people God called out of Egypt to be his own and a new covenant was established in Jesus so that salvation would be extended to all peoples. Indeed, in his teaching, Jesus alludes to divine providence, as in today's gospel passage. Elsewhere, Jesus refers to the God who cares for us (Matthew 10:29–31), who answers our prayers (Luke 11:9–13), who forgives our sins if we forgive others (Matthew 6:14–15), and who invites us to eternal life (John 6:40). Jesus' greatest teaching, however, is his own sacrifice for our sakes, opening for us the gates of paradise. Thus, the theme of a wise, loving, and caring God who extends that wisdom, love, and care to us throughout history—and definitively in Christ—dominates the writings of scripture.

God is the master of the plan of creation. But as noted above, creation is not yet perfect. Therefore, in understanding the Catholic notion of divine providence, it is necessary to touch on two related issues pertaining to the incompleteness of creation: the problem of human freedom and the scandal of evil.

Human beings have been given the ability to freely share in God's providence by collaborating with the divine will to complete the work of creation (CCC 307). God is sovereign and the first cause of all things, but to us creatures God grants not only an existence but the dignity and responsibility of cooperating and thus acting as secondary causes. Human free will means that we can choose to act as collaborators with God or we can choose evil and work against God. The Creator loves us all and offers to everyone membership in the New Jerusalem. Some individuals freely choose by their lives to turn their back on this membership and as such are judged by God as failing. This moral evil, in our Catholic view, is much worse than physical evil in the world. And yet we believe God created a world which is in a process of unfolding, of journeying toward perfection, and therefore the possibility of individuals choosing to do evil was freely allowed by the Most High in accord with creation's status as journeying toward its ultimate end.

Thus, certain individuals can choose to do wrong and sin (moral evil). In addition, we sometimes experience, through no fault of our own, the debilitation of sickness and worldly limits (physical evil). But we believe that all things will work toward creation's ultimate end (perfection) in God (CCC 313). How can human freedom, secondary causes, and the problem of evil be reconciled with a good God without asserting at the same time that all things are predetermined by the Creator?

St. Thomas Aquinas (d. 1274) provides an answer. God who is transcendent does not *foresee* (remember the derivation of the term "providence") what is to happen as something in a "future," because since God is beyond time, God sees all things as *present*. Those same things may be understood by us creatures as "future," for we exist in time. Thus, Aquinas argued that knowledge of what is present can be infallibly certain on the part of God without imposing necessity on what is known (NDictTheol 818).

Only through eyes of faith can the believer begin to comprehend the mystery of divine providence, human free will, and the problem of evil. When we see God face to face in the kingdom we will understand completely this mystery and know that ultimately in all things, in spite of evil and sin, the love of God prevails and works toward the perfection to which creation journeys.

St. Catherine of Siena said to "those who are scandalized and rebel against what happens to them": "Everything comes from love, all is ordained for the salvation of [humanity], God does nothing without this goal in mind" (Dialogue on Providence, ch. IV, 138). In the Catholic understanding of divine providence, therefore, the focus becomes less the great power of God and more the overwhelming love of God.

Catholic Culture

The mystic, Julian of Norwich, meditated, "Here I was taught by the grace of God that I should steadfastly keep me in the faith . . . and that at the same time I should take my stand on and earnestly believe in what our Lord shewed in this time— that 'all manner [of] thing shall be well' " (*The Revelations of Divine Love*, 32, trsl. James Walshe, S.J.).

At the beginning of Ordinary Time, the Church prays, referring to divine providence: "Almighty and ever-present Father, your watchful care reaches from end to end and orders all things in such power that even the tensions and tragedies of sin cannot frustrate your loving plans. Help us to embrace your will, give us the strength to follow your call, so that your truth may live in our hearts and reflect peace to those who believe in your love" (*Sacramentary*, Alt. Opening Prayer, Second Sunday in Ordinary Time).

Dismissal Catechesis (30 min.)

Getting Started

1. Prepare the space ahead of time with a circle of chairs around a table draped with a green cloth. On the table place an arrangement of flowers, fruits, and berries, and even some artificial birds.
2. Lead the candidates and catechumens to the circle and place the Lectionary on the table. Begin the session by leading all in singing Psalm 62 or the song "Only in God" (John Foley, New Dawn Music, 1976).

First Impressions

1. Invite the catechumens and candidates to close their eyes as you repeat some of the images of God from this powerful psalm, saying: *This psalm prayer contains some of the most powerful images of trust in God. Listen as I repeat some of the words used and allow their full reality to sink deep within your soul. God is my rock—God is my stronghold—In God I find hope—God is my safety—God is my refuge—God is my glory—God is my strength—I can pour out my heart to God.* After a period of silent reflection, invite the participants to share the thoughts and feelings evoked in them by these images of God.
2. Ask the participants to gather into pairs and share with one another a personal experience of God that corresponds to these images presented in the psalm. When they have finished, invite a few comments in the large group. Summarize their input by making the following observation: *We can trust in God at all times, we can pour out our hearts to God because we trust in God's steadfast love for us. This trust is based on the foundation, forged over centuries, of people who have come to know the enduring quality of God's love for us.*

Making Connections

1. Ask the participants to name some of the reasons people fail to trust in God's steadfast love. List these on newsprint or an overhead, writing large enough for everyone to read.
2. Gather them back into the same pairs and invite the candidates and catechumens to explore some of the ways they have come to know God's loving care. Ask each pair to list one of these examples on another newsprint or overhead as they conclude their discussions. When all have finished, read the examples of God's care aloud for the whole group. Encapsulate their responses by concluding: *There are many attitudes and obstacles that prevent us from believing that God could possibly care for each of us. (Here, mention some of the examples listed on the first newsprint of overhead.) However, throughout our life's experiences, there are times when we simply know that God is caring for us. (Give examples from their recorded discussion.) God not only creates all things, God continues to guide, care for, and protect all creation. There are times in our life when it takes great faith to believe and trust in God's presence and love.*

Prayer

Invite the participants to reflect in silence, calling to mind those situations in their life and in the world, which cry out for God, our rock of safety. When you feel the time is right, ask each person to name one of these situations aloud, using a brief sentence, rather than a long explanation. After each naming, ask the group to respond: *"We pour out our hearts to you, our God in whom we trust."* Conclude by praying in these or your own words:
God, our source of hope and salvation, we place our trust in you. We believe that your love is enduring. Help our disbelief. We trust that you care for us, even beyond human imagining. Help us when we despair. We hope that your presence will become more apparent as we journey in faith. Heal our blindness when we fail to see you. Creator, you gave us your Son to show us the length, breadth and depth of your love. We pray all this in Jesus' name. Amen.

Extended Catechesis

SESSION FOCUS: *Divine Providence*

Gathering

A. Sunday:

1. Greet and welcome the sponsors and team members as they arrive. Invite them to join the circle of catechumens and candidates.
2. Encourage everyone to reflect upon the centerpiece and offer them a sense of its symbolism in the light of today's scriptures. When they have finished, lead all in singing the Gathering Song from this morning's liturgy.
3. Ask a sponsor to proclaim the first reading from Isaiah 49:14—15. Invite a catechumen or candidate to present a brief summary of the Dismissal Catechesis; then open the sharing by asking anyone who wishes to comment on the assurance we can offer one another that our God is indeed trustworthy and caring. Then proclaim the gospel, Matthew 6:24—34.

B. Weekday:

1. Use the same centerpiece as described for the Dismissal Catechesis.
2. As the participants gather in the circle, greet and warmly welcome each person. Encourage everyone to reflect upon the centerpiece and offer them a sense of its symbolism in the light of today's scriptures.
3. Lead this celebration of the Word:
   • Song: Gathering Song used at Sunday's liturgy
   • First Reading: Isaiah 49:14—15
   • Sharing as described in A
   • Second Reading: 1 Corinthians 4:1—5
   • Gospel: Matthew 6:24—34

The Word (30 min.)

1. Distribute large sheets of paper and glue-sticks to each participant. Have a variety of magazine pictures cut and spread out on a side table or on the floor within the bounds of the circle. Ask each person to complete this sentence: *God is like . . .* by selecting a picture or pictures to depict their sense of God and gluing it on their paper. When most have finished, encourage everyone to briefly explain their picture in small groups.

2. Present the background on the first reading in these or your own words:

   In the first passage from Isaiah, the prophet had the difficult task of giving new hope to the broken spirits of the returning exiles. The people had been displaced in Babylon for a long time. When the benevolent Persian king, Cyrus, freed them to return to their homeland, the work of rebuilding their destroyed temple and beloved land began. But they needed deeper reassurance that God was still with them, faithful to Israel in covenant love. In using the image of a mother's love for her infant, the prophet offers them and us one of the most touching expressions of love.

3. Invite the small groups to gather again to discuss this question: *What does this image of mother and infant reveal to you about the nature of God?* In the large group, invite a few of the participants to offer their insights.

4. Continue to explain the gospel in these or similar words:

   At first glance, this passage and its admonition that we stop worrying may sound naive and simplistic. If we look into the context of chapter 6 of Matthew, we discover that the disciples were asking how to pray the Lord's Prayer. Therefore, many scholars believe that the admonition not to worry and the statement that it is impossible to serve two masters are a commentary on the fourth petition in that prayer, "Give us this day our daily bread." Ultimately, the gospel emphasizes the radical choice one must make to follow Jesus. Jesus demands that his disciples must rely completely on God's care in their daily living. This radical dependence on God is very difficult. The sense of power we derive from having money, taking control of our lives and competing at all costs is extremely difficult to shed. Yet, to follow Jesus, we must "let go and let God."

5. Gather the participants back into the same small groups to discuss these questions: *How would you live out the radical call to surrender your worries, your concerns, and your life completely into God's care? What would have to change in your lifestyle?*

Catholic Teaching (30 min.)

1. When the small group discussions seem to be concluding, ask some of the groups to summarize their responses for everyone to hear.

2. Present the Church's teaching on divine providence using the information found in the Catholic Doctrine section in Understanding this Sunday. Emphasize these points:
   - Divine providence refers to the teaching that God not only creates but also guides all of creation to fullness and perfection throughout the course of history.
   - This teaching is at the core of the sacred scriptures; the Old Testament is based upon the covenant between God and Israel; the New Testament reveals the fulfillment of this covenant—salvation through the ministry, death, and resurrection of Jesus. Jesus came to reveal the love and care of God, who answers our prayers, forgives our sins, and invites us to eternal life.
   - Humankind is free to share in God's providence by collaborating with God's plan in completing the work of creation—bringing all things to fullness and perfection. Evil, working against God's plan, is the option open to those who deliberately choose to turn their backs on God.
   - Illness, human limitations, and tragedies are part of the human condition through no fault of our own. Yet we believe that God works all things to the good for those who love God. Only through the eyes of faith can the believer begin to comprehend the mystery of divine providence, human freedom, and the problem of evil.

3. Ask the participants to reflect on the questions found in their Participant Book on page 68 and share their insights in their small groups. Gather the attention of the groups when they are finished talking and invite a few to offer their thoughts and reflections.

Putting Faith into Practice

1. Encourage everyone to refer back to page 68 in the Participant Book and complete the exercise described in the Reflection section. When they have had time to reflect upon the scriptures and write their prayer of surrender, invite all to give their attention to the large gathering.

2. Invite a parishioner or team member to present a witness on a personal experience of surrendering to God's provident care during a troubling or worrisome time. Encourage this person to stress the outcome of this act of trust in God, rather than the details of their struggle.

3. Invite the participants to respond to the witness with further questions or by relating similar experiences.

Prayer

Focus the attention of the group on the centerpiece, inviting them to think about God's care for creation evidenced in the natural world. Play some instrumental music from "Vision" (Angel Records, 1994), the contemporary album attributed to Hildegard of Bingen's music. This mystic found God through the natural world. Invite people to pray their own prayer of surrender (written in the Participant Book) in silence. Then invite each person who wishes to call out a place, a situation, or a person he or she would like to commit to God's providence. Conclude the session by praying:

Almighty and ever-present God, your watchful care reaches across the expanse of the universe. Who am I that you should care for me? I am a speck of little significance in the vastness of the cosmos. Yet your love for me is like that of a mother for her infant. Your love goes far beyond the capacity of human love, for you constantly reassure me that you will never forget; you will never abandon me. I surrender my life, my concerns, and my struggles to your unfathomable love. Take and receive me into your loving

Ninth Sunday in Ordinary Time

Understanding this Sunday:
Background for Catechesis

The Word in Liturgy

Deuteronomy 11:18, 26–28, 32
Psalm 31:2–3, 3–4, 17, 25
Romans 3:21–25, 28
Matthew 7:21–27

Ostensibly a farewell speech of Moses before the Israelites enter Canaan, the Book of Deuteronomy contains traditional material spanning many centuries. Most scholars believe that the final version reflects the concerns of a seventh-century editor, but it is not known whether the literal observance of this command to wear phylacteries (or prayer boxes, in which texts of the Torah were placed) was in force at that time or came about only later. In the theological vision of the deuteronomic school, the blessing and curse set before Israel had to do with their decision to observe the Law or not. Disobedience to the prescriptions of the Covenant brought down divine retribution; observance of the Law resulted in divine blessings. Many of the historical books of the Bible are written with this presupposition in mind and attempt to understand Jewish history from this perspective. Despite the danger of mere external compliance that this view can foster, authentic deuteronomic theology clearly seeks to instill a deeply internalized love, not fear, as the motive for observance of the Law (cf. 6:8). The opening verse of today's first reading is a partial quote from the Shema (cf. Deuteronomy 6:8), one of the most important prayers of the Jewish people from ancient times up to the present day, enjoining them to love God and keep the commandments. In view of today's reading from Romans, it is also worth mentioning that Deuteronomy regards observance of the Law both as possible and as fruitful.

Psalm 31 gives voice to the prayer of one undergoing trial and distress. The verses selected for today express the supplicant's unshakable faith in God, a "rock of safety." Mention of God's "justice" (v. 2) and the repeated references to God's saving action ("refuge . . . rescue . . . deliver . . . safety . . . fortress") may have dictated the choice of this psalm as a fitting preparation for the reading from Romans.

With today's reading from Romans we begin a fifteen-week semi-continuous series of readings from that letter that will continue until the twenty-fourth Sunday in Ordinary Time. The theme of Romans, first announced in 1:16–17, is here restated, namely that "the justice of God has been manifested apart from the law (v. 21) . . . that justice of God which works through faith in Jesus Christ (v. 22)." The heart of Paul's teaching is his insistence that we are all sinners, incapable of overcoming our sinfulness, and that only God can save us by the free gift of grace. That offer of grace has been revealed to us in the person of Jesus Christ, and it is our faith in Christ, not our observance of the Law, that opens us to the justice of God. The focus of today's catechesis on the doctrine of justification draws heavily on a proper understanding of Paul's nuanced theology found in Romans 3:21–4:25. Centuries of polemic since the Reformation once made it seem impossible for Catholics and Protestants to agree on this central issue, but a return to the scriptural basis of the Church's understanding now has shown the considerable common ground that is actually shared by both traditions. Rather than continue to insist on the mutually exclusive "faith *versus* works" approach, today's readings (including the gospel) help us to understand that, in the concrete, it is always "faith *and* works" that characterize the experience of the believer.

The section of Matthew that we read today forms the conclusion of the great Sermon on the Mount. Jesus points to the importance of being a doer of his word, not just a hearer, much in the way that the first reading from Deuteronomy demanded a choice between blessing and curse. Jesus urges his disciples to enter the reign of God by internalizing their faith in him and by expressing that faith in action. It is the deeper motivations of the heart ("hears my words") that must form the basis for right action ("and puts them into practice"). In developing a correct understanding of the Catholic position on justification, both the emphasis of this text and of Paul's teaching in Romans must be kept in balance.

Catholic Doctrine

Justification

As we explore the Catholic viewpoint on being justified before God, it is worth noting that this doctrine article and next week's go together. Today's topic of justification is followed next week by our understanding of how justification is achieved. Justification is the theological term used by Catholics to describe our stance before God, having been saved by Jesus Christ and gifted with the Holy Spirit, such that we believers are freed from sin and given a new birth by divine grace. The key here is the utterly free and generous act of God—the bestowal of grace—so that believers are justified, that is, put into a right relationship with the divine. For us believers this is celebrated in the sacrament of baptism (CCC 1987).

The Protestant reformers emphasized the universality of sin, the absolute gratuity of justification, and insisted human freedom was destroyed by original sin. The Council of Trent (meeting for various sessions between the years 1546–53 A.D.) rejected this view. Instead, the Catholic Church proclaimed it is possible for humans to exercise their free will and cooperate with God's grace and thus be renewed inwardly. Indeed, it is possible to grow in holiness as we practice the virtues of hope and love. Unfortunately, the way in which the Catholic Church and the Reformation theologians initially spoke about justification only furthered the split in Christianity. Today, however, as a result of continuing discussions between the Roman Catholic Church and the Lutheran Church, there is much closer agreement on the basic themes of justification which is grounded in both the Old and New Testament scriptures: justification is the action of God's grace through the salvation achieved by Jesus Christ and individuals appropriate that justification by their faith-in-action.

Thus, the central linchpin of the doctrine of justification is Jesus and his life, death, and resurrection. Through the Holy Spirit we are joined to Christ's suffering and death when we die to sin and, in the same way, we are joined to Christ's resurrection when we are born again to eternal life in baptism (CCC 1988). Given this line of theological reflection, conversion is characterized as the first work of the grace given by the Holy Spirit—in keeping with the gospel message of repentance initially proclaimed by Jesus (CCC 1989). In this vein, Jesus continues to preach as he does in today's gospel passage (Matthew 7:21–27), for the believer cannot embrace the message of salvation without also putting that saving Word into practice.

Another way to approach this point is to characterize justification, as does our Catholic teaching, as the ground of cooperation between God's gift of grace and our human freedom. God holds out to us the possibility of conversion and believers accept this gift in faith. Humans, therefore, are not inactive in this drama. Individuals can choose to either accept or reject the grace of God. And yet, without God's loving grace extended to us, we cannot by our own will enter into new life and a justified stance before the divine (CCC 1993).

Finally, justification is a way of indicating the tremendous love we have been shown by God in Christ. After all, humanity did not on its own bring itself into a right relationship with God. While still in sin, God chose us, graced us, and justified us. St. Augustine (d. 430 A.D.) spoke of the justification of sinners as a greater work than the creation of heaven and earth, for the heavens and earth will pass away but the salvation of those whom God has elected will not. St. Catherine of Siena (d. 1380 A.D.) reflected upon the disobedience of Adam, the entrance of sin in the world, and the consequent loving action of God to save and justify us. Her reflection is couched as a dialogue to her from God: "Beloved daughter, everything I give to [humanity] comes from the love and care I have for [people]. I desire to show my mercy to the whole world and my protective love to all those who want it. . . . I attended to you with loving care—out of provident concern I handed over my only-begotten Son to make satisfaction for your needs. I demanded supreme obedience from him so that the human race might be freed of the poison which had infected the entire earth because of Adam's disobedience. With eager love he submitted to a shameful death on the cross and by that death he gave you life, not merely human but divine" (Cap. 134, ed. latina, Ingolstadii 1583, ff° 215v–216 found in LitHrs, vol. 4, pp. 465–66).

The bestowal of divine life is thus an emphasis found in the Catholic view of justification. By giving birth to a new interior reality that is joined to the divine, the Holy Spirit not only effects our justification but sanctifies us, that is, makes our entire being holy and graced (CCC 1995).

Catholic Culture

The Catholic posture of prayer on one's knees indicates a relationship of superior-inferior and acknowledges the supremacy of God who alone saves us. The practice of kneeling derives from oriental and medieval courts where subjects knelt before the presence of the potentate or king.

Even today, Latinos not only pray in a kneeling position, but also practice prayer walking on their knees (for example, up the aisle of a church) in answer to graces perceived from God in their lives or in order to petition God for help. The attitude which is encouraged in this type of prayer is, in Spanish, *humillarse*, "to humble oneself" before not only the majesty of God but also before the great love of God.

Dismissal Catechesis (30 min.)

Getting Started

1. Prepare the space ahead of time with the chairs arranged in a circle around a centerpiece on the floor. For the centerpiece arrange a green cloth with a candle and a very large rock. Have enough newspapers on hand for the small groups who will gather at the Extended Catechesis.
2. Lead the candidates and catechumens to the circle and prop the Lectionary up against the rock. Light the candle.
3. Open with a prayer, using these or similar words: *God, you are the rock of our safety, we take refuge in you. You rescue us in time of trouble. You are the rock of our safety. You lead and guide us in the good times and bad. You are the rock of our salvation. As we gather today, to reflect and share today's celebration of your Word, be our guide, for we depend on you, our rock of safety.*

First Impressions

1. After the catechumens and candidates are seated, invite them to recall words and phrases from the Liturgy of the Word. Slowly include such words as: *blessing and curse— my rock of safety—Lord, Lord—who enters the kingdom of God—out of my sight—house built on rock and house built on sand.*
2. Ask the group: *What feelings, thoughts, insights do such word and phrases convey?* Invite them to turn to the person next to them and share their responses.
3. Then, slowly and deliberately, proclaim Deuteronomy 11:18, 26–28. Lead the participants in naming images from first reading by beginning with these phrases:
   take these words into your heart and soul
   bind them on your wrist
   let them be a pendant on your forehead
   set before you a blessing and a curse
   Invite them to add to this list.

Making Connections

1. Ask everyone to close their eyes as you guide them in this reflective exercise: *Imagine yourself in the crowd of people whom Moses is addressing.* Pause. *What do you see? What do you feel?* Pause. *Hear Moses speaking, "I set before you a blessing and a curse. A blessing if you obey the commandments of God; a curse if you turn away from God and his commandments in order to follow false gods."* Pause. *What tone of voice is Moses using? What choices are you being offered? How do you feel? What do you think of such a choice? What results from such a choice? What do you choose?* Pause.
2. Ask each participant to find a partner and direct the pairs to share a little about the experience of being in the crowd addressed by Moses. Then ask them to discuss the passage further, using these questions as a catalyst for this time of sharing. *What choices are before you today? How will you choose?*

3. After sufficient time, gather some responses from the candidates and catechumens. Summarize these in a few sentences. Invite all to write down their choice in the Participant Book on page 71 under the heading "I want to put my faith into action by."

Prayer

Invite everyone to the quiet of the moment. Then invite them to pray the refrain, *"God, you are our rock of safety"* after you pray each verse of the responsorial psalm, Psalm 31:2–3, 3–4, 17, 25.

Extended Catechesis

SESSION FOCUS: *Justification*

Gathering

A. Sunday:
1. Greet and welcome the sponsors and team members as they arrive. Invite them to join the circle of catechumens and candidates.
2. Ask one or two of the catechumens and candidates to summarize briefly their discussion during the dismissal catechesis for those who just joined the group.
3. Invite one of the team members to slowly and deliberately proclaim Matthew 7:2–27.

B. Weekday:
1. Use the same centerpiece as described for the Dismissal Catechesis.
2. As the participants gather in the circle, greet and warmly welcome each person. Invite all to share what experience they might have had over the past few days of God as our rock of safety.
3. Lead this celebration of the Word:
   * Song: Gathering Song from Sunday's Liturgy
   * First Reading: Deuteronomy 11:18, 26–28, 32
   * Sing the Psalm refrain from Sunday
   * Second Reading: Romans 3:21–25, 28
   * Alleluia
   * Gospel: Matthew 7:21–27

The Word (30 min.)

1. Gather the participants into small groups. Invite them to take a few minutes to quietly reflect on these questions, found in the Participant Book in Part I: *What do you understand by the phrase "Be hearers and doers of the Word"? Describe a time when you witnessed someone being a doer of the spoken Word.* When they seem ready, ask them to discuss and share their responses to these questions. Giving sufficient time for this discussion, focus the attention of everyone back to the large group and invite their insights and comments.

2. Continue in the small groups, asking them to read and discuss the following scenarios in the light of the gospel. Direct them to turn to page 70 in the Participant Book, Part II, to read through the scenarios, then guide them through the exercise in the following words: *Describe in what way the person is building a house on rock and retell the story from the perspective of a house built on sand.*

3. In the large group, invite the participants to share insights gained about the message of the gospel from the discussion of the scenarios.

Catholic Teaching (30 min.)

1. Slowly and deliberately proclaim Romans 3:21–25, 28. Explore Romans 3:21–25, 28 in these or similar words: *The heart of Paul's teaching is his insistence that we are all sinners, incapable of overcoming our sinfulness. Paul is clear in that only God can save us by the free gift of grace. That offer of grace has been revealed to us in the person of Jesus Christ, and it is our faith in Christ, not our observance of the Law, that opens us to the justice of God.*

When you are finished, lead the group in singing the first verse of "Amazing Grace."

2. Continue to present the Church's teaching on justification in these words: *The Catholic Church teaches that justification, our coming into a right relationship with God, is brought about by the action of God's grace through the salvation achieved by Jesus Christ. Individuals appropriate that justification by their faith-in-action.* Briefly tell the story of St. Francis of Assisi, emphasizing his response to God's invitation (grace) to give up his worldly ways to freely live a life of poverty.

3. Move deeper into the teaching by expanding on the following points. (The Catholic Doctrine section of Understanding this Sunday will be of help as you prepare this presentation.)

- The central lynchpin of the doctrine of justification is Jesus and his life, death, and resurrection. Through the Holy Spirit we are joined to Christ's suffering and death when we die to sin. In the same way, we are joined to Christ's resurrection when we are born again to eternal life in baptism. Conversion is characterized as the first work of the grace given by the Holy Spirit.
- The believer cannot embrace the message of salvation without also putting that Word into practice.

- Another approach to characterize justification is to describe it as the ground of cooperation between God's gift of grace and our human freedom.
- God holds out for us the possibility of conversion and believers accept this gift in faith.
- Individuals can choose to either accept or reject the grace of God.
- We need God's loving grace extended to us in order to enter into new life.
- Through God's grace, a free and generous act of God, believers are justified, that is, put into right relationship with the divine.

Conclude this teaching by leading all in singing the second verse of "Amazing Grace."

Putting Faith into Practice

1. Direct the participants back into small groups to discuss their understanding of this teaching. Then invite them to use their own words to describe God's gift of grace as it is present in their own life. Then ask them to share their thoughts on this question: *How can we, as individuals, respond to God's gift of grace?* Encourage a few groups to offer their ideas.

2. Distribute copies of a newspaper to each small group. Invite them to find at least one headline or article which demonstrates the choice that people have made to accept or reject God's gift of grace. Direct them to name the choice made and how it resulted in either a blessing or a curse. After each group has had an opportunity to share the results of their newspaper search, have them stay in their groups to ponder the gift of God's grace and our human freedom to accept or reject such grace.

3. Conclude by encouraging everyone to take time each day to describe the ways in which they are striving to put their faith into action. Suggest that each person ask herself or himself this question every evening: *Did I choose to accept all the graces God sent my way this day or did I reject his wondrous gift of love?* Propose that they write their thoughts in a journal.

Prayer

Ask the catechumens and candidates to stand in an inner circle. Sponsors and other team members stand behind and place a hand on their shoulder. After a few moments for quiet, pray the words of Minor Exorcism, (RCIA 93C). Lead them in singing the remaining verses of "Amazing Grace."

Tenth Sunday in Ordinary Time

The Word in Liturgy

Hosea 6:3–6
Psalm 50:1, 12–13, 14–15
Romans 4:18–25
Matthew 9:9–13

The prophet Hosea wrote during the eighth century, at a time of enormous turmoil in the Northern Kingdom. Today's reading is part of a longer section (5:8–6:6) in which the prophet castigates Israel for its infidelity to the covenant with Yahweh and calls for a sincere repentance and return to the Lord. Scholars situate this particular oracle in the year 734, when the Assyrians under Tiglath Pileser III were threatening Israelite territory. The people were offering prayers of entreaty for deliverance. In fact, the verses that open today's reading ("Let us know, let us strive to know the Lord") may be Hosea's parody of the empty rituals of his countrymen beseeching the Lord's intervention. Yahweh's reply ("Your piety is like a morning cloud, like the dew that early passes away") sums up the prophet's indictment of such worship that is offered without the corresponding dispositions of heart. What God wants is "love" (that is, *hesed,* the steadfast love that characterizes fidelity to the covenant—this is the verse quoted in today's gospel reading) and "knowledge of God," i.e., intimate, experiential knowledge that comes only when one is deeply involved in a relationship with the object of that knowledge, as is the case in sexual intercourse or within the intimacy of the family circle. Israel has demonstrated neither such love nor such knowledge, which is why Yahweh has "smote them through the prophets . . . slew them by the words of my mouth."

Today's psalm makes clear that it is not the fact of calling upon God in times of need that has earned the Lord's disfavor. In fact, the opposite is true. ("Call upon me in time of distress; I will rescue you.") In the spirit of Hosea's rejection of empty sacrifices, the verses used in today's liturgy are meant to relativize the value of mere ritual in God's eyes. ("Do I eat the flesh of strong bulls . . . ?") Still, Yahweh does not reject the notion of sacrifice ("Not for your sacrifices do I rebuke you"); rather, the Lord asks for the proper spirit to permeate Israel's worship ("Offer to God

praise . . ."). The point of the psalmist is identical with Hosea's: God wants our hearts, given over in love; nothing else really matters.

The focus chosen for today's catechesis springs from the gospel story of the unearned love shown by the Lord for Matthew the tax collector. Even before Matthew has repented of his sins, in fact, without any guarantee at all that he will change his ways, Matthew is loved by Jesus and called to discipleship. And, as if to underline the point that this is Jesus' ordinary way of doing business, the evangelist next describes Jesus sitting down at a table with Matthew and a host of other tax collectors and sinners. The Pharisees' shock and outrage at Jesus' welcome of the ritually impure and the outcast is put in deliberate contrast to the religious perspective of Jesus, who simply points out what he feels should be an obvious truth: "People who are in good health do not need a doctor; sick people do." Jesus even quotes Yahweh's words through Hosea, "It is mercy I desire and not sacrifice." Ritual impurity that bars one from participation in the official cult is not the issue for Jesus. Rather, his mission ("I have come to call not the self-righteous, but sinners") is to offer the gift of God—grace—to all those who are in need of it (i.e., to all of us) and to invite all people to accept that grace symbolized in his table fellowship with sinners.

Chapter 4 of Romans completes Paul's treatment of justification that began at 1:16. In this chapter Paul holds up the example of Abraham, whose "faith was credited to him as justice" (v. 22). Paul wants his Christian audience to recognize the heart of Abraham's faith, namely that his belief "that God could do whatever he had promised" (v. 21) corresponds with their own belief "in him who raised Jesus our Lord from the dead" (v. 24). Both Abraham and the Christian community have been given the gift (grace) of faith, the ability to put their trust in God to bring life from what, humanly speaking, seems dead. From Abraham's body, "which was as good as dead" (v. 19), life came forth, just as from the dead body of Jesus, God raised up new life. In accord with the focus of catechesis today, the catechist should point out that such faith is always God's gift (grace), not the result of any human accomplishment.

Catholic Doctrine

Grace

Justification derives from the grace of God. *Gratia* (Latin) means "favor" or "goodwill." In the broadest sense, this theological term indicates how the loving kindness of God has favored humanity. While still sinful, humanity has been offered help so that we might become adopted sons and daughters of the Most High, given a share in the divine nature and therefore receive eternal life (CCC 1996). The vocabulary of the New Testament reflects the depth of this mystery. For example, "favor," "reward," "gift," "loving kindness," "thanks," and "for the sake of" are differing descriptions used by the scriptural authors to indicate the love shown to us by God in the Son who gave himself for our sake (ColBibTheol, 399).

Theologians have long grappled with the concept of grace. Pelagius (d. 425 A.D.) espoused the view that if humans could not live good, upright lives without God's help, then they couldn't be held responsible for their sinful actions. St. Augustine (d. 430 A.D.) countered this heretical viewpoint, eloquently arguing that without Christ we could do nothing. The Church adopted St. Augustine's reasoning. This early dispute was just the beginning of the Church's reflection upon grace—scholasticism and its metaphysical turn, Trent and the Counter-Reformation, and modern writers such as Karl Rahner and Bernard Lonergan all helped to develop the Catholic understanding of God's favor shown to us in Jesus.

What, then, is the Catholic contemporary understanding of grace? The gift of God's favor enables humans to participate or share in the intimate love of Trinitarian life. Baptism incorporates us into the mystery of Christ whereby we adopted children of the Most High are enabled to call God our "Father" and Jesus our "brother," receiving new life from the Holy Spirit who immerses us in divine love (CCC 1997).

This sharing in divine love is further elaborated by several theological concepts: (1) sanctifying (or habitual) grace, (2) actual grace, and (3) sacramental grace. Each of these concepts builds one upon the other.

One's initiation into the love of God and new life is characterized as supernatural, beyond human nature, relying only on the gift of God. This gift given to us by God in Christ that heals and makes holy our souls once broken by sin is described as sanctifying grace. Sanctifying grace is a habitual gift, a stable, ongoing reality that makes us who we are in accordance with God's love. Sanctifying or habitual grace differs from actual grace—which is the special help or intervention God grants to us (CCC 2000). In addition, each sacrament gives the grace of God in a particular way proper to that sacrament which helps the believer to continue to grow in holiness and build up the body of Christ, the Church (CCC 2003).

What are the implications of all these theological terms? There are four main directions of the contemporary Catholic understanding of grace (ColBibTheol 400–01).

First, grace is understood as an experience of the present whose fullness will only be found in the future. That is, the way in which we are gifted in Jesus here and now is but a foretaste of that which will be fulfilled at the end of time. Thus, the early Christians prayed, "Let grace come and let this world pass away" (Didache 10:6, found in *The Heart of Catholicism*, Theodore E. James, ed., Our Sunday Visitor, Inc., Huntington, Indiana, 1997, p. 58).

Second, grace is universally offered to all, even those who are not yet explicit members of the Church. Thus, the Second Vatican Council affirmed, ". . . we must hold that the Holy Spirit offers to all the possibility of being made partners, in a way known to God, in the paschal mystery" (GS 22).

Third, grace transforms. Christ died for sinners, justifying us before God. Thus, because of God's utterly gratuitous gift we are changed for the better.

Fourth, grace opens us to participation or communion with divine life. What sin severed and scattered, Jesus reunites through his sacrifice and the Holy Spirit. Jesus acted not because we merited it, but because God has favored us.

Catholic Culture

The *Baltimore Catechism* taught that sacraments were channels of God's grace and compared the sacraments to ordinary experiences of human life to exemplify how they conferred sacramental grace. For example, the birth of a baby was compared to the new birth in Christ we have by baptism, the human need for bodily sustenance found in food was compared to the meal of the Eucharist that sustains our life in God's grace, and bodily sickness and wounds healed by medicine was compared with the sacrament of reconciliation that heals souls wounded by sin.

The cornucopia is a symbol deriving from pagan times depicting the "horn of plenty" overflowing with flowers, fruit, and corn sometimes associated with the goddess Ceres. In Christian art it symbolizes the bountiful and abundant grace we have from God the Father in Jesus which overflows through the power of the Spirit and makes of us a new creation.

Dismissal Catechesis (30 min.)

Getting Started

1. Prepare the space ahead of time with a circle of chairs around a table. Cover the table with a green cloth and place a candle on the table. Place fresh flowers and a cornucopia with various kinds of fruit and vegetables near the centerpiece. Provide a space for the Lectionary.

2. Invite the catechumens and candidates to gather and be seated in silence within the circle. Light the candle and pray in these or similar words: *Gracious God, you entered Matthew's life through your own goodness and love. Enter our lives more deeply. Move our hearts through the initiative of your grace. Speak your word ever more deeply in us. We ask this through Christ, our Savior. Amen.*

First Impressions

1. Invite the participants to gather in pairs to share their insights into the following: *What did you find inspiring about the celebration of the Word today? What can you recall from the sacred scriptures that touched your heart?* After they have shared, ask each pair to share some of their responses with everyone.

2. Draw the attention of the group to the following similarity in today's first and third readings in these or similar words: *The first reading from the prophet Hosea includes a sentence that appears several places in the Old Testament, "It is love that I desire, not sacrifice." Matthew's gospel passage that we heard today expresses a similar sentiment, "It is mercy I desire and not sacrifice."* Then ask them to discuss this question in the same pairs: *In what way do these statements connect with your experience and image of God?* After sufficient time, invite each pair to give a summary of their discussion in the light of this question to everyone.

Making Connections

1. Invite the large group to reflect upon and share their responses to the following question, saying: *Consider your experience and image of the God who desires love and mercy more than sacrifice, that is, the ritual offerings that were given to God as part of the religion of the people. God received these offerings that were supposed to be an expression of the people's true love for God, but in reality their hearts were far from him. How do you react when you receive a material gift, but know it was not given with love?* Briefly summarize the variety of examples that are shared.

2. Continue the discussion using the following words to deepen the understanding of the participants: *God's mercy and love are freely given, as certain as the dawn. The best way to respond is to freely give our love and mercy to others in turn. Yet we may fall into the trap of only giving when we expect that we will get something back.* Then ask the pairs to share: *What are some of the ways that you are called to show mercy to others freely, out of love, without expecting anything in return?*

3. After this discussion, distribute pieces of paper and ask the participants to write down some of the unearned favors of God they have received.

Prayer

Create a litany of thanksgiving by asking the participants to read aloud the favors they have received from God. Direct the group to respond, *"God has done great things for us, we are grateful,"* after each favor is named. Conclude by leading the participants in singing the first and second verses of "For the Beauty of the Earth" (Folliet S. Pierpoint, text, Lucerna Laudoniae, melody).

Extended Catechesis

SESSION FOCUS: *Grace*

Gathering

A. Sunday:

1. Welcome sponsors and other team members as they arrive. Invite them to join the circle of catechumens and candidates. Offer to the group a brief summary of the Dismissal Catechesis.

2. Begin by leading the group in singing several verses of "All You Works of God" (Marty Haugen, GIA Publications, 1989). Pray in these or similar words: *Gracious God, you are full of gifts and surprises. You are wonderful, full of love, overflowing with what is good for us. Help us be aware of all of the ways you gift us. Give us now the grace to share your Word. We pray through Jesus, your gift to us. Amen.*

3. Then invite the participants to enter today's gospel scene with these or similar meditative words: *Imagine yourself in Jerusalem with a crowd of people walking here and there in the afternoon sun. You notice a man near a government building. He is known to be a tax collector for the Romans. Jewish people were generally irritated that they had to abide by Roman rule and pay taxes. Their anger was directed at all tax collectors because of the injustices of the Roman rule, which they endured. Then you observe that Jesus approaches this despicable tax collector.* Proclaim the Gospel, Matthew 9:9–13.

B. Weekday:

1. As the group gathers in the circle, greet and welcome each person. Invite everyone to share a way they experienced the "favor" of the Lord in the past few days.
2. Lead this celebration of the Word:
   - Song: "All You Works of God"
   - Sign of the Cross, Greeting
   - First Reading: Hosea 6:3–6
   - Sing Psalm 50 or the Psalm sung at Sunday's liturgy
   - Introduce the gospel as in section A
   - Gospel: Matthew 9:9–13
   - Silent Reflection

The Word (30 min.)

1. Ask the participants to discuss this question in small groups: *What about this gospel passage most attracts your attention?* When the discussion is complete, ask each small group to present a brief report of the responses to everyone. Highlight or mention that Matthew did nothing to earn or deserve Jesus' invitation.
2. Then, ask the participants to respond aloud in the large gathering to these questions, asking them one at a time: *How do you think Matthew felt when Jesus said, "Follow me"? When have you had a similar feeling or experience?*
3. Present the following background to the scriptures: *Today's readings from Hosea and from the gospel speak of God's desire for love rather than sacrifice. The word used for love is* hesed, *which means "the steadfast love that characterizes fidelity to covenant." This love involves an intimate, experiential knowledge of God that is attained through a close relationship. In the gospel, it is striking that Jesus is eating with tax collectors and sinners. The Pharisees, good people who know and keep the law, are irritated with Jesus for offering his love to these tax collectors and sinners.*
4. When you have finished, ask the participants to reflect on the following questions: (They may write their responses to these questions in their Participant Book, page 73.) *In what ways do you identify with the self-righteous, who complain when the unworthy are blessed? In what ways do you identify with the tax collectors and sinners who receive the favor of Jesus?* When they are ready, have them share their responses in small groups. Then invite a brief sharing of their insights in the large group.

Catholic Teaching (30 min.)

1. Invite the whole group to think about the term "grace." After a short time, ask anyone who wishes to describe grace in a few words or by using an image.
2. Present the Catholic teaching on grace, making sure to include the following points:
   - Matthew experienced God's grace—in Latin, *gratia*—thanks or favor. Jesus simply entered his life. Grace is a free gift of God and is never the result of any human accomplishment.
   - Grace is the self-gift of God's life within us. Through grace we share in the intimate love of the Trinity. Because of grace we are able to call God our "Father" and Jesus our "brother."
   - Over the course of history, the Church has struggled to identify the relationship between grace and good works. From the time of St. Augustine (d. 430) the Church has held that the good we do is through, with, and in Christ, rather than from our own power.
   - The Church identifies three types of grace. Sanctifying grace is an ongoing, habitual gift that makes us who we are in accordance with God's love. It is supernatural or beyond human nature. Actual grace is given to us as a special help at particular times or for special acts. In participating in the sacraments we encounter God's gift of life or grace in particular ways proper to that sacrament; this is called sacramental grace.
   - Four aspects of grace characterize its Catholic understanding. Grace is experienced in the present and will be brought to fulfillment at the end of time. Grace is universally offered to all. Grace transforms us into the living body of Christ. Grace opens up the way for our communion with divine life.
3. Ask the participants to share an experience of being "graced" by God in their small groups.

Or . . .

Invite someone from the parish to share their experience of God's abundant grace with the group.

Putting Faith into Practice

1. Ask the participants to brainstorm ways to be more attentive to God's grace in their ordinary daily lives. These might include prayer, silence and reflection, thanking God each night for the gifts of the day, journaling, reading scriptures. Encourage them to choose one or two ways they will commit to being attentive to God's grace this week. Ask everyone to write this commitment in the section "I want to put my faith into action by" on page 73 of the Participant Book.
2. Direct the participants to share their choices with their small group.

Prayer

Gathering back to the large group, invite participants into a moment of quiet, asking them to be present to the grace of being called to follow Jesus. Celebrate the Minor Exorcism found in *RCIA #941*, asking the catechumens and candidates to bow or kneel as their sponsors and godparents place a hand on their shoulder. When this minor rite is finished, invite each person to take a piece of fruit, a vegetable, or a flower from the cornucopia as a sign of God's free gift of grace. Lead all in singing "Amazing Grace" as they come to the center of the circle in a prayerful openness to the gifts of the earth.

Eleventh Sunday in Ordinary Time

Understanding this Sunday:
Background for Catechesis

The Word in Liturgy

Exodus 19:2–6
Psalm 100:1–2, 3, 5
Romans 5:6–11
Matthew 9:36–10:8

Chapter 19 of Exodus begins the story of the *theophany* on Mount Sinai, a story that continues throughout the remainder of this book, the entire book of Leviticus, and concludes at Numbers 10:10. The story is a substantial one, not only in terms of its literary size but also for its impact on Israelite history and identity. Today's beginning of that story captures the essence of its significance both for the Jewish people and for us in the Christian dispensation. The figure of Moses is established as the mediator between God and the people, and God's offer to enter into a covenant with the people is rooted in the events of the Exodus ("You have seen for yourselves . . ."). The conditions of the covenant are set forth (to listen to God's voice and to follow the prescriptions of the Law) as are the rewards of doing so ("You shall be my special possession . . . a kingdom of priests").

All of these themes are reworked in a Christian ecclesiology that sees the Church as the new Israel of God. Christ is the new Moses (an emphasis found especially in the gospel of Matthew), mediator between God and the new chosen people. The Passover of Jesus from death to life is the new Exodus which grounds our sacred history and forges our core identity. The demands and benefits of the ancient covenant with Moses are all reinterpreted in Christian terms by the royal priesthood (1 Peter 2:9) of the baptized, who are still charged to hear God's Word and put it into practice (cf. Matthew 7:21–27, and the Beatitudes read earlier this year).

Psalm 100 is a thanksgiving psalm used on the occasion of a "thank offering" in the temple, a joyous occasion when the people gathered for feasting and worship. The imagery of the people as God's flock is frequent in both the Jewish and Christian scriptures and always evokes the abiding care and protection that Yahweh shows toward his chosen ones. The choice of this psalm here is undoubtedly guided by the gospel's reference to the crowds "like sheep without a shepherd" (9:36) and the disciples being sent to the "lost sheep of the house of Israel" (10:6).

The opening verses of today's gospel reading provide us with the motivation (compassion) for the ministry of Jesus, a ministry which Matthew has described at length in the section just concluded (4:23–9:35) as consisting of teaching and miracles of healing. Beginning this new section at 9:36, Matthew establishes Jesus' will to share his ministry with his disciples, entrusting to those he has chosen a mission whose contours are virtually identical to his own ministry. The restriction of their activity to the children of Israel may reflect the actual chronology of the Christian mission after the resurrection, or the particular missionary thrust of the community for which Matthew was writing. This week's catechetical focus on the mystery of the Church can certainly find in this rich ecclesiological text ample material for reflection. Matthew's description of the call of the Twelve and the mission entrusted to them have been highly significant for the self-understanding of every subsequent generation of Christians.

The theme of grace chosen for last week's catechesis finds a powerful echo in today's reading from Romans. Paul is passionate about the undeserved quality of God's love for us "while we were still sinners" (v. 8). The word Paul uses here for love is *agape*, selfless love, which is based not on the attractiveness of its object (us sinners) but on the goodness of the one offering the gift. It is important to note the concrete form that love has taken in the death of Jesus, offered for our salvation. This passage is a key text for understanding Paul's opposition to justification based on fulfillment of the Law. Justification is the undeserved, freely given gift of God's love, revealed in the death and resurrection of Jesus, that has saved us ("justified by his blood . . . reconciled to him by the death of his son . . . saved by his life").

Catholic Doctrine

The Mystery of the Church

The Latin term for church, *ecclesia*, derives from the Greek (*ek ka lein*), which means "to call out of," referring to an assembly of people or a gathering together. While the term "church" can indicate a special building designated for worship, as in "St. Patrick's Church," the reality that we will explore in this doctrine essay is the deeper meaning of the word "Church," that is, the people of God who are constituted in Christ by the work of the Holy Spirit. This Church is a visible reality, an organized society that can be seen and heard in this world and our history, and yet it is also a spiritual reality which transcends this world and time as the medium of divine life (CCC 770).

As God's medium bearing divine life, the Church has been described, first and foremost, by the Second Vatican Council as a mystery, "in the nature of sacrament—a sign and instrument, that is, of communion with God and of unity among all. . ." (LG 1). The depths of this mystery are founded upon Christ and the work of the Holy Spirit, and therefore this mystery which is the Church continues to grow toward maturity as it longs for the fullness of the completed kingdom of God (LG 5). This mystery is so rich that the Council invoked five key scriptural images in its reflection upon the Church.

Thus, the Council described the Church as a *sheepfold*, the "sole and necessary gateway to which is Christ." It also used the image of a *cultivated field* or the tillage of God—a choice vineyard wherein Christ is the vine and we are the branches—to describe the Church. The Council described the Church as the *building of God* whose foundation is Jesus Christ, the stone rejected by the builders but which is now the cornerstone of the whole edifice of the house of God, the dwelling place of the divine among people, and the holy temple come down from heaven. Furthermore, the Council described the Church as *that Jerusalem which is above*, clearly referring to the spiritual nature of the new Jerusalem described in the book of Revelation, whose roots are embedded in the Old Testament people of God. Finally, the Council described the Church as *our mother*, the spotless spouse of the spotless Lamb of God whom Christ loves and sacrifices himself for that we might be made holy (LG 6).

The whole purpose of the Church can be summarized as serving the plan of God to bring all people into communion with the divine. This missionary mandate is at the heart of the good news proclaimed by the Church in all its activities, sacraments, and outreach (CCC 849 and AG 1). Our Catholic understanding of the goal of the Church, therefore, is that it is called to make holy the members of Christ's body (CCC 772). Thus, the gift of love given to the Church by its spouse, Jesus Christ, is received and the members of the Church respond in love. This is also the reason why the Council and subsequent Church teaching refers to the Church itself as a kind of sacrament, for the grace of God is both contained within and communicated by the mystery of the Church (CCC 774).

In dedicating a new church building for worship, St. Augustine (d. 430) preached to the people, referring to both the visible and invisible realities of the body founded by Christ's love. He reflected, "We are gathered together to celebrate the dedication of a house of prayer. This is our house of prayer, but we too are a house of God. If we are a house of God, its construction goes on in time so that it may be dedicated at the end of time. . . . What was done when this church was being built is similar to what is done when believers are built up into Christ. When they first come to believe they are like timber and stone taken from woods and mountains. In their instruction, baptism and formation they are, so to speak, shaped, leveled and smoothed by the hands of carpenters and craftsmen. But Christians do not make a house of God until they are one in charity. The timber and stone must fit together in an orderly plan, must be joined in perfect harmony, must give each other the support as it were of love, or no one would enter the building. . . . The work we see complete in this building is physical; it should find its spiritual counterpart in your hearts. We see here the finished product of stone and wood; so too your lives should reveal the handiwork of God's grace" (Sermon 336, 1.6: PL 38 [edit. 1861], 1471–72. 1475 found in LitHrs, vol. 4, pp. 1607–08).

Catholic Culture

In the ritual for dedicating a house of worship, the Church prays, "Here is foreshadowed the mystery of your true temple; this church is the image on earth of your heavenly city. For you made the body of your Son born of the Virgin a temple consecrated to your glory, the dwelling place of your godhead in all its fullness. You have established the Church as your holy city, founded on the apostles, with Jesus Christ its cornerstone. You continue to build your Church with chosen stones, enlivened by the Spirit, and cemented together by love. In that holy city you will be all in all for endless ages, and Christ will be its light for ever" (*Sacramentary*, Appendix VIII, Preface for Dedication of a Church).

The very shape of Catholic church buildings indicates the mystery of the Church assembled therein. Some are built in the shape of a cross to remind people of the loving sacrifice of Jesus made on our behalf. Some are eight-sided to emphasize the "eighth day" of creation (that is, the eternal "day" of new life with God that never ends). Some are round, symbolizing universality.

Dismissal Catechesis (30 min.)

Getting Started

1. Prepare the space ahead of time with a circle of chairs around a table, draped with a green cloth, upon which is placed a candle. Have a processional cross or another large cross on a stand in a prominent place near the table.
2. Invite the catechumens and candidates to be seated in the circle. Place the Lectionary on the table and light the candle. Pause for a moment of quiet and then pray in these or your own words: *God of the covenant, you have made us your holy people, a kingdom of priests, a holy nation. You speak your living Word to our hearts. You care for us tenderly as a shepherd. Open our ears and hearts that we become more attentive to your call. Speak your word in our midst this day. Amen.* Sing a setting of Psalm 100, such as *"We Are God's People"* (David Haas, GIA Publications, 1983), or whatever version was sung in today's liturgy.

First Impressions

1. Begin the discussion by offering this background on the first reading from Exodus 19:2–6:
   In the nineteenth chapter of the Book of Exodus that was proclaimed today, the story of Moses' encounter with God on Mount Sinai was heard in our midst. Moses was the mediator between God and the people of Israel. God entered into a covenant relationship with the Jewish people and this covenant is ours through Jesus, the new Moses. Listen closely to this reading, noticing the images and phrases that engage your imagination.
   Proclaim Exodus 19:2–6. Then invite them to share aloud the images and phrases that touched them.
2. Summarize their responses in a few sentences. Be sure to include in your summary the words: *"I bore you up on eagle wings," "you shall be my special possession, dearer to me than all other people,"* and *"kingdom of priests, a holy nation."*
3. Then ask the participants to discuss the following questions with a partner: *What message do you perceive regarding God's relationship with you in these images and phrases? How does this passage affect your life, as you journey toward initiation in this community of faith?* When they are finished, invite each pair to share their responses with everyone.

Making Connections

1. Once again, gather the participants into pairs to share their responses to these questions: *What feelings arise in you as you realize that the God of Israel desires to be in a covenant relationship with you? What is your reaction to the fact that the Creator of this universe thinks of you as holy? A special possession?* Encourage each pair to share some of their discussion with everyone.

2. Deepen their understanding of this passage by emphasizing the fact that God did not only invite people as individuals but, indeed, gathered and formed a whole people. In the large group initiate a discussion on the significance of this for the communities of faith and the peoples of the world by raising this question: *What does it mean for you that you are part of a Church, a whole nation of people, whom God invites into this close relationship?* As the discussion winds down, summarize their responses.
3. Ask the participants to share their response to this question: *What is one thing you want to remember from today's sharing?* Encourage them to write this down in the Participant Book on page 75 under the section "I want to remember."

Prayer

Introduce the prayer by saying: *As we pray, sense inside yourselves that you, along with many other people, are God's people. As God's people, let us listen once again as God speaks the words of the covenant to our lives.* Proclaim or ask a team member to proclaim the Exodus reading, beginning with verse 4, God's words, *"You have seen for yourselves,"* and ending at verse 6 with the words *"a holy nation"* (Exodus 19:4–6). Lead all in singing the refrain of Psalm 100, "We Are God's People" (David Haas, GIA, 1983), or whatever setting was sung in the liturgy, inviting them to stand as they sing.

Extended Catechesis

SESSION FOCUS: *The Mystery of the Church*

Gathering

A. **Sunday:**
1. Greet and welcome the sponsors and team members as they arrive. Invite them to join the circle of catechumens and candidates.
2. Begin the prayer by leading the group in the hymn *"The Church's One Foundation"* (Samuel John Stone, text, and Samuel Sebastian Wesley, melody). Provide songbooks so that all may join in singing. Then together pray Psalm 100. Provide copies of the psalm printed in verses as indicated in the Lectionary. Invite all to join in singing the refrain, *"We Are God's People"* (or some other setting of the psalm refrain) after each verse.
3. Prepare the participants to hear the gospel using these or your own words: *In today's passage from Matthew's gospel, the names of the twelve apostles are enumerated. The word "apostle" means one who is sent. Listen closely to this reading, aware of the meanings and insights that emerge in you as you hear God's Word once again.* Proclaim Matthew 9:36–10:8.

B. Weekday:

1. As the group gathers in the circle, greet each participant and light the candle. Invite everyone to think about the past few days and share a situation in which they were aware of being part of God's people.
2. Lead this celebration of the Word:
   - Song: "The Church's One Foundation," verses 1 and 2
   - Greeting, Sign of the Cross
   - First Reading: Exodus 19:2–6
   - Sing Psalm 100
   - Introduction to today's gospel as above in A
   - Gospel: Matthew 9:36–10:8
   - Song: "The Church's One Foundation," verses 3 and 4

The Word (30 min.)

1. Ask the participants to name the phrases that stand out for them from the gospel passage. Add these phrases if they are not mentioned: *Jesus was moved with pity—the people were like sheep without a shepherd—laborers are needed for the harvest—the disciples were given authority to cast out unclean spirits and cure disease—the disciples are sent to preach to the lost sheep of Israel—the reign of God is at hand.*
2. Invite the participants to reflect on the following questions: *What are some examples of how you experience being part of the mission of Jesus? In what ways do you help to bring about the reign of God?* Page 74 in the Participant Book is designed to help their contemplation of the gospel. When they are finished, invite them to discuss their responses in small groups.
3. Elicit in the large group examples of ways they experience participating in Jesus' mission. Make these points: *Jesus' mission consists of preaching the Good News, healing the sick, and expelling demons. This same mission is entrusted to his disciples. We, today's disciples, continue to carry out the mission of Jesus.* Then ask this question: *What is your response to the task of carrying out Jesus' mission today?* Allow time for discussion about these feelings and reactions.

Catholic Teaching (30 min.)

1. Begin to share the teaching on the mystery of the Church with this statement and question: *God sends us, the Church, to continue the mission of Christ in the world today. When you think of the word "Church," what associations come to mind?* Elicit their responses and list them on newsprint.
2. Then, referring to their insights, present the following points about the Church. Write the words in italics on newsprint or an overhead transparency before the presentation:
   - The Latin term for "Church," *ecclesia,* refers to an assembly or gathering together of people, rather than the building designated for worship. The Second Vatican Council defined the Church as the *People of God,* who are constituted in Christ through the Holy Spirit.

- The Church is both a *visible reality,* an organized society that exists in our world and history, and a timeless *spiritual reality* that transcends this world and time.
- The Church is a *mystery,* and it is a *sacrament,* that is, a sign and instrument of a deeper reality. As a sacrament, the Church both contains within itself and communicates the grace of God.
- The Church's goal is to make holy the members of Christ's body through the gift of love given by its spouse, Jesus Christ. Thus, the Church continues the *mission of Christ* to bring about the reign of God in this world.
- Vatican Council II uses five images to describe the Church. The Church is a *sheepfold* or gateway to Christ. It is a cultivated *field* or *vineyard* with Christ as the vine and people as the branches. The Church is a *building of God* whose foundation and cornerstone is Jesus Christ. The Church is also the *New Jerusalem* described in the Book of Revelation. And, finally, the Church is *our mother,* the spotless spouse of the spotless Lamb of God, Christ, who sacrificed himself that we might be made holy.

3. Invite the participants back to the same small groups to share their understanding of the Church's teaching on the mystery of the Church by directing them in this exercise: *Choose one of the images from the newsprint (or overhead transparency) that appeals to you. Express your understanding of this term and its significance for you.* When they are finished, invite each small group to share their insights with the large gathering.
4. Then ask the participants to brainstorm, giving concrete examples to illustrate what it means for them to be "Church."

Putting Faith into Practice

Ask the participants to reflect on this question: *What is one action you are willing to commit to this week as a way of living your identity and mission as Church?* Encourage participants to write their responses in the "I want to put my faith into action by" section of the Participant Book on page 75. When they are finished reflecting, ask them to share their commitment in their small group.

Prayer

Focus the attention of the group on the cross, and make this statement:
We the Church have as our foundation Jesus Christ. On the day of our baptism, for those of us already baptized, or at the Rite of Acceptance for those who are catechumens, we were claimed for Christ by the sign of the cross. I invite sponsors once again to trace the cross on the one you are sponsoring, from head to foot, and shoulder to shoulder. Celebrate the Minor Exorcism found in RCIA 94H. Have the catechumens bow or kneel with their sponsors placing a hand on their shoulders. Conclude by singing together "We Are Called" (David Haas, GIA Publications, 1988).

Twelfth Sunday in Ordinary Time

Understanding this Sunday:
Background for Catechesis

The Word in Liturgy

Jeremiah 20:10–13
Psalm 69:8–10, 14, 17, 33–35
Romans 5:12–15
Matthew 10:26–33

More than those of any other prophet, Jeremiah's writings reveal a wealth of autobiographical insight that allow us to understand the human drama of the man and his calling. His vocation to be a prophet (ca. 627 B.C., during the reign of Josiah) was accepted only reluctantly (Jeremiah 1:6), and with God's assurance of divine protection (1:8). The reality of his life, however, was that Jeremiah endured years of rejection and overt persecution as a result of the unpopular message he was sent to deliver. Today's selection comes from one of the so-called "Confessions" of Jeremiah, an intensely personal outpouring of anguish at a time following his conflict with the priest Pashur, when attempts were being made on his life in order to silence him. The verses chosen for today's reading allude to the betrayal and plotting of those close to him, and give voice as well to the prophet's unshakable conviction that Yahweh will ultimately vindicate him. His confidence in God's deliverance was held up by Christian authors as an image of Jesus' own trust in God and as an example to be followed by Jesus' disciples. Jeremiah's prayer to see vengeance wreaked on his persecutors was replaced, however, by Jesus' call for forgiveness of one's enemies.

Psalm 69 is a lament which would have been used during a worship service by an individual undergoing a time of personal suffering. In form and content it is reminiscent of Psalm 22. The details of the author's suffering are not spelled out with clarity, but these verses surely would have fit Jeremiah's circumstances. The final verses quoted (vv. 33–35) are the concluding section which contains words of praise in view of God's anticipated intervention. Like Jeremiah, the psalmist's confidence is absolute that Yahweh will bring deliverance.

Last Sunday, we heard Jesus send his disciples out on mission. His mandate is accompanied by a series of instructions in chapter 10 that should characterize the Christian missionary effort. This week and next, we continue to read from those instructions. Today's text contains a threefold admonition not to be afraid. Reflecting the Matthean community's firsthand knowledge of persecution and even martyrdom, Jesus' words acknowledge the reality that many may meet with death because they are his disciples. Nonetheless, in the spirit of Jeremiah and Psalm 69, Jesus uses the homey images of sparrows being watched over and the hairs on one's head being counted by the Father to point out that God's care and providence will sustain his followers. Matthew makes a point of including Jesus' warning that his disciples must witness publicly to him before those who would persecute them. One can understand the pastoral importance of such a warning in the climate of persecution in which Matthew's community lived.

In Romans 5:12, Paul begins to compare the first man, Adam, with Jesus. Through the one man (Adam) sin and death entered the world, while through the other (Jesus) came obedience and life. But before Paul gets to complete the second part of his comparison, he digresses in verses 13–14 on death reigning from Adam to the time of Moses and then to the time of the Messiah. (Paul is reflecting a common rabbinic division of time into three 2,000-year eras.) Then, in verse 15, Paul returns to complete his previous thought that through Jesus the gift ("the grace of God") was given, a gift "much more" powerful than the death brought through Adam. Augustine and the Council of Trent interpreted Paul as referring to what came later to be called the doctrine of original sin; but we note that Paul's primary intent here is a positive exposition of the work of grace wrought by God in Christ, not a dogmatic statement on original sin.

Catholic Doctrine

Persecution and Suffering

The deprivation and pain involved in mental, physical, spiritual, or emotional suffering is an inevitable part of the human experience. In addition, those believers who stand up for gospel values and the message of the kingdom of God may find themselves persecuted for their stance. Meaning, significance, and a transforming purpose can be found in these trials, however, when they are undergone in union with Christ. God does not promise to take away all pain and suffering, yet the affirmation that God is our deliverance is a thread running throughout both Old and New Testaments. The deliverance of God is often experienced as an abiding presence to the faithful in their suffering.

Both Old and New Testament scriptural figures undergo pain and suffering because they are faithfully following God's call, such as the prophet Jeremiah and the Suffering Servant of Isaiah. Saint Stephen is stoned to death for his faith in the Christ. Saints Peter and Paul are persecuted and eventually put to death for their devotion to the Son of God.

The history of the early Christian Church too is replete with the example of martyrs who witnessed to the faith through the shedding of their blood. Catholics celebrate this witness even today in the liturgical cycle. Our Church calendar contains feasts and solemnities in observance of the deaths of the martyrs whose blood was the seed of the early Christian community. Through the eyes of faith we see their deaths as triumphs and victories, testimonies of God's love overcoming evil, sin, and the difficulty of human suffering. On these feast days, the Church prays to God, "[Their] death reveals your power shining through our human weakness. You choose the weak and make them strong in bearing witness to you, through Jesus Christ our Lord" (*Sacramentary*, Preface 66). The word itself, *martyr*, in Greek means "witness." This witness to the faith is not limited to the early history of the Church. From those foundational days to the present, martyrs have shed their blood in faithfulness to the God who loves us.

There is, of course, a certain tension involved theologically and existentially, in this contemplation of persecution and suffering when there are so many scriptural texts that emphasize God's providence and protection. However, it is important to note that God is not the author of suffering and pain. Suffering is linked to natural, worldly processes and, in a biblical and theological view, to the misuse of free will resulting in the fall of humanity from its original graced state. Thus, God in Jesus plunged into our human experience and endured what we ourselves endure, that is, suffering and death, in order to offer us salvation. God's mercy holds out to us the salve (from the same Latin root word for "salvation")

for our wounded natures. The love God bears for us in Jesus overcame death and, through the experience of suffering and the tomb, the "infinite force of this love has broken through even into his body, transforming him into the risen, life-giving Lord of the universe" (NDictTheol 991). Believers respond to the difficulty and pain of human suffering and persecution by personally appropriating through prayer, sacraments, and Christian solidarity the healing power of Christ's resurrection, understanding that what one suffers may ultimately be redemptive.

John Paul II has written in an encyclical concerning the difficulty believers may endure as a result of living faithfully in the modern world. He cites the example of events in Eastern Europe prior to the year 1989, as communism eroded and countless members of the Church suffered together as a result of their peaceful resistance to totalitarianism. He notes, "Undoubtedly, the struggle which led to the changes of 1989 called for clarity, moderation, suffering and sacrifice. In a certain sense, it was a struggle born of prayer, and it would have been unthinkable without immense trust in God, the Lord of history, who carries the human heart in his hands. It is by uniting their own sufferings, for the sake of truth and freedom, to the sufferings of Christ on the Cross that [they were] able to accomplish the miracle of peace . . ." (*Centesimus annus*, May 1, 1991, 25.1 found in *The Encyclicals of John Paul II*, J. Michael Miller, C.S.B., ed., Our Sunday Visitor, Inc., Huntington, Indiana, p. 612).

Not every persecuted or suffering believer can claim such signs of success in the world. The true miracle and sign of success will always remain God's love poured out for us in Jesus.

Catholic Culture

The traditional Catholic color for Mass vestments on a martyr's feast day is red, denoting blood shed for the sake of the faith. Red is also, however, the liturgical color signifying the Holy Spirit. As such, there is a double meaning in the use of red on martyrs' feast days, for it is only in the Spirit that the martyr could endure the pain of suffering.

The text of the sacrament of the sick reminds the person enduring sickness and pain of the love and power of God in their life. Indeed, the *Roman Ritual* even contains a prayer of blessing to assist those suffering from addiction or substance abuse. The text of the prayer not only calls upon God to heal the condition of the person who is addicted but refers to those who in solidarity with that person work for restoration and recovery: "Lord, look with compassion on all those who have lost their health and freedom. Restore to them the assurance of your unfailing mercy, and strengthen them in the work of recovery. To those who care for them, grant patient understanding and a love that perseveres" (BB 422).

Dismissal Catechesis (30 min.)

Getting Started

1. Prepare the space ahead of time with a circle of chairs around a table draped with a green cloth. You may choose to arrange several strips of red, magenta, charcoal, and gray fabric over the green fabric in a tasteful design. Prepare a pottery or metal vessel with incense.

2. Lead the candidates and catechumens to the circle and place the Lectionary on the table and light the incense. Pray in these or similar words: *Yahweh, we bring our prayers before you today. Evil surrounds us and we are terrified. Pain and sickness threaten those we hold dear, and we cry out to you. Friends have betrayed us and abandoned us, and we are brokenhearted. Nations and peoples war against one another and we feel powerless. The violence in families fills us with grief. We ask that your Word fill us with hope and confidence as we sing your praises. Amen.*

First Impressions

1. Invite the participants to share some of the details they remember from the Gathering Song, the prayers, and the scriptures in today's Liturgy of the Word.

2. Explain the intimacy of our relationship to God in these words: *God is aware of our every fear and concern. Therefore, to come before God and lament the situations that distress and make us afraid is a positive and realistic response. In today's scriptures, both Jeremiah and the psalmist present their outpouring of anguish to the Lord. They can praise God because of their confidence in Yahweh's deliverance.*

3. Ask each person to turn to the individual on their right and discuss these questions: *What evils in the world terrify you? What helps you believe that God is more powerful than any of these?* Invite a few responses from the pairs and conclude by briefly summarizing their insights.

Making Connections

1. Explain the significance of the second reading from Romans 5:12–15 in these words: *In comparing Adam with Christ, Paul is speaking in a corporate sense. For him, everything is interdependent. Adam, the first human, introduced the social effects of sin and evil (death) into the world. His choice affects all of us. Similarly, Christ, the head of the new humanity, introduced salvation (life), freeing humanity from sin and death. Christ's gift of God's grace affects all of humanity. We are comforted by the knowledge that God's grace is more powerful than sin, that goodness will never be overcome by evil.*

2. Invite the same pairs to join together to share their responses to these questions: *When have you experienced goodness as more powerful than evil? How does the Christ-event assuage your fears? Where do you find comfort in times of misunderstanding or persecution?*

3. Gather the pairs back to the large setting and invite some to share the insights gained from this discussion. Summarize their comments and invite everyone to think of one thing that they wish to remember from this session. These may be recorded in their Participant Book on page 77 in the section called "Things I want to remember."

Prayer

Re-light the incense and invite all to recall silently any situations that are frightening or troubling. Encourage them to name those situations aloud as the group prays in silence. Close by distributing copies of Psalm 69:8–10, 14, 17, 33–35 to the group and inviting all to pray this lament together as they watch the incense rising up to God with their prayers.

Extended Catechesis

SESSION FOCUS: *Persecution and Suffering*

Gathering

A. Sunday:

1. Greet and welcome everyone as they arrive. Invite them to join the circle of catechumens and candidates.

2. With the incense still burning, invite all to join in singing the Gathering Song from today's Liturgy of the Word. Pray in these or your own words: *God, we cry out to you and you hear our prayers. We seek your strength and you look with great kindness upon your people. You have showered us with the graces and blessings won for us by Jesus. Hear us now as we look to you with confidence. Your mercy is endless and your love is everlasting! Keep us ever in your caring gaze through Jesus, your Son. Amen.*

3. Invite a team member to proclaim the first reading, Jeremiah 20:10–13. Lead the group in singing the verse from Psalm 69, *"Lord, in your great love, answer me."* Invite all to stand and listen as a sponsor proclaims the gospel, Luke 10:26–33. Indicate that all be seated to reflect on this Word of God as the incense rises.

B. Weekday:

1. Use the same centerpiece as in the Dismissal Catechesis.

2. As the participants gather in the circle, greet and warmly welcome each person. Encourage anyone who wishes to share any experience they might have had of good overcoming evil during these past few days.

3. Lead this celebration of the Word:
   - Song: Gathering Song from Sunday's liturgy
   - First Reading: Jeremiah 20:10–13
   - Sing Psalm 69
   - Gospel: Luke 10:26–33
   - Silent reflection

The Word (30 min.)

1. Invite the group to share what they think it means to "trust in God for deliverance." Then ask everyone to close their eyes and bring to mind a time when they experienced great fear. After a few moments ask anyone who wishes to share what they did to overcome these fears.

2. Explain the background for the first reading and the gospel, using the information found in the Word in Liturgy, being sure to include these points:

   - The reluctant prophet Jeremiah was so frank in his "confessions" to God that he reveals quite a bit about his personality. He endured years of rejection and persecution because of the unpopular message of Yahweh he was compelled to deliver.

   - Both Psalm 69 and this first reading are an honest expression of personal torment and suffering to God, undergirded by the absolute confidence that God will intervene. The question is not "if" God will deliver the persecuted, but "when."

   - The gospel passage follows the sending of Jesus' disciples out on mission. The instructions offered to them are meant for followers of Jesus today.

   - The ministry and teaching of Jesus and, therefore, that of his followers, is countercultural. The challenge to radical living and preaching of the message of Jesus is difficult and will bring persecution and ridicule.

   - Yet we need not fear because we are watched over by a God who knows every time a sparrow "lights" on the ground. This caring God will sustain the disciples and Jesus' followers today, because God is aware of the minute details of our struggles.

3. Ask the participants to gather into small groups to share their understanding of God's Word, using these questions: *What examples can you cite that indicate the Christian way of life is countercultural? What ridicule or persecution have you had to endure because of your beliefs and values? How has this ever-watchful God sustained you in a time of suffering or anguish?* When the discussion diminishes, draw the attention of the participants back to the large gathering. Invite each group to name two new key awarenesses they have gained.

Catholic Teaching (30 min.)

1. Explain the Church's teaching on persecution and suffering in these or your own words:
   The human experience includes suffering in all its forms. The human pain of chronic illness, the emotional pain of grief, and the spiritual pain of desolation are all within the range of our daily existence. God does not cause suffering and pain. Suffering can be the result of natural, or worldly processes or of the misuse of free will. We are sometimes the cause of human suffering and we are often its recipients. Yet we profess a God of mercy who forgives us when we fail to choose the good. We believe that Jesus plunged into the human experience and endured what we endure—suffering, persecution, and death. Our wounds are the pathway of our salvation. Our sufferings lead to deeper reliance on God's power to deliver us. God's power is like a light shining through human weakness, revealing our basic

dependence upon the healing power of Christ's resurrection. Our suffering is ultimately redemptive. However, suffering and persecution could not be endured if it were not for the power of the Holy Spirit, the redemption of Jesus, and the providential care of God.

2. Encourage everyone to turn to the Reflection exercise in their Participant Book on page 76 and quietly journal their thoughts and experiences. When most seem to be finished, invite the catechumens and candidates to join with their sponsor and/or godparent to share whatever they choose.

3. Continue by asking the participants to reflect on the questions posed on the same page. Invite them to share their thoughts in the same small groups. Encourage them to share their thoughts on prayer during times of suffering and persecution with the whole group.

Putting Faith into Practice

1. Share with the group an experience with which you are familiar of people suffering for the sake of the gospel. Perhaps you know of the missionaries killed in El Salvador, the struggles of people in a totalitarian country, a family in anguish over a tragedy, or whole neighborhoods struggling with violence and crime. When you have finished, invite participants to name several other groups of people who are enduring great pain.

2. Invite the group to suggest several ways in which we can be a community of support for these people. Name some of the parish outreach programs that entail working with the grieving, the divorced, and those in physical, mental, or spiritual pain. Encourage sponsors to take their catechumen or candidate to one of the events or gatherings of these groups.

3. Encourage everyone to join together in daily prayer at a set time of day for those who are suffering in silence in the parish or neighboring community.

Prayer

Gather for prayer by lighting incense and playing soft instrumental music as a background to the reflection. Encourage the participants to pray in the silence of their hearts for someone, known or unknown, who is suffering at this moment. Close with this litany of lament, asking all to respond to the petitions with, *"God, look with compassion on your people."*

For all those families who have witnessed and suffered the pain of cancer in someone they love . . .

For those who are suffering cancer's disparaging disintegration . . .

For those who suffer torment and torture because of political or religious beliefs . . .

For people everywhere who have experienced the violence of crime or abuse . . .

For those suffering the dark unknown void of mental illness . . .

For those who cannot believe in your compassionate mercy . . .

For anyone struggling to survive persecution and ridicule. . .

For what do you wish to pray? . . .

Pause and encourage the group to name additional prayers. Close by leading all in singing a verse of the Gathering Song from Sunday's liturgy.

Thirteenth Sunday in Ordinary Time

Understanding this Sunday:
Background for Catechesis

The Word in Liturgy

2 Kings 4:8–11, 14–16
Psalm 89:2–3, 16–17, 18–19
Romans 6:3–4, 8–11
Matthew 10:37–42

The suggested catechetical focus today is based on the second reading's teaching on baptism as participation in the paschal mystery of Christ. This teaching is of particular interest to those in a catechumenal setting. To understand Paul's thought here, it is important to remember that the baptism ritual in Paul's day involved an immersion in water, not just the pouring of a slight amount of water over the head as is too often the case today. Paul deliberately uses the physical imagery of going down under the water as part of his catechesis, explaining baptism as going down into the tomb, a death to the old life of sin. Coming up out of the water was suggestive of emerging from the tomb, a symbol of Christ's resurrection from the dead.

For Paul, the ritual of baptism is the accomplishment of a deep truth, the believer's acceptance of the gift of righteousness. The transformation of the believer—from one doomed under the burden of sin, to one who has been set free to live the life of grace—happens because of the real union with Christ that is accomplished through the ritual of baptism. Paul's prepositions are crucial here: "baptized *into* Christ (v. 3), buried *with* him (v. 4), died *with* Christ, live *with* him (v. 8), alive for God *in* Christ Jesus (v. 11)." The believer actually shares in the timeless, cosmic reality that is Christ, dead and risen, and is not merely recalling or imitating something that is fundamentally irretrievable. This notion of incorporation into Christ through baptism is the basis for Paul's teaching on the Church as the Body of Christ (see especially 1 Corinthians) and is also the foundation for Paul's moral teaching that those who are "in Christ" must never again live in their former, sinful ways.

Today's first reading from 2 Kings is part of a cycle of stories about the prophet Elisha, disciple and successor to Elijah.

Written around the beginning of the eighth century before Christ, more than a hundred years after Elisha's death, these tales show evidence of the oral tradition that formed and transmitted them and of the concerns of the deuteronomic editor who incorporated them into his theological history of Israel. They were designed to reinforce a popular awareness of the prophets as instruments of the all-powerful word of Yahweh that was ever ready to reward the good deeds of the people, to rescue them in time of need, and to punish them for their infidelities. The reason for the choice of this pericope is clearly the reference in today's gospel that those who welcome a prophet will receive a prophet's reward. The responsorial psalm ("For ever I will sing the goodness of the Lord") gives voice to the feelings that the Shunemite woman surely experienced upon the birth of the child foretold by Elisha. Though written in another context, the praise and thankfulness of the psalmist is rooted in his recognition that the Lord is the source of all blessings.

Today's gospel concludes both the missionary discourse from which we have been reading the past several weeks, as well as book two (8:1–10:42) of Matthew's gospel, which dealt with Jesus' ministry and mission in Galilee. Matthew's community had already experienced the cost of discipleship in the form of the very persecutions and rejections alluded to in these verses. Matthew wants his readers to understand that these were not unpredictable aberrations from God's plan. Rather, the cross is for the disciples of Jesus, as for the Master himself, the inevitable consequence of obedience to the Father's will. The final point made is that every disciple represents Jesus and should be treated accordingly, a commonplace Semitic perspective that the disciple embodies the presence and power of the Master.

Catholic Doctrine

Sacrament of Baptism

The Pauline death-resurrection motif represented in today's second reading is not the only scriptural starting point for the early Christian Church's understanding of baptism. The early Church also made use of the scriptural episode of Jesus' own baptism by John at the Jordan river to highlight our baptism and resultant mission. Various Pentecost and Spirit texts also develop a more pneumatic understanding of baptism. In addition, there is also the Johannine new birth imagery found in the dialogue between Nicodemus and Jesus (John 3).

We Catholics hold that the celebration of this sacrament is the gateway to the spiritual life, and, as such, its effects can be detailed in a number of ways. To begin with, baptism (along with confirmation and Eucharist) initiates one as a member into the Church. Claimed by Christ in baptism, each initiate is given a share in the priesthood of all believers. Thus, by baptism we belong to one another, a community whose members pour out their lives in service to one another, each using their unique gifts and abilities to build up the whole (CCC 1268–69). In addition, because we also believe that the Church is not merely a social collection of individual people but the living, mystical body of Christ, baptism also joins one to the Lord.

The newly baptized have died with Christ, all past sinfulness cleansed and destroyed, in order to rise with Christ to newness of life. The new life given in baptism endures as an indelible spiritual mark—for our belonging to Christ can never be taken away or revoked, even though we may, in the future, commit mortal sin. (The sacrament of reconciliation is needed by the sinner to address this sin.) Thus, the fruitfulness of baptism may be blocked or hurt by serious sin, but its indelible mark is never destroyed (CCC 1272).

While we Catholics believe that faith and baptism are closely linked, and that a first faith is required as evidence before one can go into the life-giving waters, we also affirm that what is being professed and offered in the sacrament is the faith of the Church itself. This is the theological reasoning behind the baptism of infants. Every individual who is baptized, regardless of chronological age, is called to grow in maturity and develop the practice of the faith with the help of the entire household of the faithful (CCC 1253).

Finally, the Catholic Church understands baptism as our incorporation into Christ's mission. Believers step forth from the baptismal font, washed and reborn, indeed, reinvigorated so that they might proclaim the good news of salvation by their words and deeds in every circumstance of life that they will meet. This baptismal understanding underlies the Second Vatican Council's teaching on the vocation of the laity. The Council affirmed, ". . . the faithful who by baptism are incorporated into Christ . . . in their own way share the priestly, prophetic and kingly office of Christ, and to the best of their ability carry on the mission of the whole Christian people in the Church and in the world. . . . [The laity] live in the world, that is, they are engaged in each and every work and business of the earth and in the ordinary circumstances of social and family life which, as it were, constitute their very existence. There they are called by God that, being led by the spirit of the Gospel, they may contribute to the sanctification of the world, as from within like leaven, by fulfilling their own particular duties" (LG 31).

St. Gregory of Nazianzus (d. 390 A.D.) reflected on this sacrament, saying, "Baptism is God's most beautiful and magnificent gift. . . . We call it gift, grace, anointing, enlightenment, garment of immortality, bath of rebirth, seal, and most precious gift. It is called gift because it is conferred on those who bring nothing of their own; grace since it is given even to the guilty; Baptism because sin is buried in the water; anointing for it is priestly and royal as are those who are anointed; enlightenment because it radiates light; clothing since it veils our shame; bath because it washes; and seal as it is our guard and the sign of God's Lordship" (Oratio 40, 3–4: PG 36, 361C).

Catholic Culture

The word "baptism" in Greek (*baptizein*) means to "plunge" or "immerse" and refers to the ritual action that takes place when the sacrament is celebrated: the one being baptized is immersed into the waters or water is poured over them, completely drenching them. The immersion or drenching takes place three times as the Trinitarian formula is spoken, "I baptize you in the name of the Father, and of the Son, and of the Holy Spirit."

Early Christians baptized in rivers and streams where water flowed freely (one sense of the phrase "living water," the other sense being made alive in the Spirit of the Lord). The Catholic Church encourages that fonts be constructed in such a way that they will have flowing water and an immersion pool large enough for adults to be plunged into this water (RBC 25 and RCIA 213).

When a newly built font is blessed, the Church prays, "Grant, O Lord, that the people who are reborn from this font may fulfill in their actions what they pledge by their faith and show by their lives what they begin by the power of your grace. Let the people of different nations and conditions who come forth as one from these waters of rebirth show by their love that they are brothers and sisters and by their concord that they are citizens of the one kingdom. Make them into true sons and daughters who reflect their Father's goodness, disciples who are faithful to the teaching of their one Master, temples in whom the voice of the Spirit resounds. Grant that they may be witnesses to the Gospel, doers of the works of holiness. Enable them to fill with the Spirit of Christ the earthly city where they live, until they are welcomed home in the heavenly Jerusalem" (BB 1101).

Dismissal Catechesis (30 min.)

Getting Started

1. Prepare the space ahead of time with a circle of chairs around a large cross, standing upon a green fabric arranged in the center of the floor. Upon the cloth, at the base of the cross, arrange small glass bowls of water and several candles. You may choose to use floating candles.

2. Lead the candidates and catechumens to the circle and place the Lectionary on the table and light the candles. Prepare copies of Psalm 89:2–3, 16–17, 18–19 prior to the session.

3. Begin the prayer by inviting everyone to reflect for a few moments upon the arrangement of the cross, water, and candles. When you are ready, distribute copies of the psalm and invite all to pray the psalm with their whole being. If someone in the parish knows "signing," invite that person to teach the group to sign the psalm.

First Impressions

1. Invite the participants to name evidence of the Lord's faithfulness and kindness proclaimed in the scriptures for today. Then ask each person to turn to the individual on their right to discuss these questions: *What in today's Liturgy of the Word was a source of joy and comfort to you? From the homily and the readings, what is the main message that you connected with at the liturgy? List some key words that you remember from the readings.*

2. Invite the pairs to write the key words they remember on newsprint. As you look over the list, add the following words if they are not mentioned—*prophet, cross, baptism, death, life, promise, disciple.* Ask the catechumens and candidates to look over the list and at the centerpiece and share their thoughts on this question with the whole group: *What connection can you see between today's scriptures and this centerpiece?* Listen to and affirm their responses.

3. Ask the participants to name words or phrases that come to mind when their hear the word "prophet." List their ideas on another newsprint. Continue by offering this background on the first reading from 2 Kings 4:8–11, 14–16: *The prophets of the Old Testament were involved in both the political and the personal lives of the Israelites. A true prophet received authority from Yahweh and was respected as a "man of God." These messengers of God, sent to speak a word of truth, warning, or hope to the People of God, often were not accepted. Today's passage from the second book of Kings illustrates God's care for the people of Israel in a situation of personal need. The kindness and care of the woman of Shunem was rewarded in superlatives. With no heir and an aging husband, the woman was promised that she would bear a son by the time of Elisha's next visit.* Ask the participants to gather into small groups to discuss this question: *What does this story of Elisha and the generous woman reveal about extending ourselves to one another?*

Making Connections

1. Encourage each small group to offer their response in the large gathering. Invite the participants to share their experiences of extending kindness to a stranger and the results of that hospitality.

2. Emphasize the connection between kindness toward another and our relationship with God in these words: *Today's gospel underlines the importance of extending ourselves for one another when it proclaims, "whoever welcomes you, welcomes me." The interconnection among all things is evident in the story of the woman and in the words of Jesus to his disciples. All is one! Everything we do, even our attitudes toward one another, affects the whole and indicates the depths of our connection with God.*

3. Encourage everyone to gather in the same small groups to share their insights on these questions: *What changes in attitude and behavior do we need to make in the light of this truth? To what lengths toward welcoming the messenger of God's Word is the Christian challenged to go? What are some practical actions that will open us and make us more receptive to others, even strangers?* Invite everyone to offer their responses in the large group. When they have finished, encourage the participants to think of one thing they wish to remember from this session and write it in their Participant Book on page 79 in the section "I want to remember."

Prayer

Close the session by praying in these or your own words: *God of promise and fulfillment, open us to listen and warmly receive your messengers in our day. Empower us to follow the example of the woman who welcomed Elisha into her home. For those who have spoken your word to us, those prophets of today, we give thanks. Our hearts are filled with gratitude for you have been a faithful and caring God. Let us respond by treating one another with the same unlimited kindness and care. We ask this in Jesus' name, the one we strive to follow. Amen.*

Extended Catechesis

SESSION FOCUS: *Sacrament of Baptism*

Gathering

A. Sunday:

1. Greet and welcome everyone as they arrive. Invite them to join the circle of catechumens and candidates.

2. Encourage the participants to silently reflect upon the centerpiece of the cross, water, and candles for a brief period. Then lead them in singing the Gathering Song from today's Liturgy of the Word. Ask a team member to proclaim the second reading, Romans 6:3–4, 8–11. As the group remains silent, prayerfully repeat some of the images from the passage by speaking these phrases aloud—*buried with Christ, baptized unto his death, we live with Christ, we live a new life, and we are alive for God in Christ Jesus.* Invite a sponsor to proclaim the gospel, Matthew 10:37–42.

B. Weekday:

1. Use the same centerpiece as in the Dismissal Catechesis.
2. As the participants gather in the circle, greet and warmly welcome each person and light the candles. Invite a few participants to describe an experience of extending kindness to another during the past few days.
3. Lead this celebration of the Word:
   - Song: Gathering Song from Sunday's liturgy
   - Second Reading: Romans 6:3–4, 8–11
   - Reflection: Prayerful reading of phrases as in A
   - Gospel: Matthew 10:37–42

The Word (30 min.)

1. Invite each person to reflect upon the scriptures, just proclaimed and at the cross. After a brief time, ask them to name whatever comes to mind when they think of Jesus' invitation to take up the cross. List their responses on newsprint or an overhead, writing large enough for all to read.
2. Offer this presentation on the background to the gospel: *This passage from Matthew was addressed to a Christian community that had experienced hostility for persevering in their faithfulness to Christ. Their conviction in the redemption that Jesus had accomplished in his death and resurrection resulted in persecution. In spite of this, they were determined to follow Jesus, abandoning all else. The writer encourages all believers, making three points: First, the decision to follow Jesus binds us to him in a way that surpasses all other relationships. Second, if we follow Jesus, we will inevitably follow him to the cross. Finally, if we do follow Jesus, in spite of these difficulties, we will be rewarded beyond our imagining.*
3. Gather the participants into small groups to discuss these questions: *How is the cross a symbol of life for the followers of Jesus? How does our relationship with Jesus, enhance our other relationships? What is your experience of following Jesus, thus far?* Invite some input from each small group.
4. Continue to describe the background of the second reading, Romans 6:3–4, 8–11. *The Christ-encounter in baptism draws the believer into union with him—specifically in his dying and rising, we die to sin and are raised to new life in and with Christ. This intimate spiritual union with Christ results in a new and transformed way of life. The question Paul raises, "Are you not aware?" challenges every one of us to live what we have become.* Encourage the participants to turn to page 78 in their Participant Book and spend time with the Reflection exercise. Encourage them to share their thoughts with their sponsor and/or godparent.

Catholic Teaching (30 min.)

1. Tell your own story of experiencing death in Christ (dying to self, desires, control) and how you were raised out of that difficult experience by the grace of God. Encourage the participants to answer the questions on page 78 of their Participant Book and discuss their responses in the same pairs.
2. Offer a presentation on the Church's teaching on the sacrament of baptism using the information provided in the Catholic Doctrine section found in Understanding this Sunday.

- Baptism is the gateway to the spiritual life, initiating the believer into the community of the faithful and gifting each with a share in the priesthood of all believers.
- The baptized belong to one another, pouring out their lives in service to one another and offering their baptismal gifts to build up the whole Body of Christ.
- Through this sacrament all sinfulness is wiped away and we are marked, indelibly, as belonging to Christ.
- Prior to baptism the individual must give evidence of first faith in Christ. What is being professed and offered in the sacrament of baptism is the faith of the Church—the corporate body. Thus, infants are baptized, because growth and maturity in faith occurs within the loving embrace of the entire household of the faithful.
- In baptism we are incorporated into Christ's mission, sharing his priestly, prophetic, and kingly role.

3. Invite the participants to raise any clarifying questions before you continue. Then ask them to discuss these questions in their same small groups: *What does it mean for you that we are incorporated into Christ in the sacrament of baptism? What do you understand by the Church's teaching that baptism incorporates us into one another? How are we challenged to relate to one another in the community of faith as a result of our baptism? What is our challenge for the sake of the world?*

Putting Faith into Practice

1. Ask the pairs to name some of the insights that arose as they discussed the last two questions, the baptismal challenge to the community of faith and the world, with the whole group.
2. Invite everyone to brainstorm some implications and actions that could result from this baptismal challenge. Encourage each person to write one challenge they wish to work on in the Participant Book on page 79 in the section "I want to put my faith into action by."
3. Ask a team member or parish leader to talk to the group about some of the ways the laity of your parish have responded to the baptismal challenge.

Prayer

Focus the attention of the group back to the centerpiece. Pray this litany of baptism, inviting the group to respond, *"Fill us with your Spirit that we may bring Christ to the world,"* after each invocation.

By your sacrament, we are graced and gifted to be priest, prophet, and king
By your sacrament we are plunged into death's waters
By your sacrament, we are bathed, cleansed, and transformed into new life
By your sacrament, we are clothed in Christ
By your sacrament, we are enlightened, anointed, and sealed in your Holy Spirit
By your sacrament, we are reborn in Christ
By your sacrament, we are made your sons and daughters
By your sacrament, we are incorporated into your Body
(Continue to add your own invocations)

Close the session by inviting all to join in singing, "We, The Body of Christ" (Paul Hellebrand, NALR, 1987) or a familiar song with a similar theme.

Fourteenth Sunday in Ordinary Time

The Word in Liturgy

Zechariah 9:9–10
Psalm 145:1–2, 8–9, 10–11, 13–14
Romans 8:9, 11–13
Matthew 11:25–30

Today's suggested focus on chastity is based on Paul's teaching in chapter 8 of his letter to the Romans, on the indwelling Spirit. Paul begins the chapter with an emphasis on the fact that we are "in" the Spirit. The consequence of this teaching on who we are is that we must therefore live "according to" the Spirit. Paul's thought moves from "is" to "ought," from indicative to imperative. This is an important perspective to keep in mind when dealing with commandments and the law. In chapter 7, Paul has dealt with the futility of living "under the Law." Now, in chapter 8, he contrasts the "law of the Spirit" and the "law of sin and death" (v. 2). That contrast is also expressed as the tension between "Spirit" and "flesh," the latter term being understood as a whole sphere of existence without God as its vivifying principle. "Flesh" (*sarx* in Greek) should not be understood narrowly here as a reference to human sexuality, although unruly, earthly desires certainly can manifest themselves in the sexual realm as a prime example of those who live according to the flesh. For Paul, the antithesis between Spirit and flesh is between two entirely different ways of living: the one "in Christ," the other "under the law of sin and death" (v. 2).

For Paul, the crucial change affecting the Christian's ability to follow the dictates of the commandments has come about as the result of the gift given in baptism, the indwelling Spirit of Christ that has irrevocably joined our destinies to his. So great is the impact of our being "in Christ," that believers can actually anticipate having their mortal bodies raised up after death in the same fashion as was Christ's in his resurrection (v. 11). So, too, Christians can realistically expect to be able to live "according to the Spirit" as long as they remain "in Christ."

Today's reading from Zechariah is taken from the second part of the book (cc. 9–14), which was written sometime around the third century B.C. The author envisions the triumphant arrival of a messianic king, deliberately portrayed as meek and humble (riding on an ass) rather than as an aggressive warlord (astride a horse). The spiritual importance given to the *anawim*, the "little ones" whom Jesus said would inherit the Kingdom, is brought to the fore here. The "just savior" is one who will banish the weapons of war and proclaim a universal peace within his dominion. Matthew (21:5) will quote this passage as a prelude to his account of the Passion, and it is certainly in the background of the pericope chosen as today's gospel reading. Today's psalm extols the reign and kingship of God, and in so doing offers powerful images of what one could call the "attributes" of the divinity ("gracious and merciful, slow to anger and of great kindness . . . good to all and compassionate . . . faithful in all his words and holy . . .").

In the section of Matthew we read today, Jesus is presented as the embodiment of that Wisdom which the Jewish scriptures had referred to as a "reflection of eternal light" (cf. Wisdom 7:22ff.). Jesus' words would have been revolutionary to his hearers: Not only does he present himself as Wisdom incarnate; he suggests that the attainment of Wisdom is given as gift to the lowly ("merest children"), and that it is not the result of the labors of the learned and the clever (from whom it is "hidden"). Moreover, whereas Jewish tradition held that God's revelation is contained fully in the law and the prophets, Jesus says that "everything" has been given over to him by his Father. He, in turn, echoes the offer of Lady Wisdom in Ecclesiasticus 51:25–27 ("Come, take my yoke, and find for yourselves rest"), an offer made to Israel bent low under the burdensome demands of the Law, but now offered by Jesus to his disciples as something "easy" and "light" because of its origin in an ethic of love.

Catholic Doctrine

Chastity

To understand why the Church upholds the virtue of chastity for all human beings in the expression of their sexuality, it is necessary to begin where St. Paul locates the discussion: the Spirit of God. The Loving One who has created us by the breath of the Spirit has also inscribed upon the human heart not only the capacity to love and share and reach out in communion but the vocation or calling to do so (CCC 2331). There is an integrity to the way in which God creates people, a connection between what we feel, who we are, and how we are built, that leads us to this vocation to love, to share, to reach out in communion. In other words, we are not just bodies and we are not reduced to blindly following sexual urges. Bodies, sexuality, sexual activity, spirit—all that we are—is subordinated to the ultimate end of humanity and creation itself, that is, to live in Christ.

Thus, the Church describes chastity as the integration of one's sexuality within the whole person, such that an inner unity of body, mind, spirit, and soul is attained (CCC 2337). This project of integration is seen by the Church as an apprenticeship in mastering one's self in human freedom. In other words, the human person learns to govern passions, desires, and drives, or that person is dominated and overwhelmed by those urges (CCC 2339) and acts without a true direction ordered toward the kingdom of God. This self-mastery is never really completed, but is, throughout every stage of life, sought and practiced (CCC 2342).

The Church's understanding of the virtue of chastity must be seen in the context of one's sexual identity or gender, for God created male and female, each with an equal dignity. When a man and a woman unite in marriage, the Church sees in their union and its procreative possibilities the fruitfulness and generosity of the divine Creator who has loved us into being. Indeed, the Church prays, "Father . . . [you] created [us] in love to share your divine life. We see [our] high destiny in the love of husband and wife, which bears the imprint of your own divine love" (*Sacramentary*, Preface 74).

Given this context, chastity strives to put one's identity as a sexual person at the service of others and of Christ. In other words, our whole person is ordered to the service of love. While love can be expressed without being physical, sexual relations should never be expressed without love and always within a pledged and stable marital relationship (CCC 2337). One author explains, "The promise and decision to live not only with, but also for, one's beloved are a crucial part of the truth that is proclaimed in the act of sexual intercourse. The body-giving of physical intercourse is an in-the-flesh expression of the self-giving which is the essence of love. For this reason the act cannot be entered into casually" (NDictTheol 954).

Given the Catholic understanding of chastity, the Church teaches that there are certain abuses of the gift of sexuality. Manipulating others sexually, treating them as objects, such as in rape, the use of pornography and prostitution, all degrade this gift from God (CCC 2354–56). Fornication, the physical union between unmarried men and women, is also considered as degrading the gift of sexuality (CCC 2353). Masturbation, which lacks the mutual self-giving of two people within marriage that is demanded by the gift of sexuality, also is an abuse of God's gift of sexuality; however, in evaluating such behavior pastoral sensitivity to the person's lack of maturity or ingrained habits must be taken into account (CCC 2352). While the Church also teaches that homosexual persons must be accorded respect and treated with dignity, homosexual relations are characterized as contrary to the natural law (CCC 2358). As such, this type of sexual activity is also considered an abuse of the gift of sexuality (CCC 2357).

Married couples, single individuals, those in religious life and clergy, all are called to the virtue of chastity. The way we give of ourselves to each other in friendship and love, building strong relationships, is not only enriching but necessary for our growth and maturity. Chastity flourishes and is wonderfully expressed in friendship (CCC 2347). Thus, human sexuality is a great gift and challenge whose drives the Church understands not as random factors in ourselves as persons and in our relationships but as ordered to the divine, to the kingdom and to God's plan.

Catholic Culture

In the Catholic marriage ritual, rings are given as gifts from one spouse to another and symbolize not only their binding love but the gift which each one gives the other of their whole self, as a total togetherness. The Church prays in blessing the rings, "Lord, . . . grant that those who wear them may always have a deep faith in each other. May they do your will and always live together in peace, good will, and love" (RM 110). Many Catholic Latino wedding celebrations also include additional gifts exchanged as signs of the self-giving and claiming in love of the spouses, such as the *arras* (coins, a sign of support for the upkeep of the household), the *lazo* (lasso, a sign of undivided love), the Bible, a sign of the strength they will derive from the Word of God, and a rosary, a sign of their need for prayer.

St. Augustine (d. 430) was a prolific early Christian writer and stern preacher against heresy, who himself admits in his autobiographical work *The Confessions,* that he led the life of a profligate before his conversion, and yet was—even if he did not always realize it—longing for God. Not known as a humorist, he nevertheless understood human nature. A prayer which is attributed to him is, "O God, give me chastity. But, not yet."

Dismissal Catechesis (30 min.)

Getting Started

1. Prepare the space ahead of time with a circle of chairs around a table draped with a green cloth. On the table place a large white candle.
2. Lead the candidates and catechumens to the circle and place the Lectionary on the table. After everyone is seated, light the candle and lead them in prayer with these or similar words: *O good and loving God, giver of all gifts, send the Spirit to guide and direct our reflection and discussion today. Help us to be open to the Word so that it might take deep root within us and that we might become beacons of light and hope for others. We ask this in the name of Jesus. Amen.*

First Impressions

1. From the Liturgy of the Word, ask the participants to recall a word or phrase that stands out. Invite them to speak aloud that word or phrase. Write these down on newsprint, overhead, or chalkboard. Assure the catechumens and candidates that if they cannot recall any, it is all right.
2. You may choose to add such words and phrases as *"rejoice heartily—your king shall come to you—my king and my God—gracious and merciful—God dwells in you—come to me—I will refresh you"* to the list. As you prepare, note words and phrases from the prayers, music, and the homily at your parish liturgy.
3. In the large group begin a discussion of the readings by asking: *Who would find comfort in these words and the scripture readings? How do these readings challenge you?* Allow for quiet reflection before discussing this question in the large group. Summarize their responses.

Making Connections

1. Slowly and deliberately repeat the words and phrases on the list. Pause. Ask if anyone would like to add to the list.
2. Challenge the group to think of places or groups within their community who need to hear these words and phrases today. Ask what Good News this Liturgy of the Word would convey to them. Invite everyone to freely discuss how the Word of God is a source of consolation. Summarize their thoughts and insights in a few sentences.
3. Then ask each participant to name the ways in which the scriptures are a source of strength as they journey in faith. List these as they are offered. Gather their responses in a few brief statements.

Prayer

Lead the participants in prayer with these or similar words: *Jesus, our brother, you invite us to come to you when we are weary and find life demanding and you refresh us. You do not promise to take our burdens away. Rather, you remind us that you are gentle and humble of heart and that we will find rest in you. Help us to trust in your words and to remember that our souls will find rest. Amen.*

Lead all in singing *"We Shall Rise Again"* (Jeremy Young, GIA Publications, 1987) or the Gathering Song from the Liturgy of the Word.

Extended Catechesis

SESSION FOCUS: *Chastity*

Gathering

A. Sunday:
1. Greet and welcome the sponsors and team members as they arrive. Invite them to join the circle of catechumens and candidates.
2. Ask one or two of the catechumens and candidates to summarize their discussion and sharing from the dismissal session.
3. After pausing for a few minutes of quiet, proclaim the first reading, Zechariah 9:9–10. Pause. Ask a team member to proclaim Matthew 11:25–30.

B. Weekday:
1. Use the same centerpiece as in the Dismissal Catechesis.
2. As the participants gather in the circle, warmly welcome each person. Ask them to share how God has been a source of comfort or challenge over the past few days.
3. Lead this celebration of the Word:
   - Song: Gathering Song from Sunday's liturgy
   - First Reading: Zechariah 9:9–10
   - Silence
   - Second Reading: Romans 8:9, 11–13
   - Alleluia
   - Gospel: Matthew 11:25–30
   - Alleluia

The Word (30 min.)

1. Ask the participants what came to mind when they heard the word "king" in the first reading. List their responses on newsprint, overhead, or chalkboard. Then invite everyone to discuss these questions: *How do you imagine the king referred to in the passage, "your king shall come to you"? What would this king be like?* Affirm the responses.
2. Present a background on the scriptures, expanding on the following points:
   - The triumphant arrival of the messianic king in the first reading is portrayed as meek and humble (riding an ass) rather than as an aggressive warlord (on a horse).
   - The just savior is one who will banish the weapons of war and proclaim universal peace within his dominion. Then gather the participants into small groups to share the contrasts and challenges depicted between an earthly understanding of king and the messianic king of Zechariah.
3. Continue to explore the scriptures in these or similar words: *In these readings, the* anawim, *that is, the poor and lowly, those who count for nothing, "the merest children," will grasp the message. They will understand*

and accept a messianic king sent by God who brings freedom to captives and oppressed, sight to the blind, etc. To such little ones, great wisdom is given. Invite the same groups to discuss why the little ones might readily grasp the message of Jesus.

4. Conclude the opening of God's Word by enlarging on these ideas:
   - Jewish tradition held that God's revelation is contained fully in the law and the prophets and that wisdom is not the result of the labors of the learned and the clever.
   - Jesus says that the Father has given "everything" over to him. This gift of the Father is shared freely with us; it is not earned.
   - Jesus echoes the offer of Lady Wisdom in Ecclesiasticus 51:25–27 ("Come, take my yoke, and find for yourselves rest"), an offer made to Israel bent low under the burdensome demands of the Law, and now offered by Jesus to his disciples as something "easy" and "light" because of its origin in an ethic of love.

5. Invite the participants to open their Participant Book on page 80 and to reflect on their experiences of a burden or struggle made lighter with the help of another. After writing about one such experience, ask them to share one of these experiences in their small groups.

Catholic Teaching (30 min.)

1. Slowly and deliberately proclaim the second reading, Romans 8:9, 11–13. Pause. Invite everyone to close their eyes. Lead them in this meditation: *Take a deep breath. Feel the air flow into your lungs, bringing fresh oxygen. Exhale slowly, expelling the used air of your body. Do this several times, breathing in deeply, exhaling slowly.* Pause. *You are in the Spirit. God dwells in you. The Spirit of Jesus is in you. You belong to Christ. Breathe deeply the Spirit. Live according to the Spirit. God dwells in you. You belong to Christ. Breathe deeply.* Long pause. Invite everyone to slowly open their eyes.

2. Continue with these or similar words: *St. Paul challenges us to live according to the Spirit. If we choose to live according to the flesh we will surely die. Paul's teaching is simply that to live in the Spirit is to live as Christ taught. To live according to the flesh, under the law of sin and death, is to die.* Gather everyone back to their small groups, directing them to the questions in the Participant Book on page 80. Ask them to contrast life "according to the Spirit" and life "according to the flesh." Use their insights to stimulate a discussion of life in the Spirit and life in the flesh in the small groups.

3. Continue: *The Spirit of God dwelling in each of us has inscribed upon the human heart not only the capacity to love and share and reach out in communion but the calling to do so. There is integrity to the way God created us, a connection between what we feel, who we are and how we are made, that leads us to this calling. All that we are is subordinated to the ultimate end of humanity and creation itself, that is, to live in Christ.* In their groups invite the participants to define "love" as portrayed by our culture. (A suggestion: have several magazines, tabloids, newspapers, and colored markers available. Ask them to underline the headlines that depict our culture's understanding of love.) Gather responses from the groups. Continue with these words: *The Church upholds virtuous love or chastity for all human beings. The human person learns to govern passions, desires, and drives (living according to the Spirit) or that person is dominated and overwhelmed by them and acts without true direction ordered toward the kingdom (living according to the flesh). The Church's understanding of the virtue of chastity must be seen in the context of one's sexual identity, for God created male and female, each with an equal dignity.* Then invite anyone who wishes to describe what it means to live "chastely," both as a single person and as a married person. Summarize their comments and add this teaching on chastity: *While love can be expressed without being physical, sexual relations ought never to be expressed without love and always within a pledged and stable marital relationship.*

4. In their groups, invite the participants to name what they consider abuses of the gift of sexuality. Invite a few groups to name some of these abuses for the entire gathering. Further their understanding of the Church's teaching on abuse of this gift of sexuality by stating: *Manipulating others sexually, treating the other as an object, such as rape, is a violation of chastity. Pornography, prostitution, fornication, and masturbation all degrade the gift of sexuality. While the Church teaches that homosexual persons must be accorded respect and treated with dignity, homosexual relations are characterized as contrary to the natural law. Married couples, single individuals, those in religious life and clergy all are called to the virtue of chastity. The way we give of ourselves to each other in friendship and love, building strong relationships, is not only enriching but also necessary for our growth and maturity. Chastity flourishes and is wonderfully expressed in friendship. Thus, human sexuality is a great gift and challenge whose drives the Church understands not as random factors in ourselves as persons and in our relationships but as ordered to the divine, to the kingdom and to God's plan.*

Putting Faith into Practice

1. Invite the participants to review what they wrote in their Participant Book under the headings, "life according to the Spirit" and "life according to the flesh." Encourage them to add or subtract items from their lists based on the Church's teaching on chastity and sexuality. They can share these additions in the small groups.

2. Encourage them to spend time this week reflecting on God's gift of sexuality and the ways we are enriched because of love. Encourage them also to reflect on how they are called to live a chaste life.

Prayer

Invite everyone to close their eyes and to breathe deeply. Breathe in the Spirit of God who dwells in you. Exhale all that keeps you from accepting God's great gift of love. Close with Minor Exorcism (RCIA 94B) adapted for the catechumens and candidates.

Fifteenth Sunday in Ordinary Time

The Word in Liturgy

Isaiah 55:10–11
Psalm 65:10, 11, 12–13, 14
Romans 8:18–23
Matthew 13:1–23 [or (short form) 13:1–9]

The author of Deutero-Isaiah (chapters 40–55) prophesied during the time of the Babylonian Exile, reassuring the people that God had not abandoned them and would be true to his Covenant promise to protect and care for them. In this final chapter of the prophet's work, written in poetic or hymnal style, the promise of consolation is couched in messianic and eschatological images of a banquet and of Yahweh's ultimate triumph over the nations. In verse 6, the prophet tells his audience to "seek the Lord," and then in verses 8, 9, 10, and 12, he offers a series of reasons ("for . . . for . . . for . . .") why this should be done. Today's reading is the third reason in the series and recalls the efficacious nature of God's Word. Just as God spoke an efficacious word in the beginning (Genesis 1) to accomplish the work of creation, so should Israel trust in the continuing power of God's Word to deliver them from exile. The outcome of the prophet's promise of consolation is as inexorable as the growth that occurs after a rainfall. In the context of the Lectionary's use of Jesus' parables over the next three weeks, this assurance of the power of the Lord's words takes on special significance. Psalm 65 echoes the imagery of lush abundance that is suggestive of God's lavish care for his people. The psalm refrain ("The seed that falls on good ground will yield a fruitful harvest") connects the psalm with the parable in today's gospel.

For three weeks, beginning today, we read from chapter 13 of Matthew, eventually ending at verse 52, which is the conclusion to the third "book" in the plan of his gospel. This entire unit is sometimes called the "Discourse in Parables" and offers a wonderful opportunity to deepen our appreciation for how God's Word has been spoken in the human words of both Jesus and of the Church (in the person of the early Christian community and Matthew its faithful scribe). Scripture scholars see in today's pericope evidence of how the gospels were formed (cf. CCC 126), first on the basis of a simple story spoken by Jesus (vv. 1–9), and then by its oral transmission enhanced with the further understandings (vv. 13–17 and 18–21) of the early Christian community—in this case, presumably, Matthew's community—all of which was ultimately woven together as a part of and according to the longer narrative plan of the evangelist himself.

The original point of today's parable on the lips of Jesus had to do with his proclamation of the reign of God and the miraculous "yield" that would be part of its in-breaking. Undoubtedly, Jesus also intended by his mention of the rocky ground and the thorns to challenge his hearers to commit themselves to God's reign so that they might be part of its messianic abundance. Subsequent sections of the pericope seem to reflect more the life situation of the early church, struggling to understand their generation's task of proclaiming God's reign in the face of resistance, persecutions, and defections, and adding allegorizing interpretations to the original parable as a way of accommodating its meaning to their own circumstances.

In today's reading from Romans, Paul offers a rationale for how and why the believer can cope with the reality of suffering. It is our hope in the inevitable "glory to be revealed in us" (v. 18) that allows us not to lose heart, even in the face of the groaning and "futility" of creation. Paul's vision is thoroughly realistic and at the same time optimistic. He is thinking of the effects of the fall as described in Genesis, which introduced division and alienation into the entire created order—into human experience as well as into nature itself. But all will be "freed from its slavery" (v. 21) and will experience the redemptive power of the Spirit which, even now, we have as "first fruits."

Catholic Doctrine

Sacred Scripture

In any Catholic description of sacred scripture and its role in our lives, the starting point must be the phrase "Word of God." The Hebrew term *dabar* means not only a spoken word but it also connotes "event" or "affair" or "act." Given this connotation, Catholics understand the Word as spoken by God as effective and dynamic, for God's self-revelation to us creates, produces, and ultimately redeems. The Word of God meets us in love, communicating to us nourishment and strength (CCC 104). While scripture is made up of many words, and in that sense is like human language, because we understand the Word of God to be the self-expression of the Most High to us, those many words of scripture are, in essence, a single communication, one Word which is uttered, that is, Jesus Christ (CCC 102).

We Catholics believe that God is the author of sacred scripture. The texts of both the Old and New Testaments, while composed and set down by humans, were written under the inspiration of God. Therefore, that truth which God endeavors to communicate to us, we hold, is faithfully transmitted in the books of scripture (CCC 106–07). However, we believe we are espoused to the active Word of God, which is not a written word, but incarnated and alive. The Old and New Testaments will contain only dry, insignificant, and dead letters unless the living Word, Jesus Christ, illuminates our minds and hearts to understand what truth is contained therein (CCC 108).

The Church teaches that to faithfully interpret scripture one must read it holistically and from within the tradition. What does this mean? First, in the interpretation of scripture one must be very attentive to its whole content and unity of purpose. The individual books of the Bible are different, yet there is a unity and wholeness to all of them together—given that they revolve around the center and heart of God's plan for us who is Jesus Christ (CCC 112). Second, scripture was written in the Church's heart rather than in documentary texts, and therefore it must be read and understood within the living tradition of the community of the faithful. The Second Vatican Council taught that both scripture and tradition flow out of the same font, divine revelation, and both communicate with each other—they make up one single "deposit of the Word of God, which is entrusted to the Church" (DV 10). Thus, the authentic interpretation of the Word of God, whether in its written form or in the tradition, has been given to the living teaching office of the Church alone who exercises this authority in the name of Jesus and therefore is not superior to the Word but is its servant.

In this vein, it was the living teaching office of the Church which discerned the canon of the Old and New Testaments. The canon refers to the official listing of which writings or books belong to the Bible, the inspired Word of God (CCC 120). The two Testaments, Old and New, are united in presenting the plan of God, although as Christians we read the Old Testament in the light of Jesus—seeing in these scriptures a typology which prefigures what God has effected in Christ (CCC 128).

Catholics hold that sacred scripture is food for our souls, a font from which we might draw strength for nourishing our faith. Therefore, the Second Vatican Council urged that all members of the Church should have as wide an access as possible to sacred scripture (DV 22). Through homilies, pastoral preaching, catechetics, and every other form of instruction, the ministry of the Word is carried out in the Catholic Church (CCC 132). Indeed, every member of the Church is called to a frequent reading and study of sacred scripture, for, echoing St. Jerome, the Second Vatican Council taught, "Ignorance of the scriptures is ignorance of Christ" (DV 25; cf. St. Jerome, Comm. in Isaias, Prol.: PL 24, 17).

Catholic Culture

St. Jerome (331–420 A.D.) had a great passion for learning. In 382 he became the secretary of Pope Damasus, who gave him the project of translating the scriptures. Since Greek was the only translation available then to the Church, St. Jerome went back to the original Hebrew texts and produced his Latin version (Latin being the common language of the Church at the time). Eventually, St. Jerome settled in the Holy Land and founded monasteries and a free hospice for travelers. In 410, while he was still engaged in his work, Rome was sacked by barbarians and the Holy Land was inundated with refugees. St. Jerome entered into relief work while still translating the scriptures, saying, "Today we must translate the words of the scriptures into deeds, and instead of speaking saintly words we must act them." His Latin translation of the scriptures, known as the Vulgate Bible, was the official text used by the Church for over fifteen hundred years (*All Saints*, Robert Ellsberg, Crossroad Publishing Company, New York, 1997, pp. 424–26).

When the lector at Mass reads the scripture texts, we believe the living Word of God is being communicated in that action. Thus, the ritual statement after the proclamation of the text is not "This is the scripture text," (or even) "This is the Word of the Lord," but "The Word of the Lord!" That is, neither the book itself in which the Word is contained nor the individual words are alone exalted, but rather the entire activity—the lector proclaiming and faithful who hear it—is being announced and celebrated within the worshipping assembly.

Three significant realities are "given" in a symbolic fashion to catechumens when they enter the catechumenate stage of the initiation process: they are signed with the cross, they are embraced by the community of the faithful, and they are handed the Word of God. The Lectionary, the book of lessons from sacred scripture arranged for proclamation at Mass and other occasions, will be the basis and heart of their instruction and reflection throughout the period of the catechumenate.

Dismissal Catechesis (30 min.)

Getting Started

1. Prepare the space ahead of time with a circle of chairs around a table draped with a green cloth. On the table place various sizes of seeds and a flat clay bowl of rich dark soil.
2. Lead the candidates and catechumens to the circle and place the Lectionary on the table. Begin the session by inviting all to imagine a dry desert or a land covered with cracked parched soil. As they place themselves into this dry, hot scenario, invite them to imagine the joy they might feel as a wonderful soft rainfall begins to moisten the earth, filling the cracks and sand with rivulets of water.

First Impressions

1. While the group remains quiet, with their eyes closed, repeat these words taken from today's scriptures: *Rain and snow come down from the heavens—Watering the earth—Making the land fertile and fruitful—So shall my word be—It shall not return to me void—It shall achieve the end for which I sent it—God's watercourses are filled—Drenching the furrows—Breaking up the clods—Paths overflow with a rich harvest—Fields are garmented with flocks—Valleys are blanketed with grain.*
2. Encourage the participants to turn to the person on their right to discuss these questions: *What feelings are evoked by the images from today's scriptures? What sense did you gain from the Liturgy of the Word today?* Briefly explain the background for today's first reading from Isaiah 55:10–11 in these words: *Today's passage comes out of a section called Deutero-Isaiah. These chapters 40–55 are reassuring prophesies to a people caught in what is known as the Babylonian captivity. They needed the hope and consolation that God had not abandoned them during this difficult time in their history. Today's passage comes after the prophet's call to "seek the Lord." This section explains why these struggling captives should seek God.* Ask the participants to form small groups to discuss this question: *What in this passage and in the psalm do you find is a source of consolation or reassurance?*

Making Connections

1. As the discussion in the small groups concludes, focus the attention of everyone back to the large gathering. Invite the small groups to summarize their discussion for all to hear.
2. Continue to explain how the Word of God has been a source of consolation in your life by recounting an incident where you found this to be true. Encourage any candidates or catechumens to describe their own experiences of God's reassurance through the Word.
3. Gather the participants back into their small groups to share their insights on these questions: *What are some reasons that we can seek the Lord, knowing he will respond? How do we actively "seek" the Lord?* Instruct each group to list some ways of seeking the Lord on a

blank sheet of newsprint or poster board. When they have finished, invite each group to read what they have written and post their list on the walls around the room.

Prayer

Gather the attention of the group and call them to close their eyes and listen with their whole being as you proclaim or sing Psalm 65. Encourage everyone to join together in singing the response after each psalm verse, *"The seed that falls on good ground will yield a fruitful harvest."*

Extended Catechesis

SESSION FOCUS: *Sacred Scripture*

Gathering

A. Sunday:

1. Greet and welcome the sponsors and team members as they arrive. Invite them to join the circle of catechumens and candidates.
2. Invite the participants to move to the table and take one of the seeds. Encourage them to reflect upon all the possibility that lies dormant within the seed in their hand. Then proclaim the gospel, Matthew 13:1–23, as several team members pantomime the parable: the seed falling on the footpath and the birds eating it up; the seed on rocky ground with little soil, the sun scorching it; the seed falling among the thorns, choking it out; and the seed on good soil, yielding a harvest of grain. Then ask the same team members to pantomime the parallels between the seeds and the Word of God. After the proclamation and pantomime, invite all to reflect upon the meaning of this parable in their own life.

B. Weekday:

1. Use the same centerpiece as in the Dismissal Catechesis.
2. As the participants gather in the circle, greet and warmly welcome each person. Encourage a few of the participants to share how they have found reassurance in God during these past few days.
3. Lead this celebration of the Word:
   - Greeting and reflection on the seed as in A.2
   - Song: Gathering Song from Sunday's liturgy
   - First Reading: Isaiah 55:10–11
   - Sing Psalm 65
   - Second Reading: Romans 8:18–23
   - Gospel: Matthew 13:1–23 pantomimed as in A
   - Silent reflection on the seed

The Word (30 min.)

1. Encourage the catechumens and candidates to each name one thing they remember from the Dismissal Catechesis.
2. Then invite the participants to name the parallels between the seed they hold and the Word of God. You may write these on newsprint or on an overhead. Present the background on the scriptures using these or your own words:

Both Isaiah and Psalm 65 offer imagery of lush abundance to re-echo God's lavish care for God's people. Isaiah moves even deeper to offer us the reassurance that God's Word does not leave the mouth of God without yielding fruit—that for which it was intended. God's Word was powerfully present at the moment of creation and continues to yield fruit in our lives. God's Word is Jesus, who revealed God's faithfulness and the trustworthiness of God's efficacious Word. The fruit of this Word is the reign of God, which is one of abundance, harmony, and glory. For the Romans who suffered the reality of persecution for the sake of the Word, this hope of "glory to be revealed in us" forms the basis of the second reading, Romans 8:18–23. All of creation groans in anticipation of God's reign. It is this future glory that causes us to continue in spite of suffering.

3. Invite everyone to gather into small groups to discuss the following questions: *What fruit has the Word of God yielded in your own life? Where have you seen evidence of the efficacious Word in the world? How can you prepare your mind, spirit, and whole being to receive the Word, as seed falling on fertile soil?* After sufficient time for this discussion, encourage each small group to summarize their discussion for the whole gathering.

4. Concentrate the attention of the participants on preparing to hear the Word and act upon its message by inviting them to create a circle diagram of the ripple effect of the Word. The reflection on page 82 of the Participant Book will lead them through this exercise.

Catholic Teaching (30 min.)

1. Ask the group to share what they learned about the Word of God from doing this exercise. Encourage each person to share a little of their experience with reading scripture by asking these questions: *How many of you have read the scriptures daily? How many of you do not feel comfortable reading the Bible on your own? What questions arise as you think about interpreting the scriptures?*

2. Invite the participants to name the words and phrases that come to mind as they hear these references to the "Word." When they have finished, explain the sense in which we are using the "Word" in these or similar words: *The Hebrew term* dabar *indicates not only a spoken word, but also connotes an event or an action—the Church understands the Word of God to be effective and dynamic. God's self-revelation in the Word creates, produces, and redeems all of creation. Scripture is made up of many words. Yet, in understanding the Word to be God's self-expression, the words of scripture are a single communication, one Word which is uttered, that is, Jesus the Christ. In the large gathering invite a discussion of this concept by asking, "What does the 'Word' of God now mean for you?"*

3. Take up a Bible and explain the Catholic approach to the sacred scriptures as you use the text to illustrate your words. Prepare a presentation based upon the information found in the Catholic Doctrine section of Understanding this Sunday. Include the following key points:

- The Church teaches that the author of sacred scripture is God; the texts are set down by human authors but written under the inspiration of God.
- We approach the interpretation of the scriptures by reading it holistically and from within the Catholic Tradition. While the individual books of the Bible are different, there is a unity and wholeness to all of them together. (Here you may point out the books of the Bible.) Furthermore, the living teaching office of the Church guides our interpretation. Scripture and Tradition flow out of the same revelation of God, making one "deposit of the Word of God entrusted to the Church."
- The two Testaments are united in presenting the plan of God. Christians read the Old Testament in the light of Jesus. The Church discerned the canon, the official listing of books. (Show the participants the index.)
- The scriptures are food for our souls, a font from which we might draw strength for nourishing our faith. We are all encouraged to engage in dialogue with the living Word through frequent reading and study, homilies, pastoral preaching, catechetics, and the proclamation of the Word in the community of believers.

4. Invite questions concerning the interpretation, authorship, and practice of reading the scriptures. Feel free to invite a pastoral minister or ordained minister to field questions.

Putting Faith into Practice

1. Encourage the participants to turn to the Questions on page 82 in their Participant Book and reflect on these for a brief period. They may want to jot down some ideas. When they are ready, ask them to gather in their same small groups to share their insights on these questions. Invite anyone who wishes to share one thing they want to remember from this discussion with the whole group.

2. Prepare a short witness on how the scriptures have been an enriching experience in your journey of faith. Give examples of the Word, proclaimed in the midst of the community and reflecting upon the Word in your personal prayer.

3. Suggest to the participants that they set aside time each day to pray using the scriptures. They may choose to read through a whole gospel, an epistle, or a book from the Old Testament. Or they may read the selected scriptures prescribed for the daily worship of the Church in the Lectionary. Encourage them to place themselves into the passage to help in their reflection. Present a few simple biblical commentaries that might help them in understanding the historical and theological context for the passage. Invite them to a scripture study or small Bible group to experience the scriptures in the midst of the community.

Prayer

Gather the participants in prayer, saying: *God, living Word who came to dwell among your people, open us to hear your Word. May our encounter with you in the Word be food for our souls. Plant your Word deep in our being that we might be encouraged, instructed, and formed to be your people. You have revealed yourself to us in the Word. Let us deepen our knowing that the Word might become a seed planted in fertile soil, yielding a rich and abundant harvest in us—food for a hungry world. Amen.*

Sixteenth Sunday in Ordinary Time

Understanding this Sunday:
Background for Catechesis

The Word in Liturgy

Wisdom 12:13, 16–19
Psalm 86:5–6, 9–10, 15–16
Romans 8:26–27
Matthew 13:24–43 [or (short form) 13:24–30]

The Book of Wisdom ascribes authorship to Solomon, but in actuality it was written (probably in Greek) in the first century before the birth of Jesus, most likely in Alexandria, Egypt. The book's audience, then, was the Jewish community of the diaspora, educated in Hellenistic thought, and always in danger of being won over by the erudition of pagan philosophers. The author writes to strengthen the faith of his fellow Jews, taking up many of the perennial questions of the philosophers (such as the problem of evil) from the perspective of Jewish faith as well as human reason. The section from which today's reading is taken (11:2–19:4) is part of a longer midrash (commentary) on the events of the Exodus. Here, the author digresses to consider God's treatment of sinners. Why are sinners allowed to prosper, while God's faithful ones seem to suffer? The answer that the author gives comes from a deep meditation on the Jewish scriptures which reveal a God of mercy and compassion, "slow to anger, abounding in kindness" (Psalm 86:15). God permits the sinner to survive with an eye to the possibility of repentance. Despite the divine power ("you are master of might") that could simply crush all evil, Yahweh has been shown to be a God of "much lenience" (Psalm 86:18). The responsorial psalm refrain ("Lord, you are good and forgiving") underlines this feature of Jewish faith in the God they had come to know and love as infinitely merciful ("abounding in kindness to all who call upon you," Psalm 86:5).

Today's text from Romans is the third in a series of five excerpts which we read from chapter 8, in which Paul is developing the theme that Christian life is lived in the Spirit and is destined for glory. Just as in last week's reading Paul said that we—along with all of creation—"groan," so today he refers to the Spirit making intercession for us with "groanings which cannot be expressed in speech" (v. 26). Paul is referring to the Spirit's intimate involvement in our human condition. Despite the brokenness of humanity about which Paul has spoken so powerfully in previous chapters, he is also able to stress here—by this expression of the Spirit's presence within our human finitude—the depth of our redemption "in the Spirit." In prayer the believer is led by the Spirit to intercede with the Father in a way that is in accord with the divine will. Despite the fact that "we do not know how to pray as we ought," the Spirit is able to pray within us in a way that is pleasing to the One "who searches hearts" (v. 27).

Today's gospel reading continues where last week's left off and is still part of the larger unit in Matthew 13 known as the "Discourse in Parables" in which the evangelist has collected a series of seven parables focused on the kingdom. One commentator has said that "structurally this section is the center and high point of the entire Gospel" (Viviano, in *The New Jerome Biblical Commentary*, p. 655). The three parables that are part of today's reading all address the perplexing reality that Jesus (and the kingdom he announced) seemed to tolerate the presence of moral evil. This attitude seemed scandalous to some, both in Jesus' day and in the early community of Matthew. The answer given to this "problem of evil" both by Jesus and Matthew is that God wishes to allow time for repentance and further growth. The excruciatingly gradual progress and seemingly insignificant size of the kingdom is not remarkable and in fact mirrors the natural phenomena of wheat, mustard seeds, and leaven. But all three parables promise an eschatological resolution to the dilemma, both in the fantastic growth that lies ahead and in the judgment reserved for the Lord alone in the final days.

Catholic Doctrine

The Problem of Moral Evil

What does it mean to categorize evil as moral? The Church is seeking by this terminology to distinguish between the evil we do and the physical evil that is not our personal responsibility, such as an earthquake that tragically kills innocent individuals. The particular set of scriptures the Church assigns to this Sunday emphasizes that there is a type of evil we choose to engage in, either by action or inaction, and at the end times all be judged accordingly. The idea of moral evil rests upon the foundation of free choice. The Church believes that human beings are accountable and therefore move toward their final destiny by their choice, through the exercise of their free will (CCC 311). Indeed, men and women have sinned. Any recounting of history provides ample proof that men and women sinned against God and neighbor.

While acknowledging the existence of moral evil from a very early point in Christian history, our greatest theologians have asserted that God is neither directly nor indirectly responsible for the cause of moral evil in the world. St. Thomas Aquinas (d. 1274), following St. Augustine (d. 430), upheld that God, by the divine nature, directs the human heart toward the good (*Summa Theologica*, I–II, 79, 1). The responsibility for choosing other than the good does not belong to God, but to human beings. Indeed, the Second Vatican Council declared that human beings are divided, frequently gravitating toward what is wrong and sinking into evil ways. The Council taught, "As a result, the whole life of [human beings], both individual and social, shows itself to be a struggle, and a dramatic one, between good and evil, between light and darkness." The Council went on to observe that we find we cannot of our own agency "overcome the assaults of evil successfully, so that everyone feels as though bound by chains" (GS 13).

God is neither directly nor indirectly the author or cause of evil; God is always "on our side," championing the good in us, and working for our well-being. The provident goodness of God works for good in everything, including those events and actions when we choose to do wrong. The worst wrong that humanity ever could possibly engage in, that is, the rejection, torture, and execution of God's only Son, innocent and without sin, brought about the most amazing of all goods: the glory of the anointed, the Christ, and humanity's redemption (CCC 312). God came among us in order to free us from that bondage into which we had sunk. The Second Vatican Council proclaimed, "Both the high calling and the deep misery which [humanity experiences] find their final explanation in the light of this Revelation" (GS 13). The revelation to which the Council refers is the saving death and resurrection of Jesus Christ.

In any discussion of evil, whether physical or moral evil, the question must be asked: why does evil exist at all? Why would not a good God simply create a world without the possibility of evil? The Church points out that, in the end, the resolution of this question is achieved only by the totality of faith. There is no quick or simple answer. However, the goodness of creation, the patient, merciful love of the Most High, the beauty of God's covenants with us, the Word made flesh, Jesus who saves us, the transforming fire of the Holy Spirit, the birth of the Church, the continual gathering of the faithful and the nourishment of life-giving sacraments all attest to our end and goal in the goodness of the divine One who provides for us and who seeks us out no matter how far we have fallen (CCC 309).

In one sense, the mystery of the ascension of Christ points us in the direction to which we must ultimately strive for and look—not down into the depths of sin where we once fell, but rather upward, to the light and to our salvation. The Church prays, "The Lord Jesus, the king of glory, the conqueror of sin and death, ascended to heaven while the angels sang his praises. Christ, the mediator between God and [humanity], judge of the world and Lord of all, has passed beyond our sight, not to abandon us but to be our hope. Christ is the beginning, the head of the Church; where he has gone, we hope to follow" (*Sacramentary*, Preface 26).

Catholic Culture

The Cathedral of Santiago de Compostela (Spain) is an extremely important pilgrimage site (legend has it that the remains of St. James were transferred from Jerusalem to this cathedral). The original edifice was destroyed by the Moors in 997 but rebuilt and consecrated in 1211. It is a magnificent church that incorporates various styles, both Baroque and Romanesque, in a cross-shaped structure. An ornate silver censor hangs on an immense chain from its ceiling. On the feast of St. James, and on other special occasions, the censor is filled with incense and eight or ten men pull the guide ropes to swing the censor back and forth above the heads of the assembly from one transept to the other (that is, from one arm of the cross to the other). The use of incense in our Catholic tradition has always been to give honor. In this case, as whenever the worshiping assembly is incensed, honor is being accorded to the holy gathering of the faithful. The very way in which this massive medieval censor is used in this cruciform pilgrimage cathedral seems to symbolize that by the sacrifice of Jesus the possibility of holiness is held out to us. In the very gathering of the faithful, under the sign of God's love, all forms of evil are banished.

The Old Testament records many instances where the image "lamb" is referred to as a sacrifice, oblation, or an offering for sin (Exodus 29:38–41; Leviticus; 3:6–11, 4:32, 9:3). The New Testament authors build on this image and apply it to Christ, who died for our sins. Christian iconography from the earliest times, therefore, depicted Jesus Christ as the "Lamb of God," frequently holding the banner of victory—denoting the resurrection.

Dismissal Catechesis (30 min.)

Getting Started

1. Prepare the space ahead of time with chairs in a circle and a low table draped with a green cloth upon which is set a candle. Surrounding the base of the table, place several containers of new plants such as lettuce, carrots, wheat, and whatever is available locally.
2. Lead the candidates and catechumens to the circle and place the Lectionary on the table. Light the candle and lead the group in singing "God of Day and God of Darkness" (Marty Haugen, OCP Publication, 1985).

First Impressions

1. Invite the catechumens and candidates to sit in silence to reflect on the Liturgy of the Word just celebrated. Then ask that they turn to the person on their right to share what they heard, thought, or felt during the celebration of the Word. When they seem ready, gather responses from the pairs in the large group. Then ask: *What in these readings or in the homily puzzles, challenges, or raises questions for you?* Listen and encourage each person to name their questions, drawing from them the ultimate focus of this session—dealing with moral evil. Explain that this session will attempt to help in our understanding of evil that comes from the actions of human beings.
2. Open the meaning of the first reading, Wisdom 12:13, 16–9, with these or similar words: *The Book of Wisdom is addressed to the Jewish community living outside of the promised land and in constant danger of being won over by the pagan culture. The author writes to strengthen the faith of his fellow Jews, taking up the perennial questions of the philosopher—the problem of evil and the treatment of sinners. Like us, they pondered why sinners are allowed to prosper while God's faithful ones seem to suffer. Isn't that our question?*
3. Gather everyone into small groups to compile a list of circumstances in which they consider that the person who does wrong (evil) receives all the benefits and the person who does good receives no benefits, or worse. Brainstorm this list; then ask them to name their feelings, thoughts, and responses to this problem. In the large gathering, encourage the small groups to share their lists and their feelings.

Making Connections

1. Ask the participants to share how they have solved this dilemma for themselves. Invite everyone to indicate the deeper questions that arise when they ponder the perplexity of an all-powerful, all-knowing, and all-loving God who allows suffering, tragedies, and pain in the lives of good human beings at the hands of people who do evil.
2. Retell the first parable of today's gospel, Matthew 13:24–30, in your own words. Invite the catechumens and candidates to discuss these questions in small groups: *What insights does this parable shed on the problem of evil? What experiences have you had in which an apparent evil had a good outcome?* Invite responses in the large group.

3. Continue by sharing some examples from your own life or use these examples: *Things are not always what they seem at first. For example, a person who loses his or her job can discover new priorities, change careers, and enter a less stressful job market. An individual diagnosed with terminal cancer can prepare for death by reconciling with estranged members of the family.* Invite them to describe other such examples from their own lives.

Prayer

Invite the catechumens and candidates to stand in a circle with their hands open and palms facing upward for prayer. Lead the prayer with the following intercessions or your own: (The response to each invocation is *"Lord, touch their hearts with your love."*) *For people who do not experience God's presence in their lives, we pray . . . For those who blame God for the pain and suffering in their lives, we pray . . . For young children who are often the victims of tragic events, we pray . . . For people who lose all hope in the face of difficulties, we pray . . .* Invite the participants to add intentions.

Extended Catechesis

SESSION FOCUS: *The Problem of Moral Evil*

Gathering

A. Sunday:

1. Welcome and invite the sponsors and team members to join the circle of catechumens and candidates.
2. Encourage one or two catechumens and candidates to summarize what transpired during the Dismissal Catechesis.
3. Lead all in singing a verse from the Gathering Song from the liturgy. Invite a team member to proclaim the first reading, Wisdom 12:13, 16–19. Pause for reflection. Then proclaim the gospel, Matthew 13:24–43.

B. Weekday:

1. Use the same centerpiece as in the Dismissal Catechesis.
2. As the participants gather in the circle, greet and warmly welcome each person.
3. Lead this celebration of the Word:
   - Song: Gathering Song from Sunday's Liturgy
   - First Reading: Wisdom 12:13, 16–19
   - Sing Psalm 86:5–6, 9–10, 15–16
   - Alleluia
   - Gospel: Matthew 13:24–43
   - Alleluia

The Word (30 min.)

1. Expand the background to the first reading from Wisdom in these or similar words: *The writer of Wisdom reveals a God of mercy and compassion, a God who never gives up on the sinner. God permits the sinner to survive with an eye to the possibility of repentance. Despite the divine*

power that could simply crush all evil, Yahweh has been shown to be a God of "much lenience."

2. Invite the participants into small groups with a sponsor or team member in each group. Raise these questions to initiate discussion: *Is the God you believe in merciful and compassionate? Explain. What example does our merciful God set for us?* Gather and summarize responses.

3. Continue with this background for the gospel: *This passage is part of a larger collection of parables focused on the kingdom. These three parables address the perplexing reality that Jesus seemed to tolerate the presence of moral evil. This attitude scandalized some, both in Jesus' day and in the early community of Matthew. The answer given to this problem of evil is that God wishes to allow time for repentance and further growth.*

4. Encourage the small groups to delve into the meaning of the parables: *What do the weeds sown among the wheat, the mustard seed, and the yeast symbolize in your own life? How has God's patience with your conversion yielded goodness in your life? What is your hope as you hear these parables?* Invite each group to share a summary of this discussion in the larger gathering.

Catholic Teaching (30 min.)

1. Describe the Church teaching on moral evil in these or similar words: *Today's readings emphasize that there is a type of evil which we choose to engage in, either by action or inaction, and that at the end of the world all will be judged accordingly. The idea of moral evil rests upon the foundation of free choice. The Church believes that human beings are accountable and therefore move toward their final destiny by their choice through the exercise of free will. A quick recounting of history is ample proof that human beings have chosen to do wrong, and thus sinned against God and neighbor.* Direct the participants to enumerate some examples of moral evil. If needed, prompt them with examples such as the holocaust, atomic or germ warfare, child labor.

2. Then expand the Church's teaching with these or similar words: *Our greatest theologians have asserted that God is neither directly nor indirectly responsible for the cause of moral evil in the world. Saint Augustine and Saint Thomas upheld that God, by divine nature, directs the human heart toward good. The responsibility for choosing other than the good does not belong to God, but to human beings. The Second Vatican Council declared that, in our very depths, human beings are divided, frequently gravitating toward what is wrong and sinking into evil ways. God is neither directly nor indirectly the author or cause of evil; in addition, God is always "on our side," championing the good in us, and working for our well-being.*

3. Direct the participants to respond to these questions in their small groups: *In what way is it impossible to blame God or others for the decisions that we make—for good or for evil? Why is it so difficult for us to accept responsibility for our decisions? How is it that the gift of free will engages us in the struggle between good and evil, ultimately leading to our final reward?*

4. Gather responses from their discussion, and then conclude the input on moral evil in the following words: *Why evil exists can only be resolved by the totality of faith. The goodness of creation, the patient, merciful love of the Most High, the beauty of God's covenant with us, the Word made flesh, Jesus who saves us, the transforming fire of the Holy Spirit, the birth of the Church, the continual gathering of the faithful, and the nourishment of life-giving sacraments all attest to our end and goal in the goodness of the divine One who provides for us no matter how far we have fallen.*

Putting Faith into Practice

1. Raise this question for the small group discussion: *In light of our discussion about the realities of evil and God's mercy and forgiveness, what new insights did you gain; what affirmations did you experience and what challenges were issued?* Listen to each group as they offer a summary of their insights.

2. Ask everyone to open their Participant Book to page 84 to rewrite one of the parables from today's gospel in the light of their own experience and understanding of the Church's teaching on moral evil. When they have finished, direct them to find their sponsor or candidate or catechumen to share the parable. Invite a few parables to be shared in the large group, then summarize the exercise: *God gave us free will. God doesn't make decisions for us nor does God give up on us. God is ever hopeful that we will recognize good and evil and choose the good. Thus, the weeds and wheat grow together till harvest; the mustard seed, which someone took and planted in the field, provides a place for the birds to build a nest; yeast, which is a bacteria, causes the whole mass of dough to rise.*

3. Invite everyone to close their eyes and to take a few deep breaths. Lead them in the following reflection: *Imagine you are in a favorite place. It's quiet and peaceful. Be still. Today we discuss the reality of moral evil and that each of us chooses evil—sin. Sometimes we engage in evil by doing it and sometimes by not doing something we ought. Think over the events of your own life. Name one that was or is a real struggle between good and evil for you.—Pause.—What made it a struggle? What made the evil so desirable and good less so?—Pause.—What did you freely choose to do? Why? What has happened as a result of your choice? God rejoices in the good that you do and God waits for you to accept the redemption, which Jesus accomplished, and to change. The choice is always yours. What will it be?—Pause.*

4. When the reflection is concluded, keeping the same mood of reverent silence, ask the participants to respond to the questions in the Participant Book on page 84. Encourage everyone to share their responses during the next week.

Prayer

Lead the closing prayer by distributing copies of Psalm 86:5–6, 9–10, 15–16 and inviting all to pray these words together. Encourage everyone to join in singing, "God of Day and God of Darkness" (Marty Haugen, OCP Publication, 1985).

Seventeenth Sunday in Ordinary Time

Understanding this Sunday:
Background for Catechesis

The Word in Liturgy

1 Kings 3:5, 7–12
Psalm 119:57, 72, 76–77, 127–128, 129–130
Romans 8:28–30
Matthew 13:44–52 [or (short form) 13:44–46]

Today's gospel text completes the "Discourse in Parables" in which Matthew has collected various teachings about the nature of God's reign proclaimed by Jesus. Each of the three parables we read today contributes some insight into the nature of that kingdom. The man who finds the buried treasure must put up (risk) everything he has in order to attain the treasure. Being part of the reign of God is not for the faint-hearted or fearful. It requires boldness and decisive action, a single-minded commitment of all one's resources. The second parable of the pearl is similar but, in this case, it is not a laborer (a poor man) who discovers the treasure but a merchant (a rich man) who seeks it out. God's kingdom is all-inclusive, available to rich and poor alike. Still, the merchant like the laborer must risk everything to succeed. The message is clear: discipleship is open to all but entails sacrifice. Equally clear is the outcome of the disciple's quest: a joy that exceeds imagination when he has found the only truly valuable thing in life. The final parable of the dragnet hearkens back to last week's parables that tried to explain the presence of those who seem unfit for the kingdom. The invitation of Jesus to be part of God's reign is open to rich and poor, good and bad; in fact, many of all sorts are collected into the community of disciples. But at the end there will be a sorting out of those who are worthless and those who have been proven valuable. The image of fishermen hauling in the dragnet would certainly have resonated with the early Christian community that had come to recognize the apostles as "fishers of men" (Matthew 4:19). They knew this was about their own mission as evangelizers. They must refuse the invitation to no one, regardless of whether or not they seemed "worthy" of the kingdom.

The first reading from 1 Kings was clearly chosen in view of the idea that discipleship requires a person to choose the one thing that is most important of all. The deuteronomic editor responsible for 1 Kings was concerned to trace the history of Israel's kings in a way that would demonstrate the importance of fidelity to Yahweh's covenant. A monarch's infidelity invariably brought ruin on the whole people; his obedience to Yahweh resulted in blessings. Solomon is presented here and elsewhere as the epitome of the wise ruler. God's offer to grant whatever Solomon asks for is exceptional. Solomon's request is equally extraordinary: he eschews wealth, longevity, and power over his enemies and simply asks for what he needs to fulfill the mission entrusted to him by the Lord. In return, the Lord lavishly promises that Solomon will be unsurpassed in wisdom among all the rulers of the earth.

Psalm 119 is a lengthy song of praise in honor of God's Torah (instruction or law). The refrain used today ("Lord, I love your commands") gives voice to what one might conjecture to be a sentiment found on the lips of Solomon. Desiring the right thing, for Solomon, meant wanting to be faithful to the commands of the covenant with Yahweh. The liturgy today holds up this example as valid for those of every age who wish to be part of God's reign.

Today's reading from Romans follows directly on last week's passage. Paul has alluded in several places to the "groanings" of all creation in which we share. He is keenly aware of the problem which suffering poses for the faithful disciple. Here, he underlines the fact of God's love, a love that is in no way contradicted by the reality of human suffering. In fact, it is a love in which we have been known, chosen, called, and saved from the beginning. Paul is not anticipating later generations' theological debates over technical predestination. Rather, he is looking at human history as a story of love, and he teaches that from beginning to end the unfolding process of salvation has enveloped us in a plan of divine love. In the verses that follow immediately, to be read next week, we see how intensely Paul is aware of the overwhelming reality of God's love, no matter what afflictions one might experience (e.g., trials, persecution, hunger, nakedness, etc.).

Catholic Doctrine

The Kingdom of God

The phrase "kingdom of God," also translated as "reign of God" or "dominion of God," appears 150 times in the New Testament. Two-thirds of these are found in Matthew, Mark and Luke. It is a rich metaphor that has definite roots in Old Testament scriptures, although the precise phrase "kingdom of God" is not found therein (the closest is "reign of the Lord" in some of the later Hebrew scriptures). However, the Old Testament gives God the title of "king" in numerous references to illustrate the relationship of the Most High to Israel, to history, and to all of creation.

The metaphor "kingdom of God," as used by Jesus, not only relies on this Old Testament basis but goes beyond it in a rich, unique way that has no one clear definition or description—precisely because the metaphor is less a concept and more a symbol. Yet this does not mean that the metaphor is void of content. Rather, the significance of the metaphor is layered and multidimensional, and can only be deciphered in relationship to the ministry and mission of Jesus Christ: the One who saves us, the One who is the decisive event in world history, and the One who is the invitation to union with God.

Jesus offers salvation, but not to a limited number of people. His saving mission is extended to all without limit (CCC 543). To those who are sick or broken by the power of sin and evil (CCC 545), he offers healing and exorcisms (for example, Matthew 12:28 and Luke 11:20). In addition, his saving ministry is aimed at the poor and lowly ones (CCC 545) and those who are outcasts of society, those ostracized from the community (for example, Matthew 11:19 and Luke 15:1). The gospel episodes which depict the healing worked by Jesus, his exorcisms, and his inclusion of outcasts give form to the "kingdom of God" as an experience of salvation (in its Latin root, meaning "health") for all. Jesus establishes God's kingdom as just and inclusive, without boundaries and boundless in heaven's mercy (NDictTheol 858).

Jesus is the decisive event in world history. He inaugurates his ministry by proclaiming that the kingdom of God is "at hand" (Mark 1:14–15). His disciples are promised that before they die they will witness the coming of God's kingdom in power (Mark 9:1 and Matthew 10:23). Jesus announces, as he works a healing miracle, that the kingdom of God "has come upon you" (Matthew 12:28 and Luke 11:20). Thus, the Church upholds Jesus as the fulfillment of God's love that is lavished upon the world; Christ is the decisive event that incarnates God's activity among men and women—for all time (CCC 541). And yet, if the event of the kingdom has been decisively inaugurated by Jesus and is here now among us, it is nevertheless not fully realized. Jesus' own transfiguration upon the mountain is a foretaste of the fullness of the kingdom when all those drawn to Christ will be transformed in glory. The scriptural episode of the transfiguration also is a reminder that those who follow Jesus and desire entrance into the kingdom of God must bear hardship and possibly persecution and the cross (CCC 556). Thus, the decisive "kingdom of God" metaphor contains a tension in that Jesus proclaims its advent among us while we yet wait for its fullness to be revealed.

Jesus invites us into union with God. The New Testament scriptures portray his vivid sense of God's presence (for example, calling God intimately by the term *abba*, as in Mark 14:36). Time and again in the gospel accounts, Jesus reaches out in compassion to the weak, the insignificant, the lost, and the lowly. All are being drawn into union with God through Jesus, most especially through his paschal sacrifice. As Christ is lifted up upon the cross, he will draw all to himself and thus into union with his heavenly Father (CCC 542). This is not an unthinking, automatic union—it requires personal appropriation, decision, and actions taken as a member of the family of God. In other words, the metaphor "kingdom of God" also contains this sense of the urgency of conversion. In order to belong, Jesus invites believers to a radical choice, that is, to give themselves totally to the intimate union he offers (CCC 546).

It is important to note that the Church is linked to the idea of the kingdom of God. On earth, the Church is the seedbed for the kingdom, but it is not exactly synonymous with it. Nonetheless, the Second Vatican Council taught that the mystery of the Church is founded on the inauguration of Jesus' good news of the kingdom (LG 5). Jesus is the head and lifeblood of the Church, and the depths of meaning involved in "kingdom of God" cannot be plumbed without reference to Christ. It follows, then, that Church and the kingdom are twin threads in the salvation story.

Catholic Culture

The Greek term *basileia* (meaning "kingdom") which is used in the New Testament to refer to the "kingdom of God" is also the root word for the word "basilica," which in ancient Rome was a building for certain public, official uses. The basilica style of public building was eventually adapted for use by the early Church for its larger and more lavish worship spaces. The basilica was the hall where Jesus, the king of kings, presided. Today, a basilica church is one that holds a special significance for a particular people or area. The major basilicas are located in Rome. Other church buildings throughout the world are accorded basilica status by the Vatican and these are called "minor" basilicas (EncyCath 144).

Dismissal Catechesis (30 min.)

Getting Started

1. Prepare the space ahead of time with a circle of chairs and a table covered with a green cloth in the center. Place on the table a candle, some fishing net, and a valued family "treasure," such as a piece of jewelry. You will need copies of Psalm 119:57, 72, 76–77, 122–128, 129–130 for each participant.

2. Invite the catechumens and candidates to be seated in the circle and light the candle. After a moment of quiet, pray: *Gracious God, you surround us with the gifts and treasures of your divine life. Give us wise and understanding hearts to choose you above everything else. Grace us now with the wisdom to hear and heed the gift of your Word today. Let your Word penetrate into our hearts and take root in our lives. We ask this through Jesus, our Savior. Amen.*

First Impressions

1. Ask the group to brainstorm images, phrases, or words from the gathering hymn and each of the readings from today's Liturgy of the Word. Make sure they include Solomon's wise and understanding heart and God's reign compared to a buried treasure and a valuable pearl for which everything else was sold, and the dragnet catching all sorts of fish.

2. Gather the participants into small groups to discuss these questions: *Which of these images are you most drawn to today? Which of these images speak to your heart? Why do you think this is so?* In the large group invite each group to share their initial experience of today's scripture readings.

Making Connections

1. Focus the attention of the group on the valued family "treasure" on the table. Ask the participants to name some of their family treasures and to explain why they are treasured.

2. Invite the participants to talk about the worth or value of these treasures. Point out that such items are usually irreplaceable and not able to be bought with money, and not only because of the monetary value. Rather, the items are valuable because of their connection with someone the owners treasure. Allow the participants time to express some personal connections with their treasured items.

3. Then ask the participants to discuss the following questions in small groups, saying: *Usually the way we spend our lives, what we give our time and energy to, indicates our values. Think about how you spend your time and energy. Is this expenditure of time and energy consistent with what you really value? Is it consistent with your relationship with God? Is God calling you to change in any way?*

4. When they have finished discussing, ask each group to give a summary of their responses. Then ask the participants to respond to this question: *What do you want to remember from today's sharing?* Invite them to write this in their Participant Book on page 87 in the section "I want to remember."

Prayer

Distribute printed copies of Psalm 119. As you move into prayer, invite the participants to bring to awareness their desire for God's treasure. After a moment of quiet, pray Psalm 119 together. Lead the group in singing the Psalm refrain, or the refrain of the song "Lord, You Have the Words" (David Haas, GIA Publications, 1983) between verses.

Extended Catechesis

SESSION FOCUS: *The Kingdom of God*

Gathering

A. **Sunday:**
   1. Greet and welcome the sponsors, team members, and other participants as they join the group.
   2. Invite everyone into a moment of quiet. Lead them in singing "The Summons" (Iona Community, GIA Publications, 1987), verses 1 through 4. Pray in these or similar words: *Lord Jesus, we hear your invitation to live in God's kingdom. We hear you proclaim that being part of God's reign is everything. Bring us along with you. Direct our hearts to what is truly important. Keep our hearts focused on you. We pray in your name. Amen.* Proclaim Matthew 13:44–52.

B. **Weekday:**
   1. Welcome and greet the participants and team members. Invite them to gather in the circle with the same centerpiece as the Dismissal Catechesis.
   2. Ask everyone to reflect on the last few days and briefly share a valued experience they had with another.
   3. Lead this celebration of the Word:
      • Gathering Song: "The Summons" (Iona Community, GIA Publications, 1987)
      • Greeting, Sign of the Cross
      • First Reading: 1 Kings 3:5, 7–12
      • Sing Psalm 119:57, 76–77, 127–128, 129–130
      • Gospel: Matthew 13:44–52
      • Silent Reflection

The Word (30 min.)

1. Ask a catechumen or candidate to briefly summarize the Dismissal Catechesis. Encourage the sponsors and team members to offer their insights on the scripture passages.

2. Introduce the gospel in these or your own words: *Today's gospel completes Matthew's teaching on the reign of God, through the use of parables. Each of today's parables expands our notions about God's reign. What three images are presented to us in this gospel?* As they are named, list these images in a column on newsprint: *The Buried Treasure, The Valuable Pearl,* and *The Dragnet.* Then invite the participants to name what each image reveals about God's reign. List these insights on newsprint under the appropriate image. Summarize their sharing in these or similar words: *The buried treasure was worth everything to the poor laborer. The pearl was worth everything to the wealthy merchant. The dragnet includes all kinds of fish.*

3. Invite the participants to turn to the questions in their Participant Book on page 86. Give them adequate time to reflect on these questions: *Have you ever given yourself completely to something or someone? Can you imagine giving yourself completely over to God? What holds you back?* They may find it helpful to write their responses in the space provided in the Participant Book. Encourage everyone to share their responses in small groups. Then, in the large gathering, invite each group to share a summary of the discussion.

4. Explain the first reading by stating: *In the first reading from 1 Kings, Solomon clearly chose fidelity to Yahweh's covenant as being the one thing that is most important. This choice is not a chore or hardship, but comes out of a relationship of love and a desire of the heart. Return to your small groups to share your stories of experiencing God calling you to let go of something else to gain the pearl or treasure of God's reign.* Allow sufficient time for this discussion. When you have gathered the attention of the large group, invite a few participants to share their experiences with everyone.

Catholic Teaching (30 min.)

1. Present the Church's teaching on the kingdom of God, making sure to include the following points:

   • The phrase "kingdom of God," also called "reign of God," "dominion of God," and "kingdom of heaven," occurs 150 times in the New Testament. With roots in the Old Testament, the term comes into use with the advent of Jesus. The metaphor "kingdom of God" is symbolic of God's reign in people and is knowable through the ministry and mission of Jesus.

   • Jesus' saving mission is extended to all people without limit. Examples in the gospel include the poor, the lowly, and the outcasts of society. Jesus' healing ministry to the sick, sinful, and ostracized give form to the kingdom of God as an experience of salvation (in its Latin root, meaning "health") for all.

   • Jesus began his ministry announcing that God's kingdom is here. Jesus is the fulfillment for all time of God's love lavished upon the world. The tension exists between the kingdom that is already present and yet not fully realized.

   • Jesus' transfiguration is a foretaste of the time when all drawn to Christ will be transformed in glory. Those transformed in glory must bear hardship and possibly persecution and the cross.

   • Jesus, who had a vivid sense of God's presence, invites us into this same union with God. This union includes compassion for the weak, the insignificant, the lost, and the lowly. This union requires personal appropriation through concrete decisions and actions, and involves radical ongoing conversion.

   • The Church, though not synonymous with the kingdom of God, is founded on God's reign. The Church's mission is an extension of the mission of Christ to preach the Good News and bring about the reign of God in this world.

2. Ask the participants to discuss this question in small groups: *What is one way that God is inviting you to live more fully as part of God's kingdom?*

Putting Faith into Practice

When they have finished sharing, invite each person to choose an action they are willing to undertake this week to live more fully as part of God's kingdom. Encourage them to write this action in the "I want to put my faith into action by" section of the Participant Book on page 87.

Prayer

Ask the participants to choose a quality from the list of people who live in God's kingdom that they wish to integrate into their lives. Invite them to pray as Solomon did, using the phrase, *"Lord, give me, your servant, . . . (name of quality)."* Go around the circle. After this litany of prayer, lead the group in singing "Amen." Then celebrate the Blessing found in RCIA 97I. Have the sponsors place a hand on the catechumen's shoulder. Conclude with all singing "We Are Called" (David Haas, GIA Publications, 1988).

Eighteenth Sunday in Ordinary Time

The Word in Liturgy

Isaiah 55:1–3
Psalm 145: 8–9, 15–16, 17–18
Romans 8:35, 37–39
Matthew 14:13–21

The story of the miraculous feeding of the multitude was extremely important in the early Church. It is recounted six times in the gospels, with each version shaped in slightly different ways according to the particular concerns of the evangelist. Matthew writes to a community for whom the ritual of the Lord's Supper had already become a venerable and central tradition, and he is eager for his audience to recognize in this story a foreshadowing of the Christian Eucharist as well as the fulfillment of ancient messianic hopes.

Matthew describes the miracle in ways clearly reminiscent of a similar story about Elisha in 2 Kings 4:42–44. Its setting in a "deserted place" also evokes the account in Exodus 16:13–14 of God's feeding the people in the wilderness. Details such as ordering the people to sit on the grass may be intended to recall Psalm 23's messianic promise of "verdant pastures" in which to lie down and God setting a table in the sight of one's foes. Commentators often point out the highly symbolic character of the meal stories in the gospels. In particular, when one sees the familiar language of Christian Eucharist ("took . . . blessed . . . broke . . . gave") used to describe the miracle, it is fairly obvious that the evangelist wishes his readers to make certain associations. Matthew is telling his audience something about their own Eucharist. The abundance of the twelve baskets of leftovers represents the twelve tribes of the New Israel (an important theme in Matthew), presided over by the twelve disciples (see Matthew 19:28). Matthew suggests that the Christian Eucharist, itself foreshadowed of old in the Jewish scriptures, is in its own way a foreshadowing of the messianic banquet still anticipated by the Christian community to whom he writes.

The metaphor of hunger and thirst and the gracious act of offering food and drink are primal symbols in the scriptures for our human dependence on God and for God's grace and care for us in every circumstance of need. By the time Deutero-Isaiah penned today's promise to the exiles in Babylon at the conclusion of his Book of Consolation, the image of a banquet set by God for the people was already an ancient symbol of Israel's hope in God. Here, the imagery is lavish in the extreme: All are invited, without exception. "Rich fare" is offered: wine and milk and bread, all without cost, so that Yahweh may "renew with you the everlasting covenant." The refrain used with today's responsorial psalm captures the experience of the exiles in Babylon to whom Deutero-Isaiah wrote, just as surely as it expresses the experience of every generation of Christians who gather at the banquet of the Eucharist: "The hand of the Lord feeds us; he answers all our needs." The verses of today's psalm exude confidence and reassurance that God is "good to all and compassionate toward all his works" (Psalm 145:9). The metaphor of God feeding the people is again prominent ("You give them their food in due season," v. 15), and again it is clear that the act of feeding is symbolic of much, much more than the fulfillment of physical need.

The Pauline text today concludes and climaxes his treatment in Romans 8 of the reality of a Christian's life in the Spirit. It is, Paul asserts, a life of divine love so intense and so complete that no human difficulty nor even superhuman powers can overcome it. Paul's list of human sufferings (v. 35) and potential obstacles to God (vv. 38–39) show that he is a realist. His audience, too, knew firsthand that Christian life entailed suffering and trials. But Paul's language fairly soars as he reminds his audience that absolutely nothing is a match for "the love of God that comes to us in Christ Jesus, our Lord." The seemingly negative—and perhaps shocking—suggestion of Paul that angels might try to separate us from the love of God can be understood to reflect the rabbinic teachings of his day which held that angels were sometimes jealous of God's favor toward lower creatures and might even act with hostility toward humans.

Catholic Doctrine

Eucharist as Meal

Eucharist, the third and final sacrament of initiation, completes the initiatory journey of the believer (CCC 1322). Coming up out of the water bath of baptism, anointed lavishly in confirmation, the newly initiated then approach the eucharistic table of the Lord in order to share in the sacred meal. The Church's wealth of understanding with regard to Eucharist is seen in the variety of ways in which this sacrament is described: as a memorial, a sacrifice, as thanksgiving, as impetus for mission, and as the Lord's Supper. This last description, which indicates the nature of the Eucharist as a meal, will be examined in this essay. (For other perspectives on the nature of the Eucharist, see the doctrinal essays for the Third Sunday of Easter and the Solemnity of the Body and Blood of Christ.)

The Eucharist perpetuates and makes present to us, here and now, the sacrifice of the cross of Jesus Christ. But the sharing of communion is likewise essential to the meaning of the Mass (CCC 1382). The Second Vatican Council was concerned to renew in the faithful a vital sense of the Eucharist as meal. This is one of the reasons why the General Instruction to the Roman Missal directs that the bread to be used for the Eucharist "appear as actual food" (GIRM 283) and why offering communion under both forms is preferable to offering communion under the form of bread alone (GIRM 240). This sacramental meal is not simply like any other act of eating and drinking. Those who eat and drink this sacred meal in faith have a share in the death and saving sacrifice of Jesus. The Church believes that eating and drinking at the table of the Lord places one in intimate communion with Christ whose loving sacrifice is made on our behalf (CCC 1382).

Partaking in the Lord's Supper also nourishes the spiritual life of the believer. Much as ordinary or material food strengthens and helps our bodies to grow, Eucharist promotes the spiritual growth begun in us at baptism. Just as we cannot hope to survive without material food, the Eucharist is necessary for our growth in the life of faith (CCC 1392). This is the reasoning behind the Church's encouragement to the faithful to receive Eucharist every Sunday (CCC 1389).

Last of all, the sacred meal of the Eucharist reminds us of the paschal feast of heaven, the banquet which awaits all the faithful at the end of their earthly pilgrimage. The image of heaven as a feast has long been revered in Catholic tradition (CCC 1027). In the liturgy, immediately before communion, we recall this eternal banquet in the words, "This is the Lamb of God who takes away the sins of the world. Happy are those who are called to his supper." The "supper of the Lamb" described in the Book of Revelation (19:9) is a "wedding banquet" uniting the faithful with Christ forever (CCC 1329). The banquet of heaven is thus an eschatological image of joy and hope.

The eating and drinking which takes place in the Eucharist is celebrated in the context of a gathering of the faithful, that is, the Mass. Catholics come together to hear the Word of God proclaimed in scripture, to reflect upon that Word and, having offered intercessions for the Church, the world, and for particular needs, the community then presents to the table of the Lord gifts of bread and wine. The gathering itself signifies the presence of Christ, for Christ is present in the assembly of his people (SC 7). Gathered around the altar, the Church enters into the action of Christ at the Last Supper who took bread and blessed, broke, and gave it, and who took a cup and shared it (CCC 1350). These elements of a people gathered together by Christ, who then "blessed, broke, gave" (Matthew 14:18) are reflected in today's gospel which clearly prefigures the Last Supper and illuminates the abundance of the gift of the Eucharist.

Sharing in the meal of the Eucharist makes us one body in Christ (CCC 1382), and thus is a sign of unity. The Church prays as it celebrates the Eucharist, "Strengthen in unity those you have called to this table. Together with . . . our pope . . . our bishop, with all your bishops, priests and deacons, and all your holy people, may we follow your paths in faith and hope and radiate our joy and trust to all the world" (Eucharistic Prayer for Masses for Various Needs and Occasions II).

Catholic Culture

A contemporary Catholic hymn which focuses on the meal aspect of the Eucharist is entitled "Table of Plenty." Its refrain and first verse invite, "Come to the feast of heaven and earth! Come to the table of plenty! God will provide for all that we need, here at the table of plenty! O, come and sit at my table where saints and sinners are friends. I wait to welcome the lost and lonely to share the cup of my love" (Schutte, OCP Publications, 1992).

The earliest depiction of the miraculous feeding of the multitude is found on the "Trinity" sarcophagus (c. 315 A.D.) now found in the Lateran museum in Rome. It is so named because the carving of the miraculous feeding is the central piece of artwork that is flanked, on the left, by the miracle at Cana, and on the right, by the raising of Lazarus. Art historians attribute this threefold work as representing early theological developments in understanding the Eucharist (the Cana miracle and the feeding of the multitude) linked with the resurrection. Another early work, the fifth-century doors of St. Sabina church in Rome, show Christ blessing the fish offered to him by the disciples while touching the bread in a basket at his feet with his staff (OxA&A 281).

Dismissal Catechesis (30 min.)

Getting Started

1. Prepare the space ahead of time with a circle of chairs around a table. Set the table as a dinner table with a white flowing cloth over the green under-cloth, signifying this season, white taper candles, a loaf of bread, and a dinner glass filled with wine.
2. Greet and welcome the catechumens and candidates as they gather. Begin by leading all in singing the refrain of "Eat This Bread" (Taize, GIA Publications, 1984) several times. Provide hymnals so that all can sing. Then pray:
Gracious God, you provide a rich feast for us. You invite us to come to your table so that you can fill our hunger. When we are hungry, direct our hearts to you, the one who gives true nourishment. Fill us now with the banquet of your word. We pray in Jesus' name. Amen.

First Impressions

1. Invite the group to listen carefully as you slowly read Isaiah 55:1–3. While they listen, invite them to take note of any words that stand out for them. Proclaim the first reading from the Book of Isaiah. Then, going around the circle, ask each person to name the words or phrases that impressed him or her.
2. Gather the participants into small groups. Ask them to discuss these questions: *As you hear these words that have stood out for each of us, what do you hear God saying over and over again? What feelings arise in you as you hear God inviting you simply to "Come"?* When they finish, ask everyone to share their responses in the large gathering.
3. Then encourage them to discuss this question in the same small groups: *What does this reading from Isaiah tell us about God's way of feeding us?* Elicit their responses. Be sure to include that God provides a banquet, all are invited, the table is set with a "rich fare" of wine, milk, and bread, and it all comes without cost.

Making Connections

1. Continue the large group sharing on the Isaiah reading by means of the following question: *What does this reading from Isaiah say to you about who God is and what God is like?* Help the group to name qualities of God that indicate God's generosity, abundance, and graciousness.
2. In the small groups invite the participants to share their hunger for God and how that hunger is satisfied. Ask them to recall a time when they felt empty or dissatisfied. Then ask: *How did God "feed" you?* Allow enough time in the small groups for each person to share their story.
3. After this sharing time, turn the attention of the participants back to the large group. Invite them to share the following: *From telling your story, what did you learn about God's desire to fill and satisfy you?* Summarize their insights.

4. Going around the circle, ask the participants to state one thing they want to remember from this session. When they have finished, encourage them to write this in their Participant Book on page 89 in the section "I want to remember."

Prayer

Prepare copies of Psalm 145 for everyone prior to the gathering. Invite the group to look at the center table as a reminder of the table God sets for them. Then, once again, proclaim Isaiah 55:1–3. Close the prayer by asking everyone to pray Psalm 145 together.

Extended Catechesis

SESSION FOCUS: *Eucharist as Meal*

Gathering

A. **Sunday:**
   1. Invite everyone to gather and welcome the sponsors, team members, and additional participants. Draw their attention to the table in the center.
   2. Begin the prayer by inviting all to become aware of the hunger for God they feel within them. Then sing several verses of "Come to the Feast" (Marty Haugen, GIA Publications, 1991). Then pray in these or similar words:
   Gracious God, you are the one who invites us to your feast. You are the one who bids us to come as we are to your abundant table. You are the one who feeds our hearts as no other can. When we are slow to respond, make our hunger for you grow. Feed us now with your word and your goodness. We pray in the name of Jesus, who fed the crowd. Amen.
   Proclaim Matthew 14:13–21.

B. **Weekday:**
   1. Welcome and greet everyone as they arrive. Invite them to gather in the circle and spend a short time in silence reflecting on the bread and wine on the table. Encourage the participants to share a way God has nourished them in the past few days.
   2. Lead this celebration of the Word:
      - Gathering Song: "Come to the Feast," (Marty Haugen, GIA Publications, 1991).
      - First Reading: Isaiah 55:1–3
      - Sing Psalm 145
      - Second Reading: Romans 8:35, 37–39
      - Sing: Alleluia
      - Gospel: Matthew 14:13–21
      - Pray the prayer stated in A.2 above.

The Word (30 min.)

1. Ask a catechumen or candidate to share a summary of the dismissal session.
2. Explain the background of the gospel in these or similar words:

   The account of the multiplication of the loaves and fishes is found in all four gospels. Matthew sets this miracle in a "deserted place" that evokes the early Jewish experience of God feeding the people in the wilderness. Matthew details Jesus inviting the people to sit on the grass, which calls to mind the messianic promise in Psalm 23 of "verdant pastures" and God setting a table in the sight of one's foes. The familiar language of the Christian Eucharist ("took . . . blessed . . . broke . . . gave") is used. The abundance of the twelve baskets of leftovers connects with the whole number twelve; the twelve tribes of the New Israel and the twelve apostles. Thus Matthew, writing for the Jewish audience, connects the Christian Eucharist with its foreshadowing in the Jewish scriptures, and its foreshadowing of the coming messianic banquet.

3. Invite the participants to listen once again to the gospel for the word or phrase that stands out for them. Then proclaim Matthew 14:13–21. Invite them to call out the word or phrase that is significant. Emphasize the facts that this feeding story occurred when Jesus wanted some time to himself after hearing of John the Baptist's death, that his heart was moved with pity for the crowd and that, rather than dismissing the crowds as the disciples suggested, Jesus told the disciples to feed them.

4. Invite the participants to share this question in small groups: *What do these actions of Jesus say to us about the meaning of Eucharist?* After a few minutes ask the participants to name their insight about Eucharist in the large group. Write their responses on newsprint.

5. Connect the gospel with the first reading from Isaiah 55:1–3: *Remember that in the first reading from Isaiah 55 God invited the Israelites to come to the table God set for them. The image of God setting a banquet for people was an ancient symbol of Israel's hope in God. Each of the gospels contains images of the banquet God provides where all of God's people are joined as one.*

   Ask the participants to reflect on the exercise presented in the Participant Book on page 88. When they have finished writing, ask them to respond to the questions presented on the same page. When they are ready, have them share their responses in the large group. List their insights on newsprint.

Catholic Teaching (30 min.)

1. Continue to delve into the meaning of Eucharist, enlarging on the following points.
   - The Eucharist, the third and final sacrament of initiation, is a memorial, a sacrifice, thanksgiving, an impetus for mission, and the Lord's Supper.
   - The Second Vatican Council renewed the Church's focus on Eucharist as meal. The Church instructs us to use bread that looks like bread, and prefers the faithful partaking of both bread and wine as a fuller experience of sharing a meal.
   - Eucharist is an intimate communion with Christ, and thus a sharing in the death and sacrifice of Christ. Eucharist is necessary to nourish the spiritual life of the believer. The Church encourages the faithful to receive Eucharist every Sunday.
   - The Eucharist is celebrated and partaken of in the midst of the gathered assembly, who signify the presence of Christ. At Mass the community gathers, hears and reflects on the Word of God, offers intercession for God's people, presents bread and wine, and shares in the action of Christ who "took, blessed, broke, and gave" (Matthew 14:18) the bread and wine of his body and blood.
   - The Eucharist draws us to the eternal heavenly banquet, the supper of the Lamb, the wedding banquet with Christ the bridegroom.
   - Sharing in the eucharistic meal makes us one body in Christ. We, then, are sent forth to share this meal with others.

   Gather the participants into small groups to share their responses to these questions: *What can we say about a Church that has a meal at the center of its faith? What does it mean for you to share in the meal of the body and blood of Jesus, who commanded the disciples to "give them something to eat yourselves?" (Matthew 14:16).* In the large group invite the participants' responses and questions regarding Eucharist as a meal.

Or . . .

Instead of gathering for this session, invite the group to work together at a soup kitchen for an evening. When you return provide adequate time for the participants to share their experiences and insights.

Putting Faith into Practice

Ask the participants to brainstorm some ways they are able to live the Eucharist by feeding others this week. List these suggested actions on newsprint. Then invite each participant to choose a way they will feed others this week. Encourage them to write this in the "I want to put my faith into action by" section of the Participant Book on page 89. Ask them to share this commitment in their small group.

Prayer

Focus the attention of the participants back to the large group. Ask the participants to turn back to the reflection exercise in their Participant Book on page 88 to read, once again, the hungers they expressed. When they are ready, beginning with you, encourage each person to express her or his prayer, using the formula, *"God, satisfy my hunger for. . . ."* Then, to recall Jesus' feeding the crowd, pass around the loaf of bread, and invite all to tear off a piece and eat it as a sign of God filling their hunger, and to share the cup of wine as well. This is not Eucharist, but simply a prayerful sharing to help the group meditate on what they have learned in the catechesis. Close by leading the group in singing several verses of "Come to the Feast" (Marty Haugen, GIA Publications, 1991).

Nineteenth Sunday in Ordinary Time

Understanding this Sunday:
Background for Catechesis

The Word in Liturgy

1 Kings 19:9, 11–13
Psalm 85:9, 10, 11–12, 13–14
Romans 9:1–5
Matthew 14:22–33

The story of Elijah's encounter with God on Horeb (an alternative name for Sinai) is part of a larger cycle of stories about the prophet that begins with chapter 17. The author's description appears to be deliberately written so as to remind the reader of the story of God's revelation of the Law to Moses on Sinai. In particular, this narrative is reminiscent of the scene recorded in Exodus 33:18–23: The prophet has journeyed forty days and nights in the wilderness; like Moses, he takes refuge in a cleft (cave) in the rock; and neither he nor Moses is allowed to see God directly. But these similarities serve only to highlight a more important difference. The heart of the story is its description of how God's presence is known. Rather than the cosmic displays that have been a standard feature of the theophany (wind, earthquake, flashes of fiery light), God's presence is revealed in what our translation calls "a tiny whispering sound" (v. 12), an enigmatic phrase which indicates the paradox of something heard within silence. The nature of this prophet's encounter with God opens up a whole new understanding of how the divine presence may be experienced and known.

Psalm 85 describes in poetic fashion the consequences of God's speaking through the prophets: "I will hear what God proclaims . . . peace" (v. 9). Then, alluding to the many ways that God's word benefits the nation, the author evokes other consequences of God's revelation with terms such as "salvation," "glory," "justice," and so forth. The psalm refrain captures the sentiments of God's people (then and now), eager for divine revelation: "Lord, let us see your kindness, and grant us your salvation."

In today's gospel, Matthew has taken material from Mark and reworked it into a sermon for the church of his day. It would have been quite easy for the disciples in Matthew's community, already facing the storms of persecution, to recognize themselves in the disciples in the storm-tossed boat. In the dark of that stormy night, the person of Jesus is revealed as the cosmic Lord, able to subdue the forces of chaos represented by the raging sea. In Peter's walk on the water and desperate grasp of Jesus' hand, Matthew presents a stunning image of how important it is to reach out in faith to Jesus. Subsequent Church teaching (cf. CCC 142–43) would describe faith as our human response to divine revelation. Matthew puts into powerful imagery that same truth, presenting the person of Jesus as the revelation or epiphany of God, and showing that faith is above all a relationship to the divine Word revealed in the human flesh of Jesus.

In chapters 9–11 of Romans, Paul deals with the question of the Jews in God's plan and with the implications in their regard of his teaching on justification by faith apart from the Torah. In this opening section, he recounts the privileges that were theirs. Indeed, throughout their history the identity and purposes of God have been revealed, even to the point of bringing forth the Messiah. The distress of Paul at the refusal of some of the Jewish people to accept Jesus as the Messiah is evident: "There is great grief and constant pain in my heart" (v. 2). His is the distress of a brother and kinsman. Although he experiences the pain of separation, he cannot speak of the benefits accorded Israel without breaking into the praise of God.

Catholic Doctrine

Revelation

The English term "revelation" derives from the Latin *revelare*, that is, "to remove the veil." The root of the word itself indicates that revelation makes known to us something that had been obscure or unknown. Revelation is an uncovering or an illumination. Classically, revelation meant a divine teaching or instruction.

All of this, however, is a limited description of what the Church means by revelation. A fuller description must refer to the personal nature of that which is being revealed, that is, God. The Catholic understanding of revelation makes reference to the way in which God reveals God's self to the world, the gift of God's own being which is revealed, and a relationship of meaning that provides an ultimate grounding for our being and our world (CCC 54).

Both the Council of Trent (1545–63) and the First Vatican Council (1869–70) addressed the subject of divine revelation. However, the Second Vatican Council provided a more comprehensive doctrine concerning the nature of divine revelation in its Dogmatic Constitution on Divine Revelation, entitled *Dei verbum* (November 18, 1965). The Council wrote, "It pleased God, in his goodness and wisdom to reveal himself and to make known the mystery of his will (cf. Ephesians 1:9). His will was that [humanity] should have access to the Father, through Christ, the Word made flesh, in the Holy Spirit, and thus become sharers in the divine nature. . . . By this revelation, then, the invisible God . . . from the fullness of his love, addresses [us] as his friends and moves among [us] . . . in order to invite and receive [us] into his own company" (DV 2). This self-disclosure of God is summed up in Christ who is proclaimed by the Church as both the mediator and fulfillment of divine revelation.

Thus, while the Church holds that God is revealed in creation (CCC 54), and in the history of the chosen people from the time of Abraham (CCC 60), and throughout the history of Israel and the first covenant (CCC 61–4), the fullness of God's Word to us is communicated in Jesus Christ (CCC 65). Thus, everything God speaks to us is spoken in Christ. The great medieval mystic, St. John of the Cross (d. 1591) wrote, "Any person questioning God or desiring some vision or revelation would be guilty not only of foolish behavior but also of offending him by not fixing his eyes entirely upon Christ and by living with the desire of some other novelty" (*The Ascent of Mount Carmel*, 2, 22, 3–5, in The Collected Works, trsl. K. Kavanaugh, OCD, and O. Rodriguez, OCD, Washington, D.C., Institute of Carmelite Studies, 1979).

The implication of Christ being the fullness of God's self-revelation is that there will be no new self-disclosure from heaven in the future. The relationship that is made possible for us in Christ with the divine will not be added to or improved upon in any new, public way (CCC 66). A key word here is "public," which the Church contrasts to private revelation. At certain times in Christian history there have been private revelations that assist living out the faith, but these private revelations do not add anything substantial to the deposit of faith and must be judged by the teaching authority of the Church to be authentically from Christ or the saints. Thus, the Catholic Church believes that no revelation whatsoever since the person of Jesus can ever correct or surpass what has been given to us in the Christ event (CCC 67).

To understand, as Catholics do, that the fullness of revelation is encompassed by Jesus who is "the way, the truth, and the life" (John 14:6) does not mean that the self-disclosure of God to us is not sometimes obscure or mysterious (CCC 157). Thus, what has been revealed and how that forms our faith is certain, but human language and thought may struggle to express and articulate what is known of the divine in the relationship of love communicated by God's self-disclosure.

The result of divine revelation is that we live now within the promise of God. Human life has as its goal the ultimate union with God who has loved us so much that the divine reaches out to us and communicates. A relationship is established that puts before us a future filled with justice, hope, love, and the vindication of faith. The eternal Word, Jesus Christ, who opens this avenue of promise, is experienced in the proclamation and study of sacred scripture, in the body of believers, the Church, and in the living Tradition that is handed on by the Church from age to age.

Catholic Culture

When the Church blesses a new pulpit, the place in a church from which the scriptures are proclaimed, it prays, "O God, who have called us out of darkness into your own wonderful light, we owe you our thanks at all times. You satisfy the hunger in our hearts with the sweet nourishment of your word. When we gather together in this church you remind us again and again of your wondrous words and works. We pray that in this church we may listen to the voice of your Son, so that, responding to the inspiration of the Holy Spirit, we may not be hearers only but doers of your word. Grant that those who proclaim your message from this lectern may show us how to direct our lives, so that we will walk in the ways of Christ, following him faithfully until we reach eternal life" (BB 1189).

In speaking of the certainty of faith, in spite of revelation being mysterious, John Henry Cardinal Newman (1801–1890) wrote, "Ten thousand difficulties do not make one doubt" (*Apologia pro Vita Sua*, London, Longman, 1878, p. 239).

Dismissal Catechesis (30 min.)

Getting Started

1. Prepare the space ahead of time with a circle of chairs around a table draped with a green cloth. On the table place several things from nature: rocks and pebbles, shells, and/or summer flowers. Use whatever is at your disposal and arrange them in a simple setting.
2. Lead the candidates and catechumens to the circle and place the Lectionary on the table. Invite them to sit in silence and reflect upon the beauty of the created world with grateful hearts. Then direct the group to name one thing from nature that reminds them of God and name it aloud as the rest of the participants listen and give thanks in the silence of their hearts. When this litany seems to be finished, lead all in singing the refrain of the Gathering Song used in today's liturgy.

First Impressions

1. Invite everyone to think about the scriptures and the homily at today's Liturgy of the Word, recalling whatever comes to mind. Ask each person to name one thing they can recall. Then ask the group: *What central image stands out for you from today's readings?* Affirm their insights as each person offers their ideas.
2. Then invite the participants to gather in small groups, directing them to share their ideas about these questions: *What did you find somewhat mysterious or "hidden" in these scriptures? What seems to be very obvious?* When they seem finished sharing, ask each small group to present a short summary of the group's discussion for everyone to hear.
3. Proclaim or sing Psalm 85:9, 10, 11–2, 13–14. Then ask the candidates and catechumens: *What does the psalmist seem to be saying in this prayer?* When they are finished commenting, conclude by saying: *This poetic song describes how God speaks a word of peace and justice through the prophets. God's Word—proclamation—yields many benefits to the nations: prosperity, justice, and truth.*

Making Connections

1. Continue to probe the meaning of the psalm in small groups, inviting all to share their feelings and thoughts on these questions: *How do we hear God's Word today? In what ways are you eager to know and understand the mystery of God?*
2. Encourage the participants to share their feelings about the desire to know God. Then invite each group to write down on newsprint the ways we hear God's Word today.
3. Conclude by asking the group to name and list on another newsprint all the consequences that result from coming to know and understand the mystery of God. Summarize what they have written in a few sentences. Direct the participants to use the "Things I want to remember" section of their Participant Book to record one thing they wish to carry with them as a result of this session.

Prayer

Invite everyone to prayer by playing gentle instrumental music or wind sounds. After a time of silent listening to the soothing sounds, pray in these or your own words:
Lord of the wind and rain, how are we to know you? We long to see your face, to hear your voice and to unveil the mystery that is your magnificence. Yet our human limits hold us back from fully recognizing you in the sunset and sunrise, the cycles of nature, the beauty of a flower, and the sounds of wind and water. Open us, free us, cleanse us that we might come to know and understand a little more of all that you can be in our lives. Amen.

Extended Catechesis

SESSION FOCUS: *Revelation*

Gathering

A. Sunday:

1. Greet and welcome the sponsors and team members as they arrive. Invite them to join the circle of catechumens and candidates.
2. Once all are seated, invite the participants to close their eyes and free themselves to meditate on the presence of God. These words will be of help in guiding the meditative prayer:
As you relax and sink into your chair, allow the breath of life, the breath of the Spirit to flow through every part of your body. Fill your lungs and imagine the breath of God coursing through your veins, your muscles, your heart and torso. Once you are relaxed, imagine that you are accompanying Elijah in his search for God. You walk with the prophet to the mountain of Horeb—another name for Mount Sinai. As you walk, you listen as he tells you of his fear and anger. In challenging the foreign Queen Jezebel's gods, Elijah was victorious over the bogus prophets and slaughtered them. Now, afraid of the queen's wrath, Elijah explains that he is running away, seeking the comfort of God. So, you both walk in the footsteps of Moses up to a small cave-like crevice in the holy mountain. Together you wait for God. When the winds roar, you listen for God, but God is not in the wind. An earthquake follows this. Surely God would be in the earthquake, but God is not there either. When the fires come, you are confident that the God of Moses—the God who spoke in the burning bush—will be revealed in the fire. God is not in the fire. You both stop. Elijah motions for silence. There it is, you hear it . . . a tiny whispering sound. God reveals God's presence in a most unusual sign— in a whisper on the wind. Encourage the participants to remain silent after this meditation. When the time seems right, invite a sponsor to proclaim the gospel, Matthew 14:22–33.

B. Weekday:

1. Use the same centerpiece as described for the Dismissal Catechesis.
2. As the participants gather in the circle, greet and warmly welcome each person. Invite a few participants to share one experience of God through nature during the past several days.
3. Lead this celebration of the Word:
   - Song: Gathering Hymn from Sunday's liturgy
   - First Reading: Meditation as in section A
   - Sing Psalm 85:9, 10, 11–2, 13–14
   - Gospel: Matthew 14:22–33

The Word (30 min.)

1. Ask a few of the catechumens and candidates to share their insights from the Dismissal Catechesis, using the newsprint lists to help them recall the session.
2. Invite the whole group to name the key events in the story of the storm at sea and Peter's walking on the water. Record their words on newsprint or an overhead transparency. Add to the list if it seems incomplete (the Reflection in the Participant Book for this session will round out the list).
3. Present a summary of the background on the first reading and the gospel in these or similar words. Use the information presented in the Word in Liturgy section of Understanding this Sunday to broaden your understanding:
   God reveals God's self to Elijah in a new way in the first reading, taken from 1 Kings—in a whispering sound. Rather than the cosmic displays that have been a standard means of God's revelation up to this point in the Old Testament, God's presence is known within the silence. This opens up a whole new understanding of how the divine presence can be perceived and known. In the gospel, Matthew's story of the storm at sea is used to enhance the faith of the early Christian community who faced the storms of persecution. Peter, a hero of faith, recognizes the Lord and steps out of the boat to walk to him. Peter is presented in sharp contrast to the other cowering, fearful apostles. Jesus is present all along, but once he manifests himself, fear is replaced by faith. Finally, all of the apostles come to recognize the presence of Jesus, declaring in faith, "Beyond doubt, you are the Son of God!" Once the apostles acknowledge Jesus' abiding presence, the storm loses its power to terrify. This story can be thought of as a faith adventure on the water. It takes great faith to recognize the presence and voice of the Lord.
4. Gather the participants into small groups, making sure a team member and/or sponsor is in each group. Ask them to discuss these questions: *What do these two scriptures reveal to you about the nature of God—the Son of God, Jesus? What role does faith place in recognizing the voice of God? What in your life is similar to either the story of Elijah or that of the apostles in the storm?* Invite a few responses in the large group.
5. Then ask the participants to turn to page 90 in the Participant Book to journal their thoughts on the exercise presented. Guide them through the directions for reflection. When they have finished, encourage them to share some of what they wrote with their small group.

Catholic Teaching (30 min.)

1. In the large group ask everyone to think about the word "revelation." Then ask them to offer their understanding of this word. Summarize their ideas and conclude by saying: *Revelation comes from a Latin word that means "to remove the veil." In the Catholic understanding of the concept of revelation there are three points of illumination: First, revelation is the way in which God reveals God's self to the world. Furthermore, Jesus is the revelation of God, that is, the gift of God's self is revealed in the person and action of Jesus in human history. Finally, revelation provides an ultimate grounding for our very existence and the existence of the world and all of creation.*
2. With that fuller definition of revelation invite the participants to name some ways in which God is revealed to us. Be sure they include nature, the history of salvation from Abraham though the nation of Israel in the whole of the Old Testament, and the fullness of God's Word communicated to us in Jesus. To further your understanding of this expansive view of revelation, refer to the Catholic Doctrine section found in Understanding this Sunday.
3. Further the participants' understanding of this teaching on revelation by guiding them through the section The Church Says in the Participant Book on page 91. Respond to any questions that emerge on this focus.

Putting Faith into Practice

1. Direct the participants to rejoin their small groups to discuss these questions: *What comfort do you find in this teaching on revelation? How does the concept of Jesus, the revelation of God enhance your faith? What is your personal experience of communicating with God?*
2. Indicate to the participants that there are several ways to enhance our ability to hear God's revelation. Stress the importance of silence and stilling our inner noise in prayer. Encourage them to read and reflect upon the scriptures, both Old and New Testaments, to discover what can be learned of God in the history of Israel and in the life of Jesus. Share the importance and the methods for using a spiritual journal to seek and know the communication of God. Conclude by expressing your amazement that God yearns to communicate with us and is always present in our daily living.

Prayer

Encourage the group to sit in silence, still their inner conversations, and listen to the God who is present. Provide a long time of silence, then conclude with this prayer or one of your own design:
God, you come to me in the stillness of the whispering wind in the trees; you are with me as I sit at this moment and as I walk through each day. When my heart is afraid you are there to quiet my fears and reassure me of your abiding presence. In the chaos and storms of my life you have reached out your hand to me and steadied my faltering steps. God, how can I express my gratitude at your desire to make yourself known to me? How can I deepen my faith and let go of my worries and weaknesses? Teach me, Lord, and excite my soul to discover more of your revelation to me through a fervor for your sacred scriptures and a commitment to the silence of prayer. Empower me with the ardor of your Holy Spirit. Amen.

Twentieth Sunday in Ordinary Time

Understanding this Sunday:

Background for Catechesis

The Word in Liturgy

Isaiah 56:1, 6–7
Psalm 67:2–3, 5, 6, 8
Romans 11:13–15, 29–32
Matthew 15:21–28

Scholars assign the third part of the Book of Isaiah, called Trito-Isaiah, to the period of restoration after the return from exile in Babylon. The post-exilic era was a time in which the prophetic voice was raised up both to exhort the Jewish people to fidelity to God's covenant and to expand their horizons to the universal proportions of the divine call. The Israelites were in constant danger of falling into a suffocating self-importance based on their sense of themselves as God's chosen people. Anti-pagan polemic was a stock feature of the rhetoric designed to shore up fidelity to the covenant. But earlier prophets had also counseled compassion for the strangers and aliens as one way of overcoming harsh and discriminatory attitudes toward the Gentiles in their midst. By the time of Trito-Isaiah, the chosen people were ready for the shocking suggestion that God's offer of salvation might even include pagans. This passage is one of the strongest statements of that universalism in the Jewish scriptures. However, it is still clear that the pagans, too, would be held to the high ethical and moral standards of the covenant ("Observe what is right; do what is just," v. 1). Henceforth, all generations of Israel would have to grapple with a prophetic word that foretold a day when God's holy temple in Jerusalem would be "a house of prayer for all peoples" (v. 7) and when God's salvation would be known "among all nations" (v. 2).

Psalm 67 reflects a liturgical usage, containing blessings, requests for divine favor, and congregational refrains. It is undoubtedly chosen today for its strong universalist perspective, supportive of both the first reading and today's gospel. After a blessing over the people that echoes the priestly prayer of Numbers 6:24–26, a prayer is made for the inclusion of the Gentiles in the worship of Yahweh. Such a remarkable phenomenon is seen as proof of Yahweh's sovereignty ("the nations on the earth you guide"), rather than a threat to or compromise of Israel's unique status.

Last week we read from the opening verses of Paul's discussion of the place of Israel in God's plan. Paul clearly struggled with the refusal of some of his fellow Jews to accept Jesus as the Messiah. He knew that "God's gifts and his call are irrevocable," (v. 29) so he had to find a way to tell his Gentile audience not to write off from God's saving plan those Jews who did not accept Christ. The answer he offers is that "God has imprisoned all in disobedience that he might have mercy on all" (v. 32).

Today's gospel reading provides yet another insight into the universality of God's offer of salvation. Matthew has reworked his Marcan material (Mark 7:24–30) in several ways that reflect the situation of his own community. He calls the woman a Canaanite, a category of people still despised by his Jewish-Christian community. There is no mention in this account of the children of Israel being fed first; rather, Jesus holds up the woman's faith as reason for her healing. Clearly, this event signals the inauguration of a new era, a new covenant of grace based on faith in Jesus rather than adherence to the Torah. The generation of believers to whom Matthew wrote apparently still struggled, as had their ancestors, with the full implications of a prophetic word that offered salvation indiscriminately to all. The act of healing in the gospels is always a sign that the messianic era has been inaugurated in the person of Jesus. Our suggested doctrinal focus today on the sacrament of anointing can be enriched with this broad understanding of God's healing activity, revealed in the person of Jesus, as a ministry that is offered to all people as a sign of the advent of God's reign. The universalism of Trito-Isaiah was an eschatological reality, only anticipated in prayerful hope; the healing of the Canaanite woman proclaims that the era of the Messiah has finally dawned in Jesus. The continuing experience of healing in the Church of Matthew's generation (and ours) reflects an awareness that we are the messianic community, charged throughout history with making God's universal offer of salvation a reality in every dimension of human existence.

Catholic Doctrine

Sacrament of Anointing of the Sick

As is clear from this Sunday's gospel reading, Jesus is sent by a loving God to be a healer for all those struck down by sickness and ill health. Indeed, Jesus extols the woman in the gospel for her faith in him, a faith that promotes wellness and healing.

The Catholic Church does not believe that sickness is a punishment from God, for the Son of God has made our pain his own (Matthew 8:17 and Isaiah 53:4). The Lamb of God, sacrificed for us, takes away the sin of the world. Thus, by the mystery of his own suffering and death, Jesus gives new meaning to our own illness and suffering whose earthly reality is transformed by the Lord. Those who are sick—and indeed all those who are healthy—can look upon the cross of Christ and know that humanity in its limitations and sickness has been configured and united to the Lord of life who is the Redeemer (CCC 1505).

Consequently, the Church supports by prayer and presence persons who are sick and invites them to faith in Jesus—in spite of the burdens and doubts occasioned by sickness. The Second Vatican Council outlined what the major thrust of this sacrament should be. They (referring to James 5:14–16; Romans 8:17; Colossians 1:24; Timothy 2:11–12; 1 Peter 4:13) declared, "By the sacred anointing of the sick and the prayer of the priests the whole Church commends those who are ill to the suffering and glorified Lord that he may raise them up and save them. And indeed she exhorts them to contribute to the good of the People of God by freely uniting themselves to the passion and death of Christ (LG 11).

The wisdom of the Council acknowledged the existential reality involved in serious sickness. This debilitating experience is a certain reminder of our human frailty, limitation and ultimate mortality, and pending despair. On the other hand, supported by the care and concern of family, friends, and the Church, a person who is sick can find an opportunity to renew and strengthen their faith in the God who will not abandon us and who has, in Jesus, suffered indignities, pain, and torture unto death.

From the earliest times, the Church has attested to an anointing for those who are sick. This prayerful action has been considered a sacrament (James 5:14–15). Bishops and priests pray over, lay hands upon, and anoint those who are sick with holy oil. Prior to the Second Vatican Council, this anointing of the sick was celebrated for only those who were perceived to be in immediate danger of death. The Council taught that this sacrament was not only for those who were in immediate danger of death but any who experienced the difficulty of physical or mental sickness, debilitation, or old age (SC 73).

The Church understands and upholds that through the celebration of this sacrament persons who are sick are strengthened through the grace of God and given peace and courage. In other words, "In this context, the sick themselves, as well as all those who participate in their sickness as social process, are . . . invited by the very nature of the act to surrender in remembrance and thanksgiving . . . they are challenged and supported by the worshipping community to entrust themselves to God in hope, in faith and in love" (NDictSacr 1170). As Catholics, we believe that suffering and sickness, through the witness of the Church to the gospel, can acquire a transforming power. It is for this reason that this sacrament should always be proceeded by the Word of God (except in an emergency) and be celebrated communally, with the sick person surrounded by family, friends, and other believers. Even if the sacrament is celebrated by a priest alone with the person who is sick, the communion of saints, the whole household of the faith, is present in prayer, consoling, reaching out, touching with this ritual action.

The Church prays in this sacrament for those who are sick, "Father in heaven, through this holy anointing grant N. comfort in her suffering. When she is afraid, give her courage, when afflicted, give her patience, when dejected, afford her hope, and when alone, assure her of the support of your holy people" (PC 125).

Catholic Culture

The anointing for those persons who are sick is done on the forehead and on the palms of the hands using the ritual formula, "Through this holy anointing, may the Lord in his love and mercy help you with the grace of the Holy Spirit. Amen. May the Lord who frees you from sin save you and raise you up. Amen" (PC 124).

The range of situations addressed by the ritual of the Church for those who are sick is indicated not only by the title of the service book for this sacrament, "The Pastoral Care of the Sick: Rites of Anointing and Viaticum" (PC), but also by its extensive contents which include prayers when visiting the sick, both adults and children, communion of the sick, anointing of the sick in various circumstances, pastoral care of the dying, prayers for the dead, and rites for exceptional circumstances.

Viaticum, one particular ritual practice for those who are sick, is the final holy communion which is provided for them. Viaticum means "food for the journey" and thus indicates our belief that life does not end in death and that those believers who suffer and die receive new life and victory in the Lord Jesus.

Dismissal Catechesis (30 min.)

Getting Started

1. Prepare the space ahead of time with a circle of chairs and a table draped with a green cloth, a blooming plant, and a vessel containing Oil of the Sick in the center.
2. Lead the candidates and catechumens to the circle and place the Lectionary on the table. Pray in these or similar words: *God of all creation, you made all that is, beautiful, that it might give glory and praise to you. You made all of us beautiful so that we, too, might give glory and praise to you. Send your Spirit to open our eyes that we might see more clearly the goodness and beauty of all creation. We ask this in the name of Jesus our brother, who lives and reigns with you in union with the Holy Spirit, one God forever and ever. Amen.*

First Impressions

1. Invite the catechumens and candidates to listen to these words and phrases from today's Liturgy of the Word. Slowly and deliberately proclaim: *observe what is right, do what is just—the sacrifice of foreigners will be acceptable—house for all peoples—all the ends of the earth—all the nations—the lost sheep of Israel—take the food of the sons and daughters, throw it to the dogs—even the dogs—great faith.*
2. Invite the participants to find a partner and ask them to name the feelings or thoughts evoked by these words and phrases. Encourage the pairs to discuss the causes of these feelings or thoughts. When they have finished, gather feedback in the large group.

Making Connections

1. With the whole group make a list of people whom society considers as marginalized or outcast. Discuss together how these people are treated.
2. Ask the candidates and catechumens to try and imagine how the Israelites would have responded to the prophet's announcement that the foreigners' sacrifice, offered on God's altar, was acceptable.
3. In the large group, ask everyone to name groups of people who today would be consoled by these readings. As they do this encourage them to explain why this is so. Then invite everyone to name groups of people who today would be challenged and/or disturbed by these readings, explaining the reasons for this.
4. Invite the pairs to compose a slogan or commercial, which captures the message of today's first reading and gospel.

Prayer

Invite everyone to join in intercessory prayer by responding *"Hear our prayer, O Lord"* to each invocation.
Forgive those who exclude others at work, play, and in the neighborhood, we pray . . .
Forgive those who make fun of those less fortunate, we pray . . .
Help those who are downtrodden, we pray . . .
For unity among all nations, we pray . . .
For acceptance by and in all races and creeds, we pray . . .
God, creator of all life, hear our prayer for unity and acceptance among all peoples. Amen.
Lead all in singing "All Are Welcome," verses 1 and 2 (Marty Haugen, GIA Publications, 1994).

Extended Catechesis

SESSION FOCUS: *Sacrament of Anointing of the Sick*

Gathering

A. Sunday:
1. Greet and welcome the sponsors and team members as they arrive. Invite them to join the circle of catechumens and candidates.
2. After everyone is seated, invite the catechumens and candidates to relate what transpired during the Dismissal Catechesis and to share their slogan and/or commercial.

B. Weekday:
1. Use the same centerpiece as described for the Dismissal Catechesis.
2. As the participants gather in the circle, greet and warmly welcome each person.
3. Lead this celebration of the Word:
   - Song: Gathering Song from Sunday's liturgy
   - First Reading: Isaiah 56:1, 6–7
   - Sing Psalm 67:2–3, 5, 6, 8
   - Sing Alleluia
   - Gospel: Matthew 15:21–28
   - Sing Alleluia

The Word (30 min.)

1. Lead the group in this reflection: *Close your eyes. Relax. Take a deep breath. Turn the pages of your life back to when you were a child in school. It is recess time and everyone wants to play baseball. The captains are chosen and one by one they pick their teams. You are chosen last.* Pause. *It's another day. . . . It's the annual school spelling bee. Everyone so far has spelled his or her word correctly. It's your turn. You're nervous and you misspell your word. You're the first one to sit down.* Pause. *There's a birthday party that you really want to go to but you don't receive an invitation.* Pause. *Recall an experience when you personally were excluded or when you observed others being excluded. What was the experience like? Who was involved? Why were you or the others excluded?*
2. Invite them to share their experiences with a partner. Gather some feedback from their sharing on the experience of being excluded.
3. Slowly and deliberately proclaim Isaiah 56:1, 6–7. Pause for a period of reflection. Then share this background on the reading in these or similar words: *The Israelites had returned*

from exile in Babylon. *They had survived that terrible experience of being outcasts in a foreign land. Finally, they had returned. God heard their cries after all; they experienced again the joy of being God's "Chosen People."*

4. Ask them to reflect on these questions found in the Participant Book on page 92: *If you had been an Israelite in this setting, how might you have responded to the prophet's words that these foreigners are also called to be God's chosen people? How would you react to the proclamation that their holocausts and sacrifices are acceptable? How do you think the Israelites responded?* After an adequate time, invite each person to share his or her responses in small groups. Then gather some feedback in the large group.

5. Slowly and deliberately proclaim Matthew 15:21–28. Expand the following points to provide a background for the gospel:
   - God's offer of salvation is universal.
   - Jesus holds up the woman's faith as reason for her healing.
   - This event signals the beginning of a new era, a new covenant of grace based on faith in Jesus Christ rather than adherence to the Torah.
   - The act of healing in the gospels is always a sign that the messianic era has been inaugurated in the person of Jesus.
   - The healing of the Canaanite woman proclaims that the era of the Messiah has finally dawned in Jesus.

   Invite the participants to discuss the significance of this passage from Matthew's gospel. This question will help initiate the discussion: *How does the background that you have just heard change your understanding of the meaning of this passage from the gospel of Matthew?* Summarize the discussion and conclude with these or similar words: *The continuing experience of healing in the Church of Matthew's generation (and ours) reflects an awareness that we are the messianic community, charged throughout history with making God's universal offer of salvation a reality in every dimension of human existence, especially in the reality of illness and its attendant forms of suffering. Jesus extols the woman for her faith in him, a faith that promotes wellness and healing.*

Catholic Teaching (30 min.)

1. Divide the participants into small groups. Lead them in discussing the following questions one by one, taking their responses to each question as you proceed: *What has been your experience or exposure to faith healers? What has been your experience visiting the sick or homebound? Has anyone witnessed a prayer time or anointing of the sick? If yes, describe it. Up to this point, what has been your understanding of sickness and its purpose?*

2. Offer a presentation on the Church teaching on the sacrament of the anointing of the sick, clarifying the following points:
   - The Catholic Church does not believe that sickness is a punishment from God. For the Son of God has made our pain his own. The Lamb of God, sacrificed for us, takes away the sin of the world. Thus, by the mystery of his own suffering and death, Jesus gives new meaning to our own illness and suffering whose earthly reality is transformed by the Lord.
   - Those who are sick—and indeed all those who are healthy—can look upon the cross of Christ and know that

humanity in its limitations and sickness has been configured and united to the Lord of life who is the Redeemer.
   - In the sacrament of anointing of the sick the Church supports, by prayer and presence, persons who are sick and invites them to faith in Jesus—in spite of the burdens and doubts occasioned by sickness.

   Invite any clarifying questions about the sacrament before you continue.

3. Describe the three elements of the sacrament of the sick in these or similar words: *Prayer over the person(s) who is sick, anointing with holy oil, and the laying on of hands by a priest or bishop are the three elements of this sacrament. The person is ordinarily anointed on the forehead and the hands with the Oil of the Sick. This sacrament is for those who are seriously impaired by sickness or old age, approaching serious surgery, chronic illness, and those persons near death.* Invite any questions regarding the actions involved in the sacrament of the anointing of the sick. Then continue: *The Church understands and upholds that through the celebration of this sacrament persons who are sick are strengthened through the grace of God and given peace and courage, even if they are not totally physically healed of their debilitating condition. As Catholics, we believe that suffering and sickness, through the witness of the Church to the gospel, can acquire a transforming power. It is for this reason that this sacrament should always be preceded by the Word of God (except in emergency) and be celebrated communally, with the sick person surrounded by family, friends, and other believers. Even if the sacrament is celebrated by a priest alone with the person who is sick, the communion of saints, the whole household of the faith, is present in prayer, consoling, reaching out, and touching with this ritual action.*

4. Show them the Oil of the Sick, a pyx (vessel used to carry the Eucharist), and the *Pastoral Care of the Sick Ritual.*

5. Invite them to discuss these questions in their groups: *How would the celebration of this rite be a sign of healing for the ill? If you have experienced a similar ritual action of the sacrament itself, describe your reactions. What new insights did you gain about the sacrament of the sick?* Invite their responses in the large gathering; then invite each group to talk about this question: *What further clarifications do you need regarding this sacrament?*

Putting Faith into Practice

1. Invite a minister of care from the parish to describe the ministry. Invite each group to present the questions that arose during the discussion.

2. Encourage the sponsors to arrange to accompany a minister of care to visit the homebound or hospitalized.

3. Announce when the next parish celebration of the anointing of the sick will be held and encourage their presence at the celebration.

Prayer

Invite everyone to gather in a circle around the table. Lead them in praying and singing the psalm for the twentieth Sunday in Ordinary Time, Psalm 67:2–3, 5, 6, 8. Then invite all to sing "All Are Welcome," verses 4 and 5 (Marty Haugen, GIA Publications, 1994).

Twenty-first Sunday in Ordinary Time

Understanding this Sunday:
Background for Catechesis

The Word in Liturgy

Isaiah 22:15, 19–23
Psalm 138:1–2, 2–3, 6, 8
Romans 11:33–36
Matthew 16:13–20

Isaiah lived at a time when competition among the powers of his day involved Israel in a considerable amount of political and military intrigue. The prophet strongly urged the king (7:4) to rely on Yahweh alone and not to make alliances with any of the pagan nations vying for military dominance. Apparently, Shebna, one of the king's top advisors, counseled the opposite, and when Israel joined Egypt in revolt against Assyria they lost disastrously. In today's passage, Isaiah pronounces God's judgment of condemnation on Shebna and foretells his disgrace and replacement by Eliakim. The oracle speaks powerfully of the trust God will place in Eliakim and refers to the "key of the House of David" that he will wield, a familiar symbol of royal power in the culture of the day. In addition to being an interesting historical narrative, the passage is about the larger issue of stewardship and the responsibility of those in authority for wielding power in accord with God's will. The Old Testament is filled with stories of leaders who failed to live up to their charge; and, with an equal number of passages expressing hopes and promises of a time to come—the messianic era—when at last the one(s) who lead the people will do so in conformity with the divine plan.

Psalm 138 is a thanksgiving hymn, very possibly a prayer said by an individual (the king, perhaps) in the context of public worship. One might imagine a ruler who has been faithful to his charge and successful in his reign, delivered by Yahweh from countless perils, who now leads the people in giving thanks to God for allowing him to minister faithfully. Even if this is a more generic expression of gratitude by the people after deliverance (from exile?), in the liturgical setting of today's first reading and gospel, the words take on added significance as an apt expression of one who has been a faithful steward of the responsibilities entrusted to him by God.

The confession of faith by Peter occupies an important place in all three synoptic gospels. In Matthew, the scene is the culmination of a section in which Jesus has been instructing his disciples on various aspects of God's reign and their role in it. For a proper understanding of the Petrine ministry within the Church, it is important to see the clear linkage that is made here between this confession of Jesus as Messiah and Son of God and the foundation of Jesus' "church" (the term is used by Jesus in the gospels only here and at 18:17) on Peter. Faith in Jesus' identity is not an individual accomplishment of Simon Peter ("No mere man has revealed this to you . . ."); it is a divine gift to the whole community of disciples. Peter's stewardship has to do with protecting and passing on the faith of an entire community, not some personal insight granted to him alone. The foundations of Vatican II's teaching on collegiality in relation to the Petrine ministry can be easily discerned in this pivotal passage. The language used as Jesus entrusts the keys to Peter must be read in connection with 18:18, where the same power is given to the entire community. This is standard language for the conferral of authority, but the linkage of this authority on earth with that in heaven conveys the extent to which we are dealing here with ultimate spiritual issues of life and death, the binding of the death of sin, and the freedom of resurrected life that comes to those who recognize Jesus as Messiah and Son of God.

Today's selection from Romans is taken from the conclusion of Paul's extended treatment of the place of Israel in God's plan (cc. 9–11). The tortured efforts that Paul has made to understand and explain Israel's rejection of Jesus as Messiah have not been entirely successful. In the end, Paul must abandon reason and simply put his faith in God's superior wisdom. ("How inscrutable [God's] judgments, how unsearchable his ways!")

Paul's final resolution of the problem is simply to break into prayer, confidently acknowledging that God's ways are worthy of praise and glory.

Catholic Doctrine

Petrine Ministry in the Church

The tradition of the Church upholds that because both St. Peter and St. Paul, two major leaders in the early community of the faithful, were martyred in Rome, the responsibility for continuing to ensure the profession of faith has been handed on to the bishop of the local Church of Rome. Thus, Catholics believe that the charge of shepherding the ever-growing universal Church has passed down from Peter to successive holders of the office of bishop of Rome.

Peter is understood by the Church as first among equals, a foundational leader. This image echoes today's gospel passage where Jesus describes Peter as "rock" (Matthew 16:18). Peter confesses his faith in Jesus as the Christ, the Son of God, the anointed Messiah. Paul takes up this same theme immediately after his conversion as he begins his own evangelizing ministry (CCC 442).

This profession that Jesus is Lord and Messiah forms the centerpiece of apostolic faith embodied in the Twelve, in which primacy of place is given to Peter. His mission, therefore, is to ensure that this profession does not waver among the college of the Twelve, that they do not lapse from it, and that they remain strong in it (CCC 552).

Although the bishop who sits in the chair of Peter presides over the entire Church in charity, responsibility for shepherding does not rest with the bishop of Rome alone. Jesus called to himself the Twelve, and this apostolic witness and function in the Church is given to all the bishops of the world who together with their head, the pope, exercise their shepherding office collegially. The Second Vatican Council, however, upheld the primacy of the pope, declaring, "For the Roman Pontiff, by reason of his office as Vicar of Christ, namely, and as pastor of the entire Church, has full, supreme and universal power over the whole Church, a power which he can always exercise unhindered. The order of bishops is the successor to the college of the apostles in their role as teachers and pastors, and in it the apostolic college is perpetuated. Together with their head, the Supreme Pontiff, and never apart from him, they have supreme and full authority over the universal Church; but this power cannot be exercised without the agreement of the Roman Pontiff" (LG 22).

While the pope exercises supreme authority in the Church, it is important to note that he does not do so as any ordinary leader or ruler in the world. His authority is spiritual, deriving from Christ who is the source of all ministry (CCC 874), and thus the papal office is exercised for the good of the whole body of the Church. The very nature of Church ministry is understood as exercised for service to others (CCC 876) because the Son of God came among us, emptying himself, taking the form of "a slave" (Philippians 2:7). Thus, the pope, as does every bishop, exercises a ministry of service in a threefold way: teaching, sanctifying and governing.

The Catholic Church deems that the papacy has, as a gift from God, the ability to proclaim definitively teaching which pertains to faith or morals. This infallibility also characterizes the teaching of all of the bishops together, especially when they are gathered at an ecumenical council (CCC 891). The pope (as does every bishop), through his prayer and preaching, through the celebration of the sacraments, and through his general work, also sanctifies the Church, offering an example of holiness of life that aims us toward the kingdom (CCC 893). The pope, as does every bishop, governs. His governance is described as proper, ordinary (not delegated), and immediate (no intermediary is necessary). But, in exercising this type of power, it must be understood that it confirms and supports the local bishop and that it does not seek to dominate as an autocrat; rather, it seeks to author life and has as its model the Good Shepherd, Christ, who is compassionate and loving (CCC 896).

Finally, the unique contribution of the papal office is best described as a center around which all the local churches gather. Thus, the pope, as successor to Peter, is the concrete expression of unity in the Church. He attempts by witnessing to Jesus and with the help of the Holy Spirit to encourage an atmosphere of love, justice, peace, and holiness throughout the entire ecclesial community.

Catholic Culture

The word "pope" comes from the Latin *papa*, an affectionate term for "father." From about the sixth century the term *papa* was applied to the bishop of Rome. Other papal titles indicate the unique position the bishop of Rome holds in the Church: Vicar of Jesus Christ, Successor of the Chief of the Apostles, Supreme Pontiff of the Universal Church, Patriarch of the West, Primate of Italy, Archbishop and Metropolitan of the Roman Province, Sovereign of the State of Vatican City, and Servant of the Servants of God.

The term "Supreme Pontiff" derives from ancient, pagan Rome at a time when the emperor was considered *Pontifex Maximus* (supreme bridge builder) of the college of priests in that city and suggests his ministry of bridging the gulf between heaven and earth, building a bridge between the two.

Including the first, Peter, and the current bishop of Rome, John Paul II, there have been, according to the annual Vatican directory, the *Annuario pontificio*, 262 holders of the Petrine office.

Dismissal Catechesis (30 min.)

Getting Started

1. Prepare the space ahead of time with a circle of chairs around a table draped with green fabric. Upon the table place a candle and a very large gold key. You may make a key out of gold paper, wrapped around a cardboard cutout of a key.
2. Lead the candidates and catechumens to the circle, place the Lectionary on the table, and light the candle. Begin the session by inviting all to quietly gather their thoughts and become aware that God is present in the midst of this gathering. Pray the prayer of Paul by proclaiming Romans 11:33–36.

First Impressions

1. Help the candidates and catechumens recall the Liturgy of the Word by inviting them to close their eyes as you repeat the following lines taken from today's music and readings, pausing between lines: (Sing or say the words to the refrain from the Gathering Song used at the liturgy.)
   "I will place the key of the House of David on his shoulder."
   "When I called, you answered me; you built up strength within me."
   "Who has known the mind of the Lord? Or who has been his counselor?"
   "I will entrust to you the keys of the kingdom of heaven."
   Repeat a line from the homily.
2. Invite the participants to gather into small groups to discuss these questions: *What is the overarching message of the Liturgy of the Word? What do you find confusing? How is your faith comforted and encouraged by this Liturgy of the Word?* As the discussion seems to be ending, invite a few groups to summarize their discussion for everyone's benefit.
3. Present the significance of the "key" in the following words: *Shebna, a royal steward or prime minister to King Hezekiah, bore the key as a sign of his influence on the king and the court. Ancient keys were large and cumbersome and were worn on the shoulder of the person of great authority. The power of the keeper of the key was significant. Isaiah condemned Shebna's authority because he advised the king to make military and political alliances with pagan nations rather than to trust single-heartedly in the faithfulness of Yahweh.*

Making Connections

1. Invite the participants to offer their insights as to the significance of the references to bestowing the "key" on Shebna, Eliakim, and later to Peter, the Rock.
2. Draw them into a deeper discussion of the responsibilities of holding the key by asking them to discuss these questions in the same small groups: *What responsibilities does entrusting a leader with the key signify? From these passages how would you define stewardship?* Ask each group to write a definition of stewardship on a large sheet of green paper. When they are ready, ask each group to present their definition to the whole gathering and to post their definition around the room.
3. Encourage a general discussion of the implications of stewardship in our own work situations, as parents and as responsible stewards of the earth. Invite each person to write one action they wish to take this week to be better stewards. This can be recorded in the Participant Book on page 95 in the section called "I want to put my faith into action by."

Prayer

Invite everyone to focus their attention back on the centerpiece as they ask God to guide them in carrying out their responsibilities as good stewards and managers. Then pray Psalm 138, either by leading the group in song or by praying the psalm verses alternately. If you choose the latter, have copies of the whole psalm available for distribution among the participants.

Extended Catechesis

SESSION FOCUS: *Petrine Ministry in the Church*

Gathering

A. **Sunday:**
1. Greet and welcome the sponsors and team members as they arrive. Invite them to join the circle of catechumens and candidates.
2. Invite the group to silent prayer as they recall the message of this morning's Liturgy of the Word. Ask a team member to proclaim the first reading, Isaiah 22:15, 19–23. Pause for a short period of silent reflection upon this word. Then proclaim the gospel, Matthew 16:13–20. Conclude this proclamation by praying in these or your own words:
   God of wisdom, who can understand or pretend to know your ways? Your knowledge is beyond our human capacity to understand. Yet throughout the ages you have guided us and proved to be faithful and trustworthy. Be with us and strengthen our faith in you. Reveal to us our responsibilities as stewards of this beautiful earth and all that you created in the universe. Give us the courage to place our trust totally in your divine ways. We confess to you and to one another that from you and through you, all things are. All glory and praise be yours. Amen.

B. **Weekday:**
1. Use the same centerpiece as described for the Dismissal Catechesis.
2. As the participants gather in the circle, greet and warmly welcome each person. Invite them to share ways in which God's ways were a surprise to them over the past few days.
3. Lead this celebration of the Word:
   - Song: Gathering Song from Sunday's liturgy
   - First Reading: Isaiah 22:15, 19–23
   - Sing Psalm 138
   - Silent Reflection on the Word
   - Gospel: Matthew 16:13–20
   - Closing Prayer: As in section A

The Word (30 min.)

1. Invite the catechumens and candidates to present a summary of the Dismissal Catechesis, focusing upon the significance of entrusting the "keys" to another and using the green sheets posted around the room as a guide. Then ask the participants to name the words or phrases that come to mind when they hear the word "stewardship." Record these on large newsprint or an overhead so that all can see the words and phrases.

2. Offer this background on the gospel in these words:
   Today's gospel from Matthew concludes the section in which Jesus has been instructing his disciples on various aspects of God's reign and their role in this reign. There is a direct link between Peter's recognition and declaration of Jesus as Messiah and his mandate to be steward over those who will come to believe in Jesus as Lord. Those charged with leading others to faith do so by the witness of their own belief. Furthermore, faith in Jesus is not Peter's accomplishment alone; it is a gift of God to and for the whole community. Therefore, Peter's responsibilities to protect and pass on the faith to an entire community form the foundation of Jesus' Church. The keys are entrusted not only to Peter, but also to the entire community. Notice that the conferral of authority—stewardship—binds earth to heaven, that is, it is a spiritual authority that deals with the ultimate spiritual issues of life and death, freedom and resurrection. The burden of the keys and their corresponding stewardship passes to all who, like Peter, lead others to Christ.
   Encourage a general discussion of the concepts presented in this background piece by asking: *What new insights does this passage offer as you think about power and authority?*

3. Explain that all authority comes from God and that we are charged with the responsibility to be true to the divine source from which it came. Invite the participants to turn to their Participant Book on page 94 and take time with the reflection exercise on authority. Gather them into the same small groups to share a few ideas about the sacred trust of one in authority.

Catholic Teaching (30 min.)

1. Ask the participants to focus their attention back to the large group. You may choose to invite a few comments from their discussion on authority. Then shift the focus to the authority of the Church by asking: *What is your understanding of authority in the Catholic Church?* Be open to both positive and negative expressions, encouraging honesty. Refrain from responding or trying to clarify at this time. Then ask: *What are some questions or needed clarifications you wish to raise about the Church authority?* List these on newsprint or an overhead so that all can see.

2. Proceed to present the Church teaching on Petrine ministry in the Church (or invite a panel to do so), including the clarifications called for by the questions of the group. Prepare for this presentation by reading the background Understanding this Sunday in the Catholic Doctrine section. Elaborate on the following points:
   - The Church teaches that the charge of stewardship for the faith of the people of God in the Catholic community is passed down from Peter to successive holders of the office of the bishop of Rome, the pope.
   - Yet this responsibility does not rest with the bishop of Rome alone. Like Peter, the pope is understood as the first among equals. Thus, all the bishops of the world exercise their responsibility as shepherd of the faithful collegially, while recognizing the primacy of the pope.
   - This authority flows from its spiritual source, Christ, the source of all ministries.
   - The pope and every bishop exercise the role of leadership by teaching, sanctifying, and governing.
   - The Catholic Church teaches that the office of pope is gifted by God to proclaim definitively teaching which pertains to faith or morals. This gift, called infallibility, characterizes the teaching authority of all the bishops, gathered together, as at an ecumenical council, as well as the pope alone under certain well-defined circumstances.
   - The pope, as successor to Peter, is a concrete expression of unity in the Church.

3. Follow this presentation or panel by encouraging the participants to raise any questions they may have about the Petrine Ministry. Prepare for this questioning by further background reading in the *Catechism of the Catholic Church* and the Vatican II document, *Lumen gentium*.

Putting Faith into Practice

1. Invite the participants to recall some of the current travels of Pope John Paul II by having some newspaper and magazine clippings of these displayed in the center of the circle. Ask the group to name some of their impressions of his ministerial role for the Church and the world. Distinguish between and list these impressions in two columns on newsprint or an overhead: "Spiritual Leader of the Catholic Church" and "Influential World Leader."

2. Encourage each person to respond to the questions posed on page 94 in the Participant Book. Ask the candidates and catechumens to gather with their sponsor and/or godparent to share their responses to these questions. When they have finished, invite the participants to offer their insights in the large gathering.

3. Explain to the group that the gathering of all the bishops of the world at the Second Vatican Council began a new era, a time when the Church truly understood herself as a world Church. Set the stage to show the opening portion of the video on Vatican II, "The Faithful Revolution," vol. 1, *Genius of the Heart* (Resources for Christian Living, Allen, TX, 1997). Discuss the importance of this council and the unifying role of the papacy.

Prayer

Invite all to pray a litany for the leaders of the Church in the following manner. Ask the participants to use the formula: *Faithful and wise God, grant your leader—(name)—the gift of—(mention gift or quality)—to faithfully carry out the stewardship of the Church.* They can name any leaders and ask for any gifts as they add their prayer. Begin the litany with your own prayer, and when they seem finished, close by praying: *Jesus, you have heard our prayers for your Church and her leaders. May we, like Peter, confess our faith in you, our Messiah and Lord of our lives. Amen.*

Twenty-second Sunday in Ordinary Time

The Word in Liturgy

Jeremiah 20:7–9
Psalm 63:2, 3–4, 5–6, 8–9
Romans 12:1–2
Matthew 16:21–27

The call of Jeremiah to be a prophet which is found at the beginning of his book (cf. 1:1ff.) describes both his initial reluctance and the Lord's insistence that he accept the call, as well as a firm reassurance of divine protection. However, we know a great many details about the life and times of the prophet which would seem to contradict the Lord's promise of protection. In the face of Jeremiah's condemnation of the leaders and the people alike for their infidelities to the covenant, he was met with resistance, rejection, and outright persecution. He was beaten and thrown into a sewer to die, an outcast from his own family and friends. In today's remarkable text from the autobiographical writings known as his "Confessions," we hear expressed the intense anguish that his sufferings have caused him. Jeremiah challenges God in bold language one might use toward a betrayer, and he admits he has even tried not to utter his message of doom to Jerusalem. But he has been unable to suppress the Word of God; keeping it in was like trying to shut up a fire burning in his bones ("I grow weary holding it in, I cannot endure it"). Christian tradition has long recognized in Jeremiah a figure for the sufferings of Christ and for the disciples of Christ. The inevitability of the suffering which awaits a true prophet or disciple of the Lord has found no more eloquent personification than Jeremiah.

Today's reading from Jeremiah offers not a glimmer of hope for any respite from suffering. In Psalm 63, however, the liturgy supplies what is lacking in the story. The psalm refrain ("My soul is thirsting for you, O Lord my God") puts on our lips words of intense longing for relief that can come only from the secure knowledge of being in God's presence. The verses of the psalm are words that could easily have been part of the prayer of Jeremiah in his suffering. But they also

contain expressions of confidence reflecting an expectation of deliverance so certain it seems already present. The palpable vindication ("your right hand upholds me") of the psalmist is a fitting image of the ultimate deliverance that Christian faith sees in the doctrine of the resurrection.

We noted last week the pivotal importance which Peter's profession of faith played in the structure of Matthew's gospel. Today's text is linked closely to that profession and, in fact, completes what Matthew wishes to say here about discipleship. For his community, already facing persecution as the cost of discipleship, Matthew wanted to be perfectly clear that what happened to Jesus on the cross and what was befalling more and more of Jesus' followers was not a random aberration. Jesus "must" go to Jerusalem to "suffer greatly" (v. 21); and so, too, if anyone wishes to be Jesus' disciple, "he must deny his very self, take up his cross, and begin to follow" in the footsteps of the Master (v. 24). For any of the members of his community who might waver at the thought of facing one of Rome's imperial tribunals, Matthew reminds his audience of the final judgment, when the Son of Man will come to repay each "according to his conduct" (v. 27).

Commentators have long noted a recurrent pattern in Paul's letters, namely that he begins with his teaching regarding doctrinal truths and only then draws from that teaching its ethical consequences. After eleven chapters in which he has set forth his understanding of the gospel, Paul finally turns in chapter 12 to some of the consequences of that gospel. As he begins this section (cc. 12–15) of exhortation, Paul makes an interesting characterization of a Christian's ethical behavior as "a living sacrifice holy and acceptable to God" (v. 1). Paul urges the community at Rome to find within themselves ("the renewal of your mind," v. 2) the basis for their behavior, rather than conforming themselves to the pagan values that surround them. It is life lived in the Spirit that constitutes the heart of Christian worship.

Catholic Doctrine

The Cross in the Life of the Disciple

The disciple of Jesus follows his example and accepts a share in the cross. The cross, that ancient and cruel Roman method of humiliation, torture, and death is for the Christian also a sign of victory and triumph. Disciples choose, in faith, to see in the way of the cross the path to resurrection and new life. As this Sunday's gospel passage clarifies, disciples of Jesus are invited to participate in the event of the cross, to share in the suffering of Christ who has united himself to every human being not only through his incarnation but through his suffering, death, and resurrection (CCC 618).

With an assassination attempt that put him in the hospital and with later surgery due to a fall, John Paul II is no stranger to the phenomenon of human suffering. Like many Christians, he chooses to see in that suffering our share in the cross of Jesus Christ. He has written that all human suffering has the potential to be transformed with the passion of Christ. Indeed, the pope wrote in an apostolic letter that in bringing about the redemption through suffering, Christ has raised human suffering to the level of the redemption (*Salvifici doloris*, 11 February 1984, 19).

Every believer can in suffering become a sharer in the redemptive suffering of Christ. The Church understands that there is a virtue in consciously uniting one's own suffering to the passion of Jesus. The paschal mystery consists of Christ's passion, death, and resurrection. The first portion of that mystery centers in the image of Christ crucified, that is, it focuses on the image of the cross. John Paul II writes, "[Jesus] dies nailed to a cross. But if at the same time in this *weakness* there is accomplished his *lifting up*, confirmed by the power of the resurrection, then this means that the weakness of all human sufferings are capable of being infused with the same power of God manifested in Christ's cross" (SD 23). The executioner's instrument has become the throne upon which Jesus is lifted up in glory (John 12:27–32). In the paschal mystery of Christ, we believe that God has therefore taken death upon the cross and turned it into our salvation (CCC 622).

The holy cross of Jesus, which is at once a horror and an honor, enables John Paul II to create a new term: the gospel of suffering. He movingly writes about Jesus who transforms our suffering and in that change the hurting person is invited to a place close to Jesus himself. "*It is He*—as the interior Master and Guide—*who reveals* to the suffering brother and sister this *wonderful interchange*, situated at the very heart of the mystery of Redemption. Suffering is, in itself, an experience of evil. But Christ has made suffering the firmest basis of the definitive good. By His suffering on the cross, Christ reached the very roots of evil, of sin and death. He conquered the author of evil, Satan, and his permanent rebellion against the Creator. To the suffering brother and sister, Christ *discloses* and gradually reveals *the horizons of the kingdom of God*: the horizons of a world converted to the Creator, of a world free from sin, a world being built on the saving power of love" (SD 26). Catholics believe that through the very heart of the experience of suffering and the cross we are led into the kingdom of God, for suffering cannot be transformed and changed from the outside, but only from within the very depths of a person through the Spirit. Thus, we believe that the way in which followers of Jesus pick up their cross and follow the Master is a matter of the heart, the interior spirit, and love.

Catholic Culture

St. Paul of the Cross (Paul Francis Danei, 1694–1775) founded a religious order commonly known as the Passionists (Congregation of the Discalced Clerks of the Most Holy Cross and Passion of Our Lord Jesus Christ). In 1720, inspired by a vision, he established his religious order that takes not only the traditional three vows of poverty, chastity, and obedience, but a fourth vow to promote devotion to the passion of Jesus (ECathHist 624). He wrote, "In naked faith and without images, clothe yourself always in the sufferings of Jesus. It is love which unites and which makes our own the sufferings of the one we love. It is through love that you will make the sufferings of Jesus your own" (*In the Heart of God: The Spiritual Teaching of Saint Paul of the Cross,* found in *The Heart of Catholicism,* Theodore E. James, ed., Our Sunday Visitor, Inc., Huntington, Indiana, 1997, p. 493).

The Way of the Cross or Stations of the Cross is a Catholic devotion that originated in the journey of pilgrims to Jerusalem where they would retrace the steps of Jesus during his passion. Franciscans originally encouraged this devotion, which became popular in the fifteenth century. The focus for the devotional practice consists of fourteen stations that can be as simple as a cross or as elaborate as wood, marble, or other artistic renditions of various aspects of the passion. Specific prayers are recited before each station as the participants meditate on that aspect of the passion of Jesus (NDictSacr 307).

As part of the Good Friday liturgy, Catholics venerate the wood of the cross. Custom varies from place to place as the cross is kissed, genuflected, bowed before, or touched reverently. In some Latino communities, flowers are placed upon the Good Friday cross, transforming it from a symbol of death to a symbol of beauty and life.

Dismissal Catechesis (30 min.)

Getting Started

1. Prepare the space ahead of time with a large cross in the center and place a green plant at its base. Near the cross, place a green cloth and a lighted candle on a table with a place for the Lectionary.

2. Invite everyone to reflect in silence upon the cross and its significance in their lives. Invite the participants to remember when they were signed with the cross at the Rite of Acceptance into the Order of Catechumens/Rite of Welcoming the Candidates. Then invite everyone to slowly and deliberately trace the cross with his or her right hand on his or her whole body, head to toe, shoulder to shoulder. When they have finished, pray in these or your own words:
Loving God, you ask us to believe that in accepting the cross, we will come to fuller life. Help us understand the mystery of the cross through the example of Jesus. Speak your Word to our hearts as we reflect and pray together during this time. We ask this through Jesus, who obediently took up his cross for us. Amen.

First Impressions

1. Ask the participants to share their prayer experience by asking: *What feelings were evoked in you as you looked at the cross and traced the cross on your body?*

2. Help the participants recall the experience of today's Liturgy of the Word by naming some of the phrases from the scriptures. Begin with these and add your own choices:
   You duped me, O Lord, and I let myself be duped
   I am an object of laughter
   O God, you are my God whom I seek
   My soul clings fast to you
   Offer your bodies as a living sacrifice, holy and acceptable to God
   Deny your very self, take up your cross, and follow in my footsteps
   Whoever loses his [her] life for my sake will find it

3. Ask the participants to state any more words or images from today's scripture, prayers, or hymns that they recall. Then invite the catechumens and candidates to find a partner to discuss this question: *What did you hear God saying to you personally in today's liturgy?* When they finish, call on each pair to share their responses in the large group.

Making Connections

1. Offer this background on the first reading, Jeremiah 20:7–9, using these or your own words:
   Jeremiah, a prophet, was called by God to condemn the leaders and the people of Israel for their infidelity to the covenant with God. Jeremiah experienced resistance, rejection, and persecution as a result of speaking out. He was beaten and thrown into a sewer to die. He was cast out even from his own family. In today's text we hear expressed the intense anguish that his sufferings have caused him. In his bold challenge to God he struggles with his own burning need to obey God's call to be a prophet for his people.

2. Ask the participants to share their response to these questions in pairs: *Describe a time when you experienced a compulsion to speak the truth in spite of possible rejection and ridicule. What happened to you? What moved you to suffer for your values, beliefs, or principles?*

3. When they have finished sharing, ask each pair to describe some of the experiences they shared. Encourage everyone to name the feelings that resulted from remaining true to their inner voice. Then ask the participants to share with another person what they want to remember from today's discussion.

Prayer

Provide copies of Psalm 63:2, 3–4, 5–6, 8–9 and distribute them to the participants. Provide this introduction to the prayer: *As we pray, let us call to mind the presence of God whom we seek, whose love is beyond all telling, and who provides the true riches of life.* After a moment of silence, invite the participants to pray Psalm 63 together. Lead them in singing the response after praying each verse.

Extended Catechesis

SESSION FOCUS: *The Cross in the Life of the Disciple*

Gathering

A. Sunday:

1. Welcome the sponsors and additional team members as they arrive. Invite them to join the circle of catechumens and candidates.

2. Focus the attention of the group on the cross, inviting them to reflect upon its significance in the life of the Christian and their own life. Begin the prayer by leading the group in singing three verses of the hymn "Lift High the Cross" (text: George W. Kitchen and Michael R. Newbolt; tune: CRUCIFER, Sydney H. Nicholson). Provide songbooks so that all may join in singing. Pray in these or your own words: *God of death and of life, you give us Jesus to show us the way. As we look at the cross, teach us to embrace the cross so as to know the life that only you can give. We ask this through Christ, our Lord. Amen.* Proclaim Matthew 16:21–27.

B. Weekday:

1. Prepare the environment as in the Dismissal Catechesis. Ask the participants to share any experiences of encountering rejection for expressing their beliefs or values during the last few days.

2. Lead this celebration of the Word:
   • Hymn: Lift High the Cross, vv. 1–3
   • Greeting, Sign of the Cross
   • First Reading: Jeremiah 20:7–9
   • Sing Psalm 63 or the psalm song used at Sunday's liturgy
   • Gospel: Matthew 16:21–27
   • Silence

The Word (30 min.)

1. After a few moments of silence ask one of the catechumens or candidates to share a summary of the Dismissal Catechesis. Invite the participants to name whatever comes to mind when they think of or see the cross. Affirm and thank each person for sharing.

2. Provide this background on the gospel, Matthew 16:21–27, using the Word in Liturgy section found in Understanding this Sunday:

   This week's gospel passage is a continuation from last week when Jesus asked the disciples, "Who do people say the Son of Man is?" When Peter professed his faith in the Messiah, Jesus went on to explain all that is involved in being a disciple. The gospel writer, Matthew, delineates the cost of discipleship. For the persecuted community of Matthew, they needed to hear that, just as Jesus journeyed to Jerusalem and the cross, the followers of Jesus could expect no less. To follow Jesus, we must deny ourselves, take up our cross, and begin to follow in the footsteps of the Master. In the final judgment, when the Son of Man will come, he will repay each "according to his conduct."

3. Invite the participants to reflect on requirements for discipleship, using the exercise on page 96 in the Participant Book. When they are finished writing, invite them to share their reflections in small groups. Then ask the participants to share some of their responses with the large group.

4. Ask everyone to respond to the questions found on the same page in the Participant Book in the large setting. Discuss each question, one at a time, encouraging the participants as they share their personal experiences:

   In your experience of taking up your cross, what feelings emerged? What new insights about the meaning of the cross did you discover in this reflection? What cross do you face at this time in your life?

Catholic Teaching (30 min.)

1. Invite everyone to look at the cross as they think about the current crosses that they are being asked to bear. Then present the Church's teaching on the cross in the life of the disciple, expanding on the following points:

   - Christians follow Jesus, who found true life by living in faithfulness to God, even when this faithfulness led to humiliation, torture, and death in the cruel Roman method of crucifixion. As Jesus' faithfulness brought him through death to the resurrection, disciples in faith know the cross as a path to resurrection and new life.

   - John Paul II, who himself shared in the suffering of Christ through an assassination attempt, stated that through the passion of Christ all human suffering has the potential to be transformed.

   - Suffering in itself is not redemptive. But consciously uniting one's own suffering with Christ's passion and death allows one to share in the new life of Christ's resurrection. The paschal mystery—Christ's passion, death, and resurrection—becomes the way of life for all Christians.

   - John Paul II created the term "the gospel of suffering." In dying on the cross Christ reached the very roots of evil, of sin and death, and makes it possible to transform suffering into good through the saving power of love. Through the heart of the experience of suffering and the cross, we are led into God's kingdom. Taking up one's cross is a matter of heart, the inner spirit, and love.

   - Catholics venerate the wood of the cross as part of the Good Friday liturgy through a kiss, genuflection, bowing, or touching the cross. Some Latino communities place flowers on this cross to show its transformation of death to beauty and life.

2. Invite the participants to give examples of ways they have seen God bring new life out of suffering.

3. Encourage everyone to share their insights on this question in the large group: *What does it mean when Jesus said we must lose our life in order to save it?*

Putting Faith into Practice

1. Ask everyone to reflect on the following: *What is the cross you are willing to embrace more fully in your life as a result of this teaching on the meaning of the cross?* Direct the participants to write their response in the section "I want to put my faith into action by" in the Participant Book on page 97. When they are ready, have them share their response in pairs.

2. Explain the Catholic devotion of praying the Stations of the Cross, using the Catholic Culture section found in Understanding this Sunday as a background for your explanation.

Prayer

Invite the participants into the Church to look at the stations and spend a time of quiet as a closing to this session. Or, proceed with this closing: In silence, invite the participants to come forward and reverence the cross in their own way through a bow, kiss, genuflection, or embrace. Then invite all to stand with hands outstretched, forming a cross with their body. Pray in these or your own words:

Loving God, we stand before you with hands outstretched, desiring to embrace the cross in our lives. Give us the grace to trust in your love. Give us faith to know that in dying you bring us to fuller life. Unite us ever more fully with Christ, who has walked the path of the cross before us, and walks with us now. We pray in the name of Jesus, who died and is risen. Amen. Lead the group in singing or listening to "Now We Remain" (David Haas, GIA Publications, 1983).

Twenty-third Sunday in Ordinary Time

Understanding this Sunday:
Background for Catechesis

The Word in Liturgy

Ezekiel 33:7–9
Psalm 95:1–2, 6–7, 8–9
Romans 13:8–10
Matthew 18:15–20

The prophet Ezekiel was active at the time of the Babylonian captivity. Scholars date this oracle to the period after he had been exiled to Babylon but before the final destruction of Jerusalem. The preaching of Ezekiel underwent a perceptible evolution as he grappled with the refusal of the nation to repent of its infidelities and its pending destruction. His focus increasingly was on individual responsibility—his own responsibility as a "watchman" charged with announcing the disaster he foresaw, as well as the responsibility to repent which belonged to every individual who heard his words of warning. His thought shows a clear development over earlier notions of corporate responsibility which consistently overlooked the individual's status before God in favor of the fate of the nation as a whole. Ezekiel's appeal was to the conversion of the individual. Behind such an appeal was the conviction that God would respond favorably to all who did indeed return to him in faithfulness to the covenant.

Psalm 95 is a hymn of praise to Yahweh and a call to worship. Its choice today is clearly based in verse 8, which is used as the responsorial refrain, "If today you hear his voice, harden not your hearts." Echoing the sentiments of Ezekiel, the psalmist calls on the people to turn toward the Lord (i.e., to convert) by hearing and responding with obedience to his voice (uttered in the words of his spokesman).

In chapter 18 of Matthew we have Jesus' discourse on the Church. This discourse follows a longer narrative section (cc. 14–17) on discipleship. It is easy to see in today's pericope

traces of the struggle of Matthew's community (and of every subsequent Christian community) to live out in harmony the Lord's command of mutual love. The focus of Matthew's concern here is how best to deal with the frictions of communal living, where members inevitably offend and sin against one another. Jesus' words reflect the pastoral approach recommended by Matthew. They also indicate the conviction that conversion of heart was indeed a possibility in such circumstances and should be actively sought by the members of the community. Perhaps Matthew had in mind the community's prayer for the conversion of recalcitrant members when he added at this point Jesus' encouraging reminder that the Father would answer the prayer of those gathered in his name. Conversion of heart, as the early Christians knew well, is ultimately a gift of God's grace.

We saw last week that Paul has begun the hortatory section (cc. 12–15) of his epistle. The importance of love as the root of all the actions of believers, reflected in today's gospel, is underlined in this teaching on love being "the fulfillment of the law" (v. 10). This teaching is not unique to Paul, or even to the Christian tradition. Rabbinic Judaism of Paul's day offers several examples of the classic question regarding which was the greatest commandment, answered in similar fashion. In contrast to those Jewish teachers whose concern was focused within their own community, however, Paul teaches as Jesus did that Christians are to love all people. Directed by an inward attitude of love, the Christian experiences true freedom in relation to the precepts of the law.

Catholic Doctrine

Conversion

The injunction to "repent" or "be converted" is the first preaching that issues forth from Jesus as he begins his public ministry and is an essential characteristic of the proclamation of the kingdom of God (CCC 1427). It is the underlying theme for all the subsequent teaching of Jesus and indeed all his healing miracles and ministerial activity that brought him to the cross and resurrection. Conversion is a constant theme in the life journey of all who follow Christ and thus who seek to put into practice the way, the truth, and the life of the kingdom which he proclaimed.

The New Testament uses two terms to speak about conversion: *metanoia* and *epistrophe.* The former indicates the internal mechanisms of thinking and willing which occasion the conversion, while the later term carries with it the sense of the outward, visible characteristics of change (NDictTheol 233). Nevertheless, both terms signal a turning around of the person who no longer pursues old ways, but has embraced a return to our true home in the holy and the divine.

Two classic stories of this Christian conversion or of turning around are found in the lives of St. Paul and St. Augustine (d. 430). Both the scriptural account of the conversion of Saul of Tarsus (who became Paul the Apostle) in the Acts of the Apostles and the account found in St. Augustine's autobiography, *The Confessions,* point to a typical pattern of conversion. This pattern can be described as (1) a perceived tension or disorientation in one's life, (2) a synthesis, learning, or insight gathered from the elements of one's past life, (3) an experience of mercy or forgiveness for failures, and (4) the gracious invitation and call from the Holy One, God, to a new, better life. The great drama involved in St. Paul's and St. Augustine's conversions may not be experienced by others, and yet the pattern may well be valid for many. There is a radical reorientation of one's whole self toward a gracious God that takes place gradually over time and eventually involves every facet of one's personality.

Besides being lifelong, the radical reorientation that describes conversion in Christ is characterized by several other important features. First, Catholics understand that conversion has an ecclesial dimension. While faith in God is a personal act, it is not an isolated act of the individual. No one comes to belief in the love of God in isolation, just as no one lives life alone. We Catholics understand that faith is received and handed on through human beings, in the Church (CCC 166). In addition, the entire body of the Church is called to conversion, for while it is holy it embraces sinners and thus is always in need of purification. (It is no accident that the third stage of adult Christian initiation is called "purification and enlightenment.") Second, Catholics understand that conversion does not remain a purely internal facet of one's being. For when one's whole self is converted to Christ, external actions necessarily issue forth. A true interior change of heart is manifested through visible signs, gestures, and works (CCC 1430). Third, Catholics understand that the way in which human beings grow and mature—along with the fact of sin, which is still present in this world—means that those who have begun the conversion journey may falter. Nevertheless, God gives us the grace and the ability to begin anew and take heart in divine love (CCC 1432). Fourth, Catholics understand that the seven sacraments are not only signs of the believer's growth and maturity in the Lord, but that they are, in effect, living symbols by which Christ acts within us to conform us more closely as adopted sons and daughters of the living God. In the sacraments, divine love heals us, transforms us (CCC 1129), and propels us further along the path of conversion.

Ultimately, Christian conversion means that the believer has embraced a living person, Jesus Christ. In other words, the change that occurs is not mere acceptance of Church teaching or fascination with the beauty of Catholic ritual, culture, or art. These things may certainly lead one to embrace the Lord, but in the final analysis the change brought about by Christian conversion is born of one's devotion toward, love of, and challenge found in the person of the Messiah, the one who suffered, died, and rose for each one of us.

Catholic Culture

St. Francis de Sales (1567–1622), bishop of Geneva, undertook in 1593 a difficult and perilous mission to preach among the Calvinists. His work among them lasted for four years and succeeded in converting many to Catholicism. He was one of the first Catholic writers to call for a spirituality of the laity reflected in their own particular circumstances of life. In his book, *Introduction to the Devout Life* (1609), he writes, "True and living devotion . . . presupposes the love of God. . . . Devotion must be practiced differently by the gentleman, the artisan, the valet, the prince, the widow, the daughter, the married woman. [Indeed,] the practice of devotion must be accommodated to the strength, the concerns and the duties of each individual. . . . It is a mistake . . . to seek to ban the devout life from the company of soldiers, the workshop of artisans, the court of princes and the household of married couples . . ." *(Introduction to the Devout Life,* found in *How to Read Church History,* vol. 2, Jean Comby with Diarmaid MacCulloch, Crossroad, New York, 1986, M. Lydamore and J. Bowden, trsl., p. 36).

When an artistic rendering of Jesus is installed in a public place of Catholic worship, the Church blesses it with a prayer which implicitly refers to conversion: "Lord, listen to our prayer. As your faithful people honor this image of your Son may they be of one mind with Christ. May they exchange the image of the old Adam of earth by being transformed into Christ, the new Adam from heaven. May Christ be the way that leads them to you, the truth that shines in their hearts, the life that animates their actions" (BB 1272).

Dismissal Catechesis (30 min.)

Getting Started

1. Prepare the space ahead of time with a circle of chairs around a table, draped with a green cloth, upon which is placed a candle. You will also need songbooks.

2. Invite the catechumens and candidates to be seated in the circle. Place the Lectionary on the table and light the candle. Pause for a moment of quiet. Pray in these words:
Loving God, you created and formed us in love. When we stray from you, you call us back. You give us one another to help us see the way to you. Fill us with your love, so that we may reach out in love and never do wrong to our brothers and sisters. Open and soften our hearts to hear your word more fully today. Amen.

First Impressions

1. Ask the catechumens and candidates to brainstorm images and phrases from the Gathering Song, the scriptures, and the homily just experienced in the Liturgy of the Word. Summarize their responses and add more images as you find necessary.

2. Invite the participants to choose an image that resonates with their lived experience as they journey in faith. Then direct everyone to turn to the person on his or her right to share this image with that person and describe its significance for them.

3. Have each pair give a summary of their responses in the large group. Highlight the variety of responses.

Making Connections

1. Offer this background on the first reading from Ezekiel:
The prophet Ezekiel wrote during the period when the Israelites were exiled in Babylon. Ezekiel announced that the nation of Israel needed to repent, and stressed that every individual has a responsibility to repent.
Invite the participants to listen closely as you proclaim Ezekiel 33:7–9 once again.

2. Ask the participants to respond to these questions or use similar questions to begin the discussion: *When you see someone doing something dangerously wrong, what is your response? Do you withdraw from the person saying "It's none of my business"? Do you become angry, striking out in retaliation for the harm that has been done? Or do you try to persuade them to do right, perhaps by warning them of the potential consequences of their actions?*
Allow sufficient discussion time in the large group.

3. Then invite the participants to talk about the following with the same partner:
Give an example of a time when out of love you tried to persuade someone to change their ways. What was the effect on the person and on your relationship with them? What feelings did you have?

4. Then ask the participants to go around the circle and respond to these questions:
What feelings arise in you today as you hear God's Word calling you to warn someone of the potentially disastrous consequences of their actions? What help do you need from God to do this?

Prayer

Lead this guided imagery prayer, using these or similar words:
Call to mind someone you know whom you feel may be in danger of hurting themselves or others, or damaging their relationship with God in some way—by doing what is against the good that God wants for them—and for whom you wish to pray. Close your eyes and picture this person in your mind's eye. Visualize God's love and light surrounding you and this person. (Pause for a couple of minutes.) In your heart pray your prayer silently for this person. Then continue to visualize the light of God's love surrounding this person and you.
After pausing another moment, say "Amen." Invite the participants to go around the circle and say one word describing their experience of this prayer.

Extended Catechesis

SESSION FOCUS: *Conversion*

Gathering

A. **Sunday:**

1. Greet and welcome the sponsors, team members, and other participants as they join the group. Invite them to gather in the circle.

2. Invite everyone into a moment of quiet. Lead the group in singing the refrain of "Change Our Hearts" (Rory Cooney, GIA Publications, 1984) several times. Then pray:
God, you are love. Your love fills us and surrounds us. You invite us to love one another, even when we do wrong. Your love calls us to change, and to live as your holy people. As we gather today, touch our hearts deeply with your love. We pray in Jesus' name. Amen.
Proclaim Matthew 18:15–20.

B. **Weekday:**

1. Welcome and greet the participants. Invite them to gather in the circle.

2. Ask everyone to respond to the following: *Give an example from the past few days of a time you felt challenged to love someone.*

3. Lead this celebration of the Word:
   - Gathering Song: "Change Our Hearts"
   - First Reading: Ezekiel 33:7–9
   - Sing Psalm 95:1–2, 6–7, 8–9
   - Second Reading: Romans 13:8–10
   - Sing: Alleluia
   - Gospel: Matthew 18:15–20
   - Silent Reflection

The Word (30 min.)

1. Ask a catechumen or candidate to briefly summarize the Dismissal Catechesis.

2. Begin with this background on the scriptures:

   All three readings this week call us to love our neighbor. This command is directly given in Romans 13:8–10. The readings from Ezekiel and Matthew put a particular twist on how we are to love our neighbor. We are to love our brothers and sisters in the community of faith enough that if one of them were to wrong us, we would go to that person in love and help them see the wrong so that they may change.

3. Invite the participants to share their thoughts in small groups, using the following directions: *Give an example of a time when you experienced someone persuading you to change out of a genuine love for you. Share how you felt and the effect of this experience on you.*

4. Then, in the large group, assemble on newsprint a list of what helped you to undergo the process of change, and a list of what hindered that process.

5. Continue to expand the background on the scriptures with this input:

   Chapter 18 of Matthew's gospel presents Jesus' discourse on the Church. Matthew recognizes that in his own community, as well as in all communities, frictions develop in communal living. Jesus teaches us that we do not come to God alone, but our life as a disciple is intrinsically linked to the lives of all in the community. We each bear the responsibility to help one another grow in God's kingdom. Note that Jesus' suggestion preserves some confidentiality, and has the person's real interest at heart.

6. Have them, individually or in pairs, reflect on a specific situation in their lives where they may be called to help someone else to make a change. Have them reflect on what concrete steps they could take to help that person, keeping in mind the insights they gained by compiling the lists in number 3 above.

Catholic Teaching (30 min.)

1. Continue with a teaching on conversion, being sure to include the following points:
   - God calls each of us, all followers of Christ, to a life of conversion. Conversion literally means a change in direction of how one lives. Conversion includes both an interior change of heart, thought and will (*metanoia*), and an exterior change in action (*epistrophe*).
   - Saint Paul and Saint Augustine (d. 430) both had significant conversions, which point to a fourfold pattern of conversion: (1) a tension in one's life, (2) a learning or insight from one's past life, (3) an experience of mercy or forgiveness, and (4) the gracious call from God to a new way of life. The experience of conversion is initiated by God's gracious action.
   - Conversion in Christ is always ecclesial. Though a personal experience, the individual's faith is affected by and affects the faith of others. Together the Church is called to walk the ongoing path of conversion, of purification and enlightenment. Living one's faith necessarily includes being involved in the conversion process of others.
   - The seven sacraments help the believer become transformed in love. After faltering through the sacrament of reconciliation the believer is able to begin the journey anew and take heart in God's saving love.
   - The aim of Christian conversion is for the believer's whole being to be converted to Christ, and manifested through visible signs, gestures, and works. For a Christian the ongoing relationship with Christ is central and continually invites the believer not only to keep the commandments, but also to embrace love even when involving self-denial.

2. Ask the participants to reflect on a time when they experienced a conversion in both heart and action. Encourage them to write about this conversion experience in the Participant Book on page 98. When they are ready, invite the participants to share their conversion experience in pairs. Then, in the large gathering, ask participants to name the elements of conversion that seemed to be similar in the shared stories. Write these elements of conversion on newsprint.

Putting Faith into Practice

1. Ask the participants to reflect on these questions: *In what way is God calling you to conversion at this time? In what way are you being asked to warn, confront, or otherwise help someone make a change that is needed?* Encourage the participants to reflect on these questions in the light of family, church, and work relationships.

2. After a few minutes, invite participants to choose a specific action they will do this week to respond to God's invitation. Participants may wish to write this action in the "I want to put my faith into action by" section of the Participant Book on page 99. When they are ready, have them share this action in pairs.

Prayer

Invite everyone to reflect on some grouping of people in the world whom we see doing wrong and endangering themselves and others. Distribute paper and pencils, and have them write this name on a piece of paper and place this paper in a basket on the center table. Invite each person to select one of the papers. Then offer this invitation to prayer:

We are invited by this week's Word to be involved in the conversion of others. Let us pray daily this week for the group of people named on the paper we hold. For our prayer together now, we will go around the circle and name the group on our paper. After every five named, we will sing the refrain of "Change our Hearts," while we pray that God's love change them and ourselves as well.

Then begin by reading the name on your paper. When this prayer is completed, celebrate the Minor Exorcism (RCIA 94K) with the sponsors placing a hand on the shoulder of the catechumen or candidate.

Twenty-fourth Sunday in Ordinary Time

Understanding this Sunday:
Background for Catechesis

The Word in Liturgy

Sirach 27:30–28:7
Psalm 103:1–2, 3–4, 9–10, 11–12
Romans 14:7–9
Matthew 18:21–35

The Book of Sirach is part of the wisdom literature, a corpus of writings dedicated to showing how the wise person can live in harmony with God's plan for the world and thus fulfill the prescriptions of the Law. The author is a sage, well traveled and well versed in the many cultures and philosophies of his day, which might seem quite attractive to his Jewish countrymen. He writes his own book of reflections on the Torah, on the wisdom of the nations, and on God's ways in the world, in order to convince his countrymen of the superiority of relying on the wisdom of Yahweh over any other source of guidance. Sirach was first written in Hebrew at the start of the second century before Christ, but the work as we know it was translated into Greek some years later following the Maccabean revolt. The translation reflects the concern of pious Judaism to counter the attractions of Hellenistic culture. Sirach was not accepted into the Jewish canon of scripture, but the Essene community was familiar with and followed many of its teachings. Protestantism considers it an apocryphal work, but Catholics regard it among the deuterocanonical, inspired books of sacred scripture. Today's selection is a remarkable anticipation of the sixth petition of the Lord's Prayer. It is an interesting speculation whether Jesus was influenced by this text in his formulation of the distinctive prayer he taught his disciples (cf. Matthew 6:9–15). Sirach bases his teaching on Israel's experience of God's unmerited and limitless forgiveness. Psalm 103 is an extended meditation on the qualities of the deity, particularly the merciful face of God that Israel had come to know so well through its history of sin and forgiveness. ("The Lord is kind and merciful; slow to anger, and rich in compassion.")

Matthew's discourse on the Church concludes with today's pericope, in which Jesus shows the extent to which community members must be willing to share with others the limitless gift of forgiveness that they themselves have received at God's hands. Peter's question evokes a response from Jesus that turns the blood vengeance of Genesis 4:24 ("If Cain is avenged sevenfold, then Lamech seventy-sevenfold") on its head. The parable illustrating this teaching is deliberately fantastic from start to finish: the amount owed by the royal official is astronomically high; the sum he demands from his debtor is absurdly little. Parables typically had but a single point, and the teaching here seems to be about total forgiveness of a debt that is impossible to repay. That, at least, is where our own experience of sinfulness intersects with divine mercy. Like Sirach before him, Matthew wants his reader to understand the connection between God's actions on our behalf and the moral imperative we are under to act likewise toward others. The stern warning at the conclusion seems to be Matthew's addition to underline for his community the urgency of heeding the Lord's teaching on forgiveness.

The section of Romans from which we read today offers yet another evidence of the frictions that beset the early Christian communities. The specific situation Paul is addressing is not exactly clear, but apparently there were differences over dietary and other practices that threatened to harm the unity of the community. His answer, perhaps quoting a familiar Christian hymn (baptismal in nature?), stresses the unity that all share in Christ as the basis for developing a greater tolerance of one another's differences. The fuller direction he gives on this matter includes an admonition to refrain from giving scandal and advice about deferring to one another in mutual love. Assuming that this letter—reflecting as it does the stresses of life in the early Christian community—was written at the same time that the gospels were developing as oral literature, one can understand how and why today's teaching from Matthew was considered important enough to be passed on and ultimately written down for wider distribution. With this text we conclude our continuous reading from Romans that has extended over the last sixteen weeks.

Catholic Doctrine

Forgiveness

As creatures that are limited and have faults, we confess our sinfulness to God and to one another. And yet, baptized into the mystery of Christ and formed anew as members of the kingdom, we also confess the limitless mercy and love of God. In Jesus, we believers have experienced this mercy and forgiveness of the Most High. It is also in Jesus that we are commanded to forgive one another inasmuch as God has forgiven us.

This Sunday's gospel passage is the crowning summary of Jesus' teaching to his Church and, as such, reflects a strong theme in his life and his ministry—forgiveness of others. This theme is also taken up in the way in which Jesus taught his disciples to pray and during his final moments upon the cross when he spoke words of forgiveness to those who tortured and killed him.

Catholics are called to emulate the example given to us in Christ. We know therefore that the mercy of God that is poured out for us in Jesus' saving life, ministry, and sacrifice will never penetrate into the depths of our hearts as long as our attitude toward those who have wronged us remains frozen in hatred and ill will (CCC 2840). Indeed, deliberately hating others and wishing them great harm is considered by the Church as a grave or mortal sin that fractures our relationship with God (CCC 2303). The Church recognizes that forgiving those who have wronged us is a daunting task, given our human nature, but it is a task that has been enjoined upon us by Jesus. The Lord is unequivocal, saying, "But I say to you, love your enemies and pray for those who persecute you, that you may be children of your heavenly Father . . ." (Matthew 5:44).

The Master not only taught his disciples to forgive and love their enemies, he also lived his own teaching perfectly. When he hung dying upon the cross, his thoughts went beyond his own pain (and what would have been justifiable anger) to pray for his torturers. Jesus interceded for them, saying, "Father, forgive them, they know not what they do" (Luke 23:34).

The Church teaches that forgiveness of one's enemies is the culmination of the disciple's prayer, for in extending mercy to those who have wronged us we are transformed—brought closer to Christ and configured to the Master who showed us the way. This path of reconciliation proves that love is stronger than sin and conquers the worst this world offers (CCC 2844). Forgiveness of enemies and those who have hurt us is not only

something upheld in the words and deeds of Jesus but is embedded by the Lord in the prayer that he has given us disciples, a prayer text that perfectly expresses the Good News of God in Jesus (CCC 2763). Thus, by truly praying this prayer every day and meditating upon its stanzas, disciples of Jesus are formed from the inside out as their hearts are attuned to the words of the Master who plants within them compassion, gratitude, and love. In the Lord's Prayer we ask the Father to "forgive us our debts, as we forgive our debtors . . ." (Matthew 6:12). The two parts of this verse turn upon that tiny word "as." As expressed in this prayer, it is not possible to keep Jesus' commandment to "love one another *as* I have loved you" (John 13:34, Matthew 5:48, and Luke 6:36) without internalizing the merciful love of God and then offering that same gift to others, including our enemies (CCC 2842).

Thus, in reflecting upon the passion and loving sacrifice of Jesus and how that impels us who have received it to live in the same manner, St. Gregory the Great preached, "If the sacrament of the Lord's passion is to work its effect in us, we must imitate what we receive and proclaim to [all] what we revere. The cry of the Lord finds a hiding place in us if our lips fail to speak of this, though our hearts believe in it. So that his cry may not lie concealed in us it remains for us all, each in [our] own measure, to make known to those around us the mystery of our new life in Christ" (*Moral Reflections on Job*, Lib.13, 21–23: PL 75, 1028–29 found in LitHrs, vol. 2, p. 259).

Finally, if we are commanded to love one another and forgive, then what of the sorry divisions among Christians? Pope John Paul II reflects, "The contemporary Church is profoundly conscious that only on the basis of the mercy of God will she be able to carry out the tasks that derive from the teaching of the Second Vatican Council, and, in the first place, the ecumenical task which aims at uniting all those who confess Christ. As she makes many efforts in this direction, the Church confesses with humility that only that *love* which is more powerful than the weakness of human divisions *can definitively bring about that unity* which Christ implored from the Father and which the Spirit never ceases to beseech for us 'with sighs too deep for words'" (DM 13.8).

Catholic Culture

In their proximate period of preparation for full initiation, Purification and Enlightenment, adults are presented with the Lord's Prayer. This presentation, for pastoral reasons, may be made during the preceding period, the Catechumenate. This prayer text, the Church believes, is proper to those who have been baptized and expresses their new spirit of adoption by God (RCIA 149). It will be prayed by the newly baptized for the first time in the eucharistic assembly, which is a gathering of those who have been redeemed and forgiven and who therefore extend this mercy of God to others.

Dismissal Catechesis (30 min.)

Getting Started

1. Prepare the space ahead of time with a circle of chairs around a table draped with a green cloth. Arrange some stones and a fireproof piece of pottery or a brass pot in which are set lighted coals for incense on the table.

2. Lead the candidates and catechumens to the circle. Place the Lectionary on the table and place some incense on the lighted coals. Invite them to reflect upon the liturgy that they just experienced as you pray in these or your own words:
   God of mercy, in your wisdom you encourage us to forgive our neighbor's injustice. We hold tight our anger and vengeful thoughts and your love compels us to let these go. We nourish anger against our enemies and yet we seek your healing. We refuse to extend mercy to those who have hurt us, yet we seek your pardon. Open our tight fists of wrath and teach us to set enmity aside, remembering that we are joined with our sisters and brothers in Christ. Strengthen us in the power of Jesus' death and resurrection, we pray. Amen.

First Impressions

1. Open up the meaning of the Liturgy of the Word by asking the group: *What is one thing that touched your conscience as you participated in the liturgy today?* Encourage each person to respond as you affirm his or her insights.

2. Gather the participants into small groups to share their experience of the liturgy using these questions as a guide: *What image or phrase stayed with you from the readings or the homily? What did you find surprising? As you listened, did the scriptures and homily inspire a new attitude in you?* Allot adequate time for this discussion, and then ask each group to offer a summary of their sharing for everyone to hear.

3. Present this insight on the background to the first reading from Sirach 27:30—28:7: *In sharp contrast to the code of just retaliation, Sirach presents a higher approach for living in the midst of diverse human interactions. Sirach indicates how the wise person is called to live in harmony with God's plan for the world. Based upon the limitless and unmerited mercy of God, the sage advises that we put enmity aside and forgive our neighbor's injustice. Listen to this motivating line: "Remember your last days, set enmity aside; remember death and decay, and cease from sin!" This first reading is indeed cause for us to stop and reflect upon our own attitudes toward those who treat us unjustly.*

Making Connections

1. Ask the whole group to discuss the implications of this passage for their lives by raising this question: *In these instructions on forgiveness, what do you find most difficult?* You may proclaim the passage from Sirach again.

2. When the sharing is winding down, encourage everyone to think of a person whom they find difficult to forgive. Then ask them to think of something they have done for which they seek God's forgiveness. Invite the participants back into their small groups to share their thoughts on these questions: *What obstacles do you find to fully forgive this person? How does your need for forgiveness compel you to try to change your inner disposition toward this person?*

3. When they have finished, ask the participants to help you form a list of the obstacles that prevent our forgiving one another. Write these on newsprint. Then encourage everyone to name some of the reasons that might move us to forgive. Write these on newsprint. Close by summarizing what you have written.

Prayer

Gather the participants' attention by leading them in singing the refrain to Psalm 103, *"The Lord is kind and merciful; slow to anger, and rich in compassion,"* or a familiar song version of this psalm. Repeat this several times, directing the participants to meditate upon the words and allow them to penetrate their hearts and spirits.

Extended Catechesis

SESSION FOCUS: *Forgiveness*

Gathering

A. Sunday:

1. Greet and welcome the sponsors and team members as they arrive. Invite them to join the circle of catechumens and candidates and be sure the incense is still burning.

2. Begin the prayer gathering by singing the psalm refrain. Ask a team member to proclaim the second reading, Romans 14:7–9, and lead the group in singing the psalm refrain once again. Indicate that all stand as you proclaim the gospel, Matthew 18:21–35. Close with a third singing of the psalm refrain.

B. Weekday:

1. Use the same centerpiece as described for the Dismissal Catechesis and light the incense.

2. As the participants gather in the circle, greet and warmly welcome each person. Invite them to reflect and then share an experience of being forgiven by another during the recent past.

3. Lead this celebration of the Word:
   - Song: Gathering Song from Sunday's liturgy
   - Call to Prayer:
     Lord, you are slow to anger and rich in compassion.
     —Lord, Have Mercy!
     Lord, your mercy is without limit and unmerited on our part.—Christ, Have Mercy!
     Lord, the debt of our transgressions is beyond our power to repay.—Lord, Have Mercy!
   - Second Reading: Romans 14:7–9
   - Sing refrain of Psalm 103
   - Gospel: Matthew 18:21–35
   - Sing refrain of Psalm 103

The Word (30 min.)

1. Ask everyone to name some words and phrases that come to mind when they hear the phrase, "forgive your neighbor's injustice." Then invite the catechumens and candidates to share some of the obstacles to forgiveness and some of the reasons given to encourage us to forgive from the lists on newsprint, written during the Dismissal Catechesis.

2. Explain the background on the second reading, Romans 14:7–9, in these or similar words: (Use the Word in Liturgy section found in Understanding this Sunday for this presentation.) *In Paul's letter to the Romans he is dealing with the issue of unity and diversity in the community of believers. Conflicts over diet, celebration of feasts, and cultural and class issues threaten to weaken and fracture this young Christian community. To preserve the unity that characterizes the love of Christ, he advises them and us to mutually respect and tolerate the multiplicity and diversity of practices among the believers. He reminds them, "In life and death we are the Lord's."* Stop and ask the participants: *What does our mutual belonging to Christ make known to us on the topic of forgiveness?* Gather and affirm their insights.

3. Provide a background on the gospel, Matthew 18:21–35, using these or similar words: *The parable of the debt owed by the wicked servant involves a debt owed to the king that is impossible to pay. The amount owed was an exaggerated amount of money, perhaps $9,000,000.00. Yet the king relented on his punishment of selling the servant's family and was moved with pity. On the other hand, the amount owed the servant was perhaps a mere $15.00. For this, he who was forgiven his dishonesty and debt jailed his fellow servant. The wicked, unforgiving servant is found out by the king and tortured for his lack of mercy. In this parable, Matthew wants us to understand the connection between God's actions on our behalf and our moral imperative to act likewise toward others.* Ask the participants to share their reactions to this understanding of the parable with a partner or their sponsors and godparents.

Catholic Teaching (30 min.)

1. Read the last sentence of the gospel: "My heavenly Father will treat you in exactly the same way unless each of you forgives his [or her] brother [or sister] from [your] heart." Ask a few participants to state for the group what this sentence means for the followers of Jesus today. You may begin by calling upon team members and sponsors first and then encourage some statements from the candidates and catechumens.

2. Present the following teaching of the Church on forgiveness. Use your own words to expand on the teaching where necessary as you consider the needs of your participants: *The ability to forgive begins with our understanding and belief of the limitless mercy and love of God. Furthermore, the Church teaches that the baptized, having experienced this mercy and forgiveness through the redemption of Jesus, are expected and commanded to forgive one another. Recall that in Jesus' teaching on prayer he instructs his followers and us to pray, "Forgive us our trespasses as we forgive those who trespass against us." It is clear that Jesus challenges us to "love even our enemies*

and pray for those who persecute us that we may be children of our heavenly Father" (Matthew 5:44 adapted). Forgiveness without limits or reservations can only begin in prayer. As we pray to become molded in the image of Christ, the path of reconciliation opens us to love, conquering even the worst injustice. Equally powerful in illuminating our hearts to forgive our enemies is meditation upon the passion and sacrifice of Jesus who could say from the cross, "Father, forgive them for they know not what they do." Thus, the unmerited and unlimited mercy of God, the desire on the part of the believer to be forgiven by God, prayer, and the passion of Jesus enliven our spirits to begin the process of forgiveness.

3. Ask the participants to open their Participant Book to page 100 and journal their experience of forgiveness in the Reflection section. When they have finished, ask them to continue by responding to the questions that follow on the same page.

Putting Faith into Practice

1. Encourage the participants to gather with the same partners to share their responses to the questions in the Participant Book with one another. After giving them sufficient time to share, ask a few to respond to this question in the large group: *Why is forgiveness vital for the community of believers?* Summarize their comments in a few sentences and encourage them to write one thing they want to remember from this session in their Participant Book in the corresponding section.

2. Using newsprint or an overhead to note the possible steps in the process of forgiveness, outline the process for initiating the practice of forgiveness: *The attitude of forgiveness begins by acknowledging the hurt or pain that another inflicts upon us or one that we love. Once named, the anger can move us to action. The action may include: praying for the perpetrator, acknowledging God's mercy and our desire to become more merciful. What else would you add to this process?* Continue writing the suggestions of the group on the newsprint or overhead. Give the participants time to record some of the steps that apply to their own lives in the section "I want to put my faith into action by" in the Participant Book.

3. Expand the notion of forgiveness to the Church and the human community by asking: *How can our commitment to forgive others bring more reconciliation to the human family?* Encourage each person to think of an example of this ripple effect that forgiveness can have upon our daily lives.

Prayer

Be sure the bowl of incense is still burning. Distribute slips of paper to each person and invite all to think about the person that they wish to forgive. Ask the participants to write the name of this person on the paper and to fold it. While they are doing this, play some instrumental music in the background. Then instruct the participants to come forward and place the paper into the lighted bowl of incense, one at a time. During this offering to God, encourage all to pray that the commitment to become like Christ, even to the point of forgiving our enemies, may transform us. Close by leading all in singing the closing song from Sunday's liturgy.

Twenty-fifth Sunday in Ordinary Time

Understanding this Sunday:
Background for Catechesis

The Word in Liturgy

Isaiah 55:6–9
Psalm 145:2–3, 8–9, 17–18
Philippians 1:20–24, 27
Matthew 20:1–16

Chapter 55 forms the conclusion of Deutero-Isaiah's Book of Consolation (cc. 40–55), written in the mid-sixth century as the Babylonian Exile was coming to an end. The glory of God's forgiveness, almost beyond belief, calls for a response from the people in the form of a return to covenant fidelity. God's ways are unfathomable; his willingness to redeem the people exceeds the prophet's ability to grasp it. What the prophet does know, however, is how urgent it is that sinners forsake their wicked ways and turn to the Lord for mercy and forgiveness. The lavish banquet described at the beginning of the chapter is set for all who are willing to "come" (repeated three times in v. 1) and taste the Lord's goodness. The joyous tenor of this passage is the perfect setting for this week's focus on the sacrament of penance. In contrast to the negative associations that many Catholics who grew up in the pre-Vatican II era had about "going to confession," the joyous mood described by Deutero-Isaiah at Israel's return from exile offers the perfect context in which to introduce catechumens and candidates to the true meaning of the sacrament of reconciliation.

The verses chosen from Psalm 145 highlight the praise of God that flows from one who has known divine forgiveness. Verse 8 ("The Lord is gracious and merciful, slow to anger and of great kindness") is a liturgical chant found in a number of other passages in the Jewish scriptures (cf. Psalms 86:15 and 103:8, Exodus 34:6, Joel 2:13, Jonah 4:2). Its Christian liturgical use is also extensive (e.g., the refrain from last week's responsorial psalm). The psalm is an extended and climactic hymn of praise for God as King. It serves as a reminder that Yahweh's greatness ("your mighty deeds," v. 12) is revealed in his mercy ("compassionate toward all his works," v. 9).

Scripture scholars have noted that Jesus' parables invariably involved a shocking "twist" which challenged conventional wisdom and invited the listener to re-think reality in an entirely new way. The reality portrayed in the parables was what Jesus called "God's reign," and it required of the listener a decision (i.e., a conversion) to be part of that kind of world. (See the Catholic Doctrine section for the Seventeenth Sunday in Ordinary Time for a fuller description of the Church's teaching on the "kingdom of God.") Jesus probably told today's parable for the benefit of his critics who objected to his offer of God's unconditional love and forgiveness to those openly recognized as sinners (and, therefore, in their eyes unfit for God's reign). That prostitutes and tax collectors should receive forgiveness without earning it was as absurd as paying all workers equal wages, regardless of how long or hard they have (or have not) worked. The "logic" of the parable is that everyone gets what they need to survive because of the owner's compassion, not because they have earned it. As an expression of the theology which underlies the Church's way of celebrating God's forgiving love, few parables can match today's for capturing the essence of the sacrament of penance.

We begin today a monthlong series of readings from Paul's letter to the Philippians. Many scholars believe our present version of the letter is actually an edited amalgam of three separate notes the apostle had sent to his beloved community at Philippi. He writes from prison, unsure of whether or not he will eventually be put to death for his faith in Christ, but steadfast in his conviction that "Christ will be exalted through me, whether I live or die" (v. 20). Paul's only wavering is in the fact that he does not know whether he should prefer the prize of martyrdom or to continue his toils spreading the gospel.

Catholic Doctrine

The Sacrament of Penance

God loves us completely and unconditionally and from this abundance flows the forgiveness of sins. It is in Jesus Christ that this divine love is fully manifested. The life, ministry, suffering, death, and resurrection of Jesus unlocks for us the font of new, risen, healed life as we are incorporated into the mystery of Christ and his Church in baptism. Those who fall into sin after baptism are not baptized again, but instead experience the bountiful mercy and forgiveness of God in the sacrament of reconciliation.

The Catholic Church describes reconciliation in a number of ways. We call it the sacrament of conversion because it celebrates change in the life of the believer who turns back to God and away from sin (CCC 1423). We call it the sacrament of confession because an essential element of this ritual encounter is the disclosing of sins (CCC 1424). We also call it the sacrament of penance because it celebrates one's steps in substituting healthy and holy actions in place of sin (CCC 1423 and 1459). We also call it the sacrament of forgiveness because by it God's loving mercy is experienced (CCC 1422). Finally, we call it the sacrament of reconciliation because it restores and reunites the sinner to God and to the Church, relationships that had been severed or damaged by sin (CCC 1440 and 1445).

How is the rupturing effect of sin repaired in the celebration of reconciliation? First of all, those who are moved by the Spirit to avail themselves of the sacrament do so marked by a radical reorientation of the inner person. In other words, prompted by God's grace, true sorrow for one's sins encourages a person to an inner change of heart and conversion and therefore leads the sinner to be reconciled (CCC 1431). Part of this inner change may also be prompted by an examination of conscience assisted by the Word of God found in scriptures or with the help of a spiritual director.

Then the believer approaches the sacrament. Catholics believe there are four parts to the celebration of the sacrament. First, the love of God, which has moved one to celebrate the sacrament, is then expressed by the believer, along with sorrow and contrition for having sinned. In addition, a firm resolution to avoid sin in the future is also expressed (CCC 1451). Second, the sins themselves are admitted. This is always done privately to a priest who presides over the celebration of this sacrament. The priest cannot make use of or reveal under any circumstances these sins (CCC 1467). This private and secret nature of confession is called "the sacramental seal." Third, the wrong that is done in sinning must be compensated and therefore satisfaction offered. This is also known as penance (CCC 1459–60). While frequently this satisfaction is observed by prayer, it can also extend to concrete activities of charitable works, service of one's neighbor, and voluntary self-sacrifice. Fourth, the priest extends his hands over the head of the believer in blessing and prays the absolution prayer. The absolution prayer expresses that it is God alone who forgives and reconciles the sinner to himself and to the Church (CCC 1441).

The Church teaches that "after having attained the age of discretion, each of the faithful is bound by an obligation faithfully to confess serious sins at least one a year" (CIC 989). Also, those who commit a serious or mortal sin may not receive Eucharist without first celebrating the sacrament of reconciliation unless a grave reason exists and the opportunity to celebrate reconciliation is not available (CIC 916). Children must first celebrate reconciliation before their first communion (CIC 914).

Reconciliation does not merely mean a detachment from sin. The healing brought about in this sacramental encounter works a real change in the person toward holiness and renewal as Christ himself places the lost sheep on his shoulders and brings them back. "The expression of all this is the sharing in the Lord's table, begun again or made more ardent; such a return from afar brings great rejoicing at the banquet of God's Church" (RPen 6d).

Catholic Culture

Catholics experience the forgiveness of God apart from the sacraments of baptism, reconciliation and Eucharist. In daily prayer, especially the Lord's Prayer, in works of mercy, and in heartfelt examination of one's conscience, believers come to know the God who forgives us and are moved to contrition. There are many prayer texts given in the ritual book for expressing this contrition. One such example expresses, "Lord Jesus, you chose to be called the friend of sinners. By your saving death and resurrection free me from my sins. May your peace take root in my heart and bring forth a harvest of love, holiness, and truth" (RPen 90).

The prayer used by the priest to absolve from sin celebrates the reality of God's love and forgiveness and the reconciliation of the believer not only to God but to the Church. This prayer states, "God, the Father of mercies, through the death and resurrection of his Son has reconciled the world to himself and sent the Holy Spirit among us for the forgiveness of sins; through the ministry of the Church may God give you pardon and peace, and I absolve you from your sins in the name of the Father, and of the Son, and of the Holy Spirit" (RPen 46).

There are two basic formats in the Catholic ritual for celebrating reconciliation. One is celebrated individually and the other communally. Even when the sacrament is celebrated communally there is time made for individual, private confession.

Dismissal Catechesis (30 min.)

Getting Started

1. Prepare the space ahead of time with chairs arranged in a circle around a green draped table, a candle, and a flowering plant.
2. Lead the candidates and catechumens to the circle and place the Lectionary on the table. Light the candle and lead them in singing "Seek the Lord" (Robert F. O'Connor, New Dawn Music, 1975).

First Impressions

1. Ask the participants to close their eyes. Slowly and deliberately recall phrases and words from the Liturgy of the Word, for example: *seek the Lord—call him—turn to the Lord—the Lord is gracious and merciful—just in all ways—life means Christ—dying is so much gain—I will pay you whatever is fair—go to the vineyard—are you envious because I am generous—the last shall be first and the first shall be last.* Include words and phrases from the songs, prayers, and homily.
2. Elicit from the participants the images, feelings, or thoughts that these words and phrases evoke for them.
3. Ask them to name groups or individuals who would take consolation from these words and phrases. Discuss why. Then ask the participants to name groups or individuals who would be challenged by these words and phrases. Discuss why these groups and individuals would be challenged.

Making Connections

1. Distribute an index card to every participant. Ask them to list on their card the ways they seek and call out to the Lord.
2. Direct the participants to exchange and read the card of another person. Discuss the commonalities as well as the unique ways we seek and call out to the Lord.
3. Lead the participants in this reflection: *Remember when you first became aware of God's nearness. How did you recognize God? What did you think? How did you feel? How do you respond to God's nearness? Recall some ways in which you have grown in your awareness of God's closeness?* Pause for quiet reflection.
4. Invite them to turn to the person on their right and share the ways they have grown in their awareness of God's intimate presence. Use the questions named in the reflection to guide their discussion. Gather responses from their sharing.
5. With the whole group, discuss these questions: *What dulls our awareness of God's presence? What pulls us away from God?* Summarize their responses in these words: *When we take the time to stop the "busy-ness" of our lives to reflect on our relationship with God—its strengths, ways we have grown, and the blessing of God's presence—we are in effect using one method of examining our conscience.*

Prayer

Lead the group in praying Psalm 145:2–3, 8–9, 17–18 from today's liturgy. Conclude by singing "Seek the Lord."

Extended Catechesis

SESSION FOCUS: *The Sacrament of Penance*

Gathering

A. Sunday:

1. Greet and welcome the sponsors and team members as they arrive. Invite them to join the circle of catechumens and candidates.
2. Ask two or three catechumens and candidates to briefly summarize the discussion from the Dismissal Catechesis. Lead them in prayer with these or similar words: *Good and gracious God, we give thanks and praise to you for the gift of life, for the gift of this day, for gift of your presence. You are near to us at all times. Help us to trust in your presence, your compassion and mercy. You are a loving God who desires that we grow in your embrace and in our acceptance of your great love for each of us. We pray this in Jesus' name. Amen.*

B. Weekday:

1. Use the same centerpiece as in the Dismissal Catechesis.
2. As the participants gather in the circle, greet and warmly welcome each person. Invite the participants to share an experience of God's presence during the past few days.
3. Lead this celebration of the Word:
   - Song: "Seek the Lord"
   - First Reading: Isaiah 55:6–9
   - Sing Psalm 145:2–3, 8–9, 17–18
   - Second Reading: Philippians 1:20–24, 27
   - Gospel: Matthew 20:1–16

The Word (30 min.)

1. Divide everyone into small groups. Invite a team member to proclaim the gospel, Matthew 20:1–16. Ask each group to discuss these questions: *How would you have felt if you had been one of the first chosen? How would you have felt if you had been one of the last chosen? Discuss your thoughts regarding the employer's hiring and wage practices.* After some time for discussion, ask each group to write an advertisement for new workers for this employer. Ask each group to share their ads in the large group.
2. Explore this gospel passage in these words: *Scripture scholars have noted that Jesus' parables invariably involved a shocking "twist" which challenged conventional wisdom.* Ask the groups to name the "twist" contained in this parable. Gather their responses before continuing: *The "twist" invited the listener to re-think reality in a new way. The reality portrayed in the parables was what Jesus called "God's reign," and it required of the listener a decision (conversion) to be part of God's world.*
3. Ask the groups to discuss what this parable requires of its listener. Gather their responses before continuing: *Jesus probably told this parable for the benefit of his critics who objected to his offer of God's unconditional love and forgiveness to those openly recognized as sinners (and,*

*therefore, in their eyes unfit for God's reign). That prosti-
tutes and tax collectors should receive forgiveness without
earning it was as absurd as paying all the workers equal
wages, regardless of how long or how hard they have or
have not worked. The "logic" of the parable is that
everyone gets what he or she needs to survive because of
the owner's compassion, not because they have earned it.*

4. Ask the groups to discuss these questions: *What does this
parable tell us about God and God's unconditional love?
Why do we find such unconditional love hard to accept?*
Gather responses from the groups. Conclude with these words:
*God's love is freely given. We do not earn it by our efforts.
It is God's gift to every person, regardless of when they
enter the vineyard.* Again, proclaim Isaiah 55:6–9.

Catholic Teaching (30 min.)

1. Comment on the Isaiah passage in these or similar words:
*The glory of God's forgiveness calls for a response from the
people in the form of a return to covenant fidelity. God's
ways are unfathomable. Just consider the gospel passage.
God's willingness to redeem the people exceeds the prophet's
and our ability to grasp it—consider the wages awarded
to the vineyard workers. What the prophet does know,
however, is how urgent it is that sinners forsake their
wicked ways and turn to the Lord for mercy and forgiveness. God loves us completely and unconditionally and
from this abundance flows the forgiveness of sins. The life,
ministry, suffering, death, and resurrection of Jesus
unlock for us the font of new, risen, healed life as we are
incorporated into the mystery of Christ and his Church in
baptism. Baptism takes away all sin. Those who fall into
sin after baptism are not baptized again but, instead,
experience the bountiful mercy and forgiveness of God in
the sacrament of reconciliation.*

2. Invite the participants to share what they already know and
what surprises or challenges them about the sacrament of
reconciliation.

3. Describe the sacrament of reconciliation:
   - Reconciliation is a sacrament of conversion—it celebrates
     change in the life of the believer who turns back to God,
     away from sin.
   - It is a sacrament of confession because an essential
     element of the ritual encounter is the disclosing of sins.
   - It is also a sacrament of penance because it celebrates the
     steps an individual must take to substitute healthy and
     holy actions for sin and weakness.
   - Reconciliation celebrates forgiveness because through it
     God's loving mercy is experienced.
   - Reconciliation restores and reunites the sinner to God and
     to the Church. It heals relationships that have been
     damaged by sin.

4. Invite one or two other team members to explain how to
approach and celebrate this sacrament. Choose a video from
the series *Echoes of Faith* (Resources for Christian Living,
Allen, TX, 1997) or use a series of illustrations to demonstrate
these points:
   - Those who are moved by the Holy Spirit to avail themselves
     of the sacrament do so marked by a reorientation of the
     inner person. Prompted by God's grace, true sorrow for

one's sins encourages a person to a change of heart and
conversion and therefore leads the sinner to be reconciled.
   - There are four parts to the celebration of the sacrament:
     (1) The love of God, which has moved one to celebrate the
     sacrament, is then expressed by the believer, along with
     sorrow and contrition for having sinned and a firm resolu-
     tion to avoid sin in the future. (2) The sins themselves are
     admitted. This is always done privately to a priest who
     presides over the celebration of this sacrament. This secret
     nature of confession is called the "sacramental seal"—the
     priest cannot reveal under any circumstances what has
     been admitted by the individual. (3) The wrong that is
     done in sinning must be compensated and therefore satis-
     faction offered. This is known as penance. While frequently
     this penance is observed through prayer, it can also extend
     to concrete activities of charitable works, service, or
     voluntary self-sacrifice. (4) The priest blesses the believer
     and prays the absolution prayer which expresses that God
     alone forgives and reconciles the sinner to himself and to
     the Church.

5. Gather insights and questions from the participants. Clarify
that anyone who has attained the age of discretion is bound to
confess serious sins at least once a year. Also, those who have
committed a serious or mortal sin must refrain from receiving
communion until they have celebrated the sacrament of
reconciliation. Summarize the teaching on this sacrament in
these words: *Reconciliation does not merely mean a
detachment from sin. The healing brought about in this
sacramental encounter works a real change in the person
toward holiness and renewal. God's love is unconditional.
Remember today's parable.*

Putting Faith into Practice

1. Invite them to visit the reconciliation chapel (room) today or
sometime this week.

2. Encourage them to spend some time each evening reviewing
their day. Suggest this format: *Ask the Holy Spirit to guide
you as you reflect over the day. Think of the blessings,
people, or events of the day. Thank God for these. Think of
actions done or not done, words spoken or unspoken,
which were sinful and ask God for forgiveness, healing,
and strength to overcome them. Think of actions done to
you or words said against you by others and forgive those
who sinned against you and pray for them. Speak to God
in the quiet of your heart or pray a favorite prayer or
psalm.*

Prayer

Gather the attention of the participants by inviting all to silence.
Then prayerfully proclaim Isaiah 55:6–9. Distribute copies of the
Confiteor from the Penitential Rite of Liturgy and invite all to
open out their hands before God as they pray together: *I confess
to almighty God, and to you, my brothers and sisters, that I
have sinned through my own fault in my thoughts and in
my words, in what I have done, and in what I have failed to
do; and I ask blessed Mary, ever virgin, all the angels and
saints, and you, my brothers and sisters, to pray for me to the
Lord our God.* Close by leading all in singing the last verse of
"Seek the Lord."

Twenty-sixth Sunday in Ordinary Time

Understanding this Sunday:
Background for Catechesis

The Word in Liturgy

Ezekiel 18:25–28
Psalm 25:4–5, 6–7, 8–9
Philippians 2:1–11 [or (short form) 2:1–5]
Matthew 21:28–32

Three weeks ago we were introduced to Ezekiel's efforts to move his fellow countrymen beyond their previous categories of thought, from an unquestioned sense of corporate solidarity to a more differentiated understanding of individual responsibility. The idea of inherited guilt, with the corollary idea of punishment and blame for the faults of ancestors and other kinfolk, was deeply ingrained in the culture of ancient Israel. The whole of chapter 18 is devoted to Ezekiel's attempts to show that each individual is held accountable for his own actions. One is not doomed and helpless before an evil fate of another's doing. The consequence of this is that one can actually repent of one's sins and be forgiven. This was a crucial message for the exiles to hear if they were not to lose heart. The prophet was convinced that restoration of the nation depended on a remnant remaining faithful, and so he preached conversion and individual responsibility as the basis of their hope ("he shall surely live, he shall not die," v. 28). Our focus today suggests that the Church's understanding of moral decision making can trace its roots to efforts such as Ezekiel's to understand more deeply the mystery of human freedom and divine judgment.

Psalm 25 is a prayer for help of various sorts (deliverance from enemies, relief from distress, forgiveness, guidance, and instruction). The refrain chosen for use today ("Remember your mercies, O Lord") and the selection of verses indicate that the liturgical emphasis is on forgiveness of sins, a theme that echoes one of the major concerns of the reading from Ezekiel.

In the gospel parable, both sons are confronted with a moral decision. There is a complex interplay of motivations, verbal responses, actions taken or not, and (on the part of the second son) ultimately a decision to reverse course. As one follows the unfolding narrative of the parable, it becomes clear that Jesus is inviting his audience to recognize their own situation in the radical choice which confronts each of the sons. How we decide whether or not to follow the Father's will for us is a matter that touches the deepest recesses of our hearts. This is about more than behavioral conformity—it is about conversion to the reign of God, a conversion open to sinners just as much as it is available to the righteous. In the plan of his gospel, Matthew undoubtedly had in mind his Jewish-Christian audience and their need to recognize that God's reign is open to the Gentiles just as much as to the children of Abraham. All that is needed is a decision for change, a conversion of mind and heart.

It is that decision to "put on Christ" which Paul refers to in verse 5 of today's reading, when he says "your attitude must be Christ's." From the fundamental decision to live one's life in Christ flows a whole new way of being in the world. When Paul tells his converts at Philippi, "let all parties think humbly of others as superior to themselves . . . looking to others' interests rather than to his own"(vv. 3–4), he is suggesting a radical de-centering of their lives from self-absorption to self-abnegation. The model of Jesus' own self-emptying becomes the basis of all Christian morality and the norm against which all decision making must be judged.

Catholic Doctrine

Moral Decision Making

Catholics look to Jesus as their first teacher in how to live a moral life. In his earthly ministry and preaching and in his faithfulness to the kingdom of God unto death, Jesus provided for us an example of goodness. But Jesus is not merely the primary teacher of the moral life, for the Christ is the source of grace, the font of goodness that enables us to live in the freedom of the children of God and choose to act in an upright and moral way (CCC 1709).

In referring to the law of love, the Second Vatican Council stood squarely in the long history of Catholic thought on moral decision making. For we believe that God reveals to us our vocation as human being (CCC 1701) and that the law which God has written on our hearts is discerned with the aid of scripture and Church tradition and the support of the teaching authority of the Church. Deep within one's conscience, God's voice echoes, calling us to love, to do good and avoid evil. The Catholic perspective on conscience and on making moral decisions is that we do not, on our own, invent this inner voice, but that we are drawn to obey it (CCC 1776).

Precisely because we are free to choose either good or evil, we are moral subjects. When a course of action is deliberately chosen, the individual is the author of those actions. Those actions can be morally evaluated as either right or wrong (CCC 1749). Traditional Catholic teaching emphasizes that the determination of the morality of a human act depends on three things: the object (the action itself, the thing which is done), the intention (the person's goal or purpose in doing the action), and the circumstances (particular features of individual situations in which an action is taken).

The object may be good or evil. For example, it is good to tell the truth, to give alms to the poor, to save a life; it is evil to lie or cheat or murder. When someone speaks of "objective evil" as in the case of murder or perjury, it is the evil action itself that is the focus of attention, irrespective of the intention or circumstances of the act.

The intention likewise may be good or evil. For example, one may give alms with the good intention of helping someone in need. One may lie with the evil intention of manipulating someone. It is important to note, however, that a good intention cannot make something evil into something good. The end does not justify the means (CCC 1753). Furthermore, a bad intention can corrupt a good action, as when a person performs a religious practice insincerely, in order to make an appearance before others.

The circumstances, including the consequences of an action, are secondary aspects of a moral decision. They do not in themselves make something good or bad, but they contribute to the degree of its goodness or evil. In other words, some wrongdoings are worse than others because of a given set of circumstances. The circumstances of an action also contribute to the degree of responsibility a person bears for an action. For example, those who act out of ignorance or fear are less responsible than those who make a deliberate choice, knowing what they are doing (CCC 1754).

Catholic moral theology holds that for an action to be judged as morally good, all three things (the object itself, the intention, and the circumstances) must be good (CCC 1755). Throughout our lives, we are faced with moral choices. Often, making moral choices is a simple matter, requiring little reflection. We decide to tell the truth rather than lie, to be kind rather than cruel, to be fair rather than cheat. At times, however, moral decisions can be complex and difficult, requiring a great deal of reflection. Then a process of reflection, prayer, listening to Church teaching, and seeking advice from individuals can help us to arrive at a good moral decision, in accord with our conscience.

Conscience enables us to act responsibly. It is that reasoned judgment by which a person recognizes the moral quality of a concrete action that is going to be performed, is currently being performed, or has been performed (CCC 1778). The Catholic perspective is that conscience is not an exercise in subjectivity. Rather, this "inner voice" must be informed. Church teaching assists us in that formation of conscience. This formation is a lifelong project where we prudently sift through our experience and the signs of the times, seek competent advice, and with the help of the Holy Spirit educate ourselves for the project of kingdom-living (CCC 1785).

The purpose of educating one's conscience is to propel the believer further along on the path of right and to help one avoid sin. Sin offends against reason, truth, and right conscience. Catholic teaching makes the distinction between mortal and venial sin. Grave sin destroys the relationship we have with God in Christ through baptism and is therefore called "mortal." Mortal sin must meet three conditions: the object is grave matter and it is committed with full knowledge and deliberate consent (CCC 1857). Venial sin does not irrevocably rupture one's relationship with God. It is defined as either having a less serious matter, or when it does, the sin is committed without full knowledge or complete consent (CCC 1862).

Catholic Culture

A Franciscan, Sister Thea Bowman (1937–1990), was a great witness to goodness in the American Catholic Church. She was of African-American descent and inspired not only her black brothers and sisters in the Church but others as well. She helped found the Institute of Black Catholic Studies at Xavier University in New Orleans and was widely traveled as a speaker and storyteller. In 1984 she was diagnosed with breast cancer and yet continued her teaching, preaching, and witnessing from her wheelchair, including a memorable witness talk given to the U.S. Conference of Catholic bishops in 1989. She constantly called on her audiences to speak the Word that is Christ, the truth, and to act upon that Word. She once said, "Maybe I'm not making big changes in the world, but if I have somehow helped or encouraged somebody along the journey then I've done what I'm called to do" (*All Saints,* Robert Ellsberg, Crossroads Publishing Company, New York, 1997, p. 142). Sr. Thea Bowman died at the age of fifty-three.

Dismissal Catechesis (30 min.)

Getting Started

1. Prepare the space ahead of time with a circle of chairs around a centerpiece, consisting of a green cloth arranged on the floor, a cross in the center, and several votive candles, arranged in a simple and satisfying pattern.

2. Lead the candidates and catechumens to the circle, place the Lectionary on the table, and light the votive candles. Open the session by praying in these or similar words: *God of all mercy, lead us on the path of goodness. Enlighten our minds to know your truth and guide our footsteps in the ways of righteousness. In your kindness remember not our faults and sins, but form us in the image of Christ. Strengthen us that we might turn away from sin and change our lives radically that we might surely live. We ask this in the power of the Holy Spirit. Amen.*

First Impressions

1. Invite the catechumens and candidates to name some of the phrases and images which they can recall from today's Liturgy of the Word. Write these down on newsprint or an overhead and add to their list when they seem finished.

2. Gather them into small groups to discuss these questions: *What words of reassurance did you hear in today's liturgy? How did the scriptures spark your inner convictions to continue this journey of faith? What was the main message of the scriptures for you today?* Allow sufficient time for this discussion. Then invite each small group to share the main message they heard in today's readings.

3. Offer this background to the first reading, Ezekiel 18:25–28: *The prophet Ezekiel is dealing with a sense of inherited guilt and punishment for the sins of one's ancestors. Knowing that this belief is deeply ingrained within the people who have suffered together as a people for the sins of the past, the prophet attempts to show that each individual is held accountable for his or her own actions. One is not doomed or helpless because of the sins and faults of parents or kinfolk or even the sins of the nation. Because of God's great mercy, the repentant sinner can enjoy a bright future with a new life, not conditioned or predetermined in any way.*

Making Connections

1. Invite the whole group to discuss this radical teaching by asking: *What do these notions of personal responsibility for sin and the mercy of God signify in our lives?*

2. Gather the participants into small groups and invite them to share stories of their own experience of the freeing effect of God's mercy and individual responsibility for one's actions. You might begin by sharing an experience from your own life to stimulate their religious awareness.

3. Then ask a few participants to share their experience with everyone. Invite the large group to discuss this question, opening a deeper sense of human freedom and accountability: *How does individual responsibility and accountability*

free us to live? Close the discussion by summarizing the input of the participants in a few sentences.

Prayer

Gather the focus of the participants by playing "Change Our Hearts" (Rory Cooney, NALR, 1984) or a song with a similar theme of conversion. Then invite all to silently pray for themselves, that they might be conformed to the ways of Christ and repent of their sins and faults. After a long time of silence, lead all in singing the psalm response *"Remember your mercies, O Lord"* after each verse of Psalm 25:4–5, 6–7, 8–9 are proclaimed.

Extended Catechesis

SESSION FOCUS: *Moral Decision Making*

Gathering

A. **Sunday:**

1. Greet and welcome the sponsors and team members as they arrive. Invite them to join the circle of catechumens and candidates.

2. Invite two team members to pantomime a modern version of the parable of the two sons sent out in the vineyard, while another team member proclaims the gospel, Matthew 21:28–32. Encourage the participants to reflect in silence upon the meaning of the parable when confronted with choices in their own lives. Then proclaim the second reading, Philippians 2:1–11.

B. **Weekday:**

1. Use the same centerpiece as in the Dismissal Catechesis.

2. Ask the participants to gather in the circle; greet and warmly welcome each person. Invite the participants who wish to share a personal experience of God's mercy over the past few days.

3. Lead this celebration of the Word:
   - Song: Gathering Song (first verse) from Sunday's liturgy
   - Gospel: Matthew 21:28–32, pantomime as in section A
   - Silent Reflection on the meaning of the parable when confronted with choices
   - Psalm: 25:4–5, 6–7, 8–9
   - Second Reading: Philippians 2:1–11
   - Song: Gathering Song (second or last verse) from Sunday's liturgy

The Word (30 min.)

1. Encourage the participants to share some of their insights as they listened to and watched the pantomime of the parable from the gospel of Matthew. Then ask the catechumens and candidates to share a summary of the Dismissal Catechesis.

2. Explain the background for the gospel in these words: *In this parable both sons are confronted with a moral decision. The motives, verbal responses, and actions deserve our attention. Through the parable, Jesus invites us to recognize our own situation in the radical choice that confronts each of the sons. As with the sons, our choice to*

follow the father involves more than behavioral confor-mity—it is about conversion to the reign of God. This parable challenges us to change our mind, heart, attitude, and actions to comply with the reign of God. Even noted sinners, like the tax collectors and prostitutes of Jesus' day, have an opportunity to choose this radical conversion. In the light of this background, invite the participants to form small groups to discuss these questions: *How does the good news that even sinners have a chance to change enlighten your understanding of God? What all is involved in making this radical change? Which son signifies your own stance toward God's reign? Why is this so?* In the large gathering listen to a summary of a few of the small discussions.

3. Move into a background on the second reading, Philippians 2:1–11, in these or similar words: *Paul's admonition to "put on Christ" offers us a sense of what it means to change our lives in conformity with the reign of God. The fundamen-tal decision to live one's life in Christ radically changes our attitudes, actions, and our heart to a new ethical base that is countercultural. The Christian is challenged to radically de-center his or her life from the self-seeking and self-absorption of modern culture, and to put on the mind of Christ, who humbled himself.* Invite the participants to name some of the characteristics of the Christian who takes on the attitude of Christ. If they have a hard time recalling the reading, proclaim it once again. Mention the following characteristics, if they are not brought up in the group: *the solace of love—fellowship in the spirit—compassion—pity—one love, united in spirit and ideals—not acting out of rivalry or conceit—looking to the interests of another.*

Catholic Teaching (30 min.)

1. Continue to move the focus to the Church's teaching on moral decision making in these or similar words:
The above characteristics present us with a guide as we make the decisions that confront us in our own lives. While it is possible that our behaviors might present a picture of the ideal Christian, there are indeed times when our inner motives and attitudes do not match our actions. Actions that flow out of love, an attitude of looking to another's interests rather than our own, find their source in the inner voice that we call conscience. God's voice within each person calls us to love, to do good and avoid evil. Most of us are in the habit of doing good, making moral choices throughout the course of our day. But there are circumstances that confront us with moral choices that are complex and difficult. These situations require a great deal of reflection. Ask the participants to move back into the same small groups to discuss this question: *What are some of the simple moral choices that you make out of love throughout the day?* Direct them to list these on newsprint, checking off similar choices named by other groups and adding the daily situations that are mentioned in their group, but are not already listed. Review the whole list with the large group.

2. Continue to expand on the three characteristics for moral decision making, giving examples of each from your own experience and reflection. These three determining factors are:

the "object" or action itself; the "intention" or attitude that motivates the action; and the "circumstances" and conse-quences of the action. Emphasize that all three things—object, intention, and circumstances—must be good.

3. Ask the participants to turn to the Reflection on page 104 in their Participant Book. Point out that there are several scenarios indicating moral dilemmas outlined. Invite each group to select a different scenario and to discuss how to make a moral choice using the criteria offered in the previous presentation. When they have finished, invite the small groups to share how they would apply the characteristics of moral decision making to each of the scenarios presented.

Putting Faith into Practice

1. After listening to the responses of the participants, present this information to them using these or your own words:
Conscience enables us to act responsibly, to choose the good. This inner voice is the echo of God's voice within, calling us to root our choices in the two great command-ments of love. As we grow and mature, our conscience develops if we continue to form it through understanding the scripture, especially the life of Jesus and his law of love, spiritual reading and direction, the witness of other Christians, the teaching of the Church, and continual religious formation through preaching and catechesis. Invite everyone to think back over their discussion of moral choices in the scenario they worked on. Direct them to respond to the questions in the Participant Book on page 104 in the light of this reflection. When they have finished, ask them to share their responses in the same small groups.

2. Invite the sponsors to bring their candidate or catechumen to one of the scripture groups, adult development sessions, or similar events taking place in your parish.

3. Explain the nature of spiritual direction and encourage all to consider finding a spiritual director or companion in the next few weeks. To present this option you will need to have in place trained spiritual directors or a network of spiritual companions. This would be a good time to discuss the role of the sponsor in walking the spiritual path with the catechumen and candidate and to encourage them to gather outside your regular meeting time for spiritual companioning.

Prayer

Ask each person to prayerfully recall a time he or she was guided by the Holy Spirit to choose a loving action, putting the needs of others above one's own self-absorption or conceit. Invite each person to vocalize a prayer of thanks to the Holy Spirit for guidance in the moral decisions we have made. They can do this by using the formula, *"Spirit of the living God, you have guided me to choose—(mention the action or attitude)—out of love for another."* When they have finished, close the prayer in these words: *Spirit of God, you give us life when we choose cooperation over competition, forgiveness over revenge, humility over conceit, and love over hate. Inspire us now to turn our lives around to follow the path of Christ, putting on his attitudes and choosing God's will over our own human weaknesses. Give us wisdom as we confront the moral dilemmas that perplex and confuse us. Help us as we surrender to your reign of justice, joy, and peace. Amen.*

Twenty-seventh Sunday in Ordinary Time

Understanding this Sunday:
Background for Catechesis

The Word in Liturgy

Isaiah 5:1–7
Psalm 80:9, 12, 13–14, 15–16, 19–20
Philippians 4:6–9
Matthew 21:33–43

The exact circumstances in which Isaiah delivered the stinging indictment represented by today's "Song of the Vineyard" are not clear. However, we know enough of the ministry of the eighth-century prophet to surmise that he is addressing the social and political injustices and infidelities that so often represented a national betrayal of the covenant with Yahweh, and that so often provoked his condemnation. The unit is a skillfully developed parable, reminiscent of popular Hebrew love poetry, but with a savage ending that forces the hearer to conclude that the nation is deserving of divine wrath. The concluding indictment (the language mimics a judicial process) in verse 7 holds a clue to the source of the prophet's ire, but there is a play on words most often lost in translation: "He looked for judgment (*mispat*), but see, bloodshed (*mispah*)! For justice (*sedaqa*), but hark, the outcry (*se'aqa*)!" In Isaiah the "justice" that the Lord seeks most often refers to social relationships grounded in fairness and equity. The absence of such conditions meant that the rich and powerful were oppressing and exploiting the weak and disadvantaged—politically, economically, or both. The prophet's ministry involved pointing out to his fellow countrymen the religious significance of such behaviors. Exploitative relationships with others destroyed their own "righteousness," i.e., their right relationship with Yahweh, whose covenant and whose consistent way of dealing with his chosen vineyard, Israel, demanded in return justice and compassion, not their opposites. Yahweh's "righteousness" and "justice" require reciprocity, not only in the people's relationship with him but with one another as well. Failing that, the people are deserving of divine judgment ("Now I will let you know what I mean to do to my vineyard . . ." v. 5).

Psalm 80 is a lament used on the occasion of a national disgrace, probably at the hands of a foreign enemy. After reminding the Lord of all that he has done for the people in the past, the psalmist questions him, asking how he can now allow his chosen ones (his vineyard) to suffer harm. Finally, the psalmist entreats the Lord to restore the fortunes of the people. In addition to the obvious choice of this psalm because of the vineyard imagery, the text represents a classic example of Israel's way of begging to be spared the divine judgment their sins have deserved.

Matthew inserts today's story of the vineyard as second in a series of three parables, within a larger section (21:23–22:14), that details Jesus' controversy with the chief priests and elders of the people. As it appears in Matthew's version, the story has become more of an allegory than a true parable, a strong indicator that Jesus' original words have been adapted to fit the situation of a later generation. In fact, the destruction of Jerusalem in the year 70 can be presumed and was considered by many Christians at the time as God's judgment on Israel's failure to accept Jesus as the Messiah. (Matthew's quotation of Psalm 118:22–23 seems to reinforce this view.) Matthew's point, however, is not this. Rather, it is a stern warning to his own community, the present tenants of the vineyard, not to fail in their responsibility to "yield a rich harvest" (v. 43; cf. also John 4:35–38). The reminder that divine justice and judgment will ultimately prevail is a message for every generation of believers.

The scholarly view that judges Philippians to be a combination of several letters sees verses 6–7 as the conclusion of one letter, verses 8–9 as the end of another. Immediately preceding these verses, Paul is urging two women members of the community to reconcile their differences peacefully. He offers some homey advice typical of the stoic philosophy of his day, but gives that advice a Christian context by wedding it to an admonition to "present your needs to God in every form of prayer" (v. 6).

Catholic Doctrine

Divine Justice and Judgment

The theological concept of divine justice and judgment is first grounded in the biblical theme that God is the ultimate source and destiny of the universe, our Creator who rules over all things. God is not random or capricious, but is good, and created the world in goodness, beauty, and order (CCC 341). Part of that arrangement, originating in God's wisdom, is moral order, by which actions are understood to be right or wrong (CCC 1954). Revelation shows us explicitly that God is just, always rejecting what is evil and embracing what is good. God is not indifferent to human behavior but, rather, is intimately aware of what we do and how it either contributes to or obstructs the good that he desires for us.

Having created the world, God continues to govern it in ways that are beyond human understanding, yet which are just and will ultimately be revealed as such (CCC 309–12). For example, God tolerates the existence of human sinfulness, which may seem unjust, yet by doing so, he gives everyone a full measure of time in which to repent. Unlike human justice, which is imperfect and variable, God's justice is eternal and surpasses all human judgments in its love and goodness (CCC 313). Although those who do evil have reason to fear the ultimate punishment that awaits them, in Jesus it is revealed that God's justice is the embodiment of mercy.

God continually offers salvation to all (CCC 74) and did not abandon us after our fall from original grace (CCC 410). Thus, the Catholic Church asserts that no one is predestined to damnation (CCC 1037). Our vocation as human beings is rather, in Jesus, our divinization and our complete union with God (CCC 27, 460). But while the reign of sin is ended because of the death and resurrection of Jesus and we are reconciled to God in Christ, nevertheless, sin still persists in the world. Why? Karl Rahner notes that we are most like God in our freedom, that ability to choose growth, goodness, and maturity in Christ. "We do this by saying 'Yes' to the world, to life, to our neighbor and, in and through all of this, to God." (ModCathE 805). But for us finite creatures, freedom means that we can possibly choose the opposite and say 'No' to goodness and engage in moral evil, committing sin.

An important theme in the preaching of Jesus is that this world will someday come to an end—it is transitory—and that our conduct in this passing world will be judged. Indeed, our attitude about our neighbor will disclose our acceptance or refusal of God's grace (CCC 678). As Matthew's parable of the final judgment (Matthew 25) illustrates, "the least" of our neighbors are precisely those with whom God has chosen to identify, and so our treatment of them will show the truth or falsity of our love for God. Christ has come in order to offer us the fullness of life in God, yet our lack of charity toward others may, in effect, by our own actions, condemn us.

Catholic teaching emphasizes that at each individual's death there is a judgment that takes place. At that judgment one is either rewarded with heaven or condemned to hell, heaven being complete and total union in joy with God and hell being total separation from God (CCC 1023 and 1033). In addition, the Church describes purgatory as that stage of final purification needed by those who are not perfectly holy at death but who nonetheless are assured of heaven after this cleansing (CCC 1030).

Created by God, the world is on a journey, moving toward ultimate perfection, guided by divine providence (CCC 310). The theological notion of divine justice and judgment supports this truth revealed to us in Christ, who is the new Adam and the summation of all human history. Thus, Christ will render a final judgment and hand over to his heavenly Father all that is subjected to the Savior, all that awaits the new heavens and new earth in which God's justice reigns supreme (CCC 314, 671).

Catholic Culture

The Catholic practice of praying for the deceased stems from an understanding of purgatory and that, by our prayers, we can intercede for those who are being purified and thus help them or assist them through these petitions. Frequently, Catholics will offer a donation for a Mass intention in observance of this type of intercessory prayer. In some parishes, this intention is then articulated near the end of the General Intercessions. If not, the intention (the name of the deceased person) may be written on a small card placed on the altar, seen, and prayed for by the priest who is presiding at Mass.

The idea of a final, divine judgment is implicitly expressed in the eucharistic prayer of the Church; for example, "Father, accept this offering from your whole family. Grant us your peace in this life, save us from final damnation, and count us among those you have chosen" (*Sacramentary*, Eucharistic Prayer I).

The Catholic Church has never identified any particular person as damned in hell, for it believes that judgment is solely up to God.

Dismissal Catechesis (30 min.)

Getting Started

1. Prepare the space ahead of time with the chairs in a circle and a green cloth spread on the floor. Place a candle and a bunch of grapes on the cloth

2. Lead the candidates and catechumens to the circle and place the Lectionary on a stand on the cloth. Pray in these words: *Source of all goodness and life, God, you have called us to this time and place on our journey of faith. Open our minds and hearts to reflect on the Liturgy of the Word we have just celebrated. Send your Spirit to guide our discussions. We ask this in the name of Jesus Christ. Amen.*

First Impressions

1. On newsprint or on a chalkboard, formulate a list of words and phrases that the catechumens and candidates recall from the liturgy just celebrated. If they need help, look over the readings and the Gathering Song beforehand and have some words and phrases ready to list.

2. Invite them to reflect upon the list of phrases and name aloud the mood or feelings expressed in these words and phrases.

3. Ask them to turn to the person on their right and ask this question for their discussion: *What do these words, phrases, moods, and feelings convey to you as to the nature of God and God's justice?* When the discussion seems to be ending, gather feedback from the pairs in the large group.

4. Remaining in the large group, ask: *What surprises or puzzles you about today's scriptures?*

Making Connections

1. Invite everyone to close their eyes and to take a few deep breaths. Lead them in the following meditation:
Imagine a warm spring day. You are out in the country-side. The air is clean and fresh. As you amble along, you observe the owner of a vineyard preparing the hillside for new vines. It's hard work but he appears to enjoy it. You stop to speak to him. He describes the choice vines that he intends to plant. He speaks of the good crop that the vines will yield. You listen intently to this man, wish him well, and go on your way. Several months later, you again are walking the road along the vineyard. The owner has indeed worked hard in the past months. The field has been well cared for but the owner is out in the field destroying his vineyard. You stop to ask why. He tells you that his vines are producing wild grapes which have no value. The vineyard is a waste. Nothing good can come of it. You listen in surprise. You can see that the owner has worked very hard and has nothing left. In a little while you continue on the road and he returns to his work.

2. Invite the participants to discuss the following questions in the large group—take one question at a time and affirm their responses: *How did you react to the fact that the owner's hard work bore no fruit? If you had been the owner, what would be your reaction to the loss of the crop to wild grapes? How would the hard work that had no*

yield make you feel? In what way(s) does this passage describe God's creation and how we human beings have responded to God's direction and guidance? Summarize their responses in a few sentences.

3. Ask them to join their partner and come up with a slogan that summarizes this passage. Share these in the large group.

Prayer

Lead the catechumens and candidates in praying aloud Psalm 80:9, 12, 13–14, 15–16, 19–20. You will need copies of the psalm to distribute to the participants. You may choose to have them pray antiphonally, that is, right side alternating with the left.

Extended Catechesis

SESSION FOCUS: *Divine Justice and Judgment*

Gathering

A. **Sunday:**

1. Greet and welcome the sponsors and team members as they arrive. Invite them to join the circle of catechumens and candidates.

2. Ask two or three catechumens and candidates to briefly summarize the discussion from the Dismissal Catechesis.

3. Ask one of the team members to proclaim the first reading, Isaiah 5:1–7. Pause and sing the refrain of Psalm 80, "The vineyard of the Lord is the house of Israel," inviting them to identify with Israel. Ask another team member or sponsor to proclaim the gospel, Matthew 21:33–43.

B. **Weekday:**

1. Use the same centerpiece as described in Dismissal Catechesis.

2. As the participants gather in the circle, greet and warmly welcome each person. Invite a few of them to give examples of how they have recently experienced God's justice.

3. Lead this celebration of the Word:
   - Song: The Gathering Song from Sunday's liturgy
   - First Reading: Isaiah 5:1–7
   - Quiet reflection
   - Sing Psalm 80
   - Sing: Alleluia
   - Gospel: Matthew 21:33–43

The Word (30 min.)

1. Use the following questions to lead the participants to recall an experience in their lives when they had made an agreement or pact with someone—use these or your own words to guide their recollection: *Think about the agreement or pact you made with another. Recall what and whom it involved. Think about why this agreement or pact was important for you.* Then request that the participants join with a partner or with their sponsor or godparent. Ask them to describe the experience of the agreement or pact. After sufficient time, gather from the pairs some key elements of an agreement or pact, such as: made in good faith, trusted the other, commitment, promises made are to be kept.

2. In pairs, lead them into a discussion of today's gospel using these or your own questions to stimulate the sharing: *Describe the agreement between the property owner and the tenant farmers. In what ways is it a fair agreement? Describe how the tenant farmers responded when payment time came. What was the property owner's response? What would you have done if you had been the property owner? What does this parable tell us about God? About Jesus? About God's justice?* Gather feedback from the pairs. Ask one or two participants to summarize the discussion.

3. Continue with these or similar words: *Both the first reading and the gospel use the image of the vineyard. In the first reading, the prophet is probably addressing the social and political injustices and infidelities that so often represented a national betrayal of the covenant with Yahweh, and so often provoked his condemnation.* Ask the group to name some of these betrayals, such as the golden calf, Jonah and the city of Nineveh, the economic injustices that Amos condemned, and the evils done by the people of Noah's time.

4. Proceed to move more deeply into the meaning of the scriptures with these or similar words:
Note the ending of the reading. Pause to read the end of Matthew's gospel aloud. *We conclude that the nation is deserving of divine wrath. For Isaiah, the justice that the Lord seeks most often refers to social relationships grounded in fairness and equity. The absence of such conditions meant that the rich and powerful were oppressing and exploiting the weak and disadvantaged. The prophet points out that exploitative relationships with others destroyed their own right relationship with Yahweh, whose covenant and whose consistent way of dealing with his chosen vineyard, Israel, demanded in return justice and compassion. If these were not present in their relationships with others, they were deserving of divine judgment.*

5. In the same pairs, ask them to discuss these questions: *How do you respond to the prophet's view of justice? What are the implications of Yahweh's justice? How does Matthew build on this sense of justice?*

6. Gather feedback from the pairs. Summarize the discussion. Include these or similar words: *For Matthew, this passage is a stern warning to his own community, the present tenants of the vineyard, not to fail in their responsibility to "yield a rich harvest." The reminder that divine justice and judgment will ultimately prevail is a message for every generation of believers.*

Catholic Teaching (30 min.)

1. In the large gathering ask the participants to offer their notions about justice; their description of God's justice and their thoughts and feelings about God's justice. Refer to the Catholic Doctrine section of Understanding This Sunday and expand on the following points:
   - God created all things and desires all to be one, now and forever.
   - God is just, always rejecting what is evil and embracing what is good.
   - God is intimately aware of what we do and how it either draws us closer or pushes us away from the oneness that God desires.

   - God tolerates human sinfulness, which may seem unjust, yet by doing so God gives everyone a full measure of time in which to repent.
   - God's justice is eternal and surpasses all human judgments in its love and goodness.

2. Ask the participants to turn to page 106 in the Participant Book to apply human and divine justice to the scenarios described in the Reflection section. Then invite them to join with their partner to share their responses.

3. Continue to expand on the Church's teaching:
   - God continually offers salvation to all. God did not abandon us after the fall from original grace.
   - The Catholic Church teaches that no one is predestined to hell. Our vocation as human beings is rather, in Jesus, our divinization and our complete union with God.
   - Though the death and resurrection of Jesus reconciled us to God and overcame the reign of sin, nevertheless, sin still persists in the world.
   - God created us in the image of God. We are most like God when in our freedom we choose goodness, right relationship with God and others, and live justly. However, we are also free to choose evil which separates us from God.

4. In the large group, ask the participants to discuss their understanding of what will happen at the end of their lives and at the end of the world. In these or similar words conclude and summarize the discussion of divine judgment: *Our lives in this world will come to an end and the way in which we have lived will be judged. The way in which we have loved God and loved our neighbor will determine our reward. At our judgment, one is either rewarded with heaven, complete union with God, or condemned to hell, total separation from God. In addition, the Church describes purgatory as that time of final purification needed by those who are not perfectly holy at death but who nonetheless are assured of heaven after a time.*

Putting Faith into Practice

1. In pairs, invite the participants to discuss these questions: *In the light of God's justice and judgment, how are we to live? What does this teaching tell you about your relationship with God? How are you to treat your neighbor?*

2. Encourage them to take time each evening to review the day; their thoughts, words, actions, and those actions which they chose not to do. (Remind them that this is referred to as an examination of conscience, which has been talked about before.) Conclude by explaining to the participants that by using this tool, we are able to review our relationships with God and our neighbor and make the necessary changes to a life of deeper faith, hope and love.

3. Teach them how to pray an Act of Contrition.

Prayer

Gather everyone in two circles around the green cloth. Catechumens and candidates form the inner circle while sponsors and team members form the outer circle. Sponsors and team members place their hands on the shoulders of the person in front of them. Light the candles. Celebrate an adaptation of the Minor Exorcism (RCIA 93G).

Twenty-eighth Sunday in Ordinary Time

Understanding this Sunday:
Background for Catechesis

The Word in Liturgy

Isaiah 25:6–10
Psalm 23:1–3, 3–4, 5, 6
Philippians 4:12–14, 19–20
Matthew 22:1–14 [or (short form) 22:1–10]

The particular selection of Isaiah that we read today has served for countless generations as a classic expression of the eschatological banquet motif, a set of images used time and again to evoke the sum of all blessings that God's people will experience on the last day, the day of vindication from the Lord. The setting for the banquet is the mountain, a place that always carries in Jewish literature symbolic connotations of encounter with the divine. The feast is lavish, and the blessings of the table are incredibly wonderful ("he will destroy death forever," v. 7).

Early Christians quickly interpreted passages such as the present one as prefiguring their gatherings for the *agape* feast on the Lord's Day. Their highly developed eschatological sense led them to identify Sunday, the day of the Lord's resurrection, as the "eighth day of creation," the long-awaited "Day of the Lord," on which judgment of evildoers and salvation for the faithful would finally be accomplished. The familiar twenty-third psalm quickly became a favorite expression of Christian confidence in the Eucharist as eschatological banquet. Today's choice of psalm refrain ("I shall live in the house of the Lord all the days of my life") reflects our continuing understanding of the eschatological dimensions of this psalm and its application to our present-day gatherings on the Lord's Day.

Jesus' table fellowship with sinners was one of the defining characteristics of his public ministry of healing and reconciliation. He was aware of and even called attention to these meals as symbolic expressions ("sacraments") of the advent of God's reign, made available in his person and ministry. Jesus' parables often used the meal as metaphor to convey

some bigger truth of the kingdom, and it is little wonder that the early Christian community continued to tell their stories of Jesus with a heavy emphasis on the symbolic importance of the table. Matthew's allegorizing hand is evident in his version of today's parable, which identifies the sending of servants first with the preaching of the prophets, secondly with the apostolic mission to Israel (along with the destruction of Jerusalem as the consequence of their refusal), and, finally, with the Church's mission to the Gentiles. Also, the work of Matthew is the juxtaposition of a second parable (vv. 11–14, [long form of the reading]), clearly aimed at warning members of his own community who were present at the banquet (i.e., participated in Christian Eucharist), but who lacked behaviors expected of the baptized. (Some commentators feel the wedding garment is probably an allusion to the white robe of baptism.) Literature such as this helps us to appreciate the importance that the early Christian community ascribed to participation in the Eucharist on the Lord's Day, even when such participation was at the risk of one's life.

Today we conclude our monthlong series of readings from Philippians. Paul, who prided himself on his policy of financial independence from those to whom he preached, has relented and allowed his beloved community at Philippi to send him a gift while he is in prison. Here he reminds them that he can still do without and survive any "hardships" (v. 14, the word has eschatological associations), but his thanks are nonetheless warm and genuine. He reminds the Philippians that God will reward them with a similar generosity "in Christ Jesus" (v. 19).

Catholic Doctrine

Keep Holy the Lord's Day

The Lord's Day refers to Sunday, the first day of the week. According to scripture, Sunday is the day when Christ rose from the dead (Matthew 28:1, Mark 16:2, Luke 24:1, and John 20:1). On this day, everything changed, in God, for the better. Thus, this day, Sunday, is the day the Lord has made. On this day, we believers rejoice.

In reflecting on the liturgical year, the Second Vatican Council declared, "By a tradition handed down from the apostles, which took its origin from the very day of Christ's resurrection, the Church celebrates the paschal mystery every eighth day, which day is appropriately called the Lord's Day or Sunday. For on this day Christ's faithful are bound to come together in one place. They should listen to the word of God and take part in the Eucharist, thus calling to mind the passion, resurrection, and the glory of the Lord Jesus, and giving thanks to God who 'has begotten them again, through the resurrection of Christ from the dead, unto a living hope' (1 Peter 1:3). The Lord's Day is the original feast day, and it should be proposed to the faithful and taught to them so that it may become in fact a day of joy and of freedom from work. Other celebrations, unless they be truly of the greatest importance, shall not have precedence over Sunday, which is the foundation and kernel of the whole liturgical year" (SC 106).

The third commandment of the Decalogue enjoins us to observe and keep holy the Sabbath. Six days were set aside for work, but the seventh day was for rest, just as God rested after having created the world. The third commandment, of course, refers to the Jewish Sabbath. But for us Christians, Sunday fulfills the injunction of the third commandment, for in Christ the old law is made complete and Sunday is associated with Christ because of his resurrection on the first day of the week (CCC 2175). St. Ignatius of Antioch (d. 107) wrote, "Those who live according to the old order of things have come to a new hope, no longer keeping the Sabbath, but the Lord's Day, in which our life is blessed by him and by his death" (*Epistula ad Magnesios* 9, 1 AFII/2, 128–30; SCh 10, 88).

From the very beginnings of the Church, the community of believers gathered on Sunday to celebrate the Eucharist, the sacrament that renews our contact with the paschal mystery and which communicates and effects life within the Church (CCC 2177) and makes us one body, one blood. Thus, the Catholic Church understands that it is necessary for believers to gather on this day, that is, to leave their homes (where they can pray as a family or as an individual) and come together to raise their minds, their hearts, and their voices in praise of the God who has made them one, uniting them in the sacrifice of Jesus. St. John Chrysostom (d. 407) preached: "You cannot pray at home as at church, where there is a great multitude, where exclamations are cried out to God as from one great heart, and where there is something more: the union of minds, the accord of souls, the bond of charity, the prayers of the priests" (*De incomprehensibili* 3, 6: PG 48, 725D).

The great significance of this day, Sunday, is shown in the precepts of the Church, for it is specified that on Sundays and the other holy days the faithful are bound to participate in the Mass except in the case of sickness or the care of the sick and infants (CCC 2181 and CIC 1247). This obligation is fulfilled by either participating at Mass during the day on Sunday or on the evening before, at a vigil Mass (in other words, Sunday as a liturgical celebration commences for us on Saturday evening and concludes at sundown on Sunday itself—reflecting our Jewish heritage).

Sunday, the Lord's Day, is the festival day when our passover in Christ from death and sin to new life and grace is celebrated. For us believers it is a markedly communal day, a day when we draw together with one voice and heart to praise the Son who has risen in our lives and illumines us with true beauty and love.

Catholic Culture

In addition to the worship that marks the Lord's Day, the actions of believers should characterize this day as a day of rest and leisure. Many Catholics also dedicate some time this day to charitable service of the sick and the elderly and other good works. Other Catholics also observe this as a day of reflection where the mind and spirit are cultivated, furthering Christian maturity and growth.

St. Justin Martyr (d. 165) wrote, "We all gather on the day of the sun, for it is the first day [after the Jewish Sabbath, but also the first day] when God, separating matter from darkness, made the world; and on this same day Jesus Christ our Savior rose from the dead" (*Apologiae* 1, 67: PG 6, 429–32).

Dismissal Catechesis (30 min.)

Getting Started

1. Prepare the space ahead of time with a circle of chairs around a table draped with a green cloth and a candle and a flowering plant at its base.

2. Lead the candidates and catechumens to the circle, place the Lectionary on the table, and light the candle. After everyone is seated lead them in prayer, using these or similar words: *Good and gracious God, you gift us, your children, with many blessings—our families, friends, faith, food for our table, shelter from the elements, clothing for our bodies, and a joy-filled heart. For all this we give you thanks and praise. Send your Spirit to guide our reflection and discussion today that we may continue to grow in our love and faith. We ask this in the name of Jesus, our brother, who lives and reigns with you now and forever. Amen.*

First Impressions

1. Invite the catechumens and candidates to close their eyes and to listen as you slowly and deliberately proclaim the first reading, Isaiah 25:6–10. Pause in silence and then invite them to picture the feast described in the passage. Use these or similar words to prod their imagination: *Smell the rich foods. Describe the mouth-watering sights and tastes. Taste the choice wines. This is a feast like none other. With whom would you want to celebrate this feast? See their faces. Hear their voices—their laughter—their stories. God invites all people to this feast. God promises that all tears will be wiped away. God has removed our sins. God has saved us.*

2. Invite the participants to turn to the person on their right and begin a discussion on this reading. Direct them to describe the feast imagined in the reflection. Then encourage them to describe their images, feelings, and the people with whom they shared this feast.

3. Gather feedback from the sharing. Perhaps ask one of the candidates or catechumens to summarize the feedback.

Making Connections

1. Help the catechumens and candidates to create a list of occasions or opportunities when they have gathered with family and friends for a feast. Encourage them to describe what precipitated these events, who participated and why such gatherings are important.

2. Explore with the catechumens and candidates a working definition of the following terms: meal, luncheon, dinner, feast, banquet. Invite them to recall and describe an experience from their own lives when they participated in a meal, luncheon, dinner, feast, and banquet.

3. Ask them to turn to the person on the right and share their experiences.

4. Based on their experiences, compare with them the feast, which God provides for all peoples.

5. Review in the large group that *God provides for all people; God destroys that which divides people; God removes the reproach of the people; God assures us that all tears will be wiped away; God promises to destroy death forever.*

Prayer

Choose of these options or create your own prayer:
Lead the group in singing a song version of Psalm 23, such as: "Psalm 23" (Conry, OCP Publications, 1988).
Or . . .
Sing the psalm refrain such as "Shepherd Me, O God," (Haugen, GIA Publications, 1986) and recite the verses of Psalm 23
Or . . .
Invite each pair to write a paraphrase of Psalm 23 and pray some of these together.

Extended Catechesis

SESSION FOCUS: *Keep Holy the Lord's Day*

Gathering

A. Sunday:
1. Greet and welcome the sponsors and team members as they arrive. Invite them to join the circle of catechumens and candidates.
2. Encourage one or two of the catechumens and candidates to briefly describe the discussion from the Dismissal Catechesis.
3. Invite a team member to proclaim the gospel: Matthew 22:1–14.

B. Weekday:
1. Use the same centerpiece as described for the Dismissal Catechesis.
2. As the participants gather in the circle, greet and warmly welcome each person. Encourage a few participants to share some of the experiences around meal sharing that they have had over the past few days.
3. Lead this celebration of the Word:
   • Song: Gathering Song from Sunday's Liturgy of the Word
   • First Reading: Isaiah 25:6–10
   • Psalm: Psalm 23:1–3, 3–4, 5, 6
   • Alleluia
   • Gospel: Matthew 22:1–14
   • Alleluia

The Word (30 min.)

1. Encourage several team members to choose a character from the gospel and role-play it for the others. The characters include: the king, servants (three or four), those invited guests who refused to come, people from the byroads, a person not dressed properly. Enjoy the role-play as a way of helping the participants enter into the passage.

2. Divide everyone into small groups. Invite them to discuss the gospel passage using the questions found in the Participant Book on page 108. Gather insights and comments from the groups.

3. Expand on the following points, providing a background to the gospel, Matthew 22:1–14:
   - Jesus' table fellowship with sinners was one of the defining characteristics of his public ministry of healing and reconciliation. He called attention to these meals as symbolic expressions (sacraments) of the coming of God's reign.
   - Matthew's allegorizing hand is evident in his version of today's parable. In the parable he identifies the sending of servants: first, with the preaching of the prophets, second, with the apostolic mission to Israel, and third, with the Church's mission to the Gentiles.
   - The gospel of Matthew juxtapositions a second parable in verses 11–14. The parable is aimed at warning members of his own community, who were present at the banquet (Eucharist), but lacked behaviors expected of the baptized.
   - Some commentators feel the wedding garment is probably an allusion to the white robe of baptism.
4. In the same small groups, invite the participants to discuss this question. *What practices, behaviors, and places today need to heed the message of these parables?* Gather their insights in the large group. Then invite the groups to role-play a modern-day version of these parables.
5. After the role-playing exercise, summarize the discussion in these or similar words: *These readings help us to appreciate the importance that the early Christian community ascribed to participation in the Eucharist on Sunday, in spite of the risk of persecution.*

Catholic Teaching (30 min.)

1. Lead the participants in the following reflection, to recall past memories: *Close your eyes and turn back the pages of your life to your earliest memories of Sundays. What did you do? Did you go to visit anyone? Who? Recall how your family marked Sundays. Consider how you spend your Sundays now. What does Sunday mean to you in this time and culture? How do you observe Sunday?* Invite them to take some time to write down their memories of Sunday in the Participant Book on page 108. Then ask the participants to gather with the same partner to share what they have written.
2. In these or similar words discuss the scriptural meaning of Sunday: *Sunday is referred to as the Lord's Day, the eighth day, the first day of the week. According to scripture, Sunday is the day Jesus rose from the dead. On this day, everything changed with Jesus' resurrection from the dead. God's promised salvation was realized on Sunday.*
3. Lead the group in singing the refrain from "This Day Was Made By The Lord," (Walker, OCP Publications, 1989).
4. Continue to present the teaching of the Church on keeping holy the Lord's Day in these or similar words: *On the Lord's Day, the Church celebrates the paschal mystery, the day the Lord rose from the dead. Thus, every Sunday is considered an Easter celebration. On Sunday, the faithful are bound to come together in one place. The faithful come to listen to the Word of God and to take part in the Eucharist, calling to mind the passion, resurrection, and the glory of the Lord Jesus and giving thanks to God that we, through baptism, are adopted sons and daughters of God and heirs to kingdom prepared for us.*

5. Ask the small groups to compile a description, naming ways to keep holy the Lord's Day. Invite each group to share their list and post it on the wall for all to read. Conclude the sharing by saying: *Sunday is kept holy by participating in the celebration of Mass. The precept (law) of the Church is that we are to participate in Mass on all Sundays and Holy Days of Obligation except in cases of illness or care of infants and the sick.* Explain that the Church marks time from sundown to sundown, reflecting our Hebrew heritage; thus, Sunday Mass may be anticipated on Saturday evening.
6. Then continue with these or similar words: *Sunday is to be observed as the Lord's Day; thus, making it a day of joy and freedom from work. No other celebrations are to take precedence over Sunday, unless they are of great importance such as Christmas. Sunday is the day when believers gather in one place to raise their minds, their hearts, and their voices in praise of God who has made them one, uniting them in the sacrifice of Jesus. Sunday, the Lord's Day, is the festival day when our passover in Christ from death and sin to new life and grace is celebrated. For us believers it is a communal day; a day when we draw together with one voice and one heart to praise the Son who has risen in our lives and illumines us with truth, beauty, and love.*

Putting Faith into Practice

1. Gather the participants into their small groups, inviting them to describe ways of keeping the Lord's Day joyful and free from work. Encourage them to also discuss the challenge that this is in our society. Gather insights and descriptions from the groups as they finish sharing.
2. Explain Holy Days of Obligation and name those that are observed in your country. The United States observes six Holy Days of Obligation:
   - December 8, The Immaculate Conception of Mary
   - December 25, Christmas
   - January 1, Solemnity of Mary, Mother of God
   - Forty days after Easter, Ascension Thursday
   - August 15, Assumption of the Blessed Virgin Mary into Heaven
   - November 1, All Saints
3. Encourage them to share with their sponsor this week some practical ways of keeping the Lord's Day holy.
4. Review the parish weekend Mass schedule. Also, discuss with them the reality that some communities do not have opportunities to celebrate Mass every weekend but the obligation to gather communally for prayer is still to be observed.

Prayer

Invite each group to compose one intercession.
Gather everyone around the table. Light the candle. Begin the Litany of Intercession with these or similar words: *Jesus, our brother, you said that wherever two or three are gathered in your name, you are present. Gathered now in prayer we acclaim your presence. Hear the prayers that we place before you today. Respond to each prayer by saying, "Lord, Hear Our Prayer."*
Close by leading the group in singing the refrain from "This Day Was Made By The Lord" (Walker, OCP Publications, 1989).

Twenty-ninth Sunday in Ordinary Time

The Word in Liturgy

Isaiah 45:1, 4–6
Psalm 96:1, 3, 4–5, 7–8, 9–10
1 Thessalonians 1:1–5
Matthew 22:15–21

In the rise to power of Cyrus, pagan king of Persia, Deutero-Isaiah sees the hand of Yahweh at work. The decision of Cyrus, after his conquest of Babylon, to repatriate all of the subject peoples within its boundaries was judged a miraculous proof that the God of Israel held power over the entire earth. In this passage, the prophet imitates the literary style of a royal decree. It was Babylonian custom to announce the king's accession to the throne by saying that the god Bel-Marduk had "grasped the king by his right hand." Here, it is Yahweh who calls Cyrus his "anointed . . . whose right hand I grasp" (v. 1). It is remarkable (only here in the entire Jewish scriptures) to hear a pagan referred to as God's "anointed" (in Hebrew, "Messiah," or Greek, "Christ"), a term used only of kings, prophets, and priests in Israel. The passage is a forceful statement of Yahweh's sovereignty over even the most powerful of earthly rulers and, by implication, over their gods. Yahweh is understood at this point in the development of Israel's religious thought to be Lord even of history, in control of the fate of nations as well as the forces of nature. This is an important passage in the consolidation of the absolute monotheism of the Jewish people ("I am the Lord and there is no other, there is no God besides me," v. 5).

Psalm 96 is a royal enthronement psalm, celebrating Yahweh as King of Israel. The center of the psalm is verse 10, a climactic expression of Israel's faith in the sovereignty of Yahweh: "Say among the nations: the Lord is king." Today's responsorial refrain captures the consequences of this faith in Yahweh's kingship: "Give the Lord glory and praise." Praise is always the proper response to the truth of faith. From authentic faith must always flow both right worship (orthodoxy) and right action (orthopraxis).

Our doctrinal focus today on the first commandment is further supported by the gospel story of Jesus' teaching regarding the competing claims of civil and religious authority. The coin which Jesus asked for (he apparently did not have one; his opponents did) would have had the image of Caesar on it, in addition to an inscription proclaiming Caesar as sovereign. For the pious Jew schooled in the prohibition of graven images, such a coin was a constant reminder of the idolatrous claims of the Caesar. Jesus scores a point against his adversaries merely by the fact that they carried such an idolatrous image. Their possession of the coin of tribute was evocative of the many ways they were collaborators with their Roman overlords. Jesus' clever response might be interpreted as saying, "Give back to Caesar his idolatrous coin; have nothing to do with it. Give to God his due—everything!" Thus, rather than engage in a superficial dispute over separation of church and state, Jesus reasserts the absolute claim of Jewish monotheism, namely, that all earthly powers are subject to Yahweh's sovereignty. This pericope is part of the larger unit of Matthew (21:23–22:14) in which he details the growing antagonism between Jesus and the Jewish religious leaders. Nothing could be more fundamental to Jewish faith than the first commandment of the Torah, and Matthew shows how vast the rift has grown between Jesus and his adversaries.

For the next five weeks, the second reading is taken from Paul's First Letter to the Thessalonians, the earliest book of the New Testament. Paul writes this letter out of pastoral concern over some of the questions that have been raised by his recent converts. In particular, a number of issues dealing with eschatology seem to have been raised and Paul's answer affords us a glimpse of his early (and still developing) thought about the end times. In this section, the warmth of his greeting gives us a sense of the affection that the apostle felt for those to whom he is writing. At the top of his list of reasons why he is thankful to God for the Church at Thessalonica, Paul mentions the triad of faith, hope, and love, indicating how fundamental he judged these virtues to be in the life of a Christian community.

Catholic Doctrine

"I Am the Lord, There Is No Other"

Catholics believe that, according to divine revelation, God is shown to be a loving God who has created the human race and brought us out of bondage. The people chosen as God's own were constituted by divine favor and, as a mark of God's love and power, were freed from slavery in Egypt (Exodus 20:2–5). The covenant God who liberated these our spiritual forebears from slavery demanded acceptance and service and worship from his people (Matthew 4:10). The first of the Ten Commandments, therefore, most fittingly concerns the unique loyalty that is due to God from the chosen people: "You shall not have other gods besides me" (Exodus 20:3).

In the fullness of time, a new covenant in Jesus was established. Christ's teaching that we sum up all our obligations and duties toward God by loving the Most High with our whole heart, soul, and mind (Matthew 22:37) echoes the great prayer and call of faith of the first covenant, "Hear, O Israel: the LORD our God is one LORD" (Deuteronomy 6:4). Based in the scriptural witness of both Old and New Testaments and based in our own experience and witness as a Church, we affirm that there are no other gods. There is only one God, the Creator and Redeemer, and to that God alone is given our service and worship (CCC 2084).

Our Catholic faith also attests that the God in whom we place our trust is constant and unchanging. God, who is perfect, remains always the same, faithful, just, and without evil. Given such perfection, it is clearly a privilege to follow and accept the covenant relationship of mercy and goodness that God offers us in Jesus. Indeed, the question becomes, who would want to reject or not follow such a God? (CCC 2086)

In our changing human history the unchanging God continues to reveal an overwhelming divine graciousness that reaches out, again and again, to save us. That divine graciousness is mirrored in our own hearts and lives by the virtues of faith, hope, and love. These three virtues help explain how we are to respond to the first commandment.

First of all, the source of our salvation, the foundation of authentic life, the impetus for our own moral and upright living, is found in God. We believe, therefore, that our first stance toward this loving God should be faith, to believe in the Most High and to proclaim that belief in our words and deeds (CCC 2087). Thus, Catholics strive to nourish one another's faith and to protect our relationship to the one God, for faith is a precious gift that underlies everything we are. The willful disregard of revealed truth, that is, voluntary doubt, is a sin against faith and offends against the first commandment (CCC 2088). This is to be distinguished from questioning and exploring the revealed truth so that a better understanding may be derived from this exploration.

Second, because of our own limited power, we humans cannot envision all that God has in store for us. We believe, therefore, that when God reveals and we are called to respond to the Almighty's revelation, we must hope that the Most High will give us the ability to love God in return (CCC 2090). Hope affords us the confident expectation of divine goodness and beatitude and helps us to resist the depths of despair or the presumption that we can rely only on ourselves for salvation (CCC 2091–92).

Third, we believe the first commandment enjoins upon us the joy of loving God above everything and all others (CCC 2093). We fail to love God, for example, when we engage in indifference to divine goodness and ingratitude for divine blessings (CCC 2094). Since Jesus linked loving God to loving neighbor (see next Sunday), the failure to love God is also shown in the same kind of indifference and ingratitude rendered toward our neighbor. In addition, our response to God in love moves us toward the virtue of religion (CCC 2095).

The word itself, "religion," derives from Latin (*re*, meaning "again," and *ligatio*, "to tie," as in "ligament"). The adoration, prayer, and sacrifice (CCC 2096–99) rendered to God by our religious attitude and actions, the promise we make as we give of ourselves to the divine by the practice of religion, ties us or binds us to God and to one another in faith, hope, and love. Superstition and idolatry (the worship of false gods) break those bonds and draw us away from the one, true God.

Catholic Culture

The frequent Old Testament title given to God, "LORD," indicates a figure who holds rightful authority over another. It denotes a superior-inferior relationship.

St. Cyril of Jerusalem (d. 386), bishop during the difficult years of the Arian heresy, helped to promote pilgrimages to the Holy Land. His primary surviving work is entitled *Catecheses*, instructions to catechumens preparing for baptism. In it, he writes, "Seeing then that many have gone astray in divers ways from the One God, some having deified the sun . . . others the moon . . . others the other parts of the world; others the arts; others their various kinds of food; others their pleasures . . . and others dazzled by the brightness of gold have deified it and the other kinds of matter—whereas if one lay as a first foundation in [one's] heart the doctrine of the unity of God, and trust to Him, [one] roots out at once the whole crop of the evils of idolatry . . . lay thou, therefore, this first doctrine of religion as a foundation in thy soul by faith" (St. Cyril of Jerusalem, Catechetical Instructions, On the Ten Points of Doctrine, found in *The Heart of Catholicism*, Theodore E. James, ed., Our Sunday Visitor, Inc., Huntington, Indiana, 1997, p. 181).

Dismissal Catechesis (30 min.)

Getting Started

1. Prepare the space ahead of time with a circle of chairs around a table draped with a green cloth. Arrange autumn leaves of various colors on the cloth and place a pillar candle on the cloth along with a pot of incense.

2. Lead the candidates and catechumens to the circle and place the Lectionary on the table, light the candle, and burn the incense. Invite the catechumens and candidates to reflect in silence, directing them to think about the question, *"Who is your God?"* When they seem ready, guide them through a litany of praise to God by encouraging them to make statements as to the nature of God, using this formula: *"I give thanks to God, who is . . ."* Invite them to notice the incense rising with our prayers of praise to God. You might begin with a statement of your own; for example, *"I give thanks to God, who is my source of hope."*

First Impressions

1. Prior to the gathering, print the following quotes from today's scripture passages on an overhead or newsprint for all to read: *"I am the Lord and there is no other, there is no God besides me." "For great is the Lord and highly to be praised; awesome is [Yahweh] beyond all gods." "Our preaching of the gospel proved not a mere matter of words for you but one of power; it was carried on in the Holy Spirit and out of complete conviction." "Then give to Caesar what is Caesar's, but give to God what is God's."* Read through the quotes with the group and invite them to recall the Liturgy of the Word in its entirety.

2. Then ask the participants to form small groups to discuss these questions: *What feelings do these phrases evoke in you? What common thread runs throughout the Liturgy of the Word (the scriptures, the homily, the prayers, and the music)? What does your inner spirit reveal to you as you recall the scriptures?* When they have finished sharing, invite each group to share some of their discussion with everyone. Summarize their comments in a few sentences and invite everyone to write down something from this discussion that they wish to remember in the appropriate section of their Participant Book on page 110.

Making Connections

1. Provide a short commentary on the second reading, 1 Thessalonians 1:1–5, in these or your own words: *In today's second reading, Paul is encouraging and affirming the community at Thessalonica with a warm greeting of affection. Notice his mention of faith, hope, and love in this passage.* Stop and proclaim the passage. *For Paul, these three virtues are the signs of and responses to the saving work of Jesus, the Christ, who is both human and divine, equal with God the Father.*

2. Ask the small groups to gather and list all the ways they have responded to God—Father, Son, and Spirit—by living out the virtues of faith, hope, and love. Distribute poster paper to each group and a marking pen, instructing them to write large enough for all to read. Provide a period of time for the small groups to talk through and list their responses to the God of life. When they are finished, invite each group to share their list with the large gathering. Post the lists around the room.

Prayer

Gather the attention of everyone by playing "Where Charity and Love Prevail" (Paul Benoit, World Library Publications, 1961) in the background. Invite everyone to reflect upon one action of faith, hope, and love which they wish to incorporate into their daily living and to pray that God will give them the inner strength to carry our their resolve. Close with this prayer: *God, you are our God. You rule the heavens and the rhythms of nature. You, Lord, are the one God, manifested in three persons, Father, Jesus, and Holy Spirit. Your dominion covers the face of the earth and all the wondrous marvels of the universe. We cannot grasp the breadth and depth of your power and your loving care. Open us that we might believe in you more fully. Mold us, that we might place our hope in you, even in difficult times. Melt our hearts that we might love all that you have created. In the name of Jesus who has redeemed us, we pray. Amen.*

Extended Catechesis

SESSION FOCUS: "I Am the Lord, There Is No Other"

Gathering

A. **Sunday:**
1. Greet and welcome the sponsors and team members as they arrive. Invite them to join the circle of catechumens and candidates.
2. Begin the prayer by leading all in singing Psalm 96:1, 3, 4–5, 7–8, 9–10. Invite a sponsor to proclaim the first reading, Isaiah 45:1, 4–6. Lead the group in singing the psalm once again. Provide this background as a way of inviting all to enter into the gospel passage:
   An ever-perennial issue among the Jews of Jesus' day and even today is the subject of taxes. This was especially significant in Jesus' day. The Jews were subjected to many taxes: an income tax, 1 percent of one's income; a ground tax, one-tenth of all grain and one-fifth of oil, and a poll tax, a denarius or one day's wages. There were other taxes, including a temple tax. All of these were collected and paid to Rome. Can you imagine the resentment these people felt toward the tax collectors and to the Roman leaders and soldiers? Keep this in mind as you listen to the gospel, centered on this controversial issue of the poll tax. Ask a team member to proclaim Matthew 22:15–21.

B. **Weekday:**
1. Use the same centerpiece as described for the Dismissal Catechesis, lighting the candle and the incense.

2. As the participants gather in the circle, greet and warmly welcome each person. Invite the participants to share one thing they discovered over the past few days regarding the vastness of our God.

3. Lead this celebration of the Word:
   - Song: Gathering Song from Sunday's liturgy
   - First Reading: Isaiah 45:1, 4–6
   - Sing Psalm 96:1, 3, 4–5, 7–8, 9–10
   - Background preparation for the gospel as in section A
   - Gospel: Matthew 22:15–21

The Word (30 min.)

1. Ask the participants to name some of their reactions to the context of the gospel and its message.

2. Present the background for the first reading from Isaiah using these or your own words: *Although as early as the time of the giving of the Ten Commandments Israel is forbidden (by the First Commandment) to worship any god but Yahweh, the Israelites' understanding of who Yahweh is continued to grow as they developed into a nation. In the time of exodus from the captivity of the Egyptians, God was a liberator, provider, guardian, and lawgiver. Yahweh was present in the desert wanderings and also remained faithful to this nation in the land of Canaan. Remember, this was during a time when gods were considered local powers. The concept of the Lord expanded, however, during the exile of the nation in Babylon. Yahweh was the one true God, wherever they were. The Lord of nature and of their nation was now understood to have power even over the pagan king Cyrus. (This is the only place in scripture where we hear of a pagan referred to as God's anointed.) This passage indicates the consolidation of the absolute monotheism of the Jewish people. "I am the Lord and there is no other, there is no God besides me."*

3. Invite the sponsors and/or godparents to gather with their catechumen or candidate to share, using these questions as a catalyst: *What do you understand about the nature of God from this background on Israel's growing sense of God's nature? Who is God for you? What are some ways that people today engage in "idolatry"? What does the verse "there is no God besides me" suggest in your own faith journey?* Elicit some responses, taking one question at a time, in the large group.

4. Present the following concepts regarding the gospel, Matthew 22:15–21—use the background found in the Word in Liturgy section of Understanding this Sunday as a guide: *The question posed to Jesus was a trap. But Jesus averts the hotbed of differences between the Herodians' and the Pharisees' opinions about the poll tax by pointing up the irrelevance of each viewpoint. Both camps had missed the point. Jesus asks for a coin, engraved with an image of Caesar as well as an inscription proclaiming Caesar as sovereign. For pious Jews, who were prohibited from possessing graven images, the fact that they carried such an idolatrous image indicated their implicit acceptance of the occupying power. Thus, Jesus underscores the status quo and unmasks those who are trying to foil him. In the famous line from this passage, Jesus averts engaging in a superficial dispute over the separation of Church and state.*

He reasserts the absolute claim of Jewish monotheism, namely, that all earthly powers are subject of Yahweh's sovereignty.

Catholic Teaching (30 min.)

1. Invite the same small groups to gather and discuss this question in the light of God's sovereignty: *What does it mean for your life that there is no other God but the Creator and Giver of Life?*

2. Ask everyone to turn to the reflection on page 110 in his or her Participant Book. When they have finished writing, encourage each person to respond to the questions posed on that same page. Invite them to share something from this reflection with the same small group.

3. Present the Church's teaching on the one, true God, expanding on these points through your own research and the Catholic Doctrine section found in Understanding this Sunday:
   - God is a loving God, who throughout our history creates, liberates, and cares for all people, all nations, and all of creation.
   - Jesus established a new covenant with God by teaching that we are to love God with our whole heart, soul, and mind, and love our neighbor as ourselves.
   - God, in whom we trust, is constant, faithful, and unchanging. We can count on God and surrender our trust and hope in God.
   - The most appropriate response to our source of life and salvation is faith, believing in the Most High in word and deed; hope in God's divine providence to carry us through the difficulties of life; and love for God as expressed in love for our neighbor, even our enemy.

Putting Faith into Practice

1. Indicate the posted lists of ways the catechumens and candidates began to reflect upon the response of faith, hope, and love due our one, true God. You may choose to have some of those present at the Dismissal Catechesis explain the lists.

2. In the large group invite everyone to add to and clarify the practical actions and attitudes that flow out of our faith, hope, and love for the God of all life.

3. Give examples of some of the early Christians mentioned in Acts and Paul's letters whose actions of faith, hope, and love offer models for loving God with our whole soul, heart, and mind. Some men and women who made God the Lord of their life include Priscilla and Aquila, Lydia, Timothy, and Stephen. Browse through your New Testament for more examples.

Prayer

Pray a Litany of Saints with the participants. Include several saints through the ages and members of your parish, as well as members of this gathering. Close by adding this prayer: *God of all, we pray that the witness of these saints, both living and dead, might be a light for us as we respond to your love for all people. Bless us with faith, hope, and love, that our lives might focus on you alone in the midst of the concerns and issues that distract us. May our hearts and minds grow in understanding your power over the entire universe. Amen.*

Thirtieth Sunday in Ordinary Time

Understanding this Sunday:
Background for Catechesis

The Word in Liturgy

Exodus 22:20–26
Psalm 18:2–3, 3–4, 47, 51
1 Thessalonians 1:5–10
Matthew 22:34–40

The compilation of the Book of Exodus was the result of a long and complex process. The second half of the work (cc. 19–40) deals with the events at Mount Sinai, the giving of the Ten Commandments and detailed prescriptions of various sorts that flow from them. The particular section from which today's reading is taken (22:18–23:19) has to do with a variety of social and cultic matters. The three issues touched on here concern groups of people who would have been particularly vulnerable in the socioeconomic system of the tribes following their settlement in Canaan. Resident aliens, widows, and orphans, as well as the poor who had to borrow to survive, were all "at risk" populations within a social milieu in which one's welfare and security depended upon being a property owner or at least being or having a breadwinner to provide for the household. Of particular note is the way the text connects its social policy imperatives both to Israel's own history and to the very nature of Yahweh. The Israelites had been treated compassionately by a God of love in their times of vulnerability. No less would be demanded of them now, if they were to remain faithful to their covenant relationship with that same God of mercy. Concern for the poor and weak is a distinguishing characteristic of Yahweh ("I will hear him; for I am compassionate," v. 26), and he in turn requires his people to refrain from exploiting the vulnerable. Jesus in the gospel will pick up and develop this teaching by demanding love for one's neighbor (remember who is "neighbor" in Jesus' eyes; cf. Matthew 5:43–48), and he will then link such love to the supreme command of the Torah, the love of God above all else.

Psalm 18 is a song of thanksgiving for (the king's?) deliverance. It seems to have been used in worship settings to keep alive the sense of Yahweh's saving actions of the past on behalf of the people and to promote hope in the continuance of that same

gracious care in the future. The reason for its choice today is not immediately clear, but most likely it serves to highlight the Lord as one who protects those in need. The vulnerable ones whom Yahweh protects by the legal prescriptions of Exodus 22 would have been able to acknowledge him as their protector in heartfelt words such as we proclaim in this text ("I love you Lord, my strength").

Today's gospel reading is another of the controversy stories collected in this place by Matthew (this entire section concludes with verses 41–46). The question put to Jesus was not remarkable; in fact, it was a commonplace query for a rabbi of the day. Nor is Jesus' reply entirely original. Other rabbis had similarly linked the two commandments of the law before (Deuteronomy 6:5 & Leviticus 19:18). But there is something important and original about the fact that Jesus puts both commandments on a par with each other. The Pharisees had categorized the 613 precepts which they observed as "light" and "heavy," depending on their perceived importance. Jesus takes the universally recognized "heavy" precept of love of God and places it on an equal footing with the Pharisees' "light" precept regarding love of one's neighbor! For Matthew's community, restating the Lord's command to love all without partiality seems to have been an extremely important teaching (cf. Matthew 5:43–48; 7:12; 9:13; 12:1–8; 18:12–35; 25:31–46).

Paul's reference to the Thessalonian Church being a model for others is no idle comment. The city, in fact, was a thriving crossroad in the empire, and the witness of this community of pagans who had accepted Christ and radically changed their lives would have been a powerful sign of the Spirit's work in spreading the gospel. The summary of Paul's message at the end of this reading (vv. 9–10) indicates the stress he must have placed in his preaching on the nearness of the last days ("the wrath to come") and the proximity of the second coming (". . . await from heaven the Son . . ." v. 10).

Catholic Doctrine

The Two Great Commandments

Jesus takes what had been two separate commandments and places them together. This new, single and greatest commandment has an enormous impact on our Catholic view of society and relationships between individuals and peoples. Modern popes have written extensively on this topic. John XXIII's *Mater et magistra* (1961) and *Pacem in terris* (1963), Paul VI's *Ecclesiam suam* (1964), and John Paul II's *Sollicitudo rei socialis* (1987) and *Cenesimus annus* (1991) all deal with the complex network of relationships defined as world society in the light of the gospel and Catholic tradition. The Second Vatican Council also examined the modern world and society, and noted, "Love of God and of one's neighbor, then, is the first and greatest commandment. . . . It goes without saying that this is a matter of the utmost importance to [human beings] who are coming to rely more and more on each other and to a world which is becoming more unified every day" (GS 24).

Indeed, the Church sees this mutual reliance as being based in the unity of the Trinity. The unity which characterizes God the Father, the Son, and the Holy Spirit is the very impetus for the members of the human community to draw closer together. Given this view, the Church affirms the gospel truth that love of God and neighbor cannot be separated (CCC 1878) and bases all its insights regarding society on this foundation. These insights can be described as: interdependence, the common good, respecting the human person, solidarity, and the requirements of peace and justice.

The Church's view on interdependence is not merely that we are social beings but that we thrive and grow by living together in society. One of the worst forms of punishment is solitary confinement. In other words, living together is not something ancillary to human nature, rather, it is by our dealings with one another, our mutual service of one another, and our fraternal dialogue that we develop and flourish (GS 25). Catholics understand, therefore, that interdependence is a requirement of our human nature and the medium by which individuals respond to their vocation and calling from God (CCC 1879).

The Church teaches that the good of the individual is related to the common good (CCC 1905). The common good is described by the Second Vatican Council as "the sum total of social conditions which allow people, either as groups or individuals, to reach their fulfillment more fully and more easily" (GS 26). Thus, the Church insists that every group that composes society must take into account and acknowledge the needs and legitimate aspirations of every other group.

Society can only be characterized as working for the common good when it is founded upon respect for the human person. Such respect means every individual be given ready access to basic necessities, such as food, clothing, housing, freedom, education, family, work, privacy, and so on (CCC 1908). Thus, as society develops, it must always uphold respect for the human person and work for more humane conditions of life for all.

In the Catholic perspective, human solidarity is an outgrowth of the avenue God has opened for us in providing holiness of life to us as a people. Jesus saves us and creates for us a Church whereby we experience the depths of our communion with God and one another. Each member of the Church gives of oneself in service to others according to the gifts given by God, and in that rendering of mutual sacrifice solidarity is increased until it is brought to fulfillment in the kingdom. This friendship is built into our very natures and echoes God's befriending of us (CCC 1939).

Finally, the common good and human solidarity require the stability of society that peace ensures, and peace, in turn, is promoted by justice. Catholics understand that we have a concrete responsibility for one another's welfare (CCC 1913). Economic inequity and wide disparities of wealth between groups is scandalous and promotes discord and instability (GS 29). Each generation must provide the next with reasons for life and optimism. As the Church prays, "Father, you have given all peoples one common origin, and your will is to gather them as one family in yourself. Fill the hearts of all . . . with the fire of your love and the desire to ensure justice for all their brothers and sisters. By sharing the good things you give us may we secure justice and equality for every human being, an end to all division, and a human society built on love and peace" (*Sacramentary*, Mass for the Progress of Peoples, Opening Prayer).

Catholic Culture

Dorothy Day (1897–1980) was cofounder along with Peter Maurin (1877–1949) of the Catholic Worker movement which promotes a gospel critique of society based on the message that we see Christ in our neighbors. Day opened the offices of the Catholic Worker as a "house of hospitality," offering food and shelter for those displaced by the Great Depression. This was one of many such houses. Day spoke of her being thrilled as a little girl reading about the lives of the saints, but she said, "I could see the nobility of giving one's life for the sick, the maimed, the leper. . . . But there was another question in my mind. Why was so much done in remedying the evil instead of avoiding it in the first place? . . . Where were the saints to try to change the social order, not just to minister to the slaves, but to do away with slavery?" (Dorothy Day quoted in *All Saints*, Robert Ellsberg, Crossroad Publishing Company, New York, 1997, p. 519).

Dismissal Catechesis (30 min.)

Getting Started

1. Prepare the space ahead of time with a circle of chairs around a green cloth spread over the floor in the center. In the circle place an icon, statue, or art piece of God and photographs of people of different backgrounds, ages, and cultures. Collect these prior to the session or cut out of magazines. A small vigil candle can be placed near the art piece representing God.
2. Lead the candidates and catechumens to the circle, place the Lectionary on the table, and light the candle. Invite the participants to respond to the petitions below by saying: *"Let us love the Lord our God and love our neighbors as we love ourselves."*

> *The strangers and aliens in our land cry out for acceptance . . .*
> *The pleas of the orphans and widows are heard across the land . . .*
> *The poor, who have nothing, shall not be exploited . . .*
> *In spite of great trials, the word of the Lord echoes forth from the Church . . .*
> *Jesus, who was raised from the dead, delivers us from the wrath to come . . .*

Add your own petitions, based upon today's reading.

First Impressions

1. Ask the participants to gather in small groups to discuss these questions: *What about today's Liturgy of the Word did you find consoling? How would you state the Good News presented in the scripture passages for today?* As the discussion concludes, invite everyone to turn their attention back to the large gathering to offer a summary of the responses.
2. Present this introduction to the second reading, 1 Thessalonians 1:5–10, using these or your own words: *This second reading continues last week's letter of Paul to this thriving community in Macedonia. Paul began a Christian community strategically located at the crossroads of trade, ensuring the spread and growth of Christianity. Paul praises the church established there, for it had become a model of Christian community. The majority of converts were former pagans who accepted Christ and changed their lives radically. For them this meant forsaking all other gods, following Jesus, who is God, and hoping for the glory of heaven in spite of great trials.* Gather the participants back into small groups to share their thoughts on these questions: *What about this community do you find impressive? What kind of faith does it take to make such radical lifestyle changes?* Invite a few groups to share their insights with everyone.

Making Connections

1. In the large group ask the participants to name some of the radical life changes that they have made in their own journey of faith. Explain that, while worship of one God does not seem difficult for us today, for these pagan peoples, to let go of the many gods they worshiped would have been very hard.

2. Invite them to think of some of the implications of loving and believing in one God in their small groups. Ask them to complete these sentences as a way of precipitating the discussion. You might write the following on an overhead or newsprint: *For me, believing in God means that I can no longer. . . . When I respond to God's unconditional love, I am compelled to change. . . . My inner attitude toward life has changed in this way . . . as I try to love God with all my heart.* Invite each group to share their responses in the ensuing discussion with the large gathering.

Prayer

Encourage the participants to look at the image or artwork in the center of your circle. As they reflect on this image, invite each person to think of God's promise to love each of us unconditionally. When they seem ready, ask them to name one simple way they might respond to God's great love during the course of each day. Then lead all in singing the response to Psalm 18, *"I love you, Lord, my strength,"* after you pray each verse.

Extended Catechesis

SESSION FOCUS: *The Two Great Commandments*

Gathering

A. Sunday:
1. Greet and welcome the sponsors and team members as they arrive. Invite them to join the circle of catechumens and candidates.
2. Ask each participant to name one thing they heard in the Dismissal Catechesis. Then pray in these or similar words: *God of compassion and love, your covenant of love compels us to love our neighbor with the same kindness and mercy which you generously lavish upon us. Yet we are blind to the stranger and alien, we forget the widow and orphan, and we hold tight our possessions and gifts. Open wide our stiff hearts and heal our blindness. We pray that we might love you and our neighbor with a wholehearted commitment and strength, knowing that you first chose and loved us. We ask this in the name of our loving Savior, Jesus. Amen.*
3. Proclaim the first reading, Exodus 22:20–26. Pause for a time of silent reflection, inviting all to think about the "at risk" people in our society. Continue by asking a team member to proclaim the gospel, Matthew 22:34–40.

B. Weekday:
1. Use the same centerpiece as in the Dismissal Catechesis.
2. As the participants gather in the circle, greet and warmly welcome each person. Invite them to share any signs of God's love they experienced in the past few days.
3. Lead this celebration of the Word:
   - Song: Gathering Song from Sunday's liturgy
   - First Reading: Exodus 22:20–26
   - Silent Reflection as described in section A

- Sing Psalm 18:2–3, 3–4, 47, 51
- Gospel: Matthew 22:34–40
- Closing prayer: use the prayer found in section A

The Word (30 min.)

1. Invite everyone to name some of the people "at risk" in today's society. Encourage them to look at the pictures in the center of the circle to help them think about these people. Then proceed to explain the background to the first reading from Exodus 22:20–26 and the gospel, Matthew 22:34–40: *The second half of Exodus details the various laws that flow out of the Ten Commandments. This passage refers to three "at risk" groups of people in the socioeconomic system of the Israelites. The law flowed out of the relationship between God and this people. Therefore, because of Yahweh's concern for the poor and bereft, those connected to God in the covenant must necessarily share the same concerns. The stranger in that culture did not have the protection of a tribe or clan and was thus vulnerable. For the widow and her children, their rights and livelihood needed the special protection of the community, for they had no rights or means of earning a living. The poor person often had to borrow money to live. Sometimes, their cloak was their only protection. These poor ones were to be treated with generosity rather than exploited. In this passage, Jesus shocks his listeners by putting love for neighbor and one's self on a par with love for God. In the light of these scriptures, who are the neighbors we are called to love?* Elicit some responses in the large group.

2. In small groups, ask the participants to share their insights on these questions: *What is the main motive for loving our neighbor, particularly the vulnerable members of our society? If love for neighbor is a barometer of our love for God, what can you say about your love for God?*

3. Invite everyone to turn to page 112 in their Participant Book and to take the time to reflect on the exercise and the questions found there. When they have finished, invite them to share whatever they are comfortable sharing with a partner. Usually the candidates and catechumens will choose to share with their sponsor and/or godparent.

Catholic Teaching (30 min.)

1. Invite the participants to discuss the last question, *What is it that connects you to others, making humankind interdependent?* in the large group.

2. Present the following concepts on the Church's teaching on the two great commandments, expanding on each from your reading of Catholic Doctrine found in Understanding this Sunday:
   - The bishops at the Second Vatican Council noted, "Love of God and of one's neighbor, then, is the first and greatest commandment. . . . It goes without saying that this is a matter of the utmost importance to [humankind] who are coming to rely more and more on each other and to a world which is becoming more unified every day" (GS 24).
   - The unity which characterizes God the Father, the Son, and the Holy Spirit is the impetus for mutual reliance and unity among peoples.
   - Interdependence is a requirement of our human nature and the medium by which individuals respond to their calling from God.
   - The Church teaches that every group that composes society must take into account and acknowledge the needs and legitimate aspirations of every other group.
   - Respect for the human person, actualized in giving every person access to the basics in life, is a necessary component of a society that has the common good as its focus.
   - Jesus saves us and creates for us a Church whereby we experience the depths of our communion with God and one another. Church communities that render mutual sacrifice increase the solidarity of the faithful members and bring to fulfillment the kingdom of God.
   - In the large group, reiterate the teaching presented by inviting the participants to define the following related terms: *interdependence, communion, common good, respect for the human person, solidarity, justice, and peace.* Write their definitions on newsprint.

3. Encourage the participants to raise questions evoked by this teaching on the two greatest commandments. Respond to the questions that you can and invite a pastoral minister from your parish staff to respond to additional questions.

Putting Faith into Practice

1. Gather everyone into small groups to look over the definitions of these characteristics. Ask each group to select two terms and to give concrete examples of how love of neighbor can be lived out based upon this characteristic. Ask each group to share their examples with everyone.

2. Encourage the participants to choose one way they will live out their faith this week by cultivating love for neighbor, based on one of these characteristics.

3. Open the discussion to further the commandment of love by asking this question: *How can we cultivate a healthy and holy love of self?* Invite everyone to determine one way they will practice love of others as we love ourselves, based on the group discussion. These resolutions can be written in the Participant Book on page 113, under the heading "I want to put my faith into action by."

Prayer

Invite the participants to begin the prayer by naming those people they encounter each day who are vulnerable in today's society. Close by praying in these or similar words:

Loving God,
  you have caused us to see human pain and injustice
  in these people at risk in our society.
While we pass them by each day,
  today you give us eyes to see their plight
  and ears to hear their cry.
Strengthen us to act on their behalf,
  bringing them a glimpse of your love,
  by loving them in some small way.
Spirit of God,
  fill us with the compassion and tenderness needed
  to love these, our neighbors and our selves,
  in order that love for God might consume us.
Amen.

Thirty-first Sunday in Ordinary Time

Understanding this Sunday:
Background for Catechesis

The Word in Liturgy

Malachi 1:14–2:2, 8–10
Psalm 131:1, 2, 3
1 Thessalonians 2:7–9, 13
Matthew 23:1–12

The author of Malachi wrote in the post-exilic period (mid-fifth century) when religious syncretism and other deviations from the covenant were still very much a problem among the Jewish people. In the section we read today (up to verse 9), the prophet's wrath is directed against the priests and their failure to maintain the purity of the cult. As leaders of the people, they bore a special responsibility for their sins ("[you] have caused many to falter by your instruction," v. 8), and so God's judgment against them will be harsh. In verse 10, a new subject is introduced, that of intermarriage. The prophet condemns this because of how easily it leads to laxity with regard to the worship of false gods. Marriage to a pagan is like a betrayal of the family unity ("Why then do we break faith with one another?" v. 10).

In Malachi's condemnation of leaders whose instruction leads astray the people, we have a powerful reminder of the great blessing God has bestowed on us by sending the Holy Spirit to guide the teaching authority (i.e., the magisterium) of the Church. Today's responsorial psalm seems to reflect the realization that only in God can we place our ultimate trust and hope. ("In you, Lord, I have found my peace.") In contrast to the arrogance of the priestly caste condemned in Malachi, the author of Psalm 131 (most likely a woman) exemplifies humble trust and reliance on God alone.

The suggested doctrinal focus for today is based on Paul's expression of gratitude to God that his message was received by the Thessalonian community, "not as the word of men, but as it truly is, the word of God at work within you who believe" (v. 13). As appears clearly later on in the letter, Paul is writing to resolve questions which had arisen in the community, questions of a doctrinal sort which held important consequences for the authenticity of the Thessalonians' faith. He reminds them here at the outset how he "preached God's good tidings" (v. 9) during his stay with them. Paul's claim to teach with authority ultimately rests on the source of his teachings, and he makes it clear that those teachings are of divine ("the word of God"), not human ("not as the word of men," v. 13) origin. In his role of nourishing the faith of the Thessalonian community, Paul compares himself to a nursing mother, an image he would later use again in 1 Corinthians 3:1ff. Behind these images are important understandings of the teaching function in the Church and its relationship to the faith of all believers.

In the gospel, Jesus accepts the traditional Jewish view regarding the teaching authority of religious leaders ("Do everything and observe everything they tell you," v. 3), but at the same time he offers a scathing critique of the disparity between the words and deeds of those who exercised that function in his day. With chapter 23, Matthew begins the final section of his narrative (23:1–25:46) prior to the saga of Jesus' death and resurrection (26:1–28:20). This is the opening of the so-called "Eschatological Discourse." Jesus begins by first warning the people against the Scribes and Pharisees (vv. 1–12) and then pronouncing his own judgment ("woe to you . . .") against them (vv. 13–36). The prohibitions at the end of today's pericope against using certain titles (Rabbi, father, teacher) seem to reflect the polemic of Matthew's community against the Jewish establishment of the time (circa 80 A.D. and after) more than specific teachings of Jesus.

Catholic Doctrine

The Role of the Magisterium

The word *magister* in classical Latin meant not only "school master" or "teacher" but also anyone who was master of a particular trade, art, or even of ships and groups of slaves. In medieval usage it indicated either the teaching authority of the university professor or of the bishop. In modern Catholic usage the term "magisterium" refers to the teaching function and authority of the hierarchy of the Church, that is, the pope and bishops. It is also used to refer directly to the whole college of bishops (headed by the pope) as one complete entity. Catholics believe that the teaching function within the Church has four dimensions: (1) a gospel rationale, (2) a hierarchical and collegial character in service to the people of God, (3) a particular twofold object, and (4) levels of articulation and assent by which it operates.

Catholic belief holds that the bishops are the successors of the apostles and, as the Second Vatican Council states, they are "endowed with the authority of Christ" authentically teaching, informing the faith of people and directing their conduct (LG 25). In other words, we believe that those who exercise magisterial or teaching authority in the Church are sent by Christ—they do not do this on their own, they do not "invent" the gospel, but are gifted by the sacrament of ordination to be Christ's emissaries (CCC 875).

The Second Vatican Council stipulated that the magisterium is not above the Word of God, but "serves it, teaching only what has been handed on, listening to it devoutly, guarding it conscientiously, and explaining it faithfully, by divine commission and with the help of the Holy Spirit" (DV 10). Thus, when conflicts or confusions arise within the Church regarding the articulation of the content of faith, it falls to the magisterium to settle those issues and questions.

The Church is constituted hierarchically, that is, each member has a proper role to fulfill in contributing to the mission of Christ. Bishops, in their magisterial or teaching ministry, lead and guide the faithful. They exercise this guidance in varying forms. Individually, within his own diocese, a bishop may issue a pastoral letter on an aspect of Church teaching. He may also promote through diocesan agencies sound catechetics and educational institutions. Bishops who have been established as a particular group, for example, a conference of bishops of a country, may also exercise guidance for their episcopal conference and, for example, issue a letter or statement or create a policy direction or pastoral plan. Catholic bishops are understood to function together as a whole worldwide college or body united to the pope, the bishop of Rome. Evidence of this is seen, in an extraordinary way, when all the bishops gathered with the pope hold an ecumenical council. No matter which forms it takes, the entire purpose of this hierarchical and collegial exercise of the bishops' teaching authority is to be of service to Christ's flock, the people of God (CCC 876).

What is the purpose of the magisterium? Its purpose is to guide people in faith and morals. In other words, the teaching authority of the bishops pertains to Christian belief or to the practice of the Christian way of life.

The Catholic Church upholds that there are various levels of articulation of teaching. Because we believe that God guarantees us the possibility of objectively professing belief without error, we understand that Christ endowed the Church with the gift of infallibility. The pope, in virtue of his ministry as supreme pastor and teacher, exercises the gift of infallibility when he proclaims by a definitive act (he describes it as such, as infallible) a doctrine pertaining to faith or morals. Ecumenical councils, together with the pope, can also exercise their teaching authority infallibly (CCC 891). It is important to note that the Church speaks of infallibility as a gift, a charism given to the Church by the Holy Spirit (LG 25). Thus, a pope or an ecumenical council infallibly define teachings that are already contained in the deposit of revelation and that serve to make the people of God "live their lives in holiness and increase their faith" (DV 8). By their nature, infallible teachings require one's obedience and the assent of faith (CCC 891). Noninfallible or the ordinary teaching of the bishops and the pope require one's religious assent (CCC 892), which means that one must be open to the teaching, give it a fair hearing, and attempt to understand its rationale in order to facilitate an intellectual acceptance of it.

Without magisterial authority, the Church could never propose that the faith be articulated in a particular way at certain points in history. In other words, we could never as a community objectively grapple with what has been revealed to us by God. The Church would not be able to adequately preach the gospel, apply it to life, or formulate creeds. The role of the magisterium is to provide surety, in Christ, of the expression of faith and how that faith is put into practice.

Catholic Culture

Three months after his election as pope, John XXIII called for an ecumenical council of the Church whose goal would be an updating or, in Italian, *aggiornamento*. John XXIII said, "The substance of the ancient deposit of faith is one thing, and the way in which it is presented is another" (*All Saints*, Robert Ellsberg, Crossroad Publishing Company, New York, 1997, p. 243).

Dismissal Catechesis (30 min.)

Getting Started

1. Prepare the space ahead of time with the chairs in a circle. Drape a small table with a green cloth. Place a candle on it and a green plant at the base of the table.
2. Lead the candidates and catechumens to the circle and place the Lectionary on the table. After everyone is seated, light the candle and lead them in prayer with these or similar words: *Come, Holy Spirit, be with us. Come, Holy Spirit, be our guide. Come, Holy Spirit, be our comforter. Come, Holy Spirit, be our source of wisdom and knowledge. Come, Holy Spirit, dwell here with us. Amen.*

First Impressions

1. Invite everyone to close their eyes and take a deep breath. Lead them in this recollection of the Liturgy of the Word: *Recall your trip to church today. What did you see? Hear? What were you feeling?* Pause. *Recall your coming into the church. Who greeted you? Whom did you greet? What did you see? Hear? What were you feeling?* Pause. *The liturgy began. Recall the words of the gathering hymn, the penitential rite, the opening prayer.* Pause. *Recall the Liturgy of the Word. "I am a great King, give glory to my name, you do not keep my ways, you show partiality, one God created us, why break faith with each other?"* Pause. Sing the refrain from the psalm. *"You believed not because of our words but because the Word of God is at work within you."* Pause. *"Observe everything they tell you but don't follow their example. Words are bold; deeds are few. One is your teacher. Call no one father but God who is in heaven."*
2. Ask the participants to turn to the person on their right and share thoughts, words, or feelings that surfaced during the reflection and the Liturgy of the Word.
3. Gather feedback from the pairs.

Making Connections

1. Ask the participants to think of short sayings or proverbs that come to mind as they hear these readings. Be ready with such sayings as *"Do as I say, not as I do,"* or *"Practice what you preach."*
2. Explore what the sayings or proverbs have in common with what they heard in the readings for today.
3. With the same partners ask everyone to discuss these questions: *In our world and country, who would be comforted by these readings and why? In our world and country, who would be challenged by these readings and why?*
4. Collect their responses to these questions. Encourage them to create their own saying or proverb from these readings.

Prayer

Invite the catechumens and candidates to close their eyes and to speak to Jesus in the quiet of their heart about how they are comforted and challenged by today's readings. Then sing the "Prayer of St. Francis" (Sebastian Temple, OCP Publication, 1967).

Extended Catechesis

SESSION FOCUS: *The Role of the Magisterium*

Gathering

A. Sunday:

1. Greet and welcome the sponsors and team members as they arrive. Invite them to join the circle of catechumens and candidates.
2. Light the candle. Pray in these or similar words: *God, source of all goodness, you are the one who faithfully and patiently invites us into a deeper and deeper relationship with you. Help us to be truthful and faith-filled in our loving response to you. We ask this in the name of Jesus, our brother. Amen.*
3. Invite a team member to proclaim Malachi 1:14—2:2, 8–10. Pause for a few moments of reflection. Invite a second team member to proclaim the second reading, 1 Thessalonians 2:7–9, 13. Pause again for a few moments of quiet. Proclaim Matthew 23:1–12 and ask the participants to remain silent as they reflect upon the scriptures.

B. Weekday:

1. Use the same centerpiece as in the Dismissal Catechesis.
2. As the participants gather in the circle, greet and warmly welcome each person and light the candle.
3. Lead this celebration of the Word:
   - Song: Gathering Song from Sunday's liturgy
   - First Reading: Malachi 1:14—2:2, 8–10
   - Sing Psalm 131:1, 2, 3
   - Second Reading: 1 Thessalonians 2:7–9, 13
   - Sing Alleluia
   - Gospel: Matthew 23:1–12

The Word (30 min.)

1. Ask one or two catechumens and candidates to briefly summarize the discussion from the Dismissal Catechesis. Invite them to repeat the sayings and proverbs which they verbalized. Invite the sponsors and team members to add other sayings or proverbs that flow from these readings.
2. Direct the participants to open the Participant Book to page 114 as you guide them through the Reflection exercise. Then gather them into pairs, asking them to share their list with one another. In the large group collect the qualities that are similar and write these on a large piece of newsprint.
3. Open the meaning of the scriptures by using these words: *In the first reading, the prophet Malachi is addressing the difficulty the Israelite community experienced in trying to be faithful to God's covenant. The prophet's anger in this instance is directed against the priests and their failure to maintain the covenant with God. As leaders they bore a special responsibility for their sins and so the prophet warns that God's judgment will be harsh.* In the same pairs, ask the participants to discuss this question: *What is the role of a religious leader as described in the reading from Malachi?* Elicit ideas from the pairs in the larger group.

4. Continue to describe the gospel, Matthew 23:1–12: *Jesus accepts the traditional view regarding the teaching authority of religious leaders but, at the same time, he offers a scathing critique of the disparity between the words and deeds of those who exercise that function in his day.*

5. Ask each pair to join with another pair to form a small group to share their insights on this question: *Why is Jesus harsh in his critique of the religious leaders of his time?* Gather feedback from their sharing.

6. Finally, open up the meaning of the second reading from 1 Thessalonians 2:2, 8–10 with these or similar words: *Paul's letter to the Thessalonians addresses doctrinal questions that arose in the community. Paul expresses his gratitude to God that his message was received by the community as the Word of God at work within the believers. In his role of nourishing the faith of the Thessalonians, Paul compares himself to a nursing mother, an image he uses again in 1 Corinthians.*

7. In the same small groups, invite the participants to take time describing and enumerating the qualities of a religious leader exhibited by Paul and this community. Invite the groups to name some of these qualities in the large gathering.

Catholic Teaching (30 min.)

1. Continue with these or similar words: *As St. Paul claims to teach with authority, his authority ultimately rests on the source of his teachings—Christ. Paul makes it clear that those teachings are of divine, not human, origin. Catholic belief holds that bishops are the successors of the apostles and that they are blessed with the authority of Jesus Christ, authentically teaching, informing the faith of people and directing their conduct. They do not create the gospel but are gifted through the sacrament of ordination to be Christ's emissaries. In their teaching function, they are referred to as the magisterium of the Church.*

   In pairs, ask them to discuss this question: *What responsibilities rest with the teaching authority of the Church?* Gather feedback from their discussion.

2. Present the teaching of the Church, stressing these points:
   - In modern Catholic usage, the term "magisterium" refers to the teaching function and authority of the hierarchy of the Church, that is, the pope and bishops.
   - The Holy Spirit directs and guides the magisterium.
   - Catholics believe that the teaching function within the Church has four dimensions: (1) a gospel rationale, (2) a hierarchical and collegial character in service to the people of God, (3) a particular twofold object, and (4) levels of articulation and assent by which it operates.
   - The purpose of the magisterium is to guide people in faith and morals. In other words, the teaching authority of the bishops pertains to Christian belief or to the practice of the Christian way of life.
   - The pope, in virtue of his ministry as supreme pastor and teacher, exercises the gift of infallibility when he proclaims by a definitive act a doctrine pertaining to faith or morals. Ecumenical councils, together with the pope, can also exercise their teaching authority infallibly (CCC 891).
   - Without magisterial authority, the Church could never propose that the faith be articulated in a particular way at

a particular time—we could never objectively grapple as a community with what has been revealed to us by God.

3. Invite everyone to gather into small groups to discuss these questions: *What do you now understand as the role of the magisterium of the Church? What confidence does this teaching offer as you struggle with questions of faith? What questions does this teaching raise for you as you continue on your journey toward full initiation into the Church?* In the large group invite responses one at a time. You may choose to invite a member of the parish staff to be present.

4. Continue with these or similar words: *Without magisterial authority, the Church could never propose that the faith be articulated in a particular way at certain points in history. In other words, we could never as a community objectively grapple with what has been revealed to us by God. The Church would not be able to adequately preach the gospel, apply it to life, or formulate creeds. The role of the magisterium is to provide surety, in Christ, of the expression of faith and how that faith is put into practice.*

5. Finally, in pairs, ask the participants to discuss what message the readings of today have for church leaders. Gather insights from the discussion.

Putting Faith into Practice

1. Explain a little about the nature of an ecumenical council such as the Second Vatican Council. Use one of the videos from "The Faithful Revolution" (Resources for Christian Living, Allen, TX, 1997) as background. Select a portion of the video to view with the participants to enhance their understanding of the significance of this gathering of Church leaders. Allow time for comments and questions.

2. Display pastoral letters, documents of Vatican II, and encyclical letters. Possibilities include: U.S. Bishops' Pastoral on Peace—U.S. Bishops' Pastoral on Economic Justice—Pope Paul VI's Letter, Evangelization in the Modern World—Pope John Paul II's Letter, Evangelization for the New Millennium—Vatican II in Plain English—Documents of the Second Vatican Council—Letters from the bishop of your diocese

3. Encourage the candidates and catechumens to borrow one or two of these church writings in order to see firsthand an example of the magisterium of the Church in action.

Prayer

Gather the participants in a circle. Light the candle. Lead them in the following intercessory prayer directing them to respond *"Come, Holy Spirit, guide your Church"* after each invocation: *For our parish leaders, we pray . . . For our diocesan leaders, we pray . . . For our bishop (Name), we pray . . . For our church leaders, we pray . . . For all who teach the Catholic faith, we pray . . . For our Holy Father, Pope (Name), we pray . . . For whom else shall we pray. . . ?*

Conclude by praying in these or similar words: *Good and gracious God, we give thanks and praise to you for our present Church leaders and for all those who have brought your Church to this point in history. We thank you for the guidance of the Holy Spirit, whom you promised would be with us till the end of time. Keep all religious leaders and ourselves faithful to your truth and your sacred Word in all we teach and in all we do. Amen.*

Thirty-second Sunday in Ordinary Time

Understanding this Sunday:
Background for Catechesis

The Word in Liturgy

Wisdom 6:12–16
Psalm 63:1, 2–3, 4–5, 6–7
1 Thessalonians 4:13–18 [or (short form) 4:13–14]
Matthew 25:1–13

As we approach the end of the liturgical year, the Lectionary assigns texts which in some way are connected to eschatological themes. This is certainly the reason why 1 Thessalonians is placed in this period of time. It is also behind the selection of today's gospel reading from Matthew's Eschatological Discourse (23:1–25:46). The choice of Wisdom today is dictated by its relationship with the gospel reading. The Book of Wisdom, attributed to Solomon, was composed sometime in the first half of the first century before Christ by an anonymous Jewish author in Alexandria, Egypt. It is thus the last of the Old Testament scriptures to be written. Wisdom does not appear in the Hebrew or Protestant canon.

Today's selection appears in an eschatological context, part of a section in which Solomon is purportedly giving advice to other rulers ("Hear, therefore, kings, and understand," 6:1). He tells them to seek Wisdom and they will not be disappointed ("She is readily perceived by those who love her, and found by those who seek her," v. 12). In fact, Wisdom herself seeks out those who are looking for her ("she makes her own rounds, seeking those worthy of her," v. 16). There are two ideas here: the notion of vigilance for one who comes and the idea of actively seeking out the good. Both are important recurring themes of Jewish and Christian eschatology.

Psalm 63 represents the motif of longing for God in one of its most classic expressions. The author's search for God has been satisfied and he rests secure in God's presence. The psalm, in a sense, demonstrates the truth of what the first reading has proclaimed—that those who seek God's Wisdom will not be disappointed. The connection to today's suggested doctrinal focus on perseverance in prayer is not hard to see.

The parable in today's gospel is unique to Matthew. In its earliest form, it was probably a simple story that Jesus told to reinforce the fact that some are ready to accept the reign of God and others are not. In the course of its oral transmission by the Christian community and in Matthew's use of it in the plan of his gospel, the parable has been highly allegorized and given a strong eschatological orientation. The wedding feast has become the messianic banquet, the coming of the bridegroom (Christ) represents the parousia with its sudden, unexpected quality, the wise and foolish virgins could be Christians and Jews or perhaps vigilant and lax members of Matthew's community. In its present form, the parable is a strong statement warning of the importance of vigilance, perseverance in prayerful watchfulness, and living in a state of readiness for the Lord's coming.

Today's reading from 1 Thessalonians gives us an understanding of the questions that were troubling the young community. Paul had preached the imminence of the Lord's coming, but members of the community were worried about the fate of those who had already died before the day had arrived. Paul, using traditional Jewish apocalyptic imagery (vv. 16-18), reassures them that the dead will also enjoy the benefits of Christ's coming. The central point is the one that Paul tells them to console one another with: "We shall be with the Lord unceasingly" (v. 18).

Catholic Doctrine

Perseverance in Prayer

The relationship that exists between God and us requires expression. Prayer is the link between ourselves and the divine, a vital necessity (CCC 2744). Prayer is also a gift which is sustained by the Holy Spirit. But there is much in this world and our lives that draws us away from this vital activity.

The Catholic tradition understands that, no matter the form of our prayer, whether it is vocalized in personal or liturgical style, whether it is meditation or whether it is contemplation, our attempt at prayer can be sidelined by innumerable distractions. Oddly enough, to attempt to root out these distractions can be to fall into the ultimate trap, for by giving credence to the distractions one falls prey to their allure. The best remedy in avoiding distractions is to turn further into the depths of one's heart, for there, in that most intimate place, is where God speaks to us (CCC 2729).

Another difficulty that our Catholic tradition warns against in the life of prayer is inner dryness. This type of barrenness is described as the experience where nothing "works" in prayer, where the person praying feels separated from God. Neither in one's thoughts, nor in one's memories, nor in one's feelings is there any inkling of God's intimate presence. This lack of presence prompts one to ask where God is. This experience is the penultimate moment of faith. Even Jesus experienced such an episode in his agony in the garden. It is the experience of the tomb where the Lord was laid to rest. It requires the faithful heart throwing itself totally upon the God of conversion, who alone will vindicate and transform it (CCC 2731).

Given these difficulties in prayer, why do we Catholics believe that we should continue to pray to God, indeed, to never stop our attempts at communicating in prayer? There are several responses to this question:

First, we persevere because we are enjoined to do so by the gospel, by the letters of St. Paul, and indeed by the whole scriptural witness and the unbroken tradition of the Church expressed in the lives of the saints and the teachings of the magisterium. All of these sources assure us that God desires our communication. God wants us to pray. As in any relationship, we must always continue to attempt to express ourselves in our relationship with God, to communicate. Whatever form that communication takes, it nourishes the relationship. Without it the relationship dies. This does not mean that if we stop expressing ourselves to God in prayer that God stops loving us or that the relationship ceases. It simply means that our link, our cooperation with God, withers and is hampered (CCC 2738).

Second, we persevere so as to purify our motives in praying and, so, deepen our devotion to God, who alone deserves all our love. For example, one particular type of prayer—the prayer of petition or intercession—asks God for certain good things to be accomplished or realized, such as the health of a loved one. When someone we love does not regain health and instead worsens or dies, sometimes we stop praying. The problem is, have we been asking in prayer for what is best or has God answered our prayers in ways that we cannot currently perceive? (CCC 2735) The ultimate prayer is simply surrender in trust to God, no matter what transpires here and now, even the cross.

In the Catholic tradition, prayer is not a manipulation of God. It is an expression of our mutual thirst, God for us and us for God (CCC 2560). It is a form of vigilance against the darkness and evil of the world (CCC 2612). Prayer is the self-expression of a heart attuned to the love of the divine, responding to that gift of heaven, not from the height of pride but from the depth, the font of humility (CCC 2559). Prayer is our communion with the one who has made life possible for us in Christ (CCC 2565).

Catholic Culture

Various postures are used by Catholics in praying. Kneeling expresses our inferior relationship to the Most High who has created and redeemed us. Standing indicates our dignity before God as creatures created in God's own image. Palms outstretched before the Almighty symbolize that we have nothing of worth to offer but ourselves. Prostration is a sign acknowledging God as supreme, that we can do nothing without the divine presence and are totally open to the animating Spirit. Standing, lying, kneeling, or prostrating ourselves with arms stretched out in the form of a cross symbolize our total reliance on the loving self-sacrifice of Jesus, embracing in faith that total abandonment of self in obedience to God's will.

A painting by Girolamo da Cremona (1483) shows six philosophers and wisdom figures, including Solomon and Aristotle, engaged in discourse. At the end of the line is St. Thomas Aquinas. While the philosophers are clothed in brilliant colors, the saint is in his Dominican habit (black and white), as if to say the only brilliance needed in his life is Christ. There is also an ape shown in the painting, the only one not paying attention to the philosophers, the artist's point being that we humans pursue knowledge and desire understanding. St. Thomas holds an open Bible in his hands. Could the artist be expressing the point of prayer, which is our letting go in the mystery of God, a mystery we humans will never totally comprehend? "All prayer, all contact with God, demands of us this profound sacrifice: we must surrender to unknowing" (*The Mystery of Love,* Sr. Wendy Beckett, Harper SanFrancisco, 1996, p. 16).

Dismissal Catechesis (30 min.)

Getting Started

1. Prepare the space ahead of time with chairs in a circle. Arrange a green cloth on the floor and place on it several small votive candles, a rosary, and a prayer book.
2. Lead the candidates and catechumens to the circle, place the Lectionary on the cloth, and light the votive candles. Indicate that the group remain standing as you play "This Alone" (Tim Manion, OCP Publications, 1981), or lead the participants in singing Psalm 63:1, 2–3, 4–5, 6–7.

First Impressions

1. Invite the candidates and catechumens to name words or phrases that they recall from the liturgy just celebrated. Encourage them to include such phrases as *"You are my God whom I seek," "Console one another," "Give us some oil," "Open the door," "You do not know the day or the hour."* Ask the large group: *What impression did these passages from scripture leave with you?*
2. Then ask the participants to spend a few moments quietly reflecting on the qualities of waiting and preparation. Ask them to name these aloud as you move around the circle.
3. Proclaim the gospel, Matthew 25:1–13.

Making Connections

1. Invite the participants to think about how they would respond to the following, stating one question at a time with time for silent reflection between each: *If you had been one of the persons with enough oil, what would you have done when asked for some? If you had been one of the persons who did not have enough oil, how would you respond to the others' refusal to share?* Form small groups and ask them to share their thoughts about these questions. In the large gathering invite a few responses. Summarize their remarks.
2. Ask the participants to return to the same small groups to offer their ideas on these questions: *Who would be consoled by this parable? Why? Who would be challenged by this parable? Why? What do you understand as the message of this gospel?* After sufficient time, gather their insights and present a few comments in summary.

Prayer

Lead the participants in the following prayerful mediation: *Close your eyes. Take a few deep breaths. Imagine you are sitting alone in a very beautiful, secluded, safe spot. Take a few minutes to notice your surroundings. What do you see, smell, and feel as you look around?* Pause. *You're waiting for a friend, Jesus. At first, it is easy sitting there; everything is so beautiful, so peaceful.* Pause. *The appointed time comes and goes and yet no sign of Jesus. You begin to wonder if you are in the right place; if it is the right day; if it's the right time. You expected Jesus to be early or at least on time. More time passes.* Pause. *You become restless. You get up and walk around. You sit back down. You ponder what to do.* Pause. *You are about to leave and go in search of Jesus, when you see him approaching. What do you do? What do you say? What does he say to you?* Pause. After a few minutes, invite everyone to come back to this space and to open his or her eyes. Invite them to share the feelings and thoughts they experienced.

Extended Catechesis

SESSION FOCUS: *Perseverance in Prayer*

Gathering

A. **Sunday:**
   1. Greet and welcome the sponsors and team members as they arrive. Invite them to join the circle of catechumens and candidates.
   2. After all are seated, re-light the votive candles. Pray in these or similar words: *God, you draw all things to yourself. You call us to this time and place to reflect on prayer and its place in our lives. Help us to grow and deepen in our desire to spend time with you in prayer. Draw us to yourself. We ask this in the name of Jesus, our brother. Amen.* Proclaim the first reading, Wisdom 6:12–16. Invite the participants to reflect on the meaning of the passage for a brief period. Then ask a team member to proclaim Matthew 25:1–13.

B. **Weekday:**
   1. Use the same centerpiece as in the Dismissal Catechesis.
   2. As the participants gather in the circle, greet and warmly welcome each person. Invite a few participants to share their experiences of waiting for something important over the past week.
   3. Lead this celebration of the Word:
      - Song: Sing the Gathering Song from last Sunday's liturgy
      - First Reading: Wisdom 6:12–16
      - Sing Psalm 63:1, 2–3, 4–5, 6–7
      - Second Reading: 1 Thessalonians 4:13–18
      - Silent reflection
      - Gospel: Matthew 25:1–13

The Word (30 min.)

1. Repeat the guided meditation from the closing of the Dismissal Catechesis or simply refer the participants to page 116 in their Participant Book. Guide them through the exercise presented there. After adequate time for this exercise, ask everyone to gather into small groups to share whatever they wish from their reflection. Gather comments about their experience of waiting in the large group.
2. Present the background to the sacred scriptures in these or similar words: *As we approach the end of the liturgical year, the Lectionary presents texts which in some way are connected to eschatological themes. Eschatology refers to matters that indicate the end times. In the second reading, 1 Thessalonians, and in the gospel, the end times are the focus of our attention. The first reading from the Book of*

Wisdom presents Solomon giving advice to rulers. He tells them to seek Wisdom and they will not be disappointed. In fact, Wisdom herself seeks out those who are looking for her. There are two ideas presented here: (1) the notion of vigilance for one who comes, and (2) the idea of actively seeking out the good. Both are recurring themes of Jewish and Christian eschatology.

3. Proclaim Wisdom 6:12–16. Invite the participants to compare their experience of waiting with that presented in the reading in the large group. Continue to explore the scriptures in these or similar words:
Waiting is not an easy task. In Paul's letter to the Thessalonians, the young community is struggling with what happens to those who die before the second coming of Christ. Paul had preached that the second coming was imminent. The Thessalonians are waiting, but Christ doesn't come. Paul assures them that the dead will also enjoy the benefits of Christ's coming. He tells them to console one another with the fact that all shall be with the Lord forever. Sometimes, we become impatient because it takes too long.

4. Direct the participants to return to the same small groups to discuss these questions: *How does this passage offer you consolation as you wait for Christ's coming?* Ask each group to present a brief summary describing their discussion.

Catholic Teaching (30 min.)

1. Invite the participants to return to their Participant Book, turning to page 116 and completing the unfinished sentences presented there. Then direct the catechumens and candidates to gather with their sponsor and/or godparent to share their responses. Then gather feedback in the large group. Summarize their discussion, concluding with these or your own words: *Prayer links us to God. Prayer is a gift which is sustained by the Holy Spirit. Our desire to pray can be sidelined by numerous distractions. Sometimes in our desire to rid ourselves of these distractions, we fall deeper into them and are unable to pray at all.* Invite the members of the team to offer suggestions on how to deal with distractions from their own experience of prayer.

2. Share additional aids to prayer, using the following words: *The best remedy in avoiding distractions is to turn further into the depths of one's heart, for there, in the most intimate place, is where God speaks to us. Be faithful to the struggle to pray in the midst of all the distractions; use the distractions as prayer. Another difficulty that our Catholic tradition warns in the life of prayer is inner dryness. Sometimes this is referred to as the "dark night of the soul" as described by St. John of the Cross. This type of barrenness is described as the experience where nothing "works" in prayer, where the person praying feels separated from God. Neither in one's thoughts, nor in one's memories, nor in one's feelings is there any inkling of God's intimate presence.* Invite the group to reflect in quiet on their own experiences of prayer. Ask, if anyone has experienced this dryness or barrenness, to describe it.

3. Continue to present the Church's teaching of prayer in these or similar words: *There are times when we feel God is no longer present to us when we pray. This lack of presence might prompt us to ask where God is. This experience is the penultimate moment of faith. Even Jesus experienced such an episode in his agony in the garden. It is the experience of the tomb where the Lord was laid to rest. It requires the faithful heart throwing itself totally upon the God of conversion, who alone will vindicate and transform it.*

4. In small groups, encourage the participants to discuss why we should continue to pray to God when we don't experience God's presence. Gather insights from the groups and then further their understanding of prayer in these words:
First, we persevere because we are enjoined to do so by the gospel, the letters of St. Paul, and, indeed, by the whole scriptural witness and the unbroken tradition of the Church expressed in the lives of the saints and the teachings of the magisterium. All of these sources assure us that God desires our communication. God wants us to pray. We must continue to attempt to express ourselves in our relationship with God. Whatever form that communication takes, it nourishes the relationship. Second, we persevere so as to purify our motives in praying, and so deepen our devotion to God, who alone deserves all our love. The ultimate prayer is simply to surrender in trust to God, no matter what transpires here and now. Often, we think God hasn't heard our prayers because we don't get what we prayed for, yet the truth is we don't always perceive the way in which God has answered the prayer.

5. Encourage the participants to share times in which God has answered their prayers in different ways and it took a while to recognize the answer. Gather insights and some experiences from the groups. Continue in these or similar words:
In the Catholic tradition, prayer is not manipulation of God. It is an expression of our mutual thirst, God for us and us for God. It is a form of vigilance against the darkness and evil of the world. Prayer is the self-expression of a heart attitude attuned to the love of the divine responding to that gift of heaven, not from the height of pride but from the depth, the font of humility. Prayer is our communion with the one who has made life possible for us in Christ. Encourage them to describe how their prayer has changed since they began this process. After sufficient time for sharing, gather some insights from the groups.

Putting Faith into Practice

1. Encourage them to turn to the Participant Book on page 117 to complete the section "For this week I want to remember" and "I want to put my faith into action by."

2. Share some of the traditional prayers of the church with the group, covering those important parts of the tradition that have not yet been explained. This might include the rosary, meditation, praying with scripture, the divine office, etc.

Prayer

Guide them in the following prayer, saying: *Close your eyes. Take several deep breaths. Slowly repeat over and over, "Jesus, I love you. Help me."* Direct the participants to be still and pray in the silence of their hearts. Then invite everyone to stand and sing "This Alone" (Tim Manion, OCP Publications, 1981).

Thirty-third Sunday in Ordinary Time

Understanding this Sunday:
Background for Catechesis

The Word in Liturgy

Proverbs 31:10–13, 19–20, 30–31
Psalm 128:1–2, 3, 4–5
1 Thessalonians 5:1–6
Matthew 25:14–30 [or (short form) 25:14–15, 19–21]

The Book of Proverbs, although it contains material that is much older, dates in its present form to the fifth century before Christ. The author seeks to reassure the post-exilic Jewish community of the abiding desire of God to offer guidance to the people of the covenant—a guidance that would be on a par with the "wisdom" available among the pagan nations. Previous generations had found in the Davidic dynasty such a guarantee, but the events of the exile had shaken the faith of many. Proverbs includes material obviously borrowed from pagan neighbors, but the process of assimilation has also thoroughly imbued the material with the theological vision of Israel. Today's passage has a clear parallel in the Egyptian wisdom text on women, the *Instruction of Ani*, but the ideal offered in Proverbs is of a praiseworthy wife who "fears the Lord" (v. 30).

The industrious woman described in this text is both mindful of the poor and an economic asset to her husband. As an example of wise stewardship of one's God-given gifts, the reading is a perfect match to the gospel parable. The psalm refrain ("Happy are those who fear the Lord") picks up on the notion of obedience to God's will, while the verses of Psalm 128 echo Proverbs' recognition of the blessings that accrue to a man with such a wife.

Today's gospel passage contains the third in a series of parables on the coming judgment that Matthew has linked together at the conclusion of his Eschatological Discourse. Like last week's parable of the bridesmaids, Jesus' original

parable of the talents has undergone a process of allegorization and has been given a strong eschatological orientation in the process of oral transmission and incorporation into Matthew's written gospel. The owner has become a figure for Christ, away for a time on a (heavenly) journey, until he returns (at the parousia) to settle accounts with his servants (early Christian believers). The settling of accounts has become an image of final judgment, and the servants' rewards and punishments are meant to remind Matthew's audience of the importance of using their gifts wisely and well.

In today's selection from 1 Thessalonians, we see Paul addressing the problem of certain Christians who were so convinced of the imminence of the Lord's return that they had ceased working and were becoming a burden on the rest of the community. Paul himself is being forced to rethink just how close the parousia may be, and has to remind the Thessalonians that no one knows just when the Day of the Lord will arrive. It is coming, he says, "like a thief in the night" (v. 2) and, in the meantime, he counsels a lifestyle that is "awake and sober" (v. 6) while they await Christ's return. Although the idea of stewardship is not explicitly mentioned here, the implication of Paul's advice is certainly that a Christian should live in the world in an industrious manner, using God's gifts wisely and well until the day of judgment. As "children of light and of the day" (v. 5), they must conduct themselves in an exemplary fashion as Christian stewards.

Catholic Doctrine

Stewardship

The Anglo-Saxon term *stigweard,* or "hall keeper," meant the person responsible for feeding the entire manor. The corresponding scriptural term is *oikonomos,* or household manager, the one responsible for managing the resources and essential functions of the whole estate or household (*oikos*) and who was accountable for this management to the *kyrios,* the lord or master/owner. Thus, in general, as theologians use the scriptural term to arrive at a concept of Christian stewardship, what is meant is the care or good management of the entire household of God, all that God gives us in creation and all of God's plan of salvation, the divine economy. Jesus himself is the model for good Christian stewardship, for Jesus illustrates in his life and ministry the obedient servant of God who gives totally of himself to effect humanity's wholeness and communion with God. What does it mean for Catholics to assert that they follow Jesus in giving totally of themselves as good stewards of God's creation?

First, Catholics understand from the gospel message and the life of Jesus that they have a responsibility for others. (See Doctrine section for the thirtieth Sunday in Ordinary Time.) We have been commanded to love God and our neighbor. Loving our neighbor is inseparable from loving God. Our gospel task in faithfulness to this commandment takes concrete form, given the needy conditions of people in the world. We strive to reverse exploitation of individuals and groups and to feed the hungry, clothe the naked, house the homeless, care for the sick, and so on, activities that in traditional Catholic teaching are called the corporal works of mercy (CCC 2447).

Second, Catholics understand that this responsibility stems from the way in which God has fashioned everything, that is, interdependence is built into the very fabric of creation. The panoply of creation is immeasurably diverse and does not exist or function in isolation (CCC 340). Indeed, given advances in science and technology that facilitate the "global village," the Second Vatican Council spoke of an increase in human interdependence in the contemporary world (GS 25). The Council then called upon existing international and regional organizations to assist in the Church's mission "to alleviate the enormity of human misery" (GS 84).

Third, there is a Catholic assumption that in following Jesus the believer develops a deep personal spirituality that funds a reverence for creation. This reverence is based in the biblical view where humanity is given dominion over creatures. But this dominion is not absolute and demands a religious respect for the integrity of what God has created (CCC 2415).

Indeed, John Paul II has articulated a spirituality of work and of labor based on Genesis and on the example of Jesus that situates human endeavors within the design of God (LE 25.6). In his encyclical on work, *Laborem exercens,* the pope's vision promotes the human activity of work as sharing "in the activity of the Creator" (LE 25.2). He specifies that the value of work is directly related to the notion of human progress toward greater justice and a right ordering of social relationships (LE 26.6). Thus, God entrusts to us the goodness of creation which must be upheld as humans benefit from it (CCC 299).

Finally, the way we Catholics understand holding property and goods reflects the notion of Christian stewardship. Thus, the Second Vatican Council taught that all property is held by individuals for the common or universal good. The Council affirmed, "God destined the earth and all it contains for all [individuals] and all peoples so that all created things would be shared fairly by all . . . under the guidance of justice tempered by charity. No matter what the structures of property are in different peoples, according to various and changing circumstances and adapted to their lawful institutions, we must never lose sight of this universal destination of earthly goods" (GS 69). Catholics see this world as transitory and believe that ultimately all things will be summed up in Christ. Jesus, in inaugurating the kingdom, proclaimed a world that is being transformed and that will one day, in God's good time, reach harmony and wholeness in Christ. To be a good steward means that the very way we hold property and utilize the limited resources of this world assists in building toward the fulfillment of God's kingdom.

Catholic Culture

St. Francis of Assisi (d. 1226) wrote hymns of praise to "brother sun and sister moon." St. Francis of Assisi and St. Philip Neri (d. 1595) both were known for the kind way in which they treated animals, seeing in them the praise of God, their Creator.

The *Roman Ritual*, in its Book of Blessings, contains many prayers for acknowledging the importance of (and blessing) such things as an office, shop or factory, centers for social communication, a gym or athletic field, boats and fishing gear, technical installations or equipment, tools for work, fields, flocks, seeds, and animals. Many of the prayers express the beauty of creation and humanity's role in preserving and protecting what God has given us. For example, the Church prays in blessing tools for work, "In your loving providence, O God, you have made the forces of nature subject to the work of our hands. Grant that by devotion to our own work we may gladly cooperate with you in the building up of creation" (BB 935).

Dismissal Catechesis (30 min.)

Getting Started

1. Prepare the space ahead of time with a circle of chairs around a green cloth arranged on the floor in the center of the circle. On the cloth place several objects from nature: leaves, stones, branches, flowers, photos—whatever is indigenous to your location. Near the arrangement place a large candle on a stand.

2. Lead the candidates and catechumens to the circle; place the Lectionary on the table and light the candle. As you begin, invite the participants to reflect on one object which fills them with awe and wonder at God's created beauty. Pray in these words: *Divine Creator, you surround us with beauty and wonder. We marvel at the growth and cycles of plants and trees. We are in awe of flowing rivers and crashing waterfalls and the variety of life in these waters. Our eyes behold the majesty of mountains and we are overwhelmed with joy. As we reflect upon your Word, keep us mindful that we are intimately connected to all of creation. Help us to understand that we are wonderfully made in your image and likeness. Grace our time together with your presence. Amen.*

First Impressions

1. Invite the participants to recall their experience at today's Liturgy of the Word. Ask everyone to close their eyes and listen as you guide them through the experience once again. Repeat a line or two of the Gathering Song. Select a line from each scripture passage and the theme of today's homily.

2. When you have finished, invite everyone to find a partner and share their experience of the liturgy by responding to these questions: *What was your overall perception as you remembered today's Liturgy of the Word? How would you express the meaning of the scriptures for you? As you worshiped this morning, what did God seem to be saying to you?* Invite the pairs to respond to the questions as you ask them in the large group, taking one question at a time.

3. In the large group, ask the catechumens and candidates this question: *Some of you may have heard the parable from today's gospel before. What is the message of the parable as you understand it?*

Making Connections

1. Continue to share in the large group, asking everyone, *What warning do you hear in today's readings?*

2. Explain the imminence of the end times in these words: *In all three readings there is an underlying suggestion that Christ, the king who went on the voyage in the parable, will return. We do not know when, but the early Church thought his return was imminent. The second reading warns us that his return will come like a thief in the night or like the onset of labor to a pregnant woman. We discover from the parable in Matthew's gospel that when Christ does return, he will judge us on how well we used our gifts to effect more beauty and goodness.*

3. Invite the same pairs to share their insights on this concept by raising these questions as a catalyst for their sharing: *What does the uncertainty of Christ's return evoke in you? What better use of your time, gifts, and possessions can you make, knowing that he will return at an unpredictable time?* When they have finished, invite a few pairs to offer their responses in the large group. Affirm their sharing and conclude the session with a brief summary of their thoughts.

Prayer

Invite the participants to reflect upon their encounter with the Creator of all of life right now, in this time and place. Remind them that Christ is in our midst whenever we gather. In the silence of their hearts encourage each person to converse with the Risen Lord about the gifts and resources that have been poured out in them. After sufficient time, begin a Litany of Gratitude by inviting everyone to name one gift or blessing for which they are grateful. After each naming, encourage all to respond, *"Come, share your Master's joy."*

Extended Catechesis

SESSION FOCUS: *Stewardship*

Gathering

A. **Sunday:**

1. Greet and welcome the sponsors and team members as they arrive. Invite them to join the circle of catechumens and candidates.

2. As the participants take their place in the circle, invite them to remain standing as you proclaim the gospel, Matthew 25:14–30. Invite all to respond to the proclamation by leading them in singing Psalm 128:1–2, 3, 4–5.

B. **Weekday:**

1. Use the same centerpiece as in the Dismissal Catechesis.

2. As the participants gather in the circle, greet each person. Invite a few participants to share an experience of God's gift of creation that they had over the past few days.

3. Lead this celebration of the Word:
   - Song: Gathering Song from Sunday's liturgy
   - Second Reading: 1 Thessalonians 5:1–6
   - Sing Psalm 128:1–2, 3, 4–5
   - Gospel: Matthew 25:14–30

The Word (30 min.)

1. Indicate that all be seated as you lead this meditation: *As you prepare to pray, look at the centerpiece and allow the objects from nature to inspire your imagination. When you are ready, close your eyes, become aware of your breathing and heartbeat, and relax your body. Sink into your deepest self, where God dwells. Pause while they relax. Imagine yourself in a beautiful meadow full of wildflowers. Colors dazzle your eyes. You hear the whispering sounds of water and follow the sound as the splashing and gurgling grows louder. You see a beautiful waterfall and are filled with wonder. Sitting near the flowing waters is a wise-looking person in faded jeans and simple jacket. This wise person's brilliant eyes penetrate you with their depth*

and wisdom. *You feel comfortable and sit beside this person when the wise one beckons. You are so entranced that you feel a desire growing within you. You yearn to learn some of the wisdom that seems to bubble over this person like the gushing waterfall. As you share your feelings and longing for wisdom, you begin to understand the true meaning of wisdom. You listen carefully and nod in agreement as the wise one explains the secrets of becoming wise. The wise one then explains to you that a wise person should emulate the qualities of a good wife.* Proclaim the first reading, Proverbs 31:10–13, 19–20, 30–31. *You leave the wise one, the waterfall, and the meadow, keeping these things carefully in your heart.* Invite the participants to take their Participant Book, turn to page 118, and write about their experience with the wise one. Ask the participants to share with a partner whatever they wish from the meditation and the reflection they wrote. The candidates and catechumens will want to join their sponsor and/or godparent for this sharing.

2. Invite the pairs to continue their sharing by responding to the following questions: *What is implied by the line, "she extends her arms to the needy"? What connections can you make between the wise one who gives of himself or herself and experiences fear (awe and wonder) of the Lord? What does it mean to have a generous heart?* In the large group invite the pairs to share a summary of their discussion on one question at a time.

3. After their input, continue by explaining the parable in Matthew 25:14–30: *In this parable about the judgment at the end of time, Matthew continues to instruct his audience about the return of the Risen Jesus. The owner is a figure for Christ, away for a time on the journey to the right hand of God the Father. Christ will return at the end of time, the* parousia, *to settle accounts with his servants, the early Christian believers and those who follow Jesus today. This final judgment is based upon the wise use of our time, gifts, and possessions—the silver pieces. With this in mind, how can we use our gifts, time, and resources wisely?* Discuss this question in the large gathering.

Catholic Teaching (30 min.)

1. Continue in the large gathering, inviting several participants to name the ideas that come to mind when they think about the word "stewardship." Summarize their comments and explain the meaning of this word: *The root of this word is the Anglo-Saxon term* stigweard *or "hall keeper," implying the person responsible for feeding the entire manor. When we connect this to the Greek word from scripture,* oikonomos, *or "household manager," we uncover the deeper Christian sense of stewardship.* Oikos *refers to household and all relations. Thus, the gospel sense of stewardship implies the care and wise management of the entire household of God—all of creation, particularly humankind.*
Invite the same pairs to share their thoughts on this question: *In the light of the parable of the silver pieces and the gospel implications of stewardship, how are we challenged to be wise stewards of this earth and its inhabitants?* Invite the participants to note their insights on page 118 in the Participant Book under the section Questions.

2. Explain the four Church teachings that flow from the gospel vision of stewardship, using these or your own words: *Love of God and neighbor requires that we use our time, gifts, and resources to help others, particularly by reversing the exploitation of the vulnerable members of our society, and practicing the corporal works of mercy, namely, feeding the hungry, clothing the naked, housing the homeless, caring for the sick, and visiting the imprisoned. Because God has fashioned us to live with one another in unity and harmony, we are interdependent with one another and the entire created universe. Thus, a wise steward works to change systems to alleviate the enormity of human misery. Reverence for the Creator requires reverence for the earth and nature. Ecological attitudes and practices and the valuing of work as an act of co-creation are implicit in the goodness of creation. Finally, our attitudes toward possessions, particularly that of owning property, must be infused with principles that promote harmony, wholeness, and generosity in building toward the fulfillment of God's kingdom.*

3. Ask the participants to respond to the remaining questions on page 118 in their Participant Book. Then encourage them to share their responses in pairs.

Putting Faith into Practice

1. Ask the pairs to list practical ways to live out this gospel stewardship, using four sheets of newsprint or poster board with the following headings: "Responsibility for Others," "Responsibility for Global Systems," "Responsibility for the Earth," and "Responsibility for Justice." Invite the pairs to discuss the implications for stewardship under each category. After sufficient time for sharing, ask the participants to list several concrete actions under each of the categories. Summarize these to conclude the discussion.

2. Invite a parishioner involved with ecological issues or justice in changing exploitative social systems to speak to the group on practical actions that are being taken in your community.

Prayer

Invite the participants to pray for God's wisdom in deciding one action they will take to live out gospel stewardship. Ask them to write this in their Participant Book on page 119, in the section "I want to put my faith into action by." Invite each person to come to the center of the circle and to take one object from nature that will serve as a reminder of his or her decision. As they come forward, play some music that conveys nature sounds. Close with this prayer:
God of this vast universe, you have created us in your image and likeness, empowering us to experience wonder and joy at the goodness of all of life. Each day the beauty of your wonderful world surrounds us. Give us the eyes to see your marvelous works, the ears to hear the music of life, and the conviction to respond to the needs of others. Give us generous and thankful hearts, that we might share all our blessings to build your kingdom here and now. We want to live in the blessed assurance that Christ will come again to embrace us. Empower us in the living Spirit, breathed into us from creation's dawn. Amen.

Thirty-fourth Sunday in Ordinary Time

CHRIST THE KING

Understanding this Sunday:

Background for Catechesis

The Word in Liturgy

Ezekiel 34:11–12, 15–17
Psalm 23:1–2, 2–3, 5–6
1 Corinthians 15:20–26, 28
Matthew 25:31–46

On this last Sunday of the liturgical year, the Church celebrates the feast of Christ the King. Instituted by Pope Pius XI in 1925 to combat the growing secularism and atheism of his time, it is one of the so-called "idea feasts" that do not celebrate an event in the life of Jesus but rather some aspect of his identity. In it we recognize and honor Christ as ruler and universal shepherd. The original feast of Christ the King is the Ascension, in which the Church celebrates the exalted Christ, crowned with glory at the right hand of God. Today's celebration should remind us of that more important feast as the liturgical year comes to a close.

The establishment of a monarchy in Israel was initially resisted and seen as a betrayal of the more ancient ideal of a theocracy with Yahweh as sole king. Eventually, a king was established but a certain ambivalence toward the institution of the monarchy can be traced throughout the history of the chosen people. David, the shepherd king, became the idealized figure of the monarchy, but the tradition maintained its awareness that Yahweh must always be the real king over his people (cf. Psalms 23, 74, and 80). The repeated failures and infidelities of the kings in both north and south only reinforced this tradition of suspicion of earthly kings.

During the Babylonian exile, Ezekiel issued a scathing denunciation of the false shepherds who had led the people astray (Ezekiel 34:1–10). Then, in what must surely have been words that brought relief and hope to the exiles, he delivers the Lord's promise to return, to shepherd the people once again himself. The mention of judgment (v. 17) adds an eschatological dimension that makes the text all the more fitting for this last day of the liturgical year. The choice of psalmody is obvious in light of Ezekiel's use of the shepherd imagery.

In today's reading from 1 Corinthians we can see how Paul's thought about the parousia has evolved in comparison to what we have been reading during the last five weeks in his first letter to the Thessalonians. Paul realizes that Christ's reign has already commenced, that it is in fact coterminous with the age of the Church, i.e., from his ascension until the parousia. This reign, already begun, is nonetheless incomplete (remember Romans 8 and Paul's references to the "groaning" of all creation). There are still enemies to be destroyed ("Christ must reign until God has put all enemies under his feet," v. 25), but the resurrection of Christ is our proof that the final outcome is not in doubt. The Adam-Christ typology was an important part of Paul's developing understanding of the importance of the resurrection for the believer, and especially how we participate in Christ's resurrection through faith and baptism. Note the liturgical context of "first fruits," a term associated with Jewish cultic usage. If Christ's resurrection makes him the "first fruits," then the entire harvest—all of us—is consecrated to the Lord and will someday enjoy fullness of glory with him.

The judgment scene in Matthew 25 is unique to his gospel and forms the climactic conclusion to his Eschatological Discourse. Only here in all of the gospels does Jesus ascribe to himself the status of a king rendering judgment. The criteria of that judgment are most striking: They are the simple acts of love and kindness directed to the "little ones" of this world. To have done these everyday works of goodness is to have touched Jesus himself; to have neglected to do them is to have neglected the needs of Christ, an omission worthy of condemnation. This implies that doing the works of goodness called for here is already to have gained access to the reign of God and to have chosen not to act in love is already a choice not to belong to God's reign.

Catholic Doctrine

"To Judge the Living and the Dead"

This phrase from the Nicene Creed expresses our Catholic belief that Christ who died and was raised up again to new life has been given the right as our Redeemer to judge the works and hearts of all (CCC 679). Christ has ascended to heaven and participates in God's power and authority and we acknowledge him as Lord not only of the universe but of the unfolding of history itself (CCC 668). Indeed, in Christ all of human history is summed up and fulfilled and, as the Second Vatican Council affirmed, "he is the key, the center and the purpose of the whole of [our] history . . ." (GS 10).

We also believe that the kingdom over which the Lord gloriously reigns is present in a mysterious way on earth in the Church (CCC 669). And while evil—definitively defeated by the cross and resurrection—still resists this reign, the final fulfillment will be accomplished for we are in the last days before final judgment (CCC 671). Thus, the Second Vatican Council taught, "Already the final age of the world is with us (cf. 1 Corinthians 10:11) and the renewal of the world is irrevocably under way; it is even now anticipated in a certain real way, for the Church on earth is endowed already with a sanctity that is real though imperfect. However, until there be realized new heavens and a new earth in which justice dwells (cf. 2 Peter 3:13) the pilgrim Church, in its sacraments and institutions, which belong to this present age, carries the mark of this world which will pass, and she herself takes her place among the creatures which groan and travail yet and await the revelation of the [children] of God (cf. Romans 8:19–22)" (LG 48).

This revelation that we await is the judgment Christ the King will render. There are two judgments that occur, particular and final. Particular judgment refers to the judging of the moral quality of one's life immediately after death (CCC 1022) and Christ determines whether the person has chosen fundamentally to either cooperate with God's grace or how one has chosen to reject God's grace. Accordingly, judgment is rendered and the person merits heaven, purgatory, or hell. Final judgment refers to that end time of history when Christ will return to this world bringing the fullness of the kingdom and sum up everything by passing definitive judgment on all people, nations, and history itself (CCC 679).

How does Christ judge, especially in light of the gospel message (John 3:17) that he has come not to condemn but that all might have life and be saved? The form of judgment is a revelation from the Lord who is the fullness of God's revelation among us. Each person will be revealed in this judgment and, thus, the judging has already been achieved by the way in which one lived. Hence, this feast's gospel image of the separation of sheep and goats indicating how one has lived in accord (or not) with the kingdom imperative of loving one's neighbor.

The final or last judgment also constitutes God's final word on all of history. Jesus Christ, the living Word, will reveal God's glorious triumph over evil and at the same time manifest the ultimate meaning of the whole work of creation. Till then, we believe that Christ is the hope of Israel and we, the Church, continue the Pentecost preaching of Peter that all embrace the Lord Jesus and his kingdom (CCC 674). Till then, we pass through trial and faith-shaking events—and yet we hold firm in the Lord (CCC 675). Only through this time of tribulation and final passover will the Church enter into the glory of the kingdom (CCC 677) when Christ will reveal our full stature as children of the Most High "so that God may be all in all" (1 Corinthians 15:28).

How then, in the light of our Catholic belief about Christ rendering judgment, are we to understand the images contained in the Book of Revelation about the end times? The images found in this last book of the New Testament are one way that the early Christian Church expressed its faith in the God who promises to deliver us, especially in times of persecution and trial as experienced by the early Christians. The message of this apocalyptic literature is not necessarily to be found in literal acceptance of its surface meaning. Rather, its meaning is perceived through eyes of faith informed by the Church. Thus, our destiny is firmly anchored in Jesus Christ's saving life, death, and resurrection, unlocked for us believers by the Church. There is no other hope or glorious summation to the hearts and lives of all but that which is found in Christ who is our King.

Catholic Culture

On this feast of Christ the King, the Church prays, "As king [Christ] claims dominion over all creation, that he may present to you, his heavenly Father, an eternal and universal kingdom: a kingdom of truth and life, a kingdom of holiness and grace, a kingdom of justice, love and peace" (*Sacramentary*, Preface 51).

The anchor was one of the most popular early Christian symbols connected to Christ and use of it refers to Hebrews 6:18–19. It is seen on early Christian graves and seals and was recommended by Clement of Alexandria (c. 200) as an image suitable for use in seal rings. The crossbar of the anchor also was understood as a symbol of Christ's cross (OxA&A 16). Sometimes, artisans depicted dolphins twined around the anchor (perhaps a sign of humanity's being saved from drowning in the seas of sin by Christ). Some modern Catholic medals shaped as anchors are also inscribed with the names of the theological virtues (faith, hope, and charity)—those virtues from God that form our lives as believers and thus "anchor" us.

St. John of the Cross (d. 1569), mystic, preacher, and reformer, wrote, "At the evening of life, we shall be judged on our love" (*Dichos de luz y amor* 64).

Dismissal Catechesis (30 min.)

Getting Started

1. Prepare the space ahead of time with a circle of chairs around a table draped with a white cloth, covered by a smaller gold strip of fabric. On the table place a cross, a picture of the Good Shepherd, or an icon of Christ the King. Arrange several white tapers on the cloth, leaving a space for the Lectionary.

2. Lead the candidates and catechumens to the circle, place the Lectionary on the table, and light the candles. Gather the participants and lead them in singing the first two verses of "To Jesus Christ, Our Sovereign King" (Martin B. Hellriegel, text, 1941; Mainz Gesangbuch, music, 1890). Pray in these or your own words:
   Christ our Shepherd King, rescue us from sin and heal our wounds. You are the first fruits of the living sacrifice made to God. Consecrate us to your saving work. Instruct and guide us as we journey in faith and love. Let your coming in glory at the end of time be a time of rejoicing for each of us, as we strive to live out your command of love in this life. Amen.

First Impressions

1. Invite the participants to close their eyes and listen with their whole being as you repeat some of the images from today's scriptures. Ask them to imagine God speaking these words directly to them: *I will rescue the scattered—I will pasture and give my sheep rest—The lost and strayed, I will seek out—The injured and sick, I will heal and bind up—I will judge between one sheep and another—I will refresh your soul—I will guide you in right paths—I will anoint you with overflowing blessings—You shall dwell in my house for all days.*

2. Ask the group this question: *What emotions do these images evoke in you?* Listen carefully to their responses and affirm their insights.

3. Then gather them into small groups to continue sharing. These questions will help start their conversations: *Which image has meaning for you at this time in your life? How have you experienced the presence of this shepherd-God in recent months? As you listened to the scriptures and homily today, what "new" meaning do you discover in your relationship with God?* Encourage the small groups to summarize their responses to these questions for everyone to hear.

Making Connections

1. Continue in the large group, asking: *In what ways can we respond to God, our Shepherd?* As they respond, begin to list several responses that are possible. Conclude the discussion by saying: *Ultimately, we are called to respond by loving God and our neighbor with our whole heart, mind, and strength. Our simple acts of love directed at those we encounter every day are the best responses we can make to a loving, caring, shepherding Lord.*

2. Invite the small groups to gather and share their insights on these questions: *What actions do you recall from the gospel that enumerate these simple acts of love? Who are the poor, hungry, thirsty, etc., that you encounter each day? What motivates you to love the weak and vulnerable in our society?* After sufficient time, gather the responses from each group. Summarize the session in a few sentences. Ask the participants to write down one way in which they commit themselves to love in their Participant Book on page 120, in the section "I want to put my faith into action by."

Prayer

Gather the attention of the group by leading them in singing the last verse of "To Jesus Christ, Our Sovereign King" (Martin B. Hellriegel, text, 1941; Mainz Gesangbuch, music, 1890).

Extended Catechesis

SESSION FOCUS: *"To Judge the Living and the Dead"*

Gathering

A. **Sunday:**
   1. Greet and welcome the sponsors and team members as they arrive. Invite them to join the circle of catechumens and candidates.
   2. Invite all to silently reflect upon the art piece or icon in the center of the circle. Proclaim the gospel, Matthew 25:31–46.

B. **Weekday:**
   1. Use the same centerpiece as described for the Dismissal Catechesis.
   2. As the participants gather in the circle, greet and warmly welcome each person. Ask a few participants to share one way in which they experienced the care of God, our loving Shepherd, over the past week.
   3. Lead this celebration of the Word:
      * Song: Gathering Hymn from Sunday's liturgy
      * First Reading: Ezekiel 34:11–12, 15–17
      * Psalm 23:1–2, 2–3, 5–6
      * Second Reading: 1 Corinthians 15:20–26, 28
      * Gospel: Matthew 25:31–46
      * Silence

The Word (30 min.)

1. Invite the catechumens and candidates to share the insights they gained through the Dismissal Catechesis.

2. Ask the participants to offer their ideas about the qualities of a shepherd king. Explain today's feast in these or similar words: *Since 1925, the Church has celebrated the feast of Christ the King on the last Sunday of the Church year. On this feast we honor and proclaim Christ as our Ruler and universal Shepherd. Christ ascended into heaven and is seated at the right hand of the Father in glory to guide and gather his flock, that is, us. The concept of a shepherd king grew in the religious imaginations of the Israelites since the reign of David. The Church has attributed this identity to Christ*

the King. Gather the participants into small groups to discuss this question: *Given the qualities of the Lord as shepherd and the identity of Christ as king, what characteristics do you ascribe to Christ the King?* Give them an adequate time to share. Then invite all to begin a list of these qualities on a large newsprint or poster.

3. Continue to unfold the meaning of the scriptures, stressing these points:
   - Ezekiel speaks a word of hope and relief to the exiles, promising the Lord will return as in the cherished days of old, to shepherd the people once again.
   - In 1 Corinthians, Paul now realizes that Christ's reign has begun. The reign of Christ parallels the age of the Church, from the ascension of Christ, until his return to judge all peoples.
   - The comparison between Adam and Christ indicates Paul's understanding the importance of the resurrection for the believer, especially how we participate in Christ's resurrection through faith and baptism.
   - Just as Christ's resurrection makes him the "first fruits," then the entire harvest—all of us—is consecrated to the Lord and will someday enjoy the fullness of glory with him.
   - The brief reference to the judgment between one sheep and another by the shepherd, God, found in Ezekiel is expanded in the gospel. Christ, our shepherd king, will render judgment on all.
   - The criteria of that judgment are significant in that they are based upon simple acts of love and kindness directed to the "little ones" of this world.

4. Ask the participants to gather with a partner. The candidates and catechumens will want to join their sponsor and/or godparent. Invite these pairs to respond to these questions: *What do you find is most significant for you in these passages? What comes to mind when you think of Christ as the "first fruit" consecrated to God? Why are the criteria Christ will judge us by so unusual?* Invite the pairs to share a few insights on the first two questions. Summarize their insights.

Catholic Teaching (30 min.)

1. Consider the last question and ask each pair to name aloud one sentence to describe why loving the little ones is so consequential. Move around the group until each pair has responded.

2. Present the teaching of the Church on the phrase from the Nicene Creed, "to judge the living and the dead":
   In Christ all of human history is summed up and fulfilled. Christ the King is the key, center, and purpose of the whole of human history. His kingdom is here, but not yet fully revealed. While the cross defeated evil, it continues to resist Christ's reign. The final fulfillment, a new heaven and a new earth in which justice dwells, will be accomplished for we are in the final age of the world. As Paul says in Romans 8:22, "We know that all creation is groaning in labor pains even until now; and not only that, but we

ourselves, who have the first fruits of the Spirit, we also groan within ourselves as we wait for adoption, the redemption of our bodies."

3. Invite the participants to offer their comments on this question in the large group: *How do you now understand the kingship of Christ, the reign of God?*
   After affirming their responses, continue to explain the Church teaching on judgment, using these or similar words:
   Christ the King will judge the living and the dead. The Church teaches that there are two judgments. The first, called particular judgment, is the judging of the moral quality of one's life immediately after death, when Christ determines whether the person has fundamentally chosen to cooperate with God's grace or to reject it. Final judgment refers to the end time in history when Christ will come again, bringing the fullness of his kingdom, and sum up everything by passing definitive judgment on all people, nations, and history itself. In the light of the gospel message, Christ judges each according to how he or she lived in accord with the kingdom imperative to loving one's neighbor, as a sign of wholehearted love for God. On the last judgment, Christ, the living Word, will reveal God's glorious triumph over evil and at the same time manifest the ultimate meaning of the whole work of creation. Until that time we pass through trial and faith-shaking events, holding firm to the Lord of hope.

4. Invite the participants to turn to page 120 in their Participant Book to reflect upon the judgment of Christ the King. When they have finished, encourage them to share their reflection in the same pairs. Then ask them to reflect upon the questions on that same page in the Participant Book.

Putting Faith into Practice

1. In the large group take one question at a time and open the discussion to everyone. When you get to the last question on hope, work with the participants to create a litany of hope, writing on newsprint. This will be used as the closing prayer.

2. Invite a parish minister, for example, one who visits the sick, distributes food to the poor, or helps the bereaved, to offer a witness talk on the blessings his or her ministry has been. Encourage the group to share real-life stories of the people they seek to love and shepherd.

3. Encourage the catechumens, candidates, and sponsors to participate in one of the parish ministries which practices the works of mercy. Guide them to share the significance of this action after participating in this experience.

Prayer

Gather the attention of the participants by playing "Whatsoever You Do" (Willard E. Jabusch, New Dawn Music, 1976). After a few verses, invite the participants to join in singing the song. Then begin the Litany of Hope, written on the newsprint, asking all to pray the litany together and responding, *"Christ the King you are our hope of future glory,"* after each invocation.

HOLY DAYS AND FEASTS

The Immaculate Conception

DECEMBER 8

The Word in Liturgy

Genesis 3:9–15, 20
Psalm 98:1, 2–3, 3–4
Ephesians 1:3–6, 11–12
Luke 1:26–38

During the Advent season Mary, the Mother of Jesus, is frequently presented to us through the scriptures and in the theological reflection of the Church embodied in our liturgical observance. Her life, her witness, her role in the economy of salvation, and her very nature are today the subject of our meditation and inform the Church's prayer in the liturgy.

Since the eighth century in the East and the eleventh century in the West, the Christian Church has set aside a day to celebrate Mary's conception in the womb of her mother Anne, thus indicating a reverence for Mary's whole person. The dogma of Mary's conception without sin, or Immaculate Conception, was not defined by the Church, however, until the mid-nineteenth century. The Church of the United States, for whom Mary of the Immaculate Conception is its patron saint, holds this day in high esteem as one of its holy days of obligation.

The reading from Genesis sets the context for this feast in the sin of our first parents and traces the disorders of nature to this primordial sin in a rich, symbolic story. The Yahwist author of Genesis presents God in very human images, walking and talking with the man and woman in the garden, and the drama of discovery of sin is one of shame and a literal hiding from God. Blame for sin is shared among the man, the woman, and the snake, with the snake bearing the greatest responsibility because of having instigated the deception. The passage focuses on the snake, who represents all the forces of evil in the world, just as the man and the woman represent the whole human race. God's judgment upon the serpent, who in the Christian tradition is later identified with the devil, is cast in terms of an ongoing conflict with humanity. Eve, the mother of all the living, stands at the head of a perpetual struggle. Her name, however, is a sign of

hope: even though she shares responsibility for the catastrophe of sin, God's promise continues through her in the offspring she will bear.

Mary's wholly exceptional exemption from the sin of Adam and Eve, which is at the heart of the theological dogma of the Immaculate Conception, is not explicitly stated in the scriptures. But, in a certain way, it is illustrated by the gospel reading. Whereas Adam and Eve sinned through their disobedience to God's command, Mary hears and freely obeys the Word of God spoken to her by the angel. The gospel reading, which tells the story of the annunciation, is the account of Mary's *fiat* (Latin for "let it be done")—her willingness to place herself fully in the hands of God, in circumstances that promised to be difficult, unusual, and requiring great faith and trust.

This Lucan story is remarkable for its focus on Mary. In contrast to Matthew's gospel in which Joseph is the more central figure, Luke's account brings to light God's high regard for Mary. No particular marks of social status are hers. She has neither husband nor child, she does not share Joseph's Davidic ancestry, and she is not described as virtuous under the Law, as was Zechariah in Luke's parallel story of the announcement of the birth of John the Baptist. Yet the Lord favors Mary, despite her youth, her poverty, and her womanhood in a society that gave preference to men. The angel greets her with an address that is both respectful and beautiful in the original Greek, and for which there is probably no adequate translation. Finally, the event that is about to take place in Mary's life is affirmed by a sign that takes place in someone else's life—the pregnancy of Elizabeth in her old age. This way of calling attention to God's faithfulness is found often in the Acts of the Apostles (also written by Luke).

Mary's freedom from original sin signifies more than her own blessedness as "highly favored" of the Lord. The relevance of the Immaculate Conception extends to all people: Because of Mary's assent to God, the incarnation and, thus, the redemption of the world became possible. Taken together, therefore, the first reading and the gospel embrace the human race's whole drama of sin and redemption. The reading from Paul's letter to the Ephesians shows that this redemption was in the plan of God from the beginning.

Catholic Doctrine

The Immaculate Conception of the Blessed Virgin Mary

The theological notion of the Immaculate Conception of Mary was opposed by St. Bernard of Clairvaux (d. 1153) and by Sts. Thomas Aquinas and Albertus Magnus in the thirteenth century. These theologians were challenged by the Franciscan John Duns Scotus (d. 1308). For his efforts he is called the "Herald of the Immaculate Conception." This feast was approved in 1476 by Pope Sixtus IV and in 1568 it was extended to the entire Church by Pope Pius V. To give a final definition of the Immaculate Conception, Pius IX launched a theological commission in 1848 to study the issue. The following year he asked bishops around the world to comment. They responded almost unanimously in favor of this doctrine. Pius then issued the document *Ineffabilis Deus* that officially stated Mary was free from sin at the first moment of her conception by a special grace from God.

What does this dogma mean for us? Paul VI in his *Guidelines for Devotion to the Blessed Virgin Mary* (1974) stipulates that the ultimate purpose of devotion to the Blessed Virgin is to glorify God and lead Christians to commit themselves to a life which conforms absolutely to his will. Mary's assent to the invitation to become the mother of God not only gives her an esteemed place in salvation history but also provides for us the model of a true disciple of Jesus—conformity to the will of God.

Louis J. Cameli explains that Mary is holy not because of her own merits and not because of something she did. She is holy because God loved her. She was drawn close to God by the action of God's grace in her life. "Since she received God's favor from 'the first moment of her conception,' there can be no doubt that the responsibility for who she was rested with God" (Louis J. Cameli, *Mary's Journey*, p. 60). Something similar

happens in our lives, too. In terms of our faith, there are no self-made people. Everything depends on a gift from God.

We are born in need of a relationship with Jesus Christ who removes the alienation between God and ourselves. Mary needed the same redemption, but it was achieved in a unique way, by her being conceived immaculately.

The *Catechism of the Catholic Church* quotes St. Irenaeus, who wrote of Mary's role in the plan of salvation, "The knot of Eve's disobedience was untied by Mary's obedience: what the virgin Eve bound through her disbelief, Mary loosened by her faith. The Fathers of the early Church called Mary 'the Mother of the living' and coined the expression: 'Death through Eve, life through Mary'" (CCC 494). Thus, this holy day celebrates that Mary was conceived without sin, she is the model for all Christian disciples, and her "yes" opened the way for our redemption.

Catholic Culture

St. Anselm, Archbishop of Canterbury and doctor of the Church (d. 1109), wrote philosophical and theological treatises. Tradition has it that the Blessed Virgin Mary appeared to him. In a sermon whose theme addressed the place of Mary in the divine plan, he preached: "To Mary God gave his only-begotten Son, whom he loved as himself. Through Mary God made himself a Son, not different but the same, by nature Son of God and Son of Mary. The whole universe was created by God, and God was born of Mary. God created all things, and Mary gave birth to God. The God who made all things gave himself form through Mary, and thus he made his own creation. He who could create all things from nothing would not remake his ruined creation without Mary. God, then, is the Father of the created world and Mary the mother of the recreated world. God is the Father by whom all things were given life, and Mary the mother through whom all things were given new life. For God begot the Son, through whom all things were made, and Mary gave birth to him as the Savior of the world. Without God's Son, nothing could exist; without Mary's Son, nothing could be redeemed." (AnselmOratio 52)

Catholics have long practiced praying short invocations, repeated over and over. One such invocation focuses on Mary whose Immaculate Conception we celebrate on this feast. The invocation implores, "Queen conceived without original sin, pray for us!" (CathHous 370)

SESSION PLAN: The Immaculate Conception

Dismissal Catechesis (30 min.)

Getting Started

1. Prepare the space ahead of time with a circle of chairs around a table draped with a blue cloth upon which is placed a large candle and an art piece of Mary's Immaculate Conception.

One well-known work is Guido Reni's "The Immaculate Conception" in which Mary is standing in the heavens with two angels upon the crest of the moon. Another depiction of the Immaculate Conception is found on the Miraculous Medal and paintings of Mary's apparition to Catherine Labouré, who had a vision of Mary standing on a globe with rays of light streaming from her hands.

2. Invite the candidates and catechumens to be seated in the circle, place the Lectionary on the table, and light the candle. Pause for a few minutes and then pray in these words:
Loving and gracious God, we thank and praise you on this day for the gift of Mary, your Mother. You honored this simple woman of faith from the moment of her conception with the favor of sinlessness. You gave Mary the privilege of conceiving and bearing your beloved Son. Her "yes" to the angel's announcement opened the way for our salvation. Send your Holy Spirit to us to be our guide as we reflect on the meaning of Mary's Immaculate Conception for us today. We pray though Christ, who lives and reigns with you and the Holy Spirit, now and forever. Amen.

3. Invite a team member to proclaim the first reading from Genesis 3:9–15, 20. Pause and invite all to stand as you proclaim the gospel from Luke 1:26–38.

First Impressions

1. Explain the meaning of holy days in these words:
Holy days are special feasts, recalling important events in the life of Jesus or of persons close to him. Catholics gather for the Eucharist on these special days during the year to celebrate and reflect on the meaning and implications of the feast for our lives. On this feast of the Immaculate Conception, the Church celebrates Mary's conception without sin in the womb of her mother Anne.

2. Invite the participants to close their eyes and listen closely as you repeat these phrases from today's scripture:
Where are you? . . . I was afraid, because I was naked, so I hid myself.
You have eaten, then, from the tree of which I had forbidden you to eat!
The woman . . . gave me the fruit . . . so I ate it.
The serpent tricked me . . . so I ate it.
The man called his wife Eve because she became the mother of all the living.
God chose us . . . before the world began, to be holy and blameless . . . to be full of love.
Rejoice, O highly favored daughter! The Lord is with you. Blessed are you among women.
You shall conceive and bear a son . . . Jesus.
I am the maidservant of the Lord. Let it be done to me as you say.

3. Ask the participants to discuss these questions in the large group: *What image or phrase seems to have importance for you? What is evoked in you upon hearing these words from today's scriptures?* Offer this presentation on the first reading from Genesis 3:9–15, 20:
The passage from Genesis sets the context for this feast in the sin of our first parents. The effects of sin are traced back from the disorders found in the human condition to this rich symbolic story of Adam and Eve, who disobeyed the command of God and hid from God in the garden. As the story gathers impetus, Adam and Eve blame one another and the snake. From this moment on, the serpent is cast in terms of an ongoing conflict with humanity, representing chaos and evil. This original sin that originates in the first people, Adam, meaning earth, and Eve, meaning the mother of all the living, is somehow passed down from generation to generation. Yet there is a note of
hope, for even though Eve shares responsibility for the catastrophe of sin, God's promise continues through her in the offspring she will bear.
Gather the participants into small groups to discuss this question: *What can you learn about the human struggle with evil from this story?* After sufficient time for discussion, invite each small group to share their thoughts with everyone.

4. Ask the participants to turn to page 124 of the Participant Book and quietly reflect, then write about their understanding of Mary's blessedness. When all have had time, invite them to share their poems, stories, or creative writing in small groups.

Making Connections

1. Gather the attention of the participants back to the large group and ask them to name some of the influences of sin that they see in their personal lives, as well as in the world. You may choose to list these on newsprint with the heading "SIN," writing large enough for all to read. Follow with this statement: *The reality of evil exists. Yet God's grace is also available to us and is more powerful than sin.* Then ask the participants to name evidence of God's graces or blessings at work in their personal lives and in the world. List these responses on another newsprint labeled "GRACE."

2. Offer a presentation on the Church doctrine of the Immaculate Conception including the following points:
   - Today's feast celebrates that, from the moment of her conception in the womb of Anne, Mary was free from original sin and all its effects. This special grace from God flows out of Mary's role in God's plan for the salvation of humankind.
   - This doctrine of the Immaculate Conception is not found in scripture. However, since the earliest days of the Church, the belief that Mary was free from the stain of original sin has been upheld. Pope Pius IX declared the doctrine of Mary's Immaculate Conception an infallible dogma on December 8, 1854.
   - Mary's "yes" to the invitation to become the mother of God gives her an esteemed place in salvation history and provides for us a model of a true disciple, that is, conformity to God's will.
   - This favor bestowed upon Mary is not a result of something she did but is the action of God upon her. This is also true in our lives. Everything depends on gift—grace from God.
   - The breach with God described in the Genesis account of Adam and Eve disobeying God's command has been made whole through the obedient submission of Mary to God's plan for the salvation of humanity.

3. Invite the participants to reflect upon the questions presented on page 124 in the Participant Book. Then gather them back into small groups to share their responses. When all have had adequate time to share, ask the small groups to offer their insights into the last question in the large group setting: *What does this doctrine of the Immaculate Conception awaken in you?* Summarize their discussion in a few sentences.

Prayer

Invite the participants to listen as you pray the twelfth-century hymn to Mary written by Hildegard of Bingen. The hymn is found in the Catholic Culture section of Understanding this Sunday. After a short time of quiet, conclude by leading all in singing "Immaculate Mary" (Traditional Pyrenean melody; text, Jeremiah Cummings).

The Solemnity of Mary, Mother of God

JANUARY 1

Understanding this Feast:
Background for Catechesis

The Word in Liturgy

Numbers 6:22–27
Psalm 67:2–3, 5, 6, 8
Galatians 4:4–7
Luke 2:16–21

Today's celebration reflects the several liturgical traditions associated with this day over the centuries: the Holy Name of Jesus, the Circumcision, the Octave of Christmas, and Mary, Mother of God. The common denominator for all of these feasts, of course, is that each in its own way expresses some aspect of the mystery of the incarnation. Modern-day popes have also designated January 1 as a World Day of Prayer for Peace, although there is only tenuous connection between that prayer intention and today's readings (cf. Numbers 6:26). Today's celebration is the most ancient and, indeed, the only Marian feast indigenous to Rome, and the calendar reform of 1969 has given it a place of prominence as a solemnity of Mary.

The most solemn benediction in the Jewish scriptures is found in the book of Numbers, today's first reading, in which the "name" of God is invoked on the people. For the ancient Jews, to invoke God's name on someone was equivalent to rendering present the Almighty. This Aaronic blessing was prayed over the people by the priests at the conclusion of prayer and eventually became incorporated into the daily prayer of the Temple in Jerusalem. Our current *Sacramentary* has guaranteed its continued use in Christian worship by including it as one of the solemn blessing prayers at the end of Mass. The prayer's threefold repetition is a Hebrew way of intensifying the sentiment expressed. This text seems unrelated to the Marian character of the celebration. Rather, it reminds us that the Christmas season is always about the blessing of God's saving grace that has been "invoked" on us in the birth of Jesus (a name which means "Yahweh is salvation").

In his letter to the Galatians, Paul is very concerned to explain that salvation comes to Jew and Gentile alike as a result of what God has done in Jesus, not from our own efforts to observe the Mosaic Law. Here, his reference to God's son, "born of a woman" (v. 4), has deep consequences for Christian belief in the full humanity and full divinity of Jesus, as well as for Mary's role in the accomplishment of God's saving plan. Christian consciousness recognized early on that authentic faith in Jesus as true God and true man demanded the proclamation that Mary is the Mother of God, just as surely as she is the mother of his full humanity. There are saving implications in what theology describes as this union of two natures in one person, achieved in the womb of the Virgin Mary. As St. Thomas Aquinas has said, Jesus took on our human nature "so that he, made man, might make men gods" (*Opusc.* 57:1–4). Paul points to the link between the human birth of Jesus and our adoption as God's children (v. 7).

Mary's role in this divine plan is proclaimed in the gospel. The infancy narratives are always christological assertions, even when they seem merely to dwell on quaint details of Jesus' birth and early childhood. Mary's role in the salvation won by Christ is presented here, first, as she is greeted by the shepherds with her newborn child in the manger and, then, as she faithfully fulfills the prescriptions of the Law regarding circumcision, naming her child "Jesus" in accord with his divine destiny. Mary, as she "treasured all these words and pondered them in her heart," is an image of how every believer can be part of God's saving plan—by contemplating and cooperating with the mystery of a God who, by virtue of his birth of Mary, has become completely one with our human condition. Mary's motherhood assures us of the full humanity of Jesus. The Christ is God incarnate in order to "redeem those who were under the law . . . [Thus, we are] no longer a slave but a child, and if a child then also an heir" (Galatians 4:5, 7).

Catholic Doctrine

He was born of the Virgin Mary and became man.

The Council of Ephesus (431) proclaimed that Mary is truly the Mother of God (*theotokos*). On the first day of the new calendar year the Church celebrates the mother who has borne into this world the 'new day' of Christ our Savior.

The Catechism notes, "In the liturgical year the various aspects of the one Paschal Mystery unfold. This is also the case with the cycle of feasts surrounding the mystery of the incarnation (Annunciation, Christmas, Epiphany). They commemorate the beginning of our salvation and communicate to us the first fruits of the Paschal mystery." (CCC 1171) On this first day of January, between Christmas and Epiphany, the Church gathers to contemplate the Paschal Mystery through this celebration focused on Mary, Mother of God.

The Second Vatican Council observed that "In celebrating this annual cycle of the mysteries of Christ, Holy Church honors the Blessed Mary, Mother of God, with a special love. She is inseparably linked with the saving work of her Son. In her the Church admires and exults the most excellent fruit of redemption and joyfully contemplates, as in a faultless image, that which she herself desires and hopes wholly to be." (SC 103)

She is thus linked to the saving work of Jesus because she is not merely passively engaged by God. Mary freely cooperates in the work of our salvation through faith and obedience (LG 56). Refer also to the materials presented in the doctrine section on the Immaculate Conception.

The prayers for this feast express in poetic fashion the sentiment of the Church on this day, for example, "Father, source of light in every age, the virgin conceived and bore your Son who is called Wonderful God, Prince of Peace. May her prayer, the gift of a mother's love, be your people's joy through all the ages. May her response, born of a humble heart, draw your Spirit to rest on your people." (*Roman Missal*, Solemnity of Mary, Mother of God, January 1.)

Catholic Culture

The *theotokos* (Greek, "Mother of God"), is a predominate theme in the Litany of the Blessed Virgin Mary. For example, some of the invocations of the Litany are, "Mother of Christ, Mother of the Church, Mother of divine grace, Mother most pure, Mother of chaste love, Mother and virgin, Sinless Mother, Dearest of Mothers, Mother of good counsel, Mother of our Creator, [and] Mother of our Savior" (CathHous 344).

Four invocations (short prayers recited repeatedly) in traditional Catholic prayer rely on the image of Mary as our Mother. The four are, (1) "Mother of sorrows, pray for us." (2) "My Mother, my hope." (3) "Holy Mother of God, ever Virgin Mary, intercede for us." (4) Pray for us, holy Mother of God, that we may become worthy of the promises of Christ." (CathHous 369–70)

Notes

Dismissal Catechesis (30 min.)

Getting Started

1. Prepare the space ahead of time with a circle of chairs around a table covered with a white cloth. On the table place a white candle and an icon of Mary holding the child Jesus. You will need to have hymnals available for the prayer.

2. Lead the candidates and catechumens to the circle, place the Lectionary on the table, and light the candle. With the participants remaining silent, pass the icon of Mary around the circle, allowing enough time for each person to thoughtfully reflect on the image. Ask a member of the team to proclaim the gospel, Luke 2:16–21. After a period of silence, lead all in singing verses 1 and 2 of "What Child is This" (melody, "Greensleeves"; text, William Chatterton Dix).

First Impressions

1. Ask the participants to recall the Liturgy of the Word. Invite them to respond to these questions: *What did you observe or hear during today's liturgy? What did you find enlightening? What message came through for you as you listened and prayed?* Encourage the participants to freely discuss their feelings and responses.

2. Explain the background for today's celebration in these or your own words:
   We gathered to celebrate several important events at today's liturgy. On the first day of the New Year, the Church celebrates the feast or holy day called the Solemnity of Mary, Mother of God. Over the centuries, the Church has celebrated various feasts on this day, including the Circumcision of Jesus, the Holy Name of Jesus, and the Octave or eighth day of Christmas. In more recent years, the Church has celebrated this day as honoring Mary, the Mother of God. On this first day of the new calendar year, the Church celebrates the mother who has borne into this world the "new day" of Christ our Savior. Recent popes have also designated January 1 as World Day of Prayer for Peace. The common denominator in all these feasts is that each expresses some aspect of the mystery of the incarnation.
   Invite the participants to share some of the ways they celebrate the first day of the New Year.

3. Offer an explanation of the gospel passage in these or your own words:
   In the gospel, Luke points to Mary's role in the salvation won by Christ. The scene describes the astonishment of the shepherds as Mary received them. Luke goes on to say that Mary "treasured all these things and reflected on them in her heart." Faithful to the Jewish prescriptions of the Law,
   Mary presented her son to the temple for circumcision and naming. By contemplating and cooperating with God's plan for our salvation, Mary is revered as the Mother of God and our mother.
   Invite the participants to discuss these questions in small groups: *What about Mary's role as Mother of God do you find inspiring? What does it mean to "treasure" all the things about the birth of Jesus in your heart? As you look back upon your life, what do you treasure in your heart?* Focus the participants' attention back to the large group and invite a few responses.

Making Connections

1. Continue to deepen the perceptions of the participants by asking: *What happens in us when we take time to ponder or reflect on something, and treasure it in our heart?* Encourage all to respond.

2. Develop a presentation on the Church's teaching on *Theotokos*—Mary, the Mother of God—emphasizing the following points:
   - During this Christmas season the Church celebrates this feast of Mary because of the vital role she played in the birth of the Messiah. Mary is inseparably linked with the saving work of her Son.
   - The Greek word *theotokos* means one who has given birth to God. The Church proclaimed that Mary is truly the Mother of God at the Council of Ephesus in 431. This council of the Church in reaffirming the divinity of Christ went on to proclaim that Mary was mother to the whole person of Jesus, not only to his humanity.
   - Mary is not merely a passive recipient of God's will. She freely and actively cooperated in the work of our salvation through her faith and obedience.

3. Ask the participants to take time contemplating the Reflection and Questions on page 126 in their Participant Book. When they have had time to respond, invite them to share their insights in the same small groups. You may choose to gather a summary of these discussions when the whole group reconvenes.

4. Encourage participants to ask questions and make comments on today's teaching. Allow sufficient time for discussion.

Prayer

Call the group to prayer by playing an instrumental version of "Evergreen" or " What Child Is This" in the background. Invite everyone to remain silent and contemplate one thing they wish to "treasure" about Mary, Mother of God, in their heart. Allow several minutes of silence and close indicating that all stand as you proclaim the first reading, Numbers 6:22–27, as a blessing prayer upon the group.

The Presentation of the Lord

FEBRUARY 2

The Word in Liturgy

Malachi 3:1–4
Psalm 24:7, 8, 9, 10
Hebrews 2:14–18
Luke 2:22–40 or 2:22–32

The feast of the Presentation, which had for some centuries in the Latin Church been known as the feast of the Purification of Mary, was restored to its original meaning as a christological feast by the Second Vatican Council. Originating in fourth-century Jerusalem as a celebration of the meeting of the old and new dispensations, the feast of the Presentation by the eighth century also came to be associated with the blessing of candles for liturgical use—an association it has kept to the present day—because of Simeon's canticle in today's gospel reading, which proclaims Christ as the light to the Gentiles.

All of today's readings involve the temple in some way. Today's first reading is from the prophet Malachi, who preached in about 460 B.C. A staunch upholder of Judaism, the prophet was critical of the corrupt and ignorant priesthood of his day, as well as of abuses in the temple that Ezra and Nehemiah were later to correct. Today's reading comes from his fourth oracle, in which a sudden visitation of God to the temple results in the purification of its sacrifices and its ministers. The "messenger of the covenant" was not originally thought of as a messianic figure, but later the image was associated with the Messiah or the precursor of the Messiah (as, for example, John the Baptist in Matthew 11:10). In the context of today's celebration, a messianic interpretation is very appropriate.

Psalm 24 is a procession hymn, describing the triumphant entrance of the king into the temple. The king is described in terms used for the ark of the covenant; he is the war hero of Israel.

Today's reading from Hebrews celebrates Christ's sharing in the frailty of human flesh and blood. Christ is the compassionate and faithful high priest (a central theme of the letter). Although the notion of the faithful high priest has many precedents in Judaism, the element of compassion is a new one to be associated with that role, and is taken no doubt from the actual experience of Jesus' life.

Luke's narrative in today's gospel makes it clear that Jesus comes into a family and a society within Judaism that is deeply ingrained with piety and lives in expectancy of the fulfillment of divine promises. The humble eloquence of Simeon, the profound piety of the elderly prophetess Anna, and even the simple poverty of the holy family (a pair of turtledoves was the sacrifice of the poor—those with greater means offered a lamb as well) combine to form a touching portrait of the manifestation of God's Son to the faithful of Israel. Simeon's canticle, like those of Mary and Zechariah, transforms a personal gift into a broad proclamation to the world. Mary here, as elsewhere, personifies Israel. The passage does not shy away from the prediction that Jesus will cause conflict and division within Israel (the sword that will pierce Mary's heart), but does at the same time proclaim that his coming is Israel's glory.

By restoring its christological focus, the Church invites us to reflect on this feast as a celebration of Jesus the Christ. Today's readings bring to our attention the humanity of Christ, who was born subject to the Law (Luke), and who is our compassionate high priest and messianic mediator (Hebrews). It also proclaims his coming as the very visitation of God (Malachi), offering salvation and light to all nations (Simeon's canticle).

Catholic Doctrine

The Two Natures

The Catholic Church confesses the belief that Jesus possesses two natures: Jesus Christ is fully human and fully divine. While this belief is based in the apostles' experience of him and is asserted by scripture, the theological understanding of this doctrine was first addressed by the Council of Chalcedon in 451 due to the Monophysite controversy (or heresy). The Monophysites charged that the human nature of Christ ceased to exist when the divine person of the Son of God assumed it.

The Council of Chalcedon proclaimed, "Following the holy Father, we unanimously teach and confess one and the same Son, our Lord Jesus Christ: the same perfect in divinity and perfect in humanity, the same truly God and truly man, composed of rational soul and body; consubstantial with the Father as to his divinity and consubstantial with us as to his humanity; 'like us in all things but sin.'" The Council then answered the Monophysites and asserted, "We confess that one and the same Christ . . . is to be acknowledged in two natures without confusion, change, division, or separation. The distinction between the natures was never abolished by their union, but rather the character proper to each of the two natures was preserved as they came together in one person . . ." (Council of Chalcedon, DS 301–02).

Another way the Church expresses this is to assert that Jesus is both the Son of God and the Son of the Virgin Mary (CCC 724). The two natures of Christ, one divine and one human, are not confused, but united. They are united in the one person of Jesus Christ (CCC 481). This union does not cease (CCC 469).

St. Sophronius, a bishop of the early Church, preached on the feast of the Presentation: "In honor of the divine mystery that we celebrate today, let us all hasten to meet Christ. Everyone should be eager to join the procession and carry a light. Our lighted candles are a sign of the divine splendor of the one who comes to expel the dark shadows of evil and to make the whole universe radiant with the brilliance of his eternal light. Our candles also show how bright our souls should be when we go to meet Christ. . . . Our eyes have seen the God incarnate, and because we have seen him present among us and have mentally received him into our arms, we are called the new Israel. Never shall we forget his presence; every year we keep a feast in its honor" (*Orat. 3 de Hypapante* 6.7: PG 87, 3, 3291–93; LH vol. III, Presentation of the Lord, Office of Readings, pp. 1350–51).

Thus, the feast of the Presentation celebrates that Jesus, the light of all peoples, is the only Messiah, "destined to be the downfall and rising of many." The Son of God is the only mediator between the Most High and humanity. How else could this be? If Jesus is not fully and truly human, how can he understand and identify totally with us? And if Jesus is not fully and truly divine, how can he ever assist us and transform us? The Council of Chalcedon and generations of faithful afterwards have answered, confessing belief in the two natures of Christ.

Catholic Culture

In the northern hemisphere, this feast is celebrated in the dead of winter darkness. The assembly gathers prior to the liturgy outside the church and candles are blessed. As these blessed candles are lit, the people process into church singing and the Mass of the Presentation of the Lord is celebrated. Customarily, enough candles are blessed on this day in order to last through the year. Thus, this feast also goes by the name "Candlemas."

A prayer which comes to us directly from the text of scripture, the *Nunc Dimittis* (Latin for "now you are dismissing") from Simeon's exclamation found in Luke 2:29–32, is prayed by Catholics in the Liturgy of the Hours at Night Prayer to close the activities of the day and retire to bed. The accompanying antiphon petitions, "Protect us, Lord, as we stay awake; watch over us as we sleep, that awake, we may keep watch with Christ, and asleep, rest in his peace" (LH, Night Prayer).

Dismissal Catechesis (30 min.)

Getting Started

1. Prepare the space ahead of time with a circle of chairs around a table covered with a white cloth.
2. In the dismissal, include a line about the candidates and catechumens going off to meet the light of Christ in the Word. Lead the procession of candidates and catechumens, carrying a lighted Christ candle. They can follow carrying lighted glass votives and singing "The King of Glory" or Psalm 24: "We Long to See Your Face" (Kevin Keil, GIA Publications, 1993).
3. Place a lighted candle on the table in the center of the circle. Pause for a time to allow the effect of the lighted candles to affect the group. Pray in these or your own words:

   Christ our Light, you have come to expel the dark shadows of sin and death. Your presence in our midst makes the whole universe radiant with the brilliance of your eternal light. You have come to refine us like gold that we might offer to God an appropriate sacrifice. May your revealing light bring light to our hearts as we prepare to open your Word today. Open the portals of our minds that the King of Glory might enter and dwell among us. Amen.

First Impressions

1. Ask the group to discuss insights about the significance of light. Explain that this feast celebrates the Presentation of the child Jesus in the temple. Invite them to share: *What did you notice that was different in today's liturgy?* If the blessing of candles was part of your parish celebration, clarify the significance of this blessing in these or your own words:

   Since the eighth century, the blessing of candles to be used in the liturgy for the following year has been part of this feast. In today's gospel, Simeon's prayer proclaims Christ as the light to the Gentiles. It is appropriate that we celebrate this joyous feast with the blessing and procession of lighted candles.

2. Invite the group to close their eyes as you recall some of the images from the first reading from Malachi 3:1–4. Slowly read these lines from this passage, allowing time for them to affect the participants.

   "Lo, I am sending my messenger to prepare the way before me."
   "For he is like the refiner's fire or like the fuller's lye."
   "He will purify the sons of Levi, refining them like gold or silver that they might offer due sacrifice to the Lord."

3. Direct the attention of the participants to small groups, asking them to discuss these questions: *What about this passage is consoling? Who is this messenger for you? Why is the messenger's refining/purifying mission so important?*
4. In the large group gather a few insights from the small group discussion.

Making Connections

1. Then ask the whole group: *What do we mean when we call Christ our "light"?* As they respond, write their insights on a large poster board or paper. Encourage them to think about Christ as illuminator of all darkness, the fire of Christ's love igniting our faith and fervor and Christ purifying us with the refiner's fire.
2. In small groups ask them to share: *When have you experienced the light of Christ in one of the ways described by the group?*
3. Invite the response of a few participants and summarize today's session in a few sentences. Ask each person to think of one way they could celebrate the feast of the Presentation by sharing the light of Christ to someone in darkness.

Prayer

Invite everyone to center their minds and hearts on Jesus our Light by pausing to look once again at the lighted candles. Ask all to stand and sing "The Light Shines On" (Carey Landry, NALR, 1985). Pray the Collect for today's feast and close by leading the following Litany of Light, asking all to respond: *"Christ, you are our Light."*

Our hearts are grateful for all those times you shone your light in our darkness . . . Response.
We are thankful for the ways you have purified our motives and refined our thoughts . . . Response.
We stand in humble awe before the fire of your love . . . Response.
King of Glory, enter our minds and hearts as we journey toward full initiation into your community of love, for this we pray. Amen.

Extended Catechesis

SESSION FOCUS: *The Two Natures*

Gathering

A. Sunday:

1. Welcome and greet the team, sponsors, and other participants as they arrive. Invite them to join the circle around the table of lighted votive candles surrounding the lit Christ candle. Allow a time of silent reflection, with instrumental music, such as a piece from Handel's "Messiah" playing softly in the background.
2. Ask the new arrivals to share their impressions of the significance of today's feast of the Presentation of the Lord.
3. Begin the prayer by inviting all to stand and join in singing the Gathering Hymn from today's liturgy. Continue by asking one of the sponsors to proclaim the gospel from Luke 2:22–40. Indicate to the group that they sit in silence to reflect upon the meaning of this passage. Close by inviting all to stand and sing the "Canticle of Isaiah" by John Foley.

B. Weekday:

1. Greet and welcome the participants as they arrive. Invite them to join the circle around the table of lighted votive candles, surrounding the lit Christ candle. Allow a time of silent reflection, with instrumental music, such as a piece from Handel's "Messiah" playing softly in the background.
2. Ask the group to share how the light of Christ has affected their experiences these past few days.
3. Lead this celebration of the Word:
   - Song: Gathering Hymn from the Liturgy of the Feast
   - First Reading: Malachi 3:1–4
   - Sing Psalm 24
   - Second Reading: Hebrews 2:14–18
   - Silence
   - Gospel: Luke 2:22–40
   - Song: "Canticle of Isaiah"

The Word (30 min.)

1. Invite the candidates and catechumens to share their insights on the "Light of Christ" from the Dismissal session.
2. Explain the background for the scriptures in these words: *The scriptures for this feast revolve around the temple. In the first reading from Malachi, the prophet calls for reform and restoration of the cult of the temple and the priesthood. He describes God's intervention first as the "messenger" who would prepare the Lord's way and, secondly, the Lord would come in person to refine and purify the sons of Levi—the priestly tribe. In retrospect, Christians have traditionally thought of the messenger as the Messiah or the precursor of the Messiah, that is, John the Baptist. The second reading from Hebrews celebrates Christ as the compassionate and faithful high priest. The Presentation of Jesus in the temple is proclaimed in today's gospel from Luke. Both the Presentation of Jesus in the temple and his later cleansing of the temple are viewed as Jesus' action of purifying the temple according to the promise of Malachi. Thus, this narrative is considered a messianic statement, that is, Jesus came to fulfill both the law and the prophets. This messianic call infiltrated the dialogue between his parents and Anna and Simeon. The object of Simeon's long wait has now been realized as he, inspired by the Spirit, declares, "my eyes have witnessed your saving deed . . . a revealing light to the Gentiles, the glory of your people Israel." The pious widow Anna gave thanks to God and spoke, "about this child to all who looked forward to the deliverance of Jerusalem."*
3. Ask the participants to spend some time reflecting on the meaning of these scriptures in their own lives by turning to the Reflection on page 128 of the Participant Book.
4. Ask the participants to share their insights as to the meaning of Jesus in their lives in pairs. Sponsors and candidates or catechumens will want to gather together.

Catholic Teaching (30 min.)

1. Invite the participants to share a few insights on the meaning of Jesus in their lives in the large group.
2. Explain the Catholic teaching on the two natures of Christ, making the following points (The Catholic Doctrine section of Understanding this Sunday will be helpful in your preparation.):
   - The Council of Chalcedon in 451 confessed the belief that Jesus is fully human and fully divine in response to the Monophysite heresy. This controversy in the early Church charged that the human nature of Christ ceased to exist when the divine person of the Son of God assumed it.
   - The teaching consists in this statement: "We unanimously teach and confess one and the same Son, our Lord Jesus Christ: at the same time perfect in divinity and perfect in humanity, the same truly God and truly man, composed of rational soul and body; consubstantial with the Father as to his divinity and consubstantial with us as to his humanity; 'like us in all things but sin.' "
   - The two natures of Christ are united in the one person of Jesus Christ.
3. Invite the participants to gather into small groups to discuss these questions: *What qualities of Jesus are manifest in his human nature? What qualities exist in Jesus as truly divine?* Ask each group to record their discussion on paper with markers, writing large enough for all to read.

Prayer

Gather the group back to the circle surrounding the lighted candles. Invite them to silence as they keep the person with whom they wish to share the Good News of Jesus. Begin the prayer with inviting all to stand and sing, "The Light Shines On." Indicate that everyone seated. Invite the participants to bring to the center of the circle those with whom they will share the Good News by prayerfully saying their first name. When all have finished, close with this prayer:

Jesus, we desire to be messengers of your Good News. There are many in this world who need to hear the message of your human and divine presence with us. In your humanity, you have walked with us, felt the pains and joys of living, and have loved much. In your divinity, you are our source of sustenance and transformation. We raise up to you not only ourselves, but those whose names are presented to this circle of prayer. You, who promised to be with us as we gather, have heard our cry. Give us the courage to share all that you have come to mean in our lives. Give us the words to speak the glory of your presence and promise—Son of God and Child of Mary. Prepare the hearts of those we bring before you that they might hear all that you have accomplished in your living, dying, and rising. Amen.

The Ascension of the Lord

Understanding this Feast:
Background for Catechesis

The Word in Liturgy

Acts 1:1–11
Psalm 47:2–3, 6–7, 8–9
Ephesians 1:17–23
Matthew 28:16–20

The earliest scriptural traditions did not distinguish the resurrection of Jesus and his ascension as two separate events. It is in the later gospel accounts—those of Luke and John—that we find these two dimensions of the paschal mystery most clearly described as separate chronological events. So, too, in the liturgical year, it was not until the fourth and fifth centuries that a separate feast of the Ascension, celebrated forty days after the resurrection in accord with Luke's chronology in Acts, became commonplace.

All three years of the lectionary cycle use today's reading from Acts to introduce the notion of Christ's ascension. Luke's description is a carefully constructed narrative, meant to be understood in light of the parallel beginning of his gospel (compare Luke 1:1–4 & Acts 1:1–2), as well as the many key themes found here and woven throughout his two-volume work. The gospel's description of John's baptism in chapter 3 is alluded to in this passage as being surpassed by the disciples' forthcoming baptism with the Holy Spirit; Jesus' forty days (always a symbolic number in Luke) in the desert are balanced here by mention of the forty days during which he appeared to the disciples after his resurrection; the conclusion of the gospel, in which Jesus commands the disciples to be his witnesses to all nations, is matched here with a similar command in virtually identical language. It is clear that the ascension, for Luke, is much more a proclamation of theological truth than mere historical remembrance. The thrust of that proclamation is captured effectively in the psalm refrain ("God mounts his throne to shouts of joy; a blare of trumpets to the Lord"). Psalm 47 is considered by scholars to be one of the so-called "enthronement psalms," presumably sung at an annual celebration marking Yahweh's kingship, which was symbolized in the reign of Israel's sovereign.

Today's reading from Ephesians reflects the sort of evolved theological understanding of the ascension which underlies Luke's deceptively simple description. Scholars suspect that the Pauline disciple who penned this letter very likely may have borrowed the opening prayer, from which our reading is taken, from an early liturgical hymn. The mention of Christ as head of the Church recalls Paul's body metaphor in 1 Corinthians 12, but here the Church is also called the "fullness" of Christ. To be noted is the fact that although Christ is described as reigning over all creation at God's right hand, he is still intimately present to and active in the Church. The ascension is not about the removal of Christ from the Church; rather, it is about a new form of his presence, a presence that is in many ways even more powerful and significant than was his earthly existence with the disciples.

The gospel reading from Matthew, known in the tradition as "the great commission," shows Jesus sending his followers out to preach and baptize in the name of the Trinity. The scope of their mission is universal. They are sent to "all nations," not only to Israel. At the opening of the passage, Jesus appears as Lord of the universe. The very sight of him dispels the last lingering doubts of his followers. He speaks in regal fashion, with a word of command. Yet his promise to remain with them always affirms the intimacy of the disciples with their Lord. On a mountaintop, with all the world and the ages before them, the last words of Jesus recall the promise made at his birth (Matthew 1:23): ". . . they shall call him Emmanuel, a name which means 'God is with us.'"

Catholic Doctrine

"He ascended into heaven and is seated at the right hand of the Father" (Nicene Creed)

Our Catholic belief in the ascension could appear as nothing more than a historical remembrance of Jesus' final departure from this earthly existence. As such, its relevance to our lives today might seem marginal at best. Nothing could be further from the truth. In fact, the ascension is a crucial dimension of the saving plan of God which we refer to as the paschal mystery. Theologically, the ascension is expressive of our conviction that Christ's death has saving ramifications for us. Moreover, it explains how it is that we can and must experience Christ's presence to and in the Church in a totally new way in the post-resurrection era.

In a famous sermon of St. Leo the Great [*Sermo* 73, 4 (CCL 138A: 453), quoted in *The Liturgical Year*, vol. 3, by Adrian Nocent, trans. Matthew J. O'Connell, Collegeville: Liturgical Press, 1977, p. 233], the doctrinal significance of this feast is succinctly captured: "The ascension of Christ thus means our own elevation as well; where the glorious Head has gone before, the Body is called to follow in hope. Let us therefore exult, beloved. . . . For on this day not only have we been confirmed in our possession of paradise, but we have even entered heaven in the person of Christ. . . ." The preface for today's Mass captures the same thought in the simple phrase, "where he has gone, we hope to follow." The CCC explains this teaching in detail in section 659. The ascension is all about our own triumph over sin, in the person of Christ the Redeemer, enthroned at God's right hand.

A second sermon of Leo [*Sermo* 74, 2 (CCL 138A: 455–57), ibid., p. 234], equally noteworthy, goes even further in explaining the importance of the ascension for our lives today: "Thus what formerly had been visible in our Redeemer now took the form of sacred rites; and in order that faith might be purer and stronger, bodily vision was replaced by teaching. . . ." In other words, in order that people of every time and place might have access to the saving presence of Christ, it is necessary that the earthly body of Jesus, limited to time and space, be replaced by his sacramental presence. And it is precisely the ascension that makes possible the gift of Christ's Spirit in the sacraments, the "sacred rites" of which St. Leo spoke.

Catholic Culture

The ascension is one of the glorious mysteries of the rosary. Belief in the ascension is professed in both the Apostles' Creed and the Nicene Creed.

Because of its central importance in the life of Christ, artistic representations of the ascension are frequently seen in churches. Two examples that have acquired a special place in the history of art are the sculpture of the ascension in the tympanum of the west portal of Chartres Cathedral (c. 1145) in France and a painting of the ascension by Giotto (d. 1336) in the Arena chapel in Italy. The oldest stained glass window in the magnificent cathedral of Le Mans, France, is an unassuming Romanesque depiction of the ascension, damaged during the French revolution (along with other parts of the cathedral) by a rioting mob who mistook the figure of Christ for an earthly king.

Dismissal Catechesis (30 min.)

Getting Started
1. Prepare the space ahead of time. Provide a prominent place for the Lectionary and a candle.
2. Ask the catechumens and candidates to gather in a circle and to pause in silence. After a moment of silence light the candle.

First Impressions
Invite the group to gather into small groups and react to the readings and the homily. Use these questions as a guide for the discussion:
What images did the readings present to you today? How did they speak to you and what meaning do they have for your life?

Making Connections
1. Begin by exploring the meaning of the feast of the Ascension. Bring out the following points:
   - After the resurrection the Risen Christ appeared to his disciples for forty days, reminiscent of the forty days in the desert.
   - We believe that Christ, raised from the dead, ascended to the Father, and now comes to us through the Holy Spirit.
   - Move them to an understanding that Jesus, once bound historically, now resurrected and ascended, knows no bounds. Christ comes to us in a new way, forever.
2. Ask the group to discuss the following questions:
   Knowing that Jesus comes to us in new ways and that as Christ he is not bound by time and history, what does this mean for them? How, then, are they called to live their lives?

Prayer
Using the refrain *"God mounts his throne to shouts of joy; a blare of trumpets to the Lord,"* recite or sing Psalm 47 from the liturgy.

Extended Catechesis

SESSION FOCUS: *Christ has died, Christ has risen, Christ will come again*

Gathering

A. Sunday:
1. Welcome any new people to the gathering. Invite silence and ask the group to recall the readings from the liturgy.
2. Begin with the following refrain:
   We remember how you loved us to your death, and still we celebrate, for you are with us here; and we believe that we will see you when you come in your glory, Lord. We remember, we celebrate, we believe (Marty Haugen, GIA Publications, 1980).
3. Lead into the following or similar prayer:
   Let us pray:
   God, our Father, we remember how, through your Son's death, resurrection, and ascension, you revealed to us the fulfillment of your promise of salvation. We know we are blessed with your presence and that full happiness will come when we can be with you forever. Guide us in your ways, show us the way to fullness of life in you. We ask this through Christ our Lord. Amen.

B. Weekday:
1. Welcome everyone to the gathering. Invite the people to silence and begin with the refrain indicated above, "We Remember." Offer a prayer such as the one above and then proclaim the Sunday readings.
   - Read Acts 1:1—1
   - Responsorial Psalm 47
   - Ephesians 1:17—23
   - Matthew 28:16—20

The Word (30 min.)

1. Invite the group to reflect on the experience of the disciples after the death of Jesus. Help them to imagine what it would have been like to have followed Jesus, lived with him, eaten with him, and now he was gone. Ask the group to move into small groups and to reflect on the following questions:
   He is not here anymore. How does that make you feel? What are you going to do now?

2. After the discussion, explore with the group how the gospel speaks about the disciples. Ask the larger group to respond to these questions:
   How are the disciples different from after the death of Jesus and now at the ascension? Why are they different?

3. Using the Word in Liturgy, explore with the group how this event, the Ascension of Christ, makes the disciples different, how they are changed, and what action results from the change. Bring out that the readings express that because of the Ascension, Christ was now present to them in a new way. The Ascension is about Christ's new presence that is a more powerful sign than his earthly existence. Their response was to go out and witness to the world.

4. Ask the group to gather in small groups and respond to the following question:
   Christ is here. What are you going to do?

Catholic Teaching (30 min.)

1. Begin by singing the refrain from "We Remember."

2. Help the participants to understand the importance of the feast of the Ascension by pointing out that the refrain we sing can be used for the Memorial Acclamation of the Mass. Explain that the Memorial Acclamation is a statement of our faith, expressing our belief that Christ died for us, was raised from the dead, and will come again. Also, point out to them that in the Creed of the Church, we state that Christ "ascended into heaven and is seated at the right hand of the Father." Both the memorial acclamation and the creed express the fullness of the paschal mystery.

3. Develop with the group the following points:
   - Christ died. The messiah suffered, died, and was buried. This death was a death for our salvation.
   - Christ is risen. For the disciples the resurrection vindicated Christ's life and revealed to them the fulfillment of God's promised kingdom.
   - Christ will come again. Because of the Ascension, Christ was no longer bound to early existence. Christ comes now in a new way and with him is the dawning of a new age, the final age promised by God. The new age we speak about is characterized by renewal, by God's presence through the Spirit.

4. Help the participants to appreciate that we live in the hope of living with God forever. The Ascension celebrates the beginning of the fulfillment of God's kingdom which is here but not completely.

5. Preparing them for the coming Sundays of the Easter season, suggest to the participants that the Ascension points to Pentecost with the coming of the gift of the Paraclete.

6. Ask the participants to reflect on the following question as a large group and write their responses on a board for all to see:
   What are the signs of God's presence now in our world, in our cities, in our neighborhoods?

Putting Faith into Practice

1. Ask the catechumens and candidates to write in their Participant Book the response to the following question:
   What are the signs of God's ongoing presence in your personal life?

2. Continue discussion that invites responses to the following questions and have them share their responses with one other person:
   The disciples' experience led them to action even in a time of waiting for the return of the Lord. How are you called to wait for God's fullness in your life? How do you hear yourself called to act?

Prayer

Sing together "We Remember" as a closing prayer.

Trinity Sunday

Understanding this Feast:
Background for Catechesis

The Word in Liturgy

Exodus 34:4–6, 8–9
Daniel 3:42–56
2 Corinthians 13:11–13
John 3:16–18

Chapter 34 of Exodus is the story of the second giving of the law after the people of Israel broke the covenant by worshiping the golden calf. Moses is asked by God to bring a second set of blank stone tablets up the mountain, and this time to come alone. Here our passage begins, with God's appearance to Moses and a revelation of the divine name—this one less ambiguous than the one given in the sight of the burning bush ("I am who I am," Exodus 3:14). For the purposes of the liturgy of Trinity Sunday, this revelation of God's name is central, and indeed throughout the whole Old Testament literature God's identity as "merciful and gracious . . . slow to anger and rich in kindness and fidelity" is recalled and celebrated. Compassion is of God's essence. In this passage, we catch a glimpse of God in the loving act of offering a restored covenant relationship to a "stiff-necked people"—a gracious response we are to see offered again and again as the witness of scripture unfolds.

Moses' response of complete obeisance, bowing down to the ground, is the fitting act of humility before so great and merciful a God. As a mediator, Moses prefigures Christ who, because he "finds favor" with God, can prevail upon God to journey with the people and "receive us as your own" (v. 9). Moses' respectful invitation to the Lord to "come along in our company" reminds us that the people are on a journey. The reestablishment of the covenant means that this God will be with them.

The responsorial psalm (Daniel 3:42–56) is taken from the beginning of the song of the three virtuous Jewish leaders in Babylon whom King Nebuchadnezzar had thrown into a fiery furnace because of their refusal to worship a golden idol at his command. There is an interesting contrast here between the heroic faithfulness of the three men in the face of martyrdom for refusing idolatry and the background setting of the first reading

which features the idolatrous worship of a golden image. More importantly, however, the psalm is a good example of the praise of a God who saves, which is very much in keeping with the spirit of the first reading. In order to understand this, one must remember that the three men are protected by God from the flames in the furnace, and sing these joyful praises right in the midst of them. First and foremost is their praise of God's "holy and glorious" name. God's temple, throne, cherubim, and firmament are all indications of God's power and glory, sustaining in words of praise our reflection on the wonder of who God is.

The passage taken from 2 Corinthians is the earliest New Testament passage which explicitly links Father, Son, and Spirit in a way that the Church later used when it came to articulate the mystery of the Trinity. The word "Trinity," first used by Tertullian (145–220) to describe the nature of God, was only defined by Church councils in the fourth and fifth centuries. Nevertheless, our concept of the Trinity has scriptural roots in the experience of the people of God, who came in a variety of ways to understand the one God in three persons which the creeds were later to define. Here, the Trinity is invoked as a presence in the community of faith, offering grace, peace, and fellowship. As in the first reading, the presence of a God of love and peace is stressed. Neither far-off, nor some sort of abstraction, this God is "with you" (v. 11). Paul calls the community to put aside divisions and greet one another with a kiss. The closing words of the passage are familiar to us from the presider's greeting at the eucharistic liturgy.

The gospel passage is taken from the end of a long discussion between Jesus and Nicodemus about rebirth through water and the Spirit. The love of God, which resulted in the gift of Jesus Christ to the world, is depicted in all its generosity. Not to judge but to save, Jesus was given to the world. The expression "given" suggests not only his incarnation, but also his suffering and death on the cross. The response called for is faith, in other words, the active acceptance of the gift which is Jesus Christ. As the author of John's gospel illustrates throughout his account, the coming of Jesus into the world provokes a crisis in human history. The encounter with Jesus results in a kind of self-judgment, wherein people by their acceptance or rejection of him decide their own fate. Here again we see the revelation of the Trinity within the drama of salvation, calling for a human response of faith that brings with it an abundance of new and eternal life.

Catholic Doctrine

The Holy Trinity

One enters into the salvation offered by God being baptized in the name of the Father, and of the Son, and of the Holy Spirit. Our faith as followers of Jesus, as Christians, rests upon the foundation of the Trinity. It is important to note that at baptism we are baptized in the name, not the "names," for we hold that there is only one God, the Father, his beloved Son, and the Holy Spirit: the Most Holy Trinity (CCC 232).

Catholic teaching describes the Trinity as the central mystery of our Christian faith and life because it is the mystery of God's very self. It is, therefore, the fount of all the other mysteries of faith, the doctrine which underpins all the rest (CCC 234).

While our Catholic articulation of this doctrine evolved in response to misunderstandings and heretical movements, it evolved fairly quickly, being fixed within the first four centuries of the Church—and rests upon not only our conviction but our experience of God as Father, Son, and Holy Spirit, one God, three divine persons (CCC 250). This experience was expressed, from the beginning, in the baptismal formula, in scripture (for example, 2 Corinthians 13:13 and Ephesians 4:4–6), in preaching, catechesis, and the prayer of the Church (CCC 249).

There is some specific doctrinal terminology associated with explanations of the Trinity: the word "substance" (also "essence" or "nature") indicates the divine being in its unity; the term "person" (also *hypostasis*) designates the Father, Son, and Spirit in the real distinction among them; and the word "relation" indicates that their distinction lies in the relationship of each to the others. In using this terminology, the Church clarifies important aspects of the teaching on the Trinity. First, the Trinity is One. We do not believe in three Gods, but one God in three persons, that is, the divinity is not divided between the three. Each of the persons of the Trinity is God, whole and complete, such that each of them is that same reality of divine substance, essence, or nature. Second, the divine persons of the Trinity are really distinct from one another, that is, God is truly one but not solitary. Thus, the person of the Father is distinct from that of the Son, the Son distinct from the Father, and the Spirit is distinct from Father and Son. Third, the divine persons of the Trinity are relative to one another. Because the divine unity is not divided by the persons, the distinction between them arises solely from the relationships which relate them to one another (CCC 252–53).

This mystery is reflected in the way in which the Church prays. All of the longer endings of the formal prayers in the *Sacramentary,* after being addressed to the Father, conclude with "We ask this through our Lord Jesus Christ, your Son, who lives and reigns with you and the Holy Spirit, one God, for ever and ever." We begin Mass in the name of the Father, Son, and Holy Spirit. The Church proclaims, "Father, . . . we joyfully proclaim our faith in the mystery of your Godhead. You have revealed your glory as the glory also of your Son and of the Holy Spirit: three Persons equal in majesty, undivided in splendor, yet one Lord, one God, ever to be adored in your everlasting glory" (*Roman Missal*, Preface for Holy Trinity, p. 43).

Catholic Culture

In Christian iconography, the Trinity is symbolized by a triangle (the Greek letter "delta"). In early Byzantine art, God the Father is not portrayed by a human figure, but rather the *dextera Domini*, the hand of God, as in the apse of St. Mark Cathedral (Venice), dating from the ninth century. Later, in western art, the Trinity is portrayed using human figures, such as in the manuscript miniatures of Jean Fouquet (d. 1481), one of the foremost French artists of his day. In the *Hours* of Etienne Chevalier, dating from 1470, he (Chantilly) represents the Trinity as three identical figures seated on identical thrones. This type of representation of the Trinity, employing human figures, is said to have been banned by Pope Urban VIII because the Holy Spirit was to be illustrated through the use of a dove or tongues of fire.

When the elect are baptized, they are immersed three times in the waters of the font—or water is poured three times over each of them—and the Trinitarian formula is spoken: "I baptize you in the name of the Father, and of the Son, and of the Holy Spirit" (RCIA 226, RBC 60).

A priest who presides at liturgy blesses the people at its end with a single sign of the cross made over the assembly invoking the Trinitarian formula. However, a bishop makes the sign of the cross three times. He also makes this threefold sign of blessing as he processes out and through the assembly (CB 169, 1119–20).

The traditional Catholic hymn "Holy God, We Praise Thy Name" (ascribed to Ignaz Franz, [d. 1790] and translated into English by Clarence Walworth [d. 1900]), has as its closing verse an acknowledgment of the Trinity: "Holy Father, Holy Son,/ Holy Spirit, Three we name thee,/ While in essence only One,/ Undivided God we claim thee,/ And adoring bend the knee,/ While we own the mystery."

Dismissal Catechesis (30 min.)

Getting Started

1. Prepare the space with a circle of chairs around a table covered with white cloth upon which is placed a candle and an icon of the Trinity or a shamrock plant. (St. Patrick used the shamrock to teach the doctrine of the Trinity.) Provide a space for the Lectionary.
2. Welcome the catechumens and candidates into the circle and place the Lectionary on the table. Light the candle and call their attention to the representation of the Trinity either in the icon or the plant. After a moment of silence, invite everyone to make the sign of the cross using both their hands and the Trinitarian formula. Continue to pray: *Gracious God, today we celebrate your feast. You have given Christ to us in his life, suffering, death, and resurrection, and draw us into your love through the Holy Spirit. Teach us to give you praise always, for you are Lord. Grant this through Jesus Christ, who lives and reigns with you and the Holy Spirit, one God, forever and ever. Amen.*

First Impressions

1. Begin the discussion by pointing out that this feast of the Holy Trinity is celebrated yearly on the Sunday after Pentecost. Ask participants to brainstorm all the images and qualities of God they noticed at the Liturgy of the Word today. You may choose to list these on an overhead or newsprint for all to read.
2. Ask the participants to share with the group one of the images or qualities of God that touched their heart in the scriptures. Affirm and summarize their comments.

Making Connections

1. Offer this background on today's feast: *The early Church experienced God in these three unique manifestations of Father, Son, and Spirit. Over time, the Church formulated the belief that there are three persons in one God. Tertullian (145–220) first used the word "Trinity." The earliest New Testament passage which explicitly links Father, Son, and Spirit was proclaimed today in 2 Corinthians and is the presider's greeting weekly as we come to Mass: "The grace of the Lord Jesus Christ, and the love of God, and the fellowship of the Holy Spirit be with you all!" This feast of the Trinity was officially celebrated in the middle ages.*
2. Ask the participants to talk about their experience of the Trinity through these questions: *Which person of the Trinity do you think about and pray to the most often? What are the times when you pray to this person, and when do you pray to the other persons of the Trinity? What changes have occurred over time in your relationship with the persons of the Trinity?* As they share, comment briefly and invite further discussion.

3. Invite participants to become aware of any questions that they have about belief in the Trinity. Encourage the expressions of their statements or questions in the large group.

Prayer

Invite the participants into prayer in the following manner: *Take a moment to experience the presence of Yahweh, our God, who created everything and who established the covenant with the people of Israel during the period of the Old Testament. Become aware that Jesus, the Christ, is present. In Jesus all was made. He is the revelation of God to us in his life, death, and resurrection. Become aware of the presence of the Spirit, the breath of God present at the time of creation, who now as the Spirit of Jesus continues to blow where it will to bring about the mission of Jesus.* Pause for a moment, then pray: *God, we experience you as Creator, Savior, and Spirit of peace and love. Open us to the fullness of your presence with us. We praise you, our loving God, now and forever. Amen.*

Extended Catechesis

SESSION FOCUS: *The Holy Trinity*

Gathering

A. **Sunday:**
   1. Greet and welcome the sponsors, team members, and other participants as they join the group.
   2. Ask a catechumen or candidate to briefly summarize the Dismissal Catechesis.
   3. Invite everyone into a moment of quiet. Lead the group in singing "Holy God, We Praise Thy Name" (Ignaz Franz, text), verses 1 and 2. Provide hymnals so all may join in singing. Then pray in these or your own words: *God, our Lord, you are loving, slow to anger, rich in kindness. We praise you for your goodness. You are Savior. We honor you for your total gift of self. You are the Spirit of life, forgiveness, and peace. We delight in your tender love. One God, three persons, be near to us who are formed in your image. Dwell in us. We ask this, Father, Son, and Holy Spirit, one God, living and true, forever and ever. Amen.* Proclaim the gospel: John 3:16–18.

B. **Weekday:**
   1. Welcome and greet the sponsors, team members, and additional participants. Invite them to gather in the circle with the same centerpiece as the Dismissal Catechesis.
   2. Ask everyone to reflect on the last few days and respond to the following: *Describe an example from the last few days when you had an experience of God, the Creator, of Jesus, or of the Holy Spirit.*

3. Lead this celebration of the Word:
- Song: "Holy God, We Praise Thy Name," verses 1 and 2
- Sign of the Cross, Greeting (from 2 Corinthians 13:13)
- First Reading: Exodus 34:4–6, 8–9
- Sing Psalm Response: Daniel 3:42–56, or a psalm of praise
- Sing Alleluia
- Gospel: John 3:16–18
- Silent Reflection
- Closing Prayer: Use the prayer from A.3 above.

The Word (30 min.)

1. Present this background on the scriptures, expanding on these words from your reading of the Word in Liturgy section found in Understanding this Sunday:

In today's first reading from Exodus, God gives us the name of "Lord." Earlier in the Book of Exodus, God simply says: "I am who I am." This reading recounts the second giving of the law, after the people of Israel broke the covenant by worshiping the golden calf. Today's gospel from John cites God's love for the world in giving us his only Son. God's Son was given not only in his incarnation, but also in his suffering and death on the cross.

2. Ask the participants to discuss these questions in small groups: *What do you hear God saying through these words of scriptures? In what ways have you experienced this God who keeps establishing covenant and giving self in love? Give concrete examples.*

3. When they are finished, invite each group to share a summary of their discussion. Then ask participants to share some examples of various ways they experience God in day-to-day life.

Catholic Teaching (30 min.)

1. List the three persons of the Trinity on newsprint. Continue with the Church's teaching on the Trinity, being sure to include the following points:
- Christian faith is founded on belief in the Trinity. Baptism is prayed, "In the name of the Father, and of the Son, and of the Holy Spirit."
- The doctrine of the Trinity, three persons in one God, is the central mystery of the Christian faith because it is the mystery of God's very self.
- The doctrine of the Trinity is found in the Apostles' Creed, and again in the Nicene Creed formulated in 325. This creed states the belief in a God of three equal persons who have no beginning or end. This belief arises out of and expresses a continuing human experience of God as Father, Son, and Spirit. From the time of Jesus the Spirit is further identified as the Spirit of Jesus who continues the mission of Jesus to bring about the reign of God in the world.

- The Church expresses this threefold experience of God in the baptismal formula in scripture (for example, 2 Corinthians 13:13 and Ephesians 4:4–6), in preaching, catechesis, and in the prayer of the Church. We begin Mass and many other prayers as we are baptized, "In the name of the Father, and of the Son, and of the Holy Spirit." The *Sacramentary* addresses prayers to God that conclude with "We ask this through our Lord Jesus Christ, your Son, who lives and reigns with you and the Holy Spirit, one God, for ever and ever."
- The words "substance," "essence" and "nature" indicate the unity of God. The term "person" designates the three—Father, Son, and Spirit—who are distinct. The word "relation" indicates that their distinction lies in the relationship of each to the others.

2. Invite the participants to brainstorm instances where each of the persons of the Trinity are found in scripture. List these on the newsprint.

3. Ask the participants to reflect on their experience of God using the following questions: *Identify the qualities and names you associate with each person of the Trinity. What for you is the significance for God to be a Trinity of persons?* Encourage the participants to write their reflection in the Participant Book on page 132. When they are finished, invite them to share their responses in the large group. As they share, list the various qualities and names associated with each person of the Trinity on newsprint.

4. Invite and respond to any questions the participants may have on the Trinity.

Putting Faith into Practice

1. Ask the participants to reflect on one concrete way they can witness to a loving, triune God by sharing this love with some of God's people this week. Participants may write this action in the "I want to put by faith into action by" section of the Participant Book on page 133. When they are ready, invite participants to share this action in their small groups.

2. Teach the group this prayer, a doxology, which gives praise to the Trinity: *Glory to the Father, and to the Son, and to the Holy Spirit. As it was in the beginning, is now, and will be forever. Amen.*

Prayer

Pray together the prayer: *"Glory to the Father. . . ."* Then sing "Holy God, We Praise Thy Name," verse 3.

The Body and Blood of Christ

Understanding this Feast:

Background for Catechesis

The Word in Liturgy

Deuteronomy 8:2–3, 14–16
Psalm 147:12–13, 14–15, 19–20
1 Corinthians 10:16–17
John 6:51–58

The reverence for the Lord's presence in the Eucharist dates from the earliest generations of Christians, as is clear from the "bread of life" discourse in John and the meal narratives with eucharistic overtones found in all the gospels. But it was not until the tenth and eleventh centuries that devotion to the Blessed Sacrament as an object of prayerful adoration developed extensively among the Christian faithful. A feast of the Blessed Sacrament was first celebrated in 1246, and within a hundred years the observance had spread throughout the Christian world. Pope Urban IV commissioned St. Thomas Aquinas in 1264 to compose the formularies for a Mass that he ordered extended to the universal Church. Those texts are still used today as the opening prayer, the prayer over the gifts, and the prayer after communion in the Roman Missal.

Each of today's readings illuminates some aspect of today's feast. Deuteronomy recalls the way in which God fed the people of Israel in the desert with manna, that miraculous food which Christians were later to see as a prefiguration of the Eucharist. In contrast with Exodus 16, however, which presents the gift of manna simply as a miracle of feeding the people, today's passage interprets this event in a more particular way. The manna is to teach Israel that God's Word is the source of life on which she must depend. As Israel relied on manna for life in the desert, so the people must continually depend on the Word of God. The latter portion of this reading is taken from Deuteronomy 8:7–20, which is composed in the style of a hymn, rich in the praise of God "who brought you out" (v. 14), "who led you" (v. 15), "who fed you" (v. 16).

Psalm 147, chosen for today's liturgy no doubt because of its imagery of wheat, is a psalm of praise. Not only has God fed the people, he has "filled" them. By the hand of God they are sated

with the finest wheat, literally the "kidney fat of wheat"—a delectable and rich portion. Again, God's Word and command are linked to the protection and fulfillment that the people are given. All these benefits signal honors accorded to none but the chosen people.

The cup of blessing to which St. Paul refers in today's reading from 1 Corinthians was a common feature of Jewish meals. After a meal, a prayer of thanksgiving was offered over this "blessing cup" of wine. Paul is speaking of the Christian Eucharist, however, when he asserts that this cup of blessing "which *we* bless" is "a sharing" (communion, participation) in the blood of Christ. One may easily see in this a reference to the believer's participation in Christ's saving and atoning death, for a cup of blood was commonly part of a sacrifice. Nevertheless, the accent of this reading is more appropriately placed on the "communal" dimension of the cup and bread. The context of the passage is a discussion of eating meat offered to idols, and the implications of Paul's reflection on the Eucharist are that participation in a ritual meal entails a communal identity which is decisive. For Paul, the Church is the body of Christ, and our sacramental participation makes us into Christ's body.

Today's pericope from John's gospel contains the climax of the "bread of life" discourse, and announces a bold promise of eternal life. Nevertheless, the sayings of Jesus contained here are some of the most difficult for his contemporaries to grasp, because the language of eating flesh and drinking blood is as graphic and as shocking as a description of cannibalism would be to us today. The passage has been interpreted variously throughout Christian history, with two main trends: understanding the flesh and blood of Jesus to be his teaching, and the ingestion of them to be the act of believing in what he has

260   *The Body and Blood of Christ*

revealed; and a eucharistic interpretation, that in consuming the bread and wine of the Eucharist the believer is made one with the Lord himself, who is fully identified with the elements. The latter interpretation is obviously the one most favored by a feast concerning the real presence of Jesus in the Eucharist. It does not, however, rule out the relevance of faith in the teachings of Jesus for obtaining eternal life, for when believers "take in" the flesh and blood of Christ, they must surely embrace his teachings as well. Again and again, the passage returns to the theme of life, promised through this bread who is Jesus. It surpasses even the gift of manna, for it brings eternal life.

Catholic Doctrine

The Real Presence

On this feast when the Church contemplates the eucharistic banquet of the Lord, we proclaim our belief that "when we eat this bread and drink this cup we proclaim your death, Lord Jesus, until you come in glory" (*Roman Missal*, Memorial Acclamation, Eucharistic Prayer). As followers of Jesus, we carry out his command to "do this in remembrance of me" (1 Corinthians 1:24–25). What we remember is the sacrifice of the Lord which in the Eucharist we offer again to the Father through the gifts of bread and wine through the power of the Holy Spirit and the words of Christ (CCC 1357).

The assembly gathers in faith, and God makes present Jesus, his body and blood in the sacred species, the bread and wine offered in the Eucharist. This sacrament is "the source and summit of the Christian life," extolled by the Second Vatican Council (LG 11). It is a memorial of Jesus' death and resurrection, a sacrament of love, a sign of unity, a bond of charity, a paschal banquet "in which Christ is consumed, the mind is filled with grace, and a pledge of future glory is given to us" (SC 47).

The emphatic proclamation of this awesome mystery is only possible because from the earliest times the Church has experienced in this sacred meal the real presence of Jesus Christ. This means that when we eat this bread and drink this cup, although we taste the fruits of the earth and our human hands (bread and wine), we experience in faith the body and blood of our Lord and Savior who sacrificed himself on our behalf. Thus, St. Ignatius describes this sacred meal as "bread of angels, bread from heaven, medicine of immortality" (St. Ignatius of Antioch, *Epistula ad Ephesios*, 20, 2: SCh 10, 76).

We believe that when the Church gathers, Mass is celebrated with the Liturgy of the Word and the Liturgy of the Eucharist, and within the Eucharist, bread and wine are presented and prayed over, the Spirit of God descends and makes those elements into the body and blood of Jesus Christ. The Church has insisted from the earliest times that this is the "real presence" of Christ, that is, real in the fullest sense a substantial presence by which Christ, both God and man, makes himself wholly and entirely present (CCC 1374). Why? Most especially because Jesus himself promised this and secondarily because the apostles and those who have followed in this Church have experienced it to be so.

A substantial change takes place within the elements of bread and wine. Indeed, the term in our tradition for the change which takes place is "transubstantiation" (CCC 1376). St. Ambrose says of this change, "Be convinced that this is not what nature has formed, but what the blessing has consecrated. The power of the blessing prevails over that of nature, because by the blessing nature itself is changed. . . . Could not Christ's word, which can make from nothing what did not exist, change existing things into what they were not before? It is no less a feat to give things their original nature than to change their nature" (St. Ambrose, *De mysteriis* 9, 50; 52: PL 16, 405–07).

Catholic Culture

Under ordinary circumstances, the faithful are expected to fast for one hour before receiving communion. This fast is a spiritual reminder of our hunger and thirst for the Lord and of the exceptional nature of the food and drink of the Eucharist. We put all other things aside so that we may focus on the sacred meal that brings us salvation.

For the first six centuries of the life of the Church, communion was routinely offered to all the faithful under the forms of bread and wine. During the middle ages, however, the practice of sharing the chalice with the laity gradually died out. In response to challenges from the Protestant reformers in the sixteenth century, the Council of Trent affirmed the practice of sharing the consecrated bread alone. In our own century, however, the Second Vatican Council restored the ancient practice of offering communion under both forms to the laity, so that, in the words of Pope Paul VI, "a fuller light" would shine on the eucharistic banquet.

Certain laypeople in the Catholic Church today are commissioned to assist in the distribution of communion at Mass and in bringing communion to the sick and homebound. These eucharistic ministers are usually well known in the local community for their sincere devotion to the Eucharist and desire for service. They are called special or extraordinary ministers of the Eucharist, because the ordinary ministers are priests and deacons. The Eucharist itself is always the same, no matter who ministers it.

The Catholic tradition has always maintained the use of a common cup in communion, in order to emphasize the communal nature of our eucharistic sharing. Whether each person takes the cup and drinks from it, or the consecrated bread is dipped in the consecrated wine (intinction), or, as in the Eastern rite Catholic Churches, the consecrated bread is soaked in the consecrated wine and placed in the mouth with a spoon, all employ a common cup.

SESSION PLAN: The Body and Blood of Christ

Dismissal Catechesis (30 min.)

Getting Started

1. Prepare the space ahead of time with a circle of chairs around a table draped with a white cloth. On the table place a loaf of bread, grapes, and a chalice or pottery cup. Include candles in the arrangement.
2. Lead the candidates and catechumens to the circle, place the Lectionary on the table and light the candles. Begin the session by praying the portion of the hymn contained in the first reading, Deuteronomy 8:14–15, beginning with the line, "Remember, the Lord, your God . . ." and ending with ". . . a food unknown to your fathers." Invite the participants to reflect on the symbols on the table as you pray.

First Impressions

1. Invite the participants to name some of the insights that came to mind as they heard the prayer from Deuteronomy and reflected upon the symbols on the table.
2. Guide them in recalling some of the images from today's Liturgy of the Word by asking these questions: *As you entered the church today, what did you notice that was different? What was the mood or spirit of the liturgy? What can you remember from the scriptures that were proclaimed? What was the message in the homily and prayers?* Take one question at a time and affirm their responses, adding comments as you move through your parish celebration.
3. Explain the significance of this feast in these or similar words, using the background provided in Understanding this Sunday as a source of information:
   Today the Church celebrates the feast of the Body and Blood of Jesus, otherwise known as Corpus Christi. This feast of the Blessed Sacrament highlights the eucharistic banquet set before us by the Lord in a provocative remembrance of the sacrifice of Christ, through the sharing of the body and blood of Christ, blessed, broken, proclaimed, and memorialized. Ask the participants to form small groups to discuss these questions: *How did the scriptures, the prayers, and the church environment proclaim and celebrate the presence of Christ? What images and actions brought to life this feast for you? What feelings emerged as you celebrated the Liturgy of the Word this morning?*

Making Connections

1. In the large gathering guide the participants through the questions, inviting a few to summarize their discussion. Point to the image of the manna and water provided by Yahweh to the hungry and thirsty Israelites as they wandered in the desert. Ask: *As you think about God's care for these people in the first reading, what can you say about God?*
2. After some responses, gather everyone back into their small groups to discuss these questions: *What does the gift of manna signify in your life? As you think about the sustenance of manna—just enough for each day—in what ways has God filled and sustained you one day at a time?* When the discussion seems to be ending, gather insights from the small groups in the large gathering.

3. Conclude the discussion by saying: *Israel in the desert relied on manna for life. They learned that they must continually depend on the Word of God for their spiritual sustenance as well. Christians have come to view the gift of manna as a prefiguration of the Eucharist.*

Prayer

Distribute copies of Psalm 147:12–13, 14–15, 19–20. Invite everyone to reflect on all that has been said as they meditate on the symbols on the table. Then invite all to stand and pray the psalm, alternating from right to left side. Close by leading all in singing the first verse of the Gathering Hymn from the liturgy.

Extended Catechesis

SESSION FOCUS: *The Real Presence*

Gathering

A. Sunday:
1. Greet and welcome the sponsors and team members as they arrive. Invite them to join the circle of catechumens and candidates.
2. Gather the attention of the participants by leading all in singing "Our Blessing Cup" (Hurd, OCP Publications, 1979). You may sing one or two verses or just repeat the refrain several times. Proclaim the gospel, John 6:51–58. Then distribute copies of the Sequence for today's liturgy (poetic form) and invite the participants to move around the circle, praying the Sequence one verse at a time. Close with another verse or the refrain to "Our Blessing Cup."

B. Weekday:
1. Use the same centerpiece as in the Dismissal Catechesis.
2. As the participants gather in the circle, greet and warmly welcome each person. Light the candles and invite a few participants to share some ways they experienced God's nurture or sustenance these past few days.
3. Lead this celebration of the Word:
   - Song: "Our Blessing Cup," first verse
   - First Reading: Deuteronomy 8:2–3, 14–16
   - Song: "Our Blessing Cup," second verse
   - Sequence: reader for each verse as described in section A
   - Gospel: John 6:51–58
   - Song: "Our Blessing Cup," third verse

The Word (30 min.)

1. Invite the participants to quickly name the words and phrases that come to mind from their experience of singing and listening to the scriptures. When finished, ask a candidate or catechumen to summarize the Dismissal Catechesis.
2. Explain the significance of the second reading, 1 Corinthians 10:16–17, saying: *In the song "Our Blessing Cup," we are reminded of Paul's first letter to the Corinthians. The cup of blessing was a common part of Jewish meals. After a meal, a prayer of thanksgiving was offered over this "blessing cup" of wine. As this practice was incorporated*

into the Christian celebration of Eucharist following Jesus' request at the Last Supper to "do this in memory of me," this cup of blessing is a sharing, a communion in the blood of Christ. The believer shares in Christ's saving, atoning death. Furthermore, this cup of blessing unites individuals in one body, the Church, as we share in the body and blood of Christ by drinking of the cup. Gather the participants into small groups to discuss the significance of the cup of blessing, using these questions as a catalyst: When you think of a common cup, blessed and shared, what feelings are evoked in you? How does this blessing cup unite us in Christ, both his sacrifice and his desire to be one with humankind?

3. Encourage the participants to share some of their responses with everyone. Then continue to offer a background on the gospel, using these or your own words: As we listen to the words of Jesus, "I am the living bread . . ." we hear a bold promise of eternal life. Yet it is difficult to grasp the meaning of this passage because of the language of eating flesh and drinking blood. The traditional interpretation of this text is the Catholic understanding that the flesh and blood of Jesus transformed from bread and wine came directly from Jesus. And as we eat and drink of these elements we become one with Christ who is fully present in them. We are reassured over and over again that when we "take in" the flesh and blood of Christ, we accept his teachings and are promised eternal life.

4. Invite the participants to turn to their Participant Book on page 134 to write their reflections on the meaning of these scriptures. The Reflection exercise is meant to draw them deeper into the mystery of Eucharist and its implications for us, as Church, today. When they have finished, invite them to gather with their sponsor/godparent to share what they have written. As they finish this sharing, encourage any questions that have arisen in the pairs to be articulated in the large group. Respond to those you can and deal with the others by inviting a pastoral minister to present the Church teaching on the real presence of Christ in the next section.

Catholic Teaching (30 min.)

1. Invite a pastoral minister to present the Church's teaching on the real presence of Christ in the Eucharist, asking him to expand on the following points. Or, present the teaching yourself and ask a panel of catechists and staff members to respond to questions after this teaching:
   - In the Eucharist we offer to God the gifts of bread and wine and remember and make present the sacrifice of the Lord on Calvary. Through the power of the Holy Spirit and the words of Christ taken from the Last Supper, the bread and wine become Christ's body and blood.
   - The Eucharist is the source and summit of Christian life.
   - When we eat this bread and drink this cup, although we taste the fruits of the earth and our human hands, we experience in faith the body and blood of our Lord and Savior who sacrificed himself on our behalf.
   - The Church has always taught that Christ is really present under the forms of bread and wine, that is, real in the fullest sense—a substantial presence by which Christ, both God and human, makes himself wholly and entirely present.
   - Although the elements of bread and wine still appear unchanged to our senses, a change of their substance takes place that we cannot see or touch or taste but which is real. The Church calls this change "transubstantiation."

2. Invite the participants to reflect upon and to write their responses to these questions, found in the Participant Book on page 134: Why does the Church continue to celebrate the sacrament of Eucharist? How would you describe the change that takes place in the elements of bread and wine? What do you believe about Eucharist, the real presence of Christ? When they have had sufficient time, invite the same pairs to gather to share their responses. In the large gathering, guide them through the teaching on Christ's real presence in the Eucharist by asking one question at a time and encouraging a few pairs to offer their insights.

3. Invite the participants to remain silent for a brief period, asking them to think back over the session to recall any questions on the Eucharist that might have come to mind. With the help of the panel, respond to their questions, summarizing the teaching on the real presence in a few sentences.

Putting Faith into Practice

1. Explain the concept of fasting prior to eating and drinking the body and blood of Jesus: Under ordinary circumstances, the faithful are expected to fast for one hour before receiving communion. This fast is a spiritual reminder of our hunger and thirst for the Lord and of the exceptional nature of the food and drink of the Eucharist. We put all other things aside so that we may focus on the sacred meal that brings us salvation. In the large gathering, invite the participants to share their feelings on this gesture indicating our hunger for the Lord of life. Invite team members to share their past memories regarding eucharistic fasting.

2. Invite a lay minister who brings Eucharist to the housebound to offer a brief witness of this ministry. Encourage this person to stress stories of hunger for the Lord and the desire to be united with the rest of the parish community in the people to whom they bring Eucharist. Use the Catholic Culture section found in Understanding this Sunday to explain the practice of commissioning lay ministers for Eucharist if needed.

Prayer

Gather the participants' attention by leading them in singing the last verse of "Our Blessing Cup." Then pray in these words: Jesus, our bread of life and cup of blessing, we long to unite ourselves with you by eating your flesh and blood blessed, broken, and shared in the sacrament of Eucharist. As we lift our hands to receive you, expand our hearts that we might understand that we are saying "yes" to opening our hearts to receive our brothers and sisters across the globe. Give us the wisdom to understand that our "amen" to your gift of yourself is our assent to join our sufferings with yours and to surrender our lives to your passion and death. Reveal to us the fullness of Eucharist that we might grow and be nourished for the work of carrying your real presence to the world. Amen.

The Birth of John the Baptist

JUNE 24

The Word in Liturgy

Isaiah 49:1–6
Psalm 139:1–3, 13–14, 14–15
Acts 13:22–26
Luke 1:57–66, 80

Our earliest record of a feast celebrating the birth of Jesus stems from the fourth century. Not long afterward, Christians began to mark the day of John the Baptist's birth as well. It is surely not coincidental that the date assigned for Christ's birth was the winter solstice—the "birth" of the sun—while the date observed for John's birth was the summer solstice six months earlier. The Church celebrates the feast of most saints on the day of their *death*, when they entered heaven. We celebrate the *birth* of only two saints, however: the Blessed Virgin Mary and John the Baptist. Mary, by virtue of her immaculate conception, entered the world sinless at her birth. Tradition has suggested that John was also freed from original sin when he "leaped for joy" in his mother's womb upon meeting the Savior (Luke 1:41, 44); and so he, too, is regarded as having entered sinless into the world at his birth.

The liturgy chooses Isaiah's second Suffering Servant Song to be read at the Mass during the day. (The Vigil Mass also has a text from Jeremiah about being called before birth.) Scholars debate the exact origin and reference intended by this collection of poems in the Book of Isaiah that speak of a mysterious figure who will redeem his people through vicarious suffering. Most often, Christians have used the Suffering Servant Songs to understand more deeply the identity and mission of Jesus. Here, however, the vocation of the precursor of Jesus is highlighted. The application of this text to John seems dictated especially by its emphasis on the prophet being chosen from the womb ("from my mother's womb he gave me my name"), an emphasis found also in today's psalm ("you knit me in my mother's womb").

The reading from the Acts of the Apostles is taken from a sermon preached by Paul to the Jews of Antioch in Pisidia during his first missionary journey. Paul first offers a quick recapitulation of God's saving history of the chosen people, down to the choice of David as king, from whose descendants God has brought forth "Jesus, a savior for Israel." He then describes the important role played by John in announcing the coming Messiah through his preaching of a "baptism of repentance" and by the way he pointed to the one who would come after him. Here as elsewhere in the New Testament, the sacred author goes to the trouble of including John's explicit statement that he was not the messiah, only the precursor. Scholars point out that the background to these statements must have been a flourishing cult of the Baptist who refused to acknowledge the superior role of Jesus in the plan of salvation. Authentic Christian faith, while recognizing John's role as secondary to Jesus, nonetheless sees in him the greatest of the prophets.

The key to a proper interpretation of Luke's infancy narratives is to remember that everything he has written in his gospel is ultimately about the identity of Jesus as the Christ, Lord, and Savior. Hence, Luke's description of the miraculous events surrounding the birth of John the Baptist is meant to contribute to the reader's conviction that a divine destiny is unfolding in this elaborate choreography. The intricately interwoven narratives of the birth of Jesus and of John reveal the links between their destinies as part of a single divine plan ("Was not the hand of the Lord upon him?"). Today's reading gives only a portion of the Lucan material on John, but enough for us to sense the significance of his birth as an essential step preparing for his role in announcing Jesus. John will later announce to his contemporaries what the angels proclaim at Bethlehem: "a savior . . . who is Messiah and Lord." (Luke 2:11)

Catholic Doctrine

Human Cooperation with Divine Grace

The portrayal of John the Baptist's birth and his ministry in the gospel exemplifies how grace and human freedom intersect to unfold the divine plan of salvation. The birth of John emphasizes divine initiative. John's ministry represents the response of freedom.

We Catholics understand grace to be the favor of God, the free, undeserved assistance that the divine imparts to us in order that we might respond to his invitation to become adopted children of the Most High, to partake in the divine nature and eternal life (CCC 1996). In a word, grace is a gift from God. And this gift is manifold. It enables us to participate in the Trinitarian life. By baptism we are incorporated into Christ and therefore as adopted children can call God our "Father," in union with the Son. In baptism we are also gifted with the life of the Spirit who breathes charity in us and who forms the Church.

Significant in an understanding of the Catholic perspective on grace is the notion that the very preparation for receiving God's favor is already the work of grace. God is the author who brings to completion the good work already begun in us (CCC 2001). St. Augustine informs us, "Indeed we also work, but we are only collaborating with God who works, for his mercy has gone before us. It has gone before us so that we may be healed, and follows us so that once healed, we may be given life; it goes before us so that we may be called, and follows us so that we may be glorified; it goes before us so that we may live devoutly, and follows us so that we may always live with God: for without him we can do nothing" (De natura et gratia, 31: PL 44, 264).

Thus, God reaches out to us. God acts. And that action of love toward us by God invites a response.

It is interesting that while the Catechism treats grace extensively in the latter part (around paragraph 2000), the very first paragraph of the entire work refers to the calling or invitation of God whose purpose is that we might seek God out, know God, and love God with all our strength (CCC 1). In other words, the first words of our Catholic compendium

of teaching refer to our vocation in God. The initiative of God invites our free response to collaborate in the divine plan of salvation for this world. This divine drama is illustrated in capsule by the birth and ministry of John the Baptist. St. Augustine instructs, "The Church observes the birth of John as a hallowed event. We have no such commemoration for any other fathers; but it is significant that we celebrate the birthdays of John and Jesus. This day cannot be passed by. . . . John was born of a woman too old for childbirth; Christ was born of a youthful virgin. The news of John's birth was met with incredulity, and his father was struck dumb. Christ's birth was believed, and he was conceived through faith. . . . Thus [John] represents times past and is the herald of the new era to come. As a representative of the past, he is born of aged parents; as a herald of the new era, he is declared to be a prophet while still in his mother's womb. For when yet unborn, he leapt in his mother's womb at the arrival of blessed Mary . . . even before he was born; it was revealed that he was to be Christ's precursor. . . . These are divine happenings, going beyond the limits of our human frailty" (Sermo 293, 1–3: PL 38, 1327–1328 found in LH, vol. 3, Birth of John the Baptist, Office of Readings, p. 1487).

Catholic Culture

A splendid early mosaic depiction of John the Baptist can be found in the dome of the Arian Baptistry at Ravenna. The very center of the dome is dominated by Jesus' baptism by John as the Spirit in the form of a dove hovers over Christ's head and the bearded Father sits opposite the Baptist, looking on. This center scene is circled by the Apostles who move in stately procession with garland crowns toward a throne upon which sits a jeweled cross (John Beckwith, Early Christian and Byzantine Art, Yale University Press, New Haven, 1979, p. 111).

An extremely detailed silver altar frontal which shows scenes from the life of the Baptist is found in the St. John the Baptist Baptistry, Florence. Commissioned in 1367, it was not finished until 1477. On the feast day of St. John, relics were displayed on this altar. The Baptist is the patron saint of the city of Florence and was considered an important civic symbol (Evelyn Welch, Art and Society in Italy 1350–1500, Oxford University Press, New York, 1997, pp. 47–8).

John the Baptist is the patron saint of Puerto Rico, and the feast of his birth is a festive occasion for Puerto Rican Catholics. The capital, San Juan, is also named for him.

Dismissal Catechesis (30 min.)

Getting Started

1. Prepare the space with a cloth and lighted candle, and place the Lectionary on the center table. Gather in a circle of chairs.

2. Invite the participants into a moment of silent prayer. Sing "You Are Near" (Schutte) or another version of today's Psalm 139. Pray in these or similar words:
God, today we celebrate the feast of John the Baptist whose voice announces the coming of your reign. May we hear your voice and live more fully in your kingdom. We pray through Christ, the true light of the world. Amen.

First Impressions

Have the participants recall their experience at the liturgy, from their awareness as they gathered with the community, to the hymn, collect, readings, sung psalm, homily, and dismissal. After a moment of reflection, invite them to go around the circle and share something that was meaningful for them.

Making Connections

1. Ask the participants to name what they sense God was saying to them personally in the liturgy today. After a moment of reflection, have them share this in pairs.

2. Ask each pair to express some of their sharing in the large group. Highlight any observations about John the Baptist that are mentioned, and relate them to Christian life today.

3. State that today's words in Isaiah 49 talk of the experience of being called from birth and named in "my mother's womb" to be not only God's servant, but "a light to the nations." Invite participants to sense themselves as being formed in their mother's womb and named by God. Suggest to the participants that God has been leading them from the time in their mother's womb through all of their life experiences to be God's servant and voice. Ask participants to talk in pairs about what it's like to be aware of God's forming, naming, leading, and sending them personally. Then invite some large group sharing.

4. Conclude by asking participants to name something they want to take with them from today's liturgy and sharing. Go around the circle for this discussion.

Prayer

Invite participants to look inside themselves and become aware of the God who has made them. After a moment of quiet, proclaim Isaiah 49:1–6. Sing the refrain of "You Are Near" or Psalm 139.

Extended Catechesis

SESSION FOCUS: *Human Cooperation with Divine Grace*

Gathering

A. Sunday:
Welcome sponsors, spouses, fiancees, and team members. Ask them to form groups of four, with two sponsor/catechumen or sponsor/candidate pairs in a group. Additional people also form groups of four. Invite everyone into a moment of silence. Briefly share the content of the dismissal catechesis. Sing "You Are Near." Proclaim the gospel from the Lectionary.

B. Weekday:
Ask each participant to name a time since Sunday when they in some way pointed another person to God and God's reign. Go around the circle for this naming. Then pray this celebration of the Word or use your own design:

- Song: "You Are Near"
- Sign of the Cross, Greeting
- Proclaim: Isaiah 49:1–6
- Sing Psalm 139
- Proclaim Luke 1:57–66, 80
- Pray: *God, John the Baptist challenges us to repent and follow Christ. May our ears and hearts hear his message. Guide us to the way of salvation and peace. We ask this through Christ, the light of the world. Amen.*

The Word (30 min.)

1. Give some background on the setting of today's gospel. State that Elizabeth and Zechariah, like Abraham and Sarah, were elderly. Note that as with Mary, an angel came and announced to Zechariah that they would have a child. Add that the angel's greeting was also, "Do not be afraid," but when Zechariah asked how this would be, he was struck mute. State that the angel said the child's name was to be "John," which means "Yahweh has shown favor." Note that people were in disbelief of Elizabeth as she named the child John because usually a male child was named after the father or some other male in the family, which was not the present situation. State that the stories surrounding John's birth, as that of Jesus, are wonderful in themselves. Ask participants to recall any feelings about God's action or important stories about a birth of a child in their own family. Invite some small group sharing. Invite some response in the large group.

2. Invite participants to hear the gospel again and notice what happened in people as a result of this amazing story, especially in seeing Zechariah being struck mute, and then speaking at the time of the child's naming. Invite some large group response. Bring out from the participants' sharing the praise of God, fear, a sense that something new is happening and that God's hand is active in this child.

3. Then ask participants to share in their small groups their experiences of sensing that God was doing something in their lives. Invite some large group response. Highlight the awakening to and anticipation of God's action. Point out that John the Baptist is a pivotal character in scripture, a transition as a prophet before Christ who makes Christ known. Note that this uniqueness is reflected in the Church's liturgical calendar that celebrates only three births, that of Jesus, Mary, and John the Baptist. State that other saints are remembered on the day of their death, their "birth" into eternal life.

4. Ask participants to become aware of this present moment in their lives as a time when something new is happening at God's hand. Besides the general sense of becoming Catholic, invite participants to notice in a concrete way the newness of what God is doing in them. Have them share this in small groups.

Catholic Teaching (30 min.)

1. Invite the participants to brainstorm everything they know about John the Baptist. Prepare a time line of his life, from conception to his beheading. Fill in events on paper as participants name them. Include the visitation with the moments between his conception and naming in the temple. Note to the participants the familial relationship between John the Baptist and Jesus. Point out that little is known about John the Baptist's life from this time in the temple until his public appearance preaching repentance and announcing that God's reign is here.

2. State that scholars believe John was an ascetic and probably associated with the Essene community near Qumran. Note that John wore camel's hair clothing and ate locusts and wild honey (Matthew 3:4). State that John spoke with fierce passion ("You brood of vipers!" Luke 3:7) and preached repentance of sins. Talk about John's role in announcing the Good News that God's reign is here now. Note the images John used from Isaiah 40:3ff. Point out that as a result of his preaching, people were baptized (hence his name of "Baptist"), but that this baptism is different from Christian baptism. Ask participants what kinds of words, e.g., strong, fearsome, comforting, usually move them to change. Invite some small and large group sharing.

3. State that John was utterly important as the messenger of Jesus who prepared the way for him. Note Jesus' words that "among those born of women no one is greater than John; yet the least in the kingdom of God is greater than he." (Luke 7:28) Also bring out the sense in the prologue of John's gospel that John has come as a witness to the light. Ask participants who for them today are messengers that remind them that God's kingdom is now, or who are witnesses to the light of Christ. Invite some large group sharing.

Putting Faith into Practice

Ask participants to name in their small group a concrete way they sense God is calling them to be a messenger to someone that God's reign is now. Encourage their commitment to an action this week.

Prayer

Invite participants to focus their eyes on the lighted candle, and recall that God, who has created and formed them, sends them into the world as a witness to the light of Christ. Ask each person to pray in their hearts for the grace they need to do this. Then pray:

God, use us as you did John the Baptist to announce the presence of Christ to the world. Make our voices strong. Guide us in your truth. We pray through Christ, the light of the world. Amen.

Sing "Prepare the Way of the Lord."

Peter and Paul, Apostles

JUNE 29

Understanding this Feast:

Background for Catechesis

The Word in Liturgy

Acts 12:1–11
Psalm 34:2–3, 4–5, 6–7, 8–9
2 Timothy 4:6–8, 17–18
Matthew 16:13–19

This solemnity honors two great saints who, between them, represent the Church's mission to both Jews (Peter's leadership was exercised from the Jerusalem church) and Gentiles (Paul is known as the "apostle to the Gentiles"). Saint Peter, who is called by Jesus "rock," and who is revered by Catholics as the progenitor of the Petrine ministry which has endured through the centuries, enjoys first place among the apostles and has a profound significance for the Church. Saint Paul is likewise a towering figure, whose theological genius, evangelical fervor, and tireless pastoral ministry were so instrumental in the founding of the Christian religion. When we honor Peter and Paul, in truth we honor the Church as well, for their contributions have forever marked the faith and life of God's people.

The first reading from Acts details Peter's miraculous escape from prison, where he had been placed by Herod Antipas after the beheading of James the Apostle. The role of the angelic messenger, plus the dreamlike effortlessness with which Peter evades multiple guards, is freed from chains, and walks through open iron gates, accentuate the element of divine intervention. The significant mention of the fervent prayer of the Christian community during this crisis makes the further point that the power of prayer outstrips that of tyrants. The wisdom psalm which follows (Psalm 34) celebrates a faith response suitable to the crisis represented by the first reading. After a hymnal introduction and reference to deliverance, the portion of the psalm included in today's liturgy consists of injunctions to trust and fear the Lord.

It is fitting that the second reading, which relates to Paul, is not a narrative, but speaks in the apostle's own voice—since most

of what we know about Paul is learned through his letters. Here, speaking from prison, he reflects on his suffering and imminent death. He uses three metaphors to express the significance of his life. He calls it a "libation," that is, being poured out. A cup of wine or oil poured on the ground at Jewish sacrifices, the libation suggests that Paul sees his death as sacrificial. The "dissolution" he speaks of (in Greek *analusis*) can refer to the unyoking of an animal from a harness. It further suggests that his death will be a release from the labors he has undertaken for the sake of the gospel. Last of all, the metaphor of the athletic contest ("fight" and "race" refer to the striving necessary to life; the "crown" a laurel wreath worn by a victorious athlete) suggests a purposeful life and death, made glorious by an ever-lasting reward in heaven. Paul confesses God's saving presence in his trials, and the passage ends with a prayer of praise—also characteristic of Paul's letters, which are frequently filled with prayer.

The gospel is Matthew's account of the confession at Caeserea Philippi, in which Peter identifies Jesus as the Messiah and Son of God, and is in turn acclaimed by Jesus. Given a new title ("rock" was not a known personal name at that time) and a mission of teaching authority through the passing of the "keys" and the power of binding and loosing, Peter is thus established by Jesus in a special role because of his confession. In the context of today's celebration, the central importance of Peter's ability to proclaim the true identity of Jesus stands out as the key element of the passage. Peter is the one who names Jesus the Messiah, and is thus named by him "the rock" on which he will build his Church.

Catholic Doctrine

Collegiality

Collegiality is a Catholic teaching that describes an essential element in the ecclesial ministry of the bishop. This essential element derives from Jesus, who at the start of his own public ministry called the Twelve to follow him. Selected by Christ and formed as a group, the disciples were sent on mission together. Today, Catholic bishops, who are successors to the apostles, exercise their individual episcopal ministry from within a similar group created by Christ, that is, the college of bishops (CCC 880). They cannot exercise this ministry, however, without also being in communion with the bishop of Rome, the successor of St. Peter and head of this college of bishops (CCC 877).

Early writings attest to collegiality. Aside from the New Testament scriptural references to the Twelve (for example, see Mark 3:14, 4:10, 6:7, 10:32, 11:11, 14:10, Acts 6:2, 1 Corinthians 15:5, and Revelation 12:14), St. Cyprian (d. 258) also spoke of the office of bishop, equality between bishops, and the episcopal college (in Latin, *collegium*). Throughout the ages, different terms have been used to describe the collective union of bishops in addition to "college," such as "order" and "body," but the sense of these other terms signifies the same meaning.

In our own times, the Second Vatican Council also addressed the reality of how the college of bishops functions. The Council reiterated that the body of bishops is the successor to the college of the apostles and affirmed that, "Together with their head, the [pope], and never apart from him, they have supreme and full authority over the universal Church; but this power cannot be exercised without the agreement of the Roman Pontiff" (LG 22).

The most concrete example of collegiality, where the whole body of bishops acts in union with the pope, is seen in the solemn workings of an ecumenical council, in its deliberations and decisions (CCC 884). It is also possible to concretely discern collegiality in the concerted action of all the bishops of the world together with the pope outside of an ecumenical council. Another form of leadership within the Church that manifests collegial workings are specific groupings of bishops organized around provinces, patriarchies, regions, or bishops' conferences by countries (CCC 887). In less concrete fashion, collegiality is also manifested by individual bishops throughout the world who show their concern for the universal Church by governing well their own local diocese (CCC 886).

In addition to these forms of collegial leadership, the Synod of Bishops created by Paul VI on September 15, 1965, also is an example of how the body of bishops works together in fraternity. This synod is a permanent group established as a consultative body to the pope. It represents the entire episcopate. The synod has been summoned to advise the pope on various issues, for example, the unfinished business of the Second Vatican Council (1967), priestly ministry and world justice (1971), evangelization (1974), catechesis (1977), the Christian family (1980), penance and reconciliation (1983), and the laity (1987). Two extraordinary synods have also been called, one which examined the very issue of collegiality and the relationship of bishops' conferences to the Holy See (1969) and another which celebrated the twentieth anniversary of the Second Vatican Council (1985). A recent synod advised John Paul II on the Americas (1998). The synod itself does not issue any authoritative documents but gives input that the pope uses in issuing letters, exhortations, or other papal pronouncements.

What, then, does our Catholic history and our current experience say about collegiality? First, it is expressive of the multiplicity and universality of the whole People of God, the Church, while at the same time it attests to the unity or communion of that people united to one head, the bishop of Rome. Second, it is expressive of the apostolicity of the Church, which traces its origins to the call of Jesus to the Twelve, a group or college of leaders sent on mission by the Lord.

Finally, it may be very difficult for modern people to accept or grasp the concept involved in a collegial leadership exercised by all the bishops who are one body and yet subject hierarchically to an individual, the pope, as universal and supreme pastor, head of the entire Church. Our Catholic understanding of collegiality relies on the analogy of the human body. It has many parts that function differently and, yet, for them to function effectively, they are attached to one head. Ultimately, though the visible, earthly head of the Church is the pope, the communion expressed by the ministry of the bishops is made possible and knit together by the sacramental gift of Christ himself (CCC 875).

Catholic Culture

At the local level, the Catholic diocese also exhibits a collegial character in the priests' council that advises the bishop. It has no authoritative power but, like the Synod of Bishops, it is formed as a consultative body for the bishop of a local diocese. The bishop, by canon (Church) law, must listen to it and seek its advice before certain significant actions can be taken, for example, the creation of a new parish or the closure of an existing parish.

According to an ancient custom of the Church, an ordaining bishop who is consecrating a new bishop must, ordinarily, be assisted by two other bishops who co-consecrate. The three of them together signify the whole body of bishops. In the liturgy for ordination, the suggested homily addresses the assembly and emphasizes collegiality: "Gladly and gratefully, therefore, receive our brother whom we are about to accept into the college of bishops by the laying on of hands. Respect him as a minister of Christ and a steward of the mysteries of God" (OB 18).

Dismissal Catechesis (30 min.)

Getting Started

1. Prepare a center table with a red cloth, a large rock that can be passed around, a candle, and a place for the Lectionary. Gather in a circle of chairs.

2. Lead the candidates and catechumens to the circle, place the Lectionary on the table, and light the candle. Invite them to reflect on the presence of Peter and Paul, strong apostles and martyrs. Pray in these or similar words:

   God, we praise you today as we honor Peter and Paul who, with deep faith in you, proclaimed your gospel without fear, even fear of death. Strengthen us with this same faith that we may proclaim your gospel to others. We ask this through Christ, our Lord. Amen.

First Impressions

1. Ask the participants to share in pairs something that caught their attention from the liturgy today.

2. Invite them to share their insights in the large group. Facilitate conversation around what each person brings forth. Comment that the liturgical color red is used for the feasts of apostles and martyrs.

3. Ask the catechumens and candidates to brainstorm all they know and have heard about Peter and Paul. Bring out the awareness that Peter, the Church's first leader in the faith, spread the faith to the people of Israel, while Paul, who was converted, taught the faith to the Gentiles from various nations. Note that both Peter and Paul received new names from God.

Making Connections

1. Invite the participants to reflect and then name who the apostles of the faith have been for them in their lives, either by what they have experienced personally or by what they have observed. After the names are shared, ask the participants to talk about ways that this same faith has spread to them.

2. Then ask them to formulate one sentence about what celebrating this feast of Peter and Paul means to them. Go around the circle for this sharing.

Prayer

Invite the participants to name something they need to be a stronger apostle of the faith. Then pray in these or your own words:

God, you give us the gift of faith and call us to share the faith we have received with others. Give each of us what we need to be your apostles in all dimensions of our lives. We pray in Jesus' name. Amen.

Extended Catechesis

SESSION FOCUS: *Collegiality*

Gathering

A. **Sunday:**

1. Greet and welcome the sponsors and team members as they arrive. Invite them to join the circle of catechumens and candidates. Invite them to sit in groups of four with two sponsor/catechumen or sponsor/candidate pairs in a group. Ask a candidate or catechumen to give a brief summary of the dismissal sharing.

2. Lead the participants in singing "We Are Called" (David Haas, GIA Publications, 1988). Then ask the participants to reflect upon the faith of Peter and Paul and the long tradition of the handing down and spreading of faith begun in them. Pass the rock around the circle and invite the participants to pray and reflect on the meaning of Jesus calling Simon "rock." Proclaim Matthew 16:13–19.

B. **Weekday:**

1. Use the same centerpiece as in the Dismissal Catechesis.

2. As the participants gather in the circle, greet and warmly welcome each person. Light the candle. Pass the rock from one person to the next, inviting them to reflect upon the meaning of our faith being handed down from Christ through the centuries. While holding the rock, ask the participants to name one way over the past few days that they did something to spread the faith or a way in which another strengthened their own faith.

3. Lead this celebration of the Word:
   - Song: "We Are Called" (David Haas, GIA Publications, 1988)
   - Sign of the Cross, Greeting
   - First Reading: Acts 12:1–11
   - Sing Psalm 34
   - Second Reading: 2 Timothy 4:6–8, 17–18
   - Sing Alleluia
   - Gospel: Matthew 16:13–19
   - Prayer: *Through the prayers of the apostles Peter and Paul, may we who received faith through their preaching share their joy in following the Lord and spreading the faith of the Church. We pray in the name of Jesus. Amen.*

The Word (30 min.)

1. Explain to the group that this event of Jesus asking his disciples "Who do people say that I am?" is found in Matthew, Mark, and Luke. Note that Matthew's gospel adds Jeremiah, an important prophet in the Jewish community, as one of the responses. Explain also that Peter, as the rock or foundation of the Church, gave his life to spread the

faith and eventually was martyred. In their small groups, ask the participants to share what they think it might have been like for Peter to be called "rock," to have the keys of the kingdom entrusted to him, and to live this out in his life. After sufficient time, invite some large group sharing.

2. Recall for the participants that in the reading from Acts 12:1–11, James had just been beheaded when Peter was taken into custody. Note that Acts says the Church, meaning the community of believers, was praying fervently for people. Bring to mind the wondrous activity of the angels who freed Peter and led him to safety. Note also that Paul was rescued from the lion's mouth. Note that this was a time of great faith in the Church. Ask the participants to name and share in their groups those times in their own lives when they experienced the presence of great faith. Invite some large group response.

3. Call to the attention of the participants the image in the second letter to Timothy, of Paul assuring the community of receiving a crown of victory, running a good race, and keeping the faith. Given the scriptural images of the Church at prayer, an angel freeing Peter from prison, running the race, a crown, the rock, and the keys, ask the participants to note their own images of faith as they live. Give time for small group sharing. Then ask the participants to name some of their images of faith.

4. Explore the ways that Peter and Paul were on fire with their faith in Christ. Note that such fire led them to give their lives to the spread of the Good News of Jesus Christ. Ask the participants to name a concrete way they are being invited to give themselves over more fully to their faith in Christ. Suggest that as they do this, the faith will necessarily spread to others. Allow time for some small group sharing.

Catholic Teaching (30 min.)

1. Prepare a presentation on the Church's teaching on collegiality, expanding on these points:
   - The faith was spread to both Jews and Gentiles through the activity of Peter and Paul.
   - Jesus handed over to Peter authority for the founding of a church. This is symbolized when Jesus gives to Peter the keys of the kingdom of heaven.
   - Jesus gives the power to bind and to loose, which is viewed as the teaching authority.
   - Jesus calls Peter "rock," the first leader to become a follower of Jesus. Peter has come to be called the first pope, and all popes are successors of Peter. The office is sometimes referred to as "the chair of Peter."

2. Ask the participants to name popes that they have heard about, including the present pontiff. You may want to specifically mention John XXIII, who is known for calling the Second Vatican Council; Paul VI, who is known for the implementation of Vatican II as well as his work for evangelization; and Pope John Paul II, one of the longest reigning popes, who is known for his many trips to make known the message of Christ as well as his youth gatherings.

3. Point out the following concepts on collegiality:
   - The pope is also the bishop of Rome, which is understood as the foundation of unity in the Church.
   - Collegiality is a Catholic teaching that describes an essential element in the ecclesial ministry of the bishop. This element derives from Jesus who at the start of his own public ministry called the Twelve to follow him. Selected by Christ and formed as a group, the disciples were sent on mission together. Thus, Catholic bishops, who are the successors to the apostles, exercise their episcopal ministry today from within a similar group created by Christ, that is, the college of bishops.
   - They cannot exercise this ministry, however, without also being in communion with the bishop of Rome, the successor of St. Peter and head of this college of bishops.
   - In our own times, the Second Vatican Council also addressed the reality of how the college of bishops functions. The Council reiterated that the body of bishops is the successor to the college of apostles and affirmed that, "Together, with their head, the pope, and never apart from him, they have supreme and full authority over the universal Church; but this power cannot be exercised without the agreement of the Roman Pontiff" (LG 22).

4. In the small groups, invite them to share what they know and have heard about the Second Vatican Council. Gather insights and comments in the large group. Summarize with these or similar words:
   An ecumenical council is the most concrete example of collegiality. The whole body of bishops acts in union with the pope in their deliberations and decisions. Another form of leadership within the Church that manifests collegial workings are specific groupings of bishops organized around provinces, patriarchies, regions, or bishops' conferences by countries. In less concrete fashion, collegiality is also manifested by individual bishops throughout the world who show their concern for the universal Church by governing well their own local diocese.
   Give examples of some of the work of the bishops' conference, such as pastoral letters in the area of faith and morals and liturgical concerns.

Putting Faith into Practice

Ask participants to share in their small group something they will do this week to spread the faith to others.

Prayer

Celebrate the Minor Exorcism (RCIA 94J). When the candidates are present, the language needs to be adapted to reflect their baptismal status. Then pray:
God has built the Church upon the rock of Peter's faith.
Raise your hands over the participants and invite the sponsors to do the same as you continue to pray. *May God bless us with a solid faith. Paul's labors and preaching were undaunted in times of trial. May Paul's example inspire us to proclaim our faith. May Peter and Paul's untiring witness and prayers lead us to full life with Christ. We ask this through Christ our Lord. Amen.*

The Transfiguration of the Lord

AUGUST 6

Understanding this Feast:

Background for Catechesis

The Word in Liturgy

Daniel 7:9–10, 13–14
Psalm 97:1–2, 5–6, 9
2 Peter 1:16–19
Matthew 17:1–9

The transfiguration celebrates an event in the life of the Lord, and thus draws the Church into a deeper appreciation of his identity and mission. When the Church proclaims the story of the transfiguration on the second Sunday of Lent, as it does each year, it looks toward the specific ways in which that event prefigures the glory of Easter, and leads the faithful to a renewal of their baptism during the Lenten season. Here, the focus is rather on the glory of God seen in Jesus. We behold God's glory through the apocalyptic vision of the prophet Daniel, we celebrate it through the psalm, we are dazzled by it along with the apostles as we behold the face of Jesus on the high mountaintop, and we affirm it along with the second letter of Peter as a promise of the second coming.

The Book of Daniel, written in the mid-second century B.C., is a combination of edifying stories and apocalyptic literature. The book promotes faithfulness to Judaism and resistance to Hellenizing influences. In it the God of Israel is presented as the Lord of all human history. Today's reading is part of an apocalyptic vision in which the Son of Man, who represents the kingdom of the holy ones of God, comes down from heaven and is given dominion by the "Ancient One," who represents God. The Son of Man in the passage was later taken to be a messianic figure. When "Son of Man" became the preferred title of Jesus, the Church interpreted this passage to point to him, and combined this apocalyptic vision with the notion of suffering. God is presented here, as in the psalm, with the typical features of a theophany (appearance of God to human beings), such as fire and light. Psalm 97 is a hymn of praise to Yahweh as king. It proclaims God, describes a theophany, and closes with a response of joy.

The second letter of Peter, written near the end of the first century or the beginning of the second, uses the name of Peter, but is too late to have been written by Peter himself. (Later authors used the name of an authoritative witness to indicate the importance of the content of the letter.) The purpose of this letter is mainly to warn against the dangers of false teachers. Thus, it reveals the continuing concerns of the early Church in the period after the death of the first apostles. Today's passage encourages the community to expect the *parousia* (second coming of Christ) because of what had been seen by the apostles in the transfiguration.

Because throughout his gospel Matthew is concerned to present Jesus as "the new Moses" delivering "the new law" to "the new Israel," it is significant that he locates the transfiguration on a "high mountain." Like Moses, whose face was shining from the theophany on Mount Sinai, Jesus is portrayed in brilliant light. The cloud overshadowing Jesus also recalls the Jewish concept of the *shekinah,* or shadow of the Almighty, as well as the pillar of cloud that led the Israelites through the desert. It is significant that Moses and Elijah, who represent the law and the prophets, give way to Jesus, who remains alone, thus suggesting that both the law and the prophets reach their culmination in him.

Significant visions of the glory of God have caused apostles, saints, and holy people throughout the centuries to experience religious awe, know their own frailty, and glimpse a future that inspires hope. The feast of the Transfiguration—that vision of Jesus that foreshadowed the resurrection—is an appropriate occasion to reflect on God's immediate and personal revelation to human beings, which may be the subject of today's catechesis.

Catholic Doctrine

Visions and Private Revelations

The starting point for our stance on visions and private revelations can be found in what we believe Jesus himself reveals. The Catholic Church teaches that Jesus Christ alone offers the fullness of God's revelation to us. The mystery of Christ illuminates the mystery of creation (CCC 280). Indeed, in his life, his mission, his suffering, death, resurrection, and ascension, God's Son reveals to us the love of the Father through the Holy Spirit. The apostles witnessed to the truth of the resurrection and, in time, the gospels were set down in writing. Together, Scripture and Tradition form one single deposit of revelation which the Church preserves, preaches from, and interprets in the light of present-day needs. [This subject is treated at greater length in the Fifth Sunday of Ordinary Time, Year C.] Thus, the Second Vatican Council, citing 1 Timothy 6:14 and Titus 2:13, taught, "The Christian economy, therefore, since it is the new and definitive covenant, will never pass away; and no new public revelation is to be expected before the glorious manifestation of our Lord Jesus Christ" (DV 4).

In other words, the Council teaches that everything that God chooses to communicate to us for our salvation has been done so in Jesus and that no new "public" revelation will be given before Christ comes a second time in glory to this world of ours. This does not mean that the content of revelation as given in Jesus cannot be understood anew or interpreted freshly given the situation of the world. It simply means that nothing will be added.

In the history of Christian mysticism there are many examples of individual mystics who have claimed a private experience which communicates or reveals the activity of God. This extraordinary phenomenon may be comprised of images, ideas, or words. This communication of God to the mystic may result in physical, psychological, or intellectual manifestations. The appearances of Mary at Lourdes and Fatima fall into this category of private revelation. Approved by the Church as credible, these apparitions are nonetheless not held by the Church to be part of the content of doctrine or teaching. The approval is stated in the negative, that there is nothing there which would harm the faith. As for the recent Marian apparitions at Medjugorje, the Church has not yet concluded its investigation, although many pilgrims have visited this site and found solace and encouragement to their faith.

As with any image or artistic rendering of the mystery of God's self-revelation to us in Jesus, none of these apparitions or mystical experiences and visions can supersede the Christ event. In that sense, both in art and in these visions, that which is communicated enhances and draws out the meaning conveyed by Jesus Christ, eternal Word of God.

Although it is difficult to precisely define mysticism, some mystics who have related in their writings or preaching the direct experiences of the divine in their personal prayer and contemplation are St. Bernard of Clairvaux (d. 1153), St. Francis of Assisi (d. 1226), Meister Eckhart (d. 1327), St. Bridget of Sweden (d. 1373), St. Catherine of Siena (d. 1380), Julian of Norwich (d. 1420), St. Joan of Arc (d. 1431), St. Teresa of Avila (d. 1582), St. John of the Cross (d. 1591), and St. Ignatius Loyola (d. 1556).

Perhaps St. John of the Cross speaks for all of the mystics down through the ages when he writes, "In giving us his son, his only Word (for he possesses no other), he spoke everything to us at once in this sole Word—and he has no more to say . . . because what he spoke before to the prophets in parts, he has now spoken all at once by giving us the All Who is His Son. Any person questioning God or desiring some vision or revelation would be guilty not only of foolish behavior but also of offending him, by not fixing [their] eyes entirely upon Christ and by living with the desire for some other novelty" (*The Ascent of Mount Carmel*, 2, 22, 3–5, in *The Collected Works*, trsl. K. Kavanaugh, OCD, and O. Rodriguez, OCD, Institute of Carmelite Studies, Washington D.C., 1979, pp. 179–80, or LH, Second Week of Advent, Office of Readings).

Catholic Culture

St. Bridget of Sweden, born into a noble family, married and had eight children, one of whom was St. Catherine of Sweden. She made a pilgrimage to St. James at Compostela, Spain, and upon her husband's death she entered religious life, eventually establishing a monastery for nuns and monks. Making further pilgrimages to the Holy Land, she claimed to have visions of the nativity and the passion from the Virgin herself. These visions were recorded and became the basis for paintings, especially of the nativity, which show Mary dressed in white, kneeling on the ground, with her cloak and shoes beside her and the naked child Jesus from which a brilliant light shines forth overpowering the candle held by Joseph. Grunewald's Isenheim altarpiece panel of the *Virgin and Child* is also associated with her visions. (*Oxford Companion to Christian Art and Architecture*, p. 66).

Dismissal Catechesis (30 min.)

Getting Started

1. Prepare the center of the circle with a lit candle and an icon of the Transfiguration (early fifteenth century, Novgorod School found in *Festal Icons of the Lord*, Sr. Helen Weier [The Liturgical Press]) before the gathering.
2. Invite all to join the circle as you welcome and greet the catechumens and candidates. Have soft instrumental music, for example, the Gregorian chant, playing in the background. Allow some time for the participants to gaze at the icon and pray in quiet.
3. Close the prayer time with the short passage from Daniel 7:9–10, 13–14 used as the first reading in today's liturgy.

First Impressions

1. Invite the group to offer their insights from the Liturgy of the Word and the quiet prayer time with this question: *What is the motif of today's feast?* Listen carefully to their ideas.
2. Continue the discussion of today's feast in small groups. These or similar questions may be used: *What images from today's scriptures are particularly meaningful for you? Where was there consolation and reassurance in these passages? What did you find confusing or difficult to understand?*

Making Connections

1. Continue the conversation in the small groups with these questions: *What do you find troubling in your own journey of faith? Have you ever experienced doubts raised by "false teachers," as did the community to whom Peter's second letter is addressed? Have you felt that God took a long time to "appear" when you needed God's consolation or God's presence?* Encourage the participants to share their experiences of doubt or waiting with one another.
2. Invite the participants to share a few stories of discouragement in the large group. Don't force the sharing, just allow those who are willing and open a short time to share.

Prayer

Close the section by praying Psalm 97. The response of the group after the leader prays two or three verses is: *"The Lord is King; let the earth rejoice."*

Extended Catechesis

SESSION FOCUS: *Visions and Private Revelations*

Gathering

A. Sunday:

1. Welcome and greet the new arrivals as they join the circle. Begin this time of prayer with the song "The Heavens Proclaim the Glory of God." Allow a time of silence for all to view the icon of the Transfiguration. Proclaim the gospel.
2. Continue to pray in these or your own words:
   God of glory and awe, you created all people out of love. You redeemed us by sending your Son Jesus, in whom both the law and the prophets found fulfillment. You sanctify us and remain constantly with us through your Spirit. Let the cloud of your presence continue to overshadow and lead us as it did when it led the Israelites through the desert. Let us never falter or lose hope, but trust that you shall come again in glory to bring your reign to fullness in the Risen Lord. Amen.

B. Weekday:

Lead the Liturgy of the Word outlined below:
- Song: Gathering Hymn from the feast day liturgy
- First Reading: Daniel 7:9–10, 13–14
- Psalm 97: Pray with the same response found in the Dismissal Catechesis
- Second Reading: 2 Peter 1:16–19
- Sing Alleluia
- Gospel: Matthew 17:1–9
- Close singing the "Gloria"

The Word (30 min.)

1. Continue in the same prayerful mode with the following centering meditation. Invite the group to close their eyes, remain quiet, and gradually sink into the depths of their beings, where God dwells. Take time to allow each person to become aware of their breathing, their heartbeat, and move inward. Then begin this imaginative scene, reading slowly and allowing for the meditation to unfold:
   You are part of the close-knit group that follows Jesus. Are you Peter . . . James . . . John? On a bright, warm day, Jesus beckons you to follow him. Your heart beats with excitement. You have been singled out from all the rest. Curious, you walk with him, climbing to the top of the highest mountain. Sweaty and hot, you rush to keep up with the Lord, who is ahead. When you and the others reach the top, you are tired and flushed. Just as you sit to listen to the Master, he is transfigured before your eyes. You are dazzled by the brightness of the light radiating from his whole being. In the bright light you also see Moses and Elijah who appear to be talking with Jesus. Peter wants to set up the festival tents, but as he speaks a cloud wraps around you and the others. You are transfixed as you hear a voice declare, "This is my beloved Son, with whom I am well pleased, listen to him." Your mind is racing, you feel . . . ? You tumble to the ground, prostrate. You are awed and filled with . . . ? Then Jesus reassures you and you stand up to discover Jesus alone. You leave the mountain, returning to this room, and taking up your book begin to journal your experience.
2. Gently invite the participants to remain silent as they take up their Participant Book, turn to the corresponding section on page 140, and begin to write their experience and feelings precipitated by the meditation.

3. Continue by presenting the background to the readings for this feast day.

The intention of the Book of Daniel is to encourage the Jews to remain faithful to their faith and traditions amidst growing persecution from the Hellenistic culture. Today's passage is part of an apocalyptic vision in which the Son of Man, who represents the kingdom of the holy ones of God, comes down from heaven and is given dominion by the "Ancient One" who represents God. An apocalyptic vision is a revelation about heaven or other hidden regions of the cosmos not normally accessible to humans. In this first reading the Jewish community is consoled and sustained by the promise that the Son of Man will share future glory with God's holy ones. In the same vein, the author of 2 Peter reassures the early Christian community that Christ will come again in glory. In the light of their confusion caused by false teachers, the community is encouraged by the eyewitness account of Jesus' glory at the transfiguration. In the gospel, the glory of God is seen in the transfigured form of Jesus on the mountain as an encouragement to his apostles and us.

4. Invite the group to discuss their reaction to these passages, in small groups, with the following questions: *What about these readings do you find encouraging? What does it mean when we speak of God's glory? How do you imagine God's holy ones will share in God's glory?*

Catholic Teaching (30 min.)

1. Continue to share with the large group the concepts found in the Catholic Doctrine section of Understanding this Feast on visions and private revelations. Use the script provided to prepare your own prior to the session:

God is fully revealed to us in the life, ministry, teaching, death, and resurrection of Jesus. We can come to understand God through the Scripture and Tradition of the Church as the primary means of revelation. In other words, everything that God chooses to communicate to us for our salvation has been done so in Jesus and no new "public" revelation will be given before Christ comes a second time in glory. However, the content of that revelation, given in the person of Jesus, can be understood anew or freshly interpreted in the context of the world. Throughout the history of the Church, Christian mystics have claimed private experiences which reveal the activity of God.

2. Invite the participants to share any stories from the lives of the saints or the Marian tradition which include private revelation or visions.

3. Take some time to present a few criteria for authenticating visions. These include: (1) The vision or private revelation may not contradict anything in scripture or the Catholic Tradition; (2) The message of the vision does not add to revelation, but enhances it; (3) The vision usually leads to some common good or builds up God's people, for example, the continued healing at Lourdes.

Putting Faith into Practice

1. Tell the story of Hildegard of Bingen. This summary will be helpful: *Hildegard had a deep spiritual awareness from her early childhood. A vision of a dazzling light came to her at the age of three and continued throughout her lifetime. But she only revealed them to Jutta, her childhood tutor, to whom her parents entrusted Hildegard from the age of eight. When she was forty-three, Hildegard received a prophetic call from God telling her to say and write what she saw and heard. Thus, today we have a record of her visions, poetry, music, and drawings in the book known as* Scivias *(Know the ways). Most of the figures who appeared in Hildegard's visions were images from the Hebrew scriptures. Each vision was interpreted with help from a voice from heaven.* Further reading on Hildegard can be found in Gloria Durka's *Praying with Hildegard of Bingen* (St. Mary's Press) and *Hildegard of Bingen: Scivias, The Classics of Western Spirituality* (Paulist Press).

2. Invite the group to listen to this description of one of her visions:

"It happened that, in the eleven hundred and forty-first year of the Incarnation of the Son of God, Jesus Christ, when I was forty-two years and seven months old, Heaven was opened and a fiery light of exceeding brilliance came and permeated my whole breast, not like a burning but like a warming flame, as the sun warms anything its rays touch. And immediately I knew the meaning of the exposition of the Scriptures. . . . I had sensed in myself wonderfully the power and mystery of secret and admirable visions from my childhood—that is, from the age of five—up to that time, as I do now. This, however, I showed to no one except a few religious persons who were living in the same manner as I." [Hildegard of Bingen, *Scivias*, tr. by Mother Columba Hart and Jane Bishop (Mahwah, NJ: Paulist Press, 1990), pp. 59–60.]

3. Ask the participants to pause and reflect on this question: *When have you experienced God as a warm, revealing light?*

Prayer

While the group is quietly reflecting you may choose to play one of Hildegard's compositions, found on the popular cassette or CD, *Visions*. Close with this prayer excerpt from "Meditations with Hildegard of Bingen":

The soul is kissed by God
in its innermost regions.
With interior yearning,
grace and blessing
are bestowed.
It is a yearning to take on God's
gentle yoke,
it is a yearning to give one's self
to God's way.

The Assumption of Mary

AUGUST 15

Understanding this Feast:
Background for Catechesis

The Word in Liturgy

Revelation 11:19; 12:1–6, 10
Psalm 45:10, 11, 12, 16
1 Corinthians 15:20–26
Luke 1:39–56

The cult of the saints developed gradually in the early Christian centuries. The earliest expressions of devotion to the saints were directed toward martyrs who had shed their blood for the faith. Later, confessors, virgins, and other ascetics gradually were included among those receiving special honor. The definition of the Council of Ephesus (431) that Mary is *Theotokos*, Mother of God, seems to have been a major impetus for the Church's Marian devotion. Today's feast grew up in Jerusalem in the fifth century and was originally called the "Dormition" (falling asleep) of the Virgin. The feast was universally observed by the end of the sixth century in the East and the seventh century in the West, where it came to be called the Assumption. On November 1, 1950, Pius XII defined the dogma of the Assumption as an article of Catholic belief.

The Book of Revelation was written to encourage the early Christian community during a time of persecution. Its exotic language and imagery were a deliberate attempt to hide from the uninitiated the full meaning of its teaching. The section read today starts with a vision of the ark of the covenant in heaven, and then shifts immediately to a woman "clothed with the sun." The ark, kept in the holy of holies of the temple, had been lost when Jerusalem was destroyed in 587 B.C. As a symbol of God's abiding presence, it is replaced here by the woman who gives birth to a child who is acclaimed God's "Anointed One." The imagery of a dragon attempting to snatch the child at its birth is borrowed from the Greek myth of Apollo, pursued by Python but rescued by Zeus. For the Roman authorities persecuting the Christian community, these visions are no more remarkable than their own myths of the gods. For the Christian reader, this was a coded tale of God's ultimate triumph over the demonic forces at work in

the world, especially the forces of the Roman state that were persecuting the Christian community. The woman in labor may be Israel, giving birth to the Messiah, or perhaps Mary, the Messiah's physical mother, or even Holy Mother Church, giving birth to offspring that form the Body of Christ. The responsorial psalm, originally composed for a royal wedding, becomes in the context of today's liturgy a song about the royal nuptials between Christ and his bride, the Church.

In Chapter 15 of Paul's first letter to the Corinthians, he addresses a number of questions that were being posed about the resurrection of the dead. He is concerned to teach clearly two crucial truths: First, Christ has risen from the dead. In the verses immediately preceding today's reading, he has shown the consequences of a denial of Christ's resurrection. Here, he states positively the truth that Christ lives and reigns now "until God has put all enemies under his feet." Second, Paul asserts that those who die in Christ will also share in his resurrection. He uses the image of first fruits to imply that others will follow Christ's lead. And, using the notion of inherited destiny found in traditional Jewish understandings of Adam, he draws a parallel between Adam and Christ, who will bring to life "all those who belong to him." The use of this text to celebrate today's feast is an obvious choice, given the Church's understanding of the dogma of the Assumption as Mary's experience of being "more fully conformed to her Son . . . conqueror of . . . death" (*Munificentissimus Deus*, 43).

Scholars are in agreement that the infancy narratives in Luke's gospel are profound theological reflections on the identity and mission of Jesus, not mere historical remembrances. The reading chosen for today's feast casts the spotlight on the great blessings enjoyed by Mary by virtue of the identity of her offspring. Hers is a reflected glory, but a glory nonetheless. The "greatness of the Lord" proclaimed in her being is the source of the extraordinary blessings she received—including her assumption, the subject of today's feast. The phrase "[God] has . . . raised the lowly to high places" may be interpreted as a poetic description of the deep truth contained in the imagery of Mary's assumption body and soul into heaven. Ultimately, what we celebrate today in Mary is a proclamation of our faith in "God who is mighty [and who] has done great things."

Catholic Doctrine

The Assumption of Mary

This feast celebrates a long-held belief of the Church which was not officially defined, however, until recent times. In his apostolic constitution of 1950, Pius XII declared as an article of faith that: "[T]he Immaculate Virgin, preserved free from all stain of original sin, when the course of her earthly life was finished, was taken up body and soul into heavenly glory, and exalted by the Lord as Queen over all things, so that she might be the more fully conformed to her Son, the Lord of lords and conqueror of sin and death" (*Munificentissimus Deus*, 1 November 1950 n. 43; AAS 42, 1950; DS 3903).

In the Western Church we generally refer to this feast and the doctrine involved as the "assumption" of Mary. In common parlance, however, "to assume" means "to put on" or "to take upon oneself" or simply "to take for granted." As the Church uses it in describing this feast and this doctrine, "assumption" means being "taken up" into heaven by God.

What is the meaning of this feast? We believe that Mary's assumption is a unique participation in Christ's resurrection (CCC 966). This doctrine declares that the resurrection we hope for, Mary now enjoys completely. The Mother of God anticipates that which will be our destiny—she has been taken up fully into the life of God which awaits us all. In a sense, this teaching of the Church says that one of us has made it and is therefore a sign for us.

This doctrine is also related to our belief that at the end of Mary's earthly life she did not cease being an intercessor for us (CCC 969). The Second Vatican Council asserted, "This

motherhood of Mary in the order of grace continues uninterruptedly from the consent which she loyally gave at the Annunciation and which she sustained without wavering beneath the cross, until the eternal fulfillment of all the elect. Taken up to heaven she did not lay aside this saving office but by her manifold intercession continues to bring us the gifts of eternal salvation. . . . Therefore, the Blessed Virgin is invoked in the Church under the titles of Advocate, Helper, Benefactress, and Mediatrix" (LG 62). And yet this role of intercessor and the doctrine of the assumption does not supersede in importance Christ, but flows from the Lord. Thus, the verse and response that concludes the Litany of the Blessed Virgin Mary begs, "Pray for us, holy Mother of God/That we may become worthy of the promises of Christ."

The Preface for this Mass sums up our belief which we celebrate today, "Father, . . . Today the virgin Mother of God was taken up into heaven to be the beginning and the pattern of the Church in its perfection, and a sign of hope and comfort for your people on their pilgrim way. You would not allow decay to touch her body, for she had given birth to your Son, the Lord of all life, in the glory of the incarnation" (*Roman Missal*, Preface for the Assumption, p. 59).

Catholic Culture

A fresco dating from the ninth century found in the Church of San Clemente, Rome, depicts the assumption. On the north side of the cathedral of Florence there is a door known as the *Porta della Mandorla* (Italian for "almond") due to the almond-shaped oval framing or enclosing the *Virgin in Glory* above the prophets, a joint work by Antonio di Banco, his son Nanni, and Donatello (c. 1414). The *mandorla* is an artistic device frequently used to highlight a figure in heavenly splendor and glory.

Zermatt, Switzerland, high in the Alps and tucked in the shadow of the Matterhorn, annually holds a gigantic festival parade on the feast of the Assumption that starts with Mass and ends about three hours later. All of the surrounding cantons are invited to send representative bands, floats, and performers. Zermatt does not allow any gas-fueled conveyances within the town limits. The parade is particularly quaint and colorful and draws tourists worldwide on this day honoring Mary.

Dismissal Catechesis (30 min.)

Getting Started

1. Prepare the space with a cloth, plant, an icon of Mary's dormition or a statue of Mary, lighted candle, and a place for the Lectionary on the center table. Gather in a circle of chairs.
2. Invite participants to imagine Mary and sense their feelings toward her and relationship with her. Sing a version of the "Magnificat."

First Impressions

Today's feast of the Assumption celebrates that upon Mary's death she was assumed both body and soul into heaven. Have participants recall the gathering hymn, the various readings, homily, and dismissal. Ask them to state something that speaks to them or catches their attention. Invite sharing in pairs. Then ask each pair to give input to the large group.

Making Connections

1. Ask participants to name what they know about Mary, about her life and death, and about the Church's view of her. Invite large group sharing. With this input, pull together some of the basic facts about Mary's life as recorded in scripture. Then ask participants to name how they think of Mary, and who she is for them. Again invite a large group sharing. Be aware that, for some participants, relationship with Mary will be new or somewhat unfamiliar, and possibly uncomfortable. Invite some discussion about Mary and her role in the life of the Church.
Then ask participants to name what images of Mary they have seen portrayed in icons, statues, or paintings. Invite them to name images that appeal to them. Note the well-known image of Mary presented in Revelation 12:1 of a heavenly woman clothed with the sun, with the moon under her feet and a crown of twelve stars on her head.
2. Conclude by inviting participants to name something they want to remember from today's liturgy. Go around the circle for this discussion.
3. Provide copies of the "Hail Mary" prayer for the participants. Point out that the second part of the prayer, "Blessed are you among women, and blessed is the fruit of your womb," comes from today's gospel from Luke at the time of Mary's visitation to Elizabeth. Note that on this feast of Mary assumed into heaven, she who is with God is asked in this prayer to "pray for us at the hour of our death."

Prayer

Pray the "Hail Mary" aloud together.

Extended Catechesis

SESSION FOCUS: *The Assumption of Mary*

Gathering

A. **Sunday:**
1. Welcome sponsors, spouses, fiancees, and team members.
2. Ask them to form groups of four, with two sponsor/catechumen or sponsor/candidate pairs in a group. Additional people also form groups of four.
3. Invite everyone into a moment of silence. Briefly share the content of the dismissal catechesis. Sing a version of the "Magnificat." Proclaim the gospel from the Lectionary.

B. **Weekday:**
1. Prepare the space as suggested in the Dismissal Catechesis.
2. Ask each participant to name a time when they thought about Mary or prayed to Mary since Sunday.
3. Then lead this celebration of the Word or use your own design:
   - Song: a version of the "Magnificat"
   - Sign of the Cross, Greeting
   - Proclaim Revelation 11:19, 12:1–6,10
   - Sing Psalm 45
   - Proclaim 1 Corinthians 15:20–26
   - Sing Alleluia
   - Proclaim Luke 1:39–56
   - Silence

   Conclude with the following words (from the introductory rite at Mass):
   Let us rejoice in the Lord and celebrate this feast in honor of the Virgin Mary, at whose assumption the angels rejoice, giving praise to the Son of God. Let us pray the Hail Mary together. Hail Mary, . . .

The Word (30 min.)

1. State that this gospel passage from Luke presents the well-known scene of Mary's visit to Elizabeth. Note especially Mary's statement which has come to be known as the "Magnificat." State that many of the words of the Magnificat are found earlier in scripture in Hannah's words in 1 Samuel 2:1–11. Ask participants to share in their small groups what this scene of the visitation and these words of the Magnificat tell them about what kind of a woman Mary was. Then invite some large group sharing.

2. Before proclaiming the gospel again, ask participants to listen for a word or phrase that stands out to them. After proclaiming the gospel, invite the participants to go around the room and simply call out the word or phrase, forming a sort of litany of verses. Then ask the participants what they hear God speaking to them through these words. Allow time for some small group sharing. Then elicit some responses in the large group.

3. Recall for the participants the reading from Revelation that pictures a sign of Mary, clothed with the sun. Note that the visitation portrays a young Mary pregnant with Jesus and already faithful to God. Point out that the reading from Corinthians talks about all who die being raised with Christ. Ask the participants to name what they hear in joining these readings together for the celebration of Mary's being assumed body and soul into heaven. Invite large group sharing.

4. Given the various images of Mary from today's scripture and today's feast of the Assumption, ask participants to name an image of Mary they want to carry with them. Ask this in the large group.

Catholic Teaching (30 min.)

1. Ask participants to name their understanding of who Mary is for the Church. With their sharing, interweave some of the historical content of this feast. Recall that on the cross Jesus said to Mary "Behold your son," and to John "Behold your mother." The Church sees in this exchange a relationship established between Mary and the Church. Note that scholars believe that Mary went with John to Ephesus and lived her final years there. Point out that Mary's death is often referred to as her "dormition," that is, her falling asleep—a once familiar way of referring to death. Note the existence of icons of Mary's dormition.

2. State that as the Church struggled to identify Mary's role, the tradition of Mary's assumption body and soul into heaven existed from early in the Church's history. Note that the liturgical remembrance of this feast on August 15 has been celebrated since the thirteenth century. Point out that the Assumption of Mary was officially promulgated as a dogma of the Church by Pius XII on November 1, 1950.

3. For the Church this feast is both a statement of Mary's honored status at God's side and a promise of what is to come for all of God's faithful people. Note that the Church sees this assumption of Mary's body as well as her soul into heaven as a special honor given to God's mother. Note that from this privileged place Mary is seen as one who is able to intercede for the Church, her children. Ask the participants to talk about how they view prayer to Mary. Talk about Mary's role as intercessor and mediatrix.

4. Ask the participants to state ways this feast gives hope for our future with God. Elicit various statements from them of this hope for living daily a faith-filled life, for living in union with Christ who has conquered all sin and death, for being fully united with God after death. Invite the participants to imagine all of God's people one day joined together with God and Mary.

Putting Faith into Practice

Ask the participants to name something they are able to do this week to live life more fully in union with God. Ask them to share this and their commitment to this action in their small groups.

Prayer

Pray the prayer from the *Sacramentary:*
Let us pray: Father in heaven, all creation rightly gives you praise, for all life and all holiness come from you. In the plan of your wisdom she who bore the Christ in her womb was raised body and soul in glory to be with him in heaven. May we follow her example in reflecting your holiness and join in her hymn of endless life and praise. We ask this through Christ our Lord. Amen.
Sing "Hail Mary: Gentle Woman" (Landry).

The Triumph of the Cross

SEPTEMBER 14

Understanding this Feast:
Background for Catechesis

The Word in Liturgy

Numbers 21:4–9
Psalm 78:1–2, 34–35, 36–37, 38
Philippians 2:6–11
John 3:13–17

Two historical events in Jerusalem stand in the background of this feast. The first is the dedication of the basilica of the Holy Sepulchre in the fifth century (on September 14). The second is the recovery of the true cross from the Persians in the seventh century. The readings of the day do not dwell on the sufferings of Christ, as one might expect, but, rather, celebrate the cross as a focus of healing and redemption.

The first reading presents a wonder worked by God through the prophet Moses to save the Israelites from illness caused by a plague of serpents. Because their bite caused inflammation, the serpents who attacked the Israelites were called *sarap,* which means "fiery." Set in a moral context—the people repent of their sin of complaining bitterly (in Hebrew, the expression is: their spirits "loathe" God and Moses)—the miraculous cure through the bronze serpent is shown to be a work of divine mercy. It is God who punishes and God who cures.

The psalm which follows is a historical psalm written in a hymn style. Most of the psalm that is included in today's liturgy pertains to the infidelity of Israel during the forty-year wandering in the wilderness, thus accentuating the background of sin and rebellion that provides the context for our redemption through the cross.

The early Christian hymn proclaimed in today's second reading from Paul's letter to the Philippians contains a beautiful and profound theology of the incarnation, centering on the cross. The *kenosis,* or "self-emptying" of Jesus, is a voluntary and intentional renunciation of divine power and majesty for the sake of identification with human beings. The hymn is perfectly balanced between the downward movement leading to Jesus' death on a cross, and the upward movement of his glorification by God and the whole cosmos. The hymn's context in the letter makes it clear that the self-emptying of Christ, which leads to the cross—and through the cross to glory—is the paradigm of the Christian life.

Although contemporary Christians tend to refer to the cross and resurrection as separate events, the early Church did not maintain such a rigid distinction, but viewed them as a single mystery to be proclaimed and lived. When today's gospel refers to Jesus being "lifted up," this same rich ambiguity is evident. Jesus is lifted up in his crucifixion. He is also lifted up in the resurrection and ascension which completes the process of his glorification. The monologue of Jesus, of which today's reading is a part, begins with a question from Nicodemus concerning Jesus' *ascension*.

To illustrate God's saving work in Jesus, John makes reference to the incident in Numbers that was the subject of the first reading. Just as looking upon the serpent brought healing to the Israelites, so looking upon Jesus will bring salvation to all who see him "lifted up." The passage closes with an affirmation of the overpowering love of God that grounds the whole mystery of Christ's self-giving, and leads the human person to faith.

Catholic Doctrine

Redemption

The crucifixion of Jesus, his humiliation, suffering, and violent death, was not a pointless, tragic end to a good man's life. It is, we believe, the triumph of Jesus' patience, love, and self-offering that follows from his whole life and mission in fulfillment of the old covenant and in accordance with God's plan of salvation (CCC 599). The cross of Jesus is characterized by believers as his exultation, and is the triumph of God's goodness over sin and death whereby our redemption is accomplished. What do we mean by "redemption"?

Redemption is a key concept in theology that explains Jesus Christ's significance for us humans. It is one of the titles we use for Christ. The Lord is the Redeemer who heals and saves us. In English, the term literally means "a buying back." Theologically, it carries the sense that we who have been "bought back" from sin have been released from that faulted or estranged condition and thus we have been changed from one state to another, that is, from bondage to liberation.

To reiterate the first point made about the crucifixion (above), it is important to note that the fullness of redemption is understood only in the light of Jesus' whole life, his teaching, his public ministry, and the consequences of his mission to proclaim the Good News among us. In other words, the redemption is not just linked to or accomplished by the cross alone, but by the triumph of Jesus' entire earthly life and heavenly exultation.

Catholics believe that the work of the redemption is continued in the experience of the Church at liturgy. Christ, the high priest, who offered himself on our behalf to his heavenly Father, continues the saving work begun in the redemption through the Church, his body. Thus, we who are incorporated into Christ by the grace of God experience in the liturgy the continuing gift of salvation made possible by Christ's sacrifice (CCC 1069).

Catholics believe that the redemption of Christ affects not only an individual's life (liberation from sin, entrance into the life of grace) but also affects all of human history and creation itself. This was an important theme first developed by St. Irenaeus (d. 200) who took as his starting point Ephesians 1:10 where God is described as having summed up all things (*anacephalaiosis*) in Christ. The redemption is reuniting what had been scattered in creation and is continuing to realize God's plan of salvation for all of humanity and our history. The image of the eighth day in Catholic teaching emphasizes this summation in Christ's redemption. Seven days is the length of time for the first creation accomplished by God, as described in the Old Testament. But by our redemption a new day has dawned, the eighth day of the new creation in Christ (CCC 349).

St. Andrew, bishop of Crete (d. 740), in reflecting on this feast and its significance for our redemption, wrote, "We are celebrating the feast of the cross which drove away darkness and brought in the light. As we keep this feast, we are lifted up with the crucified Christ, leaving behind us earth and sin so that we may gain the things above. So great and outstanding a possession is the cross that [one] who wins it has won a treasure. Rightly could I call this treasure the fairest of all fair things and the costliest, in fact as well as in name, for on it and through it and for its sake the riches of salvation that had been lost were restored to us" (Oratio 10 in *Exaltatione sanctae crucis*: PG 97, 1018–1019, found in LH, vol. 4, p. 1390).

The treasure of the redemption can be described and savored in so many ways and by so many images because it is central to the significance of Jesus Christ. Thus, we believe that the redemption achieves our entire restoration. It moves us from all that is inauthentic to a true faith. It moves us from estrangement to a proper center in life. It moves us from the burden of sin and guilt to a divine liberation. Finally, it moves us from a passive acceptance of darkness and death to an active affirmation of risen life in Christ.

Catholic Culture

The eighth day of the new creation in Christ is symbolized by eight-sided baptistries, baptismal fonts, and church buildings. Even the city water troughs and fountains in Chur, Switzerland (an ancient see city that dates from the early Middle Ages) are eight-sided.

A relic of the true cross of Christ is said to have been discovered by St. Helena (d. 330), the mother of Emperor Constantine, during a pilgrimage she made to Jerusalem in about the year 326. St. Cyril of Jerusalem (d. 386) mentions its veneration in his sermons to catechumens.

In the celebrant's introduction to the blessing of an image of the cross, he explains the meaning of the rite and the significance of Christ's cross for our redemption. This introduction echoes the doctrinal themes of the completion of his whole mission and the new creation accomplished by his saving action. The celebrant says, "Let us venerate in faith the eternal plan by which God has made the cross of Christ the preeminent sign of his mercy. As we look upon the cross, let us call to mind that on it Christ brought to completion the sacrament of his love for the Church. As we bow before the cross, let us remember that in his own blood Christ has removed all divisions and out of the many nations created the one people of God. As we venerate the cross, let us reflect that we are ourselves Christ's disciples and must therefore follow him, willingly taking up our own cross each day" (BB 1241).

Dismissal Catechesis (30 min.)

Getting Started

1. Prepare the space ahead of time with a circle of chairs. In the center of the circle place a large cross with a red cloth and a white cloth draped over the crossbar.
2. Lead the candidates and catechumens to the circle and place the Lectionary on the table. Call the catechumens and candidates to prayer with the Gospel Alleluia, praying, *"We adore you, O Christ, and we praise you, because by your cross you have redeemed the world."* Invite all to respond "Amen." Invite them to reflect on the cross and its meaning for their lives as believers. After a period of silence repeat the Gospel Alleluia.

First Impressions

1. In the large group, ask the participants: *As you reflected on the meaning of the cross in your life and the lives of all believers, what images and emotions were evoked in you?* Affirm and comment on their responses.
2. Then ask them to recall their experience of the Liturgy of the Word at this feast of the Triumph of the Cross. You might have ready a few lines from the scriptures and recall the Gathering Song and something from the homily to help their remembering.
3. After they name some of these significant images from the liturgy, invite them to find a partner to share their thoughts on these questions: *What seems to be the focal point of this feast? In what words or images did you find peace and solace? What confused or challenged you in the liturgical experience?* Invite a few pairs to share their insights in the large group.

Making Connections

1. Explain the feast of the Triumph of the Cross in these or your own words: *Two important historical events form the backdrop for this feast. The first is the dedication of the basilica of the Holy Sepulchre in the fifth century on September 14. The second is the recovery of the true cross from the Persians in the seventh century. This feast celebrates the healing and redeeming power of the cross.*
2. Invite the participants to name whatever comes to mind that indicates we have something to celebrate when we reflect upon the cross.
3. Gather them in pairs to share experiences they have had in which their struggles or difficulties led to something good and beneficial. When the pairs have finished sharing stories, invite a few participants to tell their story in the large gathering.

Prayer

Invite the participants to gather by playing some instrumental music that has a joyful theme. After a time of silence, proclaim the second reading, Philippians 2:6–11.

Extended Catechesis

SESSION FOCUS: *Redemption*

Gathering

A. Sunday:
1. Greet and welcome the sponsors and team members as they arrive. Invite them to join the circle of catechumens and candidates.
2. Invite the participants to reflect on the cross as they recall the crosses in their own life. Then direct them to remember a time when their cross turned out to be a blessing. With this recollection in mind, proclaim the gospel, John 3:13–17.

B. Weekday:
1. Use the same centerpiece as described for the Dismissal Catechesis.
2. As the participants gather in the circle, greet and warmly welcome each person.
3. Lead this celebration of the Word:
   - Song: Gathering Hymn from the liturgy of this feast
   - First Reading: Numbers 21:4–9
   - Second Reading: Philippians 2:6–11
   - Team leads the group in singing "Jesus the Lord" (Roc O'Connor, New Dawn Music, 1981)
   - Sing Alleluia
   - Gospel: John 3:13–17
   - Reflection on the cross as in section A.2

The Word (30 min.)

1. Invite the participants to share some of their experiences when their cross in life was a source of blessing. Begin this sharing by offering your own story of the blessings of the cross.
2. Present the background on the scriptures in these or your own words: *In the first reading from Numbers 21:4–9, God works a miracle through the prophet Moses. The plague of serpents, called* sarap, *attacked the Israelites, causing inflamed sores and even death. When the people repent of their sins—their complaining against the Lord—Moses is instructed by the Lord to lift high the bronze serpent or seraph, mounting it on a pole. Those who repented and looked upon the seraph were healed. In the gospel, John makes reference to this incident to illustrate God's saving work in Jesus. Jesus will bring salvation to all as he is lifted up on the cross. This "lifting up" has come to be understood as Jesus lifted up in the resurrection and ascension which completes the process of his glorification. Thus, the cross is understood as our source of salvation.*

3. Invite the participants to form small groups to share their thought on these questions: *As God uses the source of the Israelites' suffering, the serpent, to heal them, how has this occurred in your life? What do you understand to be the cause of our celebration on this feast? Why is it important to consider the cross in the light of Jesus' resurrection and ascension into glory?*

4. In the large group invite the small groups to share their insights to one question at a time. Summarize their comments and invite all to turn to the Reflection in their Participant Book on page 144. Guide them as they journal their reflection on the cross. Ask the participants to share their stories in the same small groups.

Catholic Teaching (30 min.)

1. Present the teaching of the Church on redemption, emphasizing and expanding the following points (Use the Catholic Doctrine section in Understanding this Sunday to further your understanding of this teaching.):

   • The crucifixion of Jesus became his triumph. His self-offering and love fulfilled the covenant in accordance with God's plan of salvation.

   • Through the cross Jesus won the victory over sin and death, redeeming and setting us free. We are redeemed by Christ's sacrifice and resurrection, that is, we are healed and saved—brought back from sin and released from its bondage.

   • The fullness of redemption can only be understood in the light of Jesus' whole life—his teaching, his ministry, and the consequences of his mission to proclaim the Good News among us.

   • This work of redemption is continued in the experience of the Church at liturgy, whereby Christ the high priest who offered himself on our behalf continues this saving work.

   • Redemption in Christ restores us fully, moving us to true faith, divine liberation, and a life centered wholly in Christ.

2. Ask the Participants to respond in writing to the Questions presented in their Participant Book on page 144. *How does the work of redemption in Christ set you free? What ways can you name to indicate evidence of deeper faith through Christ's death and resurrection? How have you become more centered on Christ as you journey in faith?* Gather everyone in small groups to share what they have written. As they finish sharing, ask each small group to present a summary of their discussion with everyone.

3. Invite the same small groups to role-play sharing the Good News of the cross, our redemption, with an unbeliever or someone curious about the faith. You may choose to write down typical scenarios of encounters for each role-play. Give the groups enough time to plan their scene. Then enjoy their enactment.

Putting Faith into Practice

1. From the scenarios invite the whole group to name their learnings about the paradox of the cross and the meaning of redemption. Summarize their insights in a few sentences.

2. Share with the group some Catholic practices and traditions regarding the cross. These might include the Stations of the Cross, veneration of the cross on Good Friday, the significance of the Sign of the Cross, and hanging crosses in our homes.

Prayer

Gather the participants and invite them to stand close to the foot of the cross. Then pray in the words of St. Andrew, bishop of Crete, saying: *"We are celebrating the feast of the cross which drove away darkness and brought in the light. As we keep this feast, we are lifted up with the crucified Christ, leaving behind us earth and sin so that we may gain the things above. So great and outstanding a possession is the cross that [one] who wins it has won a treasure. Rightly could I call this treasure the fairest of all fair things and the costliest, in fact as well as in name, for on it and through it and for its sake the riches of salvation that had been lost were restored to us."*

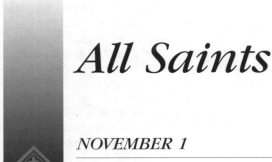

All Saints

Understanding this Feast:

Background for Catechesis

The Word in Liturgy

Revelation 7:2–4, 9–14
Psalm 24:1–2, 3–4, 5–6
1 John 3:1–3
Matthew 5:1–12

The remote origins of this feast are found in the honor that early Christians paid to the martyrs, remembering them on the anniversary of their death, often at the very place of their martyrdom. After the age of persecution had ended, other holy individuals were gradually added to the list of those commemorated annually. In the fourth century, saints were named in the Eucharistic Prayer. By the fifth century, a feast of All Saints was celebrated in certain churches of the Christian East. When Pope Boniface (d. 615) transformed the Roman pantheon into a Christian church on May 13, 610, he designated that day as a feast of All Saints. It was under Gregory IV (d. 844) that the feast was moved to November 1, and thenceforth the observance spread throughout the West.

Today's reading from the Book of Revelation contains excerpts from two visions, each portraying in vivid imagery the salvation of the just. In the first, an angel comes from the East (the place from which the Messiah was expected to come) "holding the seal of the living God." In the ancient world, a sovereign's seal was a sign both of ownership and of protection. Thus, the angel's placing of the seal on the forehead of God's servants affords them protection in the time of trial. The number 144,000 is symbolic of a vast, all-inclusive throng (the perfect number twelve squared, times one thousand). In the second vision, the survivors of the time of trial (i.e., the Roman persecutions under Domitian, 81–96) are revealed in glory, an obvious appeal to those still undergoing persecution to persevere. Their white robes are reminiscent of their baptismal garments as well as symbolic of the "washing" they have undergone in the blood of the Lamb; both references are expressive of the saving action of Christ on behalf of his faithful followers.

Scholars have helped us understand the internal struggles within the Johannine community that prompted the writing of this letter. Apparently, a split had developed to the point of some members leaving the community (see 1 John 2:19). The author warns his followers against the errors of those who have left, and reiterates key points of his own teaching. He insists here that the transformation of the believers under the power of Christ's grace is real ("children of God . . . is what we are"). But that transformation is a progressive, ongoing reality, not something that happened once and for all, freeing a person to disregard all further ethical concerns ("what we shall later be has not yet come to light"). The letter offers a classic description of what it means to be a saint, what true holiness consists in: " . . . we shall be like him [Christ]."

Matthew uses various subtle cues to underline the tremendous importance of Jesus' teaching contained in the Beatitudes. Like Moses, he ascends a mountain to proclaim the law of the (new) covenant. Unlike Moses, he speaks words on his own authority. What he says describes not only who is a member of God's kingdom; he also prescribes how those who wish to belong in that kingdom must act. The nature of Christian holiness is summed up in these idealistic yet demanding pronouncements of who is "blessed" in God's kingdom. The suffering and persecution of the "little ones" are recognized as a source of holiness; so, too, is action aimed at transforming the world to make it conform to the kingdom which Jesus announced.

Catholic Doctrine

The Communion of Saints

All Christians who follow in the way of Jesus are called to a life of holiness and witness on behalf of the kingdom of God. The Second Vatican Council stated, "It is therefore quite clear that all Christians in any state or walk of life are called to the fullness of Christian life and to the perfection of love, and by this holiness a more human manner of life is fostered also in earthly society" (LG 40). Using the strength which Christ provides, we who confess his name are given the grace to follow in his footsteps and conform ourselves more closely to the image of Jesus. Thus, we are able to devote ourselves wholeheartedly to the glory of God and serve our neighbor. The holiness which is fostered among the People of God by the grace of Christ will grow in fruitful abundance "as is clearly shown in the history of the Church through the life of so many saints" (LG 40).

The title of "saint" (from Latin *sanctus* for "holy") was initially attributed to certain individuals by popular devotion, but since about the tenth century there has been a formal papal procedure for bestowing this honor. Prior to the development of the formal procedure, in about the third century, the holy men and women understood as saints were considered as intercessors before God. Tertullian, Origen, and Cyprian supported this view in their writings and preaching (W. Beinert & F. S. Fiorenza, *Handbook of Catholic Theology*, p. 637).

Contemporary Catholic teaching asserts that we assimilate the teachings of Christ from the Word of God and obtain grace from the celebration of the sacraments, and in communion with the whole Church, the Christian vocation is fulfilled. It is from the Church that one learns the example of holiness and recognizes its model in the Virgin Mary, the Mother of God, and discovers it in the spiritual tradition and long history of the saints.

One of the credal affirmations is belief in the "communion of saints." What is meant by this phrase? The *Catechism* asserts quite simply and clearly that the communion of saints is the Church. The Church forms one body, with Christ as its head, who shares his riches with all the members through the sacraments. Those riches, governed by one and the same Spirit throughout all the members, are considered as one common fund (CCC 947). The term *communis in sacris*, therefore, indicates both a sharing in holy things (the riches of Christ) and a sharing among a holy people (we who are claimed for God in Christ).

Thus, in the New Testament, "the saints" refers to the whole body of believers, the Church. But, in terms of the formal, ecclesial procedure for the recognition of saints (canonization), the term refers to those men and women who throughout our Christian history have been outstanding in holiness, sometimes heroic in their efforts to witness to the kingdom of God.

In Catholic teaching the saints are variously described as our companions in prayer, as patrons for those individuals who take their names or who are in certain walks of life, and as intercessors for us before the throne of God (although Christ is the one mediator between God and humanity). Because of this, Catholics hold that to God alone is due our worship (Latin, *latria*), and that the saints deserve veneration (Latin, *dulia*), which is different. The Second Vatican Council teaches, "The Church has always believed that the apostles and Christ's martyrs, who gave the supreme witness of faith and charity by the shedding of their blood, are closely united with us in Christ; she has always venerated them, together with the Blessed Virgin Mary and the holy angels, with a special love, and has piously asked for the help of their intercession. Soon there were added to these others who had chosen to imitate more closely the virginity and poverty of Christ, and still others whom the outstanding practice of the Christian virtues and the wonderful graces of God recommended to the pious devotion and imitation of the faithful" (LG 50).

Catholic Culture

The Litany of Saints is prayed in Masses where churches are dedicated, at ordinations, at confirmations, at the Easter Vigil, at baptisms, and as one form of the commendation of the dying.

Catholic churches are often filled with images of the Virgin Mary and of the saints, in paintings, mosaics, stained glass, murals, and statues. The type of medium is restricted only by the genius of the artists and materials involved. The purpose of these representations is not to compete with our worship of God but to inspire us with the example of these holy men and women who have gone before us and who are yet part of the communion of all saints of the household of God.

Norwegian Catholic writer Sigrid Undset reflected on the meaning of saints in the Catholic tradition in this way: "There is an element in the veneration of the saints of which Catholics themselves are often unconscious. The cult of the saints excludes the cult of success—the veneration of people who have got on well in this world, the snobbish admiration of wealth and fame" (Sigrid Undset, *Stages on the Road,* tr. by Arthur G. Chater, NY: Alfred A. Knopf, 1934, pp. VI-VII). Frequently, the lives of saints embody terrible misfortunes, suffering, and failure, at least if one judges by how their aspirations were realized in their own lifetime. Their "success" lies in their fidelity to God, and in this alone.

Dismissal Catechesis (30 min.)

Getting Started

1. Prepare the space ahead of time with a circle of chairs. Drape a white cloth on the floor. Place a white candle and a green plant on it. Have several books of saints displayed, including the parish book of the dead.
2. Lead the candidates and catechumens to the circle and place the Lectionary on the cloth. Light the candle. Lead them in singing "Blest Are They" (David Haas, GIA Publications, 1985).

First Impressions

1. Invite the participants to share their experience of today's liturgy in the large group, asking: *What did you notice today? What did we celebrate?* Explain the concept of Holy Days if this is the first time you are gathering on this type of Church feast.
2. Name the following images to help the group recall the scriptures. Invite the participants to close their eyes as you read the list slowly and prayerfully:
   "Put the seal on the foreheads of the servants of our God"
   "wearing white robes and holding palm branches"
   "white in the blood of the Lamb"
   "called the children of God"
   "he went up the mountain"
   "Blessed are . . ."
   "Theirs is the kingdom of heaven"
   Gather the participants into small groups and ask them to discuss the following: *What about these passages did you find inspiring? What image is empowering for you? Why?*

Making Connections

1. When they have finished, turn their attention back to the large group and ask: *From these readings, how would you describe holiness?* Prepare ahead of time a poster with the word "HOLINESS" in the center with radiating lines from the word. On these lines write those qualities of holiness named by the candidates and catechumens.
2. Continue the discussion in small groups, using these questions: *What are the challenges to holiness presented in these scriptures? From these passages, how is holiness possible?*
3. Ask the small groups to share one thing they discussed. Summarize their comments to close the session.

Prayer

Prepare for prayer with a moment of quiet. Invite all to join in singing "Blest Are They" (David Haas, GIA Publications, 1985). Then pray in these or similar words: *Holy God, we praise you today for setting before us the witness of so many who have gone before us in faith: all the martyrs, virgins, widows, teachers, and holy men and women known for their actions on behalf of your kingdom.*

We join with them as they cry out, "Salvation comes from our God, who is seated on the throne, and from the Lamb" (Revelation 7:19). "Amen. Blessing and glory, wisdom and thanksgiving, honor, power, and might be to our God, forever and ever. Amen" (Revelation 7:12).

Extended Catechesis

SESSION FOCUS: *The Communion of Saints*

Gathering

A. Sunday:
1. Greet and welcome the sponsors and team members as they arrive. Invite them to join the circle of catechumens and candidates.
2. Ask one or two catechumens and candidates to briefly summarize what has been discussed in the Dismissal Catechesis.
3. Lead them in the following prayer, saying:
   Let us cry out with the assembly of white-robed saints as we respond: "Salvation comes from our God, who is seated on the throne and from the Lamb."
   Wash us in the blood of the Lamb. . . Response.
   Clothe us in your white garment of grace. . . Response.
   Protect us with the seal of kingship. . . Response.
   Call us your children, for that is what we are. . . Response.
   Purify our hearts and comfort our mourning. . . Response.
   Fill our hungering, thirsting, and longing. . . Response.
   Bless us when we suffer for the sake of your kingdom. . . Response.
   Invite all to stand as a team member proclaims Matthew 5:1–12.

B. Weekday:
1. Use the same centerpiece as described for the Dismissal Catechesis.
2. As the participants gather in the circle, greet and warmly welcome each person. Light the candle and invite all to consider the following question and then respond in the large group: *What glimmers of holiness did you observe this past week?*
3. Lead this celebration of the Word:
   • Song: Use the Gathering Song from last Sunday's liturgy
   • First Reading: Revelation 7:2–4, 9–14
   • Psalm: 24:1–2, 3–4, 5–6
   • Second Reading: 1 John 3:1–3
   • Sing Alleluia
   • Gospel: Matthew 5:1–12
   • Sing Alleluia

The Word (30 min.)

1. Lead the participants in the following reflection: *Think of people in your life who have had a positive influence on you. They may be people you have known personally or people whom you have never met. As you think of these people, remember the way(s) they have influenced you. What quality or qualities of their lives do you admire? Why?*

2. After some time for quiet reflecting, urge the participants to gather in pairs. Ask them to share something from their reflection, stressing qualities they admired in these acquaintances and friends.

3. Refer back to the holiness poster and ask these questions: *Are any of the qualities you admired in your relationships listed on the poster? What qualities would you like to add to the poster?*

4. Present this background to the scriptures to the whole group: *Today's feast celebrates our present process of conversion as we aspire toward holiness and the future realization of our sainthood. The first reading from the Book of Revelation presents two visions that describe symbolically our progress toward sanctity.* Proclaim Revelation 7:2–4, 9–14. Ask if anyone can name the two visions. Gather insights from the group. Then continue in these or similar words: *First, we are all sealed on the forehead; that is, we are under God's protection. We belong to God. In the second vision, those who persevered through trials and persecution are revealed in the glory of white robes, washed in the blood of the Lamb. These saints embody the inner attitude and moral behavior that we are challenged to live in the present time. They have entered into glory because of their conversion to Christ and their actions on behalf of the kingdom.*

5. Ask the participants to turn to their Participant Book on page 146 and to respond to the questions presented. Invite all to share their responses in pairs. After sufficient time, gather feedback from the pairs.

6. Present the background on the gospel in these or similar words: *Actions on behalf of the kingdom are described in Jesus' proclamation of the Beatitudes on the mountain. The heart of today's gospel, Matthew 5:1–12, are the Beatitudes, which offer all believers the attitudes that are normative guides for holiness. The first four Beatitudes inform us of the spiritual posture or inner attitude we are to acquire. That is, they describe the openness and simplicity of the* anawim—*the little ones of the scriptures. The last four Beatitudes hold up the moral actions for justice that need to be enacted by all who would build God's kingdom in union with all the saints.*

Catholic Teaching (30 min.)

1. In the large group discuss how the Beatitudes affirm or challenge our understanding of success. Include the point that the feast we celebrate today affirms that following the Beatitudes as a way of life is possible. Stress that success as a Christian is not determined in the public realm of commerce or in secular attributes of wealth, power, and prestige. Ask the participants: *How do you understand the challenge to be faithful to Christ by living the Beatitudes?*

2. Offer the following points in a short teaching on the Communion of Saints:
   - All Christians are called to a life of holiness, that is, to conform ourselves to the image of Christ.
   - Saints (the word is derived from the Latin word for holy) are considered to be intercessors before God. They are not worshiped but venerated for the model of holiness that they offer to those of us still on earth.
   - The Virgin Mary is venerated, with all the saints, for her witness of holiness and her constant *fiat,* that is, her "yes" to God's will in seemingly impossible circumstances.
   - The Communion of Saints celebrates the one body of the Church, with Christ as its head. Those who have gone before us, those still on earth, and those yet to come all share in the holiness of Christ as a holy people, sealed in the blood of the Lamb.

3. Invite the small groups to look through the books on the lives of the saints. Encourage them to find their namesake in one of the books. As they do so, ask them to consider once again the qualities of holiness on the poster. After some time, ask the participants to share what they have been reading/discussing about the saints.

Putting Faith into Practice

1. Invite the participants to gather in pairs to share their own stories. Direct the sharing by instructing them to describe their own experience of the Communion of Saints. Encourage them to think again of those who have had a profound experience in their lives. Encourage them to think about deceased members of their families and how their memories are kept alive through stories and events.

2. When they have finished sharing ask: *What has this understanding of the Catholic teaching on saints meant in your life as you grow in holiness?*

3. Invite two or three team members to describe the "Beatitudes" as present or modeled in the life of one of their favorite saints. Encourage all to learn more about these holy ones, suggesting several books they might wish to become familiar with, such as Alban Butler's *Lives of the Saints.*

Prayer

Close with the Litany of the Saints, found in RCIA 221.

All Souls

NOVEMBER 2

The Word in Liturgy

Readings for the feast of All Souls may be taken from any of the Masses for the dead. The choices can be found in the Lectionary, from n. 789–793. In view of the great number of possible readings (52 in all), we will not supply a scripture commentary here. Nevertheless, the scripture readings chosen for and proclaimed in your liturgy remain the foundation for catechesis. The catechist should reflect on the readings with the help of a Bible commentary, and invite the catechumens and candidates into prayerful reflection on the readings in a way similar to the method that has been used on other Sundays: first in the Dismissal Catechesis, and then in the Word section of the Extended Catechesis.

What follows is an essay on an appropriate doctrinal focus for this feast of All Souls: the Church's teaching concerning purgatory. The catechetical session gives a general outline of the catechesis based on the Sunday readings, and further attention to catechizing upon the Church teaching that is described here.

Catholic Doctrine

Purgatory

In our Catholic understanding, purgatory is a state of purification between death and heaven whereby the remaining obstacles to the full enjoyment of one's personal and eternal union with God are removed. For those justified and reconciled in Christ, this purification completes the process of sanctification such that one can enter into union with the triune God (CCC 1030).

The obstacles which are removed are venial sins not repented at the time of death and any remaining effects or consequences to one's person of repented and forgiven mortal or deadly sins committed during one's earthly life. In our Catholic understanding, purgatory is not an opportunity to reverse the course of one's earthly life. Conversion is not possible in purgatory if conversion did not take place in life before death. Since an individual judgment follows immediately upon death, purgatory is that interval after death that erases conditions preventing persons from enjoying full fellowship with God.

It is important to note that while scripture refers to a cleansing fire (1 Corinthians 3:15; 1 Peter 1:7) and burning flames figure in some artistic depictions of purgatory, the operative notion in Catholic doctrine and theology on purgatory is that it is a state of purification, not punishment (CCC 1031). This state may even last only an instant, as we count time. What the doctrine upholds is that purgatory is a transitional state which makes one ready for the experience of the beatific vision.

It is also important to note that the doctrine of purgatory upholds an unbroken liturgical practice in our Church to making intercessory prayers for the dead (CCC 1032). The Councils of Florence (1439) and Trent (1563) refer to this venerable practice which dates from the earliest times of the Church. And the Second Vatican Council observes, "In full consciousness of this communion of the whole Mystical Body of Jesus Christ, the Church in its pilgrim members, from the very earliest days of the Christian religion, has honored with great respect the memory of the dead; and, 'because it is a holy and a wholesome thought to pray for the dead that they may be loosed from their sins' (2 Maccabees 12:46) she offers her suffrages for them" (LG 50).

Thus, in the Eucharistic Prayer we pray for the dead, a practice originating in the third century. "Remember, Lord, those who have died and have gone before us marked with the sign of faith, especially those for whom we now pray . . ." and at this point in Eucharistic Prayer I names of the deceased may be inserted into the prayer (*Roman Missal*, EP I). The instruction for a blessing of a cemetery quotes Eucharistic Prayer IV, saying that "Christians therefore offer prayers to the heavenly Father for all and when they pray to him they include all, both those 'who have died in the peace of Christ and all the dead whose faith is known to God alone'" (*Book of Blessings*, *Order for the Blessing of a Cemetery*, n. 1418). Indeed, there is also the generally accepted practice of offering Mass for the deceased in the firm conviction that, as part of the communion of saints, we may "assist" them by our prayers (Order of Christian Funerals, Rite of Committal, n. 216).

St. Catherine of Genoa (1347–80) meditates, "There is no joy save that in paradise to be compared to the joy of the souls in purgatory. This joy increases day by day because of the way in which the love of God corresponds to the love of the soul, since the impediment to that love is worn away daily. This impediment is the rust of sin. As it is consumed, the soul is more and more open to God's love" (from *Catherine of Genoa: Purgation and Purgatory, the Spiritual Dialogue*, trsl. Serge Hughes, Paulist Press, New York, 1979, p. 72).

Catholic Culture

The idea that the prayers of the living could assist the dead gave rise to Chantry chapels where Masses were said for the repose of the souls of deceased family members or members of corporations and guilds. Henry VII's chapel in Westminster Abbey is one example, as is Michelangelo's Medici chapel in San Lorenzo, Florence. Work on the Medici chapel was interrupted by the sack of Rome, and it was never totally completed. Yet it is a masterpiece whose every detail contributes to the whole. Construction continued on and off from 1519 through 1534. It houses the tombs of Giuliano and Lorenzo de Medici. Michelangelo deliberately placed the windows so that the entire chapel would be bathed in a pearly radiance, meant to suggest the perpetual light shining upon the dukes in death. Masses of the Dead were still being celebrated four times daily well into the seventeenth century.

Botticelli's series of drawings illustrating Dante's *La Divina Commedia* attempts to depict the particular images of purgatory as found in those poems.

On this feast day, many Catholics visit the graves of loved ones and leave mementos and flowers. This is a significant day for Latinos. On *el dia de los muertos* (the day of the dead) food is left out on a table in the house and on the table are displayed skulls made of sugar with the names of deceased ones on the forehead of the skull. Candles are lit so that the deceased can "see" the food when they visit during the night. On this day, it is also a Hispanic custom to visit cemeteries with flowers and music to hold a picnic at the grave sites of family members and friends.

Dismissal Catechesis (30 min.)

Getting Started

1. Have a table prepared with white cloth on which is placed the parish's Book of the Dead or Book of Remembrance, a lighted candle, and a plant.

2. Invite everyone to be seated in a circle around the table. Pray in these or similar words:

"O God, giver of all life, we gather today to give thanks and praise for all those who have gone before us. We remember in a special way those members of our own families, friends, and members of this parish who have died. Bless them with the gift of eternal life, console their families. Help us to be prepared when the hour of our death is upon us. We ask this in the name of Jesus Christ, your Son, who lives and reigns with you in unity with the Holy Spirit, now and forever. Amen."

First Impressions

Recall words and phrases from the Liturgy of the Word. Include phrases from the songs and prayers as well as the readings. Spend a few minutes in quiet. Discuss with the catechumens and candidates the mood or feelings expressed in this liturgy: *How is it different; how is it the same as other liturgies? What surprised or puzzled you about today's feast?*

Making Connections

1. Elicit their remembrances of loved ones who have died. Suggest such activities as remembering anniversaries, Memorial Day, family albums, genealogy charts, and family gatherings during which stories are told. Often in families as children are growing up, adults will make comments comparing the child's behavior, looks, personality to that of someone who has died. Progeny perpetuate the family name and story.

2. Ask the participants whether they have been to a Catholic funeral. Have displayed a funeral pall, the paschal candle, and incense, and explain their symbolism. Discuss the three movements of a funeral liturgy: vigil, Mass of Resurrection, and committal rite. Explain that the white vestment—a sign of resurrection and Easter—is worn on All Souls' Day and at every funeral.

3. What does each of us believe about death and what happens to the person who has died? Proclaim 2 Maccabees 12:46. What does this reading say about death and remembering those who have died?

Prayer

Teach the prayer: *Eternal rest grant unto them, O Lord. And let perpetual light shine upon them. May their soul and all the souls of the faithful departed rest in peace. Amen.*

Extended Catechesis

SESSION FOCUS: *Purgatory*

Gathering

A. Sunday:

1. Welcome everyone and invite them to be seated in groups of three or four.

2. Invite everyone to recall a loved one who has died. After a moment of silence, pray the following prayer from the funeral liturgy:

"May the angels lead you into paradise, and the martyrs come to welcome you, and lead you into the holy city, the new and eternal Jerusalem."

Offer each person the opportunity to speak the name of a loved one who has died and direct everyone to respond with the words, *"Rest in peace."*

B. Weekday:

Welcome everyone. Begin with a celebration of the Word, such as:

- Song: "I Am the Bread of Life" (Toolan)
- Sign of the Cross and Greeting
- Reading: First Reading proclaimed on the feast
- Quiet
- Alleluia
- Gospel proclaimed on the feast
- Alleluia

The Word (30 min.)

Reflect with the group on the readings that have been proclaimed, consulting a Bible commentary, such as the Collegeville commentary, for any points that are unclear to you.

Catholic Teaching (30 min.)

1. Direct the participants to list their ideas of purgatory, including ideas they have heard as well as questions that they want to explore further regarding purgatory. Have one person from each group report key comments, observations, and questions to the whole group.

2. Delve into the common perception of purgatory as fire. Refer to 1 Corinthians 3:15 and 1 Peter 1:7. Explain that the operative notion in our Catholic doctrine and theology on purgatory is that it is a state of purification, not punishment. This state may even last only an instant, as we count time. What the doctrine upholds is that purgatory is a transitional state which makes one ready for the experience of the beatific vision.

3. Point out that purgatory is a state of purification between death and heaven whereby the remaining obstacles to the full enjoyment of one's personal and eternal union with God are removed. For those justified and reconciled in Christ, this purification completes the process of sanctification so that one can enter into union with the triune God.

4. Tell the group of the unbroken liturgical practice in our Church of making intercessory prayers for the dead. This practice dates to the earliest times of the Church: Tertullian, about 160 A.D.; St. Cyprian, bishop of Carthage, about 250 A.D.; St. Cyril of Jerusalem, about 315 A.D., just to name a few. In the Eucharistic Prayer, we pray for the dead. There is also the generally accepted practice of offering Mass for the deceased in the firm conviction that, as part of the communion of saints, we may "assist" them by our prayers.

5. Read to them the quote of St. Catherine of Genoa found in Understanding this Sunday. Invite them to discuss this quote.

6. Gather from the whole group insights and clarifications gained from this session. Mention any remaining questions or comments.

Putting Faith into Practice

1. Discuss with the participants customs for remembering the dead such as visiting the cemetery, planting flowers, requesting a Mass of Remembrance for a loved one, and memorials, as well as other cultural practices.

2. Show them the Book of the Dead or the Book of Remembrance. Invite them to write in the Book of Remembrance names of family members and friends that they would like to add.

Prayer

Gather as a large group standing around the Book of Remembrance. Spend a few moments again recalling people who have died. Sing "On Eagle Wings" (Joncas).

The Dedication of St. John Lateran

NOVEMBER 9

The Word in Liturgy

Isaiah 52:7–10
Psalm 98:1, 2–3, 3–4, 5–6
Hebrews 1:1–6
John 1:1–18 [or (short form) 1:1–5, 9–14]

Readings for the feast of the Dedication of St. John Lateran may be taken from any of the readings assigned for the dedication of a church. The choices can be found in the Lectionary, n. 701–706. In view of the great number of possible texts (22 in all), we will not supply a scripture commentary here. Nevertheless, the scripture readings chosen for and proclaimed in your liturgy remain the foundation for catechesis. The catechist should reflect on the readings with the help of a Bible commentary, and invite the catechumens and candidates into prayerful reflection on the readings in a way similar to the method that has been used on other Sundays: first in the Dismissal Catechesis, and then in the Word section of the Extended Catechesis.

What follows is an essay on an appropriate doctrinal focus for this feast: the four marks of the Church. The catechetical session gives a general outline of the catechesis based on the Sunday readings, and further attention to catechizing upon the Church teaching that is described here.

Catholic Doctrine

The Four Marks of the Church

The feast we celebrate today observes the anniversary of the dedication of the cathedral church of Rome. When the Emperor Constantine officially recognized Christianity, he made generous gifts to the Church, one of which was a palace and grounds formerly belonging to the Laterani family. In 324 he added a large church on the grounds named the Basilica of the Savior. Legend has it that the basilica was dedicated on November 9 that year. Later a baptistry was added and dedicated to St. John the Baptist. In subsequent years the entire edifice became known as St. John of the Lateran. Because it is the cathedral church of the bishop of Rome, the feast, at first observed only in Rome, was later extended to the whole Church as a sign of devotion to and of unity with the Chair of Peter.

Thus, while this feast originates in a particular edifice in a particular place, it truly celebrates the universal Church which is apostolic, catholic, holy, and one. The following is a brief summary of each of these characteristics.

We believe the Church is "apostolic" because it is founded upon the apostles, those chosen witnesses who were sent out on mission by the Lord himself and who later testified to the saving plan of God in Christ (CCC 857). Through the agency of the Holy Spirit the Church is entrusted to keep and to hand on the teaching of the apostles. Down through the ages the Church continues to be nourished in the teaching of the apostles by their successors, the college of bishops "assisted by priests, and one which [the bishops] share with the successor of St. Peter, the supreme pastor of the Church . . ." (Second Vatican Council, *Ad Gentes*, 7 November 1965, n. 5).

We believe the Church is "catholic" or universal because Christ is its head. The body, the Church, is in union with its head who has provided "the fullness of the means of salvation" to us (Second Vatican Council, *Unitatis Redintegratio*, 21 November 1964, n. 3). This fullness of the means of salvation is to be found in a correct and complete confession of faith, sacramental life, and ordained ministry in apostolic succession (CCC 830). The Church is also catholic in the sense that its mission is to the whole world. This universal Church is truly present in each local or particular church, a diocese or eparchy, that is legitimately organized around its pastor who is in communion with the Church of Rome (CCC 832–34).

We believe the Church is "holy" because Jesus, the Son of God, with the Father and the Spirit, is acknowledged as the Holy One and loved the Church so much that he sacrificed himself in order to sanctify his ecclesial body (CCC 823). Thus, the Church is called the "holy people of God" and her members "saints" (Acts 9:13; 1 Corinthians 6:l; 16:1). This holiness with which the earthly Church is endowed is real but also imperfect. Every individual within the Church, including ordained ministers, acknowledges that they are sinners. Pope Paul VI wrote, "The Church is therefore holy, though having sinners in her midst, because she herself has no other life but the life of grace" (Paul VI, *Credo of the People of God: Solemn Profession of Faith*, 30 June 1968, 19; quoted in CCC 827).

We believe the Church is "one" because of its source, the divinity, who is the supreme example of unity: the God who is three-in-one (CCC 813). The Second Vatican Council, in different documents, also asserts that the Church is one because of its founder, Jesus, the Word made flesh, who by his saving action restores unity in "one people and one body" (GS 78) and that the Church is one because of the Holy Spirit, "the principle of the Church's unity" (UR 2).

These four characteristics, which we profess in the Creed, indicate essential elements or qualities of the Church and its mission. In and of itself, the Church does not possess these elements. They are gifts given by Christ and, simultaneously, a challenge. For the Church is called to realize, appropriate, and work with this endowment.

Catholic Culture

The Lateran basilica is filled with venerable relics. The high altar itself is constructed over a wooden table at which, as legend has it, St. Peter celebrated the Eucharist with the ancient Christians of Rome (Mary Ellen Hynes, *Companion to the Calendar*, LTP, Archdiocese of Chicago, 1993, p. 166).

The famous Lateran Treaty or "Concordat" agreed upon between the Vatican and Mussolini was finalized and signed at the Lateran Palace. The agreement stipulates that the Lateran grounds are also considered part of Vatican City State.

Dismissal Catechesis (30 min.)

Getting Started

1. Before the session, prepare the meeting space with a prayer environment and enough chairs. Be sure that the room is set in a manner conducive to group discussion.
2. Gather the group and place the Lectionary in a prominent place. Invite the participants to join you in beginning with a prayer. You may use the following prayer or one of your own composition. The following prayer is from the Common of the Dedication of a Church:
   Father,
   each year we recall the dedication of this church
   to your service.
   Let our worship always be sincere
   and help us to find your saving love in this church.
   Grant this through Jesus Christ, your Son,
   who lives and reigns with you and the Holy Spirit,
   one God, for ever and ever.

First Impressions

1. Explain to the group that the Church is celebrating the feast of St. John Lateran. Share with them the significance of the basilica of St. John Lateran as a symbol of the universal Church. You may use the following words from the Catholic Doctrine section or summarize the teaching in your own words:
   The feast we celebrate today observes the anniversary of the dedication of the cathedral church of Rome. When the Emperor Constantine officially recognized Christianity, he made generous gifts to the Church, one of which was a palace and grounds formerly belonging to the Laterani family. In 324 he added a large church on the grounds named the Basilica of the Savior. Legend has it that the basilica was dedicated on November 9 that year. Later, a baptistry was added and dedicated to St. John the Baptist. In subsequent years the entire edifice became known as St. John of the Lateran. Because it is the cathedral church of the bishop of Rome, the feast, at first observed only in Rome, was later extended to the whole Church as a sign of devotion to and of unity with the Chair of Peter.
2. Invite the group to reflect on how they feel about becoming a member of a universal Church. Ask them what hesitations, concerns, or questions they have. Depending on the size of your group, you might offer the group an opportunity to discuss in small groups before sharing with the large group.

Making Connections

1. Share with the group what it means for you to be a member of a universal Church. Include in your sharing any questions it has raised for you and the blessings it has held for you as a Catholic.

2. Explore how the Church's universal dimension impacts the life of Catholics throughout the world. A simple example would be the liturgy and how it is the same throughout the world, but at the same time culturally adapted to the people. Another example would be the hierarchical structure of the pope and bishops. Explain to the group that even with a universal dimension that allows for diversity it is called to be one Church. This unity is a gift, a charism of God in Jesus Christ.
3. Invite participants to gather in small groups to discuss the following questions: *In light of the discussion, how are you challenged? What gift does being part of a universal Church offer to you?* Afterward, elicit any comments or responses from the group.

Prayer

Conclude with spontaneous prayers for the Church, such as the following:
Let us pray:
Loving God, you desire that all your people throughout the world come to know the glorious joy of your salvation. Hear our prayers for your people:
For the Church, the People of God, throughout the world, may they grow in their witness of God's love for all people. We pray to the Lord . . .
   Response: *Lord, hear our prayer.*
For the Pope, may he grow in wisdom. We pray to the Lord . . .
   Response: *Lord, hear our prayer.*
For our bishop (name), may he be faithful in his proclamation of the gospel. We pray to the Lord . . .
   Response: *Lord, hear our prayer.*
For our parish, may we grow in our witness, in God's wisdom, and in our faithful action to proclaim the gospel. We pray to the Lord . . .
   Response: *Lord, hear our prayer.*
Invite the group to offer their own prayers and then conclude with the following:
Lord, we know that you hear our prayers and we thank you for all that you are doing in our lives. We ask these prayers in Jesus' name. Amen.

Extended Catechesis

SESSION FOCUS: *The Four Marks of the Church*

Gathering

A. Sunday:
   Welcome the sponsors and team members to the expanded group. Ask the group to respond to the following question: *When God established the Church through Jesus Christ, what characteristics do you believe God intended the Church to exemplify?*

B. Weekday:

If you gather for extended catechesis during the week, be sure to begin with a celebration of the Word. For this feast day, there are twenty-two possible scripture tests. Select readings to use with a prayer format such as:

- Gathering Hymn
- Greeting and Gathering Prayer
- First Reading
- Sing the Responsorial Psalm
- Second Reading
- Sing the Gospel Acclamation
- Read the Gospel
- Pray using a prayer text from the Common Dedication of a Church

The Word (30 min.)

1. Readings for the feast of the Dedication of St. John Lateran may be taken from any of the readings assigned for the dedication of a church. The choices can be found in the Lectionary. In view of the great number of possible texts, a specific scripture commentary is not available. Prepare for catechesis with the help of a Bible commentary and invite the catechumens and candidates into prayerful reflection on the readings in a way similar to the method that has been used on other Sundays.

2. The following questions may be helpful: *What word or phrase spoke to you from the liturgy? What meaning did it have for you?* Continue with further discussion about the meaning of the scriptures for their lives. Conclude by asking: *In light of the liturgy, the scriptures, and our discussion, how do you hear yourself being called to respond to the Word in the coming week?*

Catholic Teaching (30 min.)

1. Remind the group that we are celebrating the Feast of St. John Lateran. Explain to the group, using the Catholic Doctrine section, that we are not just celebrating a particular place in Rome. Rather, the feast of St. John Lateran provides an opportunity to celebrate the universal Church which is one, holy, catholic, and apostolic.

   As a prelude to a discussion of the four marks of the Church, recite the section of the Nicene Creed that professes our belief in one, holy, catholic, and apostolic Church. Explain to the group that these marks do not belong exclusively to the Roman Catholic Church. They are marks of the Church as the body of Christ with Christ as the head. They are gifts given by Christ to the Church already present but not complete. We are challenged to fully realize, appropriate, and work toward the fullness of a Church which is one, holy, catholic, and apostolic.

2. Focus on the Church as "one." Ask the participants who have been baptized in another tradition to share their own experiences of being baptized. Ask: *What was it like and what does it mean to you?* After sharing, ask the group why we do not re-baptize people who have already been baptized in a Christian tradition. Be sure that the group understands that the Church recognizes the baptism of other Christian churches. In spite of the plurality of churches, we are one in our baptism and the source of our being one is

the Trinity. Conclude by discussing the following question: *How are we called individually and as a community to work for unity among the churches?*

3. Focus on the Church's mark of "holiness." Ask the group: *What does it mean to be holy?* Explain to the group that all people of the Church are called to holiness and that the source of this holiness is Christ. Using the Catholic Doctrine section, share how the Church shares in the holiness of Christ, albeit imperfectly because of sin. Through God's grace we are made holy. Ask the participants to share in pairs how they believe they are called to holiness.

4. Focus on the Church as "catholic." Point out to the group that catholic does not refer to Roman Catholic. Rather, this mark indicates that the Church is to be universal, which is the meaning of catholic. The source of its universality is Christ. The Church is in union with Christ, who has provided the fullness of the means to salvation for us. Explain to the group that the Church's mission is to proclaim the Good News of salvation to all the world. The universal proclamation of God's Good News is to be adapted to the situations and circumstances of the world. Share how the Church proclaims the Good News through the work of missionaries or agencies such as Catholic Relief Services or Catholic Charities.

5. Focus on the Church as "apostolic." Develop a definition of "apostle" as one who is sent by Jesus Christ and who is faithful to his message of salvation. As the early apostles were faithful, so the Church is called to be faithful to Christ. Bring out that since the earliest days, the Church in its desire to be faithful has entrusted the teachings of the gospel to its bishops. Ask the group to share in pairs the ways they believe they are called to be faithful to Jesus Christ.

Putting Faith into Practice

Ask the group to respond to the following questions with one other person: *In light of the discussion and reflection, how are you challenged? How are you hopeful?* After the pairs have finished, invite any comments or responses to be shared with the large group.

Prayer

Conclude the session with an adaptation of the reading from Ephesians 1:15–19.

Listen to the words of St. Paul's letter to the Ephesians as if they were addressed to you personally. For they are intended for you, as they are for every generation of believers:

"For my part, from the time I first heard of your faith in the Lord Jesus and your love for all the members of the Church, I have never stopped thanking God for you and recommending you in my prayers. May the God of our Lord Jesus Christ, the Father of glory, grant you a spirit of wisdom and insight to know him clearly. May he enlighten your innermost vision that you may know the great hope to which he has called you, the wealth of his glorious heritage to be distributed among members of the Church, and the immeasurable scope of his power in us who believe."

This is asked in the name of our Lord, Jesus Christ. Amen.

Index

Index of Doctrinal Themes

Ordinary Time 29	**The First Commandment: "I Am the Lord, There Is No Other"**	Body and Blood Sunday	**The Real Presence of Christ in the Eucharist**

Ordinary Time 29 **The First Commandment: "I Am the Lord, There Is No Other"**
OT and NT references
theological virtues of faith, hope, and love
first stance toward God: faith
our confident expectation of God's goodness: hope
Jesus' teaching linking God and neighbor: love
definition of word "religion" from the Latin *re ligatio*

Ordinary Time 30 **The Two Great Commandments**
society and individuals, modern papal social teaching
mutual human reliance based in unity of Trinity
interdependence required of our human nature
the common good and human solidarity
peace and justice contributes to common good

Ordinary Time 31 **The Role of the Magisterium**
Latin *magister* (master, teacher)
teaching function of the hierarchy of the Church
bishops as successors of the apostles
authentic teaching based in Word of God helped by Spirit
teaching by pope, bishops, ecumenical council, conferences
guidance in faith and morals
papal infallibility, obedience, and assent of faith

Ordinary Time 32 **Perseverance in Prayer**
our relationship to God requires communication
distractions to prayer
purpose in praying
ultimate prayer: surrender to God

Ordinary Time 33 **Stewardship of Creation**
care of the entire "household" (creation) of God
our responsibility for others
Vatican II and alleviating human misery in world
reverence for creation
John Paul II and value of work
property and goods and relationship to common good

Ordinary Time 34 **"To Judge the Living and the Dead"**
Christ, Lord of human history
final age of the world and kingdom of God
particular and final judgments
apocalyptic literature and Book of Revelation

Immaculate Conception **The Immaculate Conception of the Blessed Virgin Mary**
Pius XII and articulation of this dogma
Paul VI: devotion to Mary leads us to glorify God
Mary, model disciple and Mother of God
holiness of Mary due to God's love of her and God's grace
Mary's redemption achieved in a unique way: immaculate conception
Mary's "yes" to God

Mary, Mother of God **"He was born of the Virgin Mary and Became Man"**
Council of Ephesus and declaration of Mary as Mother of God
Mary linked to the work of the Son, Jesus
start of the calendar year and honoring Mary, contemplating paschal mystery
Mary's free cooperation with plan of God

Presentation of the Lord **The Two Natures of Jesus Christ**
Jesus Christ: fully human, fully divine
Council of Chalcedon and formulation of this doctrine
Jesus, Son of God and Son of Mary
this feast day and going to meet the Lord with lighted candles
Jesus Christ: the light of all peoples

Ascension of the Lord **"He Ascended into Heaven and Is Seated at the Right Hand of the Father"**
the ascension of Christ as part of the paschal mystery
salvation in Christ
Christ's presence to and in the Church in post-resurrection era
Christ's ascension and our call to follow in hope
ascension and Christ's Spirit in the gift of the sacraments
abuses of the gift of sexuality

Trinity Sunday **The Holy Trinity**
Baptism and entering the life of the Trinity
one God, three persons
central mystery of the faith
terminology of "substance" and "person"

Body and Blood Sunday **The Real Presence of Christ in the Eucharist**
the command of Jesus: "do this in memory of me"
God makes present Jesus in the eucharistic species through Spirit
real presence is a substantial presence
change in the bread and wine: transubstantiation
real presence totally and fully in each species

Birth of John the Baptist **Human Cooperation with Divine Grace**
grace and human freedom
grace as a gift from God
preparation to receive grace is also a gift from God
God reaches out to us; we are invited to respond
our vocation in God: illustrated by life of John the Baptist

Peter and Paul **Collegiality**
essential element in the ministry of bishop
this essential element derives from Jesus and the Twelve
the college of bishops and communion with pope, bishop of Rome
ecumenical council and collegiality
other groupings of bishops (regions/conferences) and collegiality
Synod of Bishops
characteristics of Church (universality/apostolicity) and collegiality
Petrine ministry, communion of Church as gift of Christ

Transfiguration **Visions and Private Revelations**
Jesus Christ alone is the fullness of God's revelation
the mystery of Christ and the mystery of creation
Scripture and Tradition and the deposit of revelation
no new public revelation until the second coming of Christ
mysticism and revelation
manifestation of Mary at Lourdes and Fatima enhances the meaning of Christ
God "speaking" everything to us in his Word, Jesus Christ

Assumption **The Assumption of Mary**
based in ancient Church tradition
Pius XII and articulation of this doctrine
the assumption and Mary's unique participation in Christ's resurrection
Vatican II on Mary: her work as intercessor continues

Triumph of the Cross **Redemption**
triumph of Jesus' entire mission over sin and death
redemption: key theological concept in understanding significance of Jesus
work of redemption continued in liturgy
redemption affects individuals and all of human history
human restoration and summation in Christ
our active affirmation of risen life in Christ

All Saints **The Communion of Saints**
all Christians called to holiness of life
exemplary Christians, the saints
saints, intercessors before God and companions in prayer, modeled on Mary
the communion of saints and the Church
distinction between worship (God) and veneration (saints)
apostles, martyrs, and supreme witness of shedding blood for faith
Blessed Virgin Mary, angels, and saints

All Souls **Purgatory**
state of purification between death and heaven
removal of obstacle to union with God
beatific vision
purgatory and tradition in our Church of interceding in prayer for the dead
communion of saints and praying for dead
Eucharistic Prayer and praying for dead
offering Mass for the dead

Dedication of John Lateran **The Four Marks of the Church**
John Lateran, the cathedral church of Rome
this feast celebrates the "whole Church"
Church: one, holy, catholic, and apostolic
these characteristics flow from Jesus and professed in the creed
these characteristics an endowment that challenges entire Church

Sources Consulted

The following citations are for materials quoted in the background materials entitled Catholic Doctrine and Catholic Culture.

Ecumenical Councils

The Second Vatican Council (1962-1965 A.D.)

These documents are found in *Vatican Council II,* Volume I, The Conciliar and Postconciliar Documents, New Revised Edition, Austin Flannery, O.P., gen. ed., Costello Publishing Company, Northport, New York, 1996:

AG	*Ad gentes divinitus* (Decree on the Church's Missionary Activity) 7 December 1965
AA	*Apostolicam actuositatem* (Decree on the Apostolate of Lay People) 18 November 1965
DV	*Dei verbum* (Dogmatic Constitution on Divine Revelation) 18 November 1965
GS	*Gaudium et spes* (Pastoral Constitution on the Church in the Modern World) 7 December 1965
LG	*Lumen gentium* (Dogmatic Constitution on the Church) 21 November 1964
PO	*Presbyterorum ordinis* (Decree on the Ministry and Life of Priests) 7 December 1965
SC	*Sacrosanctum concilium* (The Constitution on the Sacred Liturgy) 4 December 1963
UR	*Unitatis redintegratio* (Decree on Ecumenism) 21 November 1964

The Council of Chalcedon (451 A.D.)

SymbChal	Symbol of Chalcedon: DS 301-02 in Jacques Dupuis, S.J., ed., *The Christian Faith in the Doctrinal Documents of the Catholic Church,* 6th revised ed., Alba House, New York, 1996

Church Law

CIC	*Code of Canon Law,* tr. CLSA, Canon Law Society of America, Washington, D.C., 1983

Liturgy

BB	Book of Blessings, *The Roman Ritual,* English ed., The Liturgical Press, Collegeville, Minnesota, 1989
BOCC	Rite of Blessing of Oils and Rite of Consecrating the Chrism, The Roman Pontifical, English ed., in *The Rites of the Catholic Church,* v. 1, A Pueblo Book, The Liturgical Press, Collegeville, Minnesota, 1990
CB	*Ceremonial of Bishops,* English ed., The Liturgical Press, Collegeville, Minnesota, 1989
GIRM	General Instruction of the Roman Missal, *The Roman Missal,* English ed., Catholic Book Publishing Co., New York, 1985
HCWE	Holy Communion and Worship of the Eucharist outside Mass, *The Roman Ritual,* English ed., in The Rites of the Catholic Church, v. 1, A Pueblo Book, The Liturgical Press, Collegeville, Minnesota, 1990
LitHrs	The Liturgy of the Hours, *The Divine Office,* English ed., 4 vols. Catholic Book Publishing Co., New York, 1975, 1976
OB	Ordination of a Bishop, The Roman Pontifical, English ed., in *The Rites of the Catholic Church,* v. 2, A Pueblo Book, The Liturgical Press, Collegeville, Minnesota, 1991
OCF	Order of Christian Funerals, *The Roman Ritual,* English ed., Liturgy Training Publication, Archdiocese of Chicago, 1989
PCS	Pastoral Care of the Sick: Rites of Anointing and Viaticum, *The Roman Ritual,* English ed., in The Rites of the Catholic Church, v. 1, A Pueblo Book, The Liturgical Press, Collegeville, Minnesota, 1990
RBC	Rite of Baptism for Children, *The Roman Ritual,* English ed., Catholic Book Publishing Co., New York, 1977
RC	Rite of Confirmation, The Roman Pontifical, English ed., in *The Rites of the Catholic Church,* v. 1, A Pueblo Book, The Liturgical Press, Collegeville, Minnesota, 1990
RCIA	Rite of Christian Initiation of Adults, *The Roman Ritual,* English ed., Liturgy Training Publications, Archdiocese of Chicago, 1988
RMar	Rite of Marriage, *The Roman Ritual,* English ed., Catholic Book Publishing Co., New York, 1970
RPen	Rite of Penance, *The Roman Ritual,* English ed., in The Rites of the Catholic Church, v. 1, A Pueblo Book, The Liturgical Press, Collegeville, Minnesota, 1990
RM	The Sacramentary, *The Roman Missal,* English ed., Catholic Book Publishing Co., New York, 1985

Pontifical Documents

Pius XII (1939-1958)

MD	Apostolic Constitution, *Munificentissimus Deus,* 1 November 1950: AAS 42, DS 3903

Paul VI (1963-1978)

N	Address, Nazareth, 5 January 1964, in LitHrs v. 1, p. 426-28
CPG	Credo of the People of God: Solemn Profession of Faith, 30 June 1968
MC	Apostolic Exhortation, *Marialis cultus,* 2 February 1974

John Paul II (1978-)

The encyclical letters of John Paul II are found in J. Michael Miller, C.S.B., ed., *The Encyclicals of John Paul II,* Our Sunday Visitor Publishing Division, Huntington, Indiana, 1996

DM	Encyclical, *Dives in misericordia,* 30 November 1980
LE	Encyclical, *Laborem exercens,* 14 September 1981
FC	Encyclical, *Familiaris consortio,* 22 November 1981
RP	Apostolic Exhortation, *Reconciliatio et paenitentia,* 2 December 1984, Vatican tr., St. Paul Books & Media, Boston
SD	Apostolic Letter, *Salvifici dolores,* 11 February 984, Vatican tr., St. Paul Books & Media, Boston
DViv	Encyclical, *Dominum et vivificantem,* 18 May 1986
CL	Apostolic Exhortation, *Christifidelis laici,* 30 December 1988, Vatican tr., St. Paul Books & Media, Boston
RMi	Encyclical, *Redemptoris Missio,* 7 December 1990
CA	Encyclical, *Centesimus annus,* 1 May 1991
LF	Letter to Families from Pope John Paul II, 2 February 1994, Vatican tr., St. Paul Books & Media, Boston

Ecclesiastical Writers

Didache	Didache XII Apostolorum in Theodore E. James, ed., *The Heart of Catholicism,* Our Sunday Visitor Publishing Division, Huntington, Indiana, 1997
AmbMyst	Ambrose, St., *De mysteriis* 9, 50. 52: PL 16 (1880) 405-07
AndDis	Andrew of Crete, St., Discourse 10 (Oratio 10 in *Exaltatione sanctae crucis*): PG 97, 1018-19
AugSer	Augustine, St., *Sermones:* *Sermo 185:* PL 38, 997-99 *Sermo 186, 1:* PL 38, 999 *Sermo 293, 1-3:* PL 1327-28 *Sermo 293, 3:* PL 1328-29 *Sermo 336, 1.6:* PL 38 (1861) 1471-72
AugSerPas	Augustine, St., *Sermo in Octava paschae I,* 4: PL 46, 838
AugEvJn	Augustine, St., *In evangelium Johannis tractatus* (Tract 15, 10-12. 16-17): CCL 36, 154-6
AugNatG	Augustine, St., *De natura et gratia* 31: PL 44, 264
CathGenSD	Catherine of Genoa, St., Purgation and Purgatory, *The Spiritual Dialogue,* 72, Serge Hughes, trs., Paulist Press, New York, 1979
CathProv	Catherine of Siena, St., *Dialogue on Providence,* ch. 4, 138 & cap. 134
ClemPaed	Clement of Alexandria, St., *Paedagogus 1,* 6, 42: PG 8, 281
CyrCatI	Cyril of Jerusalem, St., *Catecheses illuminandorum* (Catechetical Instruction: On the Ten Points of Doctrine) in Theodore E. James, ed., *The Heart of Catholicism,* Our Sunday Visitor Publishing Division, Huntington, Indiana, 1997
GregGHom	Gregory the Great, St., *Homilia* (On the Gospels 14, 3-6): PL 76, 1129-30 in LitHrs v. 2

GregGJob Gregory the Great, St., *Moralia in Job* (Moral Reflections on Job, Lib. 13, 21-23): PL 75, 1028-29 in LitHrs v. 2

GregNanOr Gregory Nazianzus, St., *Orationes* (Oratio 40, 3-4): PG 36, 361C

HildBgSymp Hildegard of Bingen, *Symphonia,* 115, 141, Barbara Newman, trs. & ed., Cornell University Press, Ithica, New York, 1988

IgAEph Ignatius of Antioch, St., *Epistula ad Ephesios 20,* 2 AFII/2, 87: SCh 10, 76

IgAMag Ignatius of Antioch, St., *Epistula ad Magnesios 9,* 1 AFII/2, 128-30: SCh 10, 88

IrenAdH Irenaeus, St., *Adversus haereses 3,* 22, 4: PG 7/1, 959A

IrenDemoAp Irenaeus, St., *Demonstratio apostolica 7:* SCh 62, 41-2

JermIsa Jerome, St., *Commentariorum in Isaiam,* libri xviii, prol (Comm in Isaias, Prol): PL 24, 17

JnCyNatCon John Chrysostom, St., *De incomprehensibili dei natura seu contra Anomoeos* (De incomprehensibili 3, 6): PG 48, 725D

JnCMtCar John of the Cross, St., *Subida del Monte Carmelo* (Ascent of Mt. Carmel 2, 22, 3-5) in *The Collected Works,* K. Kavanaugh, OCD and O. Rodruquez, OCD, tr., Institute of Carmelite Studies, Washington, D.C., 1979

JnCLzAm John of the Cross, St., *Dichos de luz y amor 64* in CCC 1022

JnEudCorJ John Eudes, St., *Tractatus de admirabili corde Jesu* (Tract. de admirabili corde Jesu 1, 5): *Opera omnia* 6, 107. 113-115 in LitHrs v. 4

JNorDivLov Julian of Norwich, Revelation of Divine Love 32, 99-100, James Walshe, S.J., tr., London, 1961

JustApol Justin, St., *Apologiae 1,* 67: PG 6, 429-32

LeoGosp Leo the Great, St., *On the Gospels 14,* 3-6: PL 76, 1129-30 in LitHrs v. 2

LeoSer Leo the Great, St., *Sermones:*
Sermo 51, 3-4. 8: PL 54, 310-11 in LitHrs v. 2
Sermo 73, 4: CCL 138A, 453
Sermo 74, 2: CCL 138A, 455-57

LeoSerEpiph Leo the Great, St., *Sermo in Epiphania Domini* 1-3, 5: PL 54, 240-44 in LitHrs v. 1

LeoSerNat Leo the Great, St., *Sermo 21 in nat. Dom.,* 3: PL 54, 192C

JnNewVita Newman, John Henry, Cardinal, *Apologia pro Vita Sua,* 239, Longman, London, 1878

PaulCrHtG Paul of the Cross, St., In the Heart of God, in Theodore E. James, ed., *The Heart of Catholicism,* Our Sunday Visitor Publishing Division, Huntington, Indiana, 1997

SopOrHyp Soprohonius, St., *Oratione 3 de Hypapante* 6, 7: PG 87, 3, 3291-93 in LitHrs v. 3

Other Works Frequently Cited

BibTrad David Lyle Jeffrey, gen. ed., *A Dictionary of Biblical Tradition in English Literature,* William B. Eerdmans Publishing Company, Grand Rapids, Michigan, 1992

CathHous *Catholic Household Blessings & Prayers,* Bishops' Committee on the Liturgy, National Conference of Catholic Bishops, United States Catholic Conference, Washington, D.C., 1988

ChrByzA John Beckwith, *Early Christian and Byzantine Art,* 2nd ed., Yale University Press, New Haven, 1979

ColBibTheol Carroll Stuhlmueller, C.P., gen. ed., *The Collegeville Pastoral Dictionary of Biblical Theology,* The Liturgical Press, Collegeville, Minnesota, 1996

DictSymb Sarah Carr-Gomm, *The Dictionary of Symbols in Western Art,* Facts on File, Inc., New York, 1995

ECathHist Matthew Bunson, *Our Sunday Visitor's Encyclopedia of Catholic History,* Our Sunday Visitor Publishing Division, Huntington, Indiana, 1995

EncyCath Richard P. McBrien, gen. ed., *The HarperCollins Encyclopedia of Catholicism,* HarperCollins Publishers Inc., New York, 1995

HistItal Frederick Hartt, *History of Italian Renaissance Art,* Painting, Sculpture, Architecture, 4th ed., revised by David G. Wilkins, Harry N. Abrams, Inc., Publisher, New York, 1994

ModCathE Michael Glazier & Monika K. Hellwig, eds., *The Modern Catholic Encyclopedia,* The Liturgical Press, Collegeville, Minnesota, 1994

NDictSacr Peter E. Fink, S.J., ed., *The New Dictionary of Sacramental Worship,* The Liturgical Press, Collegeville, Minnesota, 1990

NDictSoc Judith A. Dwyer, ed., *The New Dictionary of Catholic Social Thought,* The Liturgical Press, Collegeville, Minnesota, 1994

NDictTheol Joseph A. Komonchak, Mary Collins, Dermot A. Lane, eds., *The New Dictionary of Theology,* The Liturgical Press, Collegeville, Minnesota, 1990

OxA&A Peter and Linda Murray, *The Oxford Companion to Christian Art and Architecture,* Oxford University Press, New York, 1996

Other Works Cited

Atawan, Robert, Dardess, George, Rosenthan, Peggy, eds., *Divine Inspiration: The Life of Jesus in World Poetry,* Oxford University Press, New York, 1998

Ball, Ann, *Catholic Traditions in Crafts,* Our Sunday Visitor Publishing Division, Huntington, Indiana, 1997

Beckett, Sr. Wendy, *The Mystery of Love: Saints in Art Through the Ages,* HarperCollins Publishers, San Fransisco, 1996

Beinert, Wolfgang, Fiorenza, Frances Schussler, eds., *Handbook of Catholic Theology,* Crossroad, New York, 1995

Cameli, Louis J., *Mary's Journey,* Sadlier, New York, 1982

Cavalletti, Sofia, *The Religious Potential of the Child,* Archdiocese of Chicago, Liturgy Training Publications, 1992

Celebration, An Ecumenical Worship Resource (January 1998), National Catholic Reporter, Kansas City, Missouri

Comby, Jean, MacCulloch, Diarmaid, *How to Read Church History,* v. 2, Crossroad, New York, 1986

Ferrone, Rita, *On the Rite of Election,* Archdiocese of Chicago, Liturgy Training Publications, 1994

Ellsberg, Robert, *All Saints,* The Crossroad Publishing Company, New York, 1997

Lewis, Elizabeth Bruening, *The Power of Sacred Images,* Christian Classics, Allen, Texas, 1997

Gantoy, Robert, & Swaeles, Romain, *Days of the Lord:* The Liturgical Year, v. 7, *Solemnities and Feasts,* Madeleine Beaumont & Mary Misrahi, trs., The Liturgical Press, Collegeville, Minnesota, 1994

Harrington, Daniel J., *The Gospel of Matthew,* Sacra Pagina Series, v. 1, Daniel J. Harrington, ed., The Liturgical Press, Collegeville, Minnesota, 1991

Harrington, Wilfred J., *Revelation,* Sacra Pagina Series, v. 16, Daniel J. Harrington, ed., The Liturgical Press, Collegeville, Minnesota, 1991

Hynes, Mary Ellen, *Companion to the Calendar,* Archdiocese of Chicago, Liturgy Training Publications, 1993

Koenig-Bricker, Woodeene, *Prayers of the Saints,* HarperSanFransisco, 1996

Martos, Joseph, *Doors to the Sacred,* expanded ed., Triumph Books, Liguori, Missouri, 1991

Pelikan, Jaroslav, *Mary Through the Centuries,* Yale University, New Haven, Connecticut, 1996

Undset, Sigrid, *Stages on the Road,* Arthur G. Chater, tr., Alfred A. Knopf, New York, 1934

Welch, Evelyn, *Art and Society in Italy 1350-1500,* Oxford University Press, New York, 1997

Hymnals

Today's Missal Music Issue 1998, Oregon Catholic Press, Portland, Oregon, 1998

Worship, 3rd ed., GIA Publications, Inc., Chicago, 1986